Linux® Bible
2005 Edition

Christopher Negus

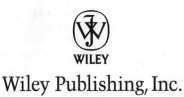

WILEY

Wiley Publishing, Inc.

Linux® Bible 2005 Edition

Published by
Wiley Publishing, Inc.
10475 Crosspoint Boulevard
Indianapolis, IN 46256
www.wiley.com

Copyright © 2005 by Wiley Publishing, Inc., Indianapolis, Indiana

Published simultaneously in Canada

ISBN: 0-7645-7949-5

Manufactured in the United States of America

10 9 8 7 6 5 4 3 2 1

1O/RZ/QR/QV/IN

For general information on our other products and services or to obtain technical support, please contact our Customer Care Department within the U.S. at (800) 762-2974, outside the U.S. at (317) 572-3993 or fax (317) 572-4002.

Wiley also publishes its books in a variety of electronic formats. Some content that appears in print may not be available in electronic books.

Library of Congress Cataloging-in-Publication Data

Negus, Chris, 1957–
  Linux bible 2005 edition/Christopher Negus.
       p. cm.
  ISBN 0-7645-7949-5 (paper/dvd)
  1. Linux. 2. Operating systems (Computers) I. Title.
  QA76.76.063N422 2005
  005.4'32- - dc22

2004028132

About the Author

Chris Negus has authored or co-authored dozens of books on Linux and UNIX, including the ***Red Hat Linux Bible*** (all editions), ***Linux Troubleshooting Bible***, and ***Linux Toys***. He worked with the organization at AT&T that developed UNIX for eight years before moving to Utah to help contribute to Novell's short-lived UnixWare project in the early 1990s. When not writing about Linux, Chris rides the 400 trail with his wife Sheree, builds things with his son Seth, and plays soccer when he can.

Contributing Authors

David Dalan is foremost a husband and a father. Although formally trained as a geologist, he now spends the bulk of his professional time writing books, making and teaching music, and earning his keep as a professional geek. David has worked on books ranging in topic from Cisco certification to Apache server administration.

Wayne Tucker is a Linux enthusiast and has been a professional system administrator for six years. He is currently a technical manager, systems administrator, and network engineer at an Internet company in Washington state. He lives in Bellingham, Washington, with his beloved wife Danielle, whom he would like to thank for her patience while he was working on this project. His future projects include continuing his education and working on the things that have recently accumulated on his "honey-do" list.

Kurt Wall is a professional technical writer by trade and a historian by training. These days, Kurt works for TimeSys Corporation in Pittsburgh, Pennsylvania. His primary responsibility is managing TimeSys' Content Group. In addition to overseeing production of the technical and end-user documentation of TimeSys' embedded Linux operating system and development tools, he writes most of the documentation for TimeSys's embedded Linux products and all of the content available on the TimeSys Network. Kurt has written all or parts of 15 books on Linux system administration and programming topics and contributes the occasional product review to LinuxPlanet. In his spare time, he has no spare time.

Kurt, who dislikes writing about himself in the third person, receives entirely too much e-mail at kwall@kurtwerks.com.

Paul Love, CISSP, CISA, CISM, Security+ has been in the IT field for 15 years. Paul holds a Master's of Science degree in Network Security and a Bachelor's in Information Systems. He has co-authored one Linux security book, contributed to another security book, and has been the technical editor for more than 10 best-selling Linux and UNIX books. Paul also ran a successful Linux portal site during the dot-com era and has been an avid UNIX/Linux user and administrator for many years. Paul is currently a security manager at a large financial services company.

Credits

Acquisitions Editor
Debra Williams Cauley

Development Editor
Maryann Steinhart

Production Editor
Gabrielle Nabi

Technical Editor
Dilip Thomas

Copy Editors
Kim Cofer
Howard Jones

Editorial Manager
Mary Beth Wakefield

Vice President & Executive Group Publisher
Richard Swadley

Vice President and Publisher
Joseph B. Wikert

Project Coordinator
Erin Smith

Graphics and Layout Technicians
Beth Brooks
Carrie Foster
Jennifer Heleine
Shelly Lea
Barry Offringa
Heather Pope
Heather Ryan

Quality Control Technicians
Laura Albert
Amanda Briggs
John Greenough
Jessica Kramer
Susan Moritz
Carl Pierce
Brian Walls

Media Development Specialist
Travis Silvers

Proofreading and Indexing
TECHBOOKS Production Services

As always, I dedicate this book to my wife Sheree.

Preface

Insert the DVD or CD that comes with this book into your PC. Within five minutes, you'll be able to try out Linux with a full range of desktop applications. Within an hour, you can have a full-blown Linux desktop or server system installed on your computer. If you are like most of us who have been bitten by the Linux bug, you won't ever look back.

The *Linux Bible 2005 Edition* is here to open your eyes to what Linux is, where it came from, and where it's going. But, most of all, the book is here to hand you Linux and help you get started. Because Linux is the operating system of free speech and free choice, the *Linux Bible* gives you choices in selecting the Linux that is right for you.

On the DVD and CD that come with this book are 10 different Linux distributions that you are free to install and try out. You learn how those distributions are alike or different, and the book leads you through the basics of installing and setting up your Linux system as:

+ **A desktop computer.** You have a full range of office, music, gaming, graphics, and other applications to use.

+ **A server computer.** Using some of the world's best server software, you can set up your computer to be a Web server, file server, mail server, or print server.

+ **A workstation.** You can draw on thousands of open source programming tools to develop your own software applications.

Unlike other books on Linux, this book doesn't tie you to one Linux distribution. The book teaches you the essentials of Linux graphical interfaces, shell commands, and basic system administration. Separate chapters break down most of the major Linux distributions available today. Then descriptions of the major software projects in most Linux distributions (KDE and GNOME desktops, Apache Web servers, Samba file and printer sharing, and so on) guide you in setting up and using those features, regardless of which Linux you choose.

Understanding the Linux Mystique

To calm your fears that "free" software can't be that good, this book guides you through the strange and circuitous path of open source software development that led to the Linux phenomenon. It also details the major companies and organizations that are behind Linux and the open source movement today.

Along the way, you learn how you can become part of the open source community, whose stars are known by a single name (like Linus) or a few initials (like rms). You'll be staggered by the number of open source projects, forums, and mailing lists that are thriving today (and always looking for more people to get involved).

How This Book Is Organized

Learn the basics of what goes into Linux and you will be able to use all sorts of devices and computers in the future. The book is organized in a way that will enable you to start off at the very beginning with Linux, but still grow to the point where you can get going with some powerful server and programming features, if you care to.

Part I assumes that someone has set up a Linux system in front of you and you want to start learning the basics of how to

♦ Use the shell (Chapter 2).

♦ Work with your graphical desktop (Chapter 3).

In Part II, you learn how to

♦ Do basic administration (Chapter 4).

♦ Attach to the Internet (Chapter 5).

♦ Secure your Linux system (Chapter 6).

If you don't have Linux installed yet, this book helps you out in a big way: the companion DVD and CD include a variety of Linux distributions you can try. Part III (Chapters 7 through 18) describe each of those distributions and how to install them. Appendix A tells you what's on the DVD and CD, how to install from the DVD or CD, and how to burn additional installation CDs from the software we provide.

In Part IV, you learn to get some fun and useful features going in Linux so that you can

♦ Play music and video (Chapter 19).

♦ Write documents and work with graphics (Chapter 20).

♦ Use Web browsers and e-mail clients (Chapter 21).

♦ Play games (Chapter 22).

Linux creates powerful servers, and in Part V you learn to

♦ Set up a Web server using Apache, MySQL, and PHP in Linux (Chapter 23).

♦ Run a mail server (Chapter 24).

♦ Share printers with a CUPS print server (Chapter 25).

♦ Share files with a Samba or NFS file server (Chapter 26).

If you are coming to Linux for its programming environment, Part VI provides chapters that describe

+ Programming environments and interfaces (Chapter 27).
+ Programming tools and utilities (Chapter 28).

In addition, Appendix B can help get you "plugged in" to the Linux community.

What You Will Get From This Book

By the time you finish this book, you'll have a good basic understanding of many of the major features in Linux and how you can use them. If you decide then that you want to go a bit deeper into any Red Hat Linux distribution, *Red Hat Fedora Linux 3 Bible* would be a good next step, with content that includes how to set up many different types of Linux servers. If you are more technically oriented, the *Linux Troubleshooting Bible* can be a good way to learn more advanced skills for securing and troubleshooting Linux systems.

Given the size of thousands of software features available for Linux systems, we can't possibly cover everything in one book. To expand our coverage in a few important areas, we created the Linux Bible 2005 Edition Web site (www.wiley.com/go/ LinuxBible2005). Refer to that site for coverage of many application and server features that didn't make it into this text.

To order the source code for Fedora, see the coupon printed at the back of the book. To order source code for any of the other Linux distributions included on the DVD or CD, go to www.wiley/go/linuxbible2005source to download a coupon with further details.

Acknowledgments

I consider anyone who has contributed to the open source community to be a contributor to the book you see in front of you. The backbone of any Linux distribution is formed by the organizations that produce the distributions, the major projects included in Linux, and the thousands of people who give their time and code to support Linux. So, thanks to you all!

For their help on understanding particular Linux distributions, I'd like to thank Patrick Volkerding (creator of Slackware), Kai Staats (CEO of Terra Soft Solutions, makers of Yellow Dog Linux), and Jesse Keating (Fedora Legacy Project), who took the time to answer my questions. Likewise, I'd like to thank Charles Mauch for helping me get started with Gentoo and Joel Parker for building my computing infrastructure so that when I work, no Linux distribution is more than a click away.

My Linux users group (TACLUG.org) was an invaluable resource. Whether on the group's mailing list or personally at meetings, the group members have been extremely valuable to me (providing direct input to this book, as well as contributing to my personal growth with Linux).

As for the contributing authors on this book, I couldn't have asked for a finer group. Without the contributions of David Dalan, Wayne Tucker, Kurt Wall, and Paul Love, this book might never have gotten done. Likewise, technical editor Dilip Thomas did a great job pointing out ways of improving the book.

Thanks to the folks at Wiley for helping me press through the project. Without Debra Williams Cauley, I would surely not have known (on a daily basis) how far behind I was on my schedule. Maryann Steinhart proved to be a tough, but kind, editor. Thanks to Margot Maley Hutchison, Kimberly Valentini, and Maureen Maloney from Waterside productions for contracting the book for me with Wiley.

And finally, special thanks to my wife Sheree. There's no way I could do the work I do without the solid support I get on the home front. I love you, and thanks for taking such good care of me, Seth, and Caleb.

Contents at a Glance

Contents

· ·

Part II: Running the Show   123

Chapter 4: Learning Basic Administration 125

Part III: Choosing and Installing a Linux Distribution 241

Chapter 7: Installing Linux 243

Chapter 8: Running Fedora Core and Red Hat Enterprise Linux . . . 273

Part V: Running Servers   593

Linux First Steps

Starting with Linux

Linux is ready for prime time. Are you ready for Linux?

Well, whether you know it or not, you probably run into Linux every day. When you buy a book from Amazon.com or search the Web with Google, you use Linux. You use Linux in your TiVo when you record TV shows, and Linux may be running the PDA in your pocket. Animations you saw in the movie *Shrek 2* were created by hundreds of Linux workstations and rendered by a server farm of hundreds of other Linux systems.

Linux truly is everywhere.

Big computer companies, such as IBM, Oracle, Novell, and Red Hat, are lining up their products behind Linux. After dismissing it for years, companies such as Microsoft and Sun Microsystems are gathering their forces to deal with it. Who would have thought that some of the world's largest computer companies would fear a computer system built from code nobody can own that is given away for free?

But despite the fact that IBM featured Mohammed Ali in commercials for Linux during the Super Bowl and that the mere mention of "Linux" for a dot-com company sent its stock through the roof in the 1990s, most people don't really know what Linux is. As Linux continues to improve exponentially, that's going to change.

The *Linux Bible 2005 Edition* brings you into the world of open source software that, through some strange twists and turns, has fallen most publicly under the "Linux" banner. Through descriptions and procedures, this book helps you to do the following:

   ✦ Understand what Linux is and where it comes from.

   ✦ Sort through the various incarnations of Linux to choose one (or more) that is right for you (you get several of them on this book's DVD and CD).

✦ Try out Linux as a desktop computer, server computer, or programmer's workstation.

✦ Become connected (if you so choose) to the open source software movement, as well as many separate high-quality software projects that are included with Linux.

Whether you are using Linux for the first time or just want to try out a new Linux distribution, the *Linux Bible 2005 Edition* is your guide to using Linux and the latest open source technology. While different Linux distributions vary in the exact software they include (you'll see why that is later), this book describes the most popular software available for Linux to

✦ Manage your desktop (menus, icons, windows, and so on).

✦ Listen to music and watch video.

✦ Use word processor, spreadsheet, and other office productivity applications.

✦ Browse the Web and send e-mail.

✦ Play games.

✦ Find thousands of other open source software packages you can get for free.

Because most Linux distributions also include features that let them act as servers (in fact, that's what Linux has always been best at), you'll also learn about software available for Linux that lets you:

✦ Connect to the Internet or other network.

✦ Use Linux as a firewall, router, and DHCP server to protect and manage your private network.

✦ Run a Web server (using Apache, MySQL, and PHP).

✦ Run a mail server (using sendmail or another mail transfer agent).

✦ Run a print server (using Samba or CUPS).

✦ Run a file server (using FTP or Samba).

This book guides you through the basics of getting started with the Linux features just mentioned plus many more features that I'll get to later. You'll go through the following basic steps:

1. **Understand Linux.** You need to know where Linux came from, how it is developed, and how it's ultimately packaged. This chapter describes the UNIX heritage on which Linux was founded, the open source software development efforts underway, and the organizations and individuals that package and produce Linux distributions.

2. **Try Linux.** In the past, an impediment to trying Linux has been getting it installed on a computer that is devoted solely to Microsoft Windows. With bootable Linux systems such as KNOPPIX (and others included with this book),

you can boot a fully functioning Linux from DVD, CD, or floppy disk without
disturbing the current contents of your computer.

3. **Install Linux.** You can install a fully functioning Linux system permanently on
   your hard disk. Disk space required varies from a few hundred megabytes for
   a minimal installation to 6 gigabytes for a full range of desktop, server, and
   programming features. Chapters in Part III, "Choosing and Installing a Linux
   Distribution," describe how to install several different Linux distributions.

4. **Use Linux.** You won't know if Linux can be used to replace your current
   desktop or server system until you start using it. This book helps you try
   OpenOffice.org software to write documents, create spreadsheets, and build
   presentations. It describes XMMS and MPlayer for playing your music and
   video content, respectively, and covers some of the best Linux tools available
   for Web browsing (for example, Mozilla and Konqueror) and managing your
   e-mail (such as Evolution and Thunderbird).

5. **Configure Linux.** Linux works very well as a desktop system, and it also can
   be configured to act as a router, a firewall, and a variety of server types. While
   there are some excellent graphical tools for administering Linux systems, most
   Linux administrators edit configuration files and run commands to configure
   Linux. Part II, "Running the Show," contains basic information for administering Linux, and Part V, "Running Servers," discusses procedures for setting up
   various types of servers.

Once you've been through the book, you should be proficient enough to track down
your more advanced questions through the volumes of man pages, FAQs, HOW-TOs,
and forums that cover different aspects of the Linux operating system.

Understanding Linux

People who don't know what Linux is sometimes ask me if it's a program that runs
on Microsoft Windows. When I tell them that Linux is, itself, an operating system
like Windows and that they can remove (or never purchase) Windows, I sometimes
get a surprised reaction: "A PC can run with nothing from Microsoft on it?"

Yes, Linux is a full-blown operating system that is a free clone of the UNIX operating
system. Start your computer with Linux, and Linux takes over the operation of your
PC and manages the following aspects of your computer:

✦ **Processor** — Because Linux can run many processes from many different users
   at the same time (even with multiple CPUs on the same machine), Linux needs
   to be able to manage those processes. The Linux scheduler sets the priorities
   for running tasks and manages which processes run on which CPUs (if multiple
   processors are present). The scheduler can be tuned differently for different
   types of Linux systems. If it's tuned properly, the most important processes get
   the quickest responses from the processor. For example, a Linux scheduler on
   a desktop system gives higher priority to things like moving a window on the
   desktop than it does to a background file transfer.

✦ **Memory** — Linux tries to keep processes with the most immediate need in RAM, while managing how processes that exceed the available memory are moved to swap space. Swap space is a defined area on your hard disk that's used to handle the overflow of running processes and data. When RAM is full, processes are placed in swap space. When swap space is full (something that you don't want to happen), new processes can't start up.

✦ **Devices** — Linux supports thousands of hardware devices, yet keeps the kernel a manageable size by including only a small set of drivers in the active kernel. Using loadable modules, the kernel can add support for other hardware as needed. Modules can be loaded and unloaded on demand, as hardware is added and removed. (The kernel, described in detail a bit later on, is the heart of the Linux operating system.)

✦ **File systems** — File systems provide the structure in which files are stored on hard disk, CD, DVD, floppy disk, or other media. Linux knows about different file system types (such as Linux ext3 and reiserfs file systems, or VFAT and NTFS from Windows systems) and how to manage them.

✦ **Security** — Like UNIX, Linux was built from the ground up to enable multiple users to access the system simultaneously. To protect each user's resources, every file, directory, and application is assigned sets of read, write, and execute permissions that define who can access them. In a standard Linux system, the root user has access to the entire system, some special logins have access to control particular services (such as Apache for Web services), and users can be assigned permission individually or in groups. Recent features, such as Security-Enhanced Linux, enable more refined tuning, and protection in highly secure computing environments.

What I have just described are components that primarily make up what is referred to as the Linux *kernel*. In fact, the Linux kernel (which was created and is still managed by Linus Torvalds) is what gives Linux its name. The kernel is the software that starts up when you boot your computer and manages the programs you use so they can communicate effectively and simply with your computer hardware.

Other components, such as administrative commands and applications, are added to the kernel from other open source projects to make Linux a complete operating system. The GNU project, in particular, contributed many components that are now in Linux. (GNU, Apache, KDE, GNOME, and other key open source projects in Linux are discussed a bit later.) Those other projects added such things as:

✦ **Graphical user interfaces (GUIs)** — Consisting of a graphical framework (typically the X Window System), window managers, panels, icons, and menus. GUIs enable you to use Linux with a keyboard and mouse combination, instead of just typing commands (as was done in the old days).

✦ **Administrative utilities** — Including hundreds (perhaps thousands) of commands and graphical windows to do such things as add users, manage disks, monitor the network, install software, and generally secure and manage your computer.

✦ **Applications** — Although no Linux distribution includes all of them, there are literally thousands of games, office productivity tools, Web browsers, chat windows, multimedia players, and other applications available for Linux.

✦ **Programming tools** — Including programming utilities for creating applications and libraries for implementing specialty interfaces.

✦ **Server features** — Enabling you to offer services from your Linux computer to another computer on the network. In other words, while Linux includes Web browsers to view Web pages, it can also be the computer that serves up Web pages to others. Popular server features include Web, mail, database, printer, file, DNS, and DHCP servers.

Once Linus Torvalds and friends had a working Linux kernel, pulling together a complete open source operating system was possible. The reason this could be done was because so much of the available "free" software was:

✦ Covered by the GNU Public License (GPL) or similar license. That allowed the entire operating system to be freely distributed, provided that some guidelines were followed relating to how the source code for that software was made available going forward.

✦ Based on UNIX-like systems. Clones of virtually all the other user-level components of a UNIX system had been created. Those and other utilities and applications were built to run on UNIX or other UNIX-like systems.

Linux has become the culmination of the open source software movement. But the traditions of sharing code and building communities that made Linux possible started years before Linux was born. You could argue that it began in a comfortable think tank known as Bell Laboratories.

What's So Cool About Linux?

If you have not used Linux before, you should expect a few things to be different from other operating systems. Here is a brief list of some features that you might find cool about using Linux:

✦ **No rebooting to install** — Uptime is valued as a matter of pride (remember, Linux and other UNIX systems are most often used as servers, which are expected to stay up 24x7). After the original installation, you can install or remove most software without having to reboot your computer.

✦ **Start/stop services without interrupting others** — You can start and stop individual services (such as Web, file, and e-mail services) without rebooting or even interrupting the work of any other users or features of the computer. In other words, you should not have to reboot your computer every time someone sneezes.

✦ **Portable software** — You can usually change to another Linux, UNIX, or BSD system and still use the exact same software! Most open source software projects were created to run on any UNIX-like system, and many also run on Windows systems, if you need them to. If it won't run where you want it to, chances are that you, or someone you hire, can port it to the computer you want.

✦ **Downloadable applications** — If the applications you want are not delivered with your version of Linux, you can often download and install them with a single command, using tools such as apt and yum.

✦ **No settings hidden in code or registries** — Once you learn your way around Linux, you'll find that (given the right permissions on your computer) most configuration is done in plain-text files that are easy to find and change.

✦ **Mature desktop** — The X Window System (providing the framework for your Linux desktop) has been around longer than Microsoft Windows. The KDE and GNOME desktop environments provide graphical interfaces (windows, menus, icons, and so forth) that rival those on Microsoft systems. Ease-of-use problems with Linux systems are rapidly evaporating.

✦ **Freedom** — Linux, in its most basic form, has no corporate agenda or bottom line to meet. You are free to choose the Linux distribution that suits you, look at the code that runs the system, add and remove any software you like, and make your computer do what you want it to do.

Some aspects of Linux make it hard for some new users to get started. One is that Linux is typically set up to be secure by default, so you need to adjust to using an administrative login (root) to make most changes that affect the whole computer system. Although this can be a bit inconvenient, trust me, it makes your computer safer than just letting anyone do anything.

For the same reason, many services are off by default, so you need to turn them on and do at least minimal configuration to get them going. Linux can be more difficult than Windows because it is just different, but because you're reading this book, I assume you want to learn about those differences.

Exploring Linux History

Some histories of Linux begin with this message posted by Linus Torvalds to the comp.os.minix newsgroup on August 25, 1991:

Hello everybody out there using minix -

I'm doing a (free) operating system (just a hobby, won't be big and professional like gnu) for 386(486) AT clones. This has been brewing since april, and is starting to get ready. I'd like any feedback on things people like/dislike in minix, as my OS resembles it somewhat (same physical layout of the file-system (due to practical reasons) among other things)... Any suggestions are welcome, but I won't promise I'll implement them :-)

Linus (torvalds@kruuna.helsinki.fi)

PS. Yes — it's free of any minix code, and it has a multi-threaded fs. It is NOT protable[sic] (uses 386 task switching etc), and it probably never will support anything other than AT-harddisks, as that's all I have :-(.

Reprinted from Linux International Web site (`www.li.org/linuxhistory.php`)

Minix was a free UNIX-like operating system that ran on PCs in the early 1990s. Like Minix, Linux was also a clone of the UNIX operating system. To truly appreciate how a free operating system could have been modeled after a proprietary system from AT&T Bell Laboratories, it helps to understand the culture in which UNIX was created and the chain of events that made the essence of UNIX possible to reproduce freely.

From a Free-Flowing UNIX Culture at Bell Labs

From the very beginning, the UNIX operating system was created and nurtured in a communal environment. Its creation was not driven by market needs but by a desire to overcome impediments to producing programs. AT&T, which owned the UNIX trademark originally, eventually made UNIX into a commercial product, but by that time, many of the concepts (and even much of the early code) that made UNIX special had fallen into the public domain.

If you are under 30 years old, you may not remember a time when AT&T was "the" phone company. Up until the early 1980s, AT&T didn't have to think much about competition because if you wanted a phone in the United States, you had to go to AT&T. It had the luxury of funding pure research projects. The Mecca for such projects was the Bell Laboratories site in Murray Hill, New Jersey.

After the failure of a project called Multics around 1969, Bell Labs employees Ken Thompson and Dennis Ritchie set off on their own to create an operating system that would offer an improved environment for developing software. Up to that time, most programs were written on punch cards that had to be fed in batches to mainframe computers. In a 1980 lecture on "The Evolution of the UNIX Time-sharing System," Dennis Ritchie summed up the spirit that started UNIX:

What we wanted to preserve was not just a good environment in which to do programming, but a system around which a fellowship could form. We knew from experience that the essence of communal computing as supplied by remote-access, time-shared machines is not just to type programs into a terminal instead of a keypunch, but to encourage close communication.

The simplicity and power of the UNIX design began breaking down barriers that impeded software developers. The foundation of UNIX was set with several key elements:

✦ **The UNIX file system** — After creating the structure that allowed levels of subdirectories (which, for today's desktop users, looks like folders inside of folders), UNIX could be used to organize the files and directories in intuitive ways. Furthermore, complex methods of accessing disks, tapes, and other devices were greatly simplified by representing those devices as individual device files that you could also access as items in a directory.

✦ **Input/output redirection** — Early UNIX systems also included the concept of input redirection and pipes. From a command line, UNIX users could direct the output of a command to a file using a right arrow key (>). Later, the concepts of pipes was added (|) where the output of one command could be directed to the input of another command. For example, the command line

```
$ cat file1 file2 | sort | pr | lpr
```

concatenates (cat) file1 and file2, sorts (sort) the lines in those files alphabetically, paginates the sorted text for printing (pr), and directs the output to the computer's default printer (lpr). This method of directing input and output enabled developers to create their own specialized utilities that could be joined together with existing utilities. This modularity made it possible for lots of code to be developed by lots of different people.

✦ **Portability** — Much of the early work in simplifying the experience of using UNIX led to its also becoming extraordinarily portable to run on different computers. By having device drivers (represented by files in the file system tree), UNIX could present an interface to applications in such a way that the programs didn't have to know about the details of the underlying hardware. To later port UNIX to another system, developers only had to change the drivers. The applications program didn't have to change for different hardware!

To make the concept of portability a reality, however, a high-level programming language was needed to implement the software needed. To that end, Brian Kernighan and Dennis Ritchie created the C programming language. In 1973, UNIX was rewritten in C. Today, C is still the primary language used to create the UNIX (and Linux) operating system kernels.

As Ritchie went on to say in his 1980 lecture:

> *Today, the only important UNIX program still written in assembler is the assembler itself; virtually all the utility programs are in C, and so are most of the applications programs, although there are sites with many in Fortran, Pascal, and Algol 68 as well. It seems certain that much of the success of UNIX follows from the readability, modifiability, and portability of its software that in turn follows from its expression in high-level languages.*

If you are a Linux enthusiast and are interested in what features from the early days of Linux have survived, an interesting read is Dennis Ritchie's reprint of the first UNIX programmer's manual (dated November 3, 1971). You can find it at Dennis Ritchie's Web site: `http://cm.bell-labs.com/cm/cs/who/dmr/1stEdman.html`. The form of this documentation is UNIX man pages—which is still the primary format for documenting UNIX and Linux operating system commands and programming tools today.

What's clear as you read through the early documentation and accounts of the UNIX system is that the development was a free-flowing process, lacked ego, and was dedicated to making UNIX excellent. This process led to a sharing of code (both inside and outside of Bell Labs) that allowed rapid development of a high-quality UNIX operating system. It also led to an operating system that AT&T would find difficult to reel back in later.

To a Commercialized UNIX

Before AT&T divestiture in 1984, when it was split up into AT&T and seven "baby Bell" companies, AT&T was forbidden to sell computer systems. Companies you now know by names such as Verizon, Qwest, SBC Communications, and Lucent Technologies were all part of AT&T. As a result of AT&T's monopoly of the telephone system, the U.S. government was concerned that an unrestricted AT&T might dominate the fledgling computer industry.

Because AT&T was restricted from selling computers directly to customers before its divestiture, UNIX source code was licensed to universities for a nominal fee. There was no UNIX operating system for sale from AT&T that you didn't have to compile yourself.

BSD Arrives

In 1975, UNIX V6 became the first version of UNIX available for widespread use outside of Bell Laboratories. From this early UNIX source code, the first major variant of UNIX was created at University of California at Berkeley. It was named the Berkeley Software Distribution (BSD).

For most of the next decade, the BSD and Bell Labs versions of UNIX headed off in separate directions. BSD continued forward in the free-flowing, share-the-code manner that was the hallmark of the early Bell Labs UNIX, while AT&T started steering UNIX toward commercialization. With the formation of a separate UNIX Laboratory, which moved out of Murray Hill and down the road to Summit, New Jersey, AT&T began its attempts to commercialize UNIX. By 1984, divestiture was behind AT&T, and it was ready to really start selling UNIX.

UNIX Laboratory and Commercialization

The UNIX Laboratory was considered a jewel that couldn't quite find a home or a way to make a profit. As it moved between Bell Laboratories and other areas of AT&T, its name changed several times. It is probably best remembered by its last name, which it had as it began its spin off from AT&T: UNIX System Laboratories (USL).

The UNIX source code that came out of USL, the legacy of which is now owned by Santa Cruz Operation (SCO), is being used as the basis for lawsuits by SCO against major Linux vendors (such as IBM and Red Hat Inc.). Because of that, I think the efforts from USL that have contributed to the success of Linux are sometimes disrespected.

You have to remember that, during the 1980s, many computer companies were afraid that a newly divested AT&T would pose more of a threat to controlling the computer industry than would an upstart company in Redmond, Washington. To calm the fears of IBM, Intel, DEC, and other computer companies, the UNIX Lab made the following commitments to ensure a level playing field:

✦ **Source code only**—Instead of producing its own boxed set of UNIX, AT&T continued to only sell source code and to make it available equally to all licensees. Each company would then port UNIX to its own equipment. It wasn't until about 1992, when the lab was spun off as a joint venture with Novell (called Univel) and then eventually sold to Novell, that a commercial boxed set of UNIX (called UnixWare) was produced directly from that source code.

✦ **Published interfaces**—To create an environment of fairness and community to its OEMs (original equipment manufacturers), AT&T began standardizing what different ports of UNIX had to be able to do to still be called UNIX. To that end, compliance with POSIX standards and the AT&T UNIX System V Interface Definition (SVID) were specifications UNIX vendors could use to create compliant UNIX systems. Those same documents also served as road maps for the creation of Linux.

Note In an early e-mail newsgroup post from Linus Torvalds, Linux makes a request for a copy, preferably online, of the POSIX standard. I think that nobody from AT&T expected someone to actually be able to write their own clone of UNIX from those interfaces without using any of its UNIX source code.

✦ **Technical approach**—Again, until the very end of USL, most decisions on the direction of UNIX were made based on technical considerations. Management was promoted up through the technical ranks, and there was never any talk that I heard of writing software to break other companies' software or otherwise restrict the success of USL's partners.

When USL eventually started taking on marketing experts and creating a desktop UNIX product for end users, Microsoft Windows already had a firm grasp on the desktop market. Also, because the direction of UNIX had always been toward source code licensing destined for large computing systems, USL had pricing difficulties for its products. For example, on software it was including with UNIX, USL found itself having to pay out per-computer licensing fees that were based on $100,000 mainframes instead of $2,000 PCs. Add to that the fact that no application programs were available with UNIXWare, and you can see why the endeavor failed.

Successful marketing of UNIX systems at the time, however, was happening with other computer companies. SCO had found a niche market, primarily selling PC versions of UNIX running dumb terminals in small offices. Sun Microsystems was selling lots of UNIX workstations (originally based on BSD but which was merged with UNIX in SVR4) for programmers and high-end technology applications (such as stock trading).

Other commercial UNIXs were also emerging by the 1980s as well. This new ownership assertion of UNIX was beginning to take its toll on the spirit of open contributions. Lawsuits were being raised to protect UNIX source code and trademarks. In 1984, this new, restrictive UNIX gave rise to an organization that eventually led a path to Linux: the Free Software Foundation.

To a GNU Free-Flowing (Not) UNIX

In 1984, Richard M. Stallman started the GNU project (www.gnu.org), recursively named by the phrase GNU is Not UNIX. As a project of the Free Software Foundation (FSF), GNU was intended to become a recoding of the entire UNIX operating system that could be freely distributed.

While rewriting millions of lines of code might seem daunting to one or two people, spreading the effort across dozens, or even hundreds, of programmers made the project possible. It turned out that not only could the same results be gained by all new code, but that in some cases that code was better than the original UNIX versions. Because everyone could see the code being produced for the project, poorly written code could be corrected quickly or replaced over time.

If you are familiar with UNIX, try searching the more than 3,400 GNU software packages for your favorite UNIX commands from the Free Software Directory (http://directory.fsf.org/GNU). Chances are you will find it there, along with many, many other software projects available as add-ons.

Over time, the term *free software* has been mostly replaced by the term *open source software*. This helps bring home the fact that, while you are free to use the software as you like, you have some responsibility to make the improvements you make to the code available to others. In that way, everyone in the community can benefit from your work as you have benefited from others'.

To clearly define how open source software should be handled, the GNU software project created the GNU Public License. Although there are many other software licenses covering slightly different approaches to protecting free software, the GPL is perhaps the most well known — and it's the one that covers the Linux kernel itself. Basic features of the GNU Public License include:

✦ **Author rights** — The original author retains the rights to his or her software.

✦ **Free distribution** — People can use the GNU software in their own software, changing and redistributing it as they please. They do, however, have to include the source code with their distribution (or make it easily available).

✦ **Copyright maintained** — Even if you were to repackage and resell the software, the original GNU agreement must be maintained with the software, which means all future recipients of the software have the opportunity to change the source code, just as you did.

There is no warranty on GNU software. If something goes wrong, the original developer of the software has no obligation to fix the problem. However, many organizations, big and small, offer paid support packages for the software when it is included in their Linux or other open source software distribution. (See the "OSI Open Source Definition" section later in this chapter for a more detailed definition of open source software.)

Despite its success producing thousands of UNIX utilities, the GNU project itself failed to produce one critical piece of code: the kernel. Its attempts to build an open source kernel with the GNU Hurd project (www.gnu.org/software/hurd) were unsuccessful.

BSD Loses Some Steam

The one software project that had a chance of beating out Linux to be the premier open source software project was the venerable old BSD project. By the late 1980s, BSD developers at UC Berkeley realized that they had already rewritten most of the UNIX source code they had received a decade earlier.

In 1989, UCB distributed its own UNIX-like code as Net/1 and later (in 1991) as Net/2. Just as UC Berkeley was preparing a complete, UNIX-like operating system that was free from all AT&T code, AT&T hit them with a lawsuit in 1992. The suit claimed that the software was written using trade secrets taken from AT&T's UNIX system.

The lawsuit was dropped when Novell bought UNIX System Laboratories from AT&T in 1994. But, during that critical time period, there was enough fear and doubt about the legality of the BSD code that the momentum BSD had gained to that point in the fledgling open source community was lost. Many people started looking for another open source alternative. The time was ripe for a college student from Finland who was working on his own kernel.

Linus Builds the Missing Piece

In 1991, Linus Torvalds, a student at the University of Helsinki, Finland, started work on a UNIX-like kernel because he wanted to be able to use the same kind of operating system on his home PC that he used at school. At the time, Linus was using Minix, but he wanted to go beyond what the Minix standards permitted.

As noted earlier, Linus announced the first public version of the Linux kernel to the comp.os.minix newsgroup on August 25, 1991. Although Linus guesses that the first version didn't actually come out until mid-September of that year (see the Linux International Web site's Linux History page: www.li.org/linuxhistory.php).

Although Torvalds stated that Linux was written for the 386 processor and probably wasn't portable, others persisted in encouraging (and contributing to) a more portable approach in the early versions of Linux. By October 5, Linux 0.02 was released with much of the original assembly code rewritten in the C programming language, which made it possible to start porting it to other machines.

The Linux kernel was the last — and the most important — piece of code that was needed to complete a whole UNIX-like operating system under the GPL. So, when people started putting together distributions, the name Linux and not GNU is what stuck. Some distributions such as Debian, however, refer to themselves as GNU/Linux distributions.

Within the next few years, commercial and noncommercial Linux distributions began to emerge. MCC Interim Linux (ftp.mcc.ac.uk/pub/linux/distributions/MCC) was released in the U.K. in February 1992. Slackware Linux (described in Chapter 14), which was first released in April 1993, is one of the oldest surviving Linux distributions.

Today, Linux can be described as an open source UNIX-like operating system that reflects a combination of SVID, POSIX, and BSD compliance. Linux continues to aim toward compliance with POSIX as well as with standards set by the new owner of the UNIX trademark, The Open Group (www.unix-systems.org).

The nonprofit Open Source Development Labs (www.osdl.org), which employs Linus Torvalds, manages the direction today of Linux development efforts. Its sponsors' list is like a who's who of commercial Linux vendors, including IBM, Red Hat, SUSE (Novell), VA Software, HP, Dell, Computer Associates, Intel, Cisco Systems, and others. OSDL's primary charter is to accelerate the growth of Linux in telecommunications and data centers.

Although much of the thrust of corporate Linux efforts is on corporate, enterprise computing, huge improvements are continuing in the desktop arena as well. The KDE and GNOME desktop environments continuously improve the Linux experience for casual users. Major efforts are underway to offer critical pieces of desktop components that are still not available in open source versions, including multimedia software and office productivity applications.

Linus continues to maintain and improve the Linux kernel.

Note   To get more detailed histories of Linux, I recommend visiting the LWN.net site. LWN.net has kept a detailed Linux timeline from 1998 to the present day. For example, the 2003 timeline is available at `http://lwn.net/Articles/Timeline2003`.

What's So Great About Linux?

Leveraging work done on UNIX and GNU projects helped to get Linux up and running quickly. The culture of sharing in the open source community and adoption of a wide array of tools for communicating on the Internet have helped Linux to move quickly through infancy and adolescence to become a mature operating system.

The simple commitment to share code is probably the single most powerful contributor to the growth of the open source software movement in general, and Linux in particular. That commitment has also encouraged involvement from the kind of people who are willing to contribute back to that community in all kinds of ways.

The following sections characterize Linux and the communities that support it.

OSI Open Source Definition

For software developers, Linux provides a platform that lets them change the operating system as they like and get a wide range of help creating the applications they need. One of the watchdogs of the open source movement is the Open Source Initiative (`www.opensource.org`). This is how the OSI Web site describes open source software:

> The basic idea behind open source is very simple: When programmers can read, redistribute, and modify the source code for a piece of software, the software evolves. People improve it, people adapt it, people fix bugs. And this can happen at a speed that, if one is used to the slow pace of conventional software development, seems astonishing.

> We in the open source community have learned that this rapid evolutionary process produces better software than the traditional closed model, in which only a very few programmers can see the source and everybody else must blindly use an opaque block of bits.

While the primary goal of open source software is to make source code available, other goals are also defined by OSI in its Open Source Definition. Most of the following rules for acceptable open source licenses are to protect the freedom and integrity of the open source code:

✦ **Free distribution** — An open source license can't require a fee from anyone who resells the software.

✦ **Source code** — The source code has to be included with the software and not be restricted from being redistributed.

✦ **Derived works** — The license must allow modification and redistribution of the code under the same terms.

✦ **Integrity of the author's source code** — The license may require that those who use the source code remove the original project's name or version if they change the source code.

✦ **No discrimination against persons or groups** — The license must allow all people to be equally eligible to use the source code.

✦ **No discrimination against fields of endeavor** — The license can't restrict a project from using the source code because it is commercial or because it is associated with a field of endeavor that the software provider doesn't like.

✦ **Distribution of license** — No additional license should be needed to use and redistribute the software.

✦ **License must not be specific to a product** — The license can't restrict the source code to a particular software distribution.

✦ **License must not restrict other software** — The license can't prevent someone from including the open source software on the same medium as non-open source software.

✦ **License must be technology-neutral** — The license can't restrict methods in which the source code can be redistributed.

Open source licenses used by software development projects must meet these criteria to be accepted as open source software by OSI. More than 40 different licenses are accepted by OSI to be used to label software as "OSI Certified Open Source Software." In addition to GPL, other popular OSI-approved licenses include:

✦ **LGPL** — The GNU Lesser General Public License (LGPL) allows people to redistribute certain software but not change its contents. This license is often used for distributing libraries that other application programs depend upon.

✦ **BSD** — The Berkeley Software Distribution License allows redistribution of source code, with the requirement that the source code keep the BSD copyright notice and not use the names of contributors to endorse or promote derived software without written permission.

✦ **MIT** — The MIT license is like the BSD license except that it doesn't include the endorsement and promotion requirement.

✦ **Mozilla** — The Mozilla license covers use and redistribution of source code associated with the Mozilla Web browser and related software. It is a much longer license than the others just mentioned because it contains more definitions of how contributors and those reusing the source code should behave. This includes submitting a file of changes when submitting modifications and that those making their own additions to the code for redistribution should be aware of patent issues or other restrictions associated with their code.

The end result of open source code is software that has more flexibility to grow and fewer boundaries in how it can be used. Many believe that the fact that many people look over the source code for a project will result in higher-quality software for everyone. As open source advocate Eric S. Raymond says in an often-quoted line, "Many eyes make all bugs shallow."

Vibrant Communities

Communities of professionals and enthusiasts have grown around Linux and its related open source projects. Many have shown themselves willing to devote their time, knowledge, and skills on public mailing lists, forums, Wikis, and other Internet venues (provided you ask politely and aren't too annoying).

Linux User Groups (LUGs) have sprung up all over the world. Many LUGs sponsor Linux installfests (where members help you install the Linux of your choice on your computer) or help nonprofit groups and schools use Linux on older computers that will no longer support the latest Microsoft Windows software. The LUG I'm a member of holds monthly meetings to give talks on Linux topics and has an active Web site, mailing list, and chat server where we can help each other with Linux questions that come up.

Free online bulletin board services have sprung up to get information on specific Linux topics. Popular general Linux forums are available from www.LinuxQuestions.org, www.LinuxForums.org, and www.LinuxHelp.net. Most of these sites are built with open source software (see www.e107.org and www.phpBB.com for examples of open source forum software).

Communities also gather around specific software projects and Linux distributions. www.Sourceforge.net is home to thousands of open source software projects. Go to the Sourceforge.net site and try keyword searches for topics that interest you (for example, image gallery or video editing). Each project provides links to project home pages, forums, and software download sites. There are always projects looking for people to help write code or documentation or just participate in discussions.

You'll find that most major Linux distributions have associated mailing lists and forums. You can go directly to the Web sites for Red Hat Fedora Linux (`www.redhat.com/fedora`), Debian (`www.debian.com`), SUSE (`www.suse.com`), Gentoo (`www.gentoo.org`), and others to learn how to participate in forums and contribute to those projects.

Major Software Projects

Some software projects have grown beyond the status of being simply a component of Linux or some other UNIX derivative. Some of these projects are sponsored and maintained by organizations that oversee multiple open source projects. This section introduces some of the most popular open source projects and organizations.

The Apache Software Foundation (`www.apache.org`) is not only the world's most popular open source Web server software, it's the most popular of all Web server software. Most Linux distributions that contain server software include Apache. The Apache Software Foundation maintains the Apache Web (HTTP) server and about a dozen other projects, including SpamAssassin (for blocking and filtering e-mail spam), Apache Portals (to provide portal software), and a bunch of projects for producing modules to use with your Apache Web server.

The Internet Systems Consortium (`www.isc.org`) supports critical Internet infrastructure projects under open source licenses. Those projects include Bind (DNS server software), DHCP (to assign IP addresses and other information to Internet clients), INN (for creating Internet news servers), and OpenReg (a tool for managing delegation of domains in a shared registry).

The Free Software Foundation (`www.fsf.org`) is the principal sponsor of the GNU Project. Most of the UNIX commands and utilities included in Linux that were not closely associated with the kernel were produced under the umbrella of the GNU project.

The Mozilla (`www.mozilla.org`) project's most well-known product is the very popular open source Web browser Mozilla Navigator, which was originally based on code released to the open source community from Netscape Communicator. Most other open source browsers incorporate Mozilla's engine. The Mozilla project also offers related e-mail, composer, IRC Chat, and address book software. New projects include the Thunderbird e-mail and news client and Firefox Web browser.

The Sendmail (`www.sendmail.org`) Consortium maintains the sendmail mail transport agent, which is the world's most popular software for transporting mail across the Internet.

There are, of course, many more open source projects and organizations that provide software included in various Linux distributions, but the ones discussed here will give you a good feel for the kind of organizations that produce open source software.

Linux Myths, Legends, and FUD

The unlikely rise in the popularity of Linux has led to rampant (and sometimes strange) speculation about all the terrible things it could lead to or, conversely, to almost manic declarations of how Linux will solve all the problems of the world. I'll try as best I can (with my own admitted bias toward Linux) to present facts to address beliefs about Linux and to combat some of the unrealistic fear, uncertainty, and doubt (FUD) being spread by those with a vested interest in seeing Linux not succeed.

Can You Stop Worrying About Viruses?

Well, you can (and should) always worry about the security of any computer connected to the Internet. At the moment, however, you are probably less likely to get a virus from infected e-mail or untrusted Web sites with standard e-mail clients and Web browsers that come with Linux systems than you would with those that come with the average Microsoft Windows system.

The most commonly cited warnings to back up that statement come in a report from the United States Computer Emergency Readiness Team (CERT) regarding a vulnerability in Microsoft Internet Explorer (www.kb.cert.org/vuls/id/713878):

> There are a number of significant vulnerabilities in technologies relating to the IE domain/zone security model, the DHTML object model, MIME type determination, and ActiveX. It is possible to reduce exposure to these vulnerabilities by using a different Web browser, especially when browsing untrusted sites. Such a decision may, however, reduce the functionality of sites that require IE-specific features such as DHTML, VBScript, and ActiveX. Note that using a different Web browser will not remove IE from a Windows system, and other programs may invoke IE, the WebBrowser ActiveX control, or the HTML rendering engine (MSHTML).
>
> —US-CERT Vulnerability Note VU#713878

While the note also recommends keeping up with patches from Microsoft to reduce your risks, it seems that the only real solutions are to disable Active scripting and ActiveX, use plain-text e-mail, and don't visit sites you don't trust with Internet Explorer. In other words, use a browser that disables insecure features included in Microsoft products.

This announcement apparently caused quite a run on the Mozilla.org site to download a Mozilla or Firefox browser and related e-mail client (described in Chapter 21 of this book). Versions of those software projects run on Windows and Mac OS X, as well as on Linux. Many believe that browsers such as Mozilla are inherently more secure because they don't allow nonstandard Web features that might do such things as automatically download unrequested software without your knowledge.

Of course, no matter what browser or e-mail client you are using, you need to follow good security practices (such as not opening attachments or downloading files you don't trust). Also, as open source browsers and e-mail clients, such as those from Mozilla.org, become more popular, the number of possible machines to infect through those applications will make it more tempting to virus writers. (At the moment, most viruses and worms are created specifically to attack Microsoft software.)

Will You Be Sued for Using Linux?

In the United States, anyone can try to sue anyone for anything. That doesn't mean that the people who bring lawsuits will win, but they can try. So far, the threat to individuals has not been substantial, but there have been some well-financed lawsuits against Linux providers. Those with litigation against Linux have gone primarily after big companies, such as IBM, Novell, and Red Hat Inc., and have made only vague threats regarding end users of Linux. Linus Torvalds himself is the rare individual who has been named in lawsuits.

The SCO Lawsuits

The lawsuits getting the most press these days are the ones involving Santa Cruz Operation (SCO). SCO is the current owner of the UNIX source code that passed from AT&T Bell Labs to UNIX System Laboratories to Univel (a lot of people don't know that one) to Novell and eventually to the company formed by joining SCO and Caldera Systems.

Although the particulars of the claims seem to change daily, SCO's basic assertion in lawsuits against IBM and others is that Linux contains UNIX System V source code that is owned by SCO, so those who sell or use Linux owe licensing fees to SCO. To a layman (I am not a lawyer!), the assertions seem weak based on the fact that:

✦ There seems to be no original UNIX code in Linux. And, even if a small amount of code that could be proved to be owned by SCO had made it in there by mistake, that code could be easily dropped and rewritten.

✦ Concepts that created UNIX all seem to be in the public domain, with public specifications of UNIX interfaces blessed by AT&T itself in the form of published POSIX and System V Interface Definition standards.

✦ AT&T dropped a similar lawsuit in 1994 against BSD, which had actually started with UNIX source code but had rewritten it completely over the years.

✦ Exactly what SCO owns has been brought into question because Novell still claims some rights to the UNIX code it sold to SCO. (In fact, SCO doesn't even own the UNIX trademark, which Novell gave away to the Open Group before it sold the source code to SCO. Attempts were underway in 2004 by SCO to trademark the name UNIX System Laboratories.)

Responses to SCO's lawsuits (which certainly hold more weight than any explanations I could offer) are available from Open Group (`www.opengroup.org`), OSDL (`www.osdl.org`), IBM (`ibm.com/linux`), and Red Hat (`www.redhat.com`). If you are interested in the paper trail relating SCO's ownership of UNIX, I recommend the Novell's Unique Legal Rights page (`www.novell.com/licensing/indemnity/legal.html`).

OSDL.org has prepared a legal defense fund to protect Linux end users and other Linux litigants (including Linus and OSDL itself). You can read about this fund at ODSL's Linux Legal Defense Fund page (`www.osdl.org/about_osdl/legal/lldf`).

Software Patents

Few will argue that it is illegal for someone to copy a software company's code and redistribute it without permission. However, the concept of being able to patent an idea that a company might incorporate in its code has become a major point of contention in recent years. Can someone patent the idea of clicking an icon to open a window?

Software companies are scrambling to file thousands of patents relating to how software is used. While those companies may never create products based on those patents, the restrictions those patents might place on other software companies or open source software development is a major issue.

The EuroLinux Alliance is a group dedicated to "protecting software freedom based on copyright, open standards, open competition, and open source software, such as Linux." EuroLinux is filing a petition in the European Parliament and European Council to warn about the dangers of software patents. To find out more, go to `http://eurolinux.org`.

Other Litigious Issues

Particularly contentious legal issues surround audio and video software. In Red Hat Linux 8, Red Hat Inc. removed support for MP3 and DVD players because of questions about licensing associated with those music and movie formats. Red Hat's advice at the time was to download and install the players yourself for personal use. Red Hat didn't want to distribute those players because companies owning patents related to certain audio and video encoders might ask Red Hat to pay licensing fees for distributing those players (see `www.redhat.com/advice/speaks_80mm.html`).

Check with an attorney about into any legal issues that concern you.

Can Linux Really Run on Everything from Handhelds to Supercomputers?

Linux is extraordinarily scalable and runs on everything from handhelds to super-computers. Features in the Linux 2.6 kernel have been particularly aimed at making the kernel easier to port to embedded Linux systems as well as large multiprocessor, enterprise-quality servers.

Will Linux Crush Microsoft?

Linux doesn't seem to be trouncing Microsoft, although the rhetoric from Microsoft has targeted Linux as a particular threat in the server area. Microsoft is still the most popular desktop operating system in the world, holding more than 90% of the desktop market, by most accounts.

Major inroads into the desktop market by Linux systems are expected to be slow in coming. However, the area where desktop Linux systems are making the greatest gains are in low-end, mass-market computers. For less than $300, you can buy a decent computer with Linspire Linux pre-installed from Wal-Mart, PC Clubs, or several other retailers. Because it is Linux, the system comes with a boatload of applications as well (not Microsoft Office, but OpenOffice.org instead). (Linspire is discussed in Chapter 15.)

So far, most of the market share that Linux has gained has been taken from other UNIX systems, such as those from Sun Microsystems. Apache Web servers running on Linux are already considered the world's most popular Web servers. With efforts underway from the likes of IBM, Oracle, Red Hat, and Novell, major pushes into the Enterprise market are already taking place. But Linux is still some distance from crushing Microsoft.

Are You on Your Own If You Use Linux?

If you are new to Linux and are concerned about support, there are several compa-nies offering well-supported versions of Linux. Those include Red Hat Enterprise Linux (from Red Hat Inc.) and SUSE Linux (from Novell, Inc.), as well as a number of other smaller players. In the corporate arena, add IBM to that list.

As noted earlier, there are also many community sites on the Internet that offer forums, mailing lists, and other venues for getting help if you get stuck.

Is Linux Only for Geeks?

It doesn't hurt to be a geek if you want to fully explore all the potential of your Linux system. However, with a good desktop Linux distribution, tremendous improvements over the past few years relating to ease of use and features have made it possible to do most things you would do on any Mac or Windows system without being a Linux expert.

Start with a Linux system that uses the KDE or GNOME desktop. Simple menus let you select word processors, Web browsers, games, and dozens of other applications you commonly use on other operating systems. In most cases, you'll get along fine just using your mouse to work with windows, menus, and forms.

With Linux distributions that offer graphical tools for basic system administration (such as configuring a printer or network connection), you can be led through most tasks you need to do. Fedora, Red Hat Enterprise Linux, and SUSE are good examples of Linux distributions that offer simplified administration tools. With a basic understanding of the Linux shell (see Chapter 2) and some help from a Linux forum, you should be able to troubleshoot almost anything that goes wrong.

How Do Companies Make Money with Linux?

Open source enthusiasts believe that better software can result from an open source software development model than from proprietary development models. So in theory, any company creating software for its own use can save money by adding its software contributions with those of others to gain a much better end product for themselves.

Companies that want to make money selling software need to be more creative than they were in the old days. While you can sell the software you create that includes GPL software, you must pass the source code of that software forward. Of course, others can then recompile that product, basically using your product without charge. Here are a few ways that companies are dealing with that issue:

✦ **Software subscriptions** — Red Hat sells its Red Hat Enterprise Linux products on a subscription basis. For a certain amount of money per year, you get binary code to run Linux (so you don't have to compile it yourself), guaranteed support, tools for tracking the hardware and software on your computer, and access to the company's knowledge base.

Although Red Hat's Fedora project includes much of the same software and is also available in binary form, there are no guarantees associated with the software or future updates of that software. A small office or personal user might take a risk on Fedora (which is itself an excellent operating system), but a big company that's running mission-critical applications will probably put down a few dollars for RHEL.

✦ **Donations** — Many open source projects accept donations from open source individuals or companies that use code from their projects. Amazingly, many open source projects support one or two developers and run exclusively on donations.

✦ **Bounties** — The concept of software bounties is a fascinating way for open source software companies to make money. Let's say that you are using XYZ software package and you need a new feature right away. By paying a software bounty to the project itself, or to other software developers, you can have your needed improvements moved to the head of the queue. The software you pay for will remain covered by its open source license, but you will have the features you need, at probably a fraction of the cost of building the project from scratch.

✦ **Boxed sets, mugs, and T-shirts** — Many open source projects have online stores where you can buy boxed sets (some people still like physical CDs and hard copies of documentation) and a variety of mugs, T-shirts, mouse pads, and other items. If you really love a project, for goodness sake, buy a T-shirt!

This is in no way an exhaustive list because more creative ways are being invented every day to support those who create open source software. Remember that many people have become contributors to and maintainers of open source software because they needed or wanted the software themselves. The contributions they make for free are worth the return they get from others who do the same.

How Different Are Linux Distributions from One Another?

Although different Linux systems will add different logos, choose some different software components to include, and have different ways of installing and configuring Linux, most people who become used to Linux can move pretty easily from one Linux to another. There are a few reasons for this.

✦ **Linux Standard Base** — There is an effort called the Linux Standard Base (www.linuxbase.org) to which most major Linux systems subscribe. The Linux Standard Base Specification (available from this site) has as one of its primary goals to ensure that applications written for one Linux system will work on other systems. To that end, the LSB will define what libraries need to be available, how software packages can be formatted, commands and utilities that must be available, and, to some extent, how the file system should be arranged. In other words, you can rely on many components of Linux being in the same place on LSB-certified Linux systems.

✦ **Open source projects** — Many Linux distributions include the same open source projects. So, for example, the most basic command and configuration files for an Apache Web server, Samba file/print server, and sendmail mail server will be the same whether you use Red Hat, Debian, or many other Linux systems. And although they can change backgrounds, colors, and other elements of your desktop, most of the ways of navigating a KDE or GNOME desktop stay the same, regardless of which Linux you use.

✦ **A shell is a shell**—Although you can put different pretty faces on it, once you open a shell command-line interpreter (such as bash or sh) in Linux, most experienced Linux or UNIX users find it pretty easy to get around on most any Linux system. For that reason, I recommend that if you are serious about using Linux, you take some time to try the shell (as described in Chapter 2). Additionally, Chapters 23 through 26 focus on command-line and configuration-file interfaces for setting up servers because learning those ways of configuring servers will make your skills most portable across different Linux systems.

Is the Linux Mascot Really a Penguin?

Figure 1-1 shows the penguin logo that Linus Torvalds approved as the official Linux mascot. His name is Tux. Use of this logo is freely available, and you find it everywhere on Linux Web sites, magazines, and other Linux venues. (I used it in my book *Linux Toys* and Linuxtoys.net Web site, for example.)

Tux was created by Larry Ewing. Different versions of Tux are available from his Web site (`www.isc.tamu.edu/~lewing/linux`). Find out more about Tux from the Linux Online Logos and Mascots page (`www.linux.org/info/logos.html`).

Figure 1-1: Tux, a gentle and pleasant penguin, is the official Linux mascot.

Running Linux

Although I've gone on a bit about Linux history and what it does, the primary goal of this book is to get you using it. To that end, I'd like to describe some things that might help you get started with Linux.

Common Mistakes When Starting with Linux

While Linux will run great on many low-end computers (even some old 486s and early Pentiums), if you are completely new to Linux, I recommend that you start with a PC that has a little more muscle. Here's why:

✦ Full-blown Linux operating systems with complete GNOME or KDE desktop environments perform poorly on slow CPUs and less than the recommended amount of RAM.

✦ You can create streamlined graphical Linux installations that will fit on small hard disks (as small as 100MB) and run fairly well on slow processors. However, putting together such a system requires some knowledge of which software packages to select and often requires some additional configuration.

If you are starting with a Pentium II, 400MHz, your desktop will run slowly in default KDE or GNOME configurations with less than 128MB of RAM. A simpler desktop system, with just X and a window manager, will work but won't give you the full flavor of a Linux desktop. (See Chapter 3 for information about different desktop choices and features.)

The good news is that, as mentioned earlier, cheap computers that you can buy from Wal-Mart or other retailers start at less than $300. Those systems will perform better than most PCs you have laying around that are more than a few years old and will come with Linux (usually Linspire) pre-installed. The bottom line is that the less you know about Linux, the more you should try to have computer hardware that is up to spec to have a pleasant experience.

Getting Started

If you already have a Linux system sitting in front of you, Chapters 2 through 6 will walk you through the Linux shell, using the desktop, and some basic system administration. If you don't have a Linux system running on your computer yet, you have a couple of choices:

✦ **Try a bootable Linux** — If you are reluctant to mess with the contents of your computer, a bootable Linux enables you to run Linux directly from a removable medium (DVD, CD, or even a floppy disk in some cases). You'll be able to try Linux without even touching the contents of your hard disk.

✦ **Install Linux on your hard disk** — If you have available disk space that's not already assigned to Windows or another system, you can install Linux on your hard disk and have a more permanent operating system. (Some Linux distributions, such as SUSE and Mandrake, let you resize your Windows hard disk to make room to install Linux.)

Linux itself is just a kernel (like the engine of a car), so to use Linux you need to select a Linux distribution. Because the distribution you choose is so critical to your Linux experience, Part III of this book is entirely devoted to understanding, choosing, and installing the most popular Linux distributions. Several of these distributions are included with this book, along with several useful bootable Linux distributions. If you don't already have a Linux system in front of you, refer to Chapter 7 to get started getting the Linux you want.

Summary

Linux is the most popular representation of the open source software model today and reflects a rich history of shared software development techniques that date back to the first UNIX systems of three decades ago. Today's Linux computer systems form the backbone of many major computing centers around the world.

In recent years, Linux has become a great choice as a desktop system as well. You will find many open source applications available for any type of application you can imagine (word processing, music playing, e-mail, games, and so on). With its powerful networking and built-in security features, Linux can provide a much safer computing environment than other desktop computing systems.

Linux gives you the freedom to create the kind of computer system you need.

✦   ✦   ✦

Running Commands from the Shell

Before icons and windows took over computer screens, you typed commands to run most computers. On UNIX systems, from which Linux was derived, the program used to interpret and manage commands was referred to as the shell.

No matter which Linux distribution you are using, you can always count on one thing being available to you: the shell. It provides a way to run programs, work with file systems, compile computer code, operate a system, and manage the computer. Although the shell is less intuitive than common GUIs (graphical user interfaces), most Linux experts consider the shell to be much more powerful than GUIs. Shells have been around a long time, and many advanced features have been built into them.

The Linux shell illustrated in this chapter is called the bash shell, which stands for Bourne Again SHell. The name is derived from the fact that bash is compatible with the first UNIX shell: the Bourne shell (represented by the sh command). Other popular shells include the C Shell (csh), which is popular among BSD UNIX users, and the Korn Shell (ksh), which is popular among UNIX System V users. Linux also has a tcsh shell (a C shell look-alike) and an ash shell (another Bourne shell look-alike). Several different shells are introduced in this chapter.

Three major reasons for learning how to use the shell are:

✦ You will know how to get around any Linux or other UNIX-like system. For example, I can log in to my Red Hat Linux MySQL server, my bootable floppy router/firewall, or my wife's iMAC and explore and use any of those computer systems from a shell.

✦ Special shell features enable you to gather data input and direct data output between commands and the Linux file system. To save on typing, you can find, edit, and repeat commands from your shell history. Many power users hardly touch a graphical interface, doing most of their work from a shell.

✦ You can gather commands into a file using programming constructs such as loops and case statements to quickly do complex operations that would be difficult to retype over and over. Programs consisting of commands that are stored and run from a file are referred to as *shell scripts*. Most Linux system administrators use shell scripts to automate tasks such as backing up data, monitoring log files, or checking system health. (See Chapter 27 for information on shell scripts.)

The shell is a command language interpreter. If you have used Microsoft operating systems, you'll see that using a shell in Linux is similar to — but generally much more powerful than — the interpreter used to run commands in DOS. You can happily use Linux from a graphical desktop interface, but as you grow into Linux you will surely need to use the shell at some point to track down a problem or administer some features.

How to use the shell isn't obvious at first, but with the right help you can quickly learn to avail yourself of many of the most important shell features. This chapter is your guide to working with the Linux system commands, processes, and file system from the shell. It describes the shell environment and helps you tailor it to your needs. It also explains how to use and move around the file system.

Starting a Shell

Several ways exist to get to a shell interface in Linux. Three of the most common are the shell prompt, Terminal window, and virtual terminal. They're discussed in the following sections.

Using the Shell Prompt

If your Linux system has no graphical user interface (or one that isn't working at the moment), you will most likely see a shell prompt after you log in. Typing commands from the shell will probably be your primary means of using the Linux system.

The default prompt for a regular user is simply a dollar sign:

$

The default prompt for the root user is a pound sign (also called a hash mark):

    #

In most Linux systems, the $ and # prompts are preceded by your username, system name, and current directory name. For example, a login prompt for the user named jake on a computer named pine with /tmp as the current directory would appear as

    [jake@pine tmp]$

You can change the prompt to display any characters you like — you can use the current directory, the date, the local computer name, or any string of characters as your prompt, for example. To configure your prompt, see the "Setting Your Prompt" section later in this chapter.

Although a tremendous number of features are available with the shell, it's easy to begin by just typing a few commands. Try some of the commands shown in the remainder of this section to become familiar with your current shell environment.

In the examples that follow, the $ and # symbols indicate a prompt. The prompt is followed by the command that you type (and then you press Enter or Return, depending on your keyboard). The lines that follow show the output resulting from the command.

Using a Terminal Window

With the desktop GUI running, you can open a terminal emulator program (sometimes referred to as a Terminal window) to start a shell. Most Linux distributions make it easy for you to get to a shell from the GUI. Here are two common ways to launch a Terminal window from a Linux desktop:

✦ **Right-click the desktop.** In the context menu that appears, look for New Terminal, Terminal Window, Xterm, or some similar item and select it.

✦ **Click the panel menu.** Many Linux desktops include a panel at the bottom of the screen from which you can launch applications. For example, in Red Hat Linux systems, you can select the Red Hat icon and then choose System Tools⇨Terminal to open a Terminal window.

In all cases, you should just be able to type a command as you would from a shell with no GUI. Different terminal emulators are available with Linux. One of the following is likely to be the default used with your Linux system:

Emulator	Description
xterm	A common terminal emulator for the X Window System (in fact, I've never seen an X Window System that didn't include xterm). Although it doesn't provide menus or many special features, it is available with most Linux distributions that support a GUI.
gnome-terminal	The default Terminal emulator window that comes with GNOME. It consumes more system resources than xterm does, and it has useful menus for cutting and pasting, opening new Terminal tabs or windows, and setting terminal profiles.
kterm	The kterm terminal emulator that comes with the KDE desktop environment. With kterm, you can display multilanguage text encoding and text in different colors.

If you don't like the terminal emulator you get by default, type a command name from the Emulator column to try out one of those instead.

Using Virtual Terminals

Many Linux systems, including Fedora and Red Hat Enterprise Linux, start multiple virtual terminals running on the computer. Virtual terminals are a way to have multiple shells open at once without having a GUI running.

You can switch between virtual terminals much the same way that you would switch between workspaces on a GUI. Press Ctrl+Alt+F1 (or F2, F3, F4, and so on up to F6 on Fedora and other Linux systems) to display one of six virtual terminals. The next virtual workspace after the virtual terminals is where the GUI is, so if there are six virtual terminals, you can return to the GUI (if one is running) by pressing Ctrl+Alt+F7. (For a system with four virtual terminals, you'd return to the GUI by pressing Ctrl+Alt+F5.)

Choosing Your Shell

In most Linux systems, your default shell is the bash shell. To find out what your current login shell is, type the following command:

```
$ echo $SHELL
/bin/bash
```

In this example, it's the bash shell. There are many other shells, and you can activate a different one by simply typing the new shell's command (ksh, tcsh, csh, sh, bash, and so forth) from the current shell.

Note Most full Linux systems include all the shells described in this section. However, some smaller Linux distributions may include only one or two shells. The best way to find out if a particular shell is available is to type the command and see if the shell starts.

You might want to choose a different shell to use because:

✦ You are used to using UNIX System V systems (often ksh by default) or Sun Microsystems and other Berkeley UNIX-based distributions (frequently csh by default), and you are more comfortable using default shells from those environments.

✦ You want to run shell scripts that were created for a particular shell environment, and you need to run the shell for which they were made so you can test or use those scripts.

✦ You might simply like features in one shell over those in another. For example, a member of my Linux Users Group prefers ksh over bash because he doesn't like the way aliases are always set up with bash.

Although most Linux users have a preference for one shell or another, when you know how to use one shell, you can quickly learn any of the others by occasionally referring to the shell's man page (for example, type **man bash**). Most people use bash just because they don't have a particular reason for using a different shell. In Chapter 4, you learn how to assign a different default shell for a user.

The following sections introduce several of the most common shells available with Linux.

Using bash (and Earlier sh) Shells

The name bash is an acronym for Bourne Again SHell, acknowledging the roots of bash coming from the Bourne shell (sh command) created by Steve Bourne at AT&T Bell Labs. Brian Fox of the Free Software foundation created bash, under the auspices of the GNU project. Development was later taken over by Chet Ramey at Case Western Reserve University.

Bash includes features originally developed for sh and ksh shells in early UNIX systems as well as some csh features. Expect bash to be the default shell in whatever Linux system you are using, with the exception of some specialized Linux systems (such as those run on embedded devices or run from a floppy disk) that may require a smaller shell that needs less memory and entails fewer features. Most of the examples in this chapter are based on the bash shell.

Bash can be run in various compatibility modes so that it behaves like different shells. It can be run to behave as a Bourne shell (sh) or as a POSIX-compliant shell (bash --posix), for example, enabling it to read configuration files that are specific to those shells and run shell scripts written directly for those shells, with a greater chance of success.

All of the Linux distributions included with this book use bash as the default shell with the exception of some bootable Linux distributions, which use the ash shell instead.

Using tcsh (and Earlier csh) Shells

The tcsh shell is the open source version of the C shell (csh). The csh shell was created by Bill Joy and used with most Berkeley UNIX systems (such as those produced by Sun Microsystems) as the default shell.

Many features of the original csh shell, such as command-line editing and its history mechanism, are included in tcsh as well as in other shells. Just as the sh command runs bash in sh compatibility mode, so does starting csh actually run the tcsh shell in csh compatibility mode.

Using ash

The ash shell is a lightweight version of the Berkeley UNIX sh shell. It doesn't include many of the sh shell's basic features and is missing such features as command histories.

The ash shell is a good shell for embedded systems that have fewer system resources available. In Fedora Core 2, the ash shell is about one-sixth the size of bash.

Using ksh

The ksh shell was created by David Korn at AT&T Bell Labs and is the predecessor of the sh shell. It became the default and most commonly used shell with UNIX System V systems. The open source version of ksh is available in many rpm-based systems (such as Fedora and Red Hat Enterprise Linux) as part of the pdksh package.

Using zsh

The zsh shell is another clone of the sh shell. It is POSIX-compliant (as is bash) but includes some different features, such as spell checking and a different approach to command editing. The first Mac OSX systems used zsh as the default shell, although now bash is used by default.

Exploring the Shell

Once you have access to a shell in Linux, you can begin by typing some simple commands. The "Using the Shell in Linux" section later in this chapter provides more details about options, arguments, and environment variables. For the time being, the following sections will help you poke around the shell a bit.

Note

> If you don't like your default shell, simply type the name of the shell you want to try out temporarily. To change your shell permanently, use the `usermod` command. For example, to change your shell to the csh shell for the user named chris, type the following as root user from a shell:
>
> ```
> # usermod -s /bin/csh chris
> ```

Checking Your Login Session

When you log in to a Linux system, Linux views you as having a particular identity, which includes your username, group name, user ID, and group ID. Linux also keeps track of your login session: It knows when you logged in, how long you have been idle, and where you logged in from.

To find out information about your identity, use the `id` command as follows:

```
$ id
  uid=501(chris) gid=105(sales) groups=105(sales),4(adm),7(lp)
```

In this example, the username is `chris`, which is represented by the numeric user ID (uid) `501`. The primary group for chris is called `sales`, which has a group ID (gid) of `105`. Chris also belongs to other groups called `adm` (gid 4) and `lp` (gid 7). These names and numbers represent the permissions that `chris` has to access computer resources. (Permissions are described in the "Understanding File Permissions" section later in this chapter.)

You can see information about your current login session by using the `who` command. In the following example, the `-u` option says to add information about idle time and the process ID and `-H` asks that a header be printed:

```
$ who -uH
NAME       LINE     TIME              IDLE     PID     COMMENT
chris      tty1     Jan 13 20:57       .       2013
```

The output from this `who` command shows that the user chris is logged in on `tty1` (which is the monitor connected to the computer) and his login session began at 20:57 on January 13. The `IDLE` time shows how long the shell has been open without any command being typed (the dot indicates that it is currently active). `PID` shows the process ID of the user's login shell. `COMMENT` would show the name of the remote computer the user had logged in from, if that user had logged in from another computer on the network, or the name of the local X display if you were using a Terminal window (such as :0.0).

Checking Directories and Permissions

Associated with each shell is a location in the Linux file system known as the *current* or *working directory*. Each user has a directory that is identified as the user's home directory. When you first log in to Linux, you begin with your home directory as the current directory.

When you request to open or save a file, your shell uses the current directory as the point of reference. Simply provide a filename when you save a file, and it is placed in the current directory. Alternatively, you can identify a file by its relation to the current directory (relative path), or you can ignore the current directory and identify a file by the full directory hierarchy that locates it (absolute path). The structure and use of the file system is described in detail later in this chapter.

To find out what your current directory is, type the pwd command:

```
$ pwd
/usr/bin
```

In this example, the current/working directory is /usr/bin. To find out the name of your home directory, type the echo command, followed by the $HOME variable:

```
$ echo $HOME
/home/chris
```

Here, the home directory is /home/chris. To get back to your home directory, just type the change directory (cd) command. (Although cd followed by a directory name changes the current directory to the directory that you choose, simply typing cd with no directory name takes you to your home directory.)

```
$ cd
```

To list the contents of your home directory, either type the full path to your home directory, or use the ls command without a directory name. Using the -a option to ls enables you to view the hidden files (dot files) as well as all other files. With the -l option, you can see a long, detailed list of information on each file. (You can put multiple single-letter options together after a single dash, for example, -la.)

```
$ ls -la /home/chris
total 158
drwxrwxrwx    2   chris   sales     4096   May 12 13:55 .
drwxr-xr-x    3   root    root      4096   May 10 01:49 ..
-rw-------    1   chris   sales     2204   May 18 21:30 .bash_history
-rw-r--r--    1   chris   sales       24   May 10 01:50 .bash_logout
-rw-r--r--    1   chris   sales      230   May 10 01:50 .bash_profile
-rw-r--r--    1   chris   sales      124   May 10 01:50 .bashrc
drw-r--r--    1   chris   sales     4096   May 10 01:50 .kde
-rw-rw-r--    1   chris   sales   149872   May 11 22:49 letter

         ^          ^      ^       ^        ^         ^              ^
       col 1     col 2  col 3   col 4    col 5     col 6          col 7
```

Displaying a long list (-l option) of the contents of your home directory shows you more about file sizes and directories. The total line shows the total amount of disk space used by the files in the list (158 kilobytes in this example). Directories such as the current directory (.) and the parent directory (..)—the directory above the current directory—are noted as directories by the letter d at the beginning of each entry (each directory begins with a d and each file begins with a -). The file and directory names are shown in column 7. In this example, a dot (.) represents /home/chris and two dots (..) represents /home. Most of the files in this example are dot (.) files that are used to store GUI properties (.kde directory) or shell properties (.bash files). The only nondot file in this list is the one named letter.

Column 3 shows the directory or file owner. The /home directory is owned by root, and everything else is owned by the user chris, who belongs to the sales group (groups are listed in column 4).

In addition to the d or -, column 1 on each line contains the permissions set for that file or directory. (Permissions and configuring shell property files are described later in this chapter.) Other information in the listing includes the number of links to the item (column 2), the size of each file in bytes (column 5), and the date and time each file was most recently modified (column 6).

Note   The number of characters shown for a directory (4,096 bytes in these examples) reflects the size of the file containing information about the directory. While this number can grow above 4,096 bytes for a directory that contains a lot of files, this number doesn't reflect the size of files contained in that directory.

Checking System Activity

In addition to being a multiuser operating system, Linux is also a multitasking system. *Multitasking* means that many programs can be running at the same time. An instance of a running program is referred to as a *process*. Linux provides tools for listing running processes, monitoring system usage, and stopping (or killing) processes when necessary.

The most common utility for checking running processes is the ps command. Use it to see which programs are running, the resources they are using, and who is running them. Here's an example of the ps command:

```
$ ps -au
USER    PID %CPU %MEM  VSZ    RSS   TTY    STAT START  TIME COMMAND
root    2146 0.0  0.8 1908   1100  ttyp0  S    14:50  0:00 login -- jake
jake    2147 0.0  0.7 1836   1020  ttyp0  S    14:50  0:00 -bash
jake    2310 0.0  0.7 2592    912  ttyp0  R    18:22  0:00 ps -au
```

In this example, the -a option asks to show processes of all users who are associated with your current terminal, and the -u option asks that usernames be shown, as well as other information such as the time the process started and memory and CPU usage. The concept of terminal comes from the old days, when people worked exclusively from character terminals, so a terminal typically represented a single person at a single screen. Now you can have many "terminals" on one screen by opening multiple Terminal windows.

On this shell session, there isn't much happening. The first process shows that the user named jake logged in to the login process (which is controlled by the root user). The next process shows that jake is using a bash shell and has just run the ps -au command. The terminal device ttyp0 is being used for the login session. The STAT column represents the state of the process, with R indicating a currently running process and S representing a sleeping process.

The USER column shows the name of the user who started the process. Each process is represented by a unique ID number referred to as a process ID (PID). (You can use the PID if you ever need to kill a runaway process.) The %CPU and %MEM columns show the percentage of the processor and random access memory, respectively, that the process is consuming. VSZ (virtual set size) shows the size of the image process (in kilobytes), and RSS (resident set size) shows the size of the program in memory. START shows the time the process began running, and TIME shows the cumulative system time used. (Many commands consume very little CPU time, as is reflected by 0:00 for processes that haven't even used a whole second of CPU time.)

Many processes running on a computer are not associated with a terminal. A normal Linux system has many processes running in the background. Background system processes perform such tasks as logging system activity or listening for data coming in from the network. They are often started when Linux boots up and run continuously until it shuts down. To page through all the processes running on your Linux system, add the pipe (|) and the less command to ps -aux, like this:

```
$ ps -aux | less
```

A pipe lets you direct the output of one command to be the input of the next command, so in this example, the output of the ps command (a list of processes) is directed to the less command, which lets you page through that information. Use the spacebar to page through and type **q** to end the list. You can also use the arrow keys to move one line at a time through the output.

Exiting the Shell

To exit the shell when you are done, either type **exit** or press Ctrl+D. If you are exiting from your login shell (the shell that started when you first logged in), type **logout** to exit the shell.

You've just seen a few commands that can help you quickly familiarize yourself with your Linux system. There are hundreds of other commands that you can try. You'll find many in the /bin and /usr/bin directories, and you can use ls to see a directory's command list: ls /bin, for example, results in a list of commands in the /bin. Then use the man command (for example, man hostname) to see what each command does. There are also administrative commands in /sbin or /usr/sbin directories.

Using the Shell in Linux

When you type a command in a shell, you can include other characters that change or add to how the command works. You can also set sequences of command or redirect input and output of a command by using control characters such as pipes (|), semicolons (;), and greater-than (>) and less-than (<) signs.

In addition to the command itself, these are some of the other items that you can type on a shell command line:

✦ **Options**— Most commands have one or more options you can add to change their behavior. Options typically consist of a single letter preceded by a dash. You can also often combine several options after a single dash. For example, the command ls -la lists the contents of the current directory. The -l asks for a detailed (long) list of information, and the -a asks that files beginning with a dot (.) also be listed. When a single option consists of a word, it is usually preceded by a double dash (--). For example, to use the help option on many commands, you enter --help on the command line.

Note   You can use the --help option with most commands to see the options and arguments that they support. For example, hostname --help.

✦ **Arguments**— Many commands also accept arguments after certain options are entered or at the end of the entire command line. An argument is an extra piece of information, such as a filename, that can be used by the command. For example, cat /etc/passwd displays the contents of the /etc/passwd file on your screen. In this case, /etc/passwd is the argument.

✦ **Environment variables**— The shell itself stores information that may be useful to the user's shell session in what are called *environment variables*. Examples of environment variables include $SHELL (which identifies the shell you are using), $PS1 (which defines your shell prompt), and $MAIL (which identifies the location of your mailbox). See the "Using Shell Environment Variables" section later in this chapter for more information.

Tip   You can check your environment variables at any time. Type **declare** to list the current environment variables. Or you can type **echo $VALUE**, where *VALUE* is replaced by the name of a particular environment variable you want to list.

✦ **Metacharacters**— These are characters that have special meaning to the shell. They can be used to direct the output of a command to a file (>), pipe the output to another command (|), and run a command in the background (&), to name a few. Metacharacters are discussed later in this chapter.

To save you some typing, there are shell features that store commands you want to reuse, recall previous commands, and edit commands. You can create aliases that enable you to type a short command to run a longer one. The shell stores previously entered commands in a history list, which you can display and from which you can recall commands. You'll see how this works a little later in the chapter.

Unless you specifically change to another shell, the bash shell is the one you use with most Linux systems. The bash shell contains most of the powerful features available in other shells. Although the description in this chapter steps you through many bash shell features, you can learn more about the bash shell by typing man bash, and the sidebar "Getting Help Using the Shell" shows you a few other ways to learn about using the shell.

Locating Commands

If you know the directory that contains the command you want to run, one way to run it is to type the full path to that command. For example, you run the date command from the /bin directory by typing

```
$ /bin/date
```

Of course, this can be inconvenient, especially if the command resides in a directory with a long path name. The better way is to have commands stored in well-known directories, and then add those directories to your shell's PATH environment variable. The path consists of a list of directories that are checked sequentially for the commands you enter. To see your current path, type the following:

```
$ echo $PATH
/bin:/usr/bin:/usr/local/bin:/usr/bin/X11:/usr/X11R6/bin:/home/chris/bin
```

The results show the default path for a regular Linux user. Directories in the path list are separated by colons. Most user commands that come with Linux are stored in the /bin, /usr/bin, or /usr/local/bin directories. Although many graphical commands (that are used with GUIs) are contained in /usr/bin, there are some special X commands that are in /usr/bin/X11 and /usr/X11R6/bin directories. The last directory shown is the bin directory in the user's home directory.

Tip If you want to add your own commands or shell scripts, place them in the bin directory in your home directory (such as /home/chris/bin for the user named chris). This directory is automatically added to your path. So as long as you add the command to your bin with execute permission (described in the "Understanding File Permissions" section later in this chapter), you can immediately begin using the command by simply typing the command name at your shell prompt.

If you are the root user, directories containing administrative commands are typically in your path. These directories include /sbin and /usr/sbin.

The path directory order is important. Directories are checked from left to right. So, in this example, if there is a command called foo located in both the /bin and /usr/bin directories, the one in /bin is executed. To have the other foo command run, you either type the full path to the command or change your PATH variable. (Changing your PATH and adding directories to it are described later in this chapter.)

Not all the commands that you run are located in directories in your PATH variable. Some commands are built into the shell. Other commands can be overridden by creating aliases that define any commands and options that you want the command to run. There are also ways of defining a function that consists of a stored series of commands. Here is the order in which the shell checks for the commands you type:

1. **Aliases** — Names set by the alias command that represent a particular command and a set of options. (Type **alias** to see what aliases are set.) Often, aliases enable you to define a short name for a long, complicated command.

2. **Shell reserved word** — Words that are reserved by the shell for special use. Many of these are words that you would use in programming-type functions, such as do, while, case, and else.

3. **Function** — A set of commands that are executed together within the current shell.

4. **Built-in command** — A command that is built into the shell. As a result, there is no representation of the command in the file system. Some of the most common commands you will use are shell built-in commands, such as cd (to change directories), echo (to echo text to the screen), exit (to exit from a shell), fg (to bring a command running in the background to the foreground), history (to see a list of commands that were previously run), pwd (to list the present working directory), set (to set shell options), and type (to show the location of a command).

5. **File system command** — This is a command that is stored in and executed from the computer's file system. (These are the commands that are indicated by the value of the PATH variable.)

To find out where a particular command is taken from, you can use the type command. (If you are using a shell other than bash, use the which command instead.) For example, to find out where the bash shell command is located, type the following:

```
$ type bash
bash is /bin/bash
```

Try these few words with the type command to see other locations of commands: which, case, and return. If a command resides in several locations, you can add the -a option to have all the known locations of the command printed.

Tip   Sometimes you run a command and receive an error message that the command was not found or that permission to run the command was denied. In the first case, check that you spelled the command correctly and that it is located in your PATH variable. In the second case, the command may be in the PATH variable but may not be executable. Adding execute permissions to a command is described later in this chapter.

Rerunning Commands

It's annoying, after typing a long or complex command line, to learn that you mis-typed something. Fortunately, some shell features let you recall previous command lines, edit those lines, or complete a partially typed command line.

The *shell history* is a list of the commands that you have entered before. Using the history command in a bash shell, you can view your previous commands. Then, using various shell features, you can recall individual command lines from that list and change them however you please.

The rest of this section describes how to do command-line editing, how to complete parts of command lines, and how to recall and work with the history list.

Command-Line Editing

If you type something wrong on a command line, the bash shell ensures that you don't have to delete the entire line and start over. Likewise, you can recall a previous command line and change the elements to make a new command.

Getting Help Using the Shell

When you first start using the shell, it can be intimidating. All you see is a prompt. How do you know which commands are available, which options they use, or how to use advanced features? Fortunately, lots of help is available. Here are some places you can look to supplement what you learn in this chapter:

✦ Check the PATH — Type **echo $PATH**. You see a list of the directories containing commands that are immediately accessible to you. Listing the contents of those directories displays most standard Linux commands.

✦ Use the help command — Some commands are built into the shell, so they do not appear in a directory. The help command lists those commands and shows options available with each of them. (Type **help | less** to page through the list.) For help with a particular built-in command, type **help *command***, replacing *command* with the name that interests you. The help command only works with the bash shell.

✦ Use --help with the command — Many commands include a --help option that you can use to get information about how the command is used. For example, type **date --help | less**. The output shows not only options, but also time formats you can use with the date command.

✦ Use the man command — To learn more about a particular command, type **man *command***. (Replace *command* with the command name you want.) A description of the command and its options appears on the screen.

By default, the bash shell uses command-line editing that is based on the emacs text editor. (Type **man emacs** to read about it, if you care to.) If you are familiar with emacs, you probably already know most of the keystrokes described here.

Tip   If you prefer the vi command for editing shell command lines, you can easily make that happen. Add the line

```
set -o vi
```

to the .bashrc file in your home directory. The next time you open a shell, you can use vi commands (as described in the tutorial later in this chapter) to edit your command lines.

To do the editing, you can use a combination of control keys, meta keys, and arrow keys. For example, Ctrl+F means to hold the Ctrl key and type F. Alt+F means to hold the Alt key and type F. (Instead of the Alt key, your keyboard may use a Meta key or the Esc key. On a Windows keyboard, you can use the Windows key.)

To try out a bit of command-line editing, type the following:

```
$ ls /usr/bin | sort -f | less
```

This command lists the contents of the /usr/bin directory, sorts the contents in alphabetical order (regardless of case), and pipes the output to less. The less command displays the first page of output, after which you can go through the rest of the output a line (press Enter) or a page (press spacebar) at a time (press Q when you are done). Now, suppose you want to change /usr/bin to /bin. You can use the following steps to change the command:

1. Press Ctrl+A. This moves the cursor to the beginning of the command line.
2. Press Ctrl+F or the right arrow (→) key. Repeat this command a few times to position the cursor under the first slash (/).
3. Press Ctrl+D. Type this command four times to delete /usr.
4. Press Enter. This executes the command line.

As you edit a command line, at any point you can type regular characters to add those characters to the command line. The characters appear at the location of your cursor. You can use right (→) and left (←) arrows to move the cursor from one end to the other on the command line. You can also press the up (↑) and down (↓) arrow keys to step through previous commands in the history list to select a command line for editing. (See the discussion on command recall for details on how to recall commands from the history list.)

There are many keystrokes you can use to edit your command lines. Table 2-1 lists the keystrokes that you can use to move around the command line.

Table 2-1
Keystrokes for Navigating Command Lines

Keystroke	Full Name	Meaning
Ctrl+F	Character forward	Go forward one character.
Ctrl+B	Character backward	Go backward one character.
Alt+F	Word forward	Go forward one word.
Alt+B	Word backward	Go backward one word.
Ctrl+A	Beginning of line	Go to the beginning of the current line.
Ctrl+E	End of line	Go to the end of the line.
Ctrl+L	Clear screen	Clear screen and leave line at the top of the screen.

The keystrokes in Table 2-2 can be used to edit command lines.

Table 2-2
Keystrokes for Editing Command Lines

Keystroke	Full Name	Meaning
Ctrl+D	Delete current	Delete the current character.
Backspace or Rubout	Delete previous	Delete the previous character.
Ctrl+T	Transpose character	Switch positions of current and previous characters.
Alt+T	Transpose words	Switch positions of current and previous characters.
Alt+U	Uppercase word	Change the current word to uppercase.
Alt+L	Lowercase word	Change the current word to lowercase.
Alt+C	Capitalize word	Change the current word to an initial capital.
Ctrl+V	Insert special character	Add a special character. For example, to add a Tab character, press Ctrl+V+Tab.

Use the keystrokes in Table 2-3 to cut and paste text on a command line.

Table 2-3
Keystrokes for Cutting and Pasting Text in Command Lines

Keystroke	Full Name	Meaning
Ctrl+K	Cut end of line	Cut text to the end of the line.
Ctrl+U	Cut beginning of line	Cut text to the beginning of the line.
Ctrl+W	Cut previous word	Cut the word located behind the cursor.
Alt+D	Cut next word	Cut the word following the cursor.
Ctrl+Y	Paste recent text	Paste most recently cut text.
Alt+Y	Paste earlier text	Rotate back to previously cut text and paste it.
Ctrl+C	Delete whole line	Delete the entire line.

Command-Line Completion

To save you a few keystrokes, the bash shell offers several different ways of completing partially typed values. To attempt to complete a value, type the first few characters, and then press Tab. Here are some of the values you can type partially:

- ✦ **Environment variable** — If the text begins with a dollar sign ($), the shell completes the text with an environment variable from the current shell.

- ✦ **Username** — If the text begins with a tilde (~), the shell completes the text with a username.

- ✦ **Command, alias, or function** — If the text begins with regular characters, the shell tries to complete the text with a command, alias, or function name.

- ✦ **Host name** — If the text begins with an at (@) sign, the shell completes the text with a host name taken from the /etc/hosts file.

Tip To add host names from an additional file, you can set the HOSTFILE variable to the name of that file. The file must be in the same format as /etc/hosts.

Here are a few examples of command completion. (When you see <Tab>, it means to press the Tab key on your keyboard.) Type the following:

```
$ echo $OS<Tab>
$ cd ~ro<Tab>
$ fing<Tab>
$ mail root@loc<Tab>
```

The first example causes $OS to expand to the $OSTYPE variable. In the next example, ~ro expands to the root user's home directory (~root/). Next, fing expands to the finger command. Finally, the address of root@loc expands to computer name localhost.

Of course, there will be times when there are several possible completions for the string of characters you have entered. In that case, you can check the possible ways text can be expanded by pressing Esc+? (or by pressing Tab twice) at the point where you want to do completion. This shows the result you would get if you checked for possible completions on $P:

```
$ echo $P<Esc+?>
$PATH $PPID $PS1 $PS2 $PS4 $PWD
$ echo $P
```

In this case, there are six possible variables that begin with $P. After possibilities are displayed, the original command line returns, ready for you to complete it as you choose.

If text you want to complete is not preceded by a $, ~, or @, you can still try to complete the text with a variable, username, or host name.

Press Key Combination	To
Alt+~	Complete the text before this point as a username.
Alt+$	Complete the text before this point as a variable.
Alt+@	Complete the text before this point as a host name.
Alt+!	Complete the text before this point as a command name (alias, reserved word, shell function, shell built-in command, and filenames are checked in that order). In other words, complete this key sequence with a command that you previously ran.
Ctrl+X+/	List possible username text completions.
Ctrl+X+$	List possible environment variable completions.
Ctrl+X+@	List possible host name completions.
Ctrl+X+!	List possible command name completions.

Command-Line Recall

After you type a command line, that entire command line is saved in your shell's history list. The list is stored in a history file, from which any command can be recalled to run again. After it is recalled, you can modify the command line, as described earlier.

To view your history list, use the `history` command. Type the command without options or followed by a number to list that many of the most recent commands. For example:

```
$ history 8
382 date
383 ls /usr/bin | sort -a | more
384 man sort
385 cd /usr/local/bin
386 man more
387 useradd -m /home/chris -u 101 chris
388 passwd chris
389 history 8
```

A number precedes each command line in the list. There are several ways to run a command immediately from this list, including:

✦ `!n` — Run command number. Replace the n with the number of the command line, and that line is run. For example, here's how to repeat the `date` command shown as command number 382 in the preceding history listing:

```
$ !382
date
Thu May 13 21:30:06 PDT 2004
```

✦ `!!` — Run previous command. Runs the previous command line. Here's how you'd immediately run that same `date` command:

```
$ !!
date
Thu May 13 21:30:39 PDT 2004
```

✦ `!?string?` — Run command containing string. This runs the most recent command that contains a particular *string* of characters. For example, you can run the `date` command again by just searching for part of that command line as follows:

```
$ !?dat?
date
Wed Oct 13 21:32:41 PDT 2004
```

Instead of just running a history command line immediately, you can recall a particular line and edit it. You can use the following keys or key combinations to do that:

Key(s)	Function Name	Description
Arrow Keys (↑ and ↓)	Step	Press the up and down arrow keys to step through each command line in your history list to arrive at the one you want. (Ctrl+P and Ctrl+N do the same functions, respectively.)
Ctrl+R	Reverse Incremental Search	After you press these keys, you enter a search string to do a reverse search. As you type the string, a matching command line appears that you can run or edit.
Ctrl+S	Forward Incremental Search	Same as the preceding function but for forward search.
Alt+P	Reverse Search	After you press these keys, you enter a string to do a reverse search. Type a string and press Enter to see the most recent command line that includes that string.
Alt+N	Forward Search	Same as the preceding function but for forward search.
Alt+<	Beginning of History List	Brings you to the first entry of the history list.
Alt+>	End of History List	Brings you to the last entry of the history list.

Another way to work with your history list is to use the fc command. Type **fc** followed by a history line number, and that command line is opened in a text editor. Make the changes that you want. When you exit the editor, the command runs. You can also give a range of line numbers (for example, fc 100 105). All the commands open in your text editor, and then run one after the other when you exit the editor.

The history list is stored in the .bash_history file in your home directory. Up to 1,000 history commands are stored for you by default.

Connecting and Expanding Commands

A truly powerful feature of the shell is the capability to redirect the input and output of commands to and from other commands and files. To allow commands to be strung together, the shell uses metacharacters. As noted earlier, a metacharacter is a typed character that has special meaning to the shell for connecting commands or requesting expansion.

Piping Commands

The pipe (|) metacharacter connects the output from one command to the input of another command. This lets you have one command work on some data and then have the next command deal with the results. Here is an example of a command line that includes pipes:

```
$ cat /etc/password | sort | less
```

This command lists the contents of the /etc/password file and pipes the output to the sort command. The sort command takes the usernames that begin each line of the /etc/password file, sorts them alphabetically, and pipes the output to the less command (to page through the output).

Pipes are an excellent illustration of how UNIX, the predecessor of Linux, was created as an operating system made up of building blocks. A standard practice in UNIX was to connect utilities in different ways to get different jobs done. For example, before the days of graphical word processors, users created plain-text files that included macros to indicate formatting. To see how the document really appeared, they would use a command such as the following:

```
$ gunzip < /usr/share/man/man1/grep.1.gz | nroff -c -man | less
```

In this example, the contents of the grep man page (grep.1.gz) are directed to the gunzip command to be unzipped. The output from gunzip is piped to the nroff command to format the man page using the manual macro (-man). The output is piped to the less command to display the output. Because the file being displayed is in plain text, you could have substituted any number of options to work with the text before displaying it. You could sort the contents, change or delete some of the content, or bring in text from other documents. The key is that, instead of all those features being in one program, you get results from piping and redirecting input and output between multiple commands.

Sequential Commands

Sometimes you may want a sequence of commands to run, with one command completing before the next command begins. You can do this by typing several commands on the same command line and separating them with semicolons (;):

```
$ date ; troff -me verylargedocument | lpr ; date
```

In this example, I was formatting a huge document and wanted to know how long it would take. The first command (date) showed the date and time before the formatting started. The troff command formatted the document and then piped the output to the printer. When the formatting was done, the date and time was printed again (so I knew how long the troff command took to complete).

Background Commands

Some commands can take a while to complete. Sometimes you may not want to tie up your shell waiting for a command to finish. In those cases, you can have the commands run in the background by using the ampersand (&).

Text formatting commands (such as nroff and troff, described earlier) are examples of commands that are often run in the background to format a large document. You also might want to create your own shell scripts that run in the background to check continuously for certain events to occur, such as the hard disk filling up or particular users logging in.

Here is an example of a command being run in the background:

```
$ troff -me verylargedocument | lpr &
```

Other ways to manage background and foreground processes are described in the "Managing Background and Foreground Processes" section later in this chapter.

Expanding Commands

With command substitution, you can have the output of a command interpreted by the shell instead of by the command itself. In this way, you can have the standard output of a command become an argument for another command. The two forms of command substitution are $(command) and `command` (backslashes, not single quotes).

The command in this case can include options, metacharacters, and arguments. Here is an example of using command substitution:

```
$ vi $(find /home | grep xyzzy)
```

In this example, the command substitution is done before the vi command is run. First, the find command starts at the /home directory and prints out all files and directories below that point in the file system. The output is piped to the grep command, which filters out all files except for those that include the string xyzzy. Finally, the vi command opens all filenames for editing (one at a time) that include xyzzy.

This particular example is useful if you want to edit a file for which you know the name but not the location. As long as the string is uncommon, you can find and open every instance of a filename existing beneath a point you choose in the file system. (In other words, don't use grep a from the root file system or you'll match and try to edit several thousand files.)

Expanding Arithmetic Expressions

There may be times when you want to pass arithmetic results to a command. There are two forms you can use to expand an arithmetic expression and pass it to the shell: $[expression] or $(expression). Here is an example:

```
$ echo "I am $[2005 - 1957] years old."
I am 48 years old.
```

The shell interprets the arithmetic expression first (2005 - 1957) and then passes that information to the echo command. The echo command displays the text, with the results of the arithmetic (48) inserted.

Here's an example of the other form:

```
$ echo "There are $(ls | wc -w) files in this directory."
There are 14 files in this directory.
```

This lists the contents of the current directory (ls) and runs the word count command to count the number of files found (wc -w). The resulting number (14 in this case) is echoed back with the rest of the sentence shown.

Expanding Environment Variables

Environment variables that store information within the shell can be expanded using the dollar sign ($) metacharacter. When you expand an environment variable on a command line, the value of the variable is printed instead of the variable name itself, as follows:

```
$ ls -l $BASH
-rwxr-xr-x 1 root  root  625516 Dec 5 11:13 /bin/bash
```

Using $BASH as an argument to ls -l causes a long listing of the bash command to be printed. The following section discusses shell environment variables.

Creating Your Shell Environment

You can tune your shell to help you work more efficiently. Your prompt can provide pertinent information each time you press Enter. You can set aliases to save your keystrokes and permanently set environment variables to suit your needs. To make each change occur when you start a shell, add this information to your shell configuration files.

Configuring Your Shell

Several configuration files support how your shell behaves. Some of the files are executed for every user and every shell, whereas others are specific to the user who creates the configuration file. Here are the files that are of interest to anyone using the bash shell in Linux:

File	Description
/etc/profile	Sets up user environment information for every user. It is executed when you first log in. This file provides values for your path, as well as setting environment variables for such things as the location of your mailbox and the size of your history files. Finally, /etc/profile gathers shell settings from configuration files in the /etc/profile.d directory.
/etc/bashrc	Executes for every user who runs the bash shell each time a bash shell is opened. It sets the default prompt and may add one or more aliases. Values in this file can be overridden by information in each user's ~/.bashrc file.
~/.bash_profile	Used by each user to enter information that is specific to their own use of the shell. It is executed only once, when the user logs in. By default it sets a few environment variables and executes the user's .bashrc file.
~/.bashrc	Contains the information that is specific to your bash shells. It is read when you log in and also each time you open a new bash shell. This is the best location to add environment variables and aliases so that your shell picks them up.
~/.bash_logout	Executes each time you log out (exit the last bash shell). By default, it simply clears your screen.

To change the /etc/profile or /etc/bashrc files, you must be the root user. Users can change the information in the $HOME/.bash_profile, $HOME/.bashrc, and $HOME/.bash_logout files in their own home directories.

The following sections provide ideas about items to add to your shell configuration files. In most cases, you add these values to the .bashrc file in your home directory. However, if you administer a system, you may want to set some of these values as defaults for all of your Linux system's users.

Setting Your Prompt

Your prompt consists of a set of characters that appears each time the shell is ready to accept a command. The PS1 environment variable sets what the prompt contains. If your shell requires additional input, it uses the values of PS2, PS3, and PS4.

When your Linux system is installed, often a prompt is set to contain more than just a dollar sign or pound sign. For example, in Linux systems from Red Hat, your prompt is set to include the following information: your username, your host name, and the base name of your current working directory. That information is surrounded by brackets and followed by a dollar sign (for regular users) or a pound sign (for the root user). Here is an example of that prompt:

```
[chris@myhost bin]$
```

If you change directories, the bin name would change to the name of the new directory. Likewise, if you were to log in as a different user or to a different host, that information would change.

You can use several special characters (indicated by adding a backslash to a variety of letters) to include different information in your prompt. These can include your terminal number, the date, and the time, as well as other pieces of information. Here are some examples (you can find more on the bash man page):

Special Character	Description
\!	Shows the current command history number. This includes all previous commands stored for your username.
\#	Shows the command number of the current command. This includes only the commands for the active shell.
\$	Shows the user prompt ($) or root prompt (#), depending on which user you are.
\W	Shows only the current working directory base name. For example, if the current working directory was /var/spool/mail, this value would simply appear as mail.
\[	Precedes a sequence of nonprinting characters. This could be used to add a terminal control sequence into the prompt for such things as changing colors, adding blink effects, or making characters bold. (Your terminal determines the exact sequences available.)
\]	Follows a sequence of nonprinting characters.
\\	Shows a backslash.
\d	Displays the day, month, and number of the date. For example: Sat Jan 23.
\h	Shows the host name of the computer running the shell.
\n	Causes a new line to occur.
\nnn	Shows the character that relates to the octal number replacing *nnn*.
\s	Displays the current shell name. For the bash shell, the value would be bash.
\t	Prints the current time in hours, minutes, and seconds (for example, 10:14:39).
\u	Prints your current username.
\w	Displays the full path to the current working directory.

Tip   If you are setting your prompt temporarily by typing at the shell, you should put the value of PS1 in quotes. For example, you could type export **PS1="[\t \w]\$ "** to see a prompt that looks like this: [20:26:32 /var/spool]$.

To make a change to your prompt permanent, add the value of PS1 to your .bashrc file in your home directory (assuming that you are using the bash shell). There may already be a PS1 value in that file that you can modify.

Adding Environment Variables

You may consider adding a few environment variables to your .bashrc file. These can help make working with the shell more efficient and effective:

✦ TMOUT—Sets how long the shell can be inactive before bash automatically exits. The value is the number of seconds for which the shell has not received input. This can be a nice security feature, in case you leave your desk while you are still logged in to Linux. So as not to be logged off while you are working, you may want to set the value to something like TMOUT=1800 (to allow 30 minutes of idle time).

✦ PATH—As described earlier, the PATH variable sets the directories that are searched for commands you use. If you often use directories of commands that are not in your PATH, you can permanently add them. To do this, add a PATH variable to your .bashrc file. For example, to add a directory called /getstuff/bin, add the following:

```
PATH=$PATH:/getstuff/bin ; export PATH
```

This example first reads all the current path directories into the new PATH ($PATH), adds the /getstuff/bin directory, and then exports the new PATH.

Caution

Some people add the current directory to their PATH by adding a directory identified simply as a dot (.), as follows:

```
PATH=.:$PATH ; export PATH
```

This lets you always run commands in your current directory (which people may be used to if they have used DOS). However, the security risk with this procedure is that you could be in a directory that contains a command that you don't intend to run from that directory. For example, a hacker could put an ls command in a directory that, instead of listing the content of your directory, does something devious.

✦ WHATEVER—You can create your own environment variables to provide shortcuts in your work. Choose any name that is not being used and assign a useful value to it. For example, if you do a lot of work with files in the /work/time/files/info/memos directory, you could set the following variable:

```
M=/work/time/files/info/memos ; export M
```

You could make that your current directory by typing cd $M. You could run a program from that directory called hotdog by typing $M/hotdog. You could edit a file from there called bun by typing **vi $M/bun**.

Adding Aliases

Setting aliases can save you even more typing than setting environment variables. With aliases, you can have a string of characters execute an entire command line. You can add and list aliases with the alias command. Here are some examples:

```
alias p='pwd ; ls -CF'
alias rm='rm -i'

alias p='pwd ; ls -CF'
alias rm='rm -i'
```

In the first example, the letter p is assigned to run the command pwd and then to run ls -CF to print the current working directory and list its contents in column form. The second runs the rm command with the -i option each time you simply type **rm**. (This is an alias that is often set automatically for the root user, so that instead of just removing files, you are prompted for each individual file removal. This prevents you from removing all the files in a directory by mistakenly typing something such as rm *.)

While you are in the shell, you can check which aliases are set by typing the alias command. If you want to remove an alias, type **unalias**. (Remember that if the alias is set in a configuration file, it will be set again when you open another shell.)

Using Shell Environment Variables

Every active shell stores pieces of information that it needs to use in what are called *environment variables*. An environment variable can store things such as locations of configuration files, mailboxes, and path directories. It can also store values for your shell prompts, the size of your history list, and type of operating system.

To see the environment variables currently assigned to your shell, type the declare command. (It will probably fill more than one screen, so type **declare | more**.) You can refer to the value of any of those variables by preceding it with a dollar sign ($) and placing it anywhere on a command line. For example:

```
$ echo $USER
chris
```

This command prints the value of the USER variable, which holds your username (chris). Substitute any other value for USER to print its value instead.

Common Shell Environment Variables

When you start a shell (by logging in or opening a Terminal window), a lot of environment variables are already set. Here are some variables that are either set when you use a bash shell or that can be set by you to use with different features.

Variable	Description
BASH	Contains the full path name of the `bash` command. This is usually `/bin/bash`.
BASH_VERSION	A number of the current version of the `bash` command.
EUID	This is the effective user ID number of the current user. It is assigned when the shell starts, based on the user's entry in the `/etc/passwd` file.
FCEDIT	If set, this variable indicates the text editor used by the `fc` command to edit `history` commands. If this variable isn't set, the `vi` command is used.
HISTFILE	The location of your history file. It is typically located at `$HOME/.bash_history`.
HISTFILESIZE	The number of history entries that can be stored. After this number is reached, the oldest commands are discarded. The default value is 1000.
HISTCMD	This returns the number of the current command in the history list.
HOME	This is your home directory. It is your current working directory each time you log in or type the `cd` command with any options.
HOSTTYPE	A value that describes the computer architecture on which the Linux system is running. For Intel-compatible PCs, the value is i386, i486, i586, i686, or something like i386-linux. For AMD 64-bit machines, the value is x86_64.
MAIL	This is the location of your mailbox file. The file is typically your username in the `/var/spool/mail directory`.
OLDPWD	The directory that was the working directory before you changed to the current working directory.
OSTYPE	A name identifying the current operating system. For Fedora Core Linux, the OSTYPE value is either linux or linux-gnu, depending on the type of shell you are using. (Bash can run on other operating systems as well.)
PATH	The colon-separated list of directories used to find commands that you type. The default value for regular users is `/bin:/usr/bin:/usr/local/bin:/usr/bin/X11:/usr/X11R6/bin:~/bin`. You need to type the full path or a relative path to a command you want to run that is not in your PATH. For the root user, the value also includes `/sbin`, `/usr/sbin`, and `/usr/local/sbin`.
PPID	The process ID of the command that started the current shell (for example, its parent process).
PROMPT_COMMAND	Can be set to a command name that is run each time before your shell prompt is displayed. Setting `PROMPT_COMMAND=date` lists the current date/time before the prompt appears.

Variable	Description
PS1	Sets the value of your shell prompt. There are many items that you can read into your prompt (date, time, username, host name, and so on). Sometimes a command requires additional prompts, which you can set with the variables PS2, PS3, and so on.
PWD	This is the directory that is assigned as your current directory. This value changes each time you change directories using the cd command.
RANDOM	Accessing this variable causes a random number to be generated. The number is between 0 and 99999.
SECONDS	The number of seconds since the time the shell was started.
SHLVL	The number of shell levels associated with the current shell session. When you log in to the shell, the SHLVL is 1. Each time you start a new bash command (by, for example, using su to become a new user, or by simply typing bash), this number is incremented.
TMOUT	Can be set to a number representing the number of seconds the shell can be idle without receiving input. After the number of seconds is reached, the shell exits. This is a security feature that makes it less likely for unattended shells to be accessed by unauthorized people. (This must be set in the login shell for it to actually cause the shell to log out the user.)
UID	The user ID number assigned to your username. The user ID number is stored in the /etc/password file.

Set Your Own Environment Variables

Environment variables can provide a handy way of storing bits of information that you use often from the shell. You can create any variables that you want (avoiding those that are already in use) so that you can read in the values of those variables as you use the shell. (The bash man page lists variables already in use.)

To set an environment variable temporarily, you can simply type a variable name and assign it to a value. Here's an example:

```
$ AB=/usr/dog/contagious/ringbearer/grind ; export AB
```

This example causes a long directory path to be assigned to the AB variable. The export AB command says to export the value to the shell so that it can be propagated to other shells you may open. With AB set, you go to the directory by typing the following:

```
$ cd $AB
```

The problem with setting environment variables in this way is that as soon as you exit the shell in which you set the variable, the setting is lost. To set variables permanently, add variable settings to a bash configuration file, as described later in this section.

If you want to have other text right up against the output from an environment variable, you can surround the variable with braces. This protects the variable name from being misunderstood. For example, if you wanted to add a command name to the AB variable shown earlier, you could type the following:

```
$ echo ${AB}/adventure
/usr/dog/contagious/ringbearer/grind/adventure
```

Remember that you must export the variable so that it can be picked up by other shell commands. You must add the export line to a shell configuration file for it to take effect the next time you log in. The export command is fairly flexible. Instead of running the export command after you set the variable, you can do it all in one step, as follows:

```
$ export XYZ=/home/xyz/bin
```

You can override the value of any environment variable. This can be temporary, by simply typing the new value, or you can add the new export line to your $HOME/.bashrc file. One useful variable to update is PATH:

```
$ export PATH=$PATH:/home/xyz/bin
```

In this example the /home/xyz/bin directory is added to the PATH, a useful technique if you want to run a bunch of commands from a directory that is not normally in your PATH, without typing the full or relative path each time.

If you decide that you no longer want a variable to be set, you can use the unset command to erase its value. For example, you could type unset XYZ, which would cause XYZ to have no value set. (Remember to remove the export from the $HOME/.bashrc file—if you added it there—or it will return the next time you open a shell.)

Managing Background and Foreground Processes

If you are using Linux over a network or from a *dumb* terminal (a monitor that allows only text input with no GUI support), your shell may be all that you have. You may be used to a windowing environment where you have a lot of programs active at the same time so that you can switch among them as needed. This shell thing can seem pretty limited.

Although the bash shell doesn't include a GUI for running many programs, it does let you move active programs between the background and foreground. In this way, you can have a lot of stuff running while selectively choosing the one you want to deal with at the moment.

You can place an active program in the background in several ways. One mentioned earlier is to add an ampersand (&) to the end of a command line. Another way is to use the at command to run commands in a way in which they are not connected to the shell.

To stop a running command and put it in the background, press Ctrl+Z. After the command is stopped, you can either bring it to the foreground to run (the fg command) or start it running in the background (the bg command).

Starting Background Processes

If you have programs that you want to run while you continue to work in the shell, you can place the programs in the background. To place a program in the background at the time you run the program, type an ampersand (&) at the end of the command line, like this:

```
$ find /usr > /tmp/allusrfiles &
```

This example command finds all files on your Linux system (starting from /usr), prints those filenames, and puts those names in the file /tmp/allusrfiles. The ampersand (&) runs that command line in the background. To check which commands you have running in the background, use the jobs command, as follows:

```
$ jobs
[1]   Stopped (tty output)  vi /tmp/myfile
[2]   Running               find /usr -print > /tmp/allusrfiles &
[3]   Running               nroff -man /usr/man2/* >/tmp/man2 &
[4]- Running                nroff -man /usr/man3/* >/tmp/man3 &
[5]+ Stopped                nroff -man /usr/man4/* >/tmp/man4
```

The first job shows a text-editing command (vi) that I placed in the background and stopped by pressing Ctrl+Z while I was editing. Job 2 shows the find command I just ran. Jobs 3 and 4 show nroff commands currently running in the background. Job 5 had been running in the shell (foreground) until I decided too many processes were running and pressed Ctrl+Z to stop job 5 until a few processes had completed.

The plus sign (+) next to number 5 shows that it was most recently placed in the background. The minus sign (-) next to number 4 shows that it was placed in the background just before the most recent background job. Because job 1 requires terminal input, it cannot run in the background. As a result, it is Stopped until it is brought to the foreground again.

Tip   To see the process ID for the background job, add a -l option to the jobs command. If you type ps, you can use the process ID to figure out which command is for a particular background job.

Using Foreground and Background Commands

Continuing with the example, you can bring any of the commands on the jobs list to the foreground. For example, to edit myfile again, type

```
$ fg %1
```

As a result, the vi command opens again, with all text as it was when you stopped the vi job.

Caution   Before you put a text processor, word processor, or similar program in the background, make sure you save your file. It's easy to forget you have a program in the background and you will lose your data if you log out or the computer reboots later on.

To refer to a background job (to cancel or bring it to the foreground), use a percent sign (%) followed by the job number. You can also use the following to refer to a background job:

✦ %—Refers to the most recent command put into the background (indicated by the plus sign). This action brings the command to the foreground.

✦ %*string*—Refers to a job where the command begins with a particular *string* of characters. The *string* must be unambiguous. (In other words, typing %vi when there are two vi commands in the background results in an error message.)

✦ %?*string*—Refers to a job where the command line contains a string at any point. The string must be unambiguous or the match will fail.

✦ %---—Refers to the previous job stopped before the one most recently stopped.

If a command is stopped, you can start it running again in the background using the bg command. For example, take job number 5 from the jobs list in the previous example:

```
[5]+ Stopped              nroff -man man4/* >/tmp/man4
```

Type the following:

```
$ bg %5
```

After that, the job runs in the background. Its jobs entry appears as follows:

```
[5]  Running              nroff -man man4/* >/tmp/man4 &
```

Working with the Linux File System

The Linux file system is the structure in which all the information on your computer is stored. Files are organized within a hierarchy of directories. Each directory can contain files, as well as other directories.

If you were to map out the files and directories in Linux, it would look like an upside-down tree. At the top is the root directory, which is represented by a single slash (/). Below that is a set of common directories in the Linux system, such as bin, dev, home, lib, and tmp, to name a few. Each of those directories, as well as directories added to the root, can contain subdirectories.

Figure 2-1 illustrates how the Linux file system is organized as a hierarchy. To demonstrate how directories are connected, the figure shows a /home directory that contains subdirectories for three users: chris, mary, and tom. Within the chris directory are subdirectories: briefs, memos, and personal. To refer to a file called inventory in the chris/memos directory, you could type the full path of /home/chris/memos/inventory. If your current directory were /home/chris/memos, you could refer to the file as simply inventory.

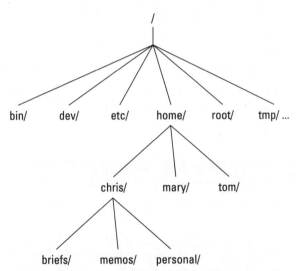

Figure 2-1: The Linux file system is organized as a hierarchy of directories.

Some of the Linux directories that may interest you include the following:

✦ /bin — Contains common Linux user commands, such as ls, sort, date, and chmod.

✦ /boot — Has the bootable Linux kernel and boot loader configuration files (GRUB).

✦ /dev — Contains files representing access points to devices on your systems. These include terminal devices (tty*), floppy disks (fd*), hard disks (hd*), RAM (ram*), and CD-ROM (cd*). (Users normally access these devices directly through the device files.)

✦ /etc — Contains administrative configuration files.

✦ `/home` — Contains directories assigned to each user with a login account.

✦ `/mnt` — Provides a location for mounting devices, such as remote file systems and removable media (with directory names of cdrom, floppy, and so on).

✦ `/proc` — Contains information about system resources.

✦ `/root` — Represents the root user's home directory.

✦ `/sbin` — Contains administrative commands and daemon processes.

✦ `/sys` (A `/proc`-like file system, new in the Linux 2.6 kernel and intended to contain files for getting hardware status and reflecting the system's device tree as it is seen by the kernel. It pulls many of its functions from `/proc`.

✦ `/tmp` — Contains temporary files used by applications.

✦ `/usr` — Contains user documentation, games, graphical files (X11), libraries (lib), and a variety of other user and administrative commands and files.

✦ `/var` — Contains directories of data used by various applications. In particular, this is where you would place files that you share as an FTP server (`/var/ftp`) or a Web server (`/var/www`). It also contains all system log files (`/var/log`).

The file systems in the DOS or Microsoft Windows operating systems differ from Linux's file structure, as the "Linux File Systems Versus Windows-Based File Systems" sidebar explains.

Linux File Systems Versus Windows-Based File Systems

Although similar in many ways, the Linux file system has some striking differences from file systems used in MS-DOS and Windows operating systems. Here are a few:

✦ In MS-DOS and Windows file systems, drive letters represent different storage devices (for example, A: is a floppy drive and C: is a hard disk). In Linux, all storage devices are fit into the file system hierarchy. So, the fact that all of `/usr` may be on a separate hard disk or that `/mnt/rem1` is a file system from another computer is invisible to the user.

✦ Slashes, rather than backslashes, are used to separate directory names in Linux. So, `C:\home\chris` in an MS system is `/home/chris` in a Linux system.

✦ Filenames almost always have suffixes in DOS (such as `.txt` for text files or `.doc` for word-processing files). Although at times you can use that convention in Linux, three-character suffixes have no required meaning in Linux. They can be useful for identifying a file type.

✦ Every file and directory in a Linux system has permissions and ownership associated with it. Security varies among Microsoft systems. Because DOS and MS Windows began as single-user systems, file ownership was not built into those systems when they were designed. Later releases added features such as file and folder attributes to address this problem.

Creating Files and Directories

As a Linux user, most of the files you save and work with will probably be in your home directory. Here are commands to create and use files and directories:

Command	Result
cd	Change to another current working directory.
pwd	Print the name of the current working directory.
mkdir	Create a directory.
chmod	Change the permission on a file or directory.
ls	List the contents of a directory.

The following steps lead you through creating directories within your home directory and moving among your directories, with a mention of setting appropriate file permissions:

1. Go to your home directory. To do this, simply type **cd**. (For other ways of referring to your home directory, see the "Identifying Directories" sidebar.)

2. To make sure that you got to your home directory, type **pwd**. When I do this, I get the following response (yours will reflect your home directory):

   ```
   $ pwd
   /home/chris
   ```

3. Create a new directory called test in your home directory, as follows:

   ```
   $ mkdir test
   ```

4. Check the permissions of the directory:

   ```
   $ ls -ld test
   drwxr-xr-x  2 chris  sales   1024  Jan 24 12:17 test
   ```

   This listing shows that test is a directory (d); followed by the permissions (rwxr-xr-x), which are explained later in the "Understanding File Permissions" section; the owner (chris); the group (sales); and that the file was most recently modified on Jan. 24 at 12:17 p.m.

Note In some Linux systems, such as Fedora Core, when you add a new user, the user is assigned to a group of the same name by default. For example, in the preceding text, the user chris would be assigned to the group chris. This approach to assigning groups is referred to as the user private group scheme. For more information on user private groups, see Chapter 4.

For now, type the following:

```
$ chmod 700 test
```

This step changes the permissions of the directory to give you complete access and everyone else no access at all. (The new permissions should read like `rwx------`.)

5. Last, make the test directory your current directory as follows:

```
$ cd test
```

Using Metacharacters and Operators

To make efficient use of your shell, the bash shell lets you use certain special characters, referred to as metacharacters and operators. Metacharacters can help you match one or more files without typing each file completely. Operators let you direct information from one command or file to another command or file.

Using File-Matching Metacharacters

To save you some keystrokes and to be able to refer easily to a group of files, the bash shell lets you use metacharacters. Anytime you need to refer to a file or directory, such as to list it, open it, or remove it, you can use metacharacters to match the files you want. Here are some useful metacharacters for matching filenames:

✦ `*` — Matches any number of characters.

✦ `?` — Matches any one character.

✦ `[...]` — Matches any one of the characters between the brackets, which can include a dash-separated range of letters or numbers.

Identifying Directories

When you need to identify your home directory on a shell command line, you can use the following:

✦ `$HOME` — This environment variable stores your home directory name.

✦ `~` — The tilde (~) represents your home directory on the command line.

You can also use the tilde to identify someone else's home directory. For example, `~chris` would be expanded to the `chris` home directory (probably `/home/chris`).

Other special ways of identifying directories in the shell include the following:

✦ `.` — A single dot (`.`) refers to the current directory.

✦ `..` — Two dots (`..`) refers to a directory directly above the current directory.

✦ `$PWD` — This environment variable refers to the current working directory.

✦ `$OLDPWD` — This environment variable refers to the previous working directory before you changed to the current one.

Try out some of these file-matching metacharacters by first going to an empty directory (such as the test directory described in the previous section) and creating some empty files:

```
$ touch apple banana grape grapefruit watermelon
```

The touch command creates empty files. The next few commands show you how to use shell metacharacters with the ls command to match filenames. Try the following commands to see if you get the same responses:

```
$ ls a*
apple
$ ls g*
grape
grapefruit
$ ls g*t
grapefruit
$ ls *e*
apple grape grapefruit watermelon
$ ls *n*
banana watermelon
```

The first example matches any file that begins with an a (apple). The next example matches any files that begin with g (grape, grapefruit). Next, files beginning with g and ending in t are matched (grapefruit). Next, any file that contains an e in the name is matched (apple, grape, grapefruit, watermelon). Finally, any file that contains an n is matched (banana, watermelon).

Here are a few examples of pattern matching with the question mark (?):

```
$ ls ????e
apple grape
$ ls g???e*
grape grapefruit
```

The first example matches any five-character file that ends in e (apple, grape). The second matches any file that begins with g and has e as its fifth character (grape, grapefruit).

Here are a couple of examples using braces to do pattern matching:

```
$ ls [abw]*
apple banana watermelon
$ ls [agw]*[ne]
apple grape watermelon
```

In the first example, any file beginning with a, b, or w is matched. In the second, any file that begins with a, g, or w and also ends with either n or e is matched. You can also include ranges within brackets. For example:

```
$ ls [a-g]*
apple banana grape grapefruit
```

Here, any filenames beginning with a letter from a through g is matched.

Using File-Redirection Metacharacters

Commands receive data from standard input and send it to standard output. Using pipes (described earlier), you can direct standard output from one command to the standard input of another. With files, you can use less-than (<) and greater-than (>) signs to direct data to and from files. Here are the file redirection characters:

✦ < — Direct the contents of a file to the command.

✦ > — Direct the output of a command to a file, deleting the existing file.

✦ >> — Direct the output of a command to a file, adding the output to the end of the existing file.

Here are some examples of command lines where information is directed to and from files:

```
$ mail root < ~/.bashrc
$ man chmod | col -b > /tmp/chmod
$ echo "I finished the project on $(date)" >> ~/projects
```

In the first example, the contents of the .bashrc file in the home directory are sent in a mail message to the computer's root user. The second command line formats the chmod man page (using the man command), removes extra back spaces (col -b) and sends the output to the file /tmp/chmod (erasing the previous /tmp/chmod file, if it exists). The final command results in the following text being added to the user's project file:

```
I finished the project on Sat Jan 22 13:46:49 PST 2005
```

Understanding File Permissions

After you've worked with Linux for a while, you are almost sure to get a "Permission denied" message. Permissions associated with files and directories in Linux were designed to keep users from accessing other users' private files and to protect important system files.

The nine bits assigned to each file for permissions define the access that you and others have to your file. Permission bits appear as rwxrwxrwx. The first three bits apply to the owner's permission, the next three apply to the group assigned to the file, and the last three apply to all others. The r stands for read, the w stands for write, and the x stands for execute permissions. If a dash appears instead of the letter, it means that permission is turned off for that associated read, write, or execute.

Because files and directories are different types of elements, read, write, and execute permissions on files and directories mean different things. Here's what you can do with each of them:

Permission	File	Directory
Read	View what's in the file.	See what files and subdirectories it contains.
Write	Change the file's content, rename it, or delete it.	Add files or subdirectories to the directory.
Execute	Run the file as a program.	Change to that directory as the current directory, search through the directory, or execute a program from the directory.

You can see the permission for any file or directory by typing the ls -ld command. The named file or directory appears as those shown in this example:

```
$ ls -ld ch3 test
-rw-rw-r--  1 chris  sales    4983  Jan 18 22:13 ch3
drwxr-xr-x  2 chris  sales    1024  Jan 24 13:47 test
```

The first line shows that the ch3 file has read and write permission for the owner and the group. All other users have read permission, which means they can view the file but cannot change its contents or remove it. The second line shows the test directory (indicated by the letter d before the permission bits). The owner has read, write, and execute permission, while the group and other users have only read and execute permissions. As a result, the owner can add, change, or delete files in that directory, and everyone else can only read the contents, change to that directory, and list the contents of the directory.

If you own a file, you can use the chmod command to change the permission on it as you please. In one method of doing this, each permission (read, write, and execute), is assigned a number — r=4, w=2, and x=1 — and you use each set's total number to establish the permission. For example, to make permissions wide open for yourself as owner, you'd set the first number to 7 (4+2+1), and to give the group and others only read permission, you'd set both the second and third numbers to 4 (4+0+0), so that the final number is 744. Any combination of permissions can result from 0 (no permission) through 7 (full permission).

Here are some examples of how to change permission on a file (named `file`) and what the resulting permission would be:

```
# chmod 777 file       rwxrwxrwx
# chmod 755 file       rwxr-xr-x
# chmod 644 file       rw-r--r-
# chmod 000 file       ---------
```

You can also turn file permissions on and off using plus (+) and minus (–) signs, respectively. This can be done for the owner user (u), owner group (g), others (o), and all users (a). For example, each time starting with a file that has all permissions open (rwxrwxrwx), here are some `chmod` examples with resulting permissions after using a minus sign:

```
chmod a-w files        r-xr-xr-x
chmod o-x files        rwsrwsrw-
chmod go-rwx files     rwx------
```

Likewise, here are some examples, starting with all permissions closed (- - - - - - - - -) where the plus sign is used with `chmod` to turn permissions on:

```
chmod u+rw files       rw-------
chmod a+x files        --x--x--x
chmod ug+rx files      r-xr-x---
```

When you create a file, it's given the permission rw-r–r– by default. A directory is given the permission rwxr-xr-x. These default values are determined by the value of `umask`. Type **umask** to see what your `umask` value is. For example:

```
$ umask
022
```

The `umask` value masks the permissions value of 666 for a file and 777 for a directory. The `umask` value of 022 results in permission for a directory of 755 (rwxr-xr-x). That same `umask` results in a file permission of 644 (rw-r–r–). (Execute permissions are off by default for regular files.)

Tip   Time saver: Use the `-R` options of `chmod` to change the permission for all of the files and directories within a directory structure at once. For example, if you wanted to open permissions completely to all files and directories in the `/tmp/test` directory, you could type the following:

```
$ chmod -R 777 /tmp/test
```

This command line runs `chmod` recursively (`-R`) for the `/tmp/test` directory, as well as any files or directories that exist below that point in the file system (for example, `/tmp/test/hat`, `/tmp/test/hat/caps`, and so on). All would be set to 777 (full read/write/execute permissions). This is not something you would do on an important directory on a read/write file system. However, you might do this before you create a directory structure on a CD-ROM that you want to be fully readable and executable to someone using the CD-ROM later.

Caution   The -R option of chmod works best if you are opening permissions completely or adding execute permission (as well as the appropriate read/write permission). The reason is that if you turn off execute permission recursively, you close off your capability to change to any directory in that structure. For example, chmod -R 644 /tmp/test turns off execute permission for the /tmp/test directory and then fails to change any files or directories below that point.

Moving, Copying, and Deleting Files

Commands for moving, copying, and deleting files are fairly straightforward. To change the location of a file, use the mv command. To copy a file from one location to another, use the cp command. To remove a file, use the rm command. Here are some examples:

```
$ mv abc def
$ mv abc ~
$ cp abc def
$ cp abc ~
$ rm abc
$ rm *
```

Of the two move (mv) commands, the first moves the file abc to the file def in the same directory (essentially renaming it), whereas the second moves the file abc to your home directory (~). The first copy command (cp) copies abc to the file def, whereas the second copies abc to your home directory (~). The first remove command (rm) deletes the abc file; the second removes all the files in the current directory (except those that start with a dot).

Note   For the root user, the mv, cp, and rm commands are aliased to each be run with the -i option. This causes a prompt to appear asking you to confirm each move, copy, and removal, one file at a time, and is done to prevent the root user from messing up a large group of files by mistake.

Another alternative with mv is to use the -b option. With -b, if a file of the same name exists at the destination, a backup copy of the old file is made before the new file is moved there.

Using the vi Text Editor

It's almost impossible to use Linux for any period of time and not need to use a text editor. This is because most Linux configuration files are plain-text files that you will almost certainly need to change manually at some point.

If you are using a GUI, you can run gedit, which is fairly intuitive for editing text. There's also a simple text editor you can run from the shell called nano. However, most Linux shell users will use either the vi or emacs command to edit text files. The advantage of vi or emacs over a graphical editor is that you can use them from any shell, a character terminal, or a character-based connection over a network (using `telnet` or `ssh`, for example)—no GUI is required. They also each contain tons of features, so you can continue to grow with them.

This section provides a brief tutorial of the vi text editor, which you can use to manually edit a configuration file from any shell. (If vi doesn't suit you, see the "Exploring Other Text Editors" sidebar for other options.)

The vi editor is difficult to learn at first, but once you know it, you never have to use a mouse or a function key—you can edit and move around quickly and efficiently within files just by using the keyboard.

Starting with vi

Most often, you start vi to open a particular file. For example, to open a file called `/tmp/test`, type the following command:

```
$ vi /tmp/test
```

If this is a new file, you should see something similar to the following:

```
    ~
    ~
    ~
    ~
    ~
    "/tmp/test" [New File]
```

The box at the top represents where your cursor is. The bottom line keeps you informed about what is going on with your editing (here you just opened a new file). In between, there are tildes (~) as filler because there is no text in the file yet. Now here's the intimidating part: There are no hints, menus, or icons to tell you what to do. On top of that, you can't just start typing. If you do, the computer is likely to beep at you. And some people complain that Linux isn't friendly.

The first things you need to know are the different operating modes: command and input. The vi editor always starts in command mode. Before you can add or change text in the file, you have to type a command (one or two letters and an optional number) to tell vi what you want to do. Case is important, so use upper- and lowercase exactly as shown in the examples! To get into input mode, type an input command. To start out, type either of the following:

  ✦ a—The add command. After it, you can input text that starts to the *right* of the cursor.

  ✦ i—The insert command. After it, you can input text that starts to the *left* of the cursor.

Type a few words and then press Enter. Repeat that a few times until you have a few lines of text. When you're finished typing, press Esc to return to command mode. Now that you have a file with some text in it, try moving around in your text with the following keys or letters:

Tip Remember the Esc key! It always places you back into command mode.

✦ **Arrow keys**—Move the cursor up, down, left, or right in the file one character at a time. To move left and right you can also use Backspace and the spacebar, respectively. If you prefer to keep your fingers on the keyboard, move the cursor with h (left), l (right), j (down), or k (up).

✦ **w**—Moves the cursor to the beginning of the next word.

✦ **b**—Moves the cursor to the beginning of the previous word.

✦ **0** *(zero)*—Moves the cursor to the beginning of the current line.

✦ **$**—Moves the cursor to the end of the current line.

✦ **H**—Moves the cursor to the upper-left corner of the screen (first line on the screen).

✦ **M**—Moves the cursor to the first character of the middle line on the screen.

✦ **L**—Moves the cursor to the lower-left corner of the screen (last line on the screen).

The only other editing you need to know is how to delete text. Here are a few vi commands for deleting text:

✦ **x**—Deletes the character under the cursor.

✦ **X**—Deletes the character directly before the cursor.

✦ **dw**—Deletes from the current character to the end of the current word.

✦ **d$**—Deletes from the current character to the end of the current line.

✦ **d0**—Deletes from the previous character to the beginning of the current line.

To wrap things up, use the following keystrokes for saving and quitting the file:

✦ **ZZ**—Save the current changes to the file and exit from vi.

✦ **:w**—Save the current file but continue editing.

✦ **:wq**—Same as ZZ.

✦ **:q**—Quit the current file. This works only if you don't have any unsaved changes.

✦ **:q!**—Quit the current file and *don't* save the changes you just made to the file.

Tip   If you've really trashed the file by mistake, the :q! command is the best way to exit and abandon your changes. The file reverts to the most recently changed version. So, if you just did a :w, you are stuck with the changes up to that point. If you just want to undo a few bad edits, press u to back out of changes.

You have learned a few vi editing commands. I describe more commands in the following sections. First, though, here are a few tips to smooth out your first trials with vi:

✦ **Esc**—Remember that Esc gets you back to command mode. (I've watched people press every key on the keyboard trying to get out of a file.) Esc followed by ZZ gets you out of command mode, saves the file, and exits.

✦ **u**—Press U to undo the previous change you made. Continue to press U to undo the change before that, and the one before that.

✦ **Ctrl+R**—If you decide you didn't want to undo the previous command, use Ctrl+R for Redo. Essentially, this command undoes your undo.

✦ **Caps Lock**—Beware of hitting Caps Lock by mistake. Everything you type in vi has a different meaning when the letters are capitalized. You don't get a warning that you are typing capitals—things just start acting weird.

✦ **:! command**—You can run a command while you are in vi using : ! followed by a command name. For example, type **:!date** to see the current date and time, type **:!pwd** to see what your current directory is, or type **:!jobs** to see if you have any jobs running in the background. When the command completes, press Enter and you are back to editing the file. You could even do that with a shell (:!bash) to run a few commands from the shell, then type **exit** to return to vi. (I recommend doing a save before escaping to the shell, just in case you forget to go back to vi.)

✦ **– INSERT**—When you are in insert mode, the word INSERT appears at the bottom of the screen.

✦ **Ctrl+G**—If you forget what you are editing, pressing these keys displays the name of the file that you are editing and the current line that you are on at the bottom of the screen. It also displays the total number of lines in the file, the percentage of how far you are through the file, and the column number the cursor is on. This just helps you get your bearings after you've stopped for a cup of coffee at 3 a.m.

Moving Around the File

Besides the few movement commands described earlier, there are other ways of moving around a vi file. To try these out, open a large file that you can't do much damage to. (Try copying /var/log/messages to /tmp and opening it in vi.) Here are some movement commands you can use:

✦ **Ctrl+F**—Page ahead, one page at a time.

✦ **Ctrl+B**—Page back, one page at a time.

✦ **Ctrl+D**—Page ahead 1/2 page at a time.

✦ **Ctrl+U**—Page back 1/2 page at a time.

✦ **G**—Go to the last line of the file.

✦ **1G**—Go to the first line of the file. (Use any number to go to that line in the file.)

Searching for Text

To search for the next occurrence of text in the file, use either the slash (/) or the question mark (?) character. Follow the slash or question mark with a pattern (string of text) to search forward or backward, respectively, for that pattern. Within the search, you can also use metacharacters. Here are some examples:

✦ /hello—Searches forward for the word *hello.*

✦ ?goodbye—Searches backward for the word *goodbye.*

✦ /The.*foot—Searches forward for a line that has the word *The* in it and also, after that at some point, the word *foot.*

✦ ?[pP]rint—Searches backward for either *print* or *Print.* Remember that case matters in Linux, so make use of brackets to search for words that could have different capitalization.

The vi editor was originally based on the ex editor, which didn't let you work in full-screen mode. However, it did enable you to run commands that let you find and change text on one or more lines at a time. When you type a colon and the cursor goes to the bottom of the screen, you are essentially in ex mode. Here is an example of some of those ex commands for searching for and changing text. (I chose the words Local and Remote to search for, but you can use any appropriate words.)

✦ :g/Local—Searches for the word Local and prints every occurrence of that line from the file. (If there is more than a screenful, the output is piped to the more command.)

✦ :s/Local/Remote—Substitutes Remote for the word Local on the current line.

✦ :g/Local/s//Remote—Substitutes the first occurrence of the word Local on every line of the file with the word Remote.

✦ :g/Local/s//Remote/g—Substitutes every occurrence of the word Local with the word Remote in the entire file.

✦ :g/Local/s//Remote/gp—Substitutes every occurrence of the word Local with the word Remote in the entire file and then prints each line so that you can see the changes (piping it through more if output fills more than one page).

Exploring Other Text Editors

Dozens of text editors are available to use with Linux. Here are a few that might be in your Linux distribution that you can try out if you find vi to be too taxing:

Text Editor	Description
gedit	The GNOME text editor that runs in the GUI.
jed	This screen-oriented editor was made for programmers. Using colors, jed can highlight code you create so you can easily read the code and spot syntax errors. Use the Alt key to select menus to manipulate your text.
joe	The joe editor is similar to many PC text editors. Use control and arrow keys to move around. Type **Ctrl+C** to exit with no save or **Ctrl+X** to save and exit.
kate	A nice-looking editor that comes in the kdebase package. It has lots of bells and whistles, such as highlighting for different types of programming languages and controls for managing word wrap.
kedit	A GUI-based text editor that comes with the KDE desktop.
mcedit	With mcedit, function keys help you get around, save, copy, move, and delete text. Like jed and joe, mcedit is screen-oriented.
nedit	An excellent programmer's editor. You need to install the optional nedit package to get this editor.

If you use ssh to log in to other Linux computers on your network, you can use any editor to edit files. A GUI-based editor will pop up on your screen. When no GUI is available, you will need a text editor that runs in the shell, such as vi, jed, or joe.

Using Numbers with Commands

You can precede most vi commands with numbers to have the command repeated that number of times. This is a handy way to deal with several lines, words, or characters at a time. Here are some examples:

Command	Description
3dw	Deletes the next three words.
5cl	Changes the next five letters (that is, removes the letters and enters input mode).
12j	Moves down 12 lines.

Putting a number in front of most commands just repeats those commands. At this point, you should be fairly proficient at using the vi command.

Note   When you invoke vi in many Linux systems, you're actually invoking the vim text editor, which runs in vi compatibility mode. Those who do a lot of programming might prefer vim because it shows different levels of code in different colors. vim has other useful features, such as the capability to open a document with the cursor at the same place where it was when you last exited that file.

Summary

Working from a shell command line within Linux may not be as simple as using a GUI, but it offers many powerful and flexible features. This chapter explains how to find your way around the shell in Linux and provides examples of running commands, including recalling commands from a history list, completing commands, and joining commands.

The chapter describes how shell environment variables can be used to store and recall important pieces of information. It also teaches you how to modify shell configuration files to tailor the shell to suit your needs. Finally, this chapter shows you how to use the Linux file system to create files and directories, use permissions, and work with files (moving, copying, and removing them), and how to edit text files from the shell using the vi command.

✦   ✦   ✦

Getting into the Desktop

In the past few years, graphical user interfaces (GUIs) available for Linux have become as easy to use as those on the Apple Mac or Microsoft Windows systems. With these improvements, even a novice computer user can start using Linux without needing to have an expert standing by.

You don't need to understand the underlying framework of the X Window System, window managers, widgets, and what-nots to get going with a Linux desktop system. That's why I start by explaining how to use the two most popular desktop environments: KDE (K desktop environment) and GNOME. After that, if you want to dig deeper, I tell you how you can put together your own desktop by discussing how to choose your own X-based window manager to run in Linux.

Understanding Your Desktop

When you install Linux distributions such as Fedora Core, SUSE, and Mandrakelinux, you have the option to choose a desktop environment. Distributions such as Gentoo and Debian GNU/Linux give you the option to go out and get what-ever desktop environment you want (without particularly prompting you for it). When you are given the opportunity to select a desktop during installation, your choices usually include one or more of the following:

✦ **K Desktop Environment** (www.kde.org) — In addition to all the features you would expect to find in a complete desktop environment (window managers, toolbars, pan-els, menus, keybindings, icons, and so on), KDE has many bells and whistles available. Applications for graphics, multimedia, office productivity, games, system adminis-tration, and many other features have been integrated to work smoothly with KDE, which is the default desktop environment for SUSE, KNOPPIX, and various other Linux distributions.

✦ **GNOME Desktop Environment** (www.gnome.org) — GNOME is a more stream-lined desktop environment. It includes a smaller feature set than KDE and runs faster in many lower-memory systems. Some think of GNOME as a more business-oriented desktop. It's the default desktop for Red Hat Linux systems such as Fedora and RHEL.

✦ **X and a window manager** (X.org or XFree86.org + WM) — You don't need a full-blown desktop environment to operate Linux from a GUI. The most basic, reasonable way of using Linux is to simply start the X Window System server and a window manager of your choice (there are dozens to choose from). Many advanced users go this route because it can offer more flexibility in how they set up their desktops.

The truth is that most X applications run in any of the desktop environments just described (provided that proper libraries are included with your Linux distribution). So you can choose a Linux desktop based on the performance, customization tools, and controls that best suit you. Each of those three types of desktop environments are described in this chapter.

Starting the Desktop

Because the way that you start a desktop in Linux is completely configurable, different distributions offer different ways of starting up the desktop. Once your Linux distribution is installed, it may just boot to the desktop, offer a graphical login, or offer a text-based login. Bootable Linux systems (which don't have to be installed at all) typically just boot to the desktop.

Boot to the Desktop

Some bootable Linux systems boot right to a desktop without requiring you to log in, so that you can immediately start working with Linux. KNOPPIX is an example of a distribution that boots straight to a Linux desktop from a CD. That desktop system usually runs as a particular username (such as knoppix, in the case of the KNOPPIX distribution). To perform system administration, you have to switch to the administrator's account temporarily (using the su or sudo command).

Boot to Graphical Login

Most desktop Linux systems that are installed on your hard disk boot up to a graphical login screen. Although the X display manager (xdm) is the basic display manager that comes with the X Window System, KDE and GNOME each have their own graphical display managers that are used as login screens (kdm and gdm, respectively). So chances are that you will see the login screen associated with KDE or GNOME (depending on which is the default on your Linux).

Note

When Linux starts up, it enters into what is referred to as a run level or system state. Typically, a system set to start at run level 5 boots to a graphical login prompt. A system set to run level 3 boots to a text prompt. The run level is set by the initdefault line in the /etc/inittab file. Change the number on the initdefault line as you please between 3 and 5 (don't use other number unless you know what you are doing, and never use 0 or 6).

Because graphical login screens are designed to be configurable, you often find that the distribution has its own logo or other graphical elements on the login screen. For example, Figure 3-1 shows a basic graphical login panel displayed by the kdm graphical display manager.

Figure 3-1: A simple KDE display manager (kdm) login screen includes a clock, login name list, and a few menu selections.

With Red Hat's Fedora Core Linux, the default login screen is based on the GNOME display manager (gdm). Figure 3-2 shows the Fedora Core graphical login screen.

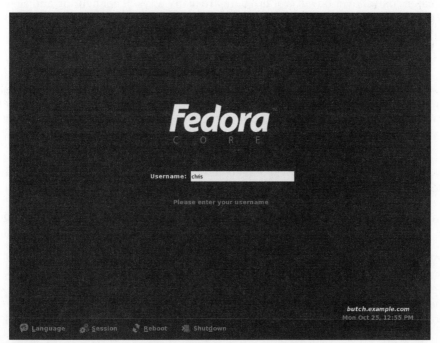

Figure 3-2: The Fedora Project login screen is based on gdm.

You can just enter your login (username) and password to start up your personal desktop environment. Your selected desktop environment — KDE or GNOME — comes up ready for you to use. Although the system defines a desktop environment by default, you can typically change desktop environments on those Linux systems, such as Fedora, that offer both KDE and GNOME.

X display managers can enable you to do a lot more than just get to your desktop. Although different graphical login screens offer different options, here are some you may encounter:

✦ **Session** — Look for a Session button on the login screen (such as the one that comes with Fedora). From there, you can choose to start your login session with a GNOME, KDE, or Failsafe environment. (Failsafe simply opens a Terminal window so, presumably, you can make a quick fix to the system without starting up a whole desktop environment.)

✦ **Language** — Linux systems that are configured to start multiple languages may give you the opportunity to choose a language (other than the default language) to boot into. For this to work, however, you must have installed support for the language you choose.

✦ **Reboot or Shutdown** — There's no need to log in if all you want to do is turn off or restart your computer. Most graphical login screens offer you the option of rebooting or shutting down the machine from that screen.

If you don't like the way the graphical login screen looks, or just want to assert greater control over how it works, there are many ways of configuring and securing X graphical login screens. Later, once you are logged in, you can use the following tools (as root user) to configure the login screen:

✦**KDE Login Manager** — From the KDE control center, you can modify your KDE display manager using the Login Manager screen (from KDE control center, select System Administration ⇨ Login Manager). You can change logos, backgrounds, color schemes, and other features related to the look-and-feel of the login screen.

✦ **GNOME Login Manager** — The GNOME display manager (gdm) comes with a Login Screen Setup utility (from the desktop run the `gdmconfig` command as root user). From the Login Screen Setup window, you can select the Graphical Greeter tab and choose a whole different theme for the login manager. On the Security tab, you may notice that all TCP connections to the X server are disallowed. Don't change this selection because no processes other than those handled directly by your display manager should be allowed to connect to the login screen.

After your login and password have been accepted, the desktop environment configured for your user account starts up. Users can modify their desktop environments to suit their tastes (even to the point of changing the entire desktop environment used).

Boot to a Text Prompt

Instead of a nice graphical screen with pictures and colors, you might see a login prompt that looks like this:

```
Welcome to XYZ Linux
yourcomputer login:
```

This is the way all UNIX and older Linux systems used to appear on the screen when they booted up. Now this is the login prompt that is typical for a system that is installed as a server or, for some reason, was configured not to start an X display manager for you to log in. Run level 3 boots to a plain-text login prompt in multiuser mode.

Just because you have a text prompt doesn't necessarily mean you can start a desktop environment. Many Linux experts boot to a text prompt because they only want to use the GUI on occasion. However, if X and the necessary other desktop components are installed on your computer, you can typically start the desktop after you log in by typing the following command:

```
$ startx
```

The default desktop environment starts up, and you should be ready to go. What you do next depends on whether you have a KDE, GNOME, or some sort of home-spun desktop environment.

Note   In most cases, the GUI configuration you do during installation for your video card and monitor gets you to a working desktop environment. If, for some reason, the screen is unusable when you start the desktop, you need to do some additional configuration. The "Configuring Your Own Desktop" section later in this chapter describes some tools you can use to get your desktop working.

K Desktop Environment (KDE)

The KDE was created to bring a high-quality desktop environment to UNIX (and now Linux) workstations. Integrated within KDE are tools for managing files, windows, multiple desktops, and applications. If you can work a mouse, you can learn to navigate the KDE desktop.

The lack of an integrated, standardized desktop environment once held back Linux and other UNIX systems from acceptance on the desktop. While individual applications ran well, you mostly could not drag-and-drop files or other items between applications. Likewise, you couldn't open a file and expect the machine to launch the correct application to deal with it or save your windows from one login session to the next. With KDE, you can do all those things and much more. For example, you can:

✦ Drag-and-drop a document from a folder window (Konqueror) to the Trash icon (to get rid of it) or on a OpenOffice.org Writer icon (to open it for editing).

✦ Right-click an image file (JPEG, PNG, etc.), and the OpenWith menu lets you choose to open the file using an image viewer (KView), editor (GIMP), slide show viewer (Kuickshow), or other application.

To make more applications available to you in the future, KDE provides a platform for developers to create programs that easily share information and detect how to deal with different data types. The things you can do with KDE grow every day.

KDE is the default desktop environment for SUSE, KNOPPIX, and several other Linux systems. It is available with Red Hat Enterprise Linux and Fedora Core but is not installed by default when they are installed as desktop systems (you need to do an Everything install or to select to add KDE specifically in those cases). KDE also has a different look-and-feel in Red Hat systems than it does from implementation on other systems that deliver KDE desktops.

The following section describes how to get started with KDE. This includes using the KDE Setup wizard, maneuvering around the desktop, managing files, and adding application launchers.

Note   In this chapter, KNOPPIX is the reference model for the KDE descriptions. Because KDE is very configurable, there may be some differences in these descriptions for KDE in other Linux systems.

Using the KDE Desktop

KDE as it's delivered with KNOPPIX uses a lot of the design elements that come from the KDE project, so it's pretty easy to distinguish from other desktop environments. The look-and-feel has similarities to both Windows and Macintosh systems. Figure 3-3 shows an example of the KDE desktop in KNOPPIX:

Some of the key elements of the KDE desktop include:

✦ **Panel** — The KDE panel (shown along the bottom of the screen) includes items that enable you to launch applications and to see minimized representations of active windows, applets, and virtual desktops. A "K" icon on the left side of the panel is used to represent the main menu on a KDE desktop. In KNOPPIX, that icon is followed by a KNOPPIX-specific menu (it looks like a squished penguin) and other icons to launch common applications (the file manager, Terminal window, Web browser, and office applications). Four virtual desktops (shown in little boxes numbered 1, 2, 3, and 4) are available by clicking on the number of the virtual desktop you want to display. Applets (on the right side of the panel) in KNOPPIX let you change your keyboard, set screen resolution, adjust audio controls, and view the time.

✦ **Desktop icons**—The icons on the desktop are usually, by default, those that enable you to access removable media (CD, floppy disk, etc.), throw out files (trash icon), and visit your home directory. In KNOPPIX, the KDE desktop also has a nice feature that lets you access your hard disk partitions directly from icons on the desktop.

✦ **Konqueror file manager**—Konqueror is the file manager window used with KDE desktops. It not only can be used to manage files but also to display Web pages. Konqueror is described in detail later in this chapter.

✦ **Desktop menu**—Right-click the desktop to see a menu of common actions to take. The menu provides a quick way to access your bookmarks; create new folders, files, or devices (with devices, you're actually choosing to mount a device on a particular part of the file system); straighten up your windows or icons; configure the desktop; and log out of your KDE session.

To navigate the KDE desktop, you can use the mouse or key combinations. The responses from the desktop to your mouse depend on which button you click and where the mouse pointer is located. Table 3-1 shows the results of clicking each mouse button with the mouse pointer placed in different locations. (You can change any of these behaviors from the Windows Behavior panel on the KDE Control Center. From the KDE menu, select Settings ➪ Control Center, and then choose the Window Behavior selection under the Desktop heading.)

Figure 3-3: The KDE desktop includes a panel, desktop icons, and menus.

Table 3-1
Single-Click Mouse Actions

Pointer Position	Mouse Button	Result
Window title bar or frame (current window active)	Left	Raises current window
Window title bar or frame (current window active)	Middle	Lowers current window
Window title bar or frame (current window active)	Right	Opens operations menu
Window title bar or frame (current window not active)	Left	Activates current window and raises it to the top
Window title bar or frame (current window not active)	Middle	Activates current window and lowers it
Window title bar or frame (current window not active)	Right	Opens operations menu without changing position
Inner window (current window not active)	Left	Activates current window, raises it to the top, and passes the click to the window
Inner window (current window not active)	Middle or Right	Activates current window and passes the click to the window
Any part of a window	Middle (plus hold Alt key)	Toggles between raising and lowering the window
Any part of a window	Right (plus hold Alt key)	Resizes the window
On the desktop area	Left (hold and drag)	Selects a group of icons
On the desktop area	Right	Opens system pop-up menu

Click a desktop icon to open it. Double-clicking a window title bar results in a window-shade action, where the window scrolls up and down into the title bar.

If you don't happen to have a mouse or you just like to keep your hands on the keyboard, there are several keystroke sequences you can use to navigate the desktop. Table 3-2 shows some examples.

Table 3-2
Keystrokes

Key Combination	Result	Directions
Ctrl+Tab	Step through the virtual desktops	To go from one virtual desktop to the next, hold down the Ctrl key and press the Tab key until you see the desktop that you want to make current. Then release the Ctrl key to select that desktop.
Alt+Tab	Step through windows	To step through each of the windows that are running on the current desktop, hold down the Alt key and press the Tab key until you see the one you want. Then release the Alt key to select it.
Alt+F2	Open Run Command box	To open a box on the desktop that lets you type in a command and run it, hold the Alt key and press F2. Next, type the command in the box and press Enter to run it. You can also type a URL into this box to view a Web page.
Alt+F4	Close current window	To close the current window, press Alt+F4.
Ctrl+Alt+Esc	Close another window	To close an open window on the desktop, press Ctrl+Alt+Esc. When a skull and crossbones appears as the pointer, move the pointer over the window you want to close and click the left mouse button. (This is a good technique for killing a window that has no borders or menu.)
Ctrl+F1, F2, F3 or F4 key	Switch virtual desktops	Go directly to a particular virtual desktop by pressing and holding the Ctrl key and pressing one of the following: F1, F2, F3, or F4. These actions take you directly to desktops one, two, three, and four, respectively. You could do this for up to eight desktops, if you have that many configured.
Alt+F3	Open window operation menu	To open the operations menu for the active window, press Alt+F3. When the menu appears, move the arrow keys to select an action (Move, Size, Minimize, Maximize, and so on), and then press Enter to select it.

Managing Files with the Konqueror File Manager

The Konqueror file manager helps elevate the KDE environment from just another
X window manager to an integrated desktop that competes with GUIs from Apple
Computing or Microsoft. The features in Konqueror rival those that are offered by
those user-friendly desktop systems. Figure 3-4 shows an example of the Konqueror
file manager window in Fedora Core.

Figure 3-4: Konqueror provides a network-ready tool for
managing files.

Some of Konqueror's greatest strengths over earlier file managers are the following:

✦ **Network desktop**— If your computer is connected to the Internet or a LAN,
features built into Konqueror enable you to create links to files (using FTP)
and Web pages (using HTTP) on the network and open them in the Konqueror
window. Those links can appear as file icons in a Konqueror window or on the
desktop. Konqueror also supports WebDAV, which can be configured to allow
local read and write access to remote folders (which is a great tool if you are
maintaining a Web server).

✦ **Web browser interface**— The Konqueror interface works like Mozilla, Internet
Explorer, or other Web browsers in the way you select files, directories, and
Web content. Because Konqueror is based on a browser model, a single click
opens a file, a link to a network resource, or an application program. You can
also open content by typing Web-style addresses in the Location box.

Tip   Web pages that contain Java and JavaScript content run by default in Konqueror. To
check that Java and JavaScript support are turned on, choose Settings ⇨ Configure
Konqueror. From the Settings window, click Java & JavaScript and select the Java
tab. To enable Java, click the Enable Java Globally box and click Apply. Repeat for
the JavaScript tab.

✦ **File types and MIME types**— If you want a particular type of file to always be
launched by a particular application, you can configure that file yourself. KDE
already has dozens of MIME types defined so that particular file and data

types can be automatically detected and opened in the correct application. There are MIME types defined for audio, image, text, video, and a variety of other content.

Of course, you can also perform many standard file manager functions with Konqueror. For example, you can manipulate files by using features such as select, move, cut, paste, and delete; search directories for files; create new items (files, folders, and links, to name a few); view histories of the files and Web sites you have opened; and create bookmarks.

Working with Files

Because most of the ways of working with files in Konqueror are quite intuitive (by intention), here's a quick rundown of how to do basic file manipulation:

To	Do This
Open a file	Double-click the file. It will open right in the Konqueror window, if possible, or in the default application set for the file type. You also can open directories, applications, and links by double-clicking them.
Open a file with a specific application	Right-click a data file, choose Open With from the pop-up menu, and then select one of the available applications to open the file. The applications listed are those that are set up to open the file.
Delete a file	Right-click the file and select Delete. You are asked if you really want to delete the file. Click Yes to permanently delete it.
Copy a file	Right-click the file and select Copy. This copies the file to your clipboard. After that, you can paste it to another folder. Click the Klipper (clipboard) icon in the panel to see a list of copied files.
	Klipper holds the seven most recent copied files, by default. Click the Klipper icon and select Configure Klipper to change the number of copied files Klipper will remember.
Paste a file	Right-click (an open area of a folder) and select Paste. A copy of the file you copied previously is pasted in the current folder.
Link a file	Drag-and-drop a file from one folder to another. When the menu appears, click Link Here. (A linked file lets you access a file from a new location without having to make a copy of the original file. When you open the link, a pointer to the original file causes it to open.)
Move a file Copy a file Create a link to a file	With the original folder and target folder both open on the desktop, click and hold the left mouse button on the file you want to move, drag the file to an open area of the new folder, and release the mouse button. From the menu that appears, click Move. (You also can use this menu to copy or create a link to the file.)

There are also several features for viewing information about the files and folders in your Konqueror windows:

✦ **View quick file information** — Positioning the mouse pointer over the file displays information such as its file name, size, and type in the window footer.

✦ **View hidden files** — Selecting View ➪ Show Hidden Files enables you to see files that begin with a dot (.). Dot files tend to be used for configuration and don't generally need to be viewed in your daily work.

✦ **View file system tree** — Selecting View ➪ View Mode ➪ Tree View provides a tree view of your folder, displaying folders above the current folder in the file system. You can click a folder in the tree view to jump directly to that folder. There are also Multicolumn, Detailed List, and Text views available.

✦ **Change icon view** — Select View ➪ Icon Size, and then choose Large, Medium, or Small to set the size of the icons that are displayed in the window. You can also choose Default Size to return to the default icon size (which is medium, unless you have changed the default through the Configure Konqueror window).

To act on a group of files at the same time, there are a couple of actions you can take. Choose Edit ➪ Selection ➪ Select. A pop-up window lets you match all (*) or any group of documents indicated by typing letters, numbers, and wildcard characters. Or, you can select a group of files by clicking in an open area of the folder and dragging the pointer across the files you want to select. All files within the box will be highlighted. When files are highlighted, you can move, copy, or delete the files as described earlier.

Searching for Files

If you are looking for a particular file or folder, you can use the Konqueror Find feature. To open a Find window to search for a file, open a local folder (such as /home/chris) and choose Tools ➪ Find File; the Find box will appear in your Konqueror window. You could also start the kfind window by typing **kfind** from a Terminal window.

Figure 3-5 shows the kfind window.

Simply type the name of the file you want to search for (in the Named text box) and the folder, including all subfolders, you want to search in (in the Look in text box). Then click the Find button. Use metacharacters, if you like, with your search. For example, search for *.rpm to find all files that end in .rpm or z*.doc to find all files that begin with z and end with .doc. You can also select to have the search be case-sensitive or click the Help button to get more information on searching.

To further limit your search, you can click the Date Range tab and then enter a date range (between), a number of months before today (during the previous x months), or the number of days before today (during the previous x days). Select the Advanced tab to choose to limit the search to files of a particular type (of Type), files that include text that you enter (Containing Text), or that are of a certain size (Size is) in kilobytes.

Figure 3-5: Search for files and folders from the kfind window.

Creating New Files and Folders

You can create a variety of file types when using the Konqueror window. Choose Edit ➪ Create New, and select Folder (to create a new folder) or one of several different types under the File or Device submenu. Depending on which version of Konqueror you are using, you might be able to create some or all of the file types that follow:

✦ **HTML File** — Opens a dialog box that lets you type the name of an HTML file to create.

✦ **Illustration Document** — Opens a dialog box that lets you create a document in kontour format (an illustration). Type the document name you want to create and click OK. The document should have a .kil extension if you want it to automatically open in kontour.

✦ **Link to Application** — Opens a window that lets you type the name of an application. Click the Permissions tab to set file permissions (Exec must be on if you want to run the file as an application). Click the Execute tab and type the name of the program to run (in the field: Execute on click) and a title to appear in the title bar of the application (in the field: Window Title). If it is a text-based command, select the Run in terminal check box. Click the check box to Run as a different user and add the user name. Click the Application tab to assign the application to handle files of particular MIME types. Click OK.

✦ **Link to Location (URL)** — Selecting this menu item opens a dialog box that lets you create a link to a Web address. Type a name to represent the address and type the name of the URL (Web address) for the site. (Be sure to add the http://, ftp://, or other prefix.)

✦ **Presentation Document** — Opens a dialog box to create a document in kpresenter format (a presentation). Type the document name you want to create and click OK. The document should have a .kpr or .kpt extension if you want it to automatically open in kpresenter.

✦ **Spread Sheet Document** — Opens a dialog box that lets you create a document in kspread format (a spreadsheet). Type the document name you want to create and click OK. The document should have a `.ksp` extension if you want it to automatically open in kspread.

✦ **Text Document** — Opens a dialog box that enables you to create a text document in KWord. Type a filename for the text file and click OK. The document should have a `.txt`, `.kwd`, or `.kwt` extension if you want it to open automatically in KWord.

✦ **Text File** — Opens a dialog box that lets you create a document in text format and place it in the Konqueror window. Type the name of the text document to create and click OK.

Under the Device submenu, you can make the following selections:

✦ **CD-ROM Device** — Opens a dialog box that lets you type a new CD-ROM device name. Click the Device tab and type the device name (`/dev/cdrom`), the mount point (such as `/mnt/cdrom` or `/media/cdrom`), and the file system type (you can use iso9660 for the standard CD-ROM file system, ext2 for Linux, or msdos for DOS). When the icon appears, you can open it to mount the CD-ROM and display its contents.

✦ **CDWRITER Device** — From the window that opens, enter the device name of your CD writer.

✦ **DVD-ROM Device** — Opens a dialog box that lets you type a new CD-ROM or DVD-ROM device name. Click the Device tab and type the device name (`/dev/cdrom`), the mount point (such as `/mnt/cdrom` or `/media/cdrecorder`), and the file system type (you can use iso9660 for the standard CD-ROM file system, ext2 for Linux, or msdos for DOS). When the icon appears, you can open it to mount the CD-ROM or DVD-ROM and display its contents.

✦ **Camera Device** — In the dialog box that opens, identify the device name for the camera devices that provides access to your digital camera.

✦ **Floppy Device** — Opens a dialog box in which you type a new floppy name. Click the Device tab and type the device name (`/dev/fd0`), the mount point (such as `/mnt/floppy`), and the file system type (you can use auto to autodetect the contents, ext2 for Linux, or msdos for DOS). When the icon appears, open it to mount the floppy and display its contents.

✦ **Hard Disc Device** — Opens a dialog box that lets you type the name of a new hard disk or hard-disk partition. Click the Device tab and type the device (`/dev/hda1`), the mount point (such as `/mnt/win`), and the file system type (you can use auto to autodetect the contents, ext2 or ext3 for Linux, or vfat for a Windows file system). When the icon appears, you can open it to mount the file system and display its contents.

Creating MIME types and applications is described later in this chapter.

Using Other Browser Features

Because Konqueror performs like a Web browser as well as a file manager, it includes several other browser features. For example, the bookmarks feature enables you to keep a bookmark list of Web sites you have visited. Click Bookmarks, and a drop-down menu of the sites you have bookmarked appears. Select from that list to return to a site. There are several ways to add and change your bookmarks list:

✦ **Add Bookmark** — To add the address of the page that is currently being displayed to your bookmark list, choose Bookmarks ➪ Add Bookmark. The next time you click Bookmarks, you will see the bookmark you just added on the Bookmarks menu. In addition to Web addresses, you can also bookmark any file or folder.

✦ **Edit Bookmarks** — Select Bookmarks ➪ Edit Bookmarks to open a tree view of your bookmarks. From the Bookmark Editor window that appears, you can change the URLs, the icon, or other features of the bookmark. There is also a nice feature that lets you check the status of the bookmark (that is, the address available).

✦ **New Bookmark Folder** — You can add a new folder of bookmarks to your Konqueror bookmarks list. To create a bookmarks folder, choose Bookmarks➪New Folder. Then type a name for the new Bookmarks folder, and click OK. The new bookmark folder appears on your bookmarks menu. You can add the current location to that folder by clicking on the folder name and selecting Add Bookmark.

Configuring Konqueror Options

You can change many of the visual attributes of the Konqueror window, including which menu bars and toolbars appear. You can have any of the following bars appear on the Konqueror window: Menubar, Toolbar, Extra Toolbar, Location Toolbar, Bookmark Toolbar. Select Settings, and then click the bar you want to have appear (or not appear). The bar appears when the check mark is shown next to it.

You can modify a variety of options for Konqueror by choosing Settings ➪ Configure Konqueror. The Konqueror Settings window appears, offering the following options:

✦ **Behavior** — Change file manager behavior.

✦ **Appearance** — Change file manager fonts and colors.

✦ **Previews & Meta-Data** — An icon in a Konqueror folder can be made to resemble the contents of the file it represents. For example, if the file is a JPEG image, the icon representing the file could be a small version of that image. Using the Previews features, you can limit the size of the file used (1MB is the default) because many massive files could take too long to refresh on the screen. You can also choose to have any thumbnail embedded in a file to be used as the icon or have the size of the icon reflect the shape of the image used.

✦ **File Associations**—Describes which programs to launch for each file type.

✦ **Web Behavior**—Click the Behavior (Browser) button to open a window to configure the Web browser features of Konqueror. By enabling Form Completion, Konqueror can save form data you type and, at a later time, fill that information into other forms. If your computer has limited resources, you can speed up page display by clearing the Automatically Load Images check box or by disabling animations.

✦ **Java and JavaScript**—Enable or disable Java and JavaScript content contained in Web pages in your Konqueror window.

✦ **Fonts**—Choose which fonts to use, by default, for various fonts needed on Web pages (standard font, fixed font, serif font, sans serif font, cursive font, and fantasy font). The serif fonts are typically used in body text, while sans serif fonts are often used in headlines. You can also set the Minimum and Medium font sizes.

✦ **Web Shortcuts**—Display a list of keyword shortcuts you can use to go to different Internet sites. For example, follow the word "ask" with a search string to search the Ask Jeeves (www.ask.com) Web site. (This feature doesn't appear to be working at the moment.)

✦ **History Sidebar**—Modify the behavior of the list of sites you have visited (the history). By default, the most recent 500 URLs are stored, and after 500 days (KNOPPIX) or 90 days (Fedora), a URL is dropped from the list. There's also a button to clear your history. (To view your history list in Konqueror, open the left side panel, then click the tiny scroll icon.)

✦ **Cookies**—Choose whether cookies are enabled in Konqueror. By default, you are asked to confirm that it is okay each time a Web site tries to create or modify a cookie. You can change that to either accept or reject all cookies. You can also set policies for acceptance or rejection of cookies based on host and domain names.

✦ **Cache**—Indicate how much space on your hard disk can be used to store the sites you have visited (based on the value in the Disk Cache Size field).

✦ **Proxy**—Click Proxy to configure Konqueror to access the Internet through a proxy server (by default, Konqueror tries to connect there directly). You need to enter the address and port number of the computer providing HTTP and/or FTP proxy services. Alternatively, you can have Konqueror try to automatically detect the proxy configuration.

✦ **Stylesheets**—Choose whether to use the default stylesheet, a user-defined stylesheet, or a custom stylesheet. The stylesheet sets the font family, font sizes, and colors that are applied to Web pages. (This won't change particular font requests made by the Web page.) If you select a custom stylesheet, click the Customize tab to customize your own fonts and colors.

✦ **Crypto** — Display a list of secure certificates that can be accepted by the Konqueror browser. By default, Secure Socket Layer (SSL) versions 2 and 3 certificates are accepted, as is TLS support (if supported by the server). You can also choose to be notified when you are entering or leaving a secure Web site.

✦ **Browser Identification** — Set how Konqueror identifies itself when it accesses a Web site. By default, Konqueror tells the Web site that it is the Mozilla Web browser. You can select Konqueror to appear as different Web browsers to specific sites. You must sometimes do this when a site denies you access because you do not have a specific type of browser (even though Konqueror may be fully capable of displaying the content).

✦ **Plugins** — Display a list of directories that Konqueror will search to find plug-ins. Konqueror can also scan your computer to find plug-ins that are installed for other browsers in other locations.

✦ **Performance** — Display configuration settings that can be used to improve Konqueror performance. You can preload an instance after KDE startup or minimize memory usage.

Managing Windows

If you have a lot of windows open at the same time, tips for organizing and managing the windows on your desktop are very helpful. KDE helps you out by maintaining window lists you can work with and shortcuts for keeping the windows in order.

Using the Taskbar

When you open a window, a button representing the window appears in the taskbar at the bottom of the screen. Here is how you can manage windows from the taskbar:

✦ **Toggle windows** — Left-click any running task in the taskbar to toggle between opening the window and minimizing it.

✦ **Move windows** — Move a window from the current desktop to any other virtual desktop. Right-click any task in the taskbar, select To Desktop, and then select any desktop number. The window moves to that desktop.

All the windows that are running, regardless of which virtual desktop you are on, appear in the taskbar. If there are multiple windows of the same type shown as a single task, you can right-click that task; then, select All to Desktop to move all related windows to the desktop you pick.

Creating an Image Gallery with Konqueror

There's a neat feature in Konqueror that lets you create a quick image gallery. The feature takes a directory of images, creates thumbnails for each one, and generates an HTML (Web) page. The HTML page includes a title you choose, all image thumbnails arranged on a page, and links to the larger images. Here's how you do it:

1. Add images you want in your gallery to any folder (for example, /home/jake/images). Make sure they are sized, rotated, and cropped the way you like before beginning. (Try The Gimp for manipulating your images by typing **gimp&** from a Terminal.)

2. Open the folder in Konqueror (for example, type **/home/knoppix/images** in the Location box).

3. Click Tools ⇨ Create Image Gallery. The Create Image Gallery window appears.

4. Type a title for the image gallery into the Page Title box. You can also select other attributes of the gallery, such as the number of rows, information about the image to appear on the page (name, size, and dimension), the fonts, and the colors to use.

5. Click OK.

Konqueror generates the thumbnails and adds them to the thumbs directory. The image gallery page itself opens and is saved to the images.html file. (Select the Folders button to save the gallery under a different name. You can also have Konqueror create galleries in recursive subfolders to a depth you choose.) You can now copy the entire contents of this directory to a Web server and publish your pictures on the Internet. Here's an example of a Konqueror image gallery:

Uncluttering the Desktop

If your windows are scattered willy-nilly all over the desktop, here are a couple of ways you can make your desktop's appearance a little neater:

✦ **Unclutter windows** — Right-click the desktop, and then click Windows ⇨ Unclutter Windows on the menu. All windows that are currently displayed on the desktop are lined up along the left side of the screen (or aligned with other windows), from the top down.

✦ **Cascade windows** — Right-click the desktop, and then click Windows ⇨ Cascade windows on the menu. The windows are aligned as they are with the Unclutter selection, except that the windows are each indented starting from the upper-left corner.

Moving Windows

The easiest way to move a window from one location to another is to place the cursor on the window's title bar, hold down the mouse button and drag the window to a new location, and release the mouse button to drop the window. Another way to do it is to click the window menu button (top-left corner of the title bar), select Move, move the mouse to relocate the window, and then click again to place it.

If somehow the window gets stuck in a location where the title bar is off the screen, you can move it back to where you want it by holding down the Alt key and clicking the left mouse button in the inner window. Then move the window where you want it and release.

Resizing Windows

To resize a window, grab anywhere on the outer edge of the window border, and then move the mouse until the window is the size you want. Grab a corner to resize vertically and horizontally at the same time. Grab a side to resize in only one direction.

You can also resize a window by clicking the window menu button (top-left corner of the title bar) and selecting Size. Move the mouse until the window is resized and click to leave it there.

Pinning Windows on Top or Bottom

You can set a window to always stay on top of all other windows or always stay under them. Keeping a window on top can be useful for a small window that you want to always refer to (such as a clock or a small TV viewing window). To pin a window on top of the desktop, click in the window title bar. From the menu that appears, select Advanced ⇨ Keep Above Others. Likewise, to keep the window on the bottom, select Advanced ⇨ Keep Below Others.

Using Virtual Desktops

To give you more space to run applications than will fit on your physical screen, KDE gives you access to several virtual desktops at the same time. Using the 1, 2, 3, and 4 buttons on the panel, you can easily move between the different desktops. Just click the one you want.

If you want to move an application from one desktop to another, you can do so from the window menu. Click the window menu button for the window you want to move, click To Desktop, and then select Desktop 1, 2, 3, or 4. The window will disappear from the current desktop and move to the one you selected.

Configuring the Desktop

If you want to change the look, feel, or behavior of your KDE desktop, the best place to start is the KDE Control Center. The Control Center window (Figure 3-6) lets you configure dozens of attributes associated with colors, fonts, backgrounds, and screen savers. You can also change attributes relating to how you work with windows and files.

To open the KDE Control Center from the desktop, select Settings ⇨ Control Center from the K menu or open a Terminal window and type **sudo kcontrol**.

Figure 3-6: Manage your KDE desktop from the KDE Control Center.

Click the plus (+) sign next to the topic you want to configure, and then select the particular item you want to configure. The following sections describe some of the features you can configure from the Control Center.

Changing the Display

You can change a lot of the look-and-feel of your desktop display. Under the Appearance & Themes topic (click the plus sign), you can change Background, Colors, Fonts, Icons, Launch Feedback, Panel, Screen Saver, Style, Theme Manager, and Window Decoration.

Here are a few of the desktop features you may want to change:

✦ **Background** — Under the Appearance & Themes heading in the KDE Control Center, select Background. By default, all of your virtual desktops use the same background. To have different backgrounds for each virtual desktop, select the box next to the Setting for Desktop heading, choose any of the four desktops, and then choose the background you want for the current desktop.

For each desktop, select Picture, Slideshow, or No Picture. For a Picture, there are several backgrounds you can choose from the pull-down menu, or you can browse your file system for a picture. To do a slide show, click Slideshow and select Setup (to choose your pictures and define how often they change).

Click Apply to apply your selections.

✦ **Screensaver** — Under the Appearance & Themes heading, select Screen Saver. From the window that appears, select from a list of screen savers. KNOPPIX only includes a blank screen saver. However, Fedora Core comes with about 160 different screen savers. My favorite is Slideshow, where you can have a slide show of images for your screen saver. Click Setup to identify an image directory or otherwise modify the behavior of the screen saver. Under settings, select how many minutes of inactivity before the screen saver turns on. You can also choose Require Password to require that a password be entered before you can access your display after the screen saver has come on.

Tip   If you are working in a place where you want your desktop to be secure, be sure to turn on the Require Password feature. This prevents others from gaining access to your computer when you forget to lock it or shut it off. If you have any virtual terminals open, switch to them and type **vlock** to lock each of them as well. (You need to install the vlock package if the `vlock` command isn't available.)

✦ **Fonts** — You can assign different fonts to different places in which fonts appear on the desktop. Under the Appearance & Themes heading, select Fonts. Select one of the categories of fonts (General, Fixed width, Toolbar, Menu, Window title, Taskbar, and Desktop fonts). Then click the Choose check box to select a font from the Select Font list box that you want to assign to that category. If the font is available, an example of the text appears in the Sample text box.

Tip   To use 100dpi fonts, you need to add an entry for 100dpi fonts to `/etc/X11/xorg.conf` file. After you make that change, you need to restart the X server for it to take effect.

Other attributes you can change for the selected fonts are size (in points) and character set (to select an ISO standard character set). Select Apply to apply the changes.

✦ **Colors** — Under the Appearance & Themes heading, select Colors. The window that appears lets you change the color of selected items on the desktop. Select a whole color scheme from the Color Scheme list box. Or select an item from the Widget color box to change a particular item. Items you can change include text, backgrounds, links, buttons, and title bars.

Changing Panel Attributes

For most people, the panel is the place where they select which desktop is active and which applications are run. You can change panel behavior from the Configure Panel window. Right-click any empty space on your panel, and then select Configure Panel. You can change these features from the Settings window that appears:

✦ **Arrangement** — Change the location of the panel by clicking Top, Left, Bottom, or Right in the Panel Location list box. The Panel Style selection lets you change the size of the Panel from Medium to Tiny, Small, or Large.

✦ **Hiding** — Certain selections enable you to autohide the panel or use hide buttons. Under the Hide Mode heading, choose whether to hide only when a panel hiding button is clicked or to hide automatically after a set number of seconds when the cursor is not in the panel area. You can also show or not show hiding buttons. Sliders let you select the delay and speed at which panels and buttons are hidden.

✦ **Menus** — Unlike with the GNOME main menu, you have the capability to manipulate the main menu from the GUI in KDE. Click the Edit K Menu button. The KDE Menu editor that appears lets you cut, copy, paste, remove, and modify submenus and applications from your main menu.

Adding Application Launchers and MIME Types

You want to be able to quickly access the applications that you use most often. One of the best ways to make that possible is to add icons to the panel or the desktop that can launch the applications you need with a single click. Procedures for adding applications to the panel and desktop are described in the following sections.

Adding Applications to the Panel

You can add any KDE application to the KDE panel quite easily. Here's how:

1. Right-click an open space on the panel.
2. Choose Add ➪ Application Button.

3. Select one of the categories of applications.

4. Select any application from that category (or select Add This Menu To Add the Whole Menu of Applications).

An icon representing the application immediately appears on the panel. (If the panel seems a bit crowded, you might want to remove some applications you don't use.)

If you decide later that you no longer want this application to be available on the panel, right-click the edge of the icon and click the Remove button. To move it to a different location on the panel, right-click it, click Move, move it to where you want it on the panel, and click again.

Adding Applications to the Desktop

To add an application to the desktop, use the desktop menu. Here's how:

1. Right-click an open area of the desktop.

2. Select Create New ⇨ File ⇨ Link to Application from the menu.

3. On the Properties window that appears, click the General tab and replace Link to Application with the name you want to appear for the application on the desktop. On that same tab, click the gear icon and select one icon from the list to represent your application.

4. Click the Application tab and add a description of the application and a comment. Then in the Command box, type the command you want to run or browse your file system (click the Browse button) to find the command to run.

5. Click OK, and the icon for the new application launcher appears on the desktop.

If you decide later that you no longer want this application to be available on the desktop, right-click the icon and click Delete or Move to Trash.

The GNOME Desktop

GNOME (pronounced *guh-nome*) provides the desktop environment that you get by default when you install Fedora Core and other Red Hat Linux systems. This desktop environment provides the software that is between your X Window System framework and the look-and-feel provided by the window manager. GNOME is a stable and reliable desktop environment, with a few cool features in it.

The new GNOME 2.8 desktop comes with the most recent version of Fedora Core. For GNOME 2.8, enhancements include a new volume manager (for managing removable media), keyring manager (for managing keys), and remote desktop preferences. To use your GNOME desktop, you should become familiar with the following components:

✦ **Metacity (window manager)** — The default window manager for GNOME in Fedora is Metacity. It provides such things as themes, and window borders and controls.

✦ **Nautilus (file manager/graphical shell)** — When you open a folder (by double-clicking the Home icon on your desktop, for example), the Nautilus window opens and displays the contents of the selected folder. Nautilus can also display other types of content, such as shared folders from Windows computers on the network (using SMB).

✦ **GNOME panel (application/task launcher)** — This panel, which lines the bottom of your screen, is designed to make it convenient for you to launch the applications you use, manage running applications, and work with multiple virtual desktops. By default, the panel contains the main menu (represented by a red hat in Red Hat Linux or a footprint icon in others), desktop application launchers (Evolution e-mail and a set of OpenOffice.org applications), a workspace switcher (for managing four virtual desktops), window list, and a clock. It also has an icon to alert you when you need software updates.

✦ **Desktop area** — The windows and icons you use are arranged on the desktop area, which supports such things a drag-and-drop between applications, a desktop menu (right-click to see it), and icons for launching applications. There is a Computer icon which consolidates CD drives, floppy drives, the file system, and shared network resources in one place.

GNOME also includes a set of Preferences windows that enable you to configure different aspects of your desktop. You can change backgrounds, colors, fonts, keyboard shortcuts, and other features relating to the look and behavior of the desktop. Figure 3-7 shows how the GNOME desktop environment appears the first time you log in, with a few windows added to the screen.

The following sections provide details on using the GNOME desktop.

Using the Metacity Window Manager

The Metacity window manager seems to have been chosen as the default window manager for GNOME in Red Hat Linux because of its simplicity. The creator of Metacity refers to it as a "boring window manager for the adult in you" — then goes on to compare other window managers to colorful, sugary cereal, while Metacity is characterized as Cheerios.

Desktop
icons

Nautilus file manager

Desktop area

Preferences window

Panel

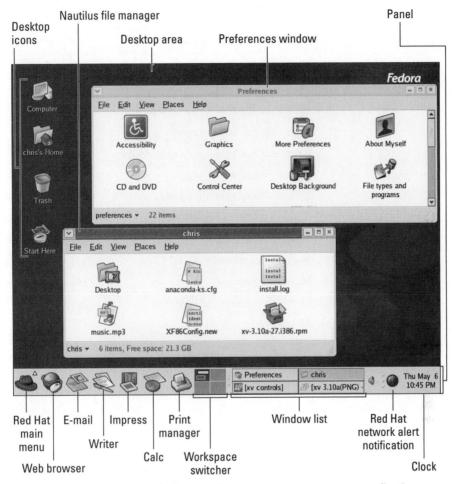

Figure 3-7: In the GNOME desktop environment, you can manage applications from the panel.

There really isn't much you can do with Metacity (except get your work done efficiently). Assigning new themes to Metacity and changing colors and window decorations is done through the GNOME preferences (and is described later). A few Metacity themes exist, but expect the number to grow.

Basic Metacity functions that might interest you are keyboard shortcuts and the workspace switcher. Table 3-3 shows keyboard shortcuts to get around the Metacity window manager.

Table 3-3
Metacity Keyboard Shortcuts

Actions	Keystrokes	
Window focus	Cycle forward, with pop-up icons	Alt+Tab
	Cycle backward, with pop-up icons	Alt+Shift+Tab
	Cycle forward, without pop-up icons	Alt+Esc
	Cycle backward, without pop-up icons	Alt+Shift+Esc
Panel focus	Cycle forward among panels	Alt+Ctrl+Tab
	Cycle backward among panels	Alt+Ctrl+Shift+Tab
Workspace focus	Move to workspace to the right	Ctrl+Alt+right arrow
	Move to workspace to the left	Ctrl+Alt+left arrow
	Move to upper workspace	Ctrl+Alt+up arrow
	Move to lower workspace	Ctrl+Alt+down arrow
	Minimize/maximize all windows	Ctrl+Alt+D
Show window menu	Alt-Space bar	
Close menu	Esc	

Another Metacity feature of interest is the workspace switcher. Four virtual workspaces appear in the workspace switcher on the GNOME panel. Here are some things to do with the workspace switcher:

✦ **Choose current workspace** — Four virtual workspaces appear in the workspace switcher. Click any of the four virtual workspaces to make it your current workspace.

✦ **Move windows to other workspaces** — Click any window, each represented by a tiny rectangle in a workspace, to drag-and-drop it to another workspace.

✦ **Add more workspaces** — Right-click the workspace switcher, and select Preferences. You can add workspaces (up to 32).

✦ **Name workspaces** — Right-click the workspace switcher and select Preferences. Click in the Workspaces pane to change names of workspaces to any names you choose.

You can view and change information about Metacity controls and settings using the gconf-editor window (type **gconf-editor** from a Terminal window). As the window says, it is not the recommended way of changing preferences, so when possible, you should change the desktop through GNOME preferences. However, gconf-editor is a good way to see descriptions of each Metacity feature.

From the gconf-editor window, select apps ➪ metacity, and then choose from general, global_keybindings, keybindings_commands, window_keybindings, and workspace_names. Click each key to see its value, along with short and long descriptions of the key.

Using the GNOME panel

The GNOME panel is the place from which you manage your desktop. From this panel you can start applications (from buttons or menus), see what programs are active, and monitor how your system is running. There are also many ways to change the panel — by adding applications or monitors, or by changing the placement or behavior of the panel, for example.

Right-click any open space on the panel to see the Panel menu (see Figure 3-8).

Figure 3-8: The GNOME panel menu.

From GNOME's Panel menu, you can perform a variety of functions, including:

✦ **Use the main menu.** The main menu (represented by a red hat in Red Hat systems) displays most of the applications and system tools you will use from the desktop.

✦ **Add to panel.** Add an applet, menu, launcher, drawer, or button.

✦ **Delete this panel.** Delete the current panel.

✦ **Properties.** Change the panel's position, size, and background properties.

✦ **New panel.** Add panels to your desktop in different styles and locations.

You can also work with items on a panel. For example, you can:

✦ **Move items.** Move items on a panel simply by dragging and dropping them to new positions.

✦ **Resize items.** Some elements, such as the Window List, can be resized by clicking an edge and dragging it to the new size.

✦ **Use the Window List.** Tasks running on the desktop appear in the Window List area. Click a task to minimize or maximize it.

The following sections describe some things you can do with the GNOME panel.

Use the Main Menu

Click the main menu icon on the panel, and you see categories of applications and system tools that you can select. Click the application you want to launch. To add an item to launch from the panel—and to view its properties—right-click it. There is currently no way to add or remove applications to or from this menu from the GUI in GNOME. However, you can manually add items to your GNOME menus.

To add to the main menu, create a `.desktop` file in the `/usr/share/applications` directory. The easiest way to do that is to copy an existing `.desktop` file that is on the menu you want and modify it. For example, to add a video player to the Sound & Video menu, you could do the following (as root user):

```
# cd /usr/share/applications
# cp gnome-cd.desktop vidplay.desktop
```

Next use any text editor to change the contents of the `vidplay.desktop` file you created by adding a comment, file to execute, icon to display, and application name. After you save the changes, the new item immediately appears on the menu (no need to restart anything).

Adding an Applet

There are several small applications, called *applets,* that you can run directly on the GNOME panel. These applications can show information you may want to see on an ongoing basis or may just provide some amusement. To see what applets are available and to add applets that you want to your panel, perform the following steps:

1. Right-click an open space in the panel so that the panel menu appears.

2. Select Add to Panel. An Add to Panel window appears.

3. Select from among several dozen applets, including a clock, dictionary lookup, stock ticker, weather report, lock screen, log out, run application, take screen shot, fortune-telling fish, eyes that follow your mouse, e-mail Inbox monitor, and modem lights monitor. The applet appears on the panel, ready for you to use.

Figure 3-9 shows (from left to right) eyes, system monitor, CD player, stock ticker, e-mail Inbox monitor, and dictionary lookup applets.

Figure 3-9: Placing applets on the Panel makes it easy to access them.

After an applet is installed, right-click it on the panel to see what options are available. For example, select Preferences for the stock ticker, and you can add or delete stocks whose prices you want to monitor. If you don't like the applet's location, right-click it, click Move, slide the mouse until the applet is where you want it (even to another panel), and click to set its location.

If you no longer want an applet to appear on the panel, right-click it, and then click Remove From Panel. The icon representing the applet disappears. If you find that you have run out of room on your panel, you can add a new panel to another part of the screen, as described in the next section.

Adding Another Panel

You can have several panels on your GNOME desktop. You can add panels that run along the entire bottom, top, or side of the screen. To add a panel, do the following:

1. Right-click an open space in the panel so that the Panel menu appears.

2. Select New Panel. A new panel appears at the top of the screen.

3. Right-click an open space in the new panel and select Properties.

4. From the Panel Properties, select where you want the panel from the Orientation box (Top, Bottom, Left or Right).

After you've added a panel, you can add applets or application launchers to it as you did to the default panel. To remove a panel, right-click it and select Delete This Panel.

Adding an Application Launcher

Icons on your panel represent a Web browser and several office productivity applications. You can add your own icons to launch applications from the panel as well. To add a new application launcher to the panel, do the following:

1. Right-click in an open space on the panel.

2. Select Add to Panel ⇨ Application Launcher from the menu. All application categories from your main desktop menu (the one under the red hat or footprint icon) appear.

3. Select the arrow next to the category of application you want, and then select Add. An icon representing the application appears.

To launch the application you just added, simply click the icon on the panel.

If the application you want to launch is not on your red hat menu, you can build a launcher yourself as follows:

1. Right-click in an open space on the panel.

2. Select Add to Panel ➪ Custom Application Launcher ➪ Add. The Create Launcher window appears.

3. Provide the following information for the application that you want to add:

   • **Name** — A name to identify the application (this appears in the tool tip when your mouse is over the icon).

   • **Generic Name** — A name to identify the type of application.

   • **Comment** — A comment describing the application. It also appears when you later move your mouse over the launcher.

   • **Command** — The command line that is run when the application is launched. Use the full path name, plus any required options.

   • **Type** — Select Application (to launch an application). (Other selections include Link, to open a Web address in a browser, or FSDevice, to open a file system.)

   • **Run in Terminal** — Click this box if the application is a character-based or ncurses application. (Applications written using the curses library run in a Terminal window but offer screen-oriented mouse and keyboard controls.)

4. Click the Icon box (it might say No Icon). Select one of the icons shown and click OK. Alternatively, you can browse the Linux file system to choose an icon.

Note Icons available to represent your application are contained in the `/usr/share/pixmaps` directory. These icons are either in `.png` or `.xpm` formats. If there isn't an icon in the directory you want to use, create your own (in one of those two formats) and assign it to the application.

5. Click OK.

The application should now appear in the panel. Click it to start the application.

Adding a Drawer

A drawer is an icon that you can click to display other icons representing menus, applets, and launchers; it behaves just like a panel. Essentially any item you can add to a panel you can add to a drawer. By adding a drawer to your GNOME panel, you can include several applets and launchers that together take up only the space of one icon. Click on the drawer to show the applets and launchers as though they were being pulled out of a drawer icon on the panel.

To add a drawer to your panel, right-click the panel and select Add to Panel ➪ Drawer. A drawer appears on the panel. Right-click it, and add applets or launchers to it as you would to a panel. Click the icon again to retract the drawer.

Figure 3-10 shows a portion of the panel with an open drawer that includes icons for launching a Terminal window, the GIMP, and the Ethereal window.

Figure 3-10: Add launchers or applets to a drawer on your GNOME panel.

Changing Panel Properties

Panel properties you can change are limited to the orientation, size, hiding policy, and background. To open the Panel Properties window that applies to a specific panel, right-click on an open space on the panel and choose Properties. The Panel Properties window that appears includes the following values:

✦ **Name** — Contains a name by which you identify this panel.

✦ **Orientation** — Move the panel to different locations on the screen by clicking on a new position.

✦ **Size** — Select the size of your panel by choosing its height in pixels (48 pixels by default).

✦ **Expand** — Click this check box to have the panel expand to fill the entire side, or unselect the check box to make the panel only as wide as the applets it contains.

✦ **AutoHide** — Select whether a panel is automatically hidden (appearing only when the mouse pointer is in the area).

✦ **Show Hide buttons** — Choose whether the Hide/Unhide buttons (with pixmap arrows on them) appear on the edges of the panel.

✦ **Arrows on hide buttons** — If you select Show Hide Buttons, you can choose to have arrows on those buttons.

✦ **Background** — From the Background tab, you can assign a color to the background of the panel, assign a pixmap image, or just leave the default (which is based on the current system theme). Click the Background Image check box if you want to select an Image for the background, and then select an image, such as a tile from `/usr/share/backgrounds/tiles` or other directory.

Tip

I usually turn on the AutoHide feature and turn off the Hide buttons. Using AutoHide gives you more desktop space to work with. When you move your mouse to the edge where the panel is, the panel pops up — so you don't need Hide buttons.

Using the Nautilus File Manager

At one time, file managers did little more than let you run applications, create data files, and open folders. These days, as the information a user needs expands beyond the local system, file managers are expected to also display Web pages, access FTP sites, and play multimedia content. The Nautilus file manager, which is the default GNOME file manager, is an example of just such a file manager.

When you open the Nautilus file manager window (from the GNOME main menu or by opening the Home icon or other folder on your desktop), you see the name of the location you are viewing (such as the folder name) and what that location contains (files, folders, and applications). Figure 3-11 is an example of the file manager window displaying the home directory of a user named chris (/home/chris).

Figure 3-11: The Nautilus file manager enables you to move around the file system, open directories, launch applications, and open Samba folders.

In GNOME 2.8, the default Nautilus window has been greatly simplified to show fewer controls and provide more space for file and directory icons. Double-click a folder to open that folder in a new window. Select your folder name in the lower-left corner of the window to see the file system hierarchy above the current folder (as shown in Figure 3-11). Whatever size, location, and other setting you had for the folder the last time you closed it, GNOME remembers and returns it to that state the next time you open it.

To see more controls, right-click a folder and select Browse Folder to open it. Icons on the toolbar of the Nautilus window let you move forward and back among the directories and Web sites you visit. To move up the directory structure, click the up arrow. To refresh the view of the folder or Web page, click the Reload button. The Home button takes you to your home page, and the Computer button lets you see the same type of information you would see from a My Computer icon on a Windows system (CD drive, floppy drive, hard disk file systems, and network folders).

Icons in Nautilus often indicate the type of data that a particular file contains. The contents or file extension of each file can determine which application is used to work with the file, or you can right-click an icon to open the file it represents with a particular application or viewer.

Here are some of the more interesting features of Nautilus:

✦ **Sidebar** — From the Browse Folder view described previously, select View ⇨ Side Pane to have a sidebar appear in the left column of the screen. From the sidebar, you can click a pull-down menu that represents different types of information you can select one at a time.

The Tree tab, for example, shows a tree view of the directory structure, so you can easily traverse your directories. The Notes tab lets you add notes that become associated with the current Directory or Web page, and the History tab displays a history of directories and Web sites you have visited, enabling you to click those items to return to the sites they represent. There is also an Emblems tab that lets you drag-and-drop emblems on files or folders to indicate something about the file or folder (emblems include icons representing drafts, urgent, bug, and multimedia).

✦ **Windows file and printer sharing** — If your computer is connected to a LAN on which Windows computers are sharing files and printers, you can view those resources from Nautilus. Type **smb:** in the Open Location box (select File ⇨ Open Location to get there) to see available workgroups. Click a workgroup to see computers from that workgroup that are sharing files and printers. Figure 3-12 shows an example of Nautilus displaying icons representing Windows computers in a workgroup called estreet (smb://estreet).

Figure 3-12: Display shared Windows file and printer servers (SMB) in Nautilus.

✦ **MIME types and file types** — To handle different types of content that may be encountered in the Nautilus window, you can set applications to respond based on MIME type and file type. With a folder being displayed, right-click a file for which you want to assign an application. Click either Open With an Application or Open With a Viewer. If no application or viewer has been assigned for the file type, click Associate Application to be able to select an application. From the Add File Types window, you can add an application based on the file extension and MIME type representing the file.

✦ **Drag-and-drop** — You can use drag-and-drop within the Nautilus window, between the Nautilus and the desktop, or among multiple Nautilus windows. As other GNOME-compliant applications become available, they are expected to also support the drag-and-drop feature.

If you would like more information on the Nautilus file manager, visit the GNOME Web site (`www.gnome.org/nautilus`).

Changing GNOME Preferences

There are many ways to change the behavior, look, and feel of your GNOME desktop. Most GNOME preferences can be modified from the Preferences window. The easiest way to access that is to type **preferences:** in the Nautilus Open Location box.

Unlike earlier versions of GNOME for Fedora Core and Red Hat Linux, boundaries between preferences relating to the window manager (Metacity), file manager (Nautilus), and the GNOME desktop itself have been blurred. Preferences for all of these features are in the Preferences window. Figure 3-13 shows the Preferences window, with icons that represent features you can change.

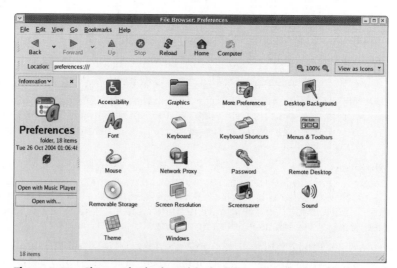

Figure 3-13: Change the look-and-feel of your desktop from the Preferences window.

The following items highlight some of the preferences you might want to change:

✦ **Accessibility** — If you have difficulty operating a mouse or keyboard, the Keyboard Accessibility Preferences (AccessX) window lets you adapt mouse and keyboard settings to make it easier for you to operate your computer. From the Preferences window, open Accessibility.

✦ **Desktop Background** — From Desktop Background Preferences, you can choose a solid color or an image to use as wallpaper. If you choose to use a solid color (by selecting No Wallpaper), click the Color box, select a color from the palette, and click OK.

To use wallpaper for your background, open the folder containing the image you want to use, and then drag the image into the Desktop Wallpaper pane on the Desktop Preferences window. You can choose from a variety of images in the /usr/share/nautilus/patterns and /usr/share/backgrounds/tiles directories. Then choose to have the wallpaper image tiled (repeated pattern), centered, scaled (in proportion), or stretched (using any proportion to fill the screen).

✦ **CD and DVD Properties** — Even if you don't change CD properties, it is important to know what happens when you insert a CD or DVD. (These properties are associated with a feature called magicdev, which is a bit controversial. You'll learn more about magicdev in Chapter 19.)

• For data CDs, the CD is mounted when it is inserted, any autorun program on the CD is run, and a file manager window opens for the CD. If you would rather mount and open the CD as you choose, you can turn off any or all of these preferences.

• For audio CDs, the gnome-cd player is launched and the CD begins playing. You can type in a different CD player, if you like, or clear the Run Command When CD Is Inserted check box so that you can choose which player to use later.

• For blank CDs, a CD-burning utility is launched through the Nautilus window. After that, you can burn audio files or data to the blank CD.

• For DVD (video), the DVD is not set to play automatically. If you have a player installed that can play the content of DVDs that you have, turn on this feature and add the command to run the player into the Command box. For a data DVD, such as the one that comes with this book, you can simply mount it to access the data.

✦ **File Types and Programs** — The File Types and Programs preferences can help you understand the different types of data files that GNOME knows about. Double-click this icon to see data types (audio, documents, images, information, and so on) that have definitions in GNOME. Then choose a particular data type (such as Audio, ogg audio).

From the Edit File Type window that appears, you can see the information assigned to the file type. For example, when data that ends with an .ogg extension appears in a Nautilus window, you can see the icon that will represent the file, the mime type assigned to the file, and the action (if any) that's taken when you open the file.

You can modify any file type that appears in these preferences windows. You can choose what applications are run and what icons represent data of that type. You can even create your own data types.

✦ **Screensaver** — Choose from dozens of screensavers from the Screensaver window. Select Random Screensaver to have your screen saver chosen randomly from those you mark with a check, or select one that you like from the list to use all the time. Next, choose how long your screen must be idle before the screensaver starts (default is 10 minutes). For random screen savers, you can select how long before cycling to the next screen saver. You can also choose to require a password or to enable power management to shut down your monitor after a set number of minutes (Advanced Tab). Figure 3-14 shows the Screensaver Preferences dialog box.

Figure 3-14: Select specific or random screen savers from the Screensaver Preferences dialog box.

✦ **Theme Selector** — Choose an entire theme of elements to be used on your desktop, if you like. A desktop theme affects not only the background but also the way that many buttons and menu selections appear. There are only a few themes available for the window manager (Metacity) in the Fedora Core distribution, but you can get a bunch of other themes from `themes.freshmeat.net` (click on Metacity).

Click Install theme, and then click the Window Border tab to select from different themes that change the title bar and other borders of your windows. Click the Icons tab to choose different icons to represent items on your desktop. Themes change immediately as you click or when you drag a theme name on the desktop.

Exiting GNOME

When you are done with your work, you can either log out from your current session or shut down your computer completely. To exit from GNOME, do the following:

1. Click the red hat menu button.

2. Select Log Out from the menu. A pop-up window appears, asking if you want to Log Out, Shut Down, or Restart the computer.

 Tip

At this point, you can also choose to save your session by clicking Save Current Setup. This is a great way to have the applications that you use all the time restart the next time you log in. Make sure you save your data before you exit, however. Most applications do not yet support the data-saving feature.

3. Select Log Out from the pop-up menu. This logs you out and returns you to either the graphical login screen or to your shell login prompt. (If you select Shut Down, the system shuts down, and if you select Reboot, the system restarts.)

4. Select OK to finish exiting from GNOME.

If you are unable to get to the Log Out button (if, for example, your Panel crashed), there are two other exit methods. Try one of these two ways, depending on how you started the desktop:

✦ If you started the desktop by typing **startx** from your login shell, press Ctrl+Alt+F1 to return to your login shell. Then press Ctrl+C to kill the desktop.

✦ If you started the desktop from a graphical login screen, first open a Terminal window (right-click the desktop and select New Terminal). In the Terminal window, type **ps x | more** to see a list of running processes. Look for a command named `gnome-session` and determine its number under the PID column. Then type **kill -9 *PID***, where *PID* is replaced by the PID number. You should see the graphical login screen.

Although these are not the most graceful ways to exit the desktop, they work. You should be able to log in again and restart the desktop.

Configuring Your Own Desktop

Today's modern desktop computer systems are made to spoon-feed you your operating system. In the name of ease of use, some desktop environments spend a lot of resources on fancy panels, complex control centers, and busy applets. In short, they can become bloated.

Many technically inclined people want a more streamlined desktop — or at least want to choose their own bells and whistles. They don't want to have to wait for windows to redraw or menus to come up. Linux enables those people to forget the complete desktop environments and configure:

✦ **X** — The X Window System provides the framework of choice for Linux and most UNIX systems. When you configure X yourself, you can choose the video driver, monitor settings, mouse configuration, and other basic features needed to get your display working properly.

✦ **Window manager** — Dozens of window managers are available to use with X on a Linux system. Window managers add borders and buttons to otherwise bare X windows. They add colors and graphics to backgrounds, menus, and windows. Window managers also define how you can use keyboard and mouse combinations to operate your desktop.

You only need to configure X directly if your desktop isn't working (the desktop may appear scrambled or just plain crash). You may choose to configure X if you want to tune it to give you higher resolutions or more colors than you get by default.

Still to come in this chapter: examining tools for tuning X and, in particular, working with the `xorg.conf` file. You'll also explore a few popular window managers that you might want to try out. Slackware Linux is used to illustrate how to choose and configure a window manager because Slackware users tend to like simple, direct ways of working with the desktop (when they need a desktop at all).

Configuring X

Before 2004, most Linux distributions used the X server from the XFree86 project (`www.xfree86.org`). Because of licensing issues, many of the major Linux vendors (including Red Hat, SUSE, and Slackware) changed to the X server from X.org (`www.X.org`). The descriptions of how to get X going on your machine assume you are using the X.org X server.

Note   To determine which X server is installed on your system, from a Terminal window type **man Xorg** and **man XFree86**. If you only have one X server installed on your computer (which you probably do) only the one installed will show a man page. While you are there, press the space bar to page through the features of your X server.

It's possible that you already did some configuration when you installed Linux. If you are able to start a desktop successfully and your mouse, keyboard, and screen all seem to be behaving, you may not have to do anything more to configure X.

However, if you can't start the desktop or you want to adjust some basic features (such as screen resolution or number of colors supported), let's look at some ideas on how to go about doing those things.

Creating a Working X Configuration File

If your desktop crashes immediately or only shows garbled text, try to create a new X configuration file. With the X.org X server, that file is /etc/X11/xorg.conf.

Note   In XFree86, the configuration file, which has basically the same format, is /etc/X11/XF86Config.

To have X try to create a sane xorg.conf file for you to use, do the following from a Terminal window as root user:

1. If Linux booted to a command prompt, go to the next step. However, if it tried to start X automatically, you might have an illegible screen. In that case, press these keys together: Ctrl+Alt+Backspace. It should kill your X server and get you back to a command prompt. If X tries to restart (and is still messed up), press Ctrl+Alt+F2. When you see the command prompt, log in as root and type **init 3**. This will temporarily bring you down to a nongraphical state.

2. To have X probe your video hardware and create a new configuration file, type:

   ```
   # Xorg -configure
   ```

3. The file x.org.conf.new should appear in your home directory. To test if this new configuration file works, type the following to start the X server:

   ```
   # X -xf86config /root/xorg.conf.new
   ```

   A gray background with an X in the middle should appear. Move the mouse to move the X pointer. If that succeeds, you have a working xorg.conf file to use.

4. Press Ctrl+Alt+Backspace to exit the X server.

5. Copy the new configuration file to where it is picked up the next time X starts.

   ```
   # cp /root/xorg.conf.new /etc/X11/xorg.conf
   ```

Chances are that you have a very basic X configuration that you may want to tune further.

Getting New X Drivers

Working video drivers are available with most video cards you can purchase today. However, to get some advanced features from your video cards (such as 3D acceleration) you may need to get proprietary drivers directly from the video manufacturers. In particular, you may want to get drivers from NVIDIA and ATI.

To get new drivers for video cards or chipsets from NVIDIA, go to the NVIDIA site (www.nvidia.com) and select the Download Drivers button. Follow the link to Linux and FreeBSD drivers. Links from the page that appears will take you to a Web page from which you can download the new driver and get instructions for installing it.

For ATI video cards and chipsets, go to www.ati.com and select Drivers & Software. Follow the links to Linux drivers and related installation instructions.

Tuning Up Your X Configuration File

The xorg.conf file might look a bit complicated when you first start working with it. However, chances are that there are only a few key elements you will need to change in it. As root user, open the /etc/X11/xorg.conf file in any text editor. Here are some things you can look for:

✦ **Mouse** — Look for an InputDevice section with a Mouse0 or Mouse1 identifier. That section for a simple two-button, PS2 mouse might look as follows:

```
Section "InputDevice"
    Identifier    "Mouse0"
    Driver        "mouse"
    Option        "Protocol" "PS/2"
    Option        "Device" "/dev/psaux"
EndSection
```

If you are unable to use some feature of the mouse, such as a middle wheel, you might be able to get it working with an entry that looks more like the following:

```
Section "InputDevice"
    Identifier    "Mouse0"
    Driver        "mouse"
    Option        "Protocol" "IMPS/2"
    Option        "Device" "/dev/psaux"
    Option        "ZAxisMapping" "4 5"
EndSection
```

Don't change the mouse identifier, but you can change the protocol and add the ZAxisMapping line to enable your wheel mouse. Try restarting X and trying your mouse wheel on something like a Web page to see if you can scroll up and down with it.

Your mouse might be connected in a different way (such as a bus or serial mouse) or may have different buttons to enable. Tools for configuring your mouse are distribution-specific. Try `mouseconfig`, `mouseadmin`, or `system-config-mouse` to reconfigure your mouse from the command line.

✦ **Monitor** — The monitor section defines attributes of your monitor. There are generic settings you can use if you don't exactly know the model of your monitor. Changing the Horizontal Sync and Vertical Refresh rates without checking your monitor's technical specifications is not recommended; you could damage the monitor. Here's an example of an entry that will work on many LCD panels:

```
Section "Monitor"
    Identifier    "Monitor0"
    VendorName    "Monitor Vendor"
    ModelName     "LCD Panel 1024x768"
    HorizSync     31.5 - 48.5
    VertRefresh   40.0 - 70.0
EndSection
```

Here's an entry for a generic CRT monitor that will work on many CRTs:

```
Section "Monitor"
    Identifier    "Monitor0"
    VendorName    "Monitor Vendor"
    ModelName     "Generic Monitor, 1280x1024 @ 74 Hz"
    HorizSync     31.5 - 79.0
    VertRefresh   50.0 - 90.0
EndSection
```

If there is a tool available to select your monitor model directly, that would be the best way to go. For example, in Red Hat systems, you would run `system-config-xfree86` to change monitor settings.

✦ **Video device** — The Device section is where you identify the driver to use with your video driver and any options to use with it. It's important to get this section right. The `Xorg` command described earlier usually does a good job detecting the driver. If you want to change to a different one, this is where to do so. Here's an example of the Device section after I added a video driver from NVIDIA to my system (the driver name is nv):

```
Section "Device"
    Identifier    "Card0"
    Driver        "nv"
    VendorName    "nVidia Corporation"
    BoardName     "Unknown Board"
    BusID         "PCI:1:0:0"
EndSection
```

✦ **Screen resolution** — The last major piece of information you may want to add is the screen resolution and color depth. There will be a screen resolution associated with each video card installed on your computer. The Screen section defines default color depths (such as 8, 16, or 24) and modes (such as 1024x768, 800x600, or 640x480). Set the DefaultDepth to the number of bits representing color depth for your system, and then add a Modes line to set the screen resolution.

To read more about how to set options in your xorg.conf file, type **man xorg.conf**. If your X server is XFree86, type **man XF86Config**.

Choosing a Window Manager

Fully integrated desktop environments have become somewhat unfriendly to changing out window managers. However, you can completely bypass KDE or GNOME, if you like, and start your desktop simply with X and a window manager of your choice.

Although I'm using Slackware as the reference distribution for describing how to change window managers, the concept is the same on other Linux systems. In general, if no desktop environment is running in Linux, you can start it by typing:

```
$ startx
```

This command starts up your desktop environment or window manager, depending on how your system is configured. Although a variety of configuration files are read and commands are run, essentially which desktop you get depends on the contents of two files:

✦ /etc/X11/xinit/xinitrc — If a user doesn't specifically request a particular desktop environment or window manager, the default desktop settings will come from the contents of this file. The xinitrc file is the system-wide X configuration file. Different Linux systems use different xinitrc files.

✦ $HOME/.xinitrc — The .xinitrc file is used to let individual users set up their own desktop startup information. Any user can add a .xinitrc file to his or her own home directory. The result is that the contents of that file will override any system-wide settings. If you do create your own .xinitrc file, it should have as its last line exec *windowmanager*, where *windowmanager* is the name of your window manager; for example:

```
exec /usr/X1R6/bin/blackbox
```

Slackware has at least seven different window managers from which you can choose, making it a good place to try out a few. It also includes a tool called xwmconfig, which lets you change the window manager system-wide (in the /etc/X11/xinit/xinitrc file). To use that tool, as the root user simply type **xwmconfig** from any shell on a Slackware system. Figure 3-15 shows an example of that screen.

Figure 3-15: In Slackware, you can change window managers using the `xwmconfig` command.

Select the window manager you want to try from that screen and select OK. That window manager will start the next time you run `startx` (provided you don't override it by creating your own `.xinitrc` file). Here are your choices:

+ **Xfce** (`www.xfce.org`) — The xfce window manager is designed to be lightweight and fast.

+ **Blackbox** (`www.blackboxwm.sourceforge.net`) — Another lightweight window manager that strives to require few library dependencies so it can run in many environments. Offers many features for setting colors and styles

+ **FluxBox** (`http://fluxbox.sourceforge.net`) — Based on Blackbox (0.61.1), FluxBox adds nice features such as window tabs (where you can join together multiple windows so they appear as multiple tabs on a single window). It also includes an icon bar and adds some useful mouse features (such as using your mouse wheel to change workspaces).

+ **Window Maker** (`www.windowmaker.org`) — Window Maker is a clone of the NEXTSTEP graphical interface, a popular UNIX workstation of the 1980s and 1990s. It is a particularly attractive window manager, with support for themes, various window decorations, and features for changing backgrounds, animations, and adding applets (called docapps).

+ **FVWM** (`www.fvwm.org`) — This window manager supports full internationalization, window manager hints, and improved font features. Interesting features include window shading in all directions (even diagonal) and side titles (including text displayed vertically).

+ **FVWM-95** (`http://fvwm95.sourceforge.net`) — A version of FVWM that was created to look and feel like Windows 95.

✦ **Twm (Tabbed Window Manager)** — Although no longer actively maintained, some people still use twm when they want a truly bare-bones desktop. Until you click the left mouse button in twm, there's nothing on the screen. Use the menu that pops up to open and close windows.

There are many other window managers available for Linux as well. To check out some more, visit the Xwinman Web site (`www.plig.org/xwinman`).

Once the system default is set for your window manager, users can set their own window manager to override that decision. The follow section describes how to do that.

Choosing Your Personal Window Manager

Simply adding an `exec` line with the name of the window manager you want to use to your own `.xinitrc` file in your home directory causes `startx` to start that window manager for you. Here is an example of the contents of a `.xinitrc` to start the Window Maker window manager:

```
exec /usr/bin/wmaker
```

Make sure that the file is executable (`chmod 755 $HOME/.xinitrc`). The Window Maker window manager should start the next time you start your desktop. Other window managers you can choose include Blackbox (`/usr/X11R6/bin/blackbox`), FluxBox (`/usr/X11R6/bin/fluxbox`), FVWM (`/usr/X11R6/bin/fluxbox`), FVWM-95 (`/usr/X11R6/bin/fvwm95`), and twm (`/usr/X11R6/bin/twm`).

Getting More Information

If you tried configuring X and you still have a server that crashes or has a garbled display, your video card may either be unsupported or may require special configuration. Here are a couple of locations you can check for further information:

✦ **X.Org** (`www.x.org`) — The latest information about the X servers that come with Fedora Core is available from the X.Org Web site. X.Org is the freeware version of X recently used by many major Linux distributions to replace the XFree86 X server.

✦ **X documentation** — README files that are specific to different types of video cards are delivered with the X.Org X server. Visit the X `doc` directory (`/usr/X11R6/lib/X11/doc`) for a README file specific to the type of video card (or more specifically, the video chipset) you are using. A lot of good information can also be found on the `xorg.conf` man page (type **man xorg.conf**).

Summary

Complete desktop environments that run in Linux can rival desktop systems from any operating system. KDE and GNOME are the most popular desktop environments available today for Linux. For people who want a sleeker, more lightweight desktop environment, a variety of simple window managers (Blackbox, FVWM, twm, FluxBox, and many others) are available to use in Linux as well.

The KDE desktop is well known for its large set of integrated applications (office productivity tools, games, multimedia, and other applications). GNOME has the reputation of being a more basic, business-oriented desktop. Most Linux distributions such as Slackware and Gentoo offer GNOME and KDE desktops that aren't changed much from how they are delivered from those desktop projects. Other Linux systems (such as Red Hat) put their own look-and-feel over GNOME and KDE desktops.

While the latest Windows systems won't run on many older 486 and Pentium machines, you can use an efficient Linux system like Slackware, add a lightweight window manager, and get reasonably good performance with your desktop system on those machines.

✦   ✦   ✦

Running the Show

Learning Basic Administration

Linux, like other UNIX systems, was intended for use by more than one person at a time. Multiuser features enable many people to have accounts on a single Linux system, with their data kept secure from others. Multitasking enables many people to run programs on the computer at the same time. Sophisticated networking protocols and applications make it possible for a Linux system to extend its capabilities to network users and computers around the world. The person assigned to manage all of this stuff is called the *system administrator*.

Even if you are the only person using a Linux system, system administration is still set up to be separate from other computer use. To do most administrative tasks, you need to be logged in as the root user (also called the *superuser*) or temporarily get root permission. Users other than root cannot change, or in some cases even see, some of the configuration information for a Linux system. In particular, security features such as stored passwords are protected from general view.

This chapter describes the general principles of Linux system administration. In particular, this chapter examines some of the basic tools you need to administer your Linux system. It also helps teach you how to work with file systems and monitor the setup and performance of your Linux system.

Graphical Administration Tools

Many Linux systems come with simplified graphical tools for administering Linux. If you are a casual user, these tools often let you do everything you need to administer your system without editing configuration files or running shell commands.

Let's examine some of the Web-based administration tools that are available to use with most Linux systems.

Using Web-Based Administration

Web-based administration tools are available with many open source projects to make those projects more accessible to casual users. Often all you need to use those tools is a Web browser (such as Mozilla), the port number of the service, and the root password. Projects such as Samba and CUPS come with their own Web administration tools. Webmin is a general-purpose tool for administering a variety of Linux system services from your Web browser.

The advantages of Web-based administration tools are that you can operate them from a familiar interface (your Web browser) and you can access them remotely.

Note   If the Linux distribution you are using comes with its own set of graphical administration tools (such as SUSE's YaST or Red Hat's system-config tools), you should generally use those instead of any Web-based interface that comes with a project because a distribution's own tools better integrate with its tools for starting and stopping services.

Open Source Projects Offering Web Administration

Several major open source projects come with Web-based interfaces for configuring those projects. Regardless of which Linux you are using, you can use your Web browser to configure the following projects:

✦ **Samba**— To set up Samba for doing file and printer sharing with Microsoft Windows systems on your LAN, use the Samba SWAT Web-based administration tools from any Web browser. With SWAT installed and running, you can access your Samba server configuration from your Web browser by typing the following URL in the location box:

```
http://localhost:901
```

The Samba project also offers other graphical tools for administering Samba. You can check them out at `http://samba.org/samba/GUI` for descriptions of those tools. Samba is described in Chapters 25 and 26.

✦ **CUPS**— The Common UNIX Printing Service (CUPS) has its own Web administration tool. With CUPS installed and configured, you can typically use CUPS Web administration by typing the following URL in your Web browser's location box:

```
http://localhost:631
```

You use the CUPS administration tool to manage printers and classes and do a variety of administration tasks. CUPS is described in Chapter 25.

Samba and CUPS are included with many Linux distributions. Other projects that offer Web-based administration that may or may not be in your Linux distribution include SquirrelMail (a webmail interface) and Mailman (a mailing list facility).

Webmin Administration Tool

The Webmin facility (www.webmin.com) offers more complete Web-based Linux and UNIX administration features. Although Webmin isn't delivered with some Linux systems that offer their own graphical administration tools (such as Red Hat's Fedora and RHEL), the Webmin project has ported Webmin to run in many different Linux distributions. Those distributions include SUSE, Red Hat (Fedora and RHEL), Debian, Slackware, Caldera OpenLinux, Mandrake, Yellow Dog, and others (see www.webmin.com/support.html for a complete list).

For Red Hat Fedora Linux 3, for example, I was able to download a Webmin RPM from Webmin.com. To start the Webmin interface, I just needed the root password after typing the following in my Web browser's location box:

```
http://localhost:10000
```

After you log in as root user, the main Webmin page displays, as shown in Figure 4-1.

Figure 4-1: Webmin offers a Web browser interface for administering Linux.

Graphical Administration with Different Distributions

Some people fear that once they've left the familiar confines of their Microsoft Windows system for Linux, they'll be stuck doing everything from a command line. To gain a wider audience, commercial Linux distributions such as Red Hat Linux and SUSE created their own sets of graphical tools to provide an easy entry point for new Linux users. The following sections describe Red Hat's system-config and SUSE's YaST graphical administration tools.

Red Hat Config Tools

A set of graphical tools that comes with Red Hat Linux systems can be launched from the red hat menu (under the System tools and System Settings submenus) or the command line. Most of the Red Hat tools that launch from the command line begin with the `system-config` string (such as `system-config-network`).

Note In Fedora Core 1 and previous versions of Red Hat Linux, the GUI administrations tools all began with `redhat-`, such as `redhat-config-network` and `redhat-logviewer`. Starting with Fedora Core 2, those names have all changed to `system-`, resulting in names like `system-config-network` and `system-logviewer`.

These administrative tasks require root permission; if you are logged in as a regular user, you must enter the root password before the GUI application's window opens. After you've entered that password, most of the system configuration tools will open without requiring you to retype the password during this login session. Look for a "keys" icon in the lower-right corner of the panel, indicating that you have root authorization. Click the keys to open a pop-up window that enables you remove authorization. Otherwise, authorization goes away when you close the GUI window.

The following list describes many of the GUI-based windows you can use to administer your Fedora or Red Hat Linux system. Start these windows from the System Settings or System Tools submenus on your red hat menu:

✦ **Server Settings** — Access the following server configuration windows:

> **Domain Name System** — Create and configure zones if your computer is acting as a DNS server.

> **HTTP** — Configure your computer as an Apache Web server.

> **NFS** — Set up directories from your system to be shared with other computers on your network using the NFS service.

> **Samba** — Configure Windows (SMB) file sharing. (To configure other Samba features, you can use the SWAT window.)

> **Services** — Display and change which services are running on your Fedora system at different run levels from this Service Configuration window (see Figure 4-2).

✦ **Add/Remove Applications** — Manage software packages in the Fedora distribution.

✦ **Authentication** — Change how users are authenticated on your system. Usually, Shadow Passwords and MD5 Passwords are selected. However, if your network supports LDAP, Kerberos, SMB, NIS, or Hesiod authentication, you can select to use any of those authentication types.

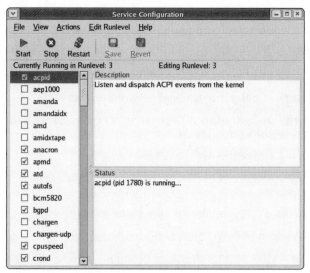

Figure 4-2: See services that start from each run level in the Service Configuration window.

✦ **Bootloader** — If you have multiple operating systems on your computer, or multiple Linux kernels available to boot in Linux, you can use the Boot Configuration screen to choose which to boot by default. For example, you might have Fedora Linux, SUSE, and Windows XP all on the same hard disk. You could choose which would start automatically (after a set number of seconds), if one wasn't selected explicitly.

✦ **Date & Time** — Set the date and time or choose to have an NTP server keep system time in sync.

✦ **Disk Management** — Mount and format removable media, such as CDs and floppy disks.

✦ **Display** — Change the settings for your X desktop, including color depth and resolution for your display. You can also choose settings for your video card and monitor.

✦ **Hardware Browser** — View information about your computer's hardware.

✦ **Internet Configuration Wizard** — Create initial configurations for connecting to the Internet via Ethernet, ISDN, modem, and other types of network equipment.

✦ **Keyboard** — Choose the type of keyboard you are using, based on language.

✦ **Kickstart** — Create a kickstart configuration file that can be used to install multiple Fedora systems without user interaction.

✦ **Language** — Select the default language used for the system.

✦ **Login Screen** — Control how your login screen appears and behaves.

✦ **Network** — Manage your current network interfaces; add interfaces as well.

✦ **Network Device Control** — Display the active profile for network devices.

✦ **Printing Manager** — Configure local and network printers.

✦ **Red Hat Network Configuration** — Register your computer with the Red Hat Network to get free software updates.

✦ **Root Password** — Change the root password.

✦ **Security Level** — Configure your firewall to allow or deny services to computers from the network.

✦ **Soundcard Detection** — Try to detect and configure your sound card.

✦ **System Logs** — View system log files, and search them for keywords.

✦ **System Monitor** — View information about running processes and resource usage.

✦ **Task Scheduler** — Schedule tasks to be run at set times.

✦ **Users & Groups** — Add, display, and change user and group accounts for your Fedora system.

SUSE YaST Tools

The YaST administrative interface is one of the strongest features of SUSE Linux. From a SUSE desktop, open the YaST Control Center by selecting System ⇨ YaST from the main menu. Figure 4-3 shows an example of the YaST Control Center that appears.

YaST has some useful tools in its Hardware section that enable you to probe your computer hardware.

On my system, for example, I could see that the CD-ROM drive that YaST detected was available through device /dev/hdc and that it supported CD-R, CD-RW, and DVD media. I could also see detailed information about my CPU, network card, PCI devices, sound card, and various storage media.

YaST also offers interfaces for configuring and starting network devices, as well as a variety of services to run on those devices. In addition, you can use YaST to configure your computer as a client for file sharing (Samba and NFS), e-mail (sendmail), and a variety of network services.

SUSE Linux Enterprise Server comes with a wider range of configuration tools that are specifically geared toward server setup, including tools for configuring a mail server, VPN tunnels, and full Samba 3.

Figure 4-3: Use the YaST Control Center to administer SUSE systems.

Using the Root Login

Every Linux system starts out with at least one administrative user account (the root user) and possibly one or more regular user accounts (given a name that you choose, or a name assigned by Linux). In most cases, you log in as a regular user and become the root user to do an administrative task.

The root user has complete control of the operation of your Linux system. That user can open any file or run any program. The root user also installs software packages and adds accounts for other people who use the system.

When you first install most Linux systems, you add a password for the root user. You must remember and protect this password — you will need it to log in as root or to obtain root permission while you are logged in as some other user. Other Linux systems (such as KNOPPIX) start you with a blank root password, so you may want to add one when you first start up by typing the following from a Terminal window or other shell:

```
# passwd root
Changing password for user root.
New UNIX password: ********
Retype new UNIX password: ********
```

Note   Some Linux distributions, such as Damn Small Linux, give you (as a regular user) the power to run commands as root. You simply have to ask for the privilege using the `sudo` command. For example, from a Terminal window, to open a shell as root, you would type:

```
$ sudo su -
#
```

You'll find out more about the `sudo` command later in this chapter.

The home directory for the root user is typically `/root`. The home directory and other information associated with the root user account are located in the `/etc/passwd` file. Here's what the root entry looks like in the `/etc/passwd` file:

```
root:x:0:0:root:/root:/bin/bash
```

This shows that for the user named root the user ID is set to 0 (root user), the group ID is set to 0 (root group), the home directory is `/root`, and the shell for that user is `/bin/bash`. (We're using a shadow password file to store encrypted password data, so the password field here contains an *x*.) You can change the home directory or the shell used by editing the values in this file. A better way to change these values, however, is to use the `useradd` command (described later in this chapter).

Becoming Root from the Shell (su Command)

Although you can become the superuser by logging in as root, sometimes that is not convenient. For example, you may be logged in to a regular user account and just want to make a quick administrative change to your system without having to log out and log back in. Or, you may need to log in over the network to make a change to a Linux system but find that the system doesn't allow root users in from over the network (a common practice in the days before secure shells were available).

The solution is to use the `su` command. From any Terminal window or shell, you can simply type

```
$ su
Password: ******
#
```

When you are prompted, type in the root user's password. The prompt for the regular user ($) changes to the superuser prompt (#). At this point, you have full permission to run any command and use any file on the system. However, one thing that the `su` command doesn't do when used this way is read in the root user's environment. As a result, you may type a command that you know is available and get the message "Command Not Found." To fix this problem, use the `su` command with the dash (-) option instead, like this:

```
$ su -
Password: ******
#
```

You still need to type the password, but after that, everything that normally happens at login for the root user happens after the su command is completed. Your current directory will be root's home directory (probably /root), and things like the root user's PATH variable will be used. If you become the root user by just typing su, rather than su -, you won't change directories or the environment of the current login session.

You can also use the su command to become a user other than root. This is useful for troubleshooting a problem that is being experienced by a particular user, but not by others on the computer (such as an inability to print or send e-mail). For example, to have the permissions of a user named jsmith, you'd type the following:

```
$ su - jsmith
```

Even if you were root user before you typed this command, afterward you would only have the permissions to open files and run programs that are available to jsmith. As root user, however, after you type the su command to become another user, you don't need a password to continue. If you type that command as a regular user, you must type the new user's password.

When you are finished using superuser permissions, return to the previous shell by exiting the current shell. Do this by pressing Ctrl+D or by typing **exit**. If you are the administrator for a computer that is accessible to multiple users, don't leave a root shell open on someone else's screen (unless you want to let that person do anything he wants to the computer)!

Allowing Limited Administrative Access

As mentioned earlier, when you run GUI tools as a regular user (from Red Hat Linux, SUSE, or some other Linux systems), you are prompted for the root password before you are able to access the tool. By entering the root password, you are given root privilege for that one task, without being root user for every task you do from that desktop session.

A particular user can also be given administrative permissions for particular tasks without being given the root password. For example, a system administrator can add a user to particular groups, such as modem, disk, users, cdrom, ftp, mail, or www, and then open group permission to use those services. Or, an administrator could add a user to the wheel group and add entries to the /etc/sudoers file to allow that user to use the sudo command to run individual commands as root. (See the description of sudo later in this chapter.)

A fairly new feature being added to some Linux distributions that are used in highly secure environments is Security Enhanced Linux (SELinux). With SELinux, instead of one all-powerful root user account, multiple roles can be defined to protect selected files and services. In that way, for example, if someone hacks into your Web server, he would not automatically have access to your mail server, user passwords, or other services running on the computer.

Exploring Administrative Commands, Configuration Files, and Log Files

You can expect to find many commands, configuration files, and log files in the same places in the file system, regardless of which Linux distribution you are using. The following sections give you some pointers on where to look for these important elements.

Administrative Commands

Only the root user is intended to use many administrative commands. When you log in as root (or use `su -` from the shell to become root), your `$PATH` variable is set to include some directories that contain commands for the root user. These include the following:

✦ `/sbin`—Contains commands for modifying your disk partitions (such as `fdisk`), checking file systems (`fsck`), and changing system states (`init`).

✦ `/usr/sbin`—Contains commands for managing user accounts (such as `useradd`) and adding mount points for automounting file systems (`automount`). Commands that run as daemon processes are also contained in this directory. (Look for commands that end in d, such as `sshd`, `pppd`, and `cupsd`.)

Some administrative commands are contained in regular user directories (such as `/bin` and `/usr/bin`). This is especially true of commands that have some options available to everyone. An example is the `/bin/mount` command, which anyone can use to list mounted file systems, but only root can use to mount file systems. (Some desktops, however, are configured to let regular users use `mount` to mount CDs, DVDs, or other removable media.)

To find commands that are intended primarily for the system administrator, check out the section 8 manual pages (usually in `/usr/share/man/man8`). They contain descriptions and options for most Linux administrative commands.

Some third-party applications will add administrative commands to directories that are not in your `PATH`. For example, an application may put commands in `/usr/local/bin`, `/opt/bin`, or `/usr/local/sbin`. In those cases, you may need to add those directories to your `PATH`.

Administrative Configuration Files

Configuration files are another mainstay of Linux administration. Almost everything you set up for your particular computer—user accounts, network addresses, or GUI preferences—is stored in plain-text files. This has some advantages and some disadvantages.

The advantage of plain-text files is that it's easy to read and change them. Any text editor will do. The downside, however, is that as you edit configuration files, no error checking is going on. You have to run the program that reads these files (such as a network daemon or the X desktop) to find out whether you set up the files correctly. A comma or a quote in the wrong place can sometimes cause a whole interface to fail.

Throughout this book you'll find descriptions of the configuration files you need to set up the different features that make up Linux systems. The two major locations of configuration files are your home directory (where your personal configuration files are kept) and the /etc directory (which holds system-wide configuration files).

Following are descriptions of directories (and subdirectories) that contain useful configuration files. (Refer to Table 4-1 for some individual configuration files in /etc that are of particular interest.) Viewing the contents of Linux configuration files can teach you a lot about administering Linux systems.

✦ $HOME — All users store information in their home directories that directs how their login accounts behave. Most configuration files in $HOME begin with a dot (.), so they don't appear as a user's directory when you use a standard ls command (you need to type ls -a to see them). There are dot files that define how each user's shell behaves, the desktop look-and-feel, and options used with your text editor. There are even files such as .ssh/* and .rhosts that configure network permissions for each user. (To see the name of your home directory, type echo $HOME from a shell.)

✦ /etc — This directory contains most of the basic Linux system-configuration files. Table 4-1 shows some /etc configuration files of interest.

✦ /etc/cron* — Directories in this set contain files that define how the crond utility runs applications on a daily (cron.daily), hourly (cron.hourly), monthly (cron.monthly), or weekly (cron.weekly) schedule.

✦ /etc/cups — Contains files that are used to configure the CUPS printing service.

✦ /etc/default — Contains files that set default values for various utilities. For example, the file for the useradd command defines the default group number, home directory, password expiration date, shell, and skeleton directory (/etc/skel) that are used when creating a new user account.

✦ /etc/httpd — Contains a variety of files used to configure the behavior of your Apache Web server (specifically, the httpd daemon process). (On some Linux systems, /etc/apache is used instead.)

✦ /etc/init.d — Contains the permanent copies of System V–style run-level scripts. These scripts are often linked to files in the /etc/rc?.d directories to have each service associated with a script started or stopped for the particular run level. The ? is replaced by the run-level number (0 through 6). (Slackware puts its run-level scripts in the /etc/rc.d directory.)

✦ /etc/mail — Contains files used to configure your sendmail mail service.

✦ /etc/pcmcia — Contains configuration files that allow you to have a variety of PCMCIA cards configured for your computer. (PCMCIA slots are those openings on your laptop that enable you to have credit card–sized cards attached to your computer. You can attach such devices as modems and external CD-ROMs.)

✦ /etc/postfix — Contains configuration files for the postfix mail transport agent.

✦ /etc/ppp — Contains several configuration files used to set up Point-to-Point Protocol (PPP) so that you can have your computer dial out to the Internet.

✦ /etc/rc?.d — There is a separate rc?.d directory for each valid system state: rc0.d (shutdown state), rc1.d (single-user state), rc2.d (multiuser state), rc3.d (multiuser plus networking state), rc4.d (user-defined state), rc5.d (multiuser, networking, plus GUI login state), and rc6.d (reboot state).

✦ /etc/security — Contains files that set a variety of default security conditions for your computer. These files are part of the pam (pluggable authentication modules) package.

✦ /etc/skel — Any files contained in this directory are automatically copied to a user's home directory when that user is added to the system. By default, most of these files are dot (.) files, such as .kde (a directory for setting KDE desktop defaults) and .bashrc (for setting default values used with the bash shell).

✦ /etc/sysconfig — Contains important system configuration files that are created and maintained by various services (including iptables, samba, and most networking services). These files are critical for Linux distributions that use GUI administration tools but not used on other Linux systems at all.

✦ /etc/xinetd.d — Contains a set of files, each of which defines a network service that the xinetd daemon listens for on a particular port. When the xinetd daemon process receives a request for a service, it uses the information in these files to determine which daemon processes to start to handle the request.

Table 4-1
/etc Configuration Files of Interest

File	Description
aliases	Can contain distribution lists used by the Linux mail service. (This file may be located in /etc/mail.)
bashrc	Sets system-wide defaults for bash shell users. (This may be called bash.bashrc on some Linux distributions.)
crontab	Sets cron environment and times for running automated tasks.
csh.cshrc (or cshrc)	Sets system-wide defaults for csh (C shell) users.
exports	Contains a list of local directories that are available to be shared by remote computers using the Network File System (NFS).

File	Description
fstab	Identifies the devices for common storage media (hard disk, floppy, CD-ROM, and so on) and locations where they are mounted in the Linux system. This is used by the mount command to choose which file systems to mount when the system first boots.
group	Identifies group names and group IDs (GIDs) that are defined on the systems. Group permissions in Linux are defined by the second of three sets of rwx (read, write, execute) bits associated with each file and directory.
gshadow	Contains shadow passwords for groups.
host.conf	Sets the locations in which domain names (for example, redhat.com) are searched for on TCP/IP networks (such as the Internet). By default, the local hosts file is searched and then any name server entries in resolv.conf.
hosts	Contains IP addresses and host names that you can reach from your computer. (Usually this file is used just to store names of computers on your LAN or small private network.)
hosts.allow	Lists host computers that are allowed to use certain TCP/IP services from the local computer.
hosts.deny	Lists host computers that are *not* allowed to use certain TCP/IP services from the local computer (doesn't exist by default).
inittab	Contains information that defines which programs start and stop when Linux boots, shuts down, or goes into different states in between. This is the most basic configuration file for starting Linux.
lilo.conf	Sets Linux boot loader (lilo) parameters to boot the computer. In particular, it lists information about bootable partitions on your computer. (If your distribution uses the GRUB boot loader, you may not see this file.)
modules.conf	Contains aliases and options related to loadable kernel modules used by your computer.
mtab	Contains a list of file systems that are currently mounted.
mtools.conf	Contains settings used by DOS tools in Linux.
named.conf	Contains DNS settings if you are running your own DNS server.
ntp.conf	Includes information needed to run the Network Time Protocol (NTP).
passwd	Stores account information for all valid users for the system. Also includes other information, such as the home directory and default shell. (Rarely includes the user passwords themselves, which are typically stored in the /etc/shadow file.)

Continued

Table 4-1 *(continued)*

File	Description
printcap	Contains definitions for the printers configured for your computer. (If the printcap file doesn't exist, look for printer information in the /etc/cups directory.)
profile	Sets system-wide environment and startup programs for all users. This file is read when the user logs in.
protocols	Sets protocol numbers and names for a variety of Internet services.
resolv.conf	Identifies the locations of DNS name server computers that are used by TCP/IP to translate Internet host.domain names into IP addresses. (When a Web browser or mail client looks for an Internet site, it checks servers listed in this file to locate the site.)
rpc	Defines remote procedure call names and numbers.
services	Defines TCP/IP services and their port assignments.
shadow	Contains encrypted passwords for users who are defined in the passwd file. (This is viewed as a more secure way to store passwords than the original encrypted password in the passwd file. The passwd file needs to be publicly readable, whereas the shadow file can be unreadable by all but the root user.)
shells	Lists the shell command-line interpreters (bash, sh, csh, and so on) that are available on the system, as well as their locations.
sudoers	Sets commands that can be run by users, who may not otherwise have permission to run the command, using the sudo command. In particular, this file is used to provide selected users with root permission.
syslog.conf	Defines what logging messages are gathered by the syslogd daemon and what files they are stored in. (Typically, log messages are stored in files contained in the /var/log directory.)
termcap	Lists definitions for character terminals, so that character-based applications know what features are supported by a given terminal. Graphical terminals and applications have made this file obsolete to most people. (Termcap was the BSD UNIX way of storing terminal information; UNIX System V used definitions in /usr/share/terminfo files.)
xinetd.conf	Contains simple configuration information used by the xinetd daemon process. This file mostly points to the /etc/xinetd.d directory for information about individual services. (Some systems use the inetd.conf file and the inetd daemon instead.)

Another directory, /etc/X11, includes subdirectories that each contain system-wide configuration files used by X and different X window managers available for Linux. The xorg.conf file (which makes your computer and monitor usable with X) and configuration directories containing files used by xdm and xinit to start X are in here.

Directories relating to window managers contain files that include the default values that a user will get if that user starts one of these window managers on your system. Window managers that may have system-wide configuration files in these directories include GNOME (gdm) and Twm (twm).

> **Note**   Some files and directories in /etc/X11 are linked to locations in the /usr/X11R6 directory.

Administrative Log Files

One of the things that Linux does well is keep track of itself. This is a good thing, when you consider how much is going on in a complex operating system. Sometimes you are trying to get a new facility to work and it fails without giving you the foggiest reason why. Other times you want to monitor your system to see if people are trying to access your computer illegally. In any of those cases, you can use log files to help track down the problem.

The main utilities for logging error and debugging messages for Linux are the syslogd and klogd daemons. General system logging is done by syslogd. Logging that is specific to kernel activity is done by klogd. Logging is done according to information in the /etc/syslog.conf file. Messages are typically directed to log files that are usually in the /var/log directory. Here are a few common log files:

+ boot.log—Contains boot messages about services as they start up.

+ messages—Contains many general informational messages about the system.

+ secure—Contains security-related messages, such as login activity.

+ XFree86.0.log or Xorg.0.log—Depending on which X server you are using, contains messages about your video card, mouse, and monitor configuration.

If you are using a Fedora or other Red Hat Linux system, the System Logs utility is a good way to step through your system's log files. From the red hat menu, select System Tools ➪ System Logs. You not only can view boot, kernel, mail, security, and other system logs, but you can also use the filter box to search for particular terms (such as a model number of a piece of hardware that's not working).

Using sudo and Other Administrative Logins

You don't hear much about other administrative logins (besides root) being used with Linux. It was a fairly common practice in UNIX systems to have several different administrative logins that allowed administrative tasks to be split among several users. For example, a person sitting near a printer could have lp permissions to move print jobs to another printer if he knew a printer wasn't working.

In any case, administrative logins are available with Linux, so you may want to look into using them. Here are some examples:

✦ **lp**—User can control some printing features. Having a separate lp administrator allows someone other than the superuser to do such things as move or remove lp logs and print spool files. The home directory for lp is /var/spool/lpd.

✦ **mail**—User can work with administrative e-mail features. The mail group has group permissions to use mail files in /var/spool/mail (which is also the mail user's home directory).

✦ **uucp**—User owns various uucp commands (once used as the primary method for dial-up serial communications) as well as log files in /var/log/uucp, spool files in /var/spool, administrative commands (such as uuchk, uucico, uuconv, and uuxqt) in /usr/sbin, and user commands (uucp, cu, uuname, uustat, and uux) in /usr/bin. The home directory for uucp is /var/spool/uucp.

✦ **bin**—User owns many commands in /bin in traditional UNIX systems. This is not the case in some Linux systems (such as Red Hat and Gentoo) because root owns most executable files. The home directory of bin is /bin.

✦ **news**—User could do administration of Internet news services, depending on how you set permission for /var/spool/news and other news-related resources. The home directory for news is /etc/news.

One way to give full or limited root privileges to any nonroot user is to set up the sudo facility, which simply entails adding the user to /etc/sudoers and defining what privilege you want that user to have. Then the user can run any command he or she is privileged to use by preceding that command with the sudo command.

Here's an example of how to use the sudo facility to cause any users that are added to the wheel group to have full root privileges:

1. As the root user, edit the /etc/sudoers file by running the visudo command:

   ```
   # /usr/sbin/visudo
   ```

   By default, the file opens in vi, unless your EDITOR variable happens to be set to some other editor acceptable to visudo (for example, export EDITOR=gedit). The reason for using visudo is that the command locks the /etc/sudoers file and does some basic sanity checking of the file to ensure it's been edited correctly.

Note If you are stuck here, refer to the vi tutorial in Chapter 2 for information on using the vi editor.

2. Uncomment the following line to allow users in the wheel group to have full root privileges on the computer:

```
%wheel      ALL=(ALL)      ALL
```

This line causes each user to provide a password to be allowed to use administrative commands. To allow users in the wheel group to have that privilege without using a password, uncomment the following line instead:

```
%wheel      ALL=(ALL)      NOPASSWD: ALL
```

3. Save the changes to the /etc/sudoers file (in vi, type **ZZ**).

4. Still as root user, open the /etc/group file in any text editor and add to the wheel line any users you want to have root privilege. For example, if you were to add the users mary and jake to the wheel group, the line would appear as follows:

```
wheel:x:10:root,mary,jake
```

Now users mary and jake can run the sudo command to run commands, or parts of commands, that are normally restricted to the root user. The following is an example of a session by the user jake after he has been assigned sudo privileges:

```
[jake]$ sudo umount /mnt/win

    We trust you have received the usual lecture
    from the local System Administrator. It usually
    boils down to these two things:

        #1) Respect the privacy of others.
        #2) Think before you type.

Password: ********
  [jake]$ umount /mnt/win
mount: only root can mount /dev/hda1 on /mnt/win
[jake]$ sudo umount /mnt/win
[jake]$
```

In this session, the user jake runs the sudo command to unmount the /mnt/win file system (using the umount command). He is given a warning and asked to provide his password (this is jake's password, *not* the root password).

Even after jake has given the password, he must still use the sudo command to run subsequent administrative commands as root (the umount fails, but the sudo umount succeeds). Notice that he is not prompted for a password for the second sudo. That's because after entering his password successfully, he can enter as many sudo commands as he wants for the next five minutes without having to enter it again. (You can change the timeout value from five minutes to however long you want by setting the passwd_timeout value in the /etc/sudoers file.)

The preceding example grants a simple all-or-nothing administrative privilege to everyone you put in the wheel group. However, the /etc/sudoers file gives you an incredible amount of flexibility in permitting individual users and groups to use individual applications or groups of applications. Refer to the sudoers and sudo man pages for information about how to tune your sudo facility.

Administering Your Linux System

Your system administrator duties don't end after you have installed Linux. If multiple people are using your Linux system, you, as administrator, must give each person his own login account. You'll use useradd and related commands to add, modify, and delete user accounts.

Configuring hardware is also on your duty list. When you add hardware to your Linux computer, that hardware is usually detected and configured automatically. In some cases, though, the hardware may not have been set up properly, and you will use commands such as lsmod, modprobe, insmod, and rmmod to configure the right modules to get the hardware working.

Note   A device driver is the code that is permanently built into the kernel to allow application programs to talk to a particular piece of hardware. A module is like a driver, but it is loaded on demand. The "Configuring Hardware" section later in this chapter includes information about using these commands to configure modules.

Managing file systems and disk space is your responsibility, too. You must keep track of the disk space being consumed, especially if your Linux system is shared by multiple users. At some point, you may need to add a hard disk or track down what is eating up your disk space (you use commands like find to do this).

Your duties also include monitoring system performance. You may have a runaway process on your system or you may just be experiencing slow performance. Tools that come with Linux can help you determine how much of your CPU and memory are being consumed.

These tasks are explored in the rest of this chapter.

Creating User Accounts

Every person who uses your Linux system should have a separate user account. Having a user account provides each person with an area in which to securely store files as well as a means of tailoring his or her user interface (GUI, path, environment variables, and so on) to suit the way that he or she uses the computer.

You can add user accounts to most Linux systems in several ways—Red Hat systems use the redhat-config-users utility, for example, and SUSE offers a user setup module in YaST. This chapter describes how to add user accounts from the command line with useradd because most Linux systems include that command.

Adding Users with useradd

The most straightforward method for creating a new user from the shell is with the useradd command. After opening a Terminal window with root permission, you simply invoke useradd at the command prompt, with details of the new account as parameters.

The only required parameter is the login name of the user, but you probably want to include some additional information ahead of it. Each item of account information is preceded by a single letter option code with a dash in front of it. Table 4-2 lists the options that are available with useradd.

Table 4-2
useradd Command Options

Option	Description
-c comment -c "comment here"	Provide a description of the new user account. Often the person's full name. Replace comment with the name of the user account (-c jake). Use quotes to enter multiple words (-c "jake jackson").
-d home_dir	Set the home directory to use for the account. The default is to name it the same as the login name and to place it in /home. Replace home_dir with the directory name to use (for example, -d /mnt/homes/jake).
-D	Rather than create a new account, save the supplied information as the new default settings for any new accounts that are created.
-e expire_date	Assign the expiration date for the account in MM/DD/YYYY format. Replace expire_date with a date you want to use (-e 05/06/2005).
-f -1	Set the number of days after a password expires until the account is permanently disabled. The default, -1, disables the option. Setting this to 0 disables the account immediately after the password has expired. Replace -1 with the number to use.

Continued

Table 4-2 *(continued)*

Option	Description
-g *group*	Set the primary group (as listed in the /etc/group file) the new user will be in. Replace *group* with the group name (-g wheel).
-G *grouplist*	Add the new user to the supplied comma-separated list of groups (-G wheel,sales,tech,lunch).
-k *skel_dir*	Set the skeleton directory containing initial configuration files and login scripts that should be copied to a new user's home directory. This parameter can only be used in conjunction with the -m option. Replace *skel_dir* with the directory name to use. (Without this option, the /etc/skel directory is used.)
-m	Automatically create the user's home directory and copy the files in the skeleton directory (/etc/skel) to it.
-M	Do not create the new user's home directory, even if the default behavior is set to create it.
-n	Turn off the default behavior of creating a new group that matches the name and user ID of the new user. This option is available with Red Hat Linux systems. Other Linux systems often assign a new user to the group named users instead.
-o	Use with -u *uid* to create a user account that has the same UID as another username. (This effectively lets you have two different usernames with authority over the same set of files and directories.)
-p *passwd*	Enter a password for the account you are adding. This must be an encrypted password. Instead of adding an encrypted password here, you can simply use the passwd *user* command later to add a password for *user*.
-s *shell*	Specify the command shell to use for this account. Replace *shell* with the command shell (-s bash).
-u *user_id*	Specify the user ID number for the account (-u 474). Without the -u option, the default behavior is to automatically assign the next available number. Replace *user_id* with the ID number (-u).

For example, let's create an account for a new user named Mary Smith with a login name of mary. First, log in as root, and then type the following command:

```
# useradd -c "Mary Smith" mary
```

Tip When you choose a username, don't begin with a number (for example, 06jsmith). Also, it's best to use all lowercase letters, no control characters or spaces, and a maximum of eight characters. The useradd command allows up to 32 characters, but some applications can't deal with usernames that long. Tools such as ps display UIDs instead of names if names are too long. Having users named Jsmith and jsmith can cause confusion with programs (such as sendmail) that don't distinguish case.

Next, set Mary's initial password using the passwd command. You're prompted to type the password twice:

```
# passwd mary
Changing password for user mary.
New password: *******
Retype new password: *******
```

(Asterisks in this example represent the password you type. Nothing is actually displayed when you type the password.)

In creating the account for Mary, the useradd command performs several actions:

✦ Reads the /etc/login.defs file to get default values to use when creating accounts.

✦ Checks command-line parameters to find out which default values to override.

✦ Creates a new user entry in the /etc/passwd and /etc/shadow files based on the default values and command-line parameters.

✦ Creates any new group entries in the /etc/group file. (Red Hat creates a group using the new user's name; Gentoo adds the user to the users group; and SUSE adds it to every group you set for new users, such as dialout, audio, video, and other services.)

✦ Creates a home directory, based on the user's name, in the /home directory.

✦ Copies any files located within the /etc/skel directory to the new home directory. This usually includes login and application startup scripts.

The preceding example uses only a few of the available useradd options. Most account settings are assigned using default values. You can set more values explicitly, if you want to; here's an example that uses a few more options to do so:

```
# useradd -g users -G wheel,sales -s /bin/tcsh -c "Mary Smith" mary
```

In this case, useradd is told to make users the primary group mary belongs to (-g), add her to the wheel and sales groups, and assign tcsh as her primary command shell (-s). A home directory in /home under the user's name (/home/mary) is created by default. This command line results in a line similar to the following being added to the /etc/passwd file:

```
mary:x:502:100:Mary Smith:/home/mary:/bin/tcsh
```

Each line in the /etc/passwd file represents a single user account record. Each field is separated from the next by a colon (:) character. The field's position in the sequence determines what it is. As you can see, the login name is first. Again, the password field contains an *x* because we are using a shadow password file to store encrypted password data. The user ID selected by useradd is 502. The primary group ID is 100, which corresponds to the users group in the /etc/group file. The comment field was correctly set to Mary Smith, the home directory was automatically assigned as /home/mary, and the command shell was assigned as /bin/tcsh, exactly as specified with the useradd options.

By leaving out many of the options (as I did in the first useradd example), defaults are assigned in most cases. For example, by not using -g users or -G wheel,sales, in Red Hat Linux a group named mary would have been created and assigned to the new user. Likewise, excluding -s /bin/tcsh causes /bin/bash to be assigned as the default shell.

The /etc/group file holds information about the different groups on your Linux system and the users who belong to them. Groups are useful for enabling multiple users to share access to the same files while denying access to others. Peek at the /etc/group file, and you find something similar to this:

```
bin:x:1:root,bin,daemon
daemon:x:2:root,bin,daemon
sys:x:3:root,bin,adm
adm:x:4:root,adm,daemon
tty:x:5:
disk:x:6:root
lp:x:7:daemon,lp
mem:x:8:
kmem:x:9:
wheel:x:10:root,joe,mary
     .
     .
     .
nobody:x:99:
users:x:100:
chris:x:500
sheree:x:501
sales:x:601:bob,jane,joe,mary
```

Each line in the group file contains the name of a group, the group ID number associated with it, and a list of users in that group. By default, each user is added to his or her own group, beginning with GID 500. Note that mary was added to the wheel and sales groups instead of having her own group.

It is actually rather significant that mary was added to the wheel group. By doing this, you grant her the capability to use the sudo command to run commands as the root user (provided that sudo is configured as described later in this chapter).

Setting User Defaults

The `useradd` command determines the default values for new accounts by reading the `/etc/login.defs` file. You can modify those defaults by either editing that file manually with a standard text editor or by running the `useradd` command with the `-D` option. Although `login.defs` is different on different Linux systems, here is an example containing many of the settings you might find in a `login.defs` file:

```
PASS_MAX_DAYS     99999
PASS_MIN_DAYS     0
PASS_MIN_LEN      5
PASS_WARN_AGE     7

UID_MIN                   500
UID_MAX                 60000
GID_MIN                   500
GID_MAX                 60000

CREATE_HOME yes
```

All uncommented lines contain keyword/value pairs. For example, the keyword `PASS_MIN_LEN` is followed by some white space and the value 5. This tells `useradd` that the user password must be at least five characters. Other lines let you customize the valid range of automatically assigned user ID numbers or group ID numbers. (Red Hat starts at UID 500; other Linuxes start with UID 100.) A comment section that explains that keyword's purpose precedes each keyword (which I edited out here to save space). Altering a default value is as simple as editing the value associated with a keyword and then saving the file.

If you want to view the defaults, type the `useradd` command with the `-D` option, as follows:

```
# useradd -D
GROUP=100
HOME=/home
INACTIVE=-1
EXPIRE=
SHELL=/bin/bash
SKEL=/etc/skel
```

You can also use the `-D` option to change defaults. When run with this flag, `useradd` refrains from actually creating a new user account; instead, it saves any additionally supplied options as the new default values in `/etc/login.defs`. Not all `useradd` options can be used in conjunction with the `-D` option. You can use only the five options listed in Table 4-3.

Table 4-3
useradd Options for Changing User Defaults

Options	Description
-b *default_home*	Set the default directory in which user home directories are created. Replace *default_home* with the directory name to use (-b garage). Usually this is /home.
-e *default_expire_date*	Set the default expiration date on which the user account is disabled. The *default_expire_date* value should be replaced with a date in the form MM/DD/YYYY (-e 10/15/2005).
-f *default_inactive*	Set the number of days after a password has expired before the account is disabled. Replace *default_inactive* with a number representing the number of days (-f 7).
-g *default_group*	Set the default group that new users will be placed in. Normally useradd creates a new group with the same name and ID number as the user. Replace *default_group* with the group name to use (-g bears).
-s *default_shell*	Set the default shell for new users. Normally this is /bin/bash. Replace *default_shell* with the full path to the shell that you want as the default for new users (-s /bin/ash).

To set any of the defaults, give the -D option first, and then add the defaults you want to set. For example, to set the default home directory location to /home/everyone and the default shell to /bin/tcsh, type the following:

```
# useradd -D -b /home/everyone -s /bin/tcsh
```

Besides setting up user defaults, an administrator can create default files that are copied to each user's home directory for use. These files can include login scripts and shell configuration files (such as .bashrc).

Other commands exist that are useful for working with user accounts, including usermod (to modify settings for an existing account) and userdel (to delete an existing user account).

Configuring Hardware

In a perfect world, after installing and booting Linux, all of your hardware is detected and available for access. Although many Linux systems are rapidly moving closer to that world, there are times when you must take special steps to get your computer hardware working.

Linux systems come with tools for configuring the drivers that stand between the programs you run (such as CD players and Web browsers) and the hardware they use (such as CD-ROM drives and network cards). The intention is to have the drivers your system needs most often built into the kernel; these are called *resident drivers*. Drivers that are added dynamically as needed are referred to as *loadable modules*.

Finding Available Modules

If you have installed the Linux kernel source code, source code files for available drivers are stored in subdirectories of the /usr/src/linux*/drivers directory. You can find information about these drivers in a couple of ways:

✦ make xconfig—With /usr/src/linux* as your current directory, type **make xconfig** from a Terminal window on the desktop. Select the category of module you want and then click Help next to the driver that interests you. The help information that appears includes a description of the driver.

✦ **Documentation**—The /usr/src/linux*/Documentation directory contains lots of plain-text files describing different aspects of the kernel and related drivers.

After modules have been built, they are installed in the /lib/modules/ subdirectories. The name of the directory is based on the current release number of the kernel. Modules that are in that directory can then be loaded and unloaded as they are needed.

Listing Loaded Modules

To see which modules are currently loaded into the running kernel on your computer, use the lsmod command. Here's an example:

Note

If you don't have a Linux system installed yet, try booting KNOPPIX and using lsmod to list your loaded modules. If all your hardware is working properly, write down this list of modules. Later, when you permanently install Fedora or some other Linux system, if your CD drive, modem, video card, or other hardware doesn't work properly, you can use your list of modules to determine which module should have been used and load it, as described in the next section.

```
# lsmod
Module                  Size   Used by
snd_seq_oss             38912  0
snd_seq_midi_event       9344  1 snd_seq_oss
snd_seq                 67728  4 snd_seq_oss,snd_seq_midi_event
snd_seq_device           8328  2 snd_seq_oss,snd_seq
  .
  .
  .
autofs                  16512  0
ne2k_pci                 9056  0
8390                    13568  1 ne2k_pci
ohci1394                41860  0
ieee1394               284464  1 ohci1394
floppy                  65712  0
sg                      36120  0
scsi_mod               124600  1 sg
parport_pc              39724  0
parport                 47336  1 parport_pc
ext3                   128424  2
jbd                     86040  1 ext3
```

This output shows a variety of modules that have been loaded on a Linux system, including several to support the ALSA sound system, some of which provide OSS compatibility (snd_seq_oss).

To find information about any of the loaded modules, use the modinfo command. For example, you could type the following:

```
# modinfo -d snd-seq-oss
"OSS-compatible sequencer module"
```

Not all modules have descriptions available. In this case, however, the snd-seq-oss module is described as an OSS-compatible sequencer module. You can also use the -a option to see the author of the module, or -n to see the object file representing the module. The author information often has the e-mail address of the driver's creator, so you can contact the author if you have problems or questions about it.

Loading Modules

You can load any module that has been compiled and installed (to the /lib/modules directory) into your running kernel using the modprobe command. A common reason for loading a module is to use a feature temporarily (such as loading a module to support a special file system on a floppy you want to access). Another reason is to identify a module that will be used by a particular piece of hardware that could not be autodetected.

Here is an example of the `modprobe` command being used to load the parport module, which provides the core functions to share parallel ports with multiple devices:

```
# modprobe parport
```

After parport is loaded, you can load the parport_pc module to define the PC-style ports available through the interface. The parport_pc module lets you optionally define the addresses and IRQ numbers associated with each device sharing the parallel port. For example:

```
# modprobe parport_pc io=0x3bc irq=auto
```

In this example, a device is identified as having an address of 0x3bc, and the IRQ for the device is autodetected.

The `modprobe` command loads modules temporarily—they disappear at the next reboot. To permanently add the module to your system, add the `modprobe` command line to one of the startup scripts that are run at boot time.

Note   An alternative to using `modprobe` is the `insmod` command. The advantage of using `modprobe`, however, is that `insmod` loads only the module you request, whereas `modprobe` tries to load other modules that the one you requested is dependent on.

Removing Modules

Use the `rmmod` command to remove a module from a running kernel. For example, to remove the module parport_pc from the current kernel, type the following:

```
# rmmod parport_pc
```

If it is not currently busy, the parport_pc module is removed from the running kernel. If it is busy, try killing any process that might be using the device. Then run `rmmod` again.

Managing File Systems and Disk Space

File systems in Linux are organized in a hierarchy, beginning from root (/) and continuing downward in a structure of directories and subdirectories. As an administrator of a Linux system, it's your duty to make sure that all the disk drives that represent your file system are available to the users of the computer. It is also your job to make sure there is enough disk space in the right places in the file system for users to store what they need.

File systems are organized differently in Linux than they are in Microsoft Windows operating systems. Instead of drive letters (for example, A:, B:, C:) for each local disk, network file system, CD-ROM, or other type of storage medium, everything fits neatly into the directory structure. It is up to an administrator to create a mount point in the file system and then connect the disk to that point in the file system.

The organization of your file system begins when you install Linux. Part of the installation process is to divide your hard disk (or disks) into partitions. Those partitions can then be assigned to:

✦ A part of the Linux file system

✦ Swap space for Linux, or

✦ Other file system types (perhaps containing other bootable operating systems)

This chapter focuses on partitions that are used for the Linux file system. To see what partitions are currently set up on your hard disk, use the fdisk command:

```
# fdisk -1

Disk /dev/hda:  40.0 GB, 40020664320 bytes
255 heads, 63 sectors/track, 4825 cylinders
Units = cylinders of 16065 * 512 bytes = 8225280 bytes

   Device Boot     Start        End      Blocks   Id  System
/dev/hda1    *         1         13         104    b  Win95 FAT32
/dev/hda2             84         89       48195   83  Linux
/dev/hda3             90        522    3478072+   83  Linux
/dev/hda4            523        554      257040    5  Extended
/dev/hda5            523        554     257008+   82  Linux swap
```

This output shows the disk partitioning for a computer capable of running both Linux and Microsoft Windows. You can see that the Linux partition on /dev/hda3 has most of the space available for data. There is a Windows partition (/dev/hda1) and a Linux swap partition (/dev/hda5). There is also a small /boot partition (46MB) on /dev/hda2. In this case, the root partition for Linux has 3.3GB of disk space and resides on /dev/hda3.

Next use the mount command (with no options) to see what partitions are actually being used for your Linux system (which available disk partitions are actually mounted and where they are mounted):

```
# mount
/dev/hda3 on / type ext3 (rw)
/dev/hda2 on /boot type ext3 (rw)
/dev/hda1 on /mnt/win type vfat (rw)
none on /proc type proc (rw)
none on /sys type sysfs (rw)
none on /dev/pts type devpts (rw,gid=5,mode=620)
```

```
none on /dev/shm type tmpfs (rw)
none on /proc/sys/fs/binfmt_misc type binfmt_misc (rw)
/dev/cdrom on /mnt/cdrom type iso9660 (ro,nosuid,nodev)
```

 Note You may notice that /proc, /sys, /dev/pts, /proc/sys/fs/binfmt_misc, /dev/shm, and other entries not relating to a partition are shown as file systems. This is because they represent different file system types (proc and devpts, and so on). The word none, however, indicates that they are not associated with a separate physical partition.

The mounted Linux partitions in this case are /dev/hda2, which provides space for the /boot directory (contains data for booting Linux), and /dev/hda3, which provides space for the rest of the Linux file system beginning from the root directory (/). This particular system also contains a Windows partition that was mounted in the /mnt/win directory and a CD that was mounted in its standard place: /mnt/cdrom. (With most GUI interfaces, the CD is typically mounted automatically when you insert it.)

After the word type, you can see the type of file system contained on the device. (See the description of different file system types later in this chapter.) Particularly on larger Linux systems, you may have multiple partitions for several reasons:

✦ **Multiple hard disks** — You may have several hard disks available to your users. In that case you would have to mount each disk (and possibly several partitions from each disk) in different locations in your file system.

✦ **Protecting different parts of the file system** — If the users on a system consume all of the file system space, the entire system can fail. For example, there may be no place for temporary files to be copied (so the programs writing to temporary files fail), and incoming mail may fail to be written to mail boxes. With multiple mounted partitions, if one partition runs out of space, the others can continue to work.

✦ **Backups** — Some fast ways exist to back up data from your computer that involve copying the entire image of a disk or partition. If you want to restore that partition later, you can simply copy it back (bit by bit) to a hard disk. With smaller partitions, this approach can be done fairly efficiently.

✦ **Protecting from disk failure** — If one disk (or part of one disk) fails, having multiple partitions mounted on your file system may enable you to continue working and just fix the one disk that fails.

When a disk partition is mounted on the file system, all directories and subdirectories below that mount point are stored on that partition. So, for example, if you were to mount one partition on / and one on /usr, everything below the /usr mount point would be stored on the second partition while everything else would be stored on the first partition. If you then mounted another partition on /usr/local, everything below that mount point would be on the third partition, while everything else below /usr would be on the second partition.

Tip
What happens if a remote file system is unmounted from your computer, and you go to save a file in that mount point directory? You will write the file to that directory and it will be stored on your local hard disk. When the remote file system is remounted, however, the file you saved will seem to disappear. To get the file back, you'll have to unmount the remote file system (causing the file to reappear), move the file to another location, remount the file system, and copy the file back there.

Mount points that are often mentioned as being candidates for separate partitions include /, /boot, /home, /usr, and /var. The root file system (/) is the catchall for directories that aren't in other mount points. The root file system's mount point (/) is the only one that is required. The /boot directory holds the images needed to boot the operating system. The /home file system is where all the user accounts are typically stored. Applications and documentation are stored in /usr. Below the /var mount point is where log files, temporary files, server files (Web, FTP, and so on), and lock files are stored (that is, items that need disk space for your computer's applications to keep running).

The fact that multiple partitions are mounted on your file system is invisible to people using your Linux system. The only times they care is when a partition runs out of space or if they need to save or use information from a particular device (such as a floppy disk or remote file system) that isn't mounted. Of course, any user can check this by typing the mount command.

Mounting File Systems

Most of your hard disks are mounted automatically for you. When you install Fedora, SUSE, and other Linux systems, you are asked to create partitions and indicate the mount points for those partitions. (Other Linux installation procedures will expect you to know that you have to partition before beginning.) When you boot Linux, all Linux partitions residing on hard disk that are listed in your /etc/fstab file are typically mounted. For that reason, this section focuses mostly on how to mount other types of devices so that they become part of your Linux file system.

The mount command is used not only to mount devices but also to mount other kinds of file systems on your Linux system. This means that you can store files from other operating systems or use file systems that are appropriate for certain kinds of activities (such as writing large block sizes). The most common use of this feature for the average Linux user, however, is to enable that user to obtain and work with files from floppy disks, CD-ROMs, or other removable media.

Supported File Systems

To see file system types that are currently available to be used on your system, type **cat /proc/filesystems**. Table 4-4 shows the file system types that are supported in Linux, although they may not be in use at the moment or they may not be built into your current kernel (so they may need to be loaded as modules).

Table 4-4
Supported File System Types

Type	Description
adfs	Acorn disk file system, which is the standard file system used on RiscOS operating systems.
befs	File system used by the BeOS operating system.
cifs	Common Internet File System (CIFS), the virtual file system used to access servers that comply with the SNIA CIFS specification. CIFS is an attempt to refine and standardize the SMB protocol used by Samba and Windows file sharing.
ext3	Ext file systems are the most common in Red Hat and many other Linux systems. The ext3 file system, also called the Third Extended file system, includes journaling features that, compared to ext2, improve a file system's capability to recover from crashes.
ext2	The default file system type for earlier Linux systems. Features are the same as ext3, except that ext2 doesn't include journaling features.
ext	This is the first version of ext3. It is not used very often anymore.
iso9660	Evolved from the High Sierra file system (the original standard for CD-ROMs). Extensions to the High Sierra standard (called Rock Ridge extensions) allow iso9660 file systems to support long filenames and UNIX-style information (such as file permissions, ownership, and links). Data CD-ROMs typically use this file system type.
kafs	AFS client file system. Used in distributed computing environments to share files with Linux, Windows, and Macintosh clients.
minix	Minix file system type, used originally with the Minix version of UNIX. It supports filenames of up to only 30 characters.
msdos	An MS-DOS file system. You can use this type to mount floppy disks that come from Microsoft operating systems.
vfat	Microsoft extended FAT (VFAT) file system.
umsdos	An MS-DOS file system with extensions to allow features that are similar to UNIX (including long filenames).
proc	Not a real file system, but rather a file-system interface to the Linux kernel. You probably won't do anything special to set up a proc file system. However, the `/proc` mount point should be a proc file system. Many utilities rely on `/proc` to gain access to Linux kernel information.
reiserfs	ReiserFS journaled file system. ReiserFS and ext3 are the most common file system types used with Linux today.
swap	Used for swap partitions. Swap areas are used to hold data temporarily when RAM is currently used up. Data is swapped to the swap area and then returned to RAM when it is needed again.

Continued

Table 8-1 (continued)

Type	Description
nfs	Network File System (NFS) type of file system. NFS is used to mount file systems on other Linux or UNIX computers.
hpfs	File system is used to do read-only mounts of an OS/2 HPFS file system.
ncpfs	This relates to Novell NetWare file systems. NetWare file systems can be mounted over a network.
ntfs	Windows NT file system. It is supported as a read-only file system (so that you can mount and copy files from it). Read-write support is available but considered unreliable (some say dangerous).
affs	File system is used with Amiga computers.
ufs	File system popular on Sun Microsystems operating systems (that is, Solaris and SunOS).

Using the fstab File to Define Mountable File Systems

The hard disks on your local computer and the remote file systems you use every day are probably set up to automatically mount when you boot Linux. The definitions for which of these file systems are mounted are contained in the /etc/fstab file. Here's an example of an /etc/fstab file:

```
LABEL=/         /            ext3      defaults                  1 1
LABEL=/boot     /boot        ext3      defaults                  1 2
none            /dev/pts     devpts    gid=5,mode=620            0 0
none            /dev/shm     tmpfs     defaults                  0 0
none            /proc        proc      defaults                  0 0
/dev/hda5       swap         swap      defaults                  0 0
/dev/cdrom      /mnt/cdrom   udf,iso9660  noauto,owner,kudzu,ro  0 0
/dev/hda1       /mnt/win     vfat      noauto                    0 0
/dev/fd0        /mnt/floppy  auto      noauto,owner              0 0
```

All file systems listed in this file are mounted at boot time, except for those set to noauto in the fourth field. In this example, the root (/) and boot (/boot) hard disk partitions are mounted at boot time, along with the /dev/pts, /dev/shm, and /proc file systems (which are not associated with particular devices). The CD-ROM (/dev/cdrom) and floppy disk (/dev/fd0) drives are not mounted at boot time. Definitions are put in the fstab file for floppy and CD-ROM drives so that they can be mounted in the future (as described later).

I also added one line for /dev/hda1, which enables me to mount the Windows (vfat) partition on my computer so I don't have to always boot Windows to get at the files on my Windows partition.

Note   To access my Windows partition, I must first create the mount point (by typing **mkdir /mnt/win**). Then I can mount it when I choose by typing (as root) **mount /mnt/win**.

Different Linux distributions will set up their `fstab` file differently. Some don't use labels and many others don't use a separate `/boot` partition by default. They will just have a swap partition and have all user data under the root partition (/).

Here is what's in each field of the `fstab` file:

✦ **Field 1** — The name of the device representing the file system. The word `none` is often placed in this field for file systems (such as `/proc` and `/dev/pts`) that are not associated with special devices. This field can include the `LABEL` option, with which you can indicate a universally unique identifier (UUID) or volume label instead of a device name. The advantage to this approach is that because the partition is identified by volume name, you can move a volume to a different device name and not have to change the `fstab` file.

✦ **Field 2** — The mount point in the file system. The file system contains all data from the mount point down the directory tree structure unless another file system is mounted at some point beneath it.

✦ **Field 3** — The file system type. Valid file system types are described in the "Supported File Systems" section earlier in this chapter.

✦ **Field 4** — Options to the `mount` command. In the preceding example, the `noauto` option prevents the indicated file system from being mounted at boot time, and `ro` says to mount the file system read-only (which is reasonable for a CD-ROM drive). Commas must separate options. See the `mount` command manual page (under the `-o` option) for information on other supported options.

Tip   Normally, only the root user is allowed to mount a file system using the `mount` command. However, to allow any user to mount a file system (such as a file system on a floppy disk), you could add the `user` option to Field 4 of `/etc/fstab`. In SUSE, read/write permissions are given to specific devices (such as disk or audio devices) by specific groups (such as the disk or audio group) so that users assigned to those groups can mount or otherwise access those devices. Choose the Security and Users selection in the YaST Control Center and look for "Secondary Groups set for New User Defaults" to see how new users are assigned to groups.

✦ **Field 5** — The number in this field indicates whether the indicated file system needs to be dumped (that is, have its data backed up). A 1 means that the file system needs to be dumped, and a 2 means that it doesn't. (I don't think this field is useful anymore because many Linux systems no longer include the `dump` command. Most often, a 0 is used.)

✦ **Field 6** — The number in this field indicates whether the indicated file system needs to be checked with `fsck`: 1 means it needs to be checked, and 2 means it doesn't.

If you want to add an additional local disk or partition, you can create an entry for it in the /etc/fstab file. See Chapter 26 for information on mounting Samba, NFS, and other remount file systems from /etc/fstab.

Using the mount Command to Mount File Systems

Linux systems automatically run mount -a (mount all file systems) each time you boot. For that reason, you generally use the mount command only for special situations. In particular, the average user or administrator uses mount in two ways:

✦ To display the disks, partitions, and remote file systems that are currently mounted.

✦ To temporarily mount a file system.

Any user can type **mount** (with no options) to see what file systems are currently mounted on the local Linux system. The following is an example of the mount command. It shows a single hard disk partition (/dev/hda1) containing the root (/) file system, and proc and devpts file system types mounted on /proc and /dev, respectively. The last entry shows a floppy disk, formatted with a standard Linux file system (ext3) mounted on the /mnt/floppy directory.

```
$ mount
/dev/hda3 on / type ext3 (rw)
none on /proc type proc (rw)
none on /sys type sysfs (rw)
none on /dev/shm type tmpfs (rw)
/dev/hda2 on /boot type ext3 (rw)
none on /dev/pts type devpts (rw,gid=5,mode=0620)
/dev/fd0 on /mnt/floppy type ext3 (rw)
```

The most common devices to mount by hand are your floppy disk and your CD-ROM. However, depending on the type of desktop you are using, CD-ROMs and floppy disks may be mounted for you automatically when you insert them. (In some cases, the autorun program may also run automatically. For example, autorun may start a CD music player or software package installer to handle the data on the medium.)

Mounting Removable Media

If you want to mount a file system manually, the /etc/fstab file helps make it simple to mount a floppy disk or a CD-ROM. In some cases, you can use the mount command with a single option to indicate what you want to mount, and information is taken from the /etc/fstab file to fill in the other options. There are probably already entries in your /etc/fstab file to let you do these quick mounts in the following two cases:

✦ **CD-ROM** — If you are mounting a CD-ROM that is in the standard ISO 9960 format (as most software CD-ROMs are), you can mount that CD-ROM by placing it in your CD-ROM drive and typing the following:

```
# mount /mnt/cdrom
```

By default, your CD-ROM is mounted on the /mnt/cdrom directory. (The file system type, device name, and other options are filled in automatically.) To see the contents, type **cd /mnt/cdrom**, and then type **ls**. Files from the CD-ROM's root directory will be displayed.

✦ **Floppy Disk** — If you want to mount a floppy in the Linux ext3 file system format (ext3), or in some cases a format that can be autodetected, mount that floppy disk by inserting it in your floppy drive and typing the following:

```
# mount /mnt/floppy
```

The file system type (ext3), device (/dev/fd0), and mount options are filled in from the /etc/fstab file. You should be able to change to the floppy disk directory (cd /mnt/floppy) and list the contents of the floppy's top directory (ls).

Note   In both of the these cases, you could give the device name (/dev/cdrom or /dev/fd0, respectively) instead of the mount point directory to get the same results.

Of course, it is possible that you may get floppy disks you want to use that are in all formats. Someone may give you a floppy containing files from a Microsoft operating system (in MS-DOS format). Or you may get a file from another UNIX system. In those cases, you can fill in your own options instead of relying on options from the /etc/fstab file. In some cases, Linux autodetects that the floppy disk contains an MS-DOS (or Windows vfat) file system and mounts it properly without additional arguments. If it doesn't, here's an example of how to mount a floppy containing MS-DOS files:

```
# mount -t msdos /dev/fd0 /mnt/floppy
```

This shows the basic format of the mount command you would use to mount a floppy disk. You can change msdos to any other supported file system type (described earlier in this chapter) to mount a floppy of that type. Instead of using floppy drive A: (/dev/fd0), you could use drive B: (/dev/fd1) or any other accessible drive. Instead of mounting on /mnt/floppy, you could create any other directory and mount the floppy there.

Here are some other useful options you could add to the mount command:

✦ -t auto — If you aren't sure exactly what type of file system is contained on the floppy disk (or other medium you are mounting), use this option to indicate the file system type. The mount command will query the disk to try to ascertain what type of file system it contains.

✦ -r — If you don't want to make changes to the mounted file system (or can't because it is a read-only medium), use this option to mount it read-only.

✦ -w — This mounts the file system with read/write permission.

Mounting a Disk Image in Loopback

Another valuable way to use the `mount` command has to do with disk images. If you download a CD or floppy disk image from the Internet and you want to see what it contains, you can do so without burning it to CD or floppy. With the image on your hard disk, create a mount point and use the `-o loop` option to mount it locally. Here's an example:

```
# mkdir /mnt/mycdimage
# mount -o loop whatever-i386-disc1.iso /mnt/mycdimage
```

In this example, the /mnt/mycdimage directory is created, and then the disk image file (`whatever-i386-disc1.iso`) residing in the current directory is mounted on it. I can now `cd` to that directory, view the contents of it, and copy or use any of its contents. This is useful for downloaded CD images from which you want to install software without having to burn the image to CD. When you are done, just type **umount /mnt/cdimage** to unmount it.

Other options to `mount` are available only for specific file system types. See the `mount` manual page for those and other useful options.

Using the umount Command

When you are done using a temporary file system, or you want to unmount a permanent file system temporarily, use the `umount` command. This command detaches the file system from its mount point in your Linux file system. To use `umount`, you can give it either a directory name or a device name. For example:

```
# umount /mnt/floppy
```

This unmounts the device (probably `/dev/fd0`) from the mount point `/mnt/floppy`. You can also unmount using the form

```
# umount /dev/fd0
```

In general, it's better to use the directory name (`/mnt/floppy`) because the `umount` command will fail if the device is mounted in more than one location. (Device names all begin with `/dev`.)

If you get the message `device is busy`, the `umount` request has failed. The reason is that either a process has a file open on the device or that you have a shell open with a directory on the device as a current directory. Stop the processes or change to a directory outside the device you are trying to unmount for the `umount` request to succeed.

An alternative for unmounting a busy device is the -l option. With umount -l (a lazy unmount), the unmount happens as soon as the device is no longer busy. To unmount a remote NFS file system that's no longer available (for example, the server went down), you can use the umount -f option to forcibly unmount the NFS file system.

Tip

A really useful tool for discovering what's holding open a device you want to unmount is the lsof command. Type **lsof** with the name of the partition you want to unmount (such as lsof /mnt/floppy). The output shows you what commands are holding open files on that partition.

Using the mkfs Command to Create a File System

You can create a file system for any supported file system type on a disk or partition that you choose. You do so with the mkfs command. While this is most useful for creating file systems on hard-disk partitions, you can create file systems on floppy disks or re-writable CDs as well.

Here is an example of using mkfs to create a file system on a floppy disk:

```
# mkfs -t ext3 /dev/fd0
mke2fs 1.34, (25-Jul-2003)
Filesystem label=
OS type: Linux
Block size=1024 (log=0)
Fragment size=1024 (log=0)
184 inodes, 1440 blocks
72 blocks (5.00%) reserved for the super user
First data block=1
1 block group
8192 blocks per group, 8192 fragments per group
184 inodes per group

Writing inode tables: done

Filesystem too small for a journal
Writing superblocks and filesystem accounting information: done

The filesystem will be automatically checked every 32 mounts or
180 days, whichever comes first. Use tune2fs -c or -i to
override.
```

You can see the statistics that are output with the formatting done by the mkfs command. The number of inodes and blocks created are output, as are the number of blocks per group and fragments per group. You could now mount this file system (mount /mnt/floppy), change to it as your current directory (cd /mnt/floppy), and create files on it as you please.

Adding a Hard Disk

Adding a new hard disk to your computer so that it can be used by Linux requires a combination of steps described in previous sections. Here's the general procedure:

1. Install the new hard disk hardware.

2. Identify the partitions on the new disk.

3. Create the file systems on the new disk.

4. Mount the file systems.

The easiest way to add a hard disk to Linux is to have the entire disk devoted to a single Linux partition. You can have multiple partitions, however, and assign them each to different types of file systems and different mount points, if you like. The following process takes you through adding a hard disk containing a single Linux partition. Along the way, it also notes which steps you need to repeat to have multiple file systems with multiple mount points.

Note   This procedure assumes that Linux is already installed and working on the computer. If this is not the case, follow the instructions for adding a hard disk on your current operating system. Later, when you install Linux, you can identify this disk when you are asked to partition your hard disk(s).

1. Follow the manufacturer's instructions for physically installing and connecting the new hard disk in your computer. If, presumably, this is a second hard disk, you may need to change jumpers on the hard disk unit itself to have it operate as a slave hard disk (if it's on the same cable as your first hard disk). You may also need to change the BIOS settings.

2. Boot your computer to Linux.

3. Determine the device name for the hard disk. As root user from a shell, type:

```
# dmesg | less
```

4. From the output, look for an indication that the new disk was found. For example, if it's a second IDE hard disk, you should see `hdb:` in the output. For a second SCSI drive, you'd see `sdb:` instead. Be sure you identify the correct disk, or you will erase all the data from disks you probably want to keep!

5. Use the `fdisk` command to create partitions on the new disk. For example, if you are formatting the second IDE disk (hdb), you could type the following:

```
# fdisk /dev/hdb1
```

Now you are in `fdisk` command mode, where you can use the `fdisk` single-letter command set to work with your partitions. If the disk had existing partitions on it, you can change or delete those partitions now. Or, you can simply reformat the whole disk to blow everything away. Use p to view all partitions and d to delete a partition.

6. To create a new partition, type the following:

n

7. Choose an extended (e) or primary partition (p). To choose a primary partition, type the following:

p

8. Type in the partition number. If you are creating the first partition (or for only one partition), type the number one:

1

Enter the first cylinder number (1 is the default). A range of cylinder numbers is displayed (for example, 1-4865 is the number of cylinders that appears for my 40GB hard drive).

9. To assign the new partition to begin at the first cylinder on the new hard disk, type the number **1**.

10. Enter the last cylinder number. If you are using the entire hard disk, use the last cylinder number shown. Otherwise, choose the ending cylinder number or indicate how many megabytes the partition should have.

11. To create more partitions on the hard disk, repeat steps 6 through 10 for each partition.

12. Type **w** to write changes to the hard disk and exit from the `fdisk` command. At this point, you should be back at the shell.

13. To create a file system on the new disk partition, use the `mkfs` command. By default, this command creates an ext2 file system, which is usable by Linux. However, in most cases you will want to use a journaling file system (such as ext3 or reiserfs). To create an ext3 file system on the first partition of the second hard disk, type the following:

```
# mkfs -t ext3 /dev/hdb1
```

If you created multiple partitions, repeat this step for each partition (such as `/dev/hdb2`, `/dev/hdb3`, and so on).

Tip

If you don't use `-t ext3`, an ext2 file system is created by default. Use other commands, or options to this command, to create other file system types. For example, use `mkfs.vfat` to create a VFAT file system, `mkfs.msdos` for DOS, or `mkfs.reiserfs` for Reiser file system type. The `tune2fs` command, described later in this section, can be used to change an ext2 file system to an ext3 file system.

14. After the file system is created, you can have the partition permanently mounted by editing the `/etc/fstab` and adding the new partition. Here is an example of a line you might add to that file:

```
/dev/hdb1    /abc          ext3    defaults    1 1
```

In this example, the partition (/dev/hdb1) is mounted on the /abc directory as an ext3 file system. The defaults keyword causes the partition to be mounted at boot time. The numbers 1 1 cause the disk to be checked for errors. Add one line like this example for each partition you created.

15. Create the mount point. For example, to mount the partition on /abc (as shown in the previous step), type the following:

   # mkdir /abc

16. Create your other mount points if you created multiple partitions. The next time you boot Linux, the new partition(s) will be automatically mounted on the /abc directory.

After you have created the file systems on your partitions, a nice tool for adjusting those file systems is the tune2fs command. You can use it to change volume labels, how often the file system is checked, and error behavior. You can also use it to change an ext2 file system to an ext3 file system so the file system can use journaling. For example:

```
# tune2fs -j /dev/hdb1
tune2fs 1.35-WIP, (07-Dec-2003)
Creating journal inode: done
This filesystem will be automatically checked every 38 mounts
or
180 days, whichever comes first. Use tune2fs -c or -i to
override.
```

By adding the -j option to tune2fs, you can change either the journal size or attach the file system to an external journal block device (essentially turning a nonjournaling ext2 file system into a journaling ext3 file system). After you use tune2fs to change your file system type, you probably need to correct your /etc/fstab file to include the file type change (from ext2 to ext3).

Checking System Space

Running out of disk space on your computer is not a happy situation. You can use tools that come with Linux to keep track of how much disk space has been used on your computer, and you can keep an eye on users who consume a lot of disk space.

Displaying System Space with df

You can display the space available in your file systems using the df command. To see the amount of space available on all the mounted file systems on your Linux computer, type **df** with no options:

```
$ df
Filesystem     1k-blocks      Used  Available  Use%  Mounted on
/dev/hda3      30645460    2958356   26130408   11%  /
/dev/hda2         46668       8340      35919   19%  /boot
/dev/fd0           1412         13       1327    1%  /mnt/floppy
```

This example output shows the space available on the hard disk partition mounted on the / (root) partition (/dev/hda1), /boot partition (/dev/hda2), and the floppy disk mounted on the /mnt/floppy directory (/dev/fd0). Disk space is shown in 1K blocks. To produce output in a more human-readable form, use the -h option:

```
$ df -h
Filesystem         Size  Used  Avail  Use%  Mounted on
/dev/hda3           29G   2.9G    24G   11%  /
/dev/hda2           46M   8.2M    25M   19%  /boot
/dev/fd0           1.4M    13k   1.2M    1%  /mnt/floppy
```

With the df -h option, output appears in a friendlier megabyte or gigabyte listing. Other options with df enable you to do the following:

✦ Print only file systems of a particular type (-t type)

✦ Exclude file systems of a particular type (-x type)

✦ Include file systems that have no space, such as /proc and /dev/pts (-a)

✦ List only available and used inodes (-i)

✦ Display disk space in certain block sizes (--block-size=#)

Checking Disk Usage with du

To find out how much space is being consumed by a particular directory (and its subdirectories), use the du command. With no options, du lists all directories below the current directory, along with the space consumed by each directory. At the end, du produces total disk space used within that directory structure.

The du command is a good way to check how much space is being used by a particular user (du /home/user1) or in a particular file system partition (du /var). By default, disk space is displayed in 1K block sizes. To make the output more friendly (in kilobytes, megabytes, and gigabytes), use the -h option as follows:

```
$ du -h /home/jake
114k    /home/jake/httpd/stuff
234k    /home/jake/httpd
137k    /home/jake/uucp/data
701k    /home/jake/uucp
1.0M    /home/jake
```

The output shows the disk space used in each directory under the home directory of the user named jake (/home/jake). Disk space consumed is shown in kilobytes (k) and megabytes (M). The total space consumed by /home/jake is shown on the last line.

Finding Disk Consumption with find

The find command is a great way to find file consumption of your hard disk using a variety of criteria. You can get a good idea of where disk space can be recovered by finding files that are over a certain size or were created by a particular person.

Note You must be root user to run this command effectively, unless you are just checking your personal files. If you are not root user, there will be many places in the file system that you will not have permission to check. Regular users can usually check their own home directories but not those of others.

In the following example, the find command searches the root file system (/) for any files owned by the user named jake (-user jake) and prints the filenames. The output of the find command is organized in a long listing in size order (ls -ldS). Finally that output is sent to the file /tmp/jake. When you view the file /tmp/jake (for example, less /tmp/jake), you will find all of the files that are owned by the user jake listed in size order. Here is the command line:

```
# find / -user jake -print -xdev | xargs ls -ldS > /tmp/jake
```

Tip The -xdev option prevents file systems other than the selected file system from being searched. This is a good way to cut out a lot of junk that may be output from the /proc file system. It could also keep large remotely mounted file systems from being searched.

Here's another example, except that instead of looking for a user's files, we're looking for files larger than 100 kilobytes (-size 100k):

```
# find / -size 100k -print -xdev | xargs ls -ldS > /tmp/size
```

You can save yourself a lot of disk space by just removing some of the largest files that are no longer needed. In this example you could see large files are sorted by size in the /tmp/size file.

Monitoring System Performance

If your Linux system is a multiuser computer, sharing the processing power of that computer can be a major issue. Likewise, anytime you can stop a runaway process or reduce the overhead of an unnecessary program running, your Linux server can do a better job serving files, Web pages, or e-mail to the people who rely on it.

Linux includes utilities that can help you monitor the performance of your Linux system. The kinds of features you want to monitor in Linux include CPU usage, memory usage (RAM and swap space), and overall load on the system. A popular tool for monitoring that information in Linux is the `top` command.

To start the top utility in a Terminal window, type **top**. The `top` command determines the largest CPU-consuming processes on your computer, displays them in descending order on your screen, and updates the list every five seconds.

By adding the `-S` option to `top`, the display shows you the cumulative CPU time for each process, as well as any child processes that may already have exited. If you want to change how often the screen is updated, you can add the `-d secs` option, where `secs` is replaced by the number of seconds between updates.

By default, processes are sorted by CPU usage. You can sort processes numerically by PID (press N), by age (press A), by resident memory usage (press M), or by time (press T). To return to CPU usage, press P. To terminate a process, type **k** and enter the PID of the process you want to kill (listed in the left column). Be careful to only kill processes you are sure you don't need or want.

Summary

Although you may be using Linux as a single-user system, many of the tasks you must perform to keep your computer running are defined as administrator tasks. A special user account called the root user is needed to do many of the things necessary to keep Linux working as you would like it to. If you are administering a Linux system that is used by lots of people, the task of administration becomes even larger. You must be able to add and support users, maintain the file systems, and ensure that system performance serves your users well.

To help the administrator, Linux comes with a variety of command-line utilities and graphical windows for configuring and maintaining your system. Commands such as `mkfs` and `mount` let you create and mount file systems, respectively. Tools like `top` let you monitor system performance.

✦　　✦　　✦

Getting on
the Internet

You won't tap into the real power of Linux until you have
connected it to a network — in particular, the Internet.
Your computer probably has an Ethernet interface built in, so
you can just plug a LAN (local area network) cable into it to
connect to a LAN (hub or switch), DSL bridge or router, or
cable modem. Some computers, particularly laptops, may
have wireless Ethernet hardware built in.

Your computer also may have a dial-up modem. If you have an
older computer that has no Ethernet card or you are in a situation in which you need to dial out over regular phone lines to
reach your Internet service provider (ISP), you'd use this
modem to get on the Internet.

This chapter describes how to connect your Linux system to
the Internet. With broadband and wireless networks becoming
more prevalent, Ethernet connections are turning out to be
the most common means of connecting to the Internet. For
dial-up connections, you'll see how to use kppp (a dialer GUI
that is often packaged with KDE desktops).

Sharing Internet connections with multiple desktop systems
or even your own mail or Web server are not that difficult to
do from a hardware perspective. However, there are some
security and configuration issues to consider when you set
out to expand how you use your Internet connection. Linux
can be used as firewalls, routers, and a variety of server types
to help you get this done.

Connecting to the Network

Linux supports a wide range of wired and wireless network devices, as well as a dizzying array of network protocols to communicate over that media. As a home or small-office Linux user, you can start evaluating how to configure your connection to the Internet from Linux by considering the following:

✦ The type of Internet account you have with your ISP (dial-up or broadband)

✦ Whether you are connecting a single computer, a bunch of desktops, and/or one or more server machines to the Internet

Connecting Via Dial-up Service

Until recently, dial-up was the most common method for an individual to get onto the Internet. Many computers had dial-up modems built into the motherboard or had serial ports where a modem could easily be connected. Many computers today do not include modems, but serial or USB modems can be purchased for just a few dollars if you need to use dial-up.

Once you have a modem (56 Kbps speed is the standard today), the only other equipment you need is a regular telephone line. Essentially, you can use a dial-up modem anywhere you can connect to a phone line. Linux contains the tools you need to configure and complete a dial-up connection. Figure 5-1 shows the setup for the connection.

Figure 5-1: Connect a modem to a serial or USB port and dial out over regular phone lines.

One difficulty with using modems in Linux is that many computers with built-in modems (especially laptops) come with what are referred to as *Winmodems*. With Winmodems, some of the processing normally done on the modem is actually implemented within the Windows system. Winmodems don't always look like real modems to Linux systems because without the code that's inside Windows they don't behave like real modems when they are connected to Linux systems.

Some Winmodems are supported in Linux, and those are sometimes referred to as *Linmodems*. If you find that Linux fails to detect your modem, check out the Linmodems Support Page (http://linmodems.technion.ac.il). It can help you determine if you have a Winmodem and, if so, help you find the right Linmodem driver (if one is available).

> **Note**   If you find that you have a Winmodem, get a real modem instead. An inexpensive external serial modem can save you the trouble of getting and loading a Linmodem driver that may or may not work. Most external modems or internal PCI modems described as being "controller-based" work well in Linux.

Connecting a Single Computer to Broadband

Increasingly, individuals have the option of signing up for broadband Internet service with cable television providers or local telephone companies. These connections typically provide transmission speeds rated at least five times greater than you can get with a dial-up connection.

The equipment you need to make broadband connections from your home or small office is typically a cable modem or Digital Subscriber Line (DSL) modem. Cable modems share the bandwidth of the cable television line coming into your location. DSL uses your house or office phone wires for both your Internet and phone services.

Because there are many ways that your ISP may be providing your Internet service, you should check with it to get the right hardware you need to connect. In particular, you should know that there are several incompatible DSL standards (ADSL, CDSL, HDSL, SDSL, etc.), so you can't just go out and buy DSL equipment without some guidance.

If you are using an external DSL or cable modem, chances are that a single connection from your Linux machine to that equipment requires only the following:

  ✦ An Ethernet port on your computer

  ✦ A LAN cable (often provided with the ISP equipment)

  ✦ The DSL router/bridge or cable modem (often provided by ISP)

Figure 5-2 illustrates a Linux computer connected to a broadband cable modem.

Broadband equipment often supplies a service called Dynamic Host Configuration Protocol (DHCP). DHCP (which is discussed in Chapter 17) provides the Internet addresses and other information that a client computer needs to connect to the network. With the cable/DSL modem acting as a DHCP server, you can literally start using the Internet without doing any special configuration in Linux. Just plug in, boot Linux, and start browsing the Web.

Figure 5-2: Connect an Ethernet card to broadband and start surfing.

Note   The DSL or cable modem often acts as a router between the ISP and your computer. Alternatively, some broadband equipment operates in a "bridging mode," in which it doesn't do routing but simply passes data through as though your computer were on the same LAN as those of the ISP. In this setup, the public IP address is assigned to your computer instead of to the DSL or cable modem.

Connecting Multiple Computers to Broadband

Instead of connecting your Linux computer directly to the cable modem or DSL equipment, you can join your machines together on a LAN, and then connect the LAN to your ISP equipment so that everyone in the house or office can share the broadband connection. It's fairly simple; you just connect your cable/DSL modem to your LAN instead of directly to your Linux box. In this configuration, though, you should consider adding a firewall/router as a buffer between your LAN and the outside world. That machine would perform such duties as:

✦ **Blocking access** — A well-configured firewall blocks access to all ports except those that you need to access the Internet the way you want, thereby minimizing the risks of intruders getting into your LAN.

✦ **NAT or IP Masquerading** — For the most part, you want the computers behind your firewall that are simply desktop systems to not be accessible to others from the Internet. By configuring your firewall to do NAT or IP Masquerading, your computers can be assigned private IP addresses. Your firewall then handles forwarding of messages between your LAN and the Internet. This is a good arrangement for several reasons. For one thing, the IP addresses of your private computers are not exposed to the outside world. Also, you can save the cost of paying your ISP for permanent IP addresses.

✦ **DHCP service** — Many firewall systems can act as a DHCP server. Those private IP addresses you can use with a NAT firewall can be assigned from the DHCP service running on your firewall system. When the client computer on your LAN starts up, besides its IP address, your DHCP service can tell the client the location of its DNS server, gateway to the Internet, or other information.

✦ **Routing**—In the home and small-office LAN environment illustrated in Figure 5-3, the firewall computer often has two Ethernet interfaces: one connected to the LAN and the other to the DSL or cable modem that leads to the ISP. Because the Ethernet interfaces are viewed as being on separate subnetworks, the firewall/router must be configured to forward packets across the two interfaces. It's not a big deal, but it does require a separate step to tell the firewall system that you want it to forward packets between the two subnetworks.

 Chapter 17 discusses setting up a firewall/router, using a Linux distribution designed specifically for the task.

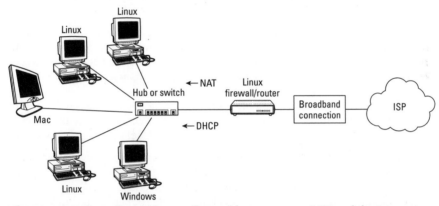

Figure 5-3: A firewall provides a safeguard between your LAN and the Internet.

In this example, the equipment you need includes:

✦ An Ethernet port on each computer

✦ A LAN cable for each computer

✦ A hub or a switch

✦ A low-end PC (as low as a 486 might do) running as a Linux firewall/router

✦ The DSL or cable modem

An alternative to this wired configuration is to replace the hub or switch with a wireless access point. Then each computer equipped with a wireless LAN card can get on the network without wires.

Connecting Servers

So far you've seen configurations that let one or more computers from your home or small business browse the Web. Letting someone from the Internet request services (Web pages, file transfers, and so forth) from your computers requires some extra thought.

After you have TCP/IP (the primary set of protocols used on the Internet) configured to connect to your ISP, requests for data can pass in either direction between your computers and the Internet unless you use a firewall to restrict traffic. So the same connection you use for Internet browsing can be used to offer services to the Internet, with a few caveats:

✦ **Permanent IP address** — Each time you reboot your computer, your ISP's DHCP server dynamically assigns your DSL/cable modem's IP address. For that reason, your IP address could change at each reboot. If you want your servers to be reachable on a permanent basis, you usually need at least one permanent IP address at which people can reach your servers. You will have to ask your ISP about a permanent IP address, and it might cost you extra money to have one.

Note A service called Dynamic DNS can be used in place of paying for a permanent IP address. With Dynamic DNS, you hire a service to constantly check whether your IP address has changed and assign your DNS host name to the new address if it does. You can search the Web for "Dynamic DNS" to find companies that offer that service.

✦ **ISP acceptable use policy** — Check that you are allowed to have incoming connections. Some ISPs, especially for inexpensive, home-use broadband service, will block incoming connections to Web servers or mail servers.

✦ **DNS hostname** — Although typing an IP address into a browser location box works just fine, most people prefer to use names (such as `www.linuxtrouble.com`) to reach a server. That requires you to purchase a DNS domain name and have an entry set up in a DNS server to resolve the name to the IP address of your server.

Although there is nothing magical about setting up an Internet server, given the few issues just mentioned, creating a public server can be a lot like opening up the doors of your house so that strangers can wander in. You want some policies in place to restrict where the strangers can go and what they can do.

For home or small-office locations that have a single Internet connection (represented by one public IP address), servers can be more exposed to the Internet than desktop systems by keeping them in one area that's referred to as the DMZ (demilitarized zone). In this configuration (illustrated in Figure 5-4), servers are directly behind the outside firewall. Desktop systems (that aren't to be accessible by people from the Internet), are behind a second, more restrictive firewall.

Whether you use Linux as your firewall machines or dedicated firewall devices, the outside firewall allows requests in for Web services (port 80), FTP services (ports 20 and 21), simple mail transfer protocol (port 25), and possibly other services. The internal firewall blocks any requests for services from the outside and allows only Internet communications that were initiated from computers behind the inside firewall.

Figure 5-4: Add servers to a DMZ where they can be more publicly accessible than your desktop systems.

Chapters 23 though 26 explain how to configure different server types, and Chapter 17 describes how to set up Linux as a router/firewall. Chapter 17 includes how to work with features such as IP Masquerading, NAT, and packet forwarding.

Connecting Other Equipment

Although I've focused on basic Ethernet equipment and dial-up modems for configuring network connections, Linux supports many, many other types of network equipment as well as different protocols for communicating over that equipment. Here are a few examples:

✦ **ISDN** — Integrated Services Digital Network (ISDN) lines were the preferred method of high-speed data lines to small businesses in the United States before DSL became widespread. It is still quite popular in Europe. ISDN4LINUX drivers and tools are available in many Linux systems for connecting to ISDN networks.

✦ **Token ring** — Support for token ring network cards is included in most Linux systems, although token rings are rarely used now. They were once popular at locations that had many IBM systems.

✦ **PLIP** — It's possible to connect two computers from their parallel ports so that they can communicate using TCP/IP protocols. Parallel Line Internet Protocol (PLIP) requires only a special cable; most Linux systems have built-in software that enables you to log in, transfer files, and perform other activities over that connection.

If your system has Linux source code installed, you can read about supported hardware devices in the documentation that comes with that source code. On Red Hat and some other Linux systems, the location of kernel documentation for various networking hardware is `/usr/src/linux*/Documentation/networking`.

Using Ethernet Connections to the Internet

Here's the general (default) way to bring up the network connection on a desktop system with Linux installed (or a bootable Linux launched):

1. Check whether you have an Ethernet card on your computer (most recent computers have one). If so, connect your Ethernet card to the equipment that gets you to the Internet (cable modem, DSL router/bridge, or network hub/switch). If not, you can purchase an Ethernet card at any retailer that sells computer hardware.

2. Ensure that appropriate drivers are available for the card and bring up the interface (typically, the first card is assigned to the eth0 interface). Usually, simply starting the computer causes the card to be detected and the appropriate driver loaded.

3. Get an IP address using DHCP if there is a DHCP server available through the interface. Most ISPs and businesses expect you to connect to their networks using DHCP, so they will have provided a DHCP server to the equipment where you connect your computer to the network.

As long as your desktop system is connected to a network that has a DHCP server willing to give it an IP address, you can be up and browsing the Web in no time.

If you find that the automatic method (DHCP) of connecting to your network doesn't work, it gets a bit trickier to connect to the Internet. Different Linux distributions offer different tools for manually configuring your Internet connection. The following sections describe a few graphical tools and some command-line and configuration-file approaches to configuring wired and wireless network connections.

Configuring Ethernet During Installation

Many Linux install processes ask you if you want to configure your network connection for your Ethernet cards. This is typically just for your Ethernet cards and not for dial-up modems or other networking equipment. Information you'll need for that process (IP address, gateway, DNS server, and so on) is explained in Chapter 7.

When you boot Linux, you can check whether you have access to the Internet by opening a Web browser (such as Mozilla or Konqueror) and typing in a Web address. If the Web site doesn't appear in your browser, you'll need to do some troubleshooting. The "Understanding Your Internet Connection" section later in this chapter provides information on how to track down problems with your Internet connection.

Configuring Ethernet from the Desktop

Most major Linux distributions offer graphical tools for configuring network interfaces. These tools step you through the information you need to enter and then start up the network interface (if you choose) to begin browsing the Web.

Here is a list of tools for configuring network interfaces in a few different Linux distributions. Some of these are graphical tools, and some are menu-based:

✦ **Red Hat/Fedora Linux** — The Network Configuration window lets you configure network connection using Ethernet, ISDN, modem, Token Ring, Wireless, and xDSL hardware. Start the Network Configuration window from the red hat menu by selecting System Settings ➪ Network or by typing **system-config-network** and entering the root password when prompted. (On older Red Hat Linux systems, the command was `redhat-config-network`.)

✦ **SUSE Linux** — The YaST Control Center that comes with SUSE contains features for configuring your network. From the SUSE menu on the panel, select System ➪ YaST, and then choose Network Devices. The YaST Control Center lets you configure a DSL, ISDN, Modem, or Network Card interface to the network. Select Network Card to configure your wired Ethernet Interface to the Internet.

✦ **Gentoo Linux** — From a shell (as root user), type **net-setup eth0** to start a menu-driven interface to configure the network connection from your first Ethernet card (eth0). The tool lets you have the interface try to start using DHCP or use static address information that you provide yourself.

✦ **KNOPPIX** — Select the squished penguin icon in the panel on the KNOPPIX desktop, and choose Networking/Internet from the menu. Select the Network card configuration menu entry to configure your network card. Or select from several other network equipment types instead (ADSL, GPRS, ISDN, Modem, or Wavelan).

Using Network Configuration in Fedora

If you did not configure your LAN connection during installation of Fedora Linux, you can do so at any time using the Network Configuration window. The IP address and host names can be assigned statically to an Ethernet interface or retrieved dynamically at boot time from a DHCP server.

Note   A computer can have more than one IP address because it can have multiple network interfaces. Each network interface must have an IP address (even if the address is assigned temporarily). So, if you have two Ethernet cards (eth0 and eth1), each needs its own IP address. Also, the address 127.0.0.1 represents the local host so that users on the local computer can access services in loopback.

Here's how to define the IP address for your Ethernet interface in Fedora Linux:

1. From the red hat menu, choose System Settings ⇨ Network or, as root user from a Terminal window, type **system-config-network**. (If prompted, type the root password.) The Network Configuration window appears.

2. Click the Devices tab. A listing of your existing network interfaces appears.

3. Double-click the eth0 interface (representing your first Ethernet card). A pop-up window titled Ethernet Device appears (see Figure 5-5), enabling you to configure your eth0 interface.

Figure 5-5: Configure and activate Ethernet devices in Fedora.

4. Select your preferences:

   • **Activate device when computer starts.** Check here to have eth0 start at boot time.

   • **Allow all users to enable and disable the device.** Check to let non-root users enable and disable the network interface.

   • **Enable IPv6 configuration for this interface.** Check here if you are connected to an IPV6 network. (Most networks are still IPV4.)

5. You also must choose whether to get your IP addresses from another computer at boot time or enter the addresses yourself:

- **Automatically obtain IP address settings with.** Select this box if you have a DHCP or BOOTP server on the network from which you can obtain your computer's IP address, netmask, and gateway. DHCP is recommended if you have more than just a couple of computers on your LAN. Optionally, you can set your own host name, which can be just a name (such as `jukebox`) or a fully qualified domain name (such as `jukebox.linuxtoys.net`).

- **Statically set IP addresses.** If there is no DHCP or other boot server on your LAN, add necessary IP address information statically by selecting this option and:

  Typing the IP address of the computer into the Address box. This number must be unique on your network. For your private LAN, you can use private IP addresses.

  Entering the netmask (described later in this chapter) in the Subnet Mask box. The netmask indicates the part of the IP address that represents the network.

  Typing the IP address of the computer into the Default Gateway Address box if a computer or router connected to your LAN provides routing functions to the Internet or other network. (Chapter 16 describes how to use NAT or IP Masquerading and how to use Fedora as a router.)

6. Click OK in the Ethernet Device window to save the configuration and close the window.

7. Click File ➪ Save to save the information you entered.

8. Click Activate in the Network Configuration window to start your connection to the LAN.

Identifying Other Computers (Hosts and DNS)

Each time you use a name to identify a computer, such as when browsing the Web or using an e-mail address, the computer name must be translated into an IP address. To resolve names to IP addresses, Fedora goes through a search order (based on the contents of three files in `/etc`: `resolv.conf`, `nsswitch.conf`, and `host.conf`). By default, it checks host names you add yourself (which end up in the `/etc/hosts` file), hosts available via NIS, and host names available via DNS.

You can use the Network Configuration window to add the following:

✦ **Host names.** You might do this to identify hosts on your LAN that are not configured on a DNS server.

✦ **DNS search path.** By adding domain names to a search path (such as `linux toys.net`), you can browse to a site by its host name (such as `jukebox`) and have Linux search the domains you added to the search path to find the host you are looking for (such as `jukebox.linuxtoys.net`).

✦ **DNS name servers.** A DNS server can resolve addresses for the domains it serves and contact other DNS servers to get addresses for all other DNS domains.

Note

If you are configuring a DNS server, you can use that server to centrally store names and IP addresses for your LAN. This saves you the trouble of updating every computer's /etc/hosts file every time you add or change a computer on your LAN.

To add host names, IP addresses, search paths, and DNS servers, follow these steps:

1. Start the Network Configuration. As root user from a Terminal window, type **system-config-network**, or from the red hat menu, click System Settings ➪ Network. The Network Configuration window appears.

2. Click the Hosts tab. A list of IP addresses, host names, and aliases appears.

3. Click New. A pop-up window (see Figure 5-6) appears.

Figure 5-6: Add an IP address, host name, and alias.

4. Type in the IP address number, host name, and, optionally, the host alias.

5. Click OK.

6. Repeat this process until you have added every computer on your LAN that cannot be reached by DNS.

7. Click the DNS tab.

8. Type the IP address of the computers that serve as your Primary and Secondary DNS servers. (You get these IP addresses from your ISP, or if you created your own DNS server, you can enter that server's IP address.)

9. Type the name of the domain (probably the name of your local domain) to be searched for host names into the DNS Search Path box.

10. Click File ⇨ Save to save the changes.

11. Click File ⇨ Quit to exit.

Now, when you use programs such as ftp, ssh, or other TCP/IP utilities, you can use any host name that is identified on your local computer, exists in your search path domain, or can be resolved from the public Internet DNS servers. (Strictly speaking, you don't have to set up your /etc/hosts file. You could use IP addresses as arguments to TCP/IP commands, but names are easier to work with.)

Understanding Your Internet Connection

If your Ethernet interface to the Internet is not working, there are ways to check what's happening that will work on many Linux distributions. Use the following procedure to find out how your network interfaces are working:

1. Open a shell (if you are using a graphical interface, open a Terminal window).

2. Type the following right after you boot your computer to verify whether Linux found your card and installed the Ethernet interface properly:

```
dmesg | grep eth
```

The dmesg command lists all the messages that were output by Linux at boot time. The grep eth command causes only those lines that contain the word *eth* to be printed. Here are a couple of examples:

```
eth0: NE2000 Compatible: port 0x300, irq3, hw_addr
00:80:C8:8C:8E:49
eth0: OEM i82557/i82558 10/100 Ethernet at 0xccc0,
00:90:27:4E:67:35, IRQ 17.
```

The first message appeared on my laptop computer with the Netgear card. It shows that a card was found at IRQ3 with a port address of 0x300 and an Ethernet hardware address of 00:80:C8:8C:8E:49. The second example is from my computer with the EtherExpress Pro/100 card. In it, the card is at IRQ 17, the port address is 0xccc0, and the Ethernet address is 00:90:27:4E:67:35.

If the eth0 interface is not found, but you know that you have a supported Ethernet card, type **lspci -vv | grep -i eth** to see if the Ethernet card is detected on the PCI bus. If it doesn't appear, check that your Ethernet card is properly seated in its slot.

3. To view which network interfaces are up and running, type the following:

```
$ /sbin/ifconfig -a
eth0      Link encap:Ethernet  HWaddr 00:D0:B7:66:9A:46
          inet addr:10.0.0.5  Bcast:10.0.0.255  Mask:255.255.255.0
          UP BROADCAST RUNNING MULTICAST  MTU:1500  Metric:1
          RX packets:326100 errors:0 dropped:0 overruns:0 frame:0
          TX packets:215931 errors:0 dropped:0 overruns:0 carrier:0
          collisions:5919
          RX bytes:168378315 (160.5 Mb)  TX bytes:40853243 (38.9 Mb)

lo        Link encap:Local Loopback
          inet addr:127.0.0.1  Mask:255.0.0.0
          UP LOOPBACK RUNNING  MTU:16436  Metric:1
          RX packets:37435 errors:0 dropped:0 overruns:0 frame:0
          TX packets:37435 errors:0 dropped:0 overruns:0 carrier:0
          collisions:0
          RX bytes:2353172 (2.2 Mb)  TX bytes:2353172 (2.2 Mb)
```

The output shows a loopback interface (lo) and one Ethernet card (eth0). The Ethernet interface (eth0) is assigned the IP address of 10.0.0.5. In this example, the eth0 has an IP address of 10.0.0.5.

4. Communicate with another computer on the LAN. The ping command can be used to send a packet to another computer and to ask for a packet in return. You could give ping either a host name (pine) or an IP address (10.0.0.10). For example, to ping a computer on the network called pine, type the following command:

```
# ping pine
```

If the computer can be reached, the output will look similar to the following:

```
PING pine (10.0.0.10): 56(84) data bytes
64 bytes from pine (10.0.0.10): icmp_seq=1 ttl=255 time=0.351 ms
64 bytes from pine (10.0.0.10): icmp_seq=2 ttl=255 time=0.445 ms
64 bytes from pine (10.0.0.10): icmp_seq=3 ttl=255 time=0.409 ms
64 bytes from pine (10.0.0.10): icmp_seq=4 ttl=255 time=0.457 ms
64 bytes from pine (10.0.0.10): icmp_seq=5 ttl=255 time=0.401 ms
64 bytes from pine (10.0.0.10): icmp_seq=6 ttl=255 time=0.405 ms
64 bytes from pine (10.0.0.10): icmp_seq=7 ttl=255 time=0.443 ms
64 bytes from pine (10.0.0.10): icmp_seq=8 ttl=255 time=0.384 ms
64 bytes from pine (10.0.0.10): icmp_seq=9 ttl=255 time=0.365 ms
```

```
64 bytes from pine (10.0.0.10): icmp_seq=10 ttl=255 time=0.367 ms

--- pine ping statistics ---
10 packets transmitted, 10 packets received, 0% packet loss, time
9011ms
rtt min/avg/max/mdev = 0.351/0.402/0.457/0.042 ms
```

A line of output is printed each time a packet is sent and received in return. It shows how much data was sent and how long it took for each package to be received. Watch this for a while, and then press Ctrl+C to stop ping; you'll see statistics on how many packets were transmitted, received, and lost.

If the output doesn't show that packets have been received, then there's no contact with the other computer. Verify that the names and addresses of the computers that you want to reach are in your /etc/hosts file or that your DNS server is accessible. Next, confirm that the names and IP addresses you have for the other computers you are trying to reach are correct (the IP addresses are the most critical).

5. If you are able to reach an IP address on your LAN with ping but are unable to ping a host computer by name, you may not be communicating with your DNS server. Repeat the ping command with the IP address of your DNS server to see if it is up and that you are able to communicate with it.

6. Check your DHCP information. If you obtained your IP address from a DHCP server, chances are your DHCP server fed your computer other information it needed to use the network as well. Look for a file that contains information about your DHCP lease. The lease includes information about the address that has been assigned to you as well as how long you can keep it. In Fedora, lease information is held in the /var/lib/dhcp/dhclient-eth0.leases file. Here's an example of information from that file:

```
lease {
  interface "eth0";
  fixed-address 10.0.0.204;
  option subnet-mask 255.255.255.0;
  option routers 10.0.0.1;
  option dhcp-lease-time 21600;
  option dhcp-message-type 5;
  option domain-name-servers 10.0.0.2;
  option domain-name-servers 10.0.0.3;
  option dhcp-server-identifier 10.0.0.5;
  option domain-name "linuxtrouble.com";
  renew 3 2004/7/21 01:23:06;
  rebind 3 2004/7/21 04:22:48;
  expire 3 2004/7/21 05:07:48;
}
```

Here you can see that the IP address assigned to the machine is 10.0.0.204, with a subnet mask of 255.255.255.0. The machine acting as the router to the Internet (also called the *gateway*) is 10.0.0.1. The DNS servers are 10.0.0.2 and 10.0.0.3 (you can ping those numbers to see if you can reach your DNS servers).

Using Dial-up Connections to the Internet

Many individuals and even some small businesses that need to connect to the Internet still do so using modems and telephone lines. The modem connects to a serial port (COM1, COM2, and so on) on your computer and then into a telephone jack. Your computer dials a modem at your Internet service provider or business that has a connection to the Internet.

The most common protocol for making dial-up connections to the Internet (or other TCP/IP network) is Point-to-Point Protocol (PPP). Let's look at how to use PPP protocol to connect to the Internet.

Getting Information

To establish a PPP connection, you need to get some information from the administrator of the network to which you are connecting. This is either your Internet service provider (ISP) when you sign up for Internet service, or the person in your workplace who wears a pocket protector and walks around carrying cables, two or more cellular phones, and a couple of beepers (when a network goes down, these people are in demand!). Here is the kind of information you need to set up your PPP connection:

✦ **Telephone number** — Gives you access to the modem (or pool of modems) at the ISP. If it is a national ISP, make sure that you get a local or toll-free telephone number (otherwise, you'll rack up long-distance fees on top of your ISP fees).

✦ **Account name and password** — Used to verify that you have an Internet account with the ISP. This is an account name when you connect to Linux or other UNIX system but may be referred to as a system name when you connect to an NT server.

✦ **An IP number** — Most ISPs use dynamic IP numbers, which means that you are assigned an IP number temporarily when you are connected. Your ISP assigns a permanent IP number if it uses static IP addresses. If your computer or all the computers on your LAN need to have a more permanent presence on the network, you may be given one static IP number or a set of static IP addresses to use.

✦ **DNS Server IP addresses** — Your computer translates Internet host names to IP addresses by querying a Domain Name System (DNS) server. Your ISP should give you at least one IP address for a preferred (and possibly alternate) DNS server.

✦ **PAP or CHAP secrets** — You may need a PAP (Password Authentication Protocol) ID or CHAP (Challenge Handshake Authentication Protocol) ID and a secret, instead of a username and password when connecting to a Windows

NT system. These features are used with authentication on Microsoft and some other operating systems. Linux and other UNIX servers don't typically use this type of authentication, although they support PAP and CHAP on the client side. Your ISP will tell you if you are using PAP or CHAP.

Your ISP typically provides services such as news and mail servers for use with your Internet connection. To configure these useful services, you need to acquire the following information:

✦ **Mail server**—If your ISP is providing you with an e-mail account, you must know the address of the mail server, the type of mail service (such as POP3—Post Office Protocol—or IMAP—Internet Message Access Protocol), and the authentication password for the mail server so you can get your e-mail.

✦ **News server**—If your ISP provides the name of a news server so that you can participate in newsgroups, the server may require you to log on, so you will need a password. The ISP provides that password, if required.

After you've gathered this information, you're ready to set up your connection to the Internet. To configure Linux to connect to your ISP, read on.

Setting Up Dial-up PPP

PPP is used to create IP connections over serial lines. Most often, the serial connection is established over a modem; however, it also works over serial cables (null modem cables) or digital lines (including ISDN and DSL).

Although one side must dial out and the other side must receive the call to create the PPP connection over a modem, after the connection is established, information can flow in both directions. For the sake of clarity, however, I refer to the computer placing the call as the client and the computer receiving the call as the server.

To simplify the process of configuring PPP (and other network interfaces), most Linux systems include graphical tools to configure dial-up. Two such tools are:

✦ **Internet Configuration Wizard**—From the main desktop menu in Fedora, choose System Tools ➪ Internet Configuration Wizard. The Select Device Type window that appears enables you to configure and test your dial-up PPP connection.

✦ **KDE PPP (KPPP) Window**—From the KDE desktop, select Internet ➪ KPPP, or from a Terminal window run the kppp command. From the KPPP window you can set up and launch a PPP dial-up connection.

Before you begin either of these procedures, physically connect your modem to your computer, plug it in, and connect it to your telephone line. If you have an internal modem, you will probably see a telephone port on the back of your computer to which you need to connect. If your modem isn't detected, you can reboot your computer or run `wvdialconf create` (as described later in this chapter) to have it detected.

Creating a Dial-up Connection with the Internet Configuration Wizard

Use the Internet Configuration Wizard to set up dial-up networking in Fedora. Here's how:

1. Choose System Tools ➪ Internet Configuration Wizard from the main menu. (Type the root password, if prompted.) A Select Device Type window appears (see Figure 5-7).

Figure 5-7: The Internet Configuration Wizard helps you set up a PPP Internet connection.

2. Select Modem connection and click Forward. The wizard searches for a modem, and then the Select Modem window appears.

3. Select the following modem properties:

   • **Modem Device** — If the modem is connected to your first serial port (COM1), you can select `/dev/ttyS0`; for the second serial port (COM2) choose `/dev/ttyS1`. (By convention, the device is often linked to `/dev/modem`. Type **ls –l /dev/modem** to see if it is linked to `/dev/ttyS0`, `/dev/ttyS1`, or another tty device.)

   • **Baud Rate** — The rate at which the computer talks to the modem (which is typically considerably faster than the modem can talk over the phone lines). The default is 115200 bits per second, which is probably fine for dial-up connections.

- **Flow Control** — Check the modem documentation to see if the modem supports hardware flow control (CRTSCTS). If it doesn't, select software flow control (XON/XOFF). Flow control prevents more data than the modem can handle from being sent to it.

- **Modem Volume** — This is off by default because the noise can be annoying, but if you select medium while you're setting up the modem, the sound can give you a sense of where things are stopping if you can't get a connection. You can turn it off after everything's working.

- **Use touch tone dialing** — Leave this check box on in most cases. If for some reason your phone system doesn't support touch-tone dialing, you can turn it off.

4. Click Forward. The Select Provider window appears. Enter the following provider information:

- **Internet Provider** — If you are using Internet service in any of the countries shown in the Internet Provider window, select the plus sign next to that country's name. If your Internet service provider appears in the National list, select it. Information is automatically filled in for that provider. Otherwise, you need to fill in the rest of the dialog window.

- **Phone Number** — The telephone number of the ISP you want to dial in to. (An optional prefix is available in case you need to dial 9 or some other number to get an outside dial tone.)

- **Provider Name** — The name of the Internet service provider. In the current release of Fedora, there is a bug that causes the dial-up to fail if you use any provider name other than ppp0. If that has not been fixed, please use ppp0 here as the provider name. (For multiple dial-up accounts, use ppp1, ppp2, and so on.)

- **Login Name** — The login name assigned to you by the ISP. The ISP may have called the login name a login ID or something similar.

- **Password** — The password associated with the login name.

5. Click Forward, and the IP Settings window appears. With a dial-up connection, you would typically select Automatically Obtain IP Address Settings. However, if the ISP has assigned a static IP address that you can use, click the Statically Set IP Addresses check box, and then enter your IP address, subnet mask, and default gateway address in the appropriate fields. Click Forward to continue.

6. The Create Dialup Connection window appears, displaying the information you just entered. If all the information looks correct, click Apply (otherwise, click the Back button, correct your information, and click Forward again to return to this window).

7. After you click Apply, the Network Configuration window appears, ideally with a new PPP connection of modem type appearing in the window. (If it doesn't appear, select System Settings ➪ Network.)

8. Select the new dial-up entry (so it is highlighted), and choose File ➪ Save to save its new dial-up configuration.

Now select the PPP device name and click the Activate button. The Internet dialer starts up and dials your ISP. (If you have sound turned on, you should hear your modem dialing out.) If everything is working properly, your login and password are accepted, and the PPP connection is completed.

Try opening Mozilla or another Web browser to see if you can access a Web site on the Internet. If this doesn't work the first time, don't be discouraged. Skip ahead to the "Checking Your PPP Connection" section to see what to check to get your dial-up PPP connection working.

Launching Your PPP Connection

Your dial-up connection is now configured, but it is not set to connect automatically. One way to start the connection is to set it up to launch manually from the desktop panel. Here's how:

From the GNOME desktop:

1. Right-click the panel and choose Add to Panel ➪ Launcher from Menu ➪ System Settings ➪ Network from the main menu. An icon appears on the panel that you can click to open the Network Configuration window.

2. Select the new icon from the panel. A Network Configuration window appears.

3. Select the dial-up interface you added (probably ppp0) and click Activate to connect.

From the KDE desktop:

1. Right-click the panel and choose Add ➪ Application Button ➪ System Settings ➪ Network from the main menu.

2. Select the new icon from the panel (type the root password, if prompted). A Network Configuration window appears.

3. Select the dial-up interface you added (probably ppp0) and click Activate to connect.

From this point forward, icons appear on your desktop that you can click to immediately connect to your ISP over the dial-up connection you configured.

Launching Your PPP Connection on Demand

Instead of starting a dial-up PPP connection manually each time you want to contact the Internet from Fedora, you can set your dial-up connection to start automatically when an application (such as a Web browser or e-mail program) tries to use the connection. On-demand dialing is particularly useful if

✦ The dial-up connection on your Linux system is acting as the gateway for other computers in your home or office. You don't have to run over to your Linux box to start the connection when another computer needs the dial-up connection.

✦ Programs that you run during off hours, such as remote backups, require an Internet connection.

✦ You don't want to be bothered clicking an extra icon when you just want to browse the Web a bit.

The risk of on-demand dialing is that because it gets going automatically, the dial-up connection can start up when you don't want it to. (Some people get worried when their computers start dialing by themselves in the middle of the night.)

Here is an example of settings you can add to your dial-up configuration file (probably/ `etc/sysconfig/network-scripts/ifcfg-ppp0`) to configure on-demand dialing:

```
ONBOOT=yes
DEMAND=yes
IDLETIMEOUT=600
RETRYTIMEOUT=30
```

The `ONBOOT=yes` starts the `pppd` daemon (but doesn't immediately begin dialing because `DEMAND` is set to `yes`). Also, because `DEMAND=yes`, a dial-up connection attempt is made anytime traffic tries to use your dial-up connection. With `IDLE TIMEOUT` set to `600`, the connection is dropped after 600 seconds (10 minutes) with no traffic on the connection. With `RETRYTIMEOUT` set to `30`, a dropped connection is retried after 30 seconds (unless the connection was dropped by an idle timeout, in which case there is no retry). You can change the timeout values as it suits you.

Note   Because it can take a bit of time for dial-up connections to be established, operations may fail while dialing occurs. In particular, DNS requests can time out in 30 seconds, which may not be long enough to establish a dial-up connection. If you have three DNS servers configured for each client, you have a 90-second timeout period. As a result, the modem connection may be running before the request fails.

Checking Your PPP Connection

The following information will help you debug your PPP connection or simply better understand how it works.

It is possible that your modem is not supported under Linux. If that is the case, your PPP connection might be failing because the modem was not detected at all. To scan your serial ports to see where your modem might be, type the following (as root user):

```
$ wvdialconf /etc/wvdial.conf.new
```

The `wvdialconf` command is really to build a configuration file (the `/etc/wvdial.conf` file) that is used by the dialer command (`wvdial`). (You only need this file if you use `wvdial` to do your dial-up.) Its first action, however, is to scan the serial ports on your computer and report where it finds modems. If it tells you that "no modem was detected," it's likely that either your modem isn't connected properly or no driver is available to support the modem.

If the modem wasn't detected, you should determine whether it is a modem supported in Linux. You can do this by finding out what type of chip set is used in the modem. This is even more important than finding out the manufacturer of the modem because the same manufacturer can use chips from different companies. (This applies primarily to internal modems because most external serial modems and many USB modems are supported in Linux.)

After you have determined the chip set being used, check the Linmodems.org Web site (`www.linmodems.org`), which contains information on so-called Winmodems that have only recently begun to be supported in Linux. Search for the chip set on your modem from this site. In many cases, the site tells you if there is a driver available for your modem.

Summary

Many different tools are available for configuring network connections in the various Linux distributions. Fedora and other Red Hat Linux systems use a graphical Network Configuration. SUSE Linux uses its YaST administrative interface to configure network equipment. For dial-up networks, the KDE desktop includes the KPPP GUI tool for configuring modems. If your network connection doesn't start up automatically (as it does in many cases), this chapter explains how to use some of these network configuration tools to configure it manually.

By adding your computer to a public network, such as the Internet, you open it to possible intruders. The next chapter describes ways in which you can secure your

Securing Linux

Since the dawn of interconnected networks, some user has been trying to break into other users' systems. As the Internet has grown and broadband Internet access has spread, the problem has only become more severe. A home computer running an insecure configuration can be used as a powerful mail relay, storage for traffic in pirated data, allow the user's personal information to become compromised, or any number of other such horrors.

Once upon a time network attacks required some effort and skill on the part of the attacker. Today automated tools can get even the most novice user up and running trying to compromise network-attached systems in an alarmingly short time. Additionally, worms have the capability to turn large numbers of insecure Win32 systems into an army of "zombies" usable for massive coordinated Denial of Service attacks.

Why should you care about security? According to the Internet Storm Center (http://isc.sans.org), a computer connected to the Internet has 16 minutes before it falls under some form of attack. Securing any computer system is not hugely difficult; it simply requires some common sense and careful application of good security practices.

In many cases, good practices for setting and protecting passwords, monitoring log files, and creating good firewalls will keep out many would-be intruders. Sometimes, more proactive approaches are needed to respond to break-ins. Use this chapter to familiarize yourself, as a Linux administrator, with the security dangers that exist and the tools necessary to protect your system.

Protecting Your Computer

Just as closing and locking the doors and windows of your house helps keep burglars from wandering in off the street, so will some basic security precautions keep most intruders out of your computer system. There are also some simple techniques for monitoring your system (like watching system log files and checking for people scanning your ports) that enable you to take an active role in responding to intrusions.

If you think that nobody will break into your computer because there's nothing on it worth stealing, think again. Often, a system is broken into solely to gain use of it as a jumping-off point to launch further attacks on other systems. And crackers might try to hijack your computer to serve up copyrighted materials or pornography from your system.

Linux (and similar UNIX and BSD systems) were designed to give you the tools to protect your computers from intruders. Your job is to learn a bit about those tools and utilize them in ways to keep your computer safe. You can start by applying a few rules for your own personal computer use:

✦ Use strong passwords (discussed later in this chapter). Simple "dictionary word" passwords (even those using number-to-letter substitution) are woefully easy to crack with freely available automated tools.

✦ Be skeptical of unsolicited e-mail. Don't open and run executable files that come to you in e-mail attachments that you don't know to be trustworthy. If an e-mail comes in telling you that you need a critical update (and tells you "click here to get it"), make sure that the message came from a valid source.

✦ Know the source of the software you allow on your computer. Download software only from valid mirror sites associated with the Linux distribution you use or from a reputable project site. Be sure to check the md5sum of iso images you download to be sure the image isn't corrupted or hasn't been tampered with.

The following tips will help you as the network administrator (which you are if you connect your computer to the Internet) prevent the majority of malicious network activity from taking you out of order:

✦ Always place a firewall between your systems and public or unsecured networks such as the Internet. Ideally this should be a standalone device, but that is not essential. If your Linux system is directly connected to the Internet, the firewall features covered in detail in Chapter 17 will help you configure Linux to only allow requests for services you want to provide to the Internet and filter out other traffic trying to get into your system.

✦ Keep tabs on the kinds of activity to which your system is exposed. Regularly monitoring your log files helps make you better able to identify the beginnings of suspicious activity. You can even monitor network ports on your system to watch for attempts by intruders to scan those ports to find vulnerabilities. (Refer to the Syslog and Portsentry sections later in this chapter for information on tools for watching your system.)

✦ Get security updates regularly. All major Linux distributions offer tools and software repositories for getting fixes for security vulnerabilities to you as they are discovered and patched. Getting those critical patches is often as simple as running a single command that downloads and installs the patches.

Tip Several Web sites provide excellent vulnerability, outbreak, and mitigation information including `www.isc.sans.org` (general Internet attack information), `www.sarc.com` (virus outbreak information), `www.cert.org` (software security information), and `www.securityfocus.com` (general security Web site).

✦ Disable network services you do not need. Any service that isn't actively being used is just a liability. Shut it down and rest easier knowing that there's one less route of entry into your systems.

Understanding Attack Techniques

Attacks on computing systems take on different forms, depending on the goal and resources of the attacker. Some attackers want to be disruptive, while others want to infiltrate your machines and utilize your resources for their own nefarious purposes. Still others are targeting your data for financial gain or blackmail. Some common attacks that are described in this section include Denial of Service, Distributed Denial of Service, and intrusion attacks.

Denial of Service (DoS) attacks are the easiest to perpetrate. The primary purpose of these attacks is to disrupt the activities of a remote site by overloading it with irrelevant data. DoS attacks can be as simple as sending thousands of page requests per second to a Web site. These types of attacks are fairly easy to resolve: after you get a handle on where the attack is coming from, a simple phone call to the perpetrator's ISP gets the problem solved.

Advanced DoS attacks are called *Distributed Denial of Service (DDoS) attacks*. They are much harder to execute and nearly impossible to stop. The attacker takes control of hundreds or even thousands of weakly secured Internet-connected computers and then directs them in unison to send a stream of irrelevant data to a single Internet host. The result is that the power of one attacker is magnified thousands of times. Instead of an attack coming from one direction, as in the usual DoS, it comes from thousands of directions at once. The best defense against a DDoS attack is to contact your own ISP to see if it can filter traffic at its border routers.

Many people use the excuse "I have nothing on my machine anyone would want" to avoid considering security. The problem with this argument is that attackers have a lot of reasons to use your machine. The attacker can turn your machine into an agent for later use in a DDoS attack. More than once, authorities have shown up at the door of a dumbfounded computer user asking questions about threats originating from the user's computer. By ignoring security, owners have opened themselves up to a great deal of liability.

Although DoS attacks are disruptive, intrusion-type attacks are the most damaging. The reasons are varied, but the result is always the same: An uninvited guest takes up residence on your machine and uses it in a way over which you have no control. To remotely use the resources of a target machine, an attacker must first look for an opening to exploit. In the absence of inside information such as passwords or encryption keys, he must scan the target machine to see what services are offered. Perhaps one of the services is weakly secured, and the attacker can use some known exploit to finagle his way in.

A tool called `nmap` is generally considered the best way to scan a host for services. Once the attacker has a list of the available services running on his target, he needs to find a way to trick one of those services into letting him have privileged access to the system. This is usually done with a program called an *exploit,* which uses known vulnerabilities in a service to ask the service to run an alternate program, change a configuration file, or give out information about the system.

Note   Besides being used as an intrusion tool, nmap can be used by a computer's own system administrator to check the security of the machine. You can use nmap on your own machine to see what an attacker would see if he scanned your system, enabling you to fill potential security holes.

Protecting Against Denial of Service Attacks

As explained earlier, a Denial of Service attack attempts to crash your computer or at least degrade its performance to an unusable level. There are a variety of DoS exploits. Most try to overload some system resource, such as your available disk space or your Internet connection. Some common attacks and defenses are discussed in the following sections.

Mailbombing

Mailbombing is the practice of sending so much e-mail to a particular user or system that the computer's hard drive becomes full. There are a couple of ways to protect yourself from mailbombing: Use the Procmail e-mail-filtering tool or configure your sendmail daemon.

Blocking Mail with Procmail

The Procmail e-mail-filtering tool is available in many Linux distributions and is tightly integrated with the sendmail e-mail daemon. This integration allows Procmail to selectively block or filter out specific types of e-mail. You can learn more about it at `www.procmail.org`.

To enable Procmail for your user account, create a `.procmailrc` file in your home directory. The file should be mode 0600 (readable by you but nobody else). Type the following, replacing *evilmailer* with the actual e-mail address that is mail-bombing you.

```
# Delete mail from evilmailer
:0
* ^From.*evilmailer
/dev/null
```

The Procmail recipe looks for the `From` line at the start of each e-mail to see if it includes the string *evilmailer*. If it does, the message is sent to `/dev/null` (effectively throwing it away).

Blocking Mail with Sendmail

The Procmail e-mail tool works quite well when only one user is being mailbombed. If, however, the mailbombing affects many users, you should probably configure your `sendmail` daemon to block all e-mail from the mailbomber. Do this by adding the mailbomber's e-mail address or system name to the `access` file located in the `/etc/mail` directory.

Each line of the `access` file contains an e-mail address, host name, domain, or IP address followed by a tab and then a keyword specifying what action to take when that entity sends you a message. Valid keywords are `OK`, `RELAY`, `REJECT`, `DISCARD`, and `ERROR`. The `REJECT` keyword causes a sender's e-mail to be bounced back with an error message. The keyword `DISCARD` causes the message to be silently dropped without sending an error back. You can even return a custom error message by using the `ERROR` keyword.

Here's an example `/etc/mail/access` file:

```
# Check the /usr/share/doc/sendmail/README.cf file for a description
# of the format of this file. (search for access_db in that file)
# The /usr/share/doc/sendmail/README.cf is part of the sendmail-doc
# package.
#
# by default we allow relaying from localhost...
localhost.localdomain           RELAY
localhost                       RELAY
127.0.0.1                       RELAY
#
# Senders we want to Block
#
evilmailer@yahoo.com    REJECT
stimpy.glaci.com        REJECT
cyberpromo.com          DISCARD
199.170.176.99          ERROR:"550 Die Spammer Scum!"
199.170.177             ERROR:"550 Email Refused"
```

As with most Linux configuration files, lines that begin with a # pound sign are comments. The list of blocked spammers is at the end of this example file. Note that the address to block can be a complete e-mail address, a full host name, a domain only, an IP address, or a subnet.

To block a particular e-mail address or host from mailbombing you, log in to your system as root, edit the /etc/mail/access file, and add a line to DISCARD mail from the offending sender.

After saving the file and exiting the editor, you must convert the access file into a hash-indexed database called access.db. The database is updated automatically the next time sendmail starts. Or you can convert the database immediately, as follows:

```
# cd /etc/mail
# make
```

Sendmail should now discard e-mail from the addresses you added.

Spam Relaying

Another way in which your e-mail services can be abused is by having your system used as a spam relay. *Spam* refers to the unsolicited junk e-mail that has become a common occurrence on the Internet. Spammers often deliver their annoying messages from a normal dial-up Internet account. They need some kind of high-capacity e-mail server to accept and buffer the payload of messages. They deliver the spam to the server all in one huge batch and then log off, letting the server do the work of delivering the e-mail to the many victims.

Naturally, no self-respecting Internet service provider (ISP) cooperates with this action, so spammers resort to hijacking servers at another ISP to do the dirty work. Having your mail server hijacked to act as a spam relay can have a devastating effect on your system and your reputation. There are even Internet "blacklists" that are used to ban communications with servers that allow open relay.

If your system is used to forward mass mailing, you could find your mail server unable to deliver e-mail to some other e-mail servers because you have been blacklisted. On many Linux installations, open mail relay is disabled by default. You can either upgrade to the latest build of sendmail, which does not allow open mail relay by default, or you can simply disable sendmail if you are not using it for host e-mail services. Open mail relaying is typically one security issue that you will not have to worry about with a recent distribution of Linux.

Note   Abuse of open mail relays is not limited to small businesses and home users. One cable Internet provider in my area had several of its mail servers added to a blacklist. I contacted my ISP, and it was totally unaware that the abuses were going on let alone that it had been blacklisted.

You can allow specific hosts or domains to relay mail through your system by adding those senders to your /etc/mail/access file with keyword RELAY. By default, relaying is allowed only from the local host. Refer to the sendmail documentation for more information.

Tip One package you might consider using to filter out spam on your mail server is spamassassin, which examines the text of incoming mail messages and attempts to filter out messages that it determines to be spam. Spamassassin is described in Chapter 24.

Smurf Amplification Attack

Smurfing refers to a particular type of Denial of Service attack aimed at flooding your Internet connection. It can be a difficult attack to defend against because it isn't easy to trace it back to the attacker.

The attack makes use of the ICMP protocol, a service intended for checking the speed and availability of network connections. Using the ping command, you can send a network packet from your computer to another computer on the Internet. The remote computer recognizes the packet as an ICMP request and echoes a reply packet to your computer, which can then print a message revealing that the remote system is up and telling you how long it took to reply to the ping.

A smurfing attack uses a malformed ICMP request to bury your computer in network traffic. The attacker bounces a ping request off an unwitting third party in such a way that the reply is duplicated dozens or even hundreds of times. An organization with a fast Internet connection and a large number of computers is used as the relay. The destination address of the ping is set to an entire subnet instead of a single host. The return address is forged to be your machine's address instead of the actual sender's. When the ICMP packet arrives at the unwitting relay's network, every host on that subnet replies to the ping! Furthermore, they reply to your computer instead of to the actual sender. If the relay's network has hundreds of computers, your Internet connection can be quickly flooded.

The best fix is to contact the organization being used as a relay, informing it of the abuse. That organization usually need only reconfigure its Internet router to stop any future attacks. If the organization is uncooperative, you can minimize the effect of the attack by blocking the ICMP protocol on your router, which at least keeps the traffic off your internal network. It helps even more if you can persuade your ISP to block ICMP packets aimed at your network.

Protecting Against Distributed DoS Attacks

A DDoS attack is much harder to initiate and nearly impossible to stop. It begins with the penetration of hundreds or even thousands of weakly secured machines. These machines are then directed to attack a single host based on the desire of the attacker.

With the advent of DSL and cable modems, millions of people are enjoying Internet access with virtually no speed restrictions. In their rush to get online, many of those people neglect even the most basic security. Because the vast majority of these people run Microsoft operating systems, they tend to get hit with worms and viruses rather quickly. Until very recently, it was common practice for Microsoft systems to have many services open to the network of which users were unaware and very little emphasis placed on using firewall features to block intruders.

After a machine has been infiltrated, quite often the worm or virus installs a program on the victim's machine that instructs it to quietly call home and announce that it is now ready to do the master's bidding. At the whim of the master, the infected machines can now be used to focus a concentrated stream of garbage data at a selected host. In concert with thousands of other infected machines, an attacker now has the power to take down nearly any site on the Internet.

Detecting a DDoS is similar to detecting a DoS attack. One or more of the following signs are likely to be present:

✦ Sustained saturated data link

✦ No reduction in link saturation during off-peak hours

✦ Hundreds or even thousands of simultaneous network connections

✦ Extremely slow system performance

Pinging an outside host can tell you a lot about your data link saturation: Much higher than usual latency is a dead giveaway. Normal ping latency (that is, the time it takes for a ping response to come back from a remote host) looks like the following:

```
# ping www.example.com
PING www.example.com (192.0.34.166) from 10.0.0.11: 56(84)
bytes of data
64 bytes from 192.0.34.166: icmp_seq=1 ttl=49 time=40.1 ms
64 bytes from 192.0.34.166: icmp_seq=2 ttl=49 time=42.5 ms
64 bytes from 192.0.34.166: icmp_seq=3 ttl=49 time=39.5 ms
64 bytes from 192.0.34.166: icmp_seq=4 ttl=49 time=38.4 ms
64 bytes from 192.0.34.166: icmp_seq=5 ttl=49 time=39.0 ms

--- www.example.com ping statistics ---
5 packets transmitted, 5 received, 0% loss, time 4035ms
rtt min/avg/max/mdev = 38.472/39.971/42.584/1.432 ms
```

In this example, the average time for a ping packet to make the round trip was about 39 thousandths of a second.

A ping to a nearly saturated link will look like the following:

```
# ping www.example.com
PING www.example.com (192.0.34.166): from 10.0.0.11:
56(84)bytes of data
64 bytes from 192.0.34.166: icmp_seq=1 ttl=62 time=1252 ms
64 bytes from 192.0.34.166: icmp_seq=2 ttl=62 time=1218 ms
64 bytes from 192.0.34.166: icmp_seq=3 ttl=62 time=1290 ms
64 bytes from 192.0.34.166: icmp_seq=4 ttl=62 time=1288 ms
64 bytes from 192.0.34.166: icmp_seq=5 ttl=62 time=1241 ms

--- www.example.com ping statistics ---
6 packets transmitted, 5 received, 0% loss, time 5032ms
rtt min/avg/max/mdev = 1218.059/1258.384/1290.861/28.000 ms
```

In this example, a ping packet took, on average, 1.3 seconds to make the round trip. From the first example to the second example, latency increased by a factor of 31! A data link that goes from working normally to slowing down by a factor of 31 is a clear sign that link utilization should be investigated.

For a more accurate measure of data throughput, a tool such as ttcp can be used. To test your connection with ttcp, you must have installed the ttcp package on machines inside *and* outside your network. If you are not sure if the package is installed, simply type **ttcp** at a command prompt. You should see something like the following:

```
# ttcp
Usage: ttcp -t [-options] host [ < in ]
       ttcp -r [-options > out]
Common options:
  -l ##   length of bufs read from or written to network (default 8192)
  -u   use UDP instead of TCP
  -p ##   port number to send to or listen at (default 5001)
  -s   -t: source a pattern to network
     -r: sink (discard) all data from network
  -A   align the start of buffers to this modulus (default 16384)
  -O   start buffers at this offset from the modulus (default 0)
  -v   verbose: print more statistics
  -d   set SO_DEBUG socket option
  -b ##   set socket buffer size (if supported)
  -f X   format for rate: k,K = kilo{bit,byte}; m,M = mega; g,G = giga
Options specific to -t:
  -n##   number of source bufs written to network (default 2048)
  -D   don't buffer TCP writes (sets TCP_NODELAY socket option)
Options specific to -r:
  -B   for -s, only output full blocks as specified by -l (for TAR)
  -T   "touch": access each byte as it's read
```

The first step is to start up a receiver process on the server machine:

```
# ttcp -rs
ttcp-r: buflen=8192, nbuf=2048, align=16384/0, port=5001  tcp
ttcp-r: socket
```

The -r flag denotes that the server machine will be the receiver. The -s flag, in conjunction with the -r flag, tells ttcp to ignore any received data.

Have someone outside your data link, with a network link close to the same speed as yours, set up a ttcp sending process:

```
# ttcp -ts server.example.com
ttcp-t: buflen=8192, nbuf=2048, align=16384/0, port=5001  tcp
-> server.example.com
ttcp-t: socket
ttcp-t: connect
```

Let the process run for a few minutes and then press Ctrl+C on the transmitting side to stop the testing. The receiving side will then take a moment to calculate and present the results:

```
# ttcp -rs
ttcp-r: buflen=8192, nbuf=2048, align=16384/0, port=5001  tcp
ttcp-r: socket
ttcp-r: accept from 64.223.17.21
ttcp-r: 2102496 bytes in 70.02 real seconds = 29.32 KB/sec +++
ttcp-r: 1226 I/O calls, msec/call = 58.49, calls/sec = 17.51
ttcp-r: 0.0user 0.0sys 1:10real 0% 0i+0d 0maxrss 0+2pf 0+0csw
```

In this example, the average bandwidth between the two hosts was 29.32 kilobytes per second. On a link suffering from a DDoS, this number would be a fraction of the actual bandwidth for which the data link is rated.

If the data link is indeed saturated, the next step is to determine where the connections are coming from. A very effective way of doing this is with the netstat command. Type the following to see connection information:

```
# netstat -tupn
```

Table 6-1 describes each of the netstat parameters used here.

Table 6-1 netstat Parameters	
Parameter	**Description**
-t, --tcp	Shows TCP socket connections.
-u, --udp	Shows UDP socket connections.
-p, --program	Shows the PID and name of the program to which each socket belongs.
-n, --numeric	Shows numerical address instead of trying to determine symbolic host, port, or usernames.

The following is an example of what the output might look like:

```
Active Internet connections (w/o servers)
Proto Recv-Q Send-Q Local Address    Foreign Address     State        PID/Program name
tcp     0      0 65.213.7.96:22      13.29.132.19:12545   ESTABLISHED  32376/sshd
tcp     0    224 65.213.7.96:22      13.29.210.13:29250   ESTABLISHED  13858/sshd
tcp     0      0 65.213.7.96:6667    13.29.194.190:33452  ESTABLISHED  1870/ircd
tcp     0      0 65.213.7.96:6667    216.39.144.152:42709 ESTABLISHED  1870/ircd
tcp     0      0 65.213.7.96:42352   67.113.1.99:53       TIME_WAIT    -
tcp     0      0 65.213.7.96:42354   83.152.6.9:113       TIME_WAIT    -
tcp     0      0 65.213.7.96:42351   83.152.6.9:113       TIME_WAIT    -
tcp     0      0 127.0.0.1:42355     127.0.0.1:783        TIME_WAIT    -
tcp     0      0 127.0.0.1:783       127.0.0.1:42353      TIME_WAIT    -
tcp     0      0 65.213.7.96:42348   19.15.11.1:25        TIME_WAIT    -
```

The output is organized into columns defined as follows:

✦ **Proto** — Protocol used by the socket.

✦ **Recv-Q** — The number of bytes not yet copied by the user program attached to this socket.

✦ **Send-Q** — The number of bytes not acknowledged by the host.

✦ **Local Address** — Address and port number of the local end of the socket.

✦ **Foreign Address** — Address and port number of the remote end of the socket.

✦ **State** — Current state of the socket. Table 6-2 provides a list of socket states.

✦ **PID/Program name** — Process ID and program name of the process that owns the socket.

Table 6-2 Socket States	
State	*Description*
ESTABLISHED	Socket has an established connection.
SYN_SENT	Socket actively trying to establish a connection.
SYN_RECV	Connection request received from the network.
FIN_WAIT1	Socket is closed and the connection is shutting down.
FIN_WAIT2	Socket is waiting for remote end to shut down.
TIME_WAIT	Socket is waiting after closing to handle packets still in the network.
CLOSED	Socket is not being used.
CLOSE_WAIT	The remote end has shut down, waiting for the socket to close.

Continued

State	Description
LAST_ACK	The remote end has shut down, and the socket is closed, waiting for acknowledgment.
LISTEN	Socket is waiting for an incoming connection.
CLOSING	Both sides of the connection are shut down, but not all of your data has been sent.
UNKNOWN	The state of the socket is unknown.

During a DoS attack, the foreign address is usually the same for each connection, in which case it's a simple matter of typing the foreign IP address into the search form at www.arin.net/whois/ so you can alert your ISP.

During a DDoS attack, the foreign address is likely to be different for each connection, which makes it impossible to track down all the offenders because there are probably thousands of them. The best way to defend yourself is to contact your ISP to see if it can filter the traffic at its border routers.

Protecting Against Intrusion Attacks

Crackers have a wide variety of tools and techniques to assist them in breaking into your computer. Intrusion attacks focus on exploiting weaknesses in your security, so crackers can take more control of your system (and potentially do more damage) than they could from the outside.

Fortunately, there are many tools and techniques for combating intrusion attacks. Let's explore some of the most common break-in methods and the tools available to protect your system.

Evaluating Access to Network Services

Linux systems provide many network services and therefore many avenues for cracker attacks. You should know these services and how to limit access to them.

What is a network service? Basically, it's any task that the computer performs that requires it to send and receive information over the network using some predefined set of rules. Routing e-mail is a network service. So is serving Web pages. Your Linux box has the potential to provide thousands of services. Many of them are listed in the /etc/services file. Look at a snippet of that file:

```
# /etc/services:
# service-name  port/protocol  [aliases ...]    [# comment]
chargen         19/tcp           ttytst source
chargen         19/udp           ttytst source
ftp-data        20/tcp
ftp-data        20/udp
# 21 is registered to ftp, but also used by fsp
ftp             21/tcp
ftp             21/udp          fsp fspd
ssh             22/tcp                      # SSH Remote Login Protocol
ssh             22/udp                      # SSH Remote Login Protocol
telnet          23/tcp
telnet          23/udp
# 24 - private mail system
smtp            25/tcp          mail
```

There are three columns of information after comment lines. The left column contains the name of each service, the middle column defines the port number and protocol type used for that service, and the right column contains an optional alias or list of aliases for the service. The last entry in this example, for instance, describes the SMTP (Simple Mail Transfer Protocol) service, which is the service used for delivering e-mail over the Internet. The middle column tells you that the SMTP protocol uses port 25 and uses the Transmission Control Protocol (TCP) as its protocol type.

What exactly is a port number? It is a unique number that's been set aside for a particular network service. It allows network connections to be properly routed to the software that handles that service. For example, when an e-mail message is delivered from some other computer to your Linux box, the remote system must first establish a network connection with your system. Your computer receives the connection request, examines it, sees it labeled for port 25, and knows that the connection should be handed to the program that handles e-mail (which happens to be sendmail).

Note A program that runs quietly in the background handling service requests (such as sendmail) is called a daemon. Daemons are usually started automatically when your system boots up, and they keep running until your system is shut down. Daemons may also be started on an as-needed basis by xinetd, a special daemon that listens on a large number of port numbers, and then launches the service that is registered with that port number.

SMTP uses the TCP protocol; some other services use UDP, the User Datagram Protocol. For this security discussion, all you really need to know about TCP and UDP is that they provide different ways of packaging the information sent over a network connection. A TCP connection provides error detection and retransmission of lost data. UDP doesn't check to ensure that the data arrived complete and intact; it is meant as a fast way to send noncritical information.

Disabling Network Services

Although there are hundreds of services potentially available and subject to attack on your Linux system, in reality only a few dozen services are installed, and only a handful of those are on by default. Most network services are started by either the xinetd process (named inetd on some Linux distributions) or by a startup script in the /etc/init.d directory.

Xinetd is a daemon that listens on a great number of network port numbers. When a connection is made to a particular port number, xinetd automatically starts the appropriate program for that service and hands the connection to it.

The configuration file /etc/xinetd.conf is used to provide default settings for the xinetd server. (If the daemon is called inetd, look for an /etc/inetd.conf file instead.) The directory /etc/xinetd.d contains files telling xinetd what ports to listen on and what programs to start. Each file contains configuration information for a single service, and the file is usually named after the service it configures. For example, to enable the rsync service, edit the rsync file in the /etc/xinetd.d directory and look for a section similar to the following:

```
service rsync
{
    disable = yes
    socket_type        = stream
    wait               = no
    user               = root
    server             = /usr/bin/rsync
    server_args        = --daemon
    log_on_failure     += USERID
}
```

The first line of this example identifies the service as rsync, which exactly matches the service name listed in the /etc/services file, causing the service to listen on port 873 for TCP and UDP protocols. You can see that the service is off by default (disable = yes). To enable the rsync services, change the line to read disable = no:

```
service rsync
{
    disable = no
    socket_type        = stream
    wait               = no
    user               = root
    server             = /usr/bin/rsync
    server_args        = --daemon
    log_on_failure     += USERID
}
```

Tip   The rsync service is a nice one to turn on if your machine is an FTP server. It enables people to use an rsync client (which includes a checksum-search algorithm) to download files from your server. With that feature, users can restart a disrupted download without having to start from the beginning.

Because most services are disabled by default, your computer is only as insecure as you make it. You can double-check that insecure services, such as rlogin and rsh (which are included in the rsh-server package), are also disabled by making sure that `disabled = yes` is set in the `/etc/xinetd.d/rlogin` and `rsh` files.

Tip   You can make the remote login service active but disable the use of the `/etc/host.equiv` and `.rhosts` files, requiring `rlogin` to always prompt for a password. Rather than disabling the service, locate the server line in the `rsh` file (`server = /usr/sbin/in.rshd`) and add a space followed by `-L` at the end.

You now need to send a signal to the xinetd process to tell it to reload its configuration file. The quickest way to do that is to restart the service. As the root user, type the following from a shell:

```
# service xinetd restart
Stopping xinetd:        [ OK ]
Starting xinetd:        [ OK ]
```

That's it — you have enabled the ipop3 service. Provided that you have properly configured your mail server, clients should now be able to get their mail from your computer.

Using TCP Wrappers

Completely disabling an unused service is fine, but what about the services that you really need? How can you selectively grant and deny access to these services? With most current Linux distributions, TCP wrapper support has been integrated into the xinetd daemon. Xinetd will look at the `/etc/hosts.allow` and `/etc/hosts.deny` files to determine when a particular connection should be granted or refused for services such as rlogin, rsh, telnet, finger, and talk.

When a service that relies on TCP wrappers is requested, the `hosts.allow` and `hosts.deny` files are scanned and checked for an entry that matches the IP address of the connecting machine. The following checks are made when connection attempts occur:

✦ If the address is listed in the `hosts.allow` file, the connection is allowed, and `hosts.deny` is not checked.

✦ Otherwise, if the address is in `hosts.deny`, the connection is denied.

✦ Finally, if the address is in neither file, the connection is allowed.

It is not necessary (or even possible) to list every single address that may connect to your computer. The `hosts.allow` and `hosts.deny` files enable you to specify entire subnets and groups of addresses. You can even use the keyword ALL to specify all possible addresses. You can also restrict specific entries in these files so they only apply to specific network services. Take a look at an example of a typical pair of `hosts.allow` and `hosts.deny` files. Here's the `/etc/hosts.allow` file:

```
#
# hosts.allow    This file describes the names of the hosts which are
#                allowed to use the local INET services, as decided
#                by the '/usr/sbin/tcpd' server.
#

cups-lpd: 199.170.177.
in.telnetd: 199.170.177., .linuxtoys.net
vsftpd: ALL
```

Here's the `/etc/hosts.deny` file:

```
#
# hosts.deny     This file describes the names of the hosts which are
#                *not* allowed to use the local INET services, as
#                decided by the '/usr/sbin/tcpd' server.
#

ALL: ALL
```

This example is a rather restrictive configuration. It allows connections to the cups-lpd and telnet services from certain hosts, but then denies all other connections. It also allows connections to the FTP service (vsftp) to all hosts. Let's examine the files in detail.

As usual, lines beginning with a # character are comments and are ignored by xinetd when it parses the file. Each noncomment line consists of a comma-separated list of daemons followed by a colon (`:`) character and then a comma-separated list of client addresses to check (for example, `tftpd,fingerd: .linuxtoys.net, .fedora trouble.com`.) In this context, a client is any computer that attempts to access a network service on your system.

A client entry can be a numeric IP address (such as `199.170.177.25`) or a host name (such as `jukebox.linuxtoys.net`) but is more often a wildcard variation that specifies an entire range of addresses. A client entry can take four different forms. The online manual page for the `hosts.allow` file describes them as follows:

✦ A string that begins with a dot character (`.`). A host name is matched if the last components of its name match the specified pattern. For example, the pattern `.tue.nl` matches the host name `wzv.win.tue.nl`.

✦ A string that ends with a dot character (`.`). A host address is matched if its first numeric fields match the given string. For example, the pattern `131.155.`

matches the address of nearly every host on the Eindhoven University of Technology network (`131.155.x.x`).

✦ A string that begins with an at sign (@)is treated as an NIS (formerly YP) net-group name. A host name is matched if it is a host member of the specified netgroup. Netgroup matches are not supported for daemon process names or for client user names.

✦ An expression of the form *n.n.n.n/m.m.m.m* is interpreted as a *net/mask* pair. A host address is matched if *net* is equal to the bitwise *and* of the address and the mask. For example, the net/mask pattern `131.155.72.0/255.255.254.0` matches every address in the range `131.155.72.0` through `131.155.73.255`.

The example `host.allow` contains the first two types of client specification. The entry `199.170.177.` will match any IP address that begins with that string, such as `199.170.177.25`. The client entry `.linuxtoys.net` will match host names such as `jukebox.linuxtoys.net` or `picframe.linuxtoys.net`.

Take a look at what happens when a host named `jukebox.linuxtoys.net` (with IP address `199.170.179.18`) connects to your Linux system using the Telnet protocol:

1. Xinetd receives the connection request.

2. Xinetd begins comparing the address and name of `jukebox.linuxtoys.net` to the rules listed in `/etc/hosts.allow`. It starts at the top of the file and works its way down the file until finding a match. Both the daemon (the program handling the network service on your Linux box) and the connecting client's IP address or name must match the information in the `hosts.allow` file. In this case, the second rule that is encountered matches the request:

   ```
   in.telnetd: 199.170.177., .linuxtoys.net
   ```

3. The jukebox host is not in the `199.170.177` subnet, but it is in the `linuxtoys.net` domain. Xinetd stops searching the file as soon as it finds this match.

What if jukebox connects to your box using the IMAP protocol? Requests from jukebox for the IMPA service matches none of the rules in `hosts.allow`; the only line that refers to the imapd daemon does not refer to the `199.170.179` subnet or to the `linuxtoys.net` domain. Xinetd continues on to the `hosts.deny` file. The entry `ALL: ALL` matches anything, so tcpd denies the connection.

The `ALL` wildcard was also used in the `hosts.allow` file, telling xinetd to permit absolutely any host to connect to the FTP service on the Linux box. This is appropriate for running an anonymous FTP server that anyone on the Internet can access. If you are not running an anonymous FTP site, you probably should not use the `ALL` flag.

A good rule of thumb is to make your `hosts.allow` and `hosts.deny` files as restrictive as possible and to explicitly enable only those services that you really need. Also, grant access only to those systems that really need access. Using the `ALL` flag to grant universal access to a particular service may be easier than typing in a long list of subnets or domains, but better a few minutes spent on proper security measures than many hours recovering from a break-in.

Tip   You can further restrict access to services by using various options within the /etc/xinetd.conf file, even to the point of limiting access to certain services to specific times of the day. Read the manual page for xinetd (by typing **man xinetd** at a command prompt) to learn more about these options.

Detecting Intrusions from Log Files

If you make use of good firewalling practices as described in Chapter 17, you will be well prepared to mitigate and prevent most cracker attacks. If your firewall should fail to stop an intrusion, you must be able to recognize the attack when it is occurring. Understanding the various (and numerous) log files in which Linux records important events is critical to this goal. The log files for your Linux system can be found in the /var/log directory.

Most Linux systems make use of log-viewing tools, either provided with the desktop environment (such as GNOME) or as a command you can execute from a terminal window. Fedora Core and Red Hat Enterprise Linux come with a System Logs window (system-logviewer command) that you can use to view and search critical system log files from the GUI. To open the System Logs window in Fedora, from the main desktop menu, select System Tools ➪ System Logs. Figure 6-1 shows an example of the System Logs window.

Figure 6-1: Display system log files in the System Logs window.

To view a particular log file, click the log name in the left column. If you are looking for a particular message or problem, type a keyword into the Filter For box, and click Filter. Only lines containing that keyword are displayed. Case matters, so searching for "Mem" won't find "mem" when you use the filter. Click Reset to display the whole file again.

Table 6-3 contains a listing of log files displayed in the System Logs window, along with other files in the /var/log directory that may interest you. Many of these files are included with most Linux systems.

Table 6-3 Log Files in the /var/log Directory		
System Logs Name	**Filename**	**Description**
Boot Log	boot.log	Contains messages indicating which systems services have started and shut down successfully and which (if any) have failed to start or stop. The most recent bootup messages are listed near the end of the file.
Cron Log	cron	Contains status messages from the crond, a daemon that periodically runs scheduled jobs, such as backups and log file rotation.
Kernel Startup Log	dmesg	A recording of messages printed by the kernel when the system boots.
FTP Log	xferlog	Contains information about files transferred using the wu-ftpd FTP service.
Apache Access Log	httpd/access_log	Logs requests for information from your Apache Web server.
Apache Error Log	httpd/error_log	Logs errors encountered from clients trying to access data on your Apache Web server.
Mail Log	maillog	Contains information about addresses to which and from which e-mail was sent. Useful for detecting spamming.
MySQL Server Log	mysqld.log	Includes information related to activities of the MySQL database server (mysqld).
News Log	spooler	Directory containing logs of messages from the Usenet News server if you are running one.
RPM Packages	rpmpkgs	Contains a listing of RPM packages that are installed on your system.

Continued

Table 6-3 *(continued)*

System Logs Name	Filename	Description
Security Log	`secure`	Records the date, time, and duration of login attempts and sessions.
System Log	`messages`	A general-purpose log file to which many programs record messages.
Update Agent Log	`up2date`	Contains messages resulting from actions by the Red Hat Update Agent.
X.Org X11 Log	`Xorg.0.log`	Includes messages output by the X.Org X server.
*	`gdm/:0.log`	Holds messages related to the login screen (GNOME display manager).
*	`samba/log.smbd`	Shows messages from the Samba SMB file service daemon.
*	`squid/access.log`	Contains messages related to the squid proxy/caching server.
*	`vsftpd.log`	Contains messages relating to transfers made using the vsFTPd daemon (FTP server).
*	`sendmail`	Shows error messages recorded by the `sendmail` daemon.
*	`uucp`	Shows status messages from the UNIX to UNIX Copy Protocol daemon.

* Indicates a log file that is not contained in the System Logs window. Access these files directly from `/var/log`.

The Role of Syslogd

Most of the files in the `/var/log` directory are maintained by the syslogd service. The syslogd daemon is the System Logging Daemon. It accepts log messages from a variety of other programs and writes them to the appropriate log files. This is better than having every program write directly to its own log file because it enables you to centrally manage how log files are handled. It is possible to configure syslogd to record varying levels of detail in the log files. It can be told to ignore all but the most critical messages, or it can record every detail.

The syslogd daemon can even accept messages from other computers on your network. This is particularly handy because it enables you to centralize the management and reviewing of the log files from many systems on your network. There is also a major security benefit to this practice. If a system on your network is broken into, the cracker cannot delete or modify the log files because those files are stored on a separate computer. It is important to remember, though, that those log messages are not, by default, encrypted. Anyone tapping into your local network can eavesdrop on those messages as they pass from one machine to another. Also, although the cracker may not be able to change old log entries, he can affect the system such that any new log messages should not be trusted.

It is not uncommon to run a dedicated `loghost`, a computer that serves no other purpose than to record log messages from other computers on the network. Because this system runs no other services, it is unlikely that it will be broken into. This makes it nearly impossible for a cracker to erase his or her tracks, but it does not mean that all of the log entries are accurate after a cracker has broken into a machine on your network.

Redirecting Logs to a Loghost with syslogd

To redirect your computer's log files to another computer's syslogd, you must make some changes to your local syslogd's configuration file, `/etc/syslog.conf`. Become root using the `su -` command and then load the `/etc/syslog.conf` file in a text editor (such as vi). You should see something similar to this:

```
# Log all kernel messages to the console.
# Logging much else clutters up the screen.
#kern.*                                 /dev/console

# Log anything (except mail) of level info or higher.
# Don't log private authentication messages!
*.info;mail.none;news.none;authpriv.none;cron.none   /var/log/messages

# The authpriv file has restricted access.
authpriv.*                             /var/log/secure

# Log all the mail messages in one place.
mail.*                                 /var/log/maillog

# Log cron stuff
cron.*                                 /var/log/cron

# Everybody gets emergency messages
*.emerg                                        *

# Save news errors of level crit and higher in a special file.
uucp,news.crit                         /var/log/spooler

# Save boot messages also to boot.log
local7.*                               /var/log/boot.log

#
# INN
#
news.=crit                             /var/log/news/news.crit
news.=err                              /var/log/news/news.err
news.notice                            /var/log/news/news.notice
```

The lines beginning with a # character are comments. Other lines contain two columns of information. The left field is a semicolon-separated list (spaces won't work) of message types and message priorities. The right field is the log file to which those messages should be written.

To send the messages to another computer (the loghost) instead of a file, simply replace the log filename with the @ character followed by the name of the loghost. For example, to redirect the output normally sent to the messages, secure, and mail log log files, make these changes to the preceding file:

```
# Log anything (except mail) of level info or higher.
# Don't log private authentication messages!
*.info;mail.none;news.none;authpriv.none;cron.none  @loghost

# The authpriv file has restricted access.
authpriv.*                              @loghost

# Log all the mail messages in one place.
mail.*                                  @loghost
```

The messages will now be sent to the syslogd running on the computer named loghost. The name loghost was not an arbitrary choice. It is customary to create such a host name and make it an alias to the actual system acting as the loghost. That way, if you ever need to switch the loghost duties to a different machine, you only need to change the loghost alias; you do not need to reedit the syslog.conf file on every computer.

Understanding the messages Log File

Because of the many programs and services that record information to the messages log file, it is important that you understand the format of this file. You can get a good early warning of problems developing on your system by examining this file. Each line in the file is a single message recorded by some program or service. Here is a snippet of an actual messages log file:

```
Feb 25 11:04:32 toys network: Bringing up loopback interface:  succeeded
Feb 25 11:04:35 toys network: Bringing up interface eth0:  succeeded
Feb 25 13:01:14 toys vsftpd(pam_unix)[10565]: authentication failure;
     logname= uid=0 euid=0 tty= ruser= rhost=10.0.0.5 user=chris
Feb 25 14:44:24 toys su(pam_unix)[11439]: session opened for
     user root by chris(uid=500)
```

This is really very simple when you know what to look for. Each message is divided into five main parts. From left to right they are:

✦ The date and time that the message was logged.

✦ The name of the computer from which the message came.

✦ The program or service name to which the message pertains.

✦ The process number (enclosed in square brackets) of the program sending the message.

✦ The actual text message.

Take another look at the preceding file snippet. In the first two lines, you can see that the network was restarted. The next line shows that the user named chris tried and failed to get to the FTP server on this system from a computer at address 10.0.0.5 (he typed the wrong password and authentication failed). The last line shows chris using the su command to become root user.

By occasionally reviewing the messages and secure files, it's possible to catch a cracking attempt before it is successful. If you see an excessive number of connection attempts for a particular service, especially if they are coming from systems on the Internet, you may be under attack.

Using Password Protection

Passwords are the most fundamental security tool of any modern operating system and consequently, the most commonly attacked security feature. It is natural to want to choose a password that is easy to remember, but very often this means choosing a password that is also easy to guess. Crackers know that on any system with more than a few users, at least one person is likely to have an easily guessed password.

By using the "brute force" method of attempting to log in to every account on the system and trying the most common passwords on each of these accounts, a persistent cracker has a good shot of finding a way in. Remember that a cracker can automate this attack, so thousands of login attempts are not out of the question. Obviously, choosing good passwords is the first and most important step to having a secure system.

Here are some things to avoid when choosing a password:

✦ Do not use any variation of your login name or your full name. Even if you use varied case, append or prepend numbers or punctuation, or type it backwards, this will still be an easily guessed password.

✦ Do not use a dictionary word, even if you add numbers or punctuation to it.

✦ Do not use proper names of any kind.

✦ Do not use any contiguous line of letters or numbers on the keyboard (such as "qwerty" or "asdfg").

Choosing Strong Passwords

A strong password is one that is not easily guessed. It should contain a mixture of uppercase and lowercase letters, numbers, and possibly even punctuation, yet still be something you can remember.

A good way to choose a strong password is to take the first letter from each word of an easily remembered sentence. The password can be made even better by adding numbers, punctuation, and varied case. The sentence you choose should have meaning only to you, and should not be publicly available (choosing a sentence on your personal Web page is a bad idea). Table 6-4 lists examples of strong passwords and the tricks used to remember them.

Table 6-4 Ideas for Good Passwords	
Password	*How to Remember It*
Mrci7yo!	My rusty car is 7 years old!
2emBp1ib	2 elephants make BAD pets, 1 is better
ItMc?Gib	Is that MY coat? Give it back

The passwords look like gibberish, but are actually rather easy to recall. Placing emphasis on words that stand for capital letters, for example, make them simple to remember.

Use the passwd command to change your password. Type **passwd** in a command shell; you're prompted to enter your old password. To protect against someone "shoulder surfing" and learning your password, the password is not displayed as you type.

If you typed your old password correctly, you are prompted to type in your new password. The passwd command checks the new password against cracklib to determine if it is a good or bad password. Non-root users are required to try a different password if the one they have chosen is not a good password. The root user is the only user who is permitted to assign bad passwords. Once the password has been accepted by cracklib, the passwd command will ask you to enter the new password a second time to make sure there are no typos (which are hard to detect when you can't see what you are typing).

When running as root, it is possible to change a user's password by supplying that user's login name as a parameter to the passwd command. For example, typing

```
# passwd joe
```

results in the `passwd` command prompting you for joe's new password. It does not prompt you for the user's old password so that root can reset a user's password when that user has forgotten it (an event that happens all too often).

Using a Password File

In early versions of UNIX, all user account and password information was stored in a file that all users could read (although only root could write to it). This was generally not a problem because the password information was encrypted using a *trapdoor algorithm*, meaning that the clear text password was encoded into a scrambled string of characters before it was stored in the file, and that the string could not be translated back to the nonencoded password.

How does the system check your password in this case? When you log in, the system encodes the password you entered, compares the resulting scrambled string with the scrambled string that is stored in the password file, and grants you access only if the two match. Have you ever asked a system administrator what the password on your account is, only to hear "I don't know" in response? If so, this is why: The administrator really doesn't have the password, only the encrypted version. The nonencoded password exists only at the moment you type it.

Breaking Encrypted Passwords

There is a problem with people being able to see encrypted passwords, however. Although it may be difficult (or even impossible) to reverse the encryption of a trapdoor algorithm, it is very easy to encode a large number of password guesses and compare them to the encoded passwords in the password file. This is, in order of magnitude, more efficient than trying actual login attempts for each user name and password. If a cracker can get a copy of your password file, the cracker has a much better chance of breaking into your system.

Fortunately, Linux and all modern UNIX systems support a `shadow` password file by default. The `shadow` file is a special version of the `passwd` file that only root can read. It contains the encrypted password information, so passwords can be left out of the `passwd` file, which any user on the system can read. Linux supports the older, single-password file method as well as the newer, shadow password file. You should always use the shadow password file (it is the default).

Checking for the Shadow Password File

The password file is named `passwd` and can be found in the `/etc` directory. The shadow password file is named `shadow` and is also located in `/etc`. If your `/etc/shadow` file is missing, then it is likely that your Linux system is storing the password information in the `/etc/passwd` file instead. Verify this by displaying the file with the `less` command:

```
# less /etc/passwd
```

Something similar to the following should be displayed:

```
root:DkkS6Uke799fQ:0:0:root:/root:/bin/bash
bin:*:1:1:bin:/bin:
daemon:*:2:2:daemon:/sbin:
    .
    .
    .
mary:KpRUp2ozmY5TA:500:100:Mary Smith:/home/mary:/bin/sh
joe:OsXrzvKnQaksI:501:100:Joe Johnson:/home/joe:/bin/sh
jane:ptNoiueYEjwX.:502:100:Jane Anderson:/home/jane:/bin/sh
bob:Ju2vY7AOX6Kzw:503:100:Bob Renolds:/home/bob:/bin/sh
```

Each line in this listing corresponds to a single user account on the Linux system. Each line is made up of seven fields separated by colon (:) characters. From left to right the fields are the login name, the encrypted password, the user ID, the group ID, the description, the home directory, and the default shell. Looking at the first line, you see that it is for the root account and has an encrypted password of DkkS6Uke799fQ. You can also see that root has a user ID of zero, a group ID of zero, and a home directory of /root, and root's default shell is /bin/sh.

All of these values are quite normal for a root account, but seeing that encrypted password between the first and second colon on each line should set off alarm bells in your head. It confirms that your system is not using the shadow password file. At this point, you should immediately use the pwconv command to convert your password file to /etc/shadow to store the password information. Simply log in as root (or use the su command to become root) and enter the pwconv command at a prompt. It will print no messages, but when your shell prompt returns, you should have a /etc/shadow file and your /etc/passwd file that looks like this:

```
root:x:0:0:root:/root:/bin/bash
bin:x:1:1:bin:/bin:
daemon:x:2:2:daemon:/sbin:
    .
    .
    .
mary:x:500:100:Mary Smith:/home/mary:/bin/sh
joe:x:501:100:Joe Johnson:/home/joe:/bin/sh
jane:x:502:100:Jane Anderson:/home/jane:/bin/sh
bob:x:503:100:Bob Renolds:/home/bob:/bin/sh
```

Encrypted password data is replaced with an *x*. The password data is moved to /etc/shadow.

There is also a screen-oriented command called authconfig that you can use to manage shadow passwords and other system authentication information. This tool also has features that enable you to work with MD5 passwords, LDAP authentication, and Kerberos 5 authentication. Type **authconfig** and step through the screens to use it.

To work with passwords for groups, you can use the `grpconv` command to convert passwords in `/etc/groups` to shadowed group passwords in `/etc/gshadow`. If you change passwords or group passwords and something breaks (you are unable to log in to the accounts), you can use the `pwunconv` and `grpunconv` commands, respectively, to reverse password conversion.

Using the shadow password file and picking good passwords are a great start toward securing your system. You may have noticed by now that security is not just a one-time job. It is an ongoing process, as much about policies as programs. Keep reading to learn more.

Using Encryption Techniques

The previous sections told you how to lock the doors to your Linux system to deny access to crackers. The best lock is useless, however, if you are mugged in your own driveway and have your keys stolen. Likewise, the best computer security can be for naught if you are sending passwords and other critical data unprotected across the Internet.

A savvy cracker can use a tool called a *protocol analyzer* or a *network sniffer* to peek at the data flowing across a network and pick out passwords, credit card data, and other juicy bits of information. The cracker does this by breaking into a poorly protected system on the same network and running software, or by gaining physical access to the same network and plugging in his or her own equipment.

You can combat this sort of theft by using encryption. The two main types of encryption in use today are symmetric cryptography and public-key cryptography.

Symmetric Cryptography

Symmetric cryptography, also called private-key cryptography, uses a single key to both encrypt and decrypt a message. This method is generally inappropriate for securing data that will be used by a third party because of the complexity of secure key exchange. Symmetric cryptography is generally useful for encrypting data for one's own purposes.

A classic use of symmetric cryptography is for a personal password vault. Anyone who has been using the Internet for any amount of time has accumulated a quantity of user names and passwords for accessing various sites and resources. A personal password vault lets you store this access information in an encrypted form. The end result is that you only have to remember one password to unlock all of your access information.

Until recently, the United States government was standardized on a symmetric encryption algorithm called DES (Data Encryption Standard) to secure important information. There's no direct way to crack DES-encrypted data, so to decrypt the data without a password requires an unimaginable amount of computing power to try to guess the password — the brute force method of decryption.

As personal computing power has increased nearly exponentially, the DES algorithm has had to be retired. In its place, after a very long and interesting search, the U.S. government has accepted the Rijndael algorithm as what it calls the *AES* (Advanced Encryption Standard). Although the AES algorithm is also subject to brute-force attacks, it requires significantly more computing power to crack than the DES algorithm does.

Go to `http://aescrypt.sourceforge.net/` for more information on AES, including a command line implementation of the algorithm.

Public-Key Cryptography

Public-key cryptography does not suffer from key distribution problems, and that is why it is the preferred encryption method for secure Internet communication. This method uses multiple keys (usually two), one to encrypt the message and another to decrypt the message. The key used to encrypt the message is called the *public key* because it is made available for all to see. The key used to decrypt the message is the private key and is kept hidden.

Say, for example, that you want to send me a secure message using public-key encryption. Here's how the process works:

1. I must have a public and private key pair. Depending on the circumstances, I may generate the keys myself (using special software) or obtain the keys from a key authority.

2. You want to send me a message, so you first look up my public key (or more accurately, the software you are using looks it up).

3. You encrypt the message with the public key. At this point, the message can only be decrypted with the private key (the public key cannot be used to decrypt the message).

4. I receive the message and use my private key to decrypt it.

Secure Socket Layer

A classic implementation of public-key cryptography is with SSL (secure socket layer) communication. This is the technology that enables you to securely submit your credit card information to an online merchant. The elements of an SSL encrypted session are:

✦ SSL-enabled Web browser (Mozilla, Internet Explorer, Opera, Konquerer, etc.)

✦ SSL-enabled Web server (Apache)

✦ SSL certificate

To initiate an SSL session, a Web browser first makes contact with a Web server on port 443, also known as the HTTPS (Hypertext Transport Protocol Secure) port. After a socket connection has been established between the two machines, the following occurs:

1. Server sends SSL certificate to browser.

2. Browser verifies identity of server through SSL certificate.

3. Browser generates symmetric encryption key.

4. Browser uses SSL certificate to encrypt symmetric encryption key.

5. Browser sends encrypted key to the server.

6. Server decrypts the symmetric key with its private key counterpart of the public SSL certificate.

7. Browser and server can now encrypt and decrypt traffic based on a common knowledge of the symmetric key.

Secure data interchange can now occur.

Creating SSL Certificates

To create your own SSL certificate for secure HTTP data interchange, you must first have an SSL-capable Web server such as the Apache Web server (httpd package), which comes with virtually every Linux distribution. Once you have a server ready to go, familiarize yourself with the important server-side components of an SSL certificate:

Note The following example is from a Fedora Core system. A similar procedure for using SSL certificates with an Apache server on a Debian system is contained in Chapter 23.

```
# ls -l /etc/httpd/conf
-rw-r--r--  1 root      root         36010 Jul 14 15:45 httpd.conf

lrwxrwxrwx  1 root      root         37 Aug 12 23:45 Makefile ->
../../../usr/share/ssl/certs/Makefile
drwx------  2 root      root         4096 Aug 12 23:45 ssl.crl
drwx------  2 root      root         4096 Aug 12 23:45 ssl.crt
drwx------  2 root      root         4096 Jul 14 15:45 ssl.csr
drwx------  2 root      root         4096 Aug 12 23:45 ssl.key
drwx------  2 root      root         4096 Jul 14 15:45 ssl.prm

# ls -l /etc/httpd/conf.d/ssl.conf
-rw-r--r--  1 root      root         11140 Jul 14 15:45 ssl.conf
```

The /etc/httpd/conf and /etc/httpd/conf.d directories contain all of the components necessary to create your SSL certificate. Here are descriptions of the components:

Component	Description
httpd.conf	Web server configuration file
Makefile	Certificate building script
ssl.crl	Certificate revocation list directory
ssl.crt	SSL certificate directory
ssl.csr	Certificate service request directory
ssl.key	SSL certificate private key directory
ssl.prm	SSL certificate parameters
ssl.conf	Primary Web server SSL configuration file

Now take a look at the tools used to create SSL certificates:

```
# cd /etc/httpd/conf
# make
This makefile allows you to create:
  o public/private key pairs
  o SSL certificate signing requests (CSRs)
  o self-signed SSL test certificates

To create a key pair, run "make SOMETHING.key".
To create a CSR, run "make SOMETHING.csr".
To create a test certificate, run "make SOMETHING.crt".
To create a key and a test certificate in one file, run "make
SOMETHING.pem".

To create a key for use with Apache, run "make genkey".
To create a CSR for use with Apache, run "make certreq".
To create a test certificate for use with Apache, run "make
testcert".

Examples:
  make server.key
  make server.csr
  make server.crt
  make stunnel.pem
  make genkey
  make certreq
  make testcert
```

The `make` command utilizes the Makefile to create SSL certificates. Without any arguments the `make` command simply prints the information as just shown. The following are the arguments you can give to `make`:

Argument	Description
`make server.key`	Creates generic public/private key pairs.
`make server.csr`	Generates a generic SSL certificate service request.
`make server.crt`	Generates a generic SSL test certificate.
`make stunnel.pem`	Generates a generic SSL test certificate, but puts the private key in the same file as the SSL test certificate.
`make genkey`	Same as `make server.key` except it places the key in the `ssl.key` directory.
`make certreq`	Same as `make server.csr` except it places the certificate service request in the `ssl.csr` directory.
`make testcert`	Same as **make** `server.crt` except it places the test certificate in the `ssl.crt` directory.

Using Third-Party Certificate Signers

In the real world, I know who you are because I recognize your face, your voice, and your mannerisms. On the Internet, I cannot see these things and must rely on a trusted third party to vouch for your identity. To ensure that a certificate is immutable, it has to be signed by a trusted third party (certificate authority) when the certificate is issued and validated every time an end user taking advantage of your secure site loads it. The following are trusted third-party certificate signers:

- ✦ GlobalSign (`www.globalsign.net`)
- ✦ Baltimore (`www.baltimore.com`)
- ✦ GeoTrust (`www.geotrust.com`)
- ✦ VeriSign (`www.verisign.com`)
- ✦ FreeSSL (`www.freessl.com`)
- ✦ Thawte (`www.thawte.com`)
- ✦ EnTrust (`www.entrust.com`)
- ✦ ipsCA (`www.ipsca.com`)
- ✦ COMODO Group (`www.comodogroup.com`)

Each of these certificate authorities has a chunk of cryptographic code embedded into nearly every Web browser in the world. This chunk of cryptographic code allows a Web browser to determine whether an SSL certificate is authentic. Without this validation, it would be trivial for crackers to generate their own certificates and dupe people into thinking they are giving sensitive information to a reputable source.

Each certificate authority has different deals, prices, and products. Check out each of the CAs in the preceding list to determine which works best for you.

Certificates that are not validated are called *self-signed certificates*. If you come across a site that has not had its identity authenticated by a trusted third party, your Web browser will display a message similar to the one shown in Figure 6-2.

Figure 6-2: A pop-up window alerts you when a site is not authenticated.

This does not necessarily mean that you are encountering anything illegal, immoral, or fattening. Many sites opt to go with self-signed certificates, not because they are trying to pull a fast one on you, but because there may not be any reason to validate the true owner of the certificate and they do not want to pay the cost of getting a certificate validated. Some reasons for using a self-signed certificate include:

✦ **The Web site accepts no input.** In this case, you as the end user have nothing to worry about—no one is trying to steal your information because you aren't giving out any information. The certificate simply secures the Web transmission from the server to you. The data in and of itself may not be sensitive, but, being a good netizen ('net citizen), the site has enabled you to secure the transmission to keep third parties from sniffing the traffic.

✦ **The Web site caters to a small clientele.** If you run a Web site that has a very limited set of customers, such as an Application Service Provider (ASP), you can simply inform your users that you have no certificate signer and that they can browse the certificate information and validate it with you over the phone or in person.

✦ **Testing.** It makes no sense to pay for an SSL certificate if you are only testing a new Web site or Web-based application. Use a self-signed certificate until you are ready to go live.

Each signing authority has different deals, prices, and products. Check out each of the signing authorities listed in the "Using Third-Party Certificate Signers" section earlier in this chapter to determine which works best for you. The following are areas where signing authorities differ:

✦ Credibility and stability

✦ Pricing

✦ Browser recognition

✦ Warranties

✦ Support

✦ Certificate strength

For good comparisons, studies, and inside information to make the job of finding an SSL signer easier, go to www.whichssl.org.

Creating a Certificate Service Request

To create a third-party validated SSL certificate, you start with a Certificate Service Request (CSR). To create a CSR, do the following on your Web server:

```
# cd /etc/httpd/conf
# make certreq
umask 77 ; \
/usr/bin/openssl genrsa -des3 1024 >
/etc/httpd/conf/ssl.key/server.key
        .
        .
        .
```

You are asked to enter a password to secure your private key. This password should be at least eight characters long, and should not be a dictionary word or contain numbers or punctuation. The characters you type do not appear on the screen to prevent someone from shoulder surfing your password. Enter the password once again to verify. The certificate generation process now begins.

At this point, it is time to start adding some identifying information to the certificate that the third-party source will later validate. Before you can do this, you must unlock the private key you just created. Do so by typing the password you just created. Then enter information as you are prompted. Here's an example of a session for adding information for a certificate:

```
Enter pass phrase for /etc/httpd/conf/ssl.key/server.key:
You are about to be asked to enter information that will be incorporated
into your certificate request.
What you are about to enter is what is called
a Distinguished Name or a DN.
```

```
There are quite a few fields but you can leave some blank
For some fields there will be a default value,
If you enter '.', the field will be left blank.
-----
Country Name (2 letter code) [GB]:US
State or Province Name (full name) [Berkshire]: Connecticut
Locality Name (eg, city) [Newbury]: Mystic
Organization Name (eg, company) [My Company Ltd]:Acme Marina, Inc.
Organizational Unit Name (eg, section) []:InfoTech
Common Name (eg, your name or your server's hostname) []:www.acmemarina.com
Email Address []: webmaster@acmemarina.com
```

To complete the process, you are asked if you want to add any extra attributes to your certificate. Unless you have a reason to provide more information, simply press Enter at each of the prompts to leave them blank:

```
Please enter the following 'extra' attributes
to be sent with your certificate request
A challenge password []:
An optional company name []:
```

Getting the CSR Signed

After your CSR is created, select a certificate authority (from the list in the "Using Third-Party Certificate Signers" section earlier in this chapter).

Then send your CSR to the CA for validation. Instructions at each CA's Web site describe where to send your CSR for validation.

You will have to go through some validation steps. Each signer has a different method of validating identity and certificate information. Some require that you fax articles of incorporation, while others require that a company officer be made available to talk to a validation operator. At some point in the process you are asked to copy and paste the contents of the CSR you created into the signer's Web form.

```
# cd /etc/httpd/conf/ssl.csr
# cat server.csr
-----BEGIN CERTIFICATE REQUEST-----
MIIB6jCCAVMCAQAwgakxCzAJBgNVBAYTAlVTMRQwEgYDVQQIEwtDb25uZWN0aWN1
dDEPMAOGA1UEBxMGTX1zdGljMRowGAYDVQQKExFBY211IE1hcmluYSwgSW5jLjER
MA8GA1UECxMISW5mb1R1Y2gxGzAZBgNVBAMTEnd3dy5hY211bWFyaW5hLmNvbTEn
MCUGCSqGSIb3DQEJARYYd2VibWFzdGVyQGFjbWVtYXJpbmEuY29tMIGfMAOGCSqG
SIb3DQEBAQUAA4GNADCBiQKBgQDcYH4pjMxKMldyXRmcoz8uBVOvwlNZHyRWw8ZG
u2eCbvgi6w4wXuHwaDuxbuDBmw//Y9DMI2MXg4wDq4xmPi35EsOlOfw4ytZJn1yW
aU6cJVQro46OnXyaqXZOPiRCxUSnGRU+OnsqKGjf7LPpXv29S3QvMIBTYWzCkNnc
gWBwwwIDAQABoAAwDQYJKoZIhvcNAQEEBQADgYEANv6eJOaJZGzopNR5h2YkR9Wg
18oBl3mgoPH60Sccw3pWsoW4qbOWq7on8dS/++QOCZWZI1gefgaSQMInKZ1II7Fs
YIwYBgpoPTMC4bpOZZtURCyQWrKIDXQBXw7BlU/3A25nvkRY7vgNL9Nq+7681EJ8
W9AJ3PX4vb2+ynttcBI=
-----END CERTIFICATE REQUEST-----
```

You can use your mouse to copy and paste the CSR into the signer's Web form.

Within 48 to 72 hours after you complete the validation and have paid for the signing, you should receive an e-mail with your shiny new SSL certificate in it. The certificate will look similar to the following:

```
-----BEGIN CERTIFICATE-----
MIIEFjCCA3+gAwIBAgIQMI262Zd6njZgN97tJAVFODANBgkqhkiG9w0BAQQFADCB
ujEfMBOGA1UEChMWVmVyaVNpZ24gVHJ1c3QgTmV0d29yazEXMBUGA1UECxMOVmVy
aVNpZ24sIEluXy4xMzAxBgNVBAsTK1Z1cmlTaWduIEludGVybmF0aW9uYWwgU2Vy
dmVyIENBIC0gZ2xhc3MgMzFMEcG1OrY2g0Dd3d3LnZlcmlzaWduLmNvbS9DUFMg
SW5jb3JwLmJ51FJlZi4gTE1BQk1SVRZIExURC4oY3yk5NyBWZXJpU2lnbjAeFw0w
MzAxMTUwMDAwMDBaFwOwNDAxMTUyMzU5NTlaMIGuMQswCQYDVQQGEwJVUzETMBEG
A1UECBMKV2FzaGluZ3RvbiHiThErE371UEBxQLRmVkZXJhbCBXYXkxGzAZBgNVBAoU
EklETSBTZXJ2aWWlcywgSW5jLjEMMAoGA1UECxQDd3d3MTMwMQYDVQQLFCpUZXJt
cyBvZiB1c2UgYXQgd3d3LnZlcmlzaWduLmNvbS9ycGGgKGMpMDAxFDASBgNVBAMU
C21kbXN1cnYuY29tMIGfMAOGCSqGSIb3DQEBAQUAA4GNADCBiQKBgQDaHSk+uzOf
7jjDFEnqT8UBa1L3yFILXFjhj3XpMXLGWzLmkDmdJjXsa4x7AhEpr1ubuVNhJVIO
FnLDopsx4pyr4n+P8FyS4M5grbcQzy2YnkM2jyqVF/7yOW2pD13Ot4eacYYaz4Qg
q9pTxhUzjEG4twvKCAFWfuhEoGu1CMV2qQ1DAQABo4IBJTCCASEwCQYDVROTBAIw
ADBEBgNVHSAEPTA7MDkGC2CGSAGG+EUBBxcDMCOwKAYIKwYBBQUHAgEWGHHGhOdHBz
Oi8vd3d3LnZlcmlzaWduLmNvbS9ycGEwCwYDVRRPBAQDAgWgMCgGA1UdJQQhMB8G
CWCGSAGG+EIEMOOcOwIYBQUHAwEGCCsGAQUFBwmCMDQGCCsGAQUFBwEBBCgwJjAk
BggrBgEFBQcwAYYYaHROcDovL29jc2AudmVyaXNpZ24uY29tMEYGA1UdHwQ/MDOw
O6A5oDeGNWhOdHA6Ly9jcmwudmVyaxNpZ24uY29tLONsYXNzMO1udGVybmF0aW9u
YWxxTZXJ2ZXIuY3JsMBkGCmCGSAgG+E+f4Nfc3zYJODA5NzMwMMTEyMA0GCSqGSIb3
DQEBBAUAA4GBAJ/PsVttm1DkQai5nLeudLceb1F4isXP17B68wXLkIeRu4Novu13
81LZXnaR+acHuCkWO1b3rQPjgv2y1mwjkPmC1WJoeYfdxH7+Mbg/6fomnK9auWAT
WFOiFW/+a8OWRYQJLMA2VQOVhX4znjpGcVNY9AQSHm1UiESJy7vtd1iX
-----END CERTIFICATE-----
```

Copy and paste this certificate into an empty file called `server.crt`, which must reside in the `/etc/httpd/conf/ssl.crt` directory, and restart your Web server. In Fedora Core, you restart your Web server by typing:

```
# service httpd restart
```

Assuming your Web site was previously working fine, you can now view it in a secure fashion by placing an `s` after the `http` in the Web address. So if you previously viewed your Web site at `http://acmemarina.com`, you can now view it in a secure fashion by going to `https://acmemarinacom`.

Creating Self-Signed Certificates

Generating and running a self-signed SSL certificate is much easier than having a signed certificate. To generate a self-signed SSL certificate, do the following:

1. Remove the key and certificate that currently exist:

```
# cd /etc/httpd/conf
# rm ssl.key/server.key ssl.crt/server.crt
```

2. Create your own server key:

```
# /usr/bin/openssl genrsa 1024 > ssl.key/server.key
```

3. Make the server.key file readable and writable only by root:

```
# chmod 600 ssl.key/server.key
```

4. Create the self-signed certificate by typing the following:

```
# make testcert
umask 77 ; \
/usr/bin/openssl req -new -key
/etc/httpd/conf/ssl.key/server.key
      -x509 -days 365 -out /etc/httpd/conf/ssl.key/server.crt
      .
      .
      .
```

At this point, it is time to start adding some identifying information to the certificate that the third-party source will later validate. Before you can do this, you must unlock the private key you just created. Do so by typing the password you typed earlier. Then follow this sample procedure:

```
You are about to be asked to enter information that will be
   incorporated into your certificate request.
What you are about to enter is what is called
a Distinguished Name or a DN.
There are quite a few fields but you can leave some blank
For some fields there will be a default value,
If you enter '.', the field will be left blank.
-----
Country Name (2 letter code) [GB]:US
State or Province Name (full name) [Berkshire]: Ohio
Locality Name (e.g., city) [Newbury]: Cincinnati
Organization Name (e.g., company) [My Company Ltd]:Industrial
Press, Inc.
Organizational Unit Name (e.g., section) []:IT
Common Name (e.g., your name or your server's hostname)
[]:www.industrialpressinc.com
Email Address []: webmaster@industrialpressinc.com
```

This generation process places all files in the proper place. All you need to do is restart your Web server and add https instead of http in front of your URL. (The https protocol is used when you want transmissions to be encrypted.) Remember, you'll get a certificate validation message from your Web browser, which you can safely ignore.

Restarting Your Web Server

Your Web server requires you to enter your certificate password every time it is started. This is to prevent someone from breaking into your server, stealing your private key, and masquerading as you. Should someone manage to break in and take your key, you are safe in the knowledge that the private key is a jumbled mess.

If you just cannot stand having to enter a password every time your Web server starts and are willing to accept the increased risk, you can remove the password encryption on your private key. Simply do the following:

```
# cd /etc/hhtpd/conf/ssl.key
# /usr/bin/openssl rsa -in server.key -out  server.key
```

Troubleshooting Your Certificates

If you are having problems with your SSL certificate, here are some troubleshooting tips:

- ✦ Only one SSL certificate per IP address is allowed. If you want to add more than one SSL-enabled Web site to your server, you must bind another IP address to the network interface.

- ✦ Make sure the permission mask on the /etc/httpd/conf/ssl.* directories and their contents is 700 (rwx------).

- ✦ Make sure you aren't blocking port 443 on your Web server. All https requests come in on port 443. If you are blocking it, you will not be able to get secure pages.

- ✦ The certificate only lasts for one year, and then you must renew it with your certificate authority. Each CA has a different renewal procedure, so check your CA's Web site for details.

- ✦ Make sure you have the mod_ssl package installed. You will not be able to serve any SSL-enabled traffic without it.

Using the Secure Shell Package

The Secure Shell package (SSH) provides shell services similar to the rsh, rcp, and rlogin commands, but encrypts the network traffic. It uses private-key cryptography, so it is ideal for use with Internet-connected computers.

Starting the SSH Service

If you have installed the openssh-server software package, the SSH server is automatically configured to start. The SSH daemon is started from the /etc/init.d/sshd startup script. To make sure the service is set up to start automatically, type the following (as root user) on a Fedora Core system:

```
# chkconfig --list sshd
sshd       0:off   1:off   2:on   3:on   4:on   5:on   6:off
```

This result shows that the sshd service is set to run in system states 2, 3, 4, and 5, which means that whenever the system is up and connected to the network, the sshd service is running. If the service is off, you can turn it on so it comes up when you boot Linux by typing the following as root user:

```
# chkconfig sshd on
```

This line turns on the SSH service when you enter run level 2, 3, 4, or 5. To start the service immediately, type the following:

```
# /etc/init.d/sshd start
```

Using the ssh, sftp, and scp Commands

The commands you can use with the SSH service are ssh, sftp, and scp. Remote users use the ssh command to log in to your system securely. The scp command lets remote users copy files to and from a system. The sftp command provides a safe way to access FTP sites.

Like the normal remote shell services, secure shell looks in the /etc/hosts.equiv file and in a user's .rhost file to determine whether it should allow a connection. It also looks in the ssh-specific files /etc/shosts.equiv and .shosts. Using the shosts.equiv and the .shosts files is preferable because it avoids granting access to the nonencrypted remote shell services. The /etc/shosts.equiv and .shosts files are functionally equivalent to the traditional hosts.equiv and .rhosts files, so the same instructions and rules apply.

Now you are ready to test the SSH service. From another computer on which SSH has been installed (or even from the same computer if another is not available), type the ssh command followed by a space and the name of the system to which you are connecting. For example, to connect to the system ratbert.glaci.com, type:

```
# ssh ratbert.glaci.com
```

If this is the first time you've ever logged in to that system using the ssh command, the command will ask you to confirm that you really want to connect:

```
Host key not found from the list of known hosts.
Are you sure you want to continue connecting (yes/no)?
```

Type **yes** and press Enter. You should be prompted for a username and password in the normal way. The connection will function like a normal telnet connection, except that the information is encrypted as it travels over the network. You should now also be able to use the ssh command to run remote commands from a shell on the local system.

The scp command is similar to the rcp command for copying files to and from Linux systems. Here is an example of using the scp command to copy a file called memo from the home directory of the user named jake to the /tmp directory on a computer called maple:

```
$ scp /home/jake/memo maple:/tmp
passwd: ********
memo            100%|***************|   153    0:00
```

Enter the password for your username (if a password is requested). If the password is accepted, the remote system indicates that the file has been copied successfully. You can name multiple files to transfer at a time. You can also use the -r option with scp to recursively copy all files from below any directories indicated.

Similarly, the sftp command starts an interactive FTP session with an FTP server that supports SSH connections. Many security-conscious people prefer sftp to other ftp clients because it provides a secure connection between you and the remote host. Here's an example:

```
$ sftp ftp.handsonhistory.com
Connecting to ftp.handsonhistory.com
passwd: ********
sftp>
```

At this point you can begin an interactive FTP session. You can use get and put commands on files as you would using any FTP client but with the comfort of knowing that you are working on a secure connection. Use the help command to learn more about supported commands.

Tip   The sftp command, as with ssh and scp, requires that the SSH service be running on the server. If you can't connect to an FTP server using sftp, the SSH service may not be available.

Using ssh, scp, and sftp Without Passwords

It's often helpful to set up machines that you use a great deal so that you do not have to use a password to log in. The following steps take you through setting up passwordless authentication from one machine to another. (In this example, the local user is named chuckw on a computer named host1, and the remote user is also chuckw, on a computer named host2. Of course, you would use your own users' and computers' names.)

1. Log in to the local computer (in this example, I log in as chuckw to host1).

Caution   Run step 2 only once as local user on your local workstation. Do not run it again unless you lose your ssh keys. When configuring subsequent remote servers, skip right to step 3.

2. Type the following to generate the ssh key:

```
$ ssh-keygen -t dsa
```

3. Accept the defaults by pressing Enter at each request.

4. Type the following to copy the key to the remote server (using your own remote user and host names):

```
$ cd ~/.ssh
$ scp id_dsa.pub chuckw@host2:/tmp
chuckw@host2's password: *******
```

Note   You will be asked for passwords in steps 4 and 5. This is okay.

5. Type the following to add the ssh key to the remote-user's authorization keys (the code should be on one line, not wrapped):

```
$ ssh chuckw@host2 'cat /tmp/id_dsa.pub >> /home/chuckw/.ssh/ \
    authorized_keys2'
```

6. Type the following to remove the key from the temporary directory:

```
$ ssh chuckw@host2 /bin/rm /tmp/id_dsa.pub
```

Note   Step 6 should not ask for a password.

Now anytime you try to log in from one machine to the other using the user account chuckw, you should connect immediately without being required to enter a password.

Once you have this working, it will work regardless of how many times the IP address changes on your local computer. IP address has nothing to do with this form of authentication.

Note   You can log in to an ssh server from a Windows system using the ssh client called PuTTY. To find out more, visit www.chiark.greenend.org.uk and click the PuTTY link.

Guarding Your Computer with PortSentry

While LogSentry gathers and sorts log messages that may represent attempts to break into your computer system, PortSentry actively watches ports for intrusion behavior. It takes a more active approach to protecting your system from network intrusions.

PortSentry is a nice complement to LogSentry. It can be installed and configured on any Linux system to monitor selected TCP and UDP ports. When PortSentry perceives an attack, it reacts to the attack (in ways that you choose) and produces log messages about the activity that can be forwarded to the system administrator by LogSentry.

PortSentry operates in several different modes, each of which can be applied to monitoring of TCP and UDP ports. The modes include:

✦ **Basic**—PortSentry's default mode. Selected UDP and TCP ports in this mode are bound by PortSentry, giving the monitored ports the appearance of offering a service to the network.

✦ **Stealth** — PortSentry listens to the ports at the socket level instead of binding the ports. This mode can detect a variety of scan techniques (strobe-style, SYN, FIN, NULL, XMAS, and UDP scans), but because it is more sensitive than basic mode, it is likely to produce more false alarms.

✦ **Advanced Stealth** — Uses the same detection method as the regular stealth mode, but instead of monitoring only the selected ports, it monitors all ports below a selected number (port number 1023, by default). You can then exclude monitoring of particular ports. This mode is even more sensitive than Stealth mode and is more likely to cause false alarms than regular stealth mode.

Note When a port is "bound" by PortSentry or any other network service daemon process, all requests that come to that port from the network are handled by the binding process. For example, when the httpd daemon binds to port 80, requests for Web services from the network are processed by httpd.

In addition to selecting the PortSentry mode and the ports that are monitored, you also can choose the response to your computer's being scanned. By default, PortSentry can log intrusion attempts and block access from the intruder. PortSentry also offers ways of using other tools to respond to intrusions, including firewall rules, route changes, and host denial configuration.

Downloading and Installing PortSentry

Portsentry is available from the SentryTools project site (`http://sourceforge.net/projects/sentrytools`). You can download it in `tar.gz` format, unzip and untar the file, and then make the binaries from source code. There are, however, PortSentry software packages available from rpmfind.net for Fedora, Yellow Dog, and other Linux systems that use RPM-based software packaging.

To install PortSentry on a Debian GNU/Linux system, use the apt-get utility (`apt get install portsentry`). For Gentoo, download and install PortSentry with the emerge command (`emerge portsentry`).

Using PortSentry As Is

As with LogSentry, you don't need to do anything to get PortSentry to work after it is installed. By default, here is what PortSentry does after you install the portsentry package:

✦ The `/etc/init.d/portsentry` startup script runs automatically when you boot to run level 3, 4, or 5 (levels 3 and 5 are most commonly used).

✦ The following port numbers are configured to be monitored by PortSentry in basic mode:

TCP: 1, 11, 15, 143, 540, 635, 1080, 1524, 2000, 5742, 6667, 12345, 12346, 20034, 31337, 32771, 32772, 32773, 32774, 40421, 49724, 54320

UDP: 1, 513, 635, 640, 641, 700, 32770, 32771, 32772, 32773, 32774, 31337, 54321

✦ In response to attacks (represented by scans of the ports being monitored), all further attempts to connect to any services for the protocol (TCP or UDP) will be blocked.

The computers that are blocked from accessing your system are listed in either the `portsentry.blocked.tcp` or `portsentry.blocked.udp` files (in the `/var/portsentry` directory), depending on which protocol was scanned (TCP or UPD). Remove entries from these files to restore access to blocked computers.

Configuring PortSentry

Chances are that you will want to make some changes to the way that PortSentry runs. To change how it behaves, modify the `/etc/portsentry/portsentry.conf` file. In that file, you can choose which ports to monitor, the mode in which to monitor, and the responses to take when a scan is detected. The responses can include:

✦ Blocking access by the remote computer.

✦ Rerouting messages from the remote computer to a dead host. (A dead host is a machine dedicated to taking unwanted network traffic, to draw that traffic away from machines doing serious work.)

✦ Adding a firewall rule to drop packets from the remote computer.

The other file you may want to change is `/etc/portsentry/portsentry.modes`, which contains the modes in which PortSentry can be run.

Changing the portsentry.conf File

To edit the `portsentry.conf` file, as root user, open the file using any text editor. The following sections describe the information that can be changed in that file.

Selecting Ports

The `portsentry.conf` file defines which ports are monitored in basic and stealth modes. By default, only basic TCP and UDP modes are active, so only those ports are monitored (unless you change to one of the stealth modes). The `TCP_PORTS` and `UDP_PORTS` options define which ports are monitored. Here is how they appear in the `portsentry.conf` file:

```
TCP_PORTS="1,11,15,143,540,635,1080,1524,2000,5742,6667,12345,12346,200
    34,31337,32771,32772,32773,32774,40421,49724,54320"
UDP_PORTS="1,513,635,640,641,700,32770,32771,32772,32773,32774,31337,
    54321"
```

Unless you are a TCP/IP expert, you're probably wondering what services these ports represent. The Internet Assigned Numbers Authority (IANA) assigns services to UDP and TCP ports. You can see these assignments at `www.iana.org/assignments/port-numbers`.

Network services obtain port number assignments from the `/etc/services` file. So, in general, you can simply check the `/etc/services` file to find out most of the services that are assigned to ports being scanned.

Ports assigned for monitoring are chosen based on a couple of different criteria. Lower port numbers (1, 11, 15, and so on) are selected to catch port scanners that begin at port 1 and scan through a few hundred ports. If the scanner is blocked after accessing port 1, it won't be able to get information about any other ports that might be open on your computer. Another criterion is to include ports that are checked specifically by intruders because those services might be vulnerable to attack. They include the systat (port 11) and netstat (port 15) services.

You will want to remove ports from the list in the `portsentry.conf` file if you are actually running the service assigned to that port. On the other hand, you might want to add ports to the list if you are paranoid about attacks and you want a bit more coverage. The file contains some examples that you can uncomment (remove the # sign) so that more ports are monitored.

If you change from basic to stealth scans (as described in the "Changing the port-sentry.modes File" section later in this chapter), the ports that are monitored are those defined by the `ADVANCED_PORTS_TCP` and `ADVANCED_PORTS_UDP` options. Here is how those two options are set by default:

```
ADVANCED_PORTS_TCP="1023"
ADVANCED_PORTS_UDP="1023"
```

These settings indicate that all ports from 1 to 1023 are monitored. Monitoring higher port numbers can result in many more false alarms, so that practice is not recommended. If you find that PortSentry is being tripped accidentally, you might want to exclude the ports being tripped by using the `ADVANCED_EXCLUDE_TCP` and `ADVANCED_EXCLUDE_UDP` options. The following example shows how these two values are set by default:

```
ADVANCED_EXCLUDE_TCP="111,113,139"
ADVANCED_EXCLUDE_UDP="520,138,137,67"
```

Ident and NetBIOS services for TCP (ports 111, 113, and 139) and route, NetBIOS, and Bootp broadcasts for UDP (ports 520, 138, 137, and 67) are excluded from the advanced scan by default because a remote computer might hit these ports without representing any misuse. If you are running in stealth mode, you should exclude any services that you are running on your system by adding their port numbers to this list.

Identifying Configuration Files

PortSentry uses several configuration files in addition to `portsentry.conf`. You can identify the locations of these other files within the `portsentry.conf` file. Here's how those files are defined:

```
# Hosts to ignore
IGNORE_FILE="/etc/portsentry/portsentry.ignore"
# Hosts that have been denied (running history)
HISTORY_FILE="/var/portsentry/portsentry.history"
# Hosts denied this session only (temporary until next restart)
BLOCKED_FILE="/var/portsentry/portsentry.blocked"
```

Here's what these files are used for:

✦ The `portsentry.ignore` file contains a list of all IP addresses that you do not want blocked (even if they improperly try to access ports on your computer). By default, all IP addresses assigned to the local computer are added to this file. You can add IP addresses of trusted computers, if you like.

✦ The `portsentry.history` file contains a list of IP addresses for computers that have been blocked from accessing your computer.

✦ The `portsentry.blocked.*` files contain a list of computers that have been blocked from accessing your computer during the current session. The `portsentry.blocked.tcp` file contains IP addresses of computers that have improperly scanned TCP ports on your computer. Addresses of computers that have been blocked after scanning UDP ports are contained in the `portsentry.blocked.udp` file.

Access to ports on your computer is only blocked during the current session (that is, until the next reboot or restart of PortSentry). To more permanently exclude remote computers, you should impose other restrictions (such as by using the `/etc/hosts.deny` file, a firewall command, or a reroute to a dead host). These methods are described later in this chapter.

Choosing Responses

Someone scanning a port can be compared to someone checking a door in your house to see if it is locked. In most cases, it indicates that someone is checking your system for weaknesses. That is why, when another computer scans your ports, the default response from PortSentry is to block further access from the other computer to your computer for the duration of the current session. No action is taken to permanently block access from that computer. The `BLOCK_UDP` and `BLOCK_TCP` options in the `portsentry.conf` file set which type of automatic response is taken when ports are scanned. Here is how these options are set by default:

```
BLOCK_UDP="2"
BLOCK_UDP="2"
```

The value in quotation marks determines how PortSentry reacts to a scan of your ports by another computer. The following list describes each of these values.

✦ A value of "2" (the default value) causes access to be temporarily blocked to services for the scanned protocol (TCP or UDP) and for the action to be logged. Also, if any commands were defined to be run by a KILL_RUN_CMD option, that command is then run. (This option is not configured by default.)

✦ A value of "0" causes port scans to be logged, but not blocked.

✦ A value of "1" causes the KILL_ROUTE and KILL_HOSTS_DENY options to be run. (See the following list for descriptions of these options.) By default, further requests from the remote computer will be rerouted to a dead host, and the remote host's IP address will be added to the /etc/hosts.deny file, thereby denying access to network services.

Following are some suggestions on options you can use to change the responses to your ports being scanned:

✦ KILL_ROUTE — Runs the /sbin/route command to reroute requests from the remote computer to a dead host. By default, this option is set to the following value, which effectively drops the request from the remote computer:

KILL_ROUTE="/sbin/route add -host $TARGET$ gw 127.0.0.1"

This ipchains rule denies all packets from the remote computer. To make this action permanent, you could add the ipchains options (from the -I to the end of the line) to the /etc/sysconfig/ipchains file, replacing the $TARGET$ with the actual IP address of the computer you want to deny access to.

Note Instead of rerouting IP packets from the remote host, you can use firewall rules to deny access. If you use ipchains firewalls, uncomment the following line to deny access from the remote host.

    KILL_ROUTE="/sbin/ipchains -I input -s $TARGET$ -j DENY
    -l"

If you are using iptables, change ipchains to iptables and create an appropriate iptables response.

✦ KILL_HOSTS_DENY — Used to deny requests for any network services that are protected by TCP wrappers. This option is set by default as follows:

KILL_HOSTS_DENY="ALL: $TARGET$"

With the preceding option set, $TARGET$ is replaced by the IP address of the intruding remote computer and the line in quotes is added to the /etc/hosts. deny file. For example, if the remote computer's IP address were 10.0.0.59, the line that appears in /etc/hosts.deny would be:

ALL: 10.0.0.59

✦ KILL_RUN_CMD — Instead of using firewalls, rerouting, or TCP wrappers to deny an intruding computer from accessing your computer, you can choose any command you like in response. With the BLOCK_TCP and BLOCK_UDP options set to "2", the value of KILL_RUN_CMD is run in response to a scan of your monitored ports.

The value of KILL_RUN_CMD should be the full path to the script you want to run, plus any options. To include the IP address of the remote computer or the port number that was scanned, you could include the $TARGET$ or $PORT$ variables, respectively. In the following example, replace /path/to/script with the full path to the script you want to run:

KILL_RUN_CMD="/path/to/script $TARGET$ $PORT$"

Caution

Do not use any KILL_RUN_CMD to retaliate against the intruding remote host. First, it is quite possible that the computer that is scanning your ports has itself been cracked and is thus not a valid target for retaliations, and second, retaliation may simply incite a cracker into further attacks on you.

✦ PORT_BANNER — You can send a message to the person who sets off the PortSentry monitor by setting the PORT_BANNER option. By default, no message is defined. However, you can uncomment the following line to use that message. (An abusive message is not recommended.)

PORT_BANNER="** UNAUTHORIZED ACCESS PROHIBITED ***
    YOUR CONNECTION ATTEMPT HAS BEEN LOGGED. GO AWAY."

The number of scans from an intruding computer that PortSentry will accept before setting off these responses can be set by using the SCAN_TRIGGER option. By default, that option is set as follows:

SCAN_TRIGGER="0"

The "0" value means that you won't accept any scans from an intruding system. In other words, the first scan will trip the PortSentry monitor. You can increase this value to be tolerant of one or more errant scans (although you probably won't want to).

Changing the portsentry.modes File

The /etc/portsentry/portsentry.modes file defines the modes in which the PortSentry command is run at boot time. Here is how that file appears by default:

```
tcp
udp
#stcp
#sudp
#atcp
#audp
```

The tcp and udp options are the basic PortSentry modes for the TCP and UDP services, respectively. Your other choices of options include stealth TCP (stcp) and advanced stealth TCP (atcp) and stealth UDP (sudp) and advanced stealth UDP (audp). Run only one TCP service and one UDP service, so if you uncomment a stealth or advanced stealth service, be sure to add a comment to the appropriate basic service.

To activate the new services, execute the following command:

```
# /etc/init.d/portsentry restart
```

The new PortSentry modes will take effect immediately, and they will also be in effect when your computer reboots.

Testing PortSentry

There are different ways to test that your ports are properly protected. What you want to do is run a program that a potential intruder would run to see if it trips the appropriate response from PortSentry. For example, you could use a port scanner to see how your ports appear to the outside world. You could also use a command, such as telnet, to try to set off a particular port. Does PortSentry catch it?

nmap is a popular tool for scanning TCP and UDP ports. You can give the nmap command a host name or IP address, and it will scan about 1,500 ports on the local computer or on a computer you can reach on the network to see which ports are open (and presumably offering services that could potentially be cracked).

With nmap installed on your system, do the following:

1. If PortSentry is running, shut it down by typing the following:

```
# /etc/init.d/portsentry stop
```

2. Type the following nmap commands to see which ports are open on the local system:

```
# nmap -sS -O 127.0.0.1
# nmap -sU -O 127.0.0.1
```

The output shows you which ports are currently offering services on your computer for TCP and UDP protocols, respectively.

3. If there are any services that you don't want open, turn off those services by using chkconfig *service* off (replacing *service* with the service name), by editing the configuration file in the /etc/xinetd.d directory that represents the service and changing disable = no to disable = yes, or by changing your firewall setup.

4. If there are services that you want to be available from your computer, make sure that the port numbers representing those services are not being monitored by PortSentry. Remove the port number from the TCP_PORTS and/or UDP_PORTS options in the /etc/portsentry/portsentry.conf file, or PortSentry will report that there is a possible stealth scan on the port.

5. Restart PortSentry as follows:

```
# /etc/init.d/portsentry start
```

6. Run nmap again:

```
# nmap -sS -O 127.0.0.1
# nmap -sU -O 127.0.0.1
```

The ports offering legitimate services, as well as the ports being monitored by PortSentry, should all appear to be open.

7. Check the /var/log/messages file to make sure that PortSentry is not trying to monitor any ports on which you are offering services.

When you have determined that PortSentry is set up the way you would like it to be, run the nmap command from another computer on your network. This time, replace 127.0.0.1 with the name or IP address of the PortSentry computer. If everything is working, the first port that the remote computer scans on your PortSentry computer should block all subsequent scans.

Never run nmap on a machine that is not yours. Running nmap to scan someone's system for open ports is considered an intrusion.

Tracking PortSentry Intrusions

In addition to taking action against intruders, PortSentry logs its activities using the syslog utility. PortSentry's startup, shutdown, and scan-detection activities are logged to your /var/log/messages file. Here are some examples of PortSentry output in that file:

```
portsentry[13259]: adminalert: Psionic PortSentry 1.0 is starting.
portsentry[13260]: adminalert: Going into listen mode on TCP port: 1
portsentry[13260]: adminalert: Going into listen mode on TCP port: 11
     .
     .
     .
portsentry[13260]: adminalert: PortSentry is active and listening.
portsentry[]: attackalert: Connect from host:10.0.0.4 to TCP port: 31337
portsentry[]: attackalert: Connect from host: 10.0.0.4 to TCP port: 11
portsentry[]: attackalert: Host: 10.0.0.4 is already blocked. Ignoring
     .
     .
     .
portsentry[13371]: securityalert: Psionic PortSentry is shutting down
portsentry[13371]: adminalert: Psionic PortSentry is shutting down
```

The first part of the output shows PortSentry starting up. As PortSentry begins listening to each port, that port is noted in a separate log message. The next messages show the computer being scanned. Someone from host 10.0.0.4 ran nmap to scan the ports on the computer. PortSentry caught the scan of port 31337 and blocked attempts to scan other ports.

Finally, the last set of messages shows PortSentry being shut down. This is a security alert because someone besides you could shut down PortSentry to hide that he had broken in. It is followed by an adminalert.

Note   If you've been running the LogSentry package (described earlier in this chapter), these messages show up in the e-mail messages you receive each hour from Logcheck.

Restoring Access

If access was cut off to a computer that you wanted to have access, there are several things you can check to correct that problem:

✦ /etc/hosts.deny — See if the computer's IP address was mistakenly added to this file. This would cause network services to be denied to the host at that IP address.

✦ /var/portsentry/portsentry.blocked — Check that an entry for the computer's IP address wasn't added to the portsentry.blocked.udp or portsentry.blocked.tcp files.

✦ route — Run the /sbin/route command to see if messages from the computer are being rerouted to a dead host (probably the localhost).

✦ iptables — Run the iptables -L command to see if a new firewall was created to block access from the computer.

Tip   To make sure that access isn't cut off again, you can add the IP address of the remote computer to the /etc/portsentry/portsentry.ignore file. Future improper scans or requests for services won't cause the remote computer to be blocked.

Security Auditing Tools

Once you have gone to all the effort of fortifying your server, you should test the strength of your defenses. There are several tools and one real handy collection of tools that can help you find the soft spots in your system configuration and network security.

Caution   Some of the tools described in this section require thorough research before you attempt to use them on a mission-critical network. Using these products often triggers alarms on intrusion detection systems, and some of the brute-force attack tools crash the servers they target. If you read up on them, you should be fine, but always experiment in a test environment before using these tools in a production environment.

Freely available network security tools were probably designed with less than noble goals in mind. The following security auditing software packages are essentially penetration tools designed to find weaknesses, report them, and ultimately exploit them if the user desires. Here's a brief rundown on each:

✦ **Nessus** — The Nessus project (`www.nessus.org`) has produced a very powerful network auditing tool. One of the key features of Nessus is that it goes beyond searching for known vulnerabilities and does a good job of hunting for *possible* vulnerabilities.

✦ **Kismet** — If you have wireless networks to manage, monitor, and protect, Kismet (`www.kismetwireless.net`) is a very useful tool for seeing just how easy it is to get on to those wireless networks. It is effective if you need to search for rogue access points on your network. Kismet also serves as an intrusion detection tool and traffic sniffer.

✦ **Ethereal** — The Ethereal tool captures and analyzes network traffic related to some 530 network protocols. Data can be evaluated in real time or stored in capture files for later analysis. Ethereal can view capture logs from a wide array of network sniffer applications as well. For more information, and to obtain a copy, go to `www.ethereal.com`.

If individual tools are not enough to satisfy your needs, there is an all-in-one tool simply called Auditor. Available from `www.moser-informatik.ch/`, this tool combines powerful applications such as Nessus, kismet, Ethereal, and about 300 others. Auditor combines all of these tools into a single, bootable CD that uses a simple GUI to launch the tools. The full spectrum of security-testing tools is included in this package from foot-printing (gathering information about the target of an attack) to brute-force password cracking.

Summary

With the rise of the Internet, security has become a critical issue for nearly all computer users. Properly using passwords, securely configuring network services, keeping on top of security issues, and monitoring log files are critical ways of keeping your computer secure.

Using encryption keys, you can help verify the authenticity of those with whom you communicate, as well as make the data you transmit more secure. With tools such as PortSentry, you can quickly identify unauthorized activity and help protect your Linux system from intrusions. Protection, in this case, can even include automatic responses to those scanning your system, such as being blocked from access or being sent a message.

Auditing software such as Nessus can be used to ensure that the security provisions you have put in place are effective against modern hacking tools. There are a variety of bootable Linux distributions that are full of security-related tools you can use to get your systems safe and running smoothly.

✦   ✦   ✦

Choosing and Installing a Linux Distribution

Installing Linux

If someone hasn't already installed and configured a Linux system for you, this chapter is going to help you get started so you can try out the Linux features described in the rest of the book. If you are a first-time Linux user, I recommend that you:

+ **Try a bootable Linux.** This book's DVD and CD include several bootable Linux systems. The advantage of a bootable Linux is that you can try out Linux without touching the contents of your computer's hard disk. In particular, KNOPPIX is a full-featured Linux system that can give you a good feel for how Linux works. Using the DVD or CD, you can boot directly to KNOPPIX or Damn Small Linux, respectively. There are also other bootable Linux distributions on the CD that you can use to create your own bootable CDs (listed in Appendix A).

+ **Install a desktop Linux system.** Choose one of the other Linux distributions and install it on your computer's hard disk. This will give you more flexibility for adding and removing software, accessing and saving data to hard disk, and more permanently customizing your system. Installing Linux as a desktop system lets you try out some useful applications and get the feel for Linux before dealing with more complex server issues.

This chapter provides you with an overview of how to choose a Linux distribution and then describes issues and topics that are common to installing most Linux distributions. Appendix A describes exactly which Linux distributions are included on this book's DVD and CD and how to either boot them from the DVD or CD or burn them to CD for installation. Each of the other chapters in this part of the book is dedicated to understanding and installing a particular Linux distribution.

After you've installed Linux, you'll want to understand how to get and manage software for your Linux system. These are important topics that are actually covered throughout the book, but this chapter describes the major packaging formats and tools to get you going.

Choosing a Linux Distribution

There are literally hundreds of Linux distributions available today. Some are generalized distributions that you can use as a desktop, server, or workstation system; others are specialized for business or computer enthusiasts. Part of the intention of this book is to help you choose which one (or ones) will suit you best.

Using the DVD that comes with this book, you can boot directly to KNOPPIX (to try out Linux without installing it on your hard disk) or to Fedora Core 3 (to install Linux on your computer's hard disk). Because the Fedora Core 3 included with the book is the complete FC3 distribution, you can install a full range of desktop interfaces and applications, programming tools, and server features. So after you've tried out KNOPPIX and are ready to install Linux on your hard disk, I recommend you try Fedora.

The CD that comes with this book boot directly to either Damn Small Linux (a compact KNOPPIX derivative) or to a Devian GNU/Linux network install (to install a customized Debian system over the network). Damn Small Linux runs well on lower-memory machines, while te Debian install we describe works well for the sample web (LAMP) and mail servers described in chapters 23 and 24.

Other Linux distributions included on the DVD are stored there in ISO images that fit on CDs, or, in some cases, mini-CDs or bootable business card-sized CDs (shaped like business cards but can be read by most CD drives). Because of space limitations on the DVD, some of the distributions contained there are intended for network installs, which means you need an Internet connection to get some of the software to complete a full install.

Linux at Work

Because I know a lot of people who use Linux, both informally and at work, I want to share my general impressions of how different Linux distributions are being used in the U.S. Most consultants I know who set up small office servers used to use Red Hat Linux but now have mostly split off to using Fedora Core or Debian GNU/Linux. Mandrakelinux has been popular with people wanting a friendly Linux desktop, but Fedora and SUSE are also well liked. The more technically inclined like to play with Gentoo (highly tunable) or Slackware (Linux in a more basic form).

For people who are transitioning to Linux with Mac hardware, Yellow Dog Linux lets them install on a PowerPC and learn skills that are useful to expand later to Red Hat Linux systems (Yellow Dog is based on Red Hat). As for the bootable Linuxes, everyone I know thinks they are great fun to try out and a good way to learn about Linux. For a bootable Linux containing desktop software that fits on a full CD (or DVD), KNOPPIX is a good choice; for a bootable mini-CD-size Linux, Damn Small Linux works well.

This book exposes you to several different Linux distributions. It gives you the advantage of being able to see the strengths and weaknesses of each distribution by actually putting your hands on it. You can also try to connect into the growing Linux user communities because strong community support results in a more solid software distribution and help when you need it (from such things as forums and online chats).

Other Distributions

There seems to be a new Linux distribution every five minutes, and I really have to stop writing this book at some point. To keep the descriptions of Linux distributions to a reasonable size (and actually have the space to describe how to use Linux), there are several interesting Linux distributions that aren't explored in this book.

Notable Linux distributions not included in this book are TurboLinux, Lycoris, and Xandros. TurboLinux (`www.turbolinux.com`) is a popular distribution in Asia Pacific countries. Lycoris (originally based on OpenLinux) and Xandros (designed to operate well in Microsoft Windows environments) are both well-regarded desktop Linux systems (see `www.lycoris.com` and `www.xandros.com`, respectively). The following sections look beyond the confines of this book for those and other Linux distributions.

Getting Your Own Linux Distribution

By packaging a handful of Linux distributions with this book, I hoped to save you the trouble of getting Linux yourself. If you have a DVD or CD drive, perhaps you can use this opportunity to at least try KNOPPIX or Damn Small Linux so you'll see better what's being discussed.

If for some reason you can't use the software on the DVD, you may want to get your own Linux distributions to use with the descriptions in this book. Reasons you might want to get your own Linux distributions include:

✦ **No DVD or CD drive** — You need a bootable DVD drive on your computer to directly use the software that comes with this book. (If you have access to a CD drive, however, you can copy Coyote Linux from the CD and create a Linux distribution, as described in chapter 17, hat runs from a floppy disk.)

✦ **Later distributions** — You may want a more recent version of a particular distribution than comes with this book.

✦ **Complete distributions** — Because there's limited space on the DVD and because some distributions require subscriptions or other fees, you may want to obtain your own, more complete distribution with which to work.

Today, there is no shortage of ways to get Linux.

Finding Another Linux Distribution

You can go to the Web site of each distribution (such as `http://fedora.redhat.com/download` or `http://slackware.com/getslack`) to get Linux software. Those sites often let you download a copy (or sample) of their distributions and give you the opportunity to purchase a boxed set.

However, a way to get a more complete view of available Linux distributions is to go to a Web site that's dedicated to spreading information about Linux distributions. Use these sites to connect to forums, download sites, and documentation about many Linux distributions. Here are some examples:

✦ **DistroWatch** (`www.distrowatch.com`) — The first place I go to find Linux distributions is DistroWatch.com. Go to the Major Distributions link to read about the top Linux distributions (most of which are included with this book). Links will take you to download sites, forums, home pages, and other sites related to each distribution.

✦ **LinuxISO** (`www.linuxiso.org`) — Like DistroWatch, this site also connects you to download sites, as well as forums, home pages, and other sites for Linux distributions. Look for the Helpful Stuff box on the LinuxISO home page for great information on getting, burning, and verifying Linux ISO images.

✦ **Linux Help** (`www.linuxhelp.net`) — Select the ISO images link from this site's home page, and you can find download links to ISO images for many of the most popular Linux distributions.

If you don't want to download and burn the CDs yourself, there are plenty of ads on those sites from places willing to sell you Linux CDs or DVDs. Distribution prices are often only a little bit higher than the cost of the media and shipping. If you really like a particular Linux distribution, it's a good idea to purchase it directly from the organization that makes it. That can ensure the health of the distribution into the future.

Books such as the *Red Hat Fedora Linux Bible* can also be a good way to get a Linux distribution. Up-to-date documentation is often a weakness when you have nothing but a CD to start out with. Standard Linux documentation (such as HOWTOs and man pages) are often out of date with the software. So, I would particularly recommend a book and distribution (such as this one or *Red Hat Fedora Linux Bible*) for first-time Linux users.

Understanding What You Need

By far, the most common way of getting Linux is on CDs, or secondarily, DVDs. The next most common way is to start with a floppy or CD that includes an installation boot image and get the parts of Linux you need live from the network as you install Linux.

The images that are burned on to the CDs are typically stored on the Internet in what are called *software repositories.* You can download them and burn them to CDs yourself. Alternatively, the software packages are usually also included separately in directories. Those separate software directories enable you to start an install process with a minimal boot disk that can grab packages over the network during the installation process. (Some of the installations we recommend with this book are done that way.)

When you follow links to Linux software repositories, here's what you look for:

✦ **Download directory** — You often have to step down a few directories from the download link that gets you to a repository. Look for subdirectories that describe the distribution, architecture, release, and medium format. For example, mirrors for the Fedora Core 3 Linux distribution might be named `fedora/linux/core/3/i386/iso`.

✦ **ISO images** — The software images you are going to burn to CD are typically stored in ISO format. Some repositories include a README file to tell you what images you need (others just assume you know). To install a distribution, you want the set of ISOs containing the Linux distribution's binary files. For example, the set of four Fedora Core 3 installation images for i386 platforms starts with FC3-i386-disc1.iso (with the others named disc2, disc3, and disc4).

Note   Although an ISO image appears as one file, it's actually like a snapshot of a file system. You can mount that image to see all the files the image contains by using the loop feature of the `mount` command. For example, with an image called `abc.iso` in the current directory, create an empty directory (`mkdir myiso`) and run the mount command as follows: `mount -o loop abc.iso myiso`. Change to the `myiso` directory, and you can view the files and directories the ISO image contains.

✦ **MD5SUM** — To verify that you got the right CDs completely intact, after you download them, look for a file named MD5SUM or ending in `.md5` in the ISO directory. You can use that file to verify the content of each CD (as described later).

Downloading the Distribution

You can download each ISO image by simply clicking the link and downloading it to a directory in your computer when prompted. You can do this on a Windows or Linux system.

If you know the location of the image you want, with a running Linux system, the `wget` command is a better way to download than just clicking a link in your browser. The advantage of using `wget` is that you can restart a download that stops in the middle for some reason. A `wget` command to download a KNOPPIX CD image (starting from the directory you want to download to) might look like this:

```
$ wget -c ftp.tux.org/pub/linux/knoppix/KNOPPIX_V3.6-2004-08-16-EN.iso
```

If the download stops before it is completed, run the command again. The `-c` option tells `wget` to begin where the download left off, so that if you are 640MB into a 650MB download when it stopped, it will just add in the last 10MB.

There is also a facility called BitTorrent (http://bitconjurer.org/BitTorrent) you might want to look into. BitTorrent lets you download a file to your computer by grabbing bits of that file from multiple computers on the network that are download-ing the file at the same time. For the privilege, you also use your upload capacity to share the same file with others as you are downloading. During times of heavy demand with a new Linux distribution, BitTorrent can be the best way to go.

If you are on a dial-up modem, you should strongly consider purchasing Linux CDs (or getting them from a friend) if the DVD or CD with this book doesn't have what you want. You might be able to download a whole 700MB CD in a couple hours on a fast DSL or cable modem connection. On a dial-up line, you might be talking a whole day or more per CD. For a large, multi-CD distribution, available disk space can also become a problem (although, with today's large hard disks, it's not as much of a problem as it used to be).

Burning the Distribution to CD

With the CD images copied to your computer, you can proceed to verify their con-tents and burn them to CD. All you really need is a CD burner on your computer.

With Linux running, you can use the md5sum command to verify the CD.

> **Note**   If you are using Windows to validate the contents of the Linux CD, you can get the MD5Summer utility (www.md5summer.org) to verify each CD image.

Assuming you downloaded the MD5 file associated with each CD image and have it in the same directory as your CD images, run the md5sum command to verify the image. For example, to verify the KNOPPIX CD shown previously in the wget example, you could type the following:

```
$ md5sum KNOPPIX_V3.6-2004-08-16-EN.iso
5bc8e9fee2a8be0b7180fcf3e49b5386 KNOPPIX_V3.6-2004-08-16-EN.iso
```

The MD5SUM file I downloaded previously from the download directory was called KNOPPIX_V3.4-2004-05-17-EN.iso.md5. It contained this content:

```
5bc8e9fee2a8be0b7180fcf3e49b5386 * KNOPPIX_V3.6-2004-08-16-EN.iso
```

As you can see, the checksum (first string of characters shown) that is output from the ISO image matches the checksum in the MD5 file. So you know that the image you downloaded is the image they put on the server. As long as you got the image from a reliable site, you should be ready to burn the CD.

With your Linux distribution in hand (either the DVD or Cd with this book or the set of CDs you got elsewhere), proceed to Appendix A for details on burning your own CDs or DVDs. After that, instructions for installing the distributions from the DVD can be found in separate chapters for each distribution (Chapters 8 through 18). Before you proceed, however, there's some information that is useful for nearly every Linux system you are installing.

Exploring Common Installation Topics

Before you begin installing your Linux distribution of choice, there is some general Linux information you should understand. Reading over this information might help you avoid problems or keep you from getting stuck when you install Linux.

Knowing Your Computer Hardware

Every Linux will not run on every computer. When installing Linux, most people use a Pentium-class PC. There are Linux systems that are compiled to run on other hardware, such as Mac PowerPCs or AMD 64-bit computers. However, the distributions provided with this book run on only 32-bit Pentium-class PCs.

Minimum hardware requirements from the Fedora Project are pretty good guidelines for most Linux systems:

✦ **Processor** — The latest version of Fedora Core recommends that you at least have a Pentium-class processor. For a text-only installation, a 200 MHz Pentium is the minimum, while a 400MHz Pentium II is the minimum for a GUI installation.

Note

If you have a 486 machine (at least 100 MHz), consider trying Slackware. The problem is that many machines that old have only floppy disks, so you can't use the CD or DVD that come with this book. In that case, you can try ZipSlack (www.slack ware.com/zipslack), which is a Slackware version that comes on about 30+ floppy disk images or a 100MB zip disk and can run on a 486 with at least 100MB of disk space.

✦ **RAM** — You should have at least 64MB of RAM to install most Linux distributions and run it in text mode. Slackware might run on 8MB of RAM, but 16MB is considered the minimum. If you are running in graphical mode, you will probably need at least 192MB. The recommended RAM for graphical mode in Fedora is 256MB. A GNOME environment generally requires a bit less memory to run than a KDE environment. If you are using a more streamlined graphical system (that runs X with a small window manager, such as Blackbox), you might get by with as little as 32MB. In that case, you might try Damn Small Linux or Slackware.

✦ **DVD or CD drive** — You need to be able to boot up the installation process from a DVD or CD. If you can't boot from a DVD or CD, there are ways to start the installation from a hard disk or using a PXE install. Some distributions, such as Slackware or Fedora (prior to Fedora Core 2), let you use floppy disks to boot installation. Once the install is booted, the software can sometimes be retrieved from different locations (over the network or from hard disk, for example).

✦ **Network card** — If you are doing an install of one of the distributions for which we provide a scaled-down boot disk, you might need to have an Ethernet card installed to get the software you need over the network. A dial-up connection won't work for network installs. You don't necessarily have to be connected to the Internet to do a network install. Some people will download the necessary software packages to a computer on their LAN and then use that as an install server.

If you're not sure about your computer hardware, there are a few ways to check what you have. If you are running Windows, the System Properties window can show you the processor you have, as well as the amount of RAM that's installed. As an alternative, you can boot KNOPPIX and let it detect and report to you the hardware you have. (Run `lspci`, `lsmod`, and `dmseg` commands in Linux to view information about your computer hardware.)

Upgrading or Installing from Scratch

If you already have a version of the Linux you are installing on your computer, many Linux distributions offer an upgrade option. This lets you upgrade all packages, for example, from version 1 of the distribution to version 2. Here are a few general rules before performing an upgrade:

✦ **Back up data** — There is a possibility that after you finish your upgrade, the operating system won't boot. It's always a good idea to back up any critical data and configuration files (in `/etc`) before doing any major changes to your operating system.

✦ **Remove extra packages** — If there are software packages you don't need, remove them before you do an upgrade. Upgrade processes typically upgrade only those packages that are on your system. Upgrades generally do more checking and comparing than clean installs do, so any package you can remove saves time during the install.

✦ **Check configuration files** — A Linux upgrade procedure often leaves copies of old configuration files. You should check that the new configuration files still work for you.

Tip

Installing Linux from scratch goes faster than an upgrade. It also results in a cleaner Linux system. So if you have the choice of backing up your data or just erasing it if you don't need it, a fresh install is usually best.

Some Linux distributions, most notably Gentoo, have taken the approach of ongoing updates. Instead of taking a new release every few months, you simply continuously grab updated packages as they become available and install them on your system.

Dual Booting with Windows or Just Linux

It is possible to have multiple, bootable operating systems on the same computer (using multiple partitions on a hard disk and/or multiple hard disks). Setting up to boot more than one operating system, however, requires some thought. It also assumes some risks.

Caution

While tools for resizing Windows partitions and setting up multiboot systems have improved in recent years, there is still considerable risk of losing data on Windows/ Linux dual-boot systems. Different operating systems often have different views of partition tables and master boot records that can cause your machine to become unbootable (at least temporarily) or lose data permanently. Always back up your data before you try to resize a Windows (NTFS or FAT) file system to make space for Linux. If you have a choice, install Linux on a machine of its own or at least on a separate hard disk.

If the computer you are using already has a Windows system on it, it's likely that that the entire hard disk is devoted to Windows. While you can run a bootable Linux such as KNOPPIX or Damn Small Linux without touching the hard disk, to do a more permanent installation you'll want to find disk space outside the Windows installation. There are a few ways to do this:

✦ **Add a hard disk** — Instead of messing with your Windows partition, you can simply add a hard disk and devote it to Linux.

✦ **Resize your Windows partition** — If you have available space on your Windows partition, you can shrink that partition so there is available free space on the disk to devote to Linux. Commercial tools such as Partition Magic (www.semantec.com/partitionmagic) or Acronis Disk Director (www.acronis.com) are available to resize your disk partitions and set up a workable boot manager. Some Linux distributions (particularly bootable Linuxes used as rescue CDs) include a tool called QTParted that is an open source clone of Partition Magic (which includes software from the Linux-NTFS project for resizing Windows NTFS partitions).

Before you try to resize your Windows partition, you might need to defragment it. To *defragment* your disk on some Windows systems, so that all your used space is put in order on the disk, open My Computer, right-click your hard disk icon (typically C:), select Properties, click Tools, and select Defragment Now.

Defragmenting your disk can be a fairly long process. The result of defragmentation is that all the data on your disk are contiguous, creating a lot of contiguous free space at the end of the partition. There are cases where you will have to do the following special tasks to make this true:

- If the Windows swap file is not moved during defragmentation, you must remove it. Then, after you defragment your disk again and resize it, you will need to restore the swap file. To remove the swap file, open the Control Panel, open the System icon, and then click the Performance tab and select Virtual Memory. To disable the swap file, click Disable Virtual Memory.

- If your DOS partition has hidden files that are on the space you are trying to free up, you need to find them. In some cases, you won't be able to delete them. In other cases, such as swap files created by a program, you can safely delete those files. This is a bit tricky because some files should not be deleted, such as DOS system files. You can use the `attrib -s -h` command from the root directory to deal with hidden files.

Once your disk is defragmented, you can use commercial tools described earlier (Partition Magic or Acronis Disk Director) to repartition your hard disk to make space for Linux. An open source alternative to those tools is QTParted.

Boot KNOPPIX or any of several other bootable Linux distributions (particularly rescue CDs) and run QTParted by selecting System Tools ➪ QTParted from the desktop main menu. From the QTParted window, select the hard disk you want to resize. Then choose Options ➪ Configuration to open a window where you can select the ntfsresize tool to resize your NTFS partition.

After you have cleared enough disk space to install Linux (see disk space requirements earlier in this chapter), you can choose your Linux distribution and install it. As you set up your boot loader during installation, you will be able to identify the Windows, Linux, and any other bootable partitions so that you can select which one to boot when your start your computer.

Using Installation Boot Options

Sometimes a Linux installation will fail because the computer has some nonfunctioning or nonsupported hardware. Sometimes you can get around those issues by passing options to the install process when it boots up. Those options can do such things as disable selected hardware (nousb, noscsi, noide, and so on) or not probe hardware when you need to select your own driver (noprobe).

Although some of these options are distribution-specific, others are simply options that can be passed to an installer environment that works from a Linux kernel. Chapter 11 includes a list of many boot options that can be used with KNOPPIX and other Linux systems.

Partitioning Hard Drives

The hard disk (or disks) on your computer provides the permanent storage area for your data files, applications programs, and the operating system itself. Partitioning is the act of dividing a disk into logical areas that can be worked with separately. In Windows, you typically have one partition that consumes the whole hard disk. However, there are several reasons you may want to have multiple partitions:

✦ **Multiple operating systems** — If you install Linux on a PC that already has a Windows operating system, you may want to keep both operating systems on the computer. For all practical purposes, each operating system must exist on a completely separate partition. When your computer boots, you can choose which system to run.

✦ **Multiple partitions within an operating system** — To protect from having your entire operating system run out of disk space, people often assign separate partitions to different areas of the Linux file system. For example, if /home and /var were assigned to separate partitions, then a gluttonous user who fills up the /home partition wouldn't prevent logging daemons from continuing to write to log files in the /var/log directory.

Multiple partitions also make it easier to do certain kinds of backups (such as an image backup). For example, an image backup of /home would be much faster (and probably more useful) than an image backup of the root file system (/).

✦ **Different file system types** — Different kinds of file systems that have different structures. File systems of different types must be on their own partitions. In most Linux systems, you need at least one file system type for / (typically ext3) and one for your swap area. File systems on CD-ROM use the iso9660 file system type.

Tip

When you create partitions for Linux, you will usually assign the file system type as Linux native (using the ext2 or ext3 type on some Linux systems and reiserfs on others). Reasons to use other types include needing a file system that allows particularly long filenames or many inodes (each file consumes an inode).

For example, if you set up a news server, it can use many inodes to store news articles. Another reason for using a different file system type is to copy an image backup tape from another operating system to your local disk (such as one from an OS/2 or Minix operating system).

If you have used only Windows operating systems before, you probably had your whole hard disk assigned to C: and never thought about partitions. With many Linux systems, you have the opportunity to view and change the default partitioning based on how you want to use the system.

During installation, systems such as SUSE and Fedora let you partition your hard disk using a graphical partitioning tool (Yast and Disk Druid, respectively). The following sections describe how to use Disk Druid (during installation) or fdisk. See the section "Tips for Creating Partitions" for some ideas about creating disk partitions.

Partitioning with Disk Druid During Installation

During installation, Fedora gives you the opportunity to change how your hard disk is partitioned using a tool called Disk Druid. The Disk Druid screen is divided into two sections. The top shows general information about each hard disk. The bottom shows details of each partition. Figure 7-1 shows an example of the Disk Druid window.

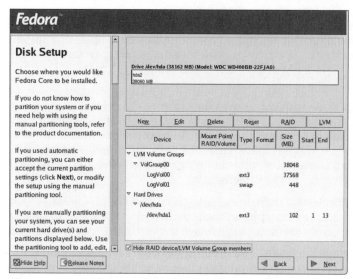

Figure 7-1: Partition your disk during Fedora installation from the Disk Setup window.

For each of the hard disk partitions, you can see:

✦ **Device** — The device name is the name representing the hard disk partition in the /dev directory. Each disk partition device begins with two letters: hd for IDE disks, sd for SCSI disks, ed for ESDI disks, or xd for XT disks. After that is a single letter representing the number of the disk (disk 1 is a, disk 2 is b, disk 3 is c, and so on). The partition number for that disk (1, 2, 3, and so on) follows that. For example, /dev/hda1 represents the first partition on the first IDE hard drive on the computer.

✦ **Mount Point/Raid/Volume** — The directory where the partition is connected into the Linux file system (if it is). You must assign the root partition (/) to a native Linux partition before you can proceed. If you are using RAID or LVM, the name of the RAID device or LVM volume appears here.

✦ **Type** — The type of file system that is installed on the disk partition. In many cases, the file system will be Linux (ext3), Win VFAT (vfat), or Linux swap. However, you can also use the previous Linux file system (ext2), physical volume (LVM), or software RAID.

✦ **Format** — Indicates whether (check mark) or not (no check mark) the installation process should format the hard disk partition. Partitions marked with a check are erased! So, on a multiboot system, be sure your Windows partitions as well as other partitions containing data are not checked!

✦ **Size (MB)** — The amount of disk space allocated for the partition. If you selected to let the partition grow to fill the existing space, this number may be much larger than the requested amount.

✦ **Start/End** — Represents the partition's starting and ending cylinders on the hard disk.

In the top section, you can see each of the hard disks that are connected to your computer. The drive name is shown first. The Geometry section (Geom) shows the numbers of cylinders, heads, and sectors, respectively, on the disk. That's followed by the model name of the disk. The total amount of disk space, the amount used, and the amount free are shown in megabytes.

Reasons for Partitioning

There are different opinions about how to divide up a hard disk. Here are some issues:

✦ **Do you want to install another operating system?** If you want Windows on your computer along with Linux, you need at least one Windows (Win95 FAT16, VFAT, or NTFS type), one Linux (Linux ext3), and one Linux swap partition.

✦ **Is it a multiuser system?** If you are using the system yourself, you probably don't need many partitions. One reason for partitioning an operating system is to keep the entire system from running out of disk space at once. That also serves to put boundaries on what an individual can use up in his or her home directory (although disk quotas are good for that as well).

✦ **Do you have multiple hard disks?** You need at least one partition per hard disk. If your system has two hard disks, you may assign one to / and one to /home (if you have lots of users) or /var (if the computer is a server sharing lots of data).

Deleting, Adding, and Editing Partitions

Before you can add a partition, there needs to be some free space available on your hard disk. If all space on your hard disk is currently assigned to one partition (as it often is in DOS or Windows), you must delete or resize that partition before you can claim space on another partition. The section on reclaiming disk space discusses how to add a partition without losing information in your existing single-partition system.

 Caution   Make sure that any data that you want to keep is backed up before you delete the partition. When you delete a partition, all its data is gone.

Disk Druid is less flexible, but more intuitive, than the fdisk utility. Disk Druid lets you delete, add, and edit partitions.

Tip   If you create multiple partitions, make sure that there is enough room in the right places to complete the installation. For example, most of the Linux software is installed in the /usr directory (and subdirectories), whereas most user data are eventually added to the /home or /var directories.

To delete a partition in Disk Druid, do the following:

1. Select a partition from the list of Current Disk Partitions on the main Disk Druid window (click it or use the arrow keys).

2. To delete the partition, click Delete.

3. When asked to confirm the deletion, click Delete.

4. If you made a mistake, click Reset to return to the partitioning as it was when you started Disk Druid.

To add a partition in Disk Druid, follow these steps from the main Disk Druid window:

1. Select New. A window appears, enabling you to create a new partition.

2. Type the name of the Mount Point (the directory where this partition will connect to the Linux file system). You need at least a root (/) partition and a swap partition.

3. Select the type of file system to be used on the partition. You can select from Linux native (ext2 or preferably ext3), software RAID, Linux swap (swap), physical volume (LVM), or Windows FAT (vfat).

Tip   To create a file system type different from those shown, leave the space you want to use free for now. After installation is complete, use fdisk to create a partition of the type you want.

4. Type the number of megabytes to be used for the partition (in the Size field). If you want this partition to grow to fill the rest of the hard disk, you can put any number in this field (1 will do fine).

5. If you have more than one hard disk, select the disk on which you want to put the partition from the Allowable Drives box.

6. Type the size of the partition (in megabytes) into the Size (MB) box.

7. Select one of the following Additional Size Options:

   • **Fixed size** — Click here to use only the number of megabytes you entered into the Size text box when you create the partition.

   • **Fill all space up to (MB)** — If you want to use all remaining space up to a certain number of megabytes, click here and fill in the number. (You may want to do this if you are creating a VFAT partition up to the 2048MB limit that Disk Druid can create.)

   • **Fill to maximum allowable size** — If you want this partition to grow to fill the rest of the disk, click here.

8. Optionally select Force to Be a Primary Partition if you want to be sure to be able to boot the partition or Check for Bad Blocks if you want to have the partition checked for errors.

9. Select OK if everything is correct. (The changes don't take effect until several steps later when you are asked to begin installing the packages.)

To edit a partition in Disk Druid from the main Disk Druid window, follow these steps:

1. Click the partition you want to edit.

2. Click the Edit button. A window appears, ready to let you edit the partition definition.

3. Change any of the attributes (as described in the add partition procedure). For a new install, you may need to add the mount point (/) for your primary Linux partition.

4. Select OK. (The changes don't take effect until several steps later, when you are asked to begin installing the packages.)

Partitioning with Fdisk

The fdisk utility is available with most every Linux system for creating and working with disk partitions in Linux. It does the same job as graphical partitioning tools such as Disk Druid, although it's no longer offered as an option during Fedora installation. However, during Fedora installation, and other Linux installations that have virtual terminals running, you can switch to a shell (press Ctrl+Alt+F2) and use fdisk manually to partition your hard disk.

The following procedures are performed from the command line as root user.

 Caution   Remember that any partition commands can easily erase your disk or make it inaccessible. Back up critical data before using any tool to change partitions! Then be very careful about the changes you do make. Keeping an emergency boot disk handy is a good idea, too.

The fdisk command is one that is available on many different operating systems (although it looks and behaves differently on each). In Linux, fdisk is a menu-based command. To use fdisk to list all your partitions, type the following (as root user):

```
# fdisk -l

Disk /dev/hda: 40.0 GB, 40020664320 bytes
255 heads, 63 sectors/track, 4865 cylinders
Units = cylinders of 16065 * 512 = 8225280 bytes

   Device Boot      Start         End      Blocks   Id  System
/dev/hda1   *           1          13      104391   83  Linux
/dev/hda2              14        4833    38716650   83  Linux
/dev/hda3            4834        4865      257040   82  Linux swap
```

To see how each partition is being used on your current system, type the following:

```
# df -h
Filesystem          Size  Used Avail Use% Mounted on
/dev/hda2            37G  5.4G   30G  16% /
/dev/hda1            99M  8.6M   86M  10% /boot
none                 61M     0   61M   0% /dev/shm
```

From the output of `df`, you can see that the root of your Linux system (/) is on the `/dev/hda2` partition and that the `/dev/hda1` partition is used for `/boot`.

Note   If this had been a dual-boot system (with Windows 98), you might have seen a Windows partition from `fdisk` that looked like the following:

```
      /dev/hda1     *      1       83           666666+
  b   Win95 FAT32
```

You could mount that partition in Linux (to get to your Windows files when Linux is booted) by typing:

 # mkdir /mnt/win

 # mount -t vfat /dev/hda1 /mnt/win

Caution   Before using `fdisk` to change your partitions, I strongly recommend running the `df -h` command to see how your partitions are currently being defined. This will help reduce the risk of changing or deleting the wrong partition.

To use `fdisk` to change your partitions, you need to identify the hard disk you are partitioning. For example, the first IDE hard disk is identified as `/dev/hda`. So, to partition your first IDE hard drive, you can begin (as root user) by typing:

```
# fdisk /dev/hda
```

For different hard drive types or numbers, `/dev/hda` is replaced by the name of the device you want to work with. For example, here are some of your choices:

Device	Description
/dev/hda	For the first IDE hard disk; hdb, hdc, and so on for other IDE disks.
/dev/sda	For the first SCSI hard disk; sdb, sdc, and so on for other SCSI disks.
/dev/rd/c0d0	For a RAID device.
/dev/ida/c0d0	Also for a RAID device.

After you have started fdisk, type **m** to see the options. Here is what you can do with `fdisk`:

✦ **Delete a partition.** Type **d** and a partition number, and then press Enter. For example, /dev/sda2 would be partition number 2. (The deletion won't take effect until you write the change—you can back out up to that point.)

✦ **Create a partition.** If you have free space, you can add a new partition. Type **n**; l for a logical partition (5 or over) or p for a primary partition (1–4); and a partition number from the available range. Then choose the first cylinder number from those available. (The output from fdisk -l shown earlier will show you cylinders being used under the Start and End columns.)

Next, enter the cylinder number the partition will end with (or type the specific number of megabytes or kilobytes you want: for example, +50M or +1024K). You just created an ext3 Linux partition. Again, this change isn't permanent until you write the changes.

✦ **Change the partition type.** Press T to choose the type of file system. Enter the partition number of the partition number you want to change. Type the number representing the file system type you want to use in hexadecimal code. (Type **L** at this point to see a list of file system types and codes.) For a Linux file system, use the number 83; for a Linux swap partition, use 82; and for a windows FAT32 file system, use the letter b.

✦ **Display the partition table.** Throughout this process, feel free to type **p** to display (print on the screen) the partition table as it now stands.

✦ **Quit or save.** Before you write your changes, display the partition table again and make sure that it is what you want it to be. If you don't like a change you make to your partitions, press **Q** to exit without saving. Nothing changes on your partition table.

If your changes are correct, write them to the partition table by pressing **W**. You are warned about how dangerous it is to change partitions, and you must confirm the change.

An alternative to the menu-driven fdisk command is sfdisk, which is a command-line oriented partitioning tool. With sfdisk, you type the full command line to list or change partitions, instead of being taken through a set of prompts (as with fdisk). See the sfdisk man page for details. Linux experts often prefer sfdisk because it can be used in combination with other commands to take and output partitioning information.

Tips for Creating Partitions

Changing your disk partitions to handle multiple operating systems can be very tricky. Part of the reason is that each different operating system has its own ideas about how partitioning information should be handled, as well as different tools for doing it. Here are some tips to help you get it right:

✦ If you are creating a dual-boot system, particularly for Windows ME or Windows XP, try to install the Windows operating system first. Otherwise, the Windows installation may make the Linux partitions inaccessible.

✦ The fdisk man page recommends that you use partitioning tools that come with an operating system to create partitions for that operating system. For example, the DOS fdisk knows how to create partitions that DOS will like, and the Linux fdisk will happily make your Linux partitions. Once your hard disk is set up for dual boot, however, you should probably not go back to Windows-only partitioning tools. Use Linux fdisk or a product made for multiboot systems (such as Partition Magic).

✦ You can have up to 63 partitions on an IDE hard disk. A SCSI hard disk can have up to 15 partitions. You won't need nearly that many partitions.

If you are using Linux as a desktop system, you probably don't need a lot of different partitions. There are, however, some very good reasons for having multiple partitions for Linux systems that are shared by a lot of users or are public Web servers or file servers. Multiple partitions within Fedora Linux, for example, offer the following advantages:

✦ **Protection from attacks.** Denial of Service attacks sometimes take action that tries to fill up your hard disk. If public areas, such as /var, are on separate partitions, a successful attack can fill up a partition without shutting down the whole computer. Because /var is the default location for Web and FTP servers, and expected to hold a lot of data, entire hard disks often are assigned to the /var file system alone.

✦ **Protection from corrupted file systems.** If you have only one file system (/), its corruption can cause the whole Fedora Linux system to be damaged. Corruption of a smaller partition can be easier to fix and often allows the computer to stay in service while the correction is made.

Here are some directories that you may want to consider making into separate file system partitions.

Directory	Explanation
/boot	Sometimes the BIOS in older PCs can access only the first 1024 cylinders of your hard disk. To make sure that the information in your /boot directory is accessible to the BIOS, create a separate disk partition (of about 100MB) for /boot and make sure that it exists below cylinder 1024. The rest of your Linux system can exist outside of that 1024-cylinder boundary if you like. Even with several boot images, there is rarely a reason for /boot to be larger than 100MB. (For newer hard disks, you can select the Linear Mode check box during installation. Then the boot partition can be anywhere on the disk.)
/usr	This directory structure contains most of the applications and utilities available to Fedora Linux users. Having /usr on a separate partition lets you mount that file system as read-only after the operating system has been installed. This prevents attackers from replacing or removing important system applications with their own versions that may cause security problems. A separate /usr partition is also useful if you have diskless workstations on your local network. Using NFS, you can share /usr over the network with those workstations.

Directory	Explanation
/var	Your FTP (/var/ftp) and Web-server (/var/www) directories are, by default in many Linux systems, stored under /var. Having a separate /var partition can prevent an attack on those facilities from corrupting or filling up your entire hard disk.
/home	Because your user account directories are located in this directory, having a separate /home account can prevent a reckless user from filling up the entire hard disk.
/tmp	Protecting /tmp from the rest of the hard disk by placing it on a separate partition can ensure that applications that need to write to temporary files in /tmp are able to complete their processing, even if the rest of the disk fills up.

Although people who use Linux systems casually rarely see a need for lots of partitions, those who maintain and occasionally have to recover large systems are thankful when the system they need to fix has several partitions. Multiple partitions can localize deliberate damage (such as Denial of Service attacks), problems from errant users, and accidental file system corruption.

Using LILO or GRUB Boot Loaders

A boot loader lets you choose when and how to boot the bootable operating systems installed on your computer's hard disks. Most Linux systems give you the opportunity to use GRUB or LILO boot loaders. The following sections describe both GRUB and LILO boot loaders.

Booting Your Computer with GRUB

With multiple operating systems installed and several partitions set up, how does your computer know which operating system to start? To select and manage which partition is booted and how it is booted, you need a boot loader. The boot loader that is installed by default with Fedora is called the GRand Unified Boot loader (GRUB).

GRUB is a GNU boot loader (www.gnu.org/software/grub) that replaced the LILO as the default boot loader in many Linux systems (including Fedora). GRUB offers the following features:

✦ Support for multiple executable formats.

✦ Support for multiboot operating systems (such as Fedora, FreeBSD, NetBSD, OpenBSD, and other Linux systems).

✦ Support for nonmultiboot operating systems (such as Windows 95, Windows 98, Windows NT, Windows ME, Windows XP, and OS/2) via a chain-loading function. Chain-loading is the act of loading another boot loader (presumably one that is specific to the proprietary operating system) from GRUB to start the selected operating system.

✦ Support for multiple file system types.

✦ Support for automatic decompression of boot images.

✦ Support for downloading boot images from a network.

For more information on how GRUB works, type **man grub** or **info grub**. The info command contains more details about GRUB.

Booting with GRUB

When you install Linux, you are typically given the option to configure the information needed to boot your computer (with one or more operating systems) into the default boot loader. With GRUB configured, when you boot your computer, the first thing you see after the BIOS loads is the GRUB boot screen (it says GRUB at the top and lists bootable partitions below it), do one of the following:

✦ **Default** — If you do nothing, the default operating system will boot automatically after a few seconds.

✦ **Select an operating system** — Use the up and down arrow keys to select any of the operating systems shown on the screen. Then press Enter to boot that operating system.

✦ **Edit the boot process** — If you want to change any of the options used during the boot process, use the arrow keys to select the operating system you want and type **e** to select it. Follow the next procedure to change your boot options temporarily.

If you want to change your boot options so that they take effect every time you boot your computer, see the section on permanently changing boot options. Changing those options involves editing the /boot/grub/grub.conf file.

Temporarily Changing Boot Options

From the GRUB boot screen, you can select to change or add boot options for the current boot session. First, select the operating system you want (using the arrow keys) and type **e** (as described earlier). You will see a graphical screen that contains information like the following:

```
GRUB version 0.94 (639K lower / 128768K upper memory)

root (hd0,0)
kernel /boot/vmlinuz-2.6.5-1.350 ro root=LABEL=/
initrd /boot/initrd-2.6.5-1.350.img

Use the↑and↓keys to select which entry is highlighted.
Press 'b' to boot, 'e' to edit the selected command in the
boot sequence, 'c' for a command-line, 'o' to open a new line
after ('O' for before) the selected line, 'd' to remove the
selected line, or escape to go back to the main menu.
```

There are three lines in the example of the GRUB editing screen that identify the boot process for the operating system you chose. The first line (beginning with `root`) shows that the entry for the GRUB boot loader is on the first partition of the first hard disk (`hd0,0`). GRUB represents the hard disk as `hd`, regardless of whether it is a SCSI, IDE, or other type of disk. You just count the drive number and partition number, starting from zero.

The second line of the example (beginning with `kernel`) identifies the boot image (`/boot/vmlinuz-2.6.5-1.350`) and several options. The options identify the partition as initially being loaded `ro` (read-only) and the location of the root file system on a partition with the label `LABEL=/`. The third line (starting with `initrd`) identifies the location of the initial RAM disk, which contains the minimum files and directories needed during the boot process.

If you are going to change any of the lines related to the boot process, you would probably change only the second line to add or remove boot options. Here is how you do that:

1. Position the cursor on the `kernel` line and type **e**.

2. Either add or remove options after the name of the boot image. You can use a minimal set of bash shell command-line editing features to edit the line. You can even use command completion (type part of a filename and press Tab to complete it). Here are a few options you may want to add or delete:

   - **Boot to a shell.** If you forgot your root password or if your boot process hangs, you can boot directly to a shell by adding `init=/bin/sh` to the boot line. (The file system is mounted read-only, so you can copy files out. You need to remount the file system with read/write permission to be able to change files.)

   - **Select a run level.** If you want to boot to a particular run level, you can add the word `linux`, followed by the number of the run level you want. For example, to have Fedora Linux boot to run level 3 (multiuser plus networking mode), add `linux 3` to the end of the boot line. You can also boot to single-user mode (1), multiuser mode (2), or X GUI mode (5). Level 3 is a good choice if your GUI is temporarily broken.

3. Press Enter to return to the editing screen.

4. Type **b** to boot the computer with the new options. The next time you boot your computer, the new options will not be saved. To add options so they are saved permanently, see the next section.

Permanently Changing Boot Options

You can change the options that take effect each time you boot your computer by changing the GRUB configuration file. In Fedora and other Linux systems, GRUB configuration centers around the `/boot/grub/grub.conf` file.

The `/boot/grub/grub.conf` file is created when you install Linux. Here's an example of that file for Fedora Core:

```
# grub.conf generated by anaconda
#
# Note that you do not have to rerun grub after making
# changes to this file
# NOTICE: You have a /boot partition.  This means that
#         all kernel and initrd paths are relative to /boot/, eg.
#         root (hd0,0)
#         kernel /vmlinuz-version ro root=/dev/hda6
#         initrd /initrd-version.img
#boot=/dev/hda
default=0
timeout=10
splashimage=(hd0,4)/grub/splash.xpm.gz
title Fedora Linux (2.6.5-1.350)
     root (hd0,4)
     kernel /vmlinuz-2.6.5-1.350 ro root=LABEL=/
     initrd /initrd-2.6.5-1.350.img
title Windows XP
     rootnoverify (hd0,0)
     chainloader +1
```

The default=0 line indicates that the first partition in this list (in this case Fedora Linux) will be the one that is booted by default. The line timeout=10 causes GRUB to pause for 10 seconds before booting the default partition. (That's how much time you have to press E if you want to edit the boot line, or to press arrow keys to select a different operating system to boot.)

The splashimage line looks in the fifth partition on the first disk (hd0,4) for the boot partition (in this case /dev/hda5, which is the /boot partition). GRUB loads splash.xpm.gz as the image on the splash screen (/boot/grub/splash.xpm.gz). The splash screen appears as the background of the boot screen.

Note   GRUB indicates disk partitions using the following notation: (hd0,0). The first number represents the disk, and the second is the partition on that disk. So, (hd0,1) is the second partition (1) on the first disk (0).

The two bootable partitions in this example are Fedora and Windows XP. The title lines for each of those partitions are followed by the name that appears on the boot screen to represent each partition.

For the Fedora Linux system, the root line indicates the location of the boot partition as the second partition on the first disk. So, to find the bootable kernel (vmlinuz-2.6.5-1.350) and the initrd initial RAM disk boot image that is loaded (initrd-2.6.5-1.350.img), GRUB looks in the root of hd0,4 (which is represented by /dev/hda5 and is eventually mounted as /boot). Other options on the kernel line set the partition as read-only initially (ro) and set the root file system to /dev/hda6.

For the Windows XP partition, the rootnoverify line indicates that GRUB should not try to mount the partition. In this case, Windows ME is on the first partition of the first hard disk (hd0,0) or /dev/hda1. Instead of mounting the partition and passing options to the new operating system, the `chainloader +1` indicates to hand control the booting of the operating system to another boot loader. The +1 indicates that the first sector of the partition is used as the boot loader.

Note Microsoft operating systems require that you use the `chainloader` to boot them from GRUB. This is because GRUB doesn't offer native support for WIndows operating sytems.

If you make any changes to the `/boot/grub/grub.conf` file, you *do not* need to load those changes. GRUB automatically picks up those changes when you reboot your computer. If you are accustomed to using the LILO boot loader, this may confuse you at first, as LILO requires you to rerun the `lilo` command for the changes to take effect.

Adding a New GRUB Boot Image

You may have different boot images for kernels that include different features. Here is the procedure for modifying the `grub.conf` file:

1. Copy the new image from the directory in which it was created (such as `/usr/src/linux-2.4/arch/i386/boot`) to the `/boot` directory. Name the file something that reflects its contents, such as `bz-2.4.21`. For example:

   ```
   # cp /usr/src/linux-2.6.5/arch/i386/boot/bzImage /boot/bz-2.6.5
   ```

2. Add several lines to the `/boot/grub/grub.conf` file so that the image can be started at boot time if it is selected. For example:

   ```
   title Fedora Linux (IPV6 build)
       root (hd0,4)
       kernel /bz-2.6.5 ro root=/dev/hda6
       initrd /initrd-2.6.5.img
   ```

3. Reboot your computer.

   When the GRUB boot screen appears, move your cursor to the title representing the new kernel and press Enter.

The advantage to this approach, as opposed to copying the new boot image over the old one, is that if the kernel fails to boot, you can always go back and restart the old kernel. When you feel confident that the new kernel is working properly, you can use it to replace the old kernel or perhaps just make the new kernel the default boot definition.

Booting Your Computer with LILO

LILO stands for LInux LOader. Like other boot loaders, LILO is a program that can stand outside the operating systems installed on the computer so you can choose which system to boot. It also lets you give special options that modify how the operating system is booted. On Slackware and other Linux systems, LILO is used instead of GRUB as the default boot loader.

If LILO is being used on your computer, it is installed in either the master boot record or the first sector of the root partition. The master boot record is read directly by the computer's BIOS. In general, if LILO is the only loader on your computer, install it in the master boot record. If there is another boot loader already in the master boot record, put LILO in the root partition.

Using LILO

When your computer boots with the Fedora version of LILO installed in the master boot record, a graphical Fedora screen appears, displaying the bootable partitions on the computer. Use the up and down arrow keys on your keyboard to select the one you want and press Enter. Otherwise, the default partition that you set at installation will boot after a few seconds.

If you want to add any special options when you boot, press Ctrl+X. You will see a text-based boot prompt that appears as follows:

```
boot:
```

LILO pauses for a few seconds and then automatically boots the first image from the default bootable partition. To see the bootable partitions again, quickly press Tab. You may see something similar to the following:

```
LILO boot:
linux linux-up dos
boot:
```

This example shows that three bootable partitions are on your computer, called linux, linux-up, and dos. The first two refer to two different boot images that can boot the Linux partition. The third refers to a bootable DOS partition (presumably containing a Windows operating system). The first bootable partition is loaded if you don't type anything after a few seconds. Or you could type the name of the other partition to have that boot instead.

If you have multiple boot images, press Shift, and LILO will ask you which image you want to boot. Available boot images and other options are defined in the /etc/lilo.conf file.

Setting Up the /etc/lilo.conf File

The /etc/lilo.conf file is where LILO gets the information it needs to find and start bootable partitions and images. By adding options to the /etc/lilo.conf file, you can change the behavior of the boot process. The following is an example of some of the contents of the /etc/lilo.conf file:

Note   Because LILO is not used by default in Fedora Core and some other Linux systems, there may be no /etc/lilo.conf file. However, the Fedora installation program creates an /etc/lilo.conf.anaconda file to suit your installation. If you change from GRUB to LILO, you can copy that file to /etc/lilo.conf.

```
prompt
timeout=50
default=linux
boot=/dev/hda
map=/boot/map
install=/boot/boot.b
message=/boot/message
linear

image=/boot/vmlinuz-2.6.5-1.327
        label=linux
        initrd=/boot/initrd-2.6.5-1.327.img
        read-only
        root=/dev/hda6
        append="root=LABEL=/"

other=/dev/hda1
        optional
        label=dos
```

With prompt on, the boot prompt appears when the system is booted without requiring that any keys are pressed. The timeout value, in this case 50 tenths of a second (5 seconds), defines how long to wait for keyboard input before booting the default boot image. The boot line indicates that the bootable partition is on the hard disk represented by /dev/hda (the first IDE hard disk).

The map line indicates the location of the map file (/boot/map, by default). The map file contains the name and locations of bootable kernel images. The install line indicates that the /boot/boot.b file is used as the new boot sector. The message line tells LILO to display the contents of the /boot/message file when booting (that contains the graphical Fedora boot screen that appears). The linear line causes linear sector addresses to be generated (instead of sector/head/cylinder addresses).

In the sample file, there are two bootable partitions. The first (image=/boot/vmlinuz-2.6.5-1.327) shows an image labeled linux. The root file system (/) for that image is on partition /dev/hda6. Read-only indicates that the file system is first mounted read-only, though it is probably mounted as read/write after a file system check. The inidrd line indicates the location of the initial RAM disk image used to start the system.

The second bootable partition, which is indicated by the word *other* in this example, is on the /dev/hda1 partition. Because it is a Windows XP system, it is labeled a DOS file system. The table line indicates the device that contains the partition.

Other bootable images are listed in this file, and you can add another boot image yourself (like one you create from reconfiguring your kernel as discussed in the next section) by installing the new image and changing lilo.conf.

After you change `lilo.conf`, you then must run the `lilo` command for the changes to take effect. You may have different boot images for kernels that include different features. Here is the procedure for modifying the `lilo.conf` file:

1. Copy the new image from the directory in which it was created (such as `/usr/src/linux-2.6/arch/i386/boot`) to the `/boot` directory. Name the file something that reflects its contents, such as `zImage-2.6.5-1`.

2. Add several lines to the `/etc/lilo.conf` file so that the image can be started at boot time if it is selected. For example:

```
image=/boot/zImage-2.6.5-1
label=new
```

3. Type the `lilo -t` command (as root user) to test that the changes were okay.

4. Type the `lilo` command (with no options) for the changes to be installed.

To boot from this new image, either select new from the graphical boot screen or type **new** and press Enter at the LILO boot prompt. If 5 seconds is too quick, increase the timeout value (such as 100 for 10 seconds).

Options that you can use in the `/etc/lilo.conf` file are divided into global options, per-image options, and kernel options. There is a lot of documentation available for LILO. For more details on any of the options described here or for other options, you can see the `lilo.conf` manual page (type `man lilo.conf`) or any of the documents in `/usr/share/doc/lilo*/doc`.

A few examples follow of global options that you can add to `/etc/lilo.conf`. Global options apply to LILO as a whole, instead of just to a particular boot image.

You can use the `default=label` option, where `label` is replaced by an image's label name, to indicate that a particular image be used as the default boot image. If that option is excluded, the first image listed in the `/etc/lilo.conf` file is used as the default. For example, to start the image labeled new by default, add the following line to `lilo.conf`:

```
default=new
```

Change the delay from 5 seconds to something greater if you want LILO to wait longer before starting the default image. This gives you more time to boot a different image. To change the value from 5 seconds (50) to 15 seconds (150), add the following line:

```
delay=150
```

You can change the message that appears before the LILO prompt by adding that message to a file and changing the message line. For example, you could create a `/boot/boot.message` file and add the following words to that file: `Choose linux, new, or dos`. To have that message appear before the boot prompt, add the following line to `/etc/lilo.conf`:

```
message=/boot/boot.message
```

All per-image options begin with either an `image=` line (indicating a Linux kernel) or `other=` (indicating some other kind of operating system, such as Windows XP). The per-image options apply to particular boot images rather than to all images (as global options do). Along with the image or other line is a `label=` line, which gives a name to that image. The name is what you would select at boot time to boot that image. Here are some of the options that you can add to each of those image definitions:

✦ `lock` — This enables automatic recording of `boot` command lines as the defaults for different boot options.

✦ `alias=name` — You can replace *name* with any name. That name becomes an alias for the image name defined in the label option.

✦ `password=password` — You can password-protect all images by adding a password option line and replacing *password* with your own password. The password would have to be entered to boot any of the images.

✦ `restricted` — This option is used with the password option. It indicates that a password should be used only if command-line options are given when trying to boot the image.

For Linux kernel images, there are specific options that you can use. These options let you deal with hardware issues that can't be autodetected, or provide information such as how the root file system is mounted. Here are some of kernel image-specific options:

✦ `append` — Add a string of letters and numbers to this option that need to be passed to the kernel. In particular, these can be parameters that need to be passed to better define the hard disk when some aspect of that disk can't be autodetected. For example: `append="hd=64,32,202"`

✦ `ramdisk` — Add the size of the RAM disk that you want to use so as to override the size of the RAM disk built into the kernel.

✦ `read-only` — Indicates to mount the root file system read-only. It is typically remounted read/write after the disk is checked.

✦ `read-write` — Indicates to mount the root file system read/write.

Changing Your Boot Loader

If you don't want to use the GRUB boot loader, or if you tried out LILO and want to switch back to GRUB, it's not hard to change to a different boot loader on Linux distributions that support both boot loaders. To switch your boot loader from GRUB to LILO, do the following:

1. Configure the /etc/lilo.conf file as described in the "Booting Your Computer with LILO" section. (On Fedora systems, you can use the contents of /etc/lilo.conf.anaconda to start.)

2. As root user from a Terminal window, type the following:

   ```
   # lilo
   ```

3. The new Master Boot Record is written, including the entries in /etc/lilo.conf.

4. Reboot your computer. You should see the LILO boot screen.

To change your boot loader from LILO to GRUB, do the following:

1. Configure the /boot/grub/grub.conf file as described in the "Booting Your Computer with GRUB" section.

2. You need to know the device on which you want to install GRUB. For example, to install GRUB on the master boot record of the first disk, type the following as root user from a Terminal window:

   ```
   # grub-install /dev/hda
   ```

   The new Master Boot Record is written to boot with the GRUB boot loader.

3. Reboot your computer. You should see the GRUB boot screen.

Configuring Networking

If you are connecting your computer to an Ethernet LAN that has a DHCP server available, you probably don't need to do anything to start up automatically on your LAN and probably be connected to the Internet. However, if there is no DHCP server on your LAN and you have to configure your TCP/IP connection manually, here is the information you will probably be prompted for during Linux installation:

✦ **IP Address**—If you set your own IP address, this is the four-part, dot-separated number that represents your computer to the network. How IP addresses are formed and how you choose them is more than can be said in a few sentences (see Chapter 5 for a more complete description). An example of a private IP address is 192.168.0.1.

✦ **Netmask**—The netmask is used to determine what part of an IP address represents the network and what part represents a particular host computer. An example of a netmask for a Class C network is 255.255.255.0. Applying this netmask to an IP address of 192.168.0.1, for example, the network address would be 192.168.0 and the host address 1. Because 0 and 255 can't be assigned to a particular host, that leaves valid host numbers between 1 and 254 available for this local network.

✦ **Activate on boot** — Some Linux install procedures ask you to indicate if you want the network to start at boot time (you probably do if you have a LAN).

✦ **Set the hostname** — This is the name identifying your computer within your domain. For example, if your computer were named "baskets" in the `handson history.com` domain, your full hostname may be `baskets.handsonhistory.com`. You can either set the domain name yourself (manually) or have it assigned automatically, if that information is being assigned by a DHCP server (automatically via DHCP).

✦ **Gateway** — This is the IP number of the computer that acts as a gateway to networks outside your LAN. This typically represents a host computer or router that routes packets between your LAN and the Internet.

✦ **Primary DNS** — This is the IP address of the host that translates computer names you request into IP addresses. It is referred to as a Domain Name System (DNS) server. You may also have Secondary and Tertiary name servers in case the first one can't be reached. (Most ISPs will give you two DNS server addresses.)

Configuring Other Administrative Features

Depending on which Linux install you are using, there are other types of information you will be asked to enter. These might involve:

✦ **Firewall** — Most Linux distributions these days use iptables to configure firewalls. Older Linux systems use ipchains. When you configure a default firewall, you typically choose which ports will be open to outside connections on your system (although there are many other things a firewall can be configured to do as well). The iptables firewall facility is described in Chapter 17 when you configure a router/firewall.

✦ **Languages** — While Linux itself doesn't include support for lots of different languages, some Linux distributions (such as Fedora) and desktop environments (such as KDE) offer support for many different languages. Nearly all Linux distributions let you configure language-specific keyboards.

✦ **Root password and additional user** — Every Linux system that uses passwords will have you add at least the root user's password when you install Linux. Some distributions require that you add at least one additional non-root user as well.

Besides the features just mentioned, every distribution needs to have some initial configuration done before you have a fully functional Linux system. See Chapter 4 for information on basic administrative tasks for Linux.

Installing from the Linux Bible DVD or CD

With the knowledge you've gained in this chapter, you're ready to select a Linux distribution to install. Read the descriptions of Linux distributions in the other chapters in Part II of this book. Each chapter includes an icon box that tells you if the distribution described there is on the DVD or CD or, if it isn't, where you can get it.

If you need more information about the DVD or CD, Appendix A describes the contents of those media. It also tells you which Linux distributions can be booted directly from the DVD or CD and which have to be burned to CD before you can boot or install the distribution.

Summary

While every Linux distribution includes a different installation method, there are many common activities you need to do, regardless of which Linux system you install. For every Linux system, you need to deal with issues of disk partitioning, network configuration, and boot loaders.

Linux Bible 2005 Edition includes a DVD and a CD with several different Linux systems you can install. If you prefer, you can instead download and burn your own CDs or DVDs to install Linux. If you go the route of burning your own CDs, this chapter helps you find Linux distributions you can download and describes tools you can use to verify their contents.

✦   ✦   ✦

CHAPTER

8

Running Fedora Core and Red Hat Enterprise Linux

◆ ◆ ◆ ◆

In This Chapter

Digging into
Fedora Core

Going forward with
Fedora Core

Installing Fedora
Core

◆ ◆ ◆ ◆

In September 2003, the world's leading Linux distribution, Red Hat Linux, disappeared.

Red Hat Inc., the company that created Red Hat Linux, divided its development efforts in two directions: the Fedora Project, which produces the Fedora Core operating system, and Red Hat Enterprise Linux. The split came from trying to better serve two diverse groups with one operating system. Wanting to make some money on the value that Red Hat Inc. adds to Linux might have had something to do with it as well.

On the
DVD-ROM

Fedora Core 3 is included on the DVD that comes with this book. You can install the entire distribution from this DVD, using descriptions in Appendix A and the "Installing Fedora Core" section later in this chapter. If you don't have a DVD drive, you can obtain the same software on four CDs by downloading them from the Internet (http://fedora. redhat.com/download) and burning them to CD as described in Appendix A.

Fedora Core and Red Hat Enterprise Linux both come from a base of code that stems from the Red Hat Linux legacy. Going forward, the two distributions have different goals and audiences and may drift farther apart over time.

Fedora Core is intended to include the latest Linux technology and be a proving ground for features slated to go into Red Hat Enterprise Linux products. It is a freely distributed operating system for the Linux community.

Although it is sponsored and directed by Red Hat Inc., the Fedora Project encourages community involvement. The latest Fedora Core will include many more features than Red Hat Enterprise Linux, but those features have less guarantee of stability and no guarantee of support.

Note   Fedora Core follows the legacy of Red Hat Linux. The final version of Red Hat Linux was version 9. Fedora Core 1 and Red Hat Enterprise Linux 3 followed Red Hat Linux 9.

Red Hat Enterprise Linux (RHEL), which is actually represented by multiple products for desktop, server, and workstation computer systems, is licensed commercially. Red Hat puts all its documentation, training, and support effort behind RHEL, which it sells to customers in the form of subscriptions. The intent is to have RHEL be a rock-solid Linux system that can be deployed across entire enterprises.

Despite the confusion it unleashed by dumping its flagship Red Hat Linux line and fears by some that Red Hat might become another Microsoft, Red Hat is still the dominant player when it comes to commercial Linux products. Many people have been happy to upgrade their critical Linux systems to Red Hat Enterprise Linux products.

To its credit, Red Hat has managed to become a profitable venture while making some remarkable contributions to the open source effort. Releasing its installer (Anaconda) and software packaging tools (RPM Package Management) under the GNU Public License (GPL), has enabled other Linux distributions to use and enhance those features. Within Red Hat Linux and now Fedora Core, Red Hat Inc. has worked hard to include only software that could be freely distributed (removing most software with patent and copyright issues).

Although Fedora is more of a testing facility than a guaranteed enterprise-quality operating system, for the purposes of this book, Fedora Core is a great way to evaluate and use technology that is in all Linux distributions from Red Hat. Features in Fedora Core 3 are in Red Hat Enterprise Linux 4. Both distributions are discussed in this chapter, so you can determine which distribution is right for you.

Digging into Features

There are many opinions on why Red Hat Linux and other distributions from Red Hat Inc. have been so popular. The following sections describe some features of Red Hat Linux distributions that are commonly believed to have led to its success and that add to the popularity of Fedora Core and Red Hat Enterprise Linux distributions.

Red Hat Installer (Anaconda)

When many Linux distributions still had you struggling from the command line to get the distribution installed, Red Hat created its own installer called Anaconda. Anaconda includes both graphical and text-based procedures for installing Linux. When you're done installing Red Hat Linux, you have the following:

✦ A set of software packages installed that suits how you want to use your computer (as a desktop, workstation, server, or some custom configuration).

✦ Standard information, such as date, time, time zone, and language set.

✦ A configured mouse, keyboard, video card, and monitor.

✦ An appropriately partitioned hard disk.

✦ A configured network card and firewall, to immediately connect to a LAN.

✦ A configured boot loader, to define how Linux starts up.

Besides being fairly intuitive to use, Anaconda is loaded with features to make it easy to manage the installation of many Red Hat systems. For example, these power features are built into the Anaconda installer:

✦ **Network installs** — After booting the install process, the actual Fedora or RHEL distribution can be on a network server that is accessible via a Web server (http), FTP server (ftp), or UNIX file server (NFS).

✦ **Kickstart installs** — It's not so bad to sit there and click through the answers to run the installation of one Fedora Core system, but if you're doing dozens or hundreds of installs (especially on similar computers), automating that task can be a major time-saver. Anaconda supports kickstart installs, for which you use a preconfigured kickstart file to answer the questions that come up during a Red Hat installation. If you answer all the questions in the file, you can launch the installation and have it run from start to finish without you in attendance.

✦ **Upgrades** — With an existing Fedora system installed, Anaconda enables you to easily upgrade to a newer Fedora system. A lot of nice features for saving backups of configuration files and logging the upgrade activities are built into that process. During an upgrade, Anaconda takes into consideration any dependency issues, so the upgraded software packages will have all the libraries and commands that the features in those packages need.

You'll find a detailed description of installing Fedora using the Anaconda installer at the end of this chapter.

RPM Package Management

All Red Hat Linux distributions use the RPM Package Management (RPM) software packaging format to store and maintain software that the distributions use. Fedora Core and RHEL contain a set of tools for installing, upgrading, maintaining, and querying software packages in RPM format. Essentially, the RPM software packages that are installed are maintained in a database, so you can list the contents of packages, view descriptions, and even check for tampering of the files in those packages.

Using RPM, add-on software can also be easily included in and maintained for Fedora systems. So users who once had to know how to deal with tarballs and makefiles to compile their own software can now simply install an RPM package to get the features they want. With other Linux distributions (such as SUSE and Mandrake) also using RPM packaging, your RPM tool skills can help you manage software on those distributions as well.

Because of the popularity of Red Hat Linux systems, lots of software repositories and third-party software management tools have been created to further automate and simplify handling software in Red Hat systems. Tools such as yum (www.linux. duke.edu/projects/yum) and apt4rpm (http://apt4rpm.sourceforge.net) are available for updating selected software. AutoRPM (www.autorpm.org) was created to automatically get RPM updates from Red Hat and install them on a single system or a cluster of machines.

Kudzu Hardware Detection

Early Linux systems required that someone installing Linux know a lot about their hardware and the Linux drivers needed for that hardware to work. The kudzu feature was created by Red Hat to detect and configure a lot of computer hardware automatically. This feature is a great boost to those who don't want to worry about finding and selecting the drivers needed for their computer hardware.

Kudzu runs during your initial Red Hat installation to detect your system's hardware. It also runs each time you start your Fedora or RHEL system so that if you add or remove hardware and restart the system, it can try to determine what the hardware is and offer you the opportunity to configure it or remove the driver, as appropriate.

 Note   The highly touted hardware detection done by the KNOPPIX bootable Linux distribution is based on the kudzu libraries from Red Hat Inc.

Red Hat Desktop Look-and-Feel

To add a level of consistency to the desktops on its Linux systems, Red Hat created a look-and-feel that is pretty much the same for both GNOME and KDE. Of course there are some differences in color and logos, but a user can expect to find menus, panels, workspaces, and other desktop features in Fedora Core and RHEL systems to be very similar.

System Configuration Tools

Red Hat created a set of simplified, graphical tools for configuring and administering many basic administrative features in Red Hat systems. Using these tools, you can add printers, configure your network, add users, set up your sound card, and tune up your video card, to name a few of the features they cover.

Red Hat's graphical configuration tools (which are described in Chapter 4) can be launched from the System Tools or Systems Settings menu or from the command line. Recently, the beginnings of these configuration tools' command names changed from `redhat-config` to `system-config`. For example, the tool to configure your network in Fedora is now called `system-config-network` (instead of `redhat-config-network`).

Going Forward with Fedora Core

With the original Red Hat Linux, you could have the exact same Linux system for free (to run in your home or small business) that was being used in large-scale enterprise deployments. For just a few dollars, you could add official Red Hat support for that system, which included official security patches and upgrade paths for the future.

Today, with the different free (Fedora Core) and subscription-based (RHEL) Linuxes from Red Hat, some of the same basic advantages hold true—if you are a bit more adventurous. Because Red Hat Linux is such a successful operating system, many who have developed skills in using and deploying Red Hat Linux have rallied to support Fedora in areas where Red Hat Inc. has bowed out. The following sections explore some of those support efforts.

Fedora Legacy Project

In April 2004, Red Hat Inc. officially ended support for Red Hat Linux 9, the last release of Red Hat Linux systems. That meant that Red Hat would no longer provide errata packages or gather bug reports for any Red Hat Linux systems. From Red Hat's perspective, you either had to upgrade to RHEL or go on your own with Fedora. The Fedora Legacy Project (`www.fedoralegacy.org`) came up with a third possibility: extend the lives of select Red Hat Linux systems.

Fedora Legacy Project's charter is to offer software patches for select Red Hat Linux and Fedora Core systems beyond the end of life set by Red Hat Inc. These critical fixes and security patches are necessary for an operating system to remain stable for at least two to three years. Without this support, companies and consultants who want to use Fedora Core to sell with their hardware or software products can't expect to have a stable OS to rely on for more than a few months.

As of this writing, Red Hat Linux 7.2, 7.3, 8, and 9 releases all have Fedora Legacy Project software repositories from which you can download available critical software updates. By following a few simple steps from the Fedora Legacy download page (www.fedoralegacy.org/download), you can use yum or apt tools to configure your system to automatically download and install selected packages.

Fedora Legacy Project's Web site provides a lot of information, from a mailing list and IRC channel you can join to overview material you can read about the project.

Fedora Software Repositories

A ton of open source software is available in the world that is not included in Fedora Core. To coordinate the gathering and testing of open source, third-party software, the Fedora Extras Project (www.fedora.us) was formed by people outside Red Hat Inc. (with Red Hat's blessing).

Unlike Fedora Legacy repositories, which consist of updates to software already in the Fedora distribution, the Fedora Extras Project encourages people to build their software into RPM packages that can easily be installed in Fedora Core and Red Hat Linux systems. Fedora Extras provides guidelines for producing these packages and then performs quality-assurance testing and security verification on them before adding them to the Fedora tree for anyone to download and use. To find sites that have packages included in Fedora Extras, check out the list of Fedora Extras mirror sites (www.fedora.us/wiki/FedoraMirrorList).

The Fedora Channels page (www.fedora.us/wiki/FedoraChannels) also includes software channels available for Fedora (and other Red Hat Linux systems).

Although there is great value in having a central organization coordinating and testing the software packages available for Fedora, the particular package you might want may not be available through Fedora Extras for one reason or another. Two other places you can check for RPM packages of third-party software available to use with Fedora are:

✦ **Fedora Tracker (**www.fedoratracker.org**)** — Use this site to search known repositories of Fedora third-party software for the packages you are interested in. You can search by package name, description, or Fedora release. The site offers clear descriptions of the different software packages available (more than 18,000 packages at the time of this writing, and many more are sure to be available by the time you read this). This site is not officially associated with the Fedora Project.

✦ **RPM Livna.org (**http://rpm.livna.org**)** — When Fedora.us merged with Red Hat Inc. to form the Fedora Project, some third-party software maintained by Fedora.us didn't meet Red Hat's standards for distribution. In particular, there are licensing and patent issues surrounding some multimedia players and codecs. Many of these contentious packages have been moved to repositories associated with the RPM Livna.org site. Most people will use rpm.livna.org in tandem with the Fedora.us repository to get a full range of Fedora Core software.

Caution   The whole issue of software patents is a sticky one. The FedoraTracker.org site does a good job of warning you when software you turn up in searches may violate DCMA restrictions in the U.S. or electronic patents. You should know that installing software that violates legitimate patents can result in the owners of those patents seeking compensation.

Forums and Mailing Lists

Since Fedora came into existence, many individuals and organizations have rallied to support Fedora going forward. If you want to get into the flow of the Fedora community, I recommend starting with the Fedora Project's own mailing lists. You can choose the Fedora mailing list that interests you from the Red Hat Mailing Lists page (`http://redhat.com/mailman/listinfo`). Start with the fedora-list or fedora-announce-list mailing list.

Many other Fedora resources are also available on the Web, and Appendix B includes a list of many of them.

Listening to the People at Red Hat

Red Hat sets out the charter for the Fedora Project on its home page (`http://fedora.redhat.com`):

> *The Fedora Project is a Red-Hat-sponsored and community-supported open-source project. It is also a proving ground for new technology that may eventually make its way into Red Hat products. It is not a supported product of Red Hat Inc.*

What that means exactly is still being sorted out more than a year after the launching of the Fedora Project. What it has meant so far has been three versions of Fedora Core that have brought in development of different technologies than were included in Red Hat Enterprise Linux distributions.

Red Hat has stuck to its plan to release Fedora two to three times per year. So far, releases have stayed closer to the two-per-year pace average that was the standard for producing Red Hat Linux releases. It has also stuck to its promise to include Fedora technology in its commercial products:

> *Each new release of our supported products will be based in part on a recent release of Fedora Core.*

Software in Red Hat Enterprise Linux 3 matched almost exactly the same packages that were in Fedora Core 1. The same is expected to be true with Fedora Core 3 software when Red Hat completes Red Hat Enterprise Linux 4. As for including the Fedora community in Fedora development, Red Hat states on the Fedora home page:

> *Red Hat will retain editorial control over Fedora Core — but will explicitly include external developers in the process of making technical decisions that align with our project objectives. This is an evolutionary, not revolutionary change; by depending on and contributing to Open Source software since the inception of Red Hat Linux, Red Hat has always shared control over the software with external developers. Red Hat will now more explicitly share control for packaging with external developers in our new project: The Fedora Project.*

Although there is no formal procedure in place as of this writing, Red Hat has stated that it expects to give people outside Red Hat more substantial roles in Fedora planning and development process based on how well they contribute to the community:

For more information on the objectives of the Fedora Project, go to `http://fedora.redhat.com/about/objectives.html`.

Listening to the Red Hat Community

As you might guess, the community of people who have hitched their wagons to the Red Hat train had some concerns about the Fedora/RHEL split. Some of the biggest concerns of the community are summed up by the following questions:

✦ **Is Fedora a real Linux distribution?** Fedora has been set up as a project for shaking bugs out of software before that software goes into Red Hat's commercial Linux products. Red Hat has gone to great lengths to make sure people know that Red Hat is not guaranteeing or supporting Fedora. If that's the case, why should Red Hat care if Fedora is a fully integrated distribution once the parts it needs are close enough to start putting into RHEL?

✦ **Who controls Fedora?** Right now, Red Hat is calling all the shots when it comes to features, schedules, and other critical parts of Fedora. Although Red Hat claims it will allow more community involvement in critical parts of the project, so far it has not. Why should the community support a Linux system over which it has no control?

The funny thing is that despite the confusing and frustrating aspects of the transition, many, many people in the open source community are still supporting the Fedora effort. I think that really is an indication of how well-regarded Red Hat's contributions to open source have been. The company is still trusted (somewhat) to offer some real value to the open source community as it also pursues its own commercial agenda.

That said, I'll end this section with an excellent and (I believe) rather realistic reflection of how the transition to Fedora looked to the open source community. The following is a post to the fedora-devel-list mailing list that includes a fictitious IRC session among the open source community, Fedora.us, and Red Hat Inc. by Konstantin Ryabitsev. (Go here for the full post: `http://lwn.net/Articles/83360`.)

```
Let me, err, relay how things are looking from outside of RH in the format
everyone will understand...

--- BEGIN IRC LOG ---
    <rh_pr> We are announcing Red Hat Project! A community-based
            distribution!
<oss_crowd> rh_pr: Neat.
   <rh_dev> rh_pr: Uh... I'm not ready.
          * rh_pr is away: promoting rhel
<oss_crowd> rh_dev: what do we do?
   <rh_dev> oss_crowd: I'm not sure.
 <rh_legal> rh_dev: don't do anything until I say it's ok.
<oss_crowd> rh_dev: what can we do to help with Red Hat Project?
   <rh_dev> oss_crowd: uh... file bugs and help test things.
<oss_crowd> rh_dev: didn't we always do that?
 <rh_sales> hey, all, if you really want a stable system, don't use
            fedora project. It will eat your brane. Buy RHEL instead.
   <rh_dev> rh_sales: stfu
        --- rh_pr removes voice from rh_sales
<fedora_us> hey, all, check out our neat community-driven system for
            red hat development
<oss_crowd> fedora_us: ooooh!
    <rh_pr> fedora_us: I like your name
        --- fedora_rh joined the channel
 <rh_legal> much better
    <rh_pr> We are announcing Fedora Project! A community-driven
            distribution!
<oss_crowd> rh_pr: Neat!
          * fedora_rh waves
<fedora_us> I'm not dead yet.
<fedora_rh> fedora_us: don't confuse things.
<fedora_us> fedora_rh: does this mean we're merging?
<fedora_rh> fedora_us: maybe
 <rh_legal> fedora_rh: don't do anything until I say it's ok.
        --- fedora_us joined #limbo
<oss_crowd> fedora_rh: so, what can we do to help?
<fedora_rh> oss_crowd: uh... file bugs and help test things.
<oss_crowd> sigh... didn't we always do that?
<fedora_rh> oss_crowd: I know, let's all go in the circle and say our
            names.
          * oss_crowd goes in the circle and says their names. This
            lasts several months.
```

```
<fedora_rh> So, there will be the following features in the next
            release of Fedora Core.
<oss_crowd> Uh... Hold on. Who gets to decide?
 <rh_sales> We do. That stuff will be neato for RHEL-4.
<oss_crowd> MMkay, then. When do _we_ get to suggest things?
<fedora_rh> oss_crowd: feel free to talk among yourselves.
          * oss_crowd talks among themselves about new features.
<fedora_rh> btw, feature X will be disabled in the release.
          * oss_crowd glares at fedora_rh
<oss_crowd> fedora_rh: nice of you to tell us while we were sitting
            here talking.
   <rh_dev> oss_crowd: sorry, it's just not happening.
<oss_crowd> rh_dev: when do we get to decide what's happening?
   <rh_dev> oss_crowd: Dunno, I'll ask rh_legal
 <rh_legal> rh_dev: ugh, /msg me
 <rh_sales> rh_dev: let's not do anything rash here.
          * fedora_us gets tired of sitting in #limbo
<oss_crowd> fedora_rh: I want to see more of the "community" part of
            the whole "community-based" thing
<oss_crowd> rh_dev: how about at least a publicly accessible CVS/SVN
            tree?
   <rh_dev> oss_crowd: Yeah, that would be cool.
<oss_crowd> rh_dev: finally, some movement. When is that going to be
            up?
          * rh_dev is away: talking to rh_legal
          * oss_crowd tries to occupy themselves and do things like
            fedoranews and fedorapeople.
<oss_crowd> Uh... ping?
<fedora_uh> oss_crowd: what's up?
<oss_crowd> fedora_rh: We're feeling kinda useless. What exactly is our
            role, again?
<fedora_rh> oss_crowd: well, it would be really helpful if you could
            test some things and file the bugs.
<oss_crowd> fedora_rh: ugh. We ALWAYS did that.
                  .
                  .
                  .
--- END IRC LOG ---
```

Even after the third release of Fedora Core, there is still no certainty about its future.

Installing Fedora Core

The Linux operating system Fedora Core, sponsored by Red Hat, is included on this book's DVD. The rest of this chapter leads you through its installation.

Before you install Fedora on your computer, ensure that your computer hardware supports it. You should also choose a method of installing Fedora Core. Those topics are discussed in the following sections.

Choosing Computer Hardware

Choosing your computer hardware may not really be a choice. You may just have an old PC lying around on which you want to try Fedora. Or you may have a killer workstation with some extra disk space and want to try Fedora out on a separate partition or whole disk. To install the PC version of Fedora (the version on the accompanying DVD) successfully, the computer must have the following:

✦ **Processor** — The Pentium-class PC needs to be at least 200 MHz for text mode and 400 MHz Pentium II for GUI.

✦ **RAM** — You need at least 64MB of RAM to install Fedora. If you are running in graphical mode, you need at least 192MB. The recommended RAM for graphical mode is 256MB.

✦ **DVD or CD drive** — You need to be able to boot up the installation process from a DVD or CD (the latter requires that you get Fedora Core installation CDs as described at `http://fedora.redhat.com/download`). If you can't boot from a DVD or CD, there are ways to start the installation from a hard disk or using a PXE install, as the following section, "Choosing an Installation Method," explains.

✦ **Hard disk** — Following is the required minimum disk space for five different installations. In each case, you will want to have more disk space than the minimums listed here:

> **Personal Desktop** — 1.9GB
>
> **Workstation** — 2.4GB
>
> **Server** — 870MB
>
> **Everything** (Custom) — 5.3GB
>
> **Minimum** (Custom) — 520MB

✦ **Keyboard and monitor** — You need a keyboard and monitor at least during installation. (You can operate Fedora quite well over a LAN using either a shell interface from a network login or an X terminal.)

Although not included with this book, Fedora Linux versions are available for the AMD64 architecture. Red Hat Enterprise Linux versions (which you have to purchase from Red Hat Inc.) are available for other hardware, such as Intel Itanium, IBM PowerPC, and IBM mainframe. The Fedora distribution that comes with this book and the installation procedures presented here are specific to PCs.

Most of the software described in this book will work the same in any of those hardware environments. (Check out `http://redhat.com/mirrors` for sites that offer Fedora Linux for different computer hardware architectures.)

Note The list of hardware supported by previous versions of Red Hat Linux is available on the Internet at `www.redhat.com/hardware`.

To begin installing Fedora Core, you also need to have the *Linux Bible 2005 Edition* DVD that comes with this book (or a set of installation CDs that you obtain yourself), and you must either be dedicating your entire hard disk (or an added hard disk) to Linux, have a preconfigured Linux partition, or have sufficient free space on your hard disk outside any existing Windows partition.

Note If you are not dedicating your whole hard disk to Fedora Core and you don't under-stand partitioning, refer to Chapter 7, which describes how to set up partitioning to allow multiple computer operating systems to coexist on the same hard drive.

Choosing an Installation Method

You can also install Fedora from any of several different types of media. You can still start the install process by booting the installation DVD. After booting the install process, however, you can type **linux askmethod** at the boot prompt, which offers you the choice of installing Fedora from the following locations:

✦ **Local CD-ROM** — This is the most common method of installing Fedora Core and the one you get by typing **linux** and pressing Enter from the Fedora instal-lation boot prompt. Use this section for both DVD and CD installs. (You may need to change the BIOS if the DVD or CD doesn't boot.) All packages needed to complete the installation are on the DVD that comes with this book.

✦ **HTTP** — Lets you install from a Web page address (http://).

✦ **FTP** — Lets you install from an FTP site (ftp://).

✦ **NFS image** — Allows you to install from any shared directory on another com-puter on your network using the Network File System (NFS) facility.

✦ **Hard drive** — If you can place a copy of the Fedora Linux distribution on your hard drive, you can install it from there. (The distribution should be on a hard drive partition to which you are *not* installing.)

Choosing Different Install Modes

Although most computers enable you to install Fedora in the default mode (graphical), there may be times when your video card does not support that mode. Also, although the install process detects most computer hardware, there may be times when your hard disk, Ethernet card, or other critical piece of hardware cannot be detected and will require you to enter special information at boot time.

The following is a list of commands that you could type at the installation boot prompt to change installation modes to start the Fedora Core install process. You would typically try these modes only if the default mode failed (that is, if the screen was garbled or installation failed at some point). For a list of other supported modes, refer to the /usr/share/doc/anaconda*/ command-line.txt file or press F2 to see short descriptions of some of these types.

Command	Description
linux text	Runs installation in a text-based mode. Do this if installation doesn't seem to recognize your graphics card.
linux lowres	Runs installation in 640×480 screen resolution for graphics cards that can't support the higher resolution.
linux nofb	Turns off frame buffer.
linux noprobe	Installation won't probe to determine your hardware; you need to load any special drivers that might be needed to install it. Normally, installation auto-probes to determine what hardware you have on your computer.
linux mediacheck	Check your DVD or CDs before installing. Because media checking is done next in the normal installation process, do this only to test the media on a computer you are not installing on.
linux rescue	Boots from CD, mounts your hard disk, and lets you access useful utilities to correct problems that are preventing your Linux system from operating properly. (Not really an installation mode.)
linux expert	Bypasses probing so you can choose your mouse, video memory, and other values that would otherwise be chosen for you. Use if you believe that the installation process is not properly auto-probing your hardware.
linux askmethod	Has the installation process ask where to install from (local CD, NFS image, FTP, HTTP, or hard disk).
linux updates	To install from an update disk.

You can add other options to the linux boot command to identify particular hardware that is not being detected properly. For example, to specify the number of cylinders, heads, and sectors for your hard disk (if you believe the boot process is not detecting these values properly), you could pass the information to the kernel as follows: linux hd=720,32,64. In this example, the kernel is told that the hard disk has 720 cylinders, 32 heads, and 64 sectors. You can find this information in the documentation that comes with your hard disk (or stamped on the hard disk itself on a sticker near the serial number).

There are also other boot options you can add to the installation prompt to instruct the installation boot prompt how to start the installation. Many of these options are described in Chapter 11.

Installing Without a Bootable CD Drive

Unlike earlier Fedora and Red Hat Linux versions, Fedora Core 3 doesn't support floppy disk boot images because the Linux 2.6 kernel is too large to fit on a floppy disk. So if you don't have a bootable CD or DVD drive, you will need to start the install process from some other medium such as a PXE server or hard drive.

Installing on Multiple Computers

If you're installing Fedora on many computers with similar configurations, you can save yourself some time by using the kickstart installation, which enables you to create a set of answers to the questions Fedora Core asks you during installation.

Installation Guides

No specific installation guide is provided with the Fedora Project. However, the Red Hat Linux Installation Guide is available from any Red Hat FTP site (such as `ftp.redhat.com`). The location on the `ftp.redhat.com` server of the Red Hat Linux 9 Installation Guide is

```
pub/redhat/linux/9/en/doc/RH-DOCS/rhl-ig-x86-en-9/index.html
```

Another document you may find useful before installing is the Fedora Linux Reference Guide (also listed in the `RH-DOCS` directory, as `rhl-rg-en-9.0`). You'll need to check for yourself to find out whether the Fedora Project eventually updates the reference guides for Fedora Core.

Choosing to Install or Upgrade

Are you doing a new install or an upgrade? If you are upgrading an existing Red Hat Linux or Fedora system to the latest version, the installation process will try to leave your data files and configuration files intact as much as possible. This type of installation takes longer than a new install. A new install simply erases all data on the Linux partitions (or whole hard disk) that you choose.

If you are upgrading an existing Fedora Linux system to this release, you should consider first removing any unwanted packages from your old Fedora Linux system. The fewer to be checked during an upgrade, the faster the upgrade installation (and the less space used).

Note   You can upgrade to Fedora Core 3 from previous Fedora or Red Hat Linux systems (such as Red Hat Linux 8 or 9). You cannot upgrade to Fedora Core 2 from a Red Hat Enterprise Linux system.

To upgrade, you must have at least a Linux 2.0 kernel installed. With an upgrade, all of your configuration files are saved as `filename.rpmsave` (for example, the hosts file is saved as `hosts.rpmsave`). The locations of those files, as well as other upgrade information, is written to `/tmp/upgrade.log`. The upgrade installs the new kernel, any changed software packages, and any packages that the installed packages depend on being there. Your data files and configuration information should remain intact. By clicking the Customize box, you can choose which packages to upgrade.

Caution   If you are installing a dual-boot system that includes a Windows operating system, install the Windows system first and the Fedora Core system afterward. Some Windows systems blow away the Master Boot Record (MBR), making the Fedora Core partition inaccessible.

If, when installing Windows or Fedora, you find that the other operating system is no longer available on your boot screen, don't panic and don't immediately reinstall. You can usually recover from the problem by booting with the Fedora Linux emergency boot disk and then using either the `grub-install` or `lilo` command to reinsert the proper MBR. If you are uncomfortable working in emergency mode, seek out an expert to help you.

Red Hat provides a description of how to configure a dual-boot system at `www.redhat.com/docs/manuals/linux/RHL-9-Manual/install-guide/ch-x86-dualboot.html`.

Beginning the Installation

Once you have selected the right type of installation for your needs, you can begin the installation procedure. Throughout most of the procedure, you can click Back to make changes to earlier screens. However, once you are warned that packages are about to be written to hard disk, there's no turning back. Most items that you configure can be changed after Fedora is installed.

Caution   It is quite possible that your entire hard disk is devoted to a Windows 95, 98, 2000, ME, NT, or XP operating system, and you may want to keep much of that information after Fedora Core is installed. Personal Desktop, Workstation, and Custom install classes retain existing partitions (by default), but they don't let you take space from existing DOS partitions without destroying them. Some good commercial products are available that you can use to resize your hard disk. In particular, I recommend Partition Magic (`www.partitionmagic.com/partitionmagic`).

Ready to install? Here's what to do:

1. **Insert the DVD into the DVD drive.** (If you are not able to boot from the DVD, obtain an installation CD set as described earlier in this chapter and continue with this procedure by inserting the first CD into the drive.)

2. **Start your computer.** If you see the Fedora installation screen, continue to the next step.

Tip   If you don't see the installation screen, your DVD or CD-ROM drive may not be bootable. You may be able to make the drive bootable, though. Here's how: Restart the computer. Immediately, you should see a message telling you how to go into setup, such as by pressing the F1, F2, or Del key. Enter setup and look for an option such as Boot Options or Boot From. If the value is `A: First, Then C:`, change it to `CD-ROM First, Then C:` or something similar. Save the changes and try to install again.

3. **Boot the install procedure.** At the boot prompt, press Enter to start the install in graphical mode. If your computer won't let you install in graphical mode (16-bit color, 800×600 resolution, framebuffer), refer to the "Choosing Different Install Modes" sidebar.

4. **Media check.** If you're asked to check your installation media, press Enter. If the DVD is damaged, this step saves you the trouble of getting deep into the install and then failing. Once the DVD is checked, select Skip to continue.

5. **Continue.** When the welcome screen appears, click Release Notes to see information about this version of Fedora Linux. Click Next when you're ready to continue.

6. **Choose an installation language.** Move the arrow keys to the language you want and then select Next. (Later, you will be able to add additional languages.)

7. **Choose a keyboard.** Some layouts enable dead keys (on by default). Dead keys enable you to use characters with special markings (such as circumflexes and umlauts).

8. **Choose install type.** Select either Install Fedora Core for a new install or Upgrade an Existing Installation to upgrade an existing version of Fedora.

9. **Select type for new install.** Choose one of the following types (also referred to as classes):

   • **Personal Desktop** — Installs software appropriate for a home or office personal computer or laptop computer. This includes the GNOME desktop (no KDE) and various desktop-related tools (word processors, Internet tools, and so on). Server tools, software development tools, and many system administration tools are not installed.

   • **Workstation** — Similar to a Personal Desktop installation but adds tools for system administration and software development. (Server software is not installed.)

Any Linux partitions or free space on your hard disk(s) will be assigned to the new installation with the Personal Desktop or Workstation types of installation. Any Windows partitions (VFAT or FAT32 file system types) will not be touched by this install. After installation, you will be able to boot Linux or Windows. If there is no free space outside your Windows partition, you must run Partition Magic, the parted utility, the FIPS program (described later) or other disk-resizing software before proceeding, or you will lose your Windows installation.

   • **Server** — Server installs the software packages that you would typically need for a Linux server (in particular, Web server, file server, and print server). It does not include many other server types (DHCP, mail, DNS, FTP, SQL, or news servers). The default server install does not include a GUI (so you'd better know how to use the shell). This install type also erases all hard disks and assigns them to Linux by default.

This is a big one. In case you didn't catch the previous paragraph, the Server type install erases the entire hard disk by default! If you have an existing Windows partition that you want to keep, change the Automatic Partitioning option that appears next either to only remove the Linux Partitions or to only use existing free space.

- **Custom System** — You are given the choice of configuring your own partitions and selecting your own software packages. Everything and Minimum installs are available under the Custom System selection.

If you are just trying out Linux, an Everything custom install gives you all the desktop, server, and development tools that come with Fedora Linux. If you have the disk space, an Everything install saves you the trouble of installing packages you need later. If you plan to use the computer as an Internet server, be selective about which packages you install. Some software packages can represent security risks if they are installed and not configured properly.

The steps will now continue through a Custom System installation. (With other installation selections, you can simply skip over steps you are not prompted for.) Although different install classes choose different partitioning methods by default, in all cases you can see and change the partitioning that was chosen for you.

10. **Choose your partitioning strategy.** You have two choices:

- **Automatically partition** — All Linux partitions on all hard disks are erased and used for the installation. The installation process automatically handles the partitioning. (It does give you a chance to review your partitioning, however.)

- **Manually partition with Disk Druid** — The Disk Druid utility is run to let you partition your hard disk.

If you select Disk Druid for partitioning, refer to the section on partitioning your hard disk in Chapter 7 for details on using those partitioning tools.

Click Next to continue.

11. **For automatic partitioning, select your partition option.** Choose from the following:

- **Remove all Linux partitions on this system** — Windows and other non-Linux partitions remain intact with this selection.

- **Remove all partitions on this system** — This erases the entire hard disk.

- **Keep all partitions and use existing free space** — This works only if you have enough free space on your hard disk that is not currently assigned to any partition.

If you have multiple hard disks, you can select which of those disks should be used for your Fedora Core installation. Turn the Review check box on to see how Linux is choosing to partition your hard disk. Click Next to continue.

12. **Review the Partitions screen.** You can change any of the partitions you choose providing you have at least one root (/) partition that can hold the entire installation and one swap partition. A small /boot partition (about 100MB) is also recommended.

The swap partition is often set to twice the size of the amount of RAM on your computer (for example, for 128MB RAM you could use 256MB of swap). Linux uses swap space when active processes have filled up your system's RAM. At that point, an inactive process is moved to swap space. You get a performance hit when the inactive process is moved to swap and another hit when that process restarts (moves back to RAM). For example, you might notice a delay on a busy system when you reopen a window that has been minimized for a long time.

When RAM and swap fill up, no other processes can start until something closes. Bottom line: Add RAM to get better performance; add swap space if processes are failing to start. Red Hat suggests a minimum of 32MB and maximum of 2GB of swap space.

Click the Next button (and select OK to accept any changes) to continue.

13. **Configure boot loader.** All bootable partitions and default boot loader options are displayed. By default, the install process uses the GRUB boot loader, installs the boot loader in the master boot record of the computer, and chooses Fedora as your default operating system to boot.

Note   If you keep the GRUB boot loader, you have the option of adding a GRUB password. The password protects your system from having potentially dangerous options sent to the kernel by someone without that password. This does not have to be the same password you use to log in later. (The GRUB boot loader is described in Chapter 7.)

The names shown for each bootable partition will appear on the boot loader screen when the system starts. Change a partition name by clicking it and selecting Edit. To change the location of the boot loader, click Configure Advanced Boot Loader Options, and continue to the next step. If you do not want to install a boot loader (because you don't want to change the current boot loader), click Change Boot Loader and select Do Not Install a Boot Loader. (If the defaults are okay, skip the next step.)

14. **Configure advanced boot loader.** To choose where to store the boot loader, select one of the following:

- **Master Boot Record (MBR)** — This is the preferred place for GRUB. It causes GRUB to control the boot process for all operating systems installed on the hard disk.

- **First Sector of Boot Partition** — If another boot loader is being used on your computer, you can have GRUB installed on your Linux partition (first sector). This lets you have the other boot loader refer to your GRUB boot loader to boot Fedora Linux.

You can choose to add kernel parameters (which may be needed if your computer can't detect certain hardware). Some of the kernel parameters you can use are described in Chapter 11 in descriptions of boot options. You can select to use linear mode (which was once required to boot from a partition on the disk that is above cylinder 1024 but is now rarely needed). Continue to the next step.

15. **Configure networking.** This applies only to a local area network. If you will use only dial-up networking, skip this section by clicking Next. If your computer is not yet connected to a LAN, you also should skip this section.

Network address information is assigned to your computer in two basic ways: statically (you type it) or dynamically (a DHCP server provides that information from the network at boot time). One Network Device appears for each network card you have installed on your computer. The first Ethernet interface is eth0, the second is eth1, and so on. Repeat the setup for each card by selecting each card and clicking Edit.

 Cross-Reference Chapter 5 discusses IP addresses, netmasks, and other information you need to set up your LAN.

With the Edit Interface eth0 dialog box displayed, add the following:

- **Configure using DHCP** — If your IP address is assigned automatically from a DHCP server, a check mark should appear here. With DHCP checked, you don't have to set other values on this page. Remove the check mark to set your own IP address.

- **IP Address** — If you set your own IP address, this is the four-part, dot-separated number that represents your computer to the network. How IP addresses are formed and how you choose them is more than can be said in a few sentences (see Chapter 5 for a more complete description). An example of a private IP address is 192.168.0.1.

- **Netmask** — The netmask is used to determine what part of an IP address represents the network and what part represents a particular host computer. An example of a netmask for a Class C network is 255.255.255.0.

- **Activate on boot** — Indicate whether you want the network to start at boot time (you probably do if you have a LAN).

Click OK, and then add the following information on the main screen:

- **Set the hostname** — The name identifying your computer within your domain. For example, if your computer were named baskets in the handsonhistory.com domain, your full hostname may be baskets. handsonhistory.com. You can either set the domain name yourself (manually) or have it assigned automatically, if that information is being assigned by a DHCP server (automatically via DHCP).

- **Gateway** — The IP number of the computer that acts as a gateway to networks outside your LAN. It represents a host computer or router that routes packets between your LAN and the Internet.

- **Primary DNS** — The IP address of the host that translates computer names you request into IP addresses. It is referred to as a Domain Name System (DNS) server. You may also have Secondary and Tertiary name servers in case the first one can't be reached. (Most ISPs will give you two DNS server addresses.)

Click Next to continue.

16. **Choose a firewall configuration.** The use of a firewall has significant impact on the security of your computer. If you are connected to the Internet or to another public network, a firewall can limit the ways an intruder may break into your Linux system. Here are your choices:

    • **No firewall** — Select this security level if you are not connected to a public network and do not want to deny requests for services from any computer on your local network. Of course, you can still restrict access to services by starting up only the services you want to offer and by using configuration files to restrict access to individual services.

    • **Enable firewall** — Select this security level if you are connecting your Linux system to the Internet for Web browsing and file downloading (FTP). By default, only services needed to enable Web browsing and basic network setup, DNS replies, and DHCP (to serve addresses) are allowed at this level.

    If you enable the firewall and you know you want to enable access to particular services, you can click the appropriate check boxes and allow incoming requests for the following services: SSH (secure shell to allow remote login), Telnet (an insecure method of remote login), WWW (act as a Web server), Mail (act as a mail server), and/or FTP (act as an FTP server). You can also add a comma-separated list of port numbers to the Other Ports box to open access to those ports, which effectively allows requests to services associated with those port numbers. (The /etc/services file lists which services are associated with which port numbers.)

    If you have a LAN that consists of trusted computers, you can click the box representing your interface to that LAN (probably eth0). Clicking the box allows access to any services you care to share with the computers on your LAN.

    Click Next to continue.

Tip   Adding firewall rules here results in rules being added to the /etc/sysconfig/ iptables file. The rules are run from the /etc/init.d/iptables startup script when you boot your system.

17. **Choose language support.** The default is your installation language. You can install support for additional languages by clicking the check boxes next to the languages you want. Click the Select All button to install all supported languages to your system. When you are done, click Next to continue.

18. **Choose a time zone.** Select one from the list. To see a more specific view of your location, click World and choose your continent. From the UTC Offset tab, you can choose a time zone according to the number of hours away from Greenwich Mean Time (GMT), known as the UTC offset.

19. **Set root password.** The root password provides complete control of your Fedora Linux system. Without it, and before you add other users, you will have no access to your own system. Enter the password, and then type it again in the Confirm box. (Remember the root user's password and keep it confidential! Don't lose it!) Click Next to continue.

Note If you are enabling Security Enhanced Linux (SELinux) on your computer, the security structure of your computer changes. The root user may no longer have complete control of the computer, but instead there may be policies set that prevent any one user from having complete control.

20. **Select Packages.** Groups of packages are selected by default depending on the type of installation you chose earlier. In general, either more workstation-oriented or server-oriented packages are selected. Pick the ones you want.

Tip You can override your package selections by choosing Mimimal or Everything install groups. Disk space requirements for those install types are described earlier in this chapter.

Because each group represents several packages, you can click the Details button next to each group to select more specifically the packages within that group. Because Workstation and Personal Desktop installations don't add any server packages, this is a good opportunity to add server packages for the services you expect to use. Click Next to continue.

21. **Decide to Install.** You can still back out now, and the disk will not have changed. Click Next to proceed. (To quit without changes, eject the CD and restart the computer.) Now the file systems are created and the packages are installed. This typically takes from 20 to 60 minutes to complete, although it can take much longer on older computers.

    If you are using the DVD, you do not need to change media. If you are installing from the four-CD set, you are prompted to insert additional installation CDs as they are needed.

22. **Configure your monitor.** You may be asked to configure your monitor. If it was probed properly, you should be able to just continue.

23. **Finish installing.** When you see the Congratulations screen, you are done. Note the links to Fedora Core information, eject the CD, and click Exit.

24. **Your computer restarts.** If you installed GRUB, you will see a graphical boot screen that displays the bootable partitions. Press the up or down arrow key to choose the partition you want to boot, and press Enter. If Linux is the default partition, you can simply wait a few moments and it will boot automatically.

The first time your system boots after installation, the Fedora Setup Agent runs to do some initial configuration of your system. The next section explains how Fedora Setup Agent works.

Running Fedora Setup Agent

The first time you boot Fedora Core after it is installed, the Fedora Setup Agent runs to configure some initial settings for your computer.

The Fedora Setup Agent runs automatically only if you have configured Fedora to boot to a graphical login prompt. To start it from a text login, log in as root and switch to init state 5 temporarily (type **init 5**). Log in to the graphical prompt. From a Terminal window, as root user, type

```
# rm /etc/sysconfig/firstboot
# /usr/sbin/firstboot
```

The Welcome screen displays. From it, step through screens to configure date and time, your monitor, user accounts, and additional software.

Summary

After throwing its devoted following into turmoil by dropping the well-known Red Hat Linux name, Red Hat Inc. has settled its development efforts into the free Fedora Project and commercial Red Hat Enterprise Linux.

Fedora Core and Red Hat Enterprise Linux distributions distinguish themselves from other Linux distributions with their simplified installer (called Anaconda), graphical configuration tools, and RPM Package Management tools. Fedora Core is freely available, whereas Red Hat Enterprise Linux is available on a paid subscription basis.

Fedora Core is included on the DVD that comes with this book. You can install the complete Fedora Core distribution by following the detailed instructions included in this chapter.

✦   ✦   ✦

Running Debian GNU/Linux

Debian GNU/Linux is a creation of the Debian Project. Founded in 1993 by Ian Murdock, the Debian Project is an association of individuals who have made a common cause to create a free, coherent, and complete operating system.

The Debian GNU/Linux network install CD is contained on the CD that comes with this book. You can install Debian from that CD as described in this chapter. You can do a minimal Debian install with just that CD or a complete Debian install with a connection to the Internet (recommended). This installation is suited for setting up a Web server (LAMP server) and a mail server (see Chapters 23 and 24, respectively).

The principles of the Debian Project are defined in the Debian Social Contract. This contract is a commitment to the free software community that basically states:

◆ All software within the Debian system will remain free, as defined in the Debian Free Software Guidelines (DFSG).

◆ The Debian Project will contribute to the free software community by licensing any software developed for the Debian system in accordance with the DFSG, developing the best system it can, and by sharing improvements and fixes with the original developers of any programs incorporated into Debian GNU/Linux.

◆ Problems will not be hidden from users, and any bug reports filed against Debian components will be made promptly available to the public through the Debian Bug Tracking System (BTS).

◆ The Debian Project will focus on the needs of its users and on the principles of free software.

◆ Provisions will be made for the support of programs that do not meet the standards in the DFSG because some users may depend on these programs to make effective use of the system. The bug tracking and support systems will always include mechanisms for handling these programs when they are provided with the Debian system.

Inside Debian GNU/Linux

Like most modern operating systems, software programs in Debian GNU/Linux are bundled into packages for easy distribution and management. The package format and management tools used in Debian GNU/Linux were created by the Debian Project and are arguably the most sophisticated of their type. Additionally, careful adherence to packaging policies and quality-control measures ensure compatibility and help make upgrades go smoothly. Debian is one of very few operating system distributions in which all components (except the kernel) can be upgraded without rebooting the system.

Debian Packages

Debian packages come in two forms: binary and source. Binary packages contain files that can be extracted directly onto the system by the package management tools. Source packages contain source code and build instructions that the Debian build tools use to create binary packages.

In addition to program data files, Debian packages contain control data that enable the package management tools to support advanced features:

✦ A main `control` file contains version and package interrelationship data. The version can be compared to an installed version of the same package to determine whether an upgrade is needed. The interrelationship data tell the package management tools which packages must or cannot be installed at the same time as this package.

Note   Package interrelationship fields include `Depends, Conflicts, Replaces,` `Provides, Recommends, Suggests,` and `Enhances.` For a complete list of control file fields, see `http://debian.org/doc/debian-policy/ch-control` `fields.html.`

✦ Optional `preinst, postinst, prerm,` and `postrm` files can instruct the packaging tools to perform functions before or after package installation or removal. Most packages containing daemons (such as Apache HTTPD) include a `postinst` script that starts the daemon automatically after installation.

✦ A `conffiles` file can designate specific files in the package as configuration files, which are not automatically overwritten during upgrades. By default, all files under the `/etc/` `directory` are configuration files.

Two special package types, meta and virtual, also exist. Meta packages are standard binary packages that depend on a number of other packages. These can be used as a convenient method for installing a set of related packages.

Virtual packages do not actually exist as files but can be referenced in the package interrelationship fields. They are most commonly used in cases where more than one package fulfills a specific requirement. Packages with this requirement can reference the virtual package in their Depends field, and packages that satisfy this dependency reference it in their Provides field. Because most programs providing a virtual package are mutually exclusive, they also include the virtual package in their Conflicts field to prevent the installation of conflicting packages.

Debian Package Management Tools

Perhaps the most interesting and well-known part of the Debian package management system is APT, the Advanced Package Tool. APT, through the apt-get binary, maintains a database of packages available in the repositories that it is configured to check and can handle automatically downloading new or upgraded packages. When installing or upgrading packages, APT downloads the necessary files to a local cache directory and then instructs the dpkg tool to take the appropriate actions.

Most basic package management functions are performed by dpkg, although not always at the direct request of the user. This tool handles medium-level package installation and removal and also manages the package status database. That database contains information about every package known to dpkg, including the package meta information and two other important fields: the package state and selection state.

As its name suggests, the package state indicates the present state of the package, which is one of the following:

✦ **not-installed** — The package is known but is not installed on the system.

✦ **half-installed** — An attempt was made to install the package, but an error prevented it from finishing.

✦ **unpacked** — The files have been extracted from the package, but any post-extract configuration steps have not yet been performed.

✦ **half-configured** — The postextract configuration was started, but an error prevented it from finishing.

✦ **installed** — The package is fully installed and configured.

✦ **config-files** — The package was removed, but the configuration files still exist on the system.

 Note

When the same version of a package that's in the config-files state is installed, any files that may have been manually removed will not be extracted. You can work around this by either purging the package (using dpkg --purge first) or by passing the --force-confmiss option to dpkg.

The package selection state indicates what state you want the package to be in. Changes to package status through `dpkg` happen immediately when using the `--install`, `--remove`, and `--purge` options on a package, but other uses and tools will instead set this flag and then process any pending changes in a batch. The package selection state is one of the following:

✦ **install** — The package should be installed.

✦ **deinstall** — The package files should be removed, with the exception of configuration files.

✦ **purge** — All package files and configuration files should be removed.

✦ **hold** — `dpkg` should not do anything with the package unless explicitly told to do so with the `--force-hold` argument.

Some packages are designed to enable you to select configuration options as they are being installed. This configuration is managed through the debconf utility. Debconf supports a number of different interfaces, including a command prompt and a menu-based interface. A database of configuration options is also maintained by debconf, allowing it to automatically answer repeated questions, such as those you might encounter while upgrading or reinstalling a package.

Examples of how to use these utilities are included in the "Managing Your Debian System" section later in this chapter.

Debian Releases

In Debian terms, a distribution is a collection of specific package versions. From time to time, a distribution is declared ready for release and becomes a release. In practice, these two terms are often used interchangeably when referring to Debian distributions that have reached the "stable" milestone.

Debian distributions are given code names (recent ones include potato, woody, and sarge) to identify their archive directory on the Debian servers and while active will be referenced by a release tag. There are three release tags, each one pointing to one of the three active releases. The tags — unstable, testing, and stable — identify the state of the release within the release cycle.

New packages, and new versions of packages, are uploaded to the Debian archive and are imported into the unstable distribution. This distribution always contains the newest version of every package, which means that changes have not yet been thoroughly tested to verify that installing them will not cause unexpected behavior.

Once a package has been in unstable for a few days and testing shows that it has not had any significant bugs filed against it, it is imported into the testing distribution. The testing distribution remains very similar to unstable until it is frozen in preparation for release as the next stable distribution. When testing is in the frozen state, only changes that are necessary to fix significant bugs are imported.

After all release-critical bugs have been fixed in the frozen testing distribution, the release manager declares the release ready and it replaces the stable distribution. The previous stable version becomes obsolete (but remains on the Debian archive for a reasonable period of time), a new testing distribution is created from the changes that went into unstable while testing was frozen, and the process begins again.

Installing Debian GNU/Linux

The CD that comes with this book contains a modified Debian network install CD and is intended for use with this tutorial. To complete more than a minimal installation, you will need an Internet connection or a local Debian software repository. You can use other CD sets, including the official ones from the Debian Project, but doing so may still result in the need for APT to download additional packages from the Internet to complete installation.

Hardware Requirements and Installation Planning

To run Debian, you need at least a 386 processor and 32MB of RAM. For a server or a graphical workstation, you should plan on having at least 128MB of memory and a Pentium-class processor.

A minimal set of packages requires 250MB of disk space, and a normal installation of desktop applications can require a few gigabytes. Additional space will be needed to store any data files that you want to keep on the system.

Most ISA and PCI network cards are supported under Linux, although ISA models are not usually detected automatically by the installer. Inexpensive cards based on RealTek 8139 chipsets can be found at most PC dealers and will work fine for low-demand applications. Intel PRO/100 and PRO/1000 adapters are supported in Linux and will work well in high-demand applications, as will cards based on the "tulip" chipsets and most 3com network cards.

Many newer systems include software-based modems that are not supported by the manufacturer under Linux. If you require a dial-up connection for Internet access, see Chapter 5 and check out `http://tldp.org/HOWTO/Modem-HOWTO-2.html` before you start the installation process.

Many other devices, such as sound and video capture cards, can also be used under Linux. For more information about hardware compatibility, see the Hardware Compatibility HOWTO at `http://tldp.org/HOWTO/Hardware-HOWTO/`.

Workstations

In most cases, workstation users will want to run the X Window System (X11). The ability to run X11 depends on compatibility with the video chipset on your video card or mainboard. Debian 3.1 includes version 4.3.0 of the XFree86 X11 System. You can find a list of video chipsets supported in this release at `http://xfree86.org/4.3.0/`.

Servers

A Linux server installation generally consists of only the minimum set of packages required to provide the service for which it was designed. In particular, this means that servers do not usually have a graphical interface installed.

Server hardware is generally more expensive than workstation hardware, although you can still run smaller servers on less-expensive desktop hardware. If you are planning to store important data on your server, then you will want to look into a RAID array for storage. A number of inexpensive ATA RAID controllers work well under Linux.

Note   More information about ATA RAID compatibility is available at `http://linux mafia.com/faq/Hardware/sata.html` **and** `http://ibiblio.org/pub/ Linux/docs/HOWTO/other-formats/html_single/Hardware-HOWTO.html #IDERAID`.

Higher-end servers will, of course, require more expensive hardware. In applications such as mail servers where you will have a lot of disk activity, plan on splitting the disk-intensive tasks across multiple arrays. When it comes to CPU and RAM, more of both is good, but most applications benefit more from extra RAM than they do from multiple CPUs.

Running the Installer

The Debian installation process consists of two stages.

Stage 1

The first stage boots from the installation medium (generally a CD); configures hardware drivers, disk partitions, and file systems; and then copies a set of essential packages known as the base system. Here's the procedure:

1. Boot the CD that comes with this book and type `debian` to begin the installation from the initial boot screen.

2. After the installer has finished booting, you are presented with the series of menus that make up the installation process. Use the arrow keys to navigate through the menus and select your language, region, and keyboard mapping.

3. Depending on whether a network card was detected in your system, you may be prompted to set up the network for your new Debian system. By default, the installer attempts to use DHCP to configure the IP addressing on the network card. If you configured it to skip DHCP, or if the DHCP configuration fails, you are prompted to enter the IP address, network mask, default gateway, and DNS server addresses.

Cross-Reference   See Chapter 7 for information about IP addresses, network masks, and other material related to setting up a network card connection.

Provide a hostname (a single-word name that you give to your system, such as debian, littlebeigebox, or yoda) and a domain name. If you do not have your own domain name, you can make one up, such as myhouse.local.

4. Configure your disk partitions for Debian. If you haven't already done so, read Chapter 7 for more information about partitioning.

   If you already have partitions on your drive and have room for more, you are given the option to use this space for your Debian system. Another option is to erase the entire disk and use the whole thing for Debian. Either of these two options takes you through the guided partitioning, which is covered in this section.

   A third option, manually editing the partition, enables you to be more exacting about your partition setup, but you should not try this without help or at least without reading Chapter 7.

   The guided partitioning section presents three partitioning schemes. Each of the options includes a suitable amount of swap space but has different benefits based on your situation. You must select one from the list before you proceed. See the "Selecting a Partition Scheme" sidebar for more information.

Note   When installing to small disk drives, use ext2 file systems instead of ext3. The journaling feature in ext3 requires that a portion of the disk be set aside for the journal, but the feature is of limited usefulness on small file systems. You can change file system types by going into the partition properties.

5. With your partition configuration chosen, select Finish Partitioning and Write Changes to Disk. This is your last chance to cancel changes that could cause damage to any other operating systems you may have on the disk, so check the screen carefully before proceeding!

   The installer writes the partitions to disk and creates the necessary file systems. After they have been prepared and mounted, the base system is extracted from the CD and installed to the target partitions.

6. The final step is to install GRUB, the boot loader. The default setting is to install to the master boot record (MBR), which is generally the best option. Accept the defaults and continue. The installer ejects the CD and prompts you to proceed with stage 2.

7. Remove the CD and continue.

Selecting a Partition Scheme

The guided partitioning feature allows you to select one of three templates to use to create your partitions. Use these guidelines to select the template that is correct for you.

✦ **All files in one partition.** Makes a single Linux partition for files. This is the easiest option to manage because you don't have to worry about balancing the sizes of your partitions. This can also be dangerous because users have the capability to fill up the entire disk, which can cause problems for the operating system. Do not use this option unless you are prepared to monitor disk space carefully.

✦ **Desktop machine.** Gives the operating system its own space and gives home directories their own space. This option is a good trade-off between the convenience of a single partition and the increased safety of the multiuser scheme. However, the /tmp/ directory is still part of the operating system partition, meaning that it is still fairly easy for people who habitually use that directory to fill up the operating system partition.

✦ **Multi-user system.** Creates separate partitions for the root file system, /usr/, /var/, /tmp/, and /home/. Use only this option when running a server on your system. It may also be a good choice for systems that will be used by more than just you, your relatives, and your close friends. The trade-off is that you may run out of room on a given partition even though the others have plenty of space, which means that you will need to plan carefully.

In some situations, you may need to adjust the partition sizes selected by the multiuser partitioning scheme to put more room where you are likely to need it:

✦ If you are planning to compile a lot of large software packages, you'll need to have plenty of space in the /usr/ partition.

✦ Active servers (especially Web and mail servers) may need extra room in /var/ for log files. Mail servers also use this space for the mail queue, and the default mail system also stores incoming mail here (you may also want to consider making /var/mail/ a separate partition in these cases).

✦ Web browsers such as Mozilla use /tmp/ for storing files while they are downloaded. This file system must be big enough to hold any large files that you want to download through there, plus any other files that may be there at the same time.

Note that with the multiuser partitioning scheme, the /home/ partition generally ends up receiving most of the space on larger disks. This usually makes it a good place to "borrow" space from when you want to make other partitions larger. However, because partman has already mapped out the partitions, you actually need to delete /home/ and then readd it after you increase the size of the other partition. If there are other partitions between /home/ and the one that you are increasing in size, you also need to delete them, and then add them back in an appropriate order.

Stage 2

The second stage boots from the newly installed packages and completes the configuration.

1. Your computer should reset on its own, and boot to the GRUB menu. GRUB should have already highlighted the default entry for Debian, so hit Enter and give the system a few moments to boot.

2. You are asked whether your system clock is set to GMT. Select Yes only if your computer will not be running any other operating systems. Then select your time zone from a list.

3. The base system includes an empty password for the root (superuser) account, which means that you want to set one here. Select a password that you will remember, but that others will not be able to easily guess.

4. Add a nonadministrative account that you can use for your day-to-day tasks on the server. Enter your name, your desired username (this should not contain any spaces or punctuation other than dashes, must not start with a number, and is generally all in lowercase), and a password for this account.

5. Select the installation medium that you want to use to install the remainder of the system. Insert your installation CD in the drive, select cdrom from the list, and press Enter. It takes a few moments to retrieve the list of packages available on the CD.

6. If you have more Debian CDs, you can have the installer check them for available packages as well.

7. You have the option of adding another APT source. If you have an Internet connection and want to do more than a minimal install or have the installer check for updated packages, choose either the HTTP or FTP methods (HTTP is recommended), and then select a country and a mirror server from the list. You are prompted for any HTTP proxy configuration, which may be necessary on some corporate or school networks. If you aren't sure, check with your support desk. If it does not apply, just leave it empty. APT retrieves a list of packages from the site that you selected.

8. The installer attempts to retrieve a list of security updates from the Debian security archive.

9. You are presented with a list of predefined package sets (known as "tasks") that you can select for installation. Package installation is covered in greater detail later, so it's recommended that you do not select any tasks from this list now.

10. APT downloads any updated packages, and debconf prompts you to configure any packages that are in the half-installed state.

11. Assuming that you did not select any tasks, the only package needing configuration is the Exim mail transfer agent. When the Configuring Exim screen appears, you choose from a list of default configurations; here are the two most likely options:

- **internet site; mail is sent and received directly using SMTP** — This option configures your server to accept incoming mail and to deliver outgoing mail directly to the servers for the recipient domain. This configuration is useful if you are running a simple mail server or if you are using mutt or pine to check your mail locally.

- **local delivery only; not on a network** — Select this option if you do not need locally generated messages to be sent to a central mail host for processing. Your system will not be configured with the capability to send messages, but this configuration still enables you to check your mail using programs such as Mozilla, Evolution, and Sylpheed that include support for sending messages using the SMTP protocol. This is also the option you want if you will soon be setting up this system to act as a mail server based on the instructions in Chapter 24.

Enter the mail name for this system (the default is generally what you want), and choose the user to whom you want system messages to go. In most cases, you want to select the user account that was added earlier.

You now have a fully functional Debian GNU/Linux system. The server does not yet have any extra packages installed but is ready to be used for the LAMP and mail server examples in this book (which you can find in Chapters 23 and 24, respectively). There's no graphical interface installed yet, which means that all interaction will be through the command line. Take some time, as needed, to browse through Chapter 2 and familiarize yourself with the command line before continuing with the next section.

Note   You can install a complete desktop for Debian using the `desktop` task. See the section on tasksel later in the chapter for more information.

Managing Your Debian System

Some of the basic tasks that you may encounter while running Debian GNU/Linux include package installation, configuration, and removal, as well as handling some special situations that you may come across.

All these steps require that you be logged in as the superuser (root). If you have just finished installing the system, you can log in as root from the login prompt.

Configuring Network Connections

Debian includes a set of tools for managing most types of network interfaces, including Ethernet, PPP, wireless, and even ATM. You may find that you need to add or change network settings after the system has been installed.

IP Networks: Ethernet and Wireless

On Debian systems, standard network connections are configured in the /etc/ network/interfaces file. If you have a network card configured to obtain an IP address automatically, this file will look like this:

```
# This file describes the network interfaces available on
# your system and how to activate them. For more information,
# see interfaces(5).

# The loopback network interface
auto lo
iface lo inet loopback

# The primary network interface
auto eth0
iface eth0 inet dhcp
```

Caution   Do not modify the loopback entry unless you are absolutely certain that you know what you are doing.

In some cases, such as when the system will be acting as a server, you want to configure your network interface with a fixed IP address. To do so, edit /etc/network/ interfaces and replace the iface eth0 inet dhcp line. Use the following block as a template, replacing the parameters with the correct settings for your network:

```
iface eth0 inet static
    address 192.168.1.220
    netmask 255.255.255.0
    gateway 192.168.1.1
```

Note   You can obtain IP network settings from your ISP or network administrator.

Wireless interfaces can also be configured using the interfaces file, but require that the wireless-tools package be installed. Use dpkg or apt-get to install the wireless-tools package. Then, add the necessary parameters to the entry for your wireless network interface. This example shows the settings for a wireless network with an access point (managed mode) set to the ESSID Home, and operating on channel 11:

```
iface eth0 inet dhcp
wireless_essid Home
wireless_mode Managed
    wireless_channel 11
```

Note If your wireless network is using encryption, you will need to specify a *wireless*_key parameter. You can find a complete list of wireless options in the iwconfig man page.

PPP Connections: Dial-up and Others

Dial-up connections can be managed using the pppconfig utility. Simply run `pppconfig`, and you are provided with a menu from which you can create, modify, and delete dial-up connection parameters. You specify connections by name when dialing, so be sure to give it a name that is easy to type.

Dial a connection using the `pon` command, replacing *peer* with the name you assigned to your connection:

```
# pon peer
```

You can disconnect using the `poff` command and can view logs (for diagnosing problems or determining status) using the `plog` command.

Some DSL and cable modem providers require that you use PPPoE (PPP over Ethernet) to connect to their systems. PPPoE connections are managed using the pppoeconf program.

Package Management Using APT

For most users, APT will be the primary tool for installing, removing, and upgrading packages. This section shows how to use the apt-get and apt-cache utilities.

Managing the List of Package Repositories

The configuration file `/etc/apt/sources.list` contains a list of Debian package repositories that APT will use. Like most configuration files on a Linux system, this file is a plain-text file that can be viewed using any text editor or pager. To view its contents, run the following:

```
# pager /etc/apt/sources.list
deb cdrom:[Debian GNU/Linux _Sarge_ NetInst]/ stable main

deb http://ftp.us.debian.org/debian/ stable main
deb-src http://ftp.us.debian.org/debian/ stable main

deb http://security.debian.org/ stable/updates main
```

Your output will differ from this example's, of course, but the kind of information remains the same. The first part of each line indicates whether the repository is to be used for binary packages (indicated by the deb prefix) or source packages (deb-src). The rest of the line defines the method (in this case, cdrom or http), the location, the distribution (stable), and the sections (main). If you want to use software from the contrib and non-free sections, you can use a text editor to add them after main.

Note   Run `man sources.list` on any Debian system for more information.

If you aren't going to have your Debian CD available all the time, you may want to remove the `cdrom:` entry from the file. Use a text editor to edit the file:

```
# editor /etc/apt/sources.list
```

Then update the package database as described in the following section.

Note   Astute readers may notice that the `pager` and `editor` commands used in this section are not standard UNIX commands. Both are pointers to programs and are managed using Debian's alternatives system, which is discussed later in this chapter.

Updating the APT Package Database

Because the lists of packages available in the Debian package repositories may change from time to time, you need to instruct APT to download these lists and update its database from time to time. To perform this process, run the following command:

```
# apt-get update
```

You generally want to run this command before installing new packages so that you do not download an older version. Run it before checking for upgrades as well.

Finding and Installing Packages

When looking for new packages to install, you may not always know what package you want. The package database maintained by APT includes package descriptions and other fields that can be searched using the apt-cache utility:

```
# apt-cache search tetris
bsdgames -- a collection of classic textual unix games
pytris -- two-player networked console tetris clone
stax -- collection of puzzle games similar to Tetris Attack.
```

Tip   Specifying multiple keywords in a search prevents it from listing packages that do not contain all of the keywords you specify. This enables you to do very specific searches such as `word processor`.

You can also use this utility to find out more information about a specific package in the repositories:

```
# apt-cache show bsdgames
Package: pytris
Priority: optional
Section: games
Installed-Size: 101
Maintainer: Radovan Garabik
```

```
Architecture: i386
Version: 0.96
Depends: python (>=2.1), libc6 (>= 2.2.4-4)
Filename: pool/main/p/pytris/pytris_0.96_i386.deb
Size: 16304
MD5sum: 70eb8ad6f5a8a901a95eb37f7336fc57
Description: two-player networked console tetris clone
 two-player networked console based tetris clone, written
 in python, similar to xtet42.
```

Note   To view information about a specific package that is already installed on your system, use dpkg, as discussed later in this chapter.

Once you know the name of the package you want to install, use the install method to download it and any packages on which it depends. For example, the ssh package is very useful for remotely accessing systems and is probably one of the first programs that you will want to install:

```
# apt-get install ssh
```

On this command, APT retrieves and installs the ssh package. If they are required, a list of additional packages is displayed by APT. If you choose to continue, APT will download and install those packages along with the package you requested.

Note   When installing packages that support automatic configuration through debconf, you're prompted to answer the appropriate configuration questions. While the Debian package developers have gone to great lengths to ensure that the default options for these questions will work in most situations, it's best to read the questions thoroughly to be sure that the defaults work for you.

Removing Packages

APT can also be used to remove packages from your system. Unlike dpkg, which removes only the package you tell it to remove, apt-get also removes any packages that depend on the package you are removing. This is best used in conjunction with the -s option to simulate what would happen if the removal were actually performed:

```
# apt-get -s remove python2.3
Reading Package Lists... Done
Building Dependency Tree... Done
The following packages will be REMOVED:
  bittornado python python2.3 python2.3-dev
0 upgraded, 0 newly installed, 4 to remove and 0 not upgraded.
Remv pytris (0.96 Debian:testing)
Remv python (2.3.4-1 Debian:testing)
Remv python2.3-dev (2.3.4-5 Debian:testing)
Remv python2.3 (2.3.4-5 Debian:testing)
```

In this example, several other packages depend on the python2.3 package and would also need to be removed. To proceed with removing python2.3 and all packages that depend on it, run the command again without the -s flag.

Upgrading Your System

As new versions of packages become available, you can instruct APT to download and install them, automatically replacing the older versions. This is as simple as updating your package list, followed by a simple command:

```
# apt-get upgrade
```

> **Note**
>
> When upgrading to a newer distribution, use dist-upgrade instead of upgrade. This will change the rules that APT uses when deciding which actions to take, making it expect major changes in dependencies and handle them appropriately.

Package Management Using dpkg

As mentioned earlier, the dpkg utility is the primary package management tool in Debian. Most other package management tools within the system, including APT, use dpkg to perform the midlevel work, and dpkg in turn uses dpkg-deb and dpkg-query to handle a number of the low-level functions.

Far too many dpkg commands exist to list in this section, but the most common ones are explained in the following sections. In most cases, there are both short and long commands to perform the same function. Use whichever is easier for you to remember.

Installing and Removing Packages

Packages can be installed with dpkg using the -i or --install flags and the path to the .deb file containing the package. The path must be accessible as a file system path (HTTP, FTP, and other methods are not supported), and more than one package can be specified:

```
# dpkg --install /home/wayne/lsof_4.71-1_i386.deb
```

Package removal through dpkg is also straightforward and is done with the -r or --remove commands. When configuration files are to be removed, the -P or --purge command can be used instead. Both commands can also be used to specify multiple packages to remove:

```
# dpkg --remove lsof
or...
# dpkg --purge lsof
```

Querying the Package Database

You will often need to obtain more information about packages that are already installed on your system. Because these operations do not modify the package database, they can be done as a non-root user.

To list all packages known to dpkg, use the -l or --list commands:

```
$ dpkg --list
```

You can restrict the list by specifying a glob pattern:

```
$ dpkg --list "*lsof*"
```

Note   The quotes are used to prevent the shell from replacing the wildcard with a list of matching files in the current directory. For more information about wildcards, see the glob man page.

To view detailed information about a specific package, use the -s or --status command:

```
$ dpkg --status lsof
Package: lsof
Status: install ok installed
Priority: standard
Section: utils
...
```

The origin package for a file can be determined using the -S or --search command:

```
$ dpkg --search /bin/ls
coreutils: /bin/ls
```

The list of files in an installed package can be viewed using the -L or --listfiles command:

```
$ dpkg --listfiles lsof
/.
/usr
/usr/sbin
/usr/bin
/usr/bin/lsof
...
```

Examining a Package File

Package files can be examined prior to installation using the --info (-I) and --contents (-c) command:

```
$ dpkg --info lsof_4.71-1_i386.deb
 new debian package, version 2.0.
 size 319058 bytes: control archive= 1534 bytes.
     557 bytes,    16 lines       control
    2246 bytes,    32 lines       md5sums
 Package: lsof
 Version: 4.71-1
 ...

$ dpkg --contents lsof_4.71-1_i386.deb
drwxr-xr-x root/root          0 2004-04-03 07:34:41 ./
drwxr-xr-x root/root          0 2004-04-03 07:34:36 ./usr/
drwxr-xr-x root/root          0 2004-04-03 07:34:39 ./usr/bin/
 ...
```

Installing Package Sets (Tasks) with Tasksel

Some package sets are too large to be managed practically through meta packages, so tasks have been created as an alternative. Tasks are installed and removed using the tasksel utility. When run without any arguments, tasksel presents a menu from which you can select tasks to install or remove.

Caution Do not install any tasks if you plan to use this system in conjunction with the server examples in Chapters 23 and 24.

Additional options are available from the command line:

✦ To see a list of known tasks, run `tasksel --list-tasks`.

✦ To list the packages that are installed by a task, run `tasksel --task-packages <task name>`.

Caution When a task is removed, all programs associated with that task, whether installed manually or as part of that task, are removed!

To install the desktop task, which includes GNOME, KDE, and XFCE environments, run the following:

```
# tasksel install desktop
```

Alternatives, Diversions, and Stat Overrides

In cases where there is more than one installed program that provides a specific function, package maintainers have the option of utilizing Debian's alternatives system. The alternatives system manages which program is executed when you run a specific command. For instance, the ed, nano, and nvi packages each provide a text editor. An alternative maintained in the system guarantees that a text editor is accessible through the generic `editor` command, regardless of which combination of these packages is installed.

The system administrator can designate which program is referenced in the alternatives database, through the use of the `update-alternatives` command:

```
# update-alternatives --config editor

These are alternatives that provide 'editor'.
  Selection    Alternative
-----------------------------------------------
        1        /bin/ed
*+      2        /bin/nano
        3        /usr/bin/nvi

Press enter to keep the default[*], or type selection number:2
```

You can also use the `--all` command with `update-alternatives` to configure
every entry in the alternatives database, one at a time. You can find more details in
the update-alternatives man page.

Note   By default, all alternatives are in automatic mode, meaning that the system automatically selects a suitable program from the available candidates. Installing a new
candidate program generally results in the automatic updating of the appropriate
alternatives. Manually configuring an alternative disables automatic mode, preventing the system from changing these settings without prior knowledge of the system
administrator.

The Debian package management tools also provide a mechanism for renaming
specific files in a package and for overriding the ownership and permission settings
on files. Unlike when these changes are made manually using `mv`, `chmod`, or `chown`,
changes made through the Debian tools remain in place across package upgrades
and re-installations.

For example, if you wanted to replace `/usr/bin/users` without modifying the core-
utils package, you could divert it to `/usr/bin/users.distrib`:

```
# dpkg-divert --local --rename --add /usr/bin/users
Adding `local diversion of /usr/bin/users to
/usr/bin/users.distrib'
```

Removing the diversion returns the original filename:

```
# dpkg-divert --remove /usr/bin/users
Removing `local diversion of /usr/bin/users to
/usr/bin/users.distrib'
```

Stat overrides are useful when you want to disable access to a program, or when
you want to make it set-UID. For instance, to disable access to the wall program:

```
# dpkg-statoverride --update --add root root 0000 /usr/bin/wall
```

This sets the owner and group of /usr/bin/wall to root and root and disables all permissions on the file.

Note You can find more information about file permissions in the "Understanding File Permissions" section of Chapter 2.

Unlike dpkg-divert, dpkg-statoverride does not keep track of the original file permissions. As a result, removing an override does not restore the old permissions. After removing the override, you need to either set the permissions manually or reinstall the package that contained the file:

```
# dpkg-statoverride --remove /usr/bin/wall
# apt-get --reinstall install bsdutils
Reading Package Lists... Done
Building Dependency Tree... Done
0 upgraded, 0 newly installed, 1 reinstalled, 0 to remove and 0
not upgraded.
Need to get 0B/62.5kB of archives.
After unpacking 0B of additional disk space will be used.
Do you want to continue? [Y/n]Y
(Reading database ... 16542 files and directories currently
installed.)
Preparing to replace bsdutils 1:2.12-10 (using
.../bsdutils_1%3a2.12-10_i386.deb) ...
Unpacking replacement bsdutils ...
Setting up bsdutils (2.12-10) ...
```

Managing Package Configuration with debconf

All packages that include support for configuration management through debconf are configured as they are being installed. If you want to change a configuration option later, you can do so using the dpkg-reconfigure utility. For instance, you can change the configuration options for ssh using the following command:

```
# dpkg-reconfigure ssh
```

Every configuration parameter is assigned a priority by the package maintainer. This allows debconf to select the default values for settings below a specific priority. By default, you will only be prompted to answer questions of medium, high, or critical priority; low-priority questions are answered automatically. You can change this by reconfiguring the debconf package:

```
# dpkg-reconfigure debconf
```

Note Advanced users who are maintaining multiple systems may want to create a database of configuration settings that can be distributed to every computer (or to sets of computers) to reduce the number of repeated steps. This process is documented in the debconf and debconf.conf man pages.

Summary

The reliability of Debian GNU/Linux, combined with the large number of high-quality packages available for it, make Debian a great choice for both workstations and servers. The carefully executed releases and the capability to upgrade most software without rebooting serve to further increase its suitability as a server operating system.

APT is a primary tool for installing, removing, and upgrading packages. This chapter explored how to use the apt-get and apt-cache utilities for package management. Also discussed were the installation of package sets (tasks) using the tasksel utility and managing package configuration with the dpkg-reconfigure utility.

✦   ✦   ✦

Running SUSE Linux

For the past few years, SUSE has been the most popular Linux distribution in Europe. Since the U.S. networking company Novell, Inc. purchased SUSE in November 2003, SUSE has been positioning itself to challenge Red Hat to become the dominant Linux distribution for large enterprise computing environments worldwide.

On the DVD-ROM The DVD that comes with this book contains the CD image of SUSE 9.2, disk 1. You can burn that image to CD as described in Appendix A and install it as described later in this chapter.

Like Red Hat Linux, SUSE is an excellent first Linux for people who prefer to work from a graphical desktop rather than from the command line. Likewise, Novell's Linux product line is geared toward enterprise computing, so the skills you gain using SUSE will scale beyond your home Linux system.

SUSE has a slick graphical installer that leads you through installation and intuitive administrative tools, consolidated under a facility called YaST. SUSE and its parent company Novell offer a range of Linux products and support plans that scale up to enterprise computing, as well as free, binary versions of SUSE that you can use with limited support.

This chapter describes the features and approach to Linux that set SUSE apart from other Linux distributions. It also explains how to install the SUSE 9.2 distribution that is included with this book.

Understanding SUSE

If you are looking for the stability and support required of a Linux system on which you can bet your business, SUSE offers impressive, stable Linux products backed by a company (Novell, Inc.) that has been selling enterprise solutions for a long time. SUSE's product offerings range from personal desktop systems to enterprise-quality servers.

SUSE began as a German version of Slackware in 1992, on 40 floppy disks, and was first officially released on CD (SUSE Linux 1.0) in 1994. Founded by Hubert Mantel, Burchard Steinbild, Roland Dyroff, and Thomas Fehr, SUSE set out as a separate distribution from Slackware to enhance the software in the areas of installation and administration.

Although SUSE had success and respect with its Linux distribution, it was not profitable, and Novell's $210 million offer for SUSE was seen as a good thing both for SUSE and for Linux in general. SUSE was running short on cash, and Novell was looking for a way to regain its stature as a growth company in the enterprise and network computing arena.

In the 1980s and early 1990s, Novell was the world's number-one computer networking company. Before the Internet took hold, Novell's NetWare servers and IPX/SPX protocols were the most popular ways of connecting PCs together on LANs. International training, support, and sales teams brought Novell products to businesses and organizations around the world.

Despite Novell's huge lead in the network computing market, file and printer sharing features in Windows and late entry into the TCP/IP (Internet) arena caused Novell to lose its market dominance in the 1990s. Although its NetWare products contained excellent features for directory services and managing network resources, Novell didn't have end-to-end computing solutions. NetWare relied on Windows for client computers and lacked high-end server products.

Novell's association with the UNIX operating system in the early 1990s makes an interesting footnote in the history of Linux. Novell purchased UNIX System V source code from AT&T and set out to make its resulting UnixWare product (a UNIX desktop product for x86 processors) a competitor to Microsoft's growing dominance on the desktop. The effort was half-hearted, and Novell soon gave the UNIX trademark to the Open Group and sold the UNIX source code to SCO.

Novell's purchase of SUSE marks its second major attempt to fill in its product line with a UNIX-like desktop and server product. From the early returns, it appears that Novell is doing a better job with Linux than it did with UNIX.

What's in SUSE

Unlike distributions geared toward more technical users, such as Gentoo and Slackware, you can configure and launch most major features of SUSE by selecting menus on the desktop. New Linux users should find SUSE to be very comfortable for daily use and basic administration.

Like Red Hat Enterprise Linux, SUSE is made to have a more cohesive look-and-feel than most Linux distributions that are geared toward Linux enthusiasts. In other words, you aren't required to put together a lot of SUSE by hand just to get it working. Although there are personal editions of SUSE that are fine for home users, SUSE is ultimately aimed more toward enterprise computing.

Let's explore what SUSE Linux offers you.

Installation and Configuration with YaST

A set of modules that can be used for configuring your SUSE system is gathered together under the YaST facility. Because many of the features needed in a Linux installer are also needed to configure a running system (network, security, software, and other setup features), YaST does double duty as an installer and an administrative tool.

YaST (which stands for Yet Another Setup Tool) was, until recently, proprietary code that was not available as open source. However, to gain wider acceptance for YaST among major computing clients as a framework for managing a range of computing services, Novell released YaST under the GNU Public License in March 2004.

YaST makes obvious what you need to do to install Linux. Hardware detection is done before your eyes. You can set up your disk partitions graphically (no need to remember options to the fdisk command). Setting up the GRUB boot loader is done for you, with the option to modify it yourself.

One of the nice features of YaST installation is that you can scan the configuration process without stepping through every feature. If you scan through the mouse, keyboard, installation mode, partitioning, and other information and they look okay, you can click Accept and just keep going. Or you can change any of those settings you choose. (The "Installing SUSE" section later in this chapter details the installation process with YaST.)

Because YaST offers both graphical (QT) and text-based (ncurses) interfaces, you can use YaST as a configuration tool from the desktop or the shell. To start YaST from the desktop, click the SUSE button on the desktop panel and select System ⇨ YaST. Figure 10-1 shows what the graphical version of the YaST utility looks like.

Figure 10-1: Configure common Linux features using the YaST utility.

Launching the YaST utility actually involves running the /sbin/yast2 command. When you run /sbin/yast2, YaST starts in text mode by default. (An alternative is to run kdesu /sbin/yast2 from a Terminal window, which starts YaST in graphical mode.) Figure 10-2 shows what YaST looks like when started in text mode from a Terminal window.

Figure 10-2: Use the arrow and Tab keys to navigate YaST in text mode.

YaST offers you some intuitive tools for configuring your system and comes preconfigured, so you start with a nice set of defaults. YaST also does a good job detecting your hardware, finding partitions, and the like, so a new user can often just accept the settings YaST chooses. Here are some examples of what YaST does for you:

✦ **Detects hardware.** You don't have to check through /etc configuration files or run lsmod to see how your hardware has been configured in SUSE. From the Hardware section, you can select icons representing your CD drives, graphics cards, printers, joysticks, scanners, sound cards, and mice. Click the Hardware information icon to see your full list of detected hardware.

✦ **Manages system configuration.** Like Red Hat Linux, SUSE stores much of the information it uses to configure services at boot time in files in the /etc/ sysconfig directory. The information in those files is in the form VARIABLE= "VALUE".

Under the YaST System icon, you can select the sysconfig Editor, which lets you select each file, and then view and possibly change each variable so that you don't have to guess what variables are available for each configuration. For more advanced system administrators, this is a great way to fine-tune the startup services for your system.

SUSE also includes a System Configuration Profile Management (SCPM) applet, which lets you store and manage a collection of system settings so it can be used again later.

✦ **Configures network devices.** YaST detects your dial-up modem, Ethernet card, DSL modem, or ISDN hardware, and gives you the opportunity to configure each piece of hardware. SUSE also does a much better job than most distributions at getting Winmodems working in Linux, which is particularly useful for using dial-up features on laptops that have cheap, built-in modems.

✦ **Defines network services.** With a connection to your LAN or WAN, YaST provides some helpful graphical tools for configuring some services that can be unintuitive to do from the command line.

✦ **Changes security settings.** Security settings in Linux are often among the most unintuitive features to configure, while at the same time being among the most important. Although features such as iptables work great for most Linux gurus for setting up a firewall, people who are accustomed to graphical interfaces may find them challenging.

From the YaST Security and Users selection, the Firewall icon enables you to step through your network interfaces and add access to those services you want by name (such as Web Server, Mail Server, and Other Services) or by port number. It even enables you to do initial setup of more complex firewall features, such as packet forwarding, IP Masquerading, and logging.

To make your way around the graphical YaST interface, you only need to click the mouse and use the Tab key to move between fields. For the text-based YaST interface, you can use the Tab and arrow keys to move among the selections and the Enter key to select the currently highlighted item.

RPM Package Management

Like Red Hat Linux, SUSE packages its software using the RPM package management file format and related tools. RPM contains a lot of features for adding, removing, and managing software in SUSE. Although software packages in the Red Hat and SUSE distributions are different, the tools you use for managing packages in those two distributions are the same.

You use the rpm utility to work with RPM software packages. Here's a list of some of its features:

✦ **Installing local or remote packages.** You can use the rpm command to add a software package to SUSE, and it doesn't care if the package is in the local directory, CD, or remote computer (providing you have network access to that computer). A remote package can be available on a Web server (http://) or FTP server (ftp://). Here's an example of using an rpm command to install a software package from an FTP server:

```
# rpm -iv ftp://ftp.linuxtoys.net/pub/suse/9.1/abc.i586.rpm
```

In this example, the -i option says to install the package, and the -v option says to give verbose output as the package is installed. The fictitious package (abc.i586.rpm) is installed from an FTP repository. If there are dependency or access issues, rpm informs you and fails. Otherwise, the package is installed. (The -U option is often used instead of the -i option to install RPMs because -U succeeds even if the package is already installed. The -U says to upgrade the package.)

✦ **Querying the RPM database.** One of the best features of the RPM facility is that you can find out a lot of information about the software packages that are installed. The query option (-q) lets you list package names, descriptions, and contents in various ways. Here are a few examples:

```
# rpm -qa xmms
# rpm -ql xmms | less
# rpm -qi xmms | less
```

The first example (-qa) searches for the xmms package and reports the current version of the package that is installed. In the second, -ql lists all files in the xmms package and then pipes that output to the less command to page through it. And finally, -qi displays a description and other information about the xmms package.

✦ **Verifying installed packages.** Use rpm to verify the contents of an RPM package. The -V option enables you to check whether any of the files in a package have been tampered with. Here is an example:

```
# rpm -V aaa_base
..5....T c /etc/inittab
S.5....T   /etc/profile.d/alias.ash
```

-V checks whether any of the contents of the aaa_base package (which contains some basic system configuration files) has been modified. The output shows that the inittab and alias.ash files have been modified from the originals. The 5 indicates that the md5sum of the files differ, while the T indicates that the time stamp on the file differs. On the alias.ash file, the S shows that the size of the file is different.

The rpm command has many other options as well. To find out more about them, type **man rpm** from any shell.

Automated Software Updates

As of version 7.1, SUSE Linux includes an automatic update agent. The YaST Online Update (YOU) utility is built right into the YaST facility and offers an easy way to get updates, security patches, and bug fixes for SUSE by downloading and installing them from software repositories over the network.

From within YaST, select YOU. YaST shows you the location of mirror sites and then enables you to begin retrieving software updates with a single click. It presents you with a list of patches from which you can choose. Security patches are in red, all recommended patches are selected, and optional patches are shown (unselected). It's easy to see all available patches and read their descriptions to determine if you want them.

After you have selected the updates you want and clicked OK, you can watch the progress as each patch and updated package is downloaded and installed. Having security-related patches and other fixes separated and being able to read all about each software update and patch right on the YaST window before you start downloading are features that set YOU apart from methods of doing upgrades from other Linux distributions.

Getting Support for SUSE

SUSE has an excellent support database and full-time support staff. You can search many of the articles on the site for free and check out the FAQs. Paid support options are available as well.

The SUSE Linux Portal (http://portal.suse.com) is the place to search for answers about using SUSE. To try the free search engine at the site, just select Search. You don't need a user account to search articles related to the SUSE Linux personal or professional editions, although you do need one to search articles related to Linux business products from SUSE.

To get an account, select the Sign Up Here link from the SUSE Linux Portal page. If you have purchased your SUSE distribution, you can use that account to register your SUSE product. Having a registered SUSE product lets you use your account to get free installation information and other support services.

Note   At the time of this writing, SUSE was offering a free 30-day evaluation for SUSE Linux Enterprise Server if you wanted to download it. That evaluation included installation support and upgrade protection. Check the Novell (`www.novell.com`) and SUSE (`www.suse.com`) Web sites to see if any evaluation specials are available at the moment.

Installing SUSE

The SUSE installation procedure described here is for the SUSE Linux Personal-CD edition. This edition is available free of charge. Functionally, it is almost exactly the same as the boxed set version that SUSE sells, with only a few items removed that are not covered under a license in which they can be redistributed.

The DVD that comes with this book includes the first CD in the SUSE Linux Personal-CD edition that you can copy and use. If you want to download the latest Personal-CD yourself, go to the SUSE download page (`www.suse.com/us/private/download/index.html`). In either case, you will have to burn the CD image to a CD yourself. (See Appendix A for information on how to do that.)

If you like SUSE and want a commercial version, select the Online Store link at the SUSE.com site. You can purchase a boxed set of the Personal edition, which includes installation support and hardcopy documentation, or you can choose one of the other editions, such as the SUSE Linux Professional or SUSE Linux Enterprise Server editions, which also include support and documentation.

Note   The installation description in this chapter covers installs on Intel x86 PCs. If you have AMD 64-bit or Intel Extended Memory 64 Technology systems, you need to purchase the SUSE Linux Professional boxed set, which includes installation media for both of those types of hardware.

Before You Begin

To install SUSE, you need at least 96MB of main memory. The entire SUSE Personal-CD installation requires about 1.8GB of disk space, although you can get by with less by deselecting packages during installation. Installation should work on any Pentium-class x86 PC.

The description here tells how to install by booting the installation CD and installing the software from that medium. If you don't have a bootable CD, you can create a boot floppy from the floppy image on the CD. To see available boot images and descriptions of how to create boot floppies, refer to the README file in the `/boot` directory on the SUSE installation CD.

Although you need a boot CD or floppy disk to begin the installation, the actual software you are installing can reside in other locations. If you have a network card installed on your computer, SUSE software can be gathered from the following types of locations:

✦ **FTP** — From the installation boot prompt, identify the location of the directory on an FTP server that contains the contents of the SUSE packages. For example, to install from the /install directory from the FTP server at 10.0.0.1, type the following at the boot prompt:

```
install=ftp://10.0.0.1/install
```

✦ **HTTP** — To use a Web (http) server instead of an FTP server, you would type the following:

```
install=http://10.0.0.1/install
```

✦ **NFS** — To use an NFS server instead of an FTP server, you would type the following:

```
install=nfs://10.0.0.1/install
```

Other installation media that are supported include hard disk (with the SUSE software installed on a different hard disk or partition on the local computer) and Samba (where the software is on an SMB share from a Windows or other Linux system).

Starting Installation

Here are the steps for installing the SUSE Linux Personal-CD edition on your hard disk:

1. **Insert the installation CD in your CD drive.** Reboot the computer. The SUSE installation boot screen appears.

2. **Installation type.** Because this install is from the local CD, highlight Installation and press Enter. The YaST screen appears to begin installation.

Note

Sometimes installation can fail because the computer hardware doesn't support certain features, such as power management (ACPI or APM) or DMA on hard drives or removable media. For those cases, you can try starting installation by selecting ACPI Disabled (which turns off ACPI) or Safe Settings (which turns off ACPI and APM as well as turning off DMA for any IDE CD, DVD, or hard drives).

3. **Language.** Select your language and click Accept. Installation Settings appear. The next few steps let you view and (optionally) change the installation settings SUSE recommends.

4. **System.** Select System to view information about the computer hardware that SUSE detected. You can select Save to File to have that information saved to a file on your hard disk. Click OK to return to Installation Settings.

5. **Mode.** New Installation is the only mode available with the Personal Edition.

6. **Keyboard layout.** Select the language/country associated with the keyboard you are using.

7. **Mouse.** If your mouse was not detected properly, select Mouse and change it to one of the mouse/connection types that appear. SUSE supports USB, serial, PS/2, and bus mouse connections. A variety of two-button, three-button, and wheel mice are supported.

8. **Partitioning.** Partitioning is very important, especially if you want to protect any data currently on your hard disk. Select Partitioning. SUSE recommends a partitioning scheme. (If your disk is already partitioned, SUSE tries to use that scheme.) You can simply accept that scheme (choose Accept Proposal As-Is and click Next) or elect to create a custom partition setup.

   The Expert partitioning selection enables you to use a partitioning interface that is very similar to Disk Druid. See the description of partitioning in Chapter 7 for information on partitioning your hard disk. If you ever plan to move your partitions around with a tool such as Partition Magic, you should assign your Linux partition to ext3 file system type. (If you are an expert and want to use the `fdisk` command described there, press Ctrl+Alt+F2 to get to a shell, run fdisk, and then press Ctrl+Alt+F7 to return to the graphical installer.)

9. **Software.** Select Software to see a list of packages available to install on your hard disk. Most of the packages in the Personal Edition are desktop-oriented. Package selections fall under these headings:

   - **Graphical Base System** — X Window System, window managers, graphics libraries, and so on.

   - **KDE Desktop Environment** — The KDE desktop and related applications.

   - **Help & Support Documentation** — The SUSE help system and related tools.

   - **Office Applications** — Office productivity tools, including wine for running MS Windows applications.

   Check boxes indicate which packages you want to install. It's a good idea to look through this list to see what you are getting. If you change any of the selections, click the Check Dependencies box to make sure that all packages other packages depend on are being installed. Figure 10-3 shows the YaST module for adding, removing, and finding out about software packages.

   The YaST software packages module used during installation is the same one used on a running SUSE system (in Figure 10-3, it's shown on a running SUSE system). In either case, you can find out a lot of information about packages that interest you. With a package selected, click tabs in the box at the bottom-right corner of the screen to see its description, technical data (its size, packager, etc.), dependencies, and version numbers.

10. **Booting.** Select Booting to see the information that is added to your boot loader (GRUB, by default, but you can use the LILO boot loader as well). The boot loader includes the information needed to boot Linux: the location of the boot loader, default operating system to boot, and other information.

Figure 10-3: Install and remove software using the YaST software module.

Caution

If you are sharing your hard disk with other operating systems (such as Windows or another version of Linux), consider putting your boot loader on floppy disk. In that way, you can test out the boot loader without actually changing the permanent master boot record on your hard disk. If the boot loader doesn't work, simply remove the floppy disk to reboot the original way.

11. **Time zone.** Select the time zone in which you're located.

12. **Language.** Select the default language to use. (You can add support for other languages later, if you like.)

13. **Default Runlevel.** Normally you'd use the default (5) to boot to a full multiuser, networked desktop system with a graphical login screen. The other common default is 3, which provides a text-based login screen but is otherwise the same. (If you choose 3, you can start the GUI after login by typing the `startx` command.)

14. **Start the install.** If the Installation settings all look okay, click Accept to begin the install process. Remember that this is your last chance to back out! When the green warning box appears, click No to abort the install process or Yes, Install to start the installation.

    If you click Yes, SUSE formats your hard disk and installs the selected packages. After installation finishes, SUSE reboots. (You can remove the CD or not, as you choose. SUSE will, by default, boot to hard disk even with the CD in.)

Although SUSE is now installed, the first time SUSE boots from hard disk you are immediately presented with a screen that asks you to do some basic configuration. With the YaST root password screen in front of you, continue to the next step.

15. **Root Password.** Enter the root password (twice). Enter up to eight characters. DES is the default encryption type used to protect your password. (You can select Expert Options to choose MD5 or Blowfish instead.) Refer to Chapter 6 for suggestions on choosing a good password.

16. **Network Configuration.** YaST probes to find any network cards, DSL connections, ISDN adapters, or modems connected to your computer. Select any of those items that appear on the screen, as appropriate, to configure it. After you are done, click Next. SUSE sets up and lets you test your network connections.

17. **User Authentication Method.** Normally, you will use your home computer in standalone mode, as it relates to user accounts. However, in a business setting, you may use NIS or LDAP to get user account lists that allow access to yours and other computers on your LAN. If the latter is the case, select Network Client and choose either NIS (a common facility used by UNIX systems to share configuration files) or LDAP (a standard directory service, used to share address books and other kinds of information on a network), depending on what your company supports. Then click Next.

18. **Add a New Local User.** You will want to add at least one user account, as prompted, for your computer. Right now, you only have the root user account set up for use on a standalone machine. Using that account for e-mail, Web browsing, or other common tasks is considered bad security practice. So you should add at least one user account for nonadministrative use of your computer. Add your full name, a short, one-word login name, and a password to protect that account. Then click Next.

When you are done, YaST writes the system configuration information to your computer. It then displays the Release Notes for your current version of SUSE. Click Next to continue.

19. **Hardware Configuration.** You now have the opportunity to configure other hardware devices to use with your system. Select to configure your graphics card, printer, sound card, or TV card. After graphics configuration, you should test your display as prompted. If the settings you choose don't work, select Ctrl+Alt+Backspace to exit and try to configure it again.

When you are done configuring hardware, click Accept. The settings are written to hard disk. An Installation Completed screen appears.

20. **Finish.** Click Finish. The system reboots and is ready for you to log in.

Starting with SUSE

If you created a user account during the preceding installation, SUSE should automatically log you in as that user and present you with the KDE desktop. (If you are presented with a graphical login screen instead, log in as that user now.) Here are a few things to help you get started using SUSE:

✦ **Desktop applications**—The desktop edition of SUSE described here includes a set of easily accessible desktop applications. On the desktop, try the Office icon to open OpenOffice.org to work with documents, spreadsheets, presentations, drawings, Web pages, or a variety of other content types. From the SUSE icon on the panel, select from among dozens of applications to try out.

✦ **Support**—A desktop icon takes you right to the SUSE Linux Portal (provided you have an Internet connection). You can search the support database for keywords relating to SUSE problems or read the FAQs without having an account. Sign up for a support account to get more benefits. Benefits include the capability to make support requests and get automatic patch support. For additional support options, visit `support.novell.com/linux`.

✦ **Network clients**—A Network Browsing icon on the desktop enables you to immediately begin browsing your LAN for Windows shared files (using Samba and SMB). On the panel, click the Web browser icon to open Mozilla Navigator or the e-mail icon to open Evolution e-mail client. SUSE also includes clients for online chat and Usenet news.

✦ **Reconfigure your computer**—Get to the YaST administration tool by selecting System ➪ YaST from the SUSE menu. You can reconfigure your system hardware and software from the YaST Control Center.

If you want to configure your desktop (change backgrounds, screensavers, or themes), use the KDE control center as you would with any KDE desktop. You can launch the control center from the SUSE menu (select Control Center).

Summary

SUSE is generally considered to be the best choice for enterprise-quality Linux systems, along with Red Hat Enterprise Linux. Its graphical installation and administrative tools (implemented in a facility called YaST) set it apart from other Linux distributions that are geared more toward technical users.

Since SUSE was acquired by Novell in 2003, SUSE Linux has become part of a larger, enterprise-ready product line. Boxed sets of SUSE are available in Personal, Professional, and Enterprise versions. Support offerings are available at many different levels. With Novell's worldwide sales and training organization, SUSE Linux has the backing it needs to compete to become the world's most popular commercial Linux system.

Because so much work has gone into the YaST installer and administrative interface, even an inexperienced user can be up and running on a newly installed SUSE system within an hour. Afterward, it's easy to begin using a variety of desktop and personal productivity applications from the SUSE desktop.

✦   ✦   ✦

Running KNOPPIX

A computer's operating system usually resides on the hard disk—but it doesn't have to. When a computer boots up, it typically checks first if there is a CD, floppy disk, or DVD in a drive and tries to boot from there (depending on BIOS settings). So, with up to 700MB (CD) or 4.7GB (DVD) of space on those media, why not use them to boot whole operating systems?

Well, that's exactly what bootable Linux distributions (also called live CDs) such as KNOPPIX do. In the case of KNOPPIX, one CD holds up to 2GB of compressed software for you to run that uncompresses on-the-fly. Start it up and you can try out all the features of a well-stocked Linux system, without touching the contents of your hard disk.

On the DVD-ROM   KNOPPIX is included on the DVD that comes with this book. In fact, it is the default option. Insert the DVD into your PC's DVD drive and, when you see the boot screen, press Enter. KNOPPIX should just start up, and you can begin using it as described in this chapter.

If you have never used Linux before, KNOPPIX gives you the chance to do so in a very safe way. If you are experienced with Linux, KNOPPIX can be used as a tool to take Linux with you everywhere, troubleshoot a computer, or check if a computer will run Linux. In any case, you can use this chapter to take a little tour of some great Linux features you can try out with KNOPPIX.

Understanding KNOPPIX

If you are impatient, you don't have to read any further. In most cases, you can just insert your DVD into your PC, reboot the computer, and start using KNOPPIX. However, if you have the time, read on a bit more.

Created by Klaus Knopper, KNOPPIX is a bootable Linux that includes a nice selection of open source software. Although it can also be delivered on DVD (as we did with this book) or other bootable media, the distribution is made to fit on a single, bootable CD. KNOPPIX is often considered to be the best bootable Linux available.

Looking Inside KNOPPIX

KNOPPIX boots right up to a full-featured desktop system complete with hundreds of desktop applications. It includes some powerful server and power user features. In fact, there are so many features, I won't even try to mention them all here, but just take a look at the following list of some of KNOPPIX's major components:

> **Note**   If you find that you are missing the NVIDIA graphics driver, Flash plug-in, or Quanta HTML editor you need, don't worry. KNOPPIX includes a KNOPPIX-Live Installer that lets you install selected software features from the network and run them live from KNOPPIX. I'll describe the KNOPPIX-Live Installer later in this chapter.

✦ **KDE**—A full-featured KDE desktop (which runs on the X Window System) that includes tools for configuring the desktop and a bunch of applications tailored for the KDE environment. (See Chapter 3 for descriptions of KDE.)

> **Note**   If you prefer the GNOME desktop environment, there are several customized versions of KNOPPIX that include GNOME. Most notable is the Gnoppix (www.gnoppix.org) distribution, which uses GNOME as its default desktop.

✦ **OpenOffice.org**—The OpenOffice.org suite of office productivity tools so that you can create documents, graphics, presentations, spreadsheets, and most anything you expect to be able to do with office applications. With KNOPPIX, I can give a presentation created in OpenOffice.org software anywhere that I have access to a PC. (See Chapter 20 for descriptions of OpenOffice.org productivity applications.)

✦ **Internet tools**—Web browsers (Mozilla browser, Konqueror, and Lynx), e-mail clients (Kmail, Mozilla mail, and mutt), a chat client (XChat IRC), a news reader (KNode), an instant messaging client (Gaim), and many more applications for using the Internet. (See Chapter 21 for descriptions of popular Web browsers and mail clients.)

✦ **Multimedia software**—Applications for playing music (xmms and KsCD), editing music (Audacity and Rosegarden), watching TV (xawtv), playing movies (xine), working with graphics (GIMP and xscanimage), using Webcams (gqcam), and displaying images (KView and Kuickshow). (Chapter 19 covers music and video players.)

✦ **Games**—A few dozen diverting board games, card games, strategy games, and puzzles to play. Try Potato Guy to keep the young ones busy, and Kasteroids for the older kids. (Chapter 22 talks about KDE and other games that you can run with KNOPPIX.)

✦ **Administrative tools** — A nice set of system and network administration tools that enables you to do some pretty advanced setup, monitoring, and debugging of your computer and network. (The Knoppix-STD distribution is configured specifically as a rescue CD to do almost anything you could imagine to check and fix your computer and network.)

✦ **Servers** — A few of the powerful server projects available for Linux, many of which don't require a lot of disk space: a Web server (Apache), FTP server (FTPd), file server (NFS), Window file/print server (Samba), proxy server (Squid), DNS server (bind9), login server (sshd), and DHCP server (dhcpd).

Note Using KNOPPIX (or any other bootable server Linux systems described in Chapter 18) as a server opens some amazing possibilities for serving the data from a Windows or other operating system to a network, while completely bypassing that operating system on the computer's hard disk.

✦ **Programming tools** — A good set of tools for developing software across a variety of programming environments.

KNOPPIX is based on Debian Linux, so a Debian user will be particularly comfortable with the selection and organization of features. KNOPPIX software packages are also done in deb package format, so you can use apt, dpkg, and related tools to list and otherwise manage the packages.

Note Refer to Chapter 9 for information on using apt and dpkg tools for managing software in Debian. Even if you don't install any new software, those tools provide an excellent way to search, list, or even upgrade software packages that are running in KNOPPIX.

What's Cool About KNOPPIX

The features just described are ones that come with many different Linux distributions. What makes them special with KNOPPIX is that you can often be up and using those features within a few minutes — without having to repartition your disk, install software, or do any configuration. For just trying out Linux or using it for some special, quick task you want to do, KNOPPIX is quite awesome.

Some features, however, are specific to KNOPPIX (as compared to a Linux system you would run from a hard disk). Many of those special features are there to help you through issues that relate to the fact that you are not working in a permanent setup. In particular, KNOPPIX includes the following:

✦ **Extraordinary hardware detection** — The capability to properly detect and configure hardware is one of the best features. During the boot-up procedure, KNOPPIX finds most common PC hardware components and loads the proper modules so it can use them. Its hwsetup tool relies on the Red Hat libkudzu facility to identify hardware, load appropriate modules, and create necessary device files.

For hardware that can't be detected, there are many boot options you can add to properly identify (or skip over) selected hardware devices. Some of them deal with particularly sticky issues related to video cards and running on laptop computers. (See Tables 11-1 through 11-3.)

✦ **Automatic desktop startup** — Instead of just dropping you to a command line, KNOPPIX does its best to start up a complete KDE desktop environment. Along the way, it adds some nice features, such as desktop icons giving you access to your computer's hard disk partitions.

✦ **Configuration tools** — Some hardware either can't be perfectly detected or requires some extra setup. You can access KNOPPIX-specific configuration tools for configuring your printer, TV card, sound card, network connections, and other features by clicking the desktop icon that looks like a squished penguin.

✦ **Save setup** — You don't have to lose the configuration you have done for KNOPPIX every time you reboot. Click the configuration icon to save your configuration — including your personal desktop configuration, files on the desktop, network settings, and graphics setup (X) — to floppy disk.

✦ **Persistent desktop** — You also can use the configuration icon to create a persistent KNOPPIX home directory on your hard disk or other medium so that you can store and reuse your desktop setup information and any data you save from session to session. (See the "Creating a Persistent Home Directory" section later in this chapter for details on setting up a persistent desktop.)

✦ **Add swap** — If you are using KNOPPIX from a computer with Linux installed, it automatically uses a swap partition that is set up there. On DOS and Windows systems, KNOPPIX enables you to create an extra swap area if you have space on an available DOS partition. (The mkdosswapfile command is used for this purpose.)

✦ **Work with Windows files** — KNOPPIX cannot include Microsoft Windows drivers for using Windows file systems (NTFS), but it provides a utility that enables you to install those drivers (providing you have legal rights to use them). The drivers enable you to safely read and write files from your hard disk if you are booting KNOPPIX from a PC with Windows installed.

For example, say that you have your entire music collection, images downloaded from your digital camera, and personal Web pages on your hard disk on a computer that was set up to be booted by Microsoft Windows XP. You boot KNOPPIX instead (notice that Microsoft Windows is not running at all). Suddenly your hard disk is just a place that holds a lot of files. You can now use applications that come with KNOPPIX to open the files on your hard disk to play the music, view or manipulate images, and display or change Web pages.

A testament to how well KNOPPIX is respected is how many other bootable Linux distributions are based on it. The KNOPPIX project even provides a KNOPPIX-customize package that lets anyone make his own customized KNOPPIX. There are specialized KNOPPIX derivatives that can be used to rescue a broken computer, play a range of multimedia content, or run a specific application.

See Chapter 17 for information on using a bootable Linux as a firewall/router and Chapter 18 for descriptions of many other bootable Linux distributions.

Examining Challenges with KNOPPIX

For most people, KNOPPIX is a special-use Linux system. It's a great way to try Linux or to access a computer that isn't set up the way you like. However, there are a few challenges with using KNOPPIX that you should keep in mind:

✦ **Reboot clears out KNOPPIX** — Unless you save your data to some other media (which you can do, as I describe later in this chapter), the entire KNOPPIX system goes away when you reboot. That means files on the desktop, installed software, system configuration, and anything else you do during your KNOPPIX session will be gone unless you explicitly save that information to a hard disk or some removable medium (floppy, CD, and so on).

✦ **Memory limitations** — KNOPPIX is made to be able to run without touching your hard disk, so when you save files to KNOPPIX, they are (by default) stored in your computer's memory (RAM). On my desktop system, which has 512MB of RAM, KNOPPIX assigned about 3MB to the root (/) partition and 396MB to ramdisk (to provide space in the /var and /home directories, where data is normally stored). So there is only about 100MB left to hold all the running applications.

✦ **Performance hits** — Even with today's faster CD and DVD drives, it's still slower getting data from CDs and DVDs than it is getting them from a local hard disk. Almost every component needed to run KNOPPIX (commands, libraries, and so on) is grabbed from the CD or DVD and decompressed on-the-fly. So it can take a bit longer to run commands with KNOPPIX than it would to run them from hard disk. (Watch the blinking light on your CD or DVD drive to see how often KNOPPIX goes there to get data.)

✦ **Uses your CD/DVD drive** — Because KNOPPIX relies so heavily on data from the CD or DVD, you can't remove it while you are using the system. So, if you have only one drive for removable media, you can't use it to access a music CD, install from another software disk, or burn data while you are using KNOPPIX.

Tiny multimedia players such as GeeXboX and MoviX can run totally from memory because they have very limited, specific functions. So you can put in a music CD or video CD or DVD to play content after the bootable Linux is loaded.

I must admit that the challenges described here are more of an explanation of how KNOPPIX works than they are problems with KNOPPIX itself. The idea that you can run a full-blown desktop and server operating system from a single CD (with nearly 2GB of available applications) is an awesome concept for someone who still remembers DOS and character terminals.

Seeing Where KNOPPIX Comes From

KNOPPIX was created by Klaus Knopper in Germany. Knopper follows in the great tradition of naming a distribution using a part of the creator's own name with "ix" or "ux" stuck on the end.

While a groundswell of interest and support has appeared for KNOPPIX in the past year or so, Knopper himself thinks of KNOPPIX more as a collection of tools he needs than as a full Linux distribution. Knopper works to provide only software that can be distributed freely, for both noncommercial and commercial use. So he doesn't even include some free software (such as browser plug-ins) that might restrict free redistribution, although he doesn't object to including non–open source software that can still be freely distributed.

There is no big company behind KNOPPIX, and development efforts continue to be headed up by Knopper himself. There are, however, many people who contribute bug reports and enhancements requests (see `www.knoppix.net/bugs`), and there are other developers who have helped create software specifically for KNOPPIX (in particular, Fabian Franz who, among other things, has contributed significant work to KNOPPIX installer-related features).

The only official KNOPPIX Web site is Knopper's own personal site: `www.knopper.net/knoppix`. The closest thing to an official community is a mailing list (`mailman.linuxtag.org/mailman/listinfo/debian-knoppix`) set up at LinuxTag.org with Knopper's blessing. LinuxTag hosts the LinuxTag Conference and Expo, which is a leading Linux and free software conference in Europe. For the 2004 conference, LinuxTag produced a special edition of KNOPPIX on DVD that held more than 5GB of software.

If you are looking for a way to get information and become involved with others who use and develop the system, the Knoppix.net site offers a very active forum and links to information about other KNOPPIX resources. It's a great place not only to get your questions answered, but also to find a wealth of links to FAQs, HOWTOs, and related projects. There is also an IRC channel (#knoppix on `irc.freenode.net`) and a Wiki used primarily to gather documentation (`www.knoppix.net/docs/`).

If you are considering creating your own customized distribution, tools for that purpose are currently under development and may be included with versions of KNOPPIX by the time you read this text. In the meantime, you can check out some remaster tools at `http://debian.tu-bs.de/knoppix/remaster/`. You can find out about versions that have already been created from the KNOPPIX Customizations page: `www.knoppix.net/docs/index.php/KnoppixCustomizations`.

Exploring Uses for KNOPPIX

Because there is so much you can do with KNOPPIX, it's hard to narrow my mind enough to give a few specific examples. So, let's start with a few concepts to help think about what you can do with KNOPPIX:

✦ **Your own, portable operating system** — You don't have to carry around a laptop or whole PC to make sure you have the software you need. Instead, you can use any PC that is available (with the exception of some unsupported hardware) and boot your whole computing environment with a single CD or floppy. By customizing your own KNOPPIX, you can add your own data and pick and choose applications as well.

✦ **A tool for managing data on any PC** — You can bypass the operating system and other software on any computer and use the applications on your KNOPPIX disk to manage the data on that computer.

Of course, these concepts are not exclusive to KNOPPIX because you could conceptually do the same thing with any boot floppy since the days of DOS (as well as any other bootable Linux). The difference is that KNOPPIX does those things so well. It lets you take over a computer, not just with a tiny rescue disk capable of running a few obtuse commands, but with at full-scale desktop, server, and administrative tool kit operating system. With that in mind, here are some ways people are using KNOPPIX:

✦ **Showing off Linux** — A demo can lack some punch when you have to spend an hour installing before you can make your point. With KNOPPIX, it can take about five minutes from the time you tell your friend about Linux to the time you have a complete desktop system running on his PC. And in the process, you don't have to worry about harming anything on his computer because you don't even need to touch his hard disk.

✦ **Testing a computer for Linux** — Instead of getting halfway through an install to see if your PC is capable of running Linux, you can boot KNOPPIX. If it works, you can check to see what drivers were loaded to deal with your hardware (type **lsmod** from a shell) and then go ahead and install any Linux you like to the hard disk.

✦ **Rescuing a computer or network** — Many tools for tracking down and fixing problems on both Linux and Windows systems are included in KNOPPIX. There is also a Knoppix-STD edition that includes dozens more tools for rescuing broken systems and tracing network problems (see www.knoppix-std.org).

✦ **Taking over a broken server** — If a Web server, file server, or firewall has been hacked or otherwise broken, you might be able to use KNOPPIX to safely server the data from a KNOPPIX boot disk while you fix the problem.

✦ **Doing anything you want** — For those of us who have gotten used to using Linux, it's a pain to go somewhere and have to do work or make a presentation on a computer that doesn't have the tools you need. By bringing the whole operating system, all your software tools and sometimes even your data (with a customized CD, separate floppy, or downloaded files), your computing environment can be the same wherever you go.

Now that you have some idea of what to do with KNOPPIX, let's get started.

Starting KNOPPIX

It's supposed to be easy to start KNOPPIX. With KNOPPIX in hand, all you really need is a PC that meets the minimum specifications.

Getting a Computer

If you are ready to start KNOPPIX, there are a few things I recommend.

✦ **A PC** — You need a PC that meets the minimal processor and memory requirements I describe a bit later. There are no hard disk space requirements since you don't need to touch the hard disk. However, to get better performance on low-RAM systems, you might want to create a swap partition on hard disk to enable you to run more processes (as described later).

✦ **Permission to reboot** — KNOPPIX is going to take over operation of the PC, so you need to be sure that it's okay to reboot it. Make sure that nobody else is currently using the computer or relying on it to be accessible over a network.

✦ **Internet connection (optional)** — It isn't necessary, but if your computer has an Ethernet card and a connection to the Internet, you can immediately start using KNOPPIX to browse the Web and otherwise take advantage of its communications tools. KNOPPIX will try to detect a DHCP server (to get an IP address and other information) and automatically configure itself to use the Internet or other network that is available.

The system requirements for running KNOPPIX are much lower than you need for most of the latest Linux systems. According to Klaus Knopper, you need:

✦ **CPU** — Intel-compatible i486 or better.

✦ **RAM** — 20MB (for text mode), 82MB (for graphics mode with KDE), or 128MB (to also run most office applications).

✦ **Bootable Drive (DVD drive to use the DVD or CD to use a CD)** — KNOPPIX is able to boot from drives that are IDE/ATAPI, Firewire, USB, or SCSI (provided that your computer can boot from those devices). Otherwise, you can create a boot floppy to start the process of booting KNOPPIX (described later). If you have a DVD drive, you can boot KNOPPIX directly from the DVD that comes with this book.

✦ **Graphics card** — Must be SVGA-compatible.

✦ **Mouse** — Supports any standard serial mouse, PS/2 mouse, or IMPS/2-compatible USB mouse.

Booting KNOPPIX

If you have a PC in front of you that meets the requirements, you can get started by following these steps:

1. Insert your KNOPPIX DVD or CD into the appropriate drive.

2. Reboot the computer. After a few moments, you will see the boot screen.

 Note Although the boot screens look different for the Linux Bible DVD and a regular KNOPPIX CD, you can proceed with the boot process the same way.

3. Press Enter. If all goes well, you should see the KNOPPIX desktop, and you can proceed to the "Using KNOPPIX" section. If KNOPPIX doesn't boot up properly or if you want to tune it further before it boots, continue on to the next section.

Correcting Boot Problems

By understanding a bit about the boot process you will, in most cases, be able to overcome any problems you might have installing KNOPPIX. Here are some things you should know:

✦ **Check boot order**— Your computer's BIOS has a particular order in which it looks for bootable operating systems. A typical order would be floppy, CD or DVD, and hard disk. If your computer skips over the KNOPPIX boot disk and boots right from hard disk, make sure that the boot order in the BIOS is set to boot from CD or DVD. To change the BIOS, restart the computer and as it first boots the hardware enter Setup (quickly) as instructed (usually by pressing F1, F2, or DEL). Look for a selection to change the boot order so that your CD or DVD boots before the hard disk.

✦ **Make boot floppies**— If your computer still can't boot from CD or DVD, you can create two floppy boot disks to start the boot process. To create the floppy boot disks from a running KNOPPIX system, run the `mkbootfloppy` command that is on the KNOPPIX disk (it automatically finds the floppy images and tells you when to put in the floppy disks). To create KNOPPIX floppy disks on other operating systems, refer to the KNOPPIX Boot Floppy How To (`www.knoppix.net/docs/index.php/BootFloppyHowTo`).

✦ **Add boot options**— Instead of just letting the boot process autodetect and configure everything about your hardware, you can add options to the boot prompt that will override what KNOPPIX autoconfiguration might do. Press F2 from the boot prompt to see additional boot options.

Some boot options are available with which you can try to overcome different issues at boot time. KNOPPIX refers to these options as *cheat codes*. For a more complete list, refer to the file knoppix-cheatcodes.txt, which you'll find in the KNOPPIX directory when you mount the CD or the DVD that comes with this book on any operating system.

Note   Many boot options can be used with different Linux systems. So if you are having trouble installing or booting a different Linux distribution, you can try any of these options to see if they work. Instead of the word "knoppix," you will probably use a different word to launch the install or boot process for other distributions (such as "linux" for Red Hat Linux systems or "morphix" for Morphix Live-CD, depending on the distribution).

When KNOPPIX first begins the boot process, you see the boot screen, with the boot: prompt at the bottom. The following tables provide boot prompt options that can help you get KNOPPIX running the way you like. Table 11-1 shows options to use when you want specific features turned on that may not be turned on by default when you boot.

Table 11-1
Boot Options to Select Features

Option	Feature
knoppix lang=??	Choose a specific language/keyboard. Replace ?? with one of the following: cn, de, da, es, fr, it, **nl**, pl, ru, sk, tr, tw, or us.
knoppix desktop=??	Instead of using the KDE desktop (kde), replace ?? with one of the following window managers: fluxbox, icewm, larswm, twm, wmaker, or xfce.
knoppix blind	Start BrailleTerminal (running without X).
knoppix brltty=type,port,table	Add parameters to use for the Braille device.
knoppix wheelmouse	For a wheel mouse, enable IMPS/2 protocol.
knoppix nowheelmouse	For a regular PS/2 mouse, force PS/2 protocol.
knoppix keyboard=us xkeyboard=us	Assign different keyboard drivers to use with text (shell) and graphical (X).
knoppix dma	Turn on DMA acceleration for all IDE drives.
knoppix alsa knoppix alsa=es1938	Select either of these two notations to select to use the ALSA driver (do at your own risk).

If there is hardware being improperly detected or configured, you can have KNOPPIX skip over that hardware. Table 11-2 contains options for skipping or turning off various hardware features:

Table 11-2	
Boot Options to Turn Off Hardware	
Option	**Result**
knoppix atapicd	No SCSI-Emulation for IDE CD-ROMs.
knoppix noagp	No detection of AGP graphics card.
knoppix noapic	Disable Advanced Programmable Interrupt Controller (can overcome some problems on SMP computers).
knoppix acpi=off	Disable Advanced Configuration and Power Interface (ACPI).
knoppix noapm	No Advanced Power Management support. (With a working acpi, apm will be off by default. Only one can be active at a time.)
knoppix noaudio	No sound support.
knoppix nodhcp	Don't try to start your network connection automatically via DHCP.
knoppix fstab	Don't read the fstab file to find file systems to mount or check.
knoppix firewire	No detection of Firewire devices.
knoppix nopcmcia	No detection of PCMCIA card slots.
knoppix noscsi	No detection of SCSI devices.
knoppix noswap	No detection of swap partitions.
knoppix nousb	No detection of USB devices.
knoppix pnpbios=off	Don't initialize plug-and-play (PnP) in the BIOS.
knoppix failsafe	Do almost no hardware detection.

Table 11-3 lists options that may help if you are having trouble with your video card. Several of these options are particularly useful if you are having trouble with X on a laptop.

Table 11-3
Boot Options to Fix Video Problems

Option	Result
knoppix noddc	No Display Data Channel (DDC) detection of monitor.
knoppix screen=??	Pick X screen resolution. Replace ?? with 640×480, 800×600, 1024×768, 1280×1024, or any other resolution supported by your video card.
knoppix xvrefresh=60	Set vertical refresh rate to 60 Hz for X (or other value as specified by monitor's manual).
knoppix xhrefresh=80	Set horizontal refresh rate to 80 Hz for X (or other value as specified by monitor's manual).
knoppix xserver=??	Replace ?? with X-Server: XFree86 or XF86_SVGA.
knoppix xmodule=??	Select the specific driver to use for your video card. Replace ?? with one of the following: ati, fbdev, i810, mga, nv, radeon, savage, s3radeon, svga, or i810.
knoppix 2	Runlevel 2, Textmode only.
knoppix vga=normal	No-framebuffer mode, but X.
knoppix fb1280x1024	Use fixed framebuffer graphics (1).
knoppix fb1024x768	Use fixed framebuffer graphics (2).
knoppix fb800x600	Use fixed framebuffer graphics (3).

Customize KNOPPIX

Several boot options exist that tell KNOPPIX to look for a customized home directory or configuration information on hard disk or floppy. See the "Customize KNOPPIX" section later in this chapter for information on how to both customize KNOPPIX and tell KNOPPIX where to look for customized information at boot time. (Unless they were created from KNOPPIX, most other Linux distributions will not use these boot options.)

Special Features and Workarounds

Other boot options are described in the knoppix-cheatcodes.txt file mentioned earlier. Things you can do with boot options include changing the splash screen when KNOPPIX boots, running in expert mode so you can load your own drivers, selecting to run either a 2.4 or 2.6 kernel, testing your computer's RAM, and trying to overcome special problems with laptop computers.

Testing the CD

If you suspect that you have a bad KNOPPIX CD, I recommend you run this from the boot prompt:

```
knoppix testcd
```

If you are still not able to boot KNOPPIX at this point, it might be that your hardware is either not supported or is broken in some way. To further pursue the problem, I recommend that you check out an appropriate forum at www.knoppix.net.

Running KNOPPIX from RAM

To improve performance, KNOPPIX offers a way to run the entire KNOPPIX distribution from RAM (provided you have enough available) or install it on hard disk and run it from there. Provided that you have more than 1GB of RAM, you can run KNOPPIX entirely from RAM (so you can remove the KNOPPIX DVD or CD and use that drive while you run KNOPPIX) by typing the following from the boot prompt:

```
knoppix toram
```

Installing KNOPPIX to Hard Disk

You can run KNOPPIX entirely from hard disk if your hard disk is either a FAT or EXT2 file system type and contains at least 800MB of space. To do this, you must know the name of the hard disk partition you are installing on. For example, to use the first partition on the first IDE drive you would use /dev/hda1. In that case, to copy KNOPPIX to that disk partition you would type this at the boot prompt:

```
knoppix tohd=/dev/hda1
```

You can watch as KNOPPIX is copied to your hard disk partition, and then boots automatically from there. The next time you want to boot KNOPPIX, you can boot it from hard disk again by inserting the KNOPPIX medium and typing the following:

```
knoppix fromhd=/dev/hda1
```

With KNOPPIX running from your hard disk, you can safely eject your CD or DVD and use it for other things (type **eject /dev/cdrom**). Refer to the knoppix-cheatcodes. txt file for information on other things you can do from the KNOPPIX boot prompt.

Using KNOPPIX

Rather than go over how to use the features in KNOPPIX that are common to many Linux systems (KDE, Internet tools, word processors, and so on), I'll give you a quick tour of the special features in KNOPPIX. If your computer booted KNOPPIX properly, you should see a screen that is similar to the one shown in Figure 11-1.

Figure 11-1: KNOPPIX boots to a full KDE desktop that is ready to run.

I've opened a couple of applications to illustrate some things, and the following sections explore what you typically get when KNOPPIX comes.

Using the KDE Desktop in KNOPPIX

KDE is the default desktop environment that comes with KNOPPIX. You can change that at the boot prompt to use one of several window managers instead, or get a Gnoppix disk instead to use the GNOME environments. But, as delivered, the desktop looks similar to what you see in Figure 11-1.

The KNOPPIX version of KDE matches pretty closely the descriptions in Chapter 3, although there are a few items related to the KNOPPIX KDE desktop that are worth noting:

> ✦ **Desktop icons** — To get information about KNOPPIX, click the KNOPPIX icon (choose a language, and then find links to FAQs, Knopper.Net, and general KNOPPIX information) or the LinuxTag icon (to read the licenses). There is also the requisite Trash icon.

> ✦ **Disk icons** — Any CD, DVD, floppy, or other removable medium drive is displayed as an icon on the desktop. Of course, this includes the drive holding the KNOPPIX disk, which you can get to directly to do such things as find boot images or KNOPPIX documentation.

Hard disk partitions are also represented by icons on your KNOPPIX desktop. Click one of those icons and you can access (read-only) the files on that hard disk partition. This is a great feature for getting the information you need without, by default, letting you change or otherwise damage the data on the computer. To make a disk writable, right-click on the disk icon and select Actions ⇨ Change read/write mode. If you are not able to write to the disk, refer to the section on making disks writable later in this chapter.

✦ **KDE Panel** — KNOPPIX loads the KDE Panel with applets and launchers for a few useful applications. Click the K button to display the menu containing most KDE applications for you to select. The Web Browser icon launches the Konqueror browser, which is the KDE file manager as well.

✦ **KNOPPIX configuration** — Click the squished penguin icon in the KDE Panel to see a menu of configuration tools specific to KNOPPIX. This is where you can tune up your TV card, configure printers, get your network connection going, and even start a few servers. I describe some of these subjects — in particular, how to save data and configuration information across sessions with this otherwise ethereal operating system — later in this chapter.

✦ **Launching games, players, and other stuff** — From the KDE menu, you can launch applications as you would from any desktop operating system. Just to illustrate that, I launched a simple game (Penguin Mastermind) and a music player (XMMS) for Figure 11-1.

Running KNOPPIX, at this point, is just like running any other Linux system with a KDE desktop, with one major exception. By default, you can't save any data permanently. There are a few ways around this issue, especially if you expect to use KNOPPIX on a regular basis. Refer to sections on creating persistent desktops and opening disks for writing later in this chapter.

Getting on the Network

If you have an Ethernet card and a connection to a network that has a DHCP server, your KNOPPIX system should just start up and offer immediate access to that network (and possibly the Internet if it offers such a connection). If not, KNOPPIX offers several tools for configuring your network connection, including:

✦ **Dial-up modem** — From the squished penguin, select Network/Internet⇨ /dev/modem connection setup. The menus that appear help you create a dial-up connection to the Internet, or other TCP/IP network, using a serial modem, USB modem, IRDA cellphone/PDA, or Bluetooth cellphone/PDA.

✦ **ADSL router** — From the squished penguin, select Network/Internet⇨ADSL /PPPOE configuration. It will help you connect your broadband ADSL router to connect to the Internet.

✦ **GPRS connection** — From the squished penguin, select Network/Internet⇨ GPRS connection to set up a connection via your cellphone provider.

✦ **Network card** — From the squished penguin, select Network/Internet⇨Network card to configure your Ethernet card (assuming you don't just want to use DHCP to get your network address).

✦ **ISDN** — From the squished penguin, select Network/Internet⇨ISDN to use ISDN to connect to the network.

✦ **Wireless Card** — From the squished penguin, select Network/Internet⇨Wavelan to use a wireless Ethernet card to connect to the network.

In addition to the interfaces available here, you can use the `wvdialconf` command to create your dial-out connection as described in Chapter 5.

Installing Software in KNOPPIX

Despite the fact that KNOPPIX includes a wide range of software applications, there may be some special software package you want to use with it that isn't included. KNOPPIX has a feature for installing software while you are running from the CD that is called the KNOPPIX-Live Installer.

To use the KNOPPIX-Live Installer, click the squished penguin on the KNOPPIX panel and select Utilities ⇨ Install software. After being warned that this is still experimental software, a list of software that you can install with KNOPPIX-Live Installer appears. The list includes software that can't be freely distributed, such as Flash plug-ins for your browser or NVIDIA drivers for your video cards.

Select the software package you want to install. KNOPPIX will try to use the Debian installer to download the selected packages and install them on your computer. Remember that the software is being installed in the version of KNOPPIX that is running in RAM. So, the software will disappear the next time you reboot, unless you do something to preserve your data (such as creating a persistent desktop before you install the software you want to keep).

Saving Files in KNOPPIX

When you reboot your computer with KNOPPIX, you not only lose KNOPPIX itself, but you lose any data and configuration information you may have created along the way. That's because, by default, KNOPPIX runs from your system's RAM and a nonwritable CD or DVD. Using tools and procedures that come with KNOPPIX, there are ways in which you can keep that information going forward.

KNOPPIX happily gives you a login name (knoppix) and a home directory (`/home/knoppix`), each time you boot from KNOPPIX. You can save files to that directory, as well as change your desktop and system configuration information (which is stored in that directory and in `/etc` files). The problem is that those directories are in RAM, so they disappear when you reboot.

The following sections give you some ideas about how to save what you do in your KNOPPIX session to use in future sessions.

Writing to Hard Disk

Although hard disk partitions are mounted read-only by default, you can make them read/write if you like. Then you can store any data you want to save on those partitions. (You can simply drag and drop files to those partitions.)

If your hard disk partitions are Linux partitions, it's pretty easy to do this. With older Windows systems that use VFAT partitions, it's not too hard either. With NTFS partitions, things get a bit trickier:

Caution   Up to this point, there's not much risk of damaging any data on your hard disk. Once you make your disks writable, you have the potential for deleting or changing that data. Keep that in mind if the computer doesn't belong to you of if you are not used to using Linux. Regardless of which user you are logged in as, KNOPPIX does not prevent you from changing any file in a writable hard disk partition.

Mounting Linux Partitions for Writing

KNOPPIX usually identifies all hard disk partitions and adds entries for each one in your /etc/fstab file. If you click the icon representing that partition, the partition is automatically mounted and a folder opens to the root of that directory.

The name of each partition (hda1, hda2, and so forth for IDE partitions; sda1, sda2, and so on for SCSI disk partitions) is shown on the desktop icon. With that information, here is how you can make any of those partitions writable:

1. Click the hard disk partition you want to write to on the KNOPPIX desktop. A folder opens, displaying the top directory in that partition.

2. When you know which partition you want to write to, close all folders or shells that have that partition open. (With the partition open, you can't remount it.)

3. Open a Terminal from the panel and become root user by typing

   ```
   $ cd
   $ su -
   #
   ```

4. Make sure that the partition you want to mount as writable is unmounted. For example, to unmount the second IDE hard disk partition (hda2), type

   ```
   # umount /dev/hda2
   ```

   If the command completes quietly or if it says "not mounted," you are fine. If it says "device is busy," there is still a shell or folder window that is holding that partition open. Before you can continue, you must close whatever is holding the partition open and make sure the umount completes.

5. Next, you need to mount the partition so it is writable. Here's how:

   ```
   # mount -orw /dev/hda2
   ```

At this point you can open the folder to the partition (hda2 in our example) or open a shell and write to that directory (/mnt/hda2 and any subdirectories). To make that change permanent (in the KNOPPIX sense), you need to change the /etc/fstab to add rw to the entry for the partition so it is mounted read/write by default. Again, with the example of /dev/hda2, an entry in /etc/fstab to mount that partition read/write could look as follows:

```
/dev/hda2 /mnt/hda2 ext3 noauto,users,exec,rw 0 0
```

With that change, simply typing **mount /dev/hda2** mounts the directory with read/write permissions. You can save that change permanently, as described in the "Keeping Your KNOPPIX Configuration" section later in this chapter.

Mounting Windows Partitions for Writing

Getting your Windows partitions mounted for writing is a bit tougher. Although using FAT and VFAT file systems works pretty much the same as described for Linux partitions (provided they are properly detected and configured in /etc/fstab), the drivers for using NTFS file systems (the current default for Windows) are unreliable for writing.

If you have legal Windows drivers on your hard disk (which you should if you are booting KNOPPIX from an otherwise-Windows machine), KNOPPIX provides a reliable way to set up your NTFS partitions to be read/write accessible from KNOPPIX. Here's how:

 Caution   You must make sure that you have the legal right to use Microsoft NTFS-related drivers to use this procedure.

1. Click the squished penguin logo in the panel, and then select Utilities ⇨ Captive NTFS. The Captive Microsoft Windows Drivers Acquire window appears.

2. Click Forward. The Local Disks Drivers Scan window appears, ready to look for the drivers KNOPPIX needs to access the NTFS partitions for writing.

3. Click Forward to look for the drivers. If the drivers are found, you can continue. If not, it asks for a location on the network where it can get the drivers. If that is not available, it offers the opportunity to get the Microsoft Windows XP Service Pack, if you are legally allowed to get that.

4. Once the necessary drivers are installed, you can mount the NTFS partition using the mount command with the captive-ntfs file system type. For example, if your NTFS partition is on hda1, you could type the following (as root user):

```
# umount /dev/hda1
# mkdir /mnt/captive-LABEL_C
# mount -t captive-ntfs /dev/hda1 /mnt/captive-Label_C
```

Now you should be able to access the NTFS partition from the `/mnt/captive-LABEL_C` directory.

Creating a Persistent Home Directory

If you are going to use the computer more than once with KNOPPIX (or if you just want more storage space for files than your computer has available in RAM) you can assign your KNOPPIX home directory (`/home/knoppix`) to use some of the available space on your hard drive. That can be done by either:

✦ Assigning an entire partition to be used for your home directory.

✦ Assigning a part of that partition for your home directory, in the form of an image file.

You can also put your persistent home directory on rewritable, removable media, such as a memory stick. Once you create that area to use as your home directory, you can tell KNOPPIX to use it every time you restart KNOPPIX. Here's what you do:

1. Click the squished penguin in the panel, and then select Configure ⇨ Create a Persistent KNOPPIX Home Directory. A window appears, asking if you are ready to create a persistent home directory.

2. Click Yes to continue. You are asked which partition you want to use for your persistent home directory.

3. Select the partition you want from the list and click OK. You are asked if you want to use the entire partition and format it as a Linux file system or just create an image.

4. Don't click Yes unless you are prepared to erase an entire partition! Click No (the safer route) to just add an image file on a directory where you have space. If you are creating the image file, you are asked how big to make it.

5. Type the number of megabytes to assign to your home directory. Be sure that that much space is available on the partition. (When the partition is mounted later, you can type `df -h` to see how much space is available on it.) You are asked if you want to save the home directory in an encrypted format.

6. Select No, to not have the directory selected as encrypted (if you choose Yes, you'll have to specify a long password that you will need to access the persistent home directory at boot time). The partition or image file should be created now.

When I ran this procedure to create a 100MB image on the hda5 partition, it created the file `/mnt/hda5/knoppix.img`, which had 97MB of available space. To see how to use that directory, see the "Restarting KNOPPIX" section later in this chapter.

Keeping Your KNOPPIX Configuration

After you have gone through all the work to configure your desktop, printer, network, disks, and other preferences for your KNOPPIX setup, it's a shame to lose all that on your next reboot. Well, KNOPPIX offers a way that you can save your configuration information and reuse if for your next session. That saved information can be stored on a floppy disk or any other medium that is accessible (such as your hard disk) the next time you reboot KNOPPIX. Here's how:

1. From the squished penguin icon on the panel, click Configure ➪ Save KNOPPIX configuration.

2. Choose the configuration files to save. You can choose to save your personal configuration (from /home/knoppix .kde and .mozilla directories), files on the desktop, your network configuration, X configuration, and other system configuration files (from /etc).

3. Choose to save your configuration files to your floppy disk or to any available disk partition that is writable. Choosing floppy can make the configuration portable, whereas using the hard disk makes the configuration easily reusable on the same machine.

4. If you are saving to floppy, insert the floppy and click OK. The data will be saved to floppy disk.

The results from this action are that the knoppix.sh and configs.tbz files are created on floppy disk. The configs.tbz file contains all the saved configuration files from your /home and /etc directories. The knoppix.sh file is a script that tells KNOPPIX how to install those files when KNOPPIX boots up. The next time you start KNOPPIX, you can use the configuration files, as described in the next section.

Note   Those who create their own customized KNOPPIX boot disks can simply add their knoppix.sh and config.tbz files to the top-level directory of the CD, so KNOPPIX will just boot to their personalized configuration without worrying about an extra floppy or other medium.

Restarting KNOPPIX

You can start KNOPPIX anytime by just inserting your KNOPPIX CD or DVD and restarting your computer. However, if you want to take advantage of the persistent desktop you set up or the saved configuration information, you need to add some options to the KNOPPIX boot prompt. Here's how:

1. Insert your KNOPPIX CD or DVD into the computer and reboot. You should see the KNOPPIX boot prompt.

2. Press F3 (before KNOPPIX boots) to see if there are any additional boot options that are required.

3. If you have a configuration floppy boot disk (or other removable media created in an earlier procedure), insert that disk now.

4. At the boot prompt, type one of the following command lines, which are different ways to load your configuration files:

```
boot: knoppix floppyconfig
boot: knoppix myconf=/dev/hda1
boot: knoppix myconf=/dev/sda1
boot: knoppix myconf=scan
```

These KNOPPIX boot commands, respectively, get configuration information from the floppy disk, look for that information on the first IDE drive partition (/dev/hda1), look for it on the first SCSI drive partition (/dev/sda1), or scan all available drives to find the information. To boot to a persistent desktop (assuming you set one up earlier), you could instead type:

```
boot: knoppix home=/dev/hda1/knoppix.img
boot: knoppix home=/dev/sda1/knoppix.img
boot: knoppix home=scan
```

The previous boot commands, respectively, assign the KNOPPIX home directory (/home/knoppix) to the /dev/hda1/knoppix.img file, to the /dev/sda1/knoppix.img file, or to the image file found by scanning all available directories for that file. You could also combine one from each of the two preceding command sets to both read your configuration files and assign a persistent desktop, as follows:

```
boot: knoppix floppyconfig home=/dev/hda1/knoppix.img
```

Now you are ready to continue your KNOPPIX session where you left off last time, with the same configuration and data files available.

Summary

KNOPPIX offers what many feel is the best bootable Linux today. It gives you a fully configured Linux desktop system available virtually anywhere you can find a bootable PC.

Besides its desktop features, KNOPPIX contains software needed to use many server, programming, and troubleshooting features of Linux as well. Despite the fact that KNOPPIX runs as a bootable system in RAM, by default, there are ways to configure it to save data and configuration information across multiple boot sessions.

KNOPPIX is particularly valuable as a tool for accessing a damaged computer so that you can troubleshoot it. With a KNOPPIX disk booted on a computer that was installed to use Microsoft Windows or other operating system, you can use KNOPPIX to access and work with data on that computer's hard disk.

✦   ✦   ✦

Running Yellow Dog Linux

Yellow Dog Linux is the premier Linux distribution for the PowerPC platform. Offered by Terra Soft Solutions (www.terrasoftsolutions.com), Yellow Dog Linux provides unparalleled concentration on the needs of the PowerPC users. Because most Linux distributions focus on the Intel/AMD (x86) platform, it's sometimes startling to realize that there's a major Linux distribution, with a passionate community of its own, providing a strong presence in the world of PowerPCs.

Yellow Dog Linux is not included on the Linux Bible DVD that comes with this book. You can purchase it from Terra Soft Solutions (www.terrasoftsolutions.com/store) or download the four-CD installation set from a Yellow Dog Linux mirror site (for a list of mirror sites, see: http://yellowdoglinux.com/resources/ftp_mirrors.shtml). See Appendix A for information on burning CDs.

Terra Soft Solutions has focused its efforts on making Yellow Dog Linux work for a wide range of Apple products, resulting in less chance of hardware incompatibilities. This is one of the distribution's strengths. Another heartening note is that Terra Soft Solutions is an Apple Authorized OEM Value Added Reseller with permission from Apple to install Linux on Apple hardware, retaining any hardware warranties provided by Apple.

Mac OS X, in the form of Aqua, is considered one of the most advanced graphical user interfaces on the market today. With a sophisticated interface available on the Apple platform, a user might question putting Linux on Apple hardware, but there are many valid reasons to install Linux on the PowerPC architecture, including:

   ✦ **Cost of applications** — Commercial applications usually have a higher price of ownership than their open source counterparts for similar functionality. For instance, the latest word processor on the Mac OS X platform can cost hundreds of dollars, whereas the open source alternatives are generally free. The free software available for Linux far exceeds that available for the Mac OS X platform.

Note   While some of the more popular open source programs are available for Mac OS X, they may require a port of the software, as opposed to a recompile. Porting applications is a more complicated process and can be very frustrating for many users. Porting is outside the sphere of this book.

✦ **Extended hardware life** — Linux is well known for its low operation requirements. You can use Yellow Dog Linux on machines that aren't necessarily supported by the latest Mac OS X version and still run the latest Linux applications.

✦ **Uniformity** — Linux is widely deployed, especially for back-office functions. By using Yellow Dog Linux (often referred to as YDL), you can mix PowerPC hardware with Intel hardware in the same production environment, with application and operating system uniformity, reducing costs associated with the support of two different operating systems. Because Linux is open source and widely available, you also reduce your dependence on one entity for your operating systems.

✦ **Security** — Yellow Dog Linux has the support of thousands of programmers who constantly develop patches and updates for software, as opposed to depending on a commercial entity to release patches.

✦ **Ease of administration/use** — Linux (and particularly Fedora Core, on which Yellow Dog Linux is based) is so widely deployed, with more installations occurring every day, that it's understood and managed by a large user/administrator group. Using a standard interface, it's often easier for system administrators and users to complete tasks on a familiar system.

✦ **Mac-on-Linux** — Mac-on-Linux software enables you to run Mac OS X (10.1-10.3.3), Mac OS 7.5.2-9.2.2, or another instance of Linux within your active Yellow Dog Linux session, so you get the best of both worlds.

A few different versions of Yellow Dog Linux are available that cover a wide spectrum of current and legacy PowerPC hardware:

✦ **Yellow Dog Linux 4.0** — Terra Soft Solutions has released version 4.0, which is aimed at the desktop users who have hardware starting from G3 Blue and White (300–450 MHz) all the way to the dual G5 Power Mac Towers. This is the 32-bit version of its distribution.

✦ **Yellow Dog Linux 3.0.1** — The prior version (October 1, 2004, and before) of Yellow Dog, which supports the beige G3 hardware (66 MHz) and below product line (Old World ROM) as well as most of the same hardware that Yellow Dog Linux 4.0 supports.

✦ **Y-HPC** — A planned variation of Yellow Dog based on the 64-bit Fedora Core version of Linux. This version is for high-performance computing and promises to offer high-performance support for Xserve G5s or cluster nodes. This is currently not available as a standalone product, but Terra Soft Solutions will preload it on hardware purchased through the company.

Digging into Yellow Dog

Yellow Dog Linux offers a Fedora Core 2, RPM-based distribution that is highly compatible with most available open source software. By basing the Yellow Dog distribution on a widely deployed and used X86 distribution such as Red Hat's Fedora Core, Terra Soft Solutions has been able to quickly deploy a very uniform, user-friendly experience for its user base. This section takes a look at some of the highlights of the Yellow Dog distribution.

Yellow Dog Linux 4.0 offers four full CDs of software with some of the following applications:

✦ 2.6.7 Linux Kernel

✦ X.org 6.6

✦ KDE 3.3 desktop (unified with GNOME to provide easy access to other desktop environments programs)

✦ GNOME 2.6.0 desktop (unified with KDE to provide easy access to other desktop environments programs)

✦ OpenOffice 1.1.1 (suite of productivity tools including a spreadsheet program, drawing program, presentation software, and a full-featured, Microsoft Word-compatible word processor)

✦ More than 1,300 other application packages from programming tools to Web browsers.

The wide range of applications included on the Yellow Dog CDs is enough to keep even the most computer-savvy person happy, but many more choices are available on the Internet, so you should be able to find an application that fits your needs.

Fedora Core is the community-supported version of what was previously the ubiquitous Red Hat Linux distribution. As a derivative of Fedora Core, Yellow Dog Linux can offer the advantages of Fedora features on a MAC platform, including:

✦ **Red Hat Package Manager (RPM) software.** Starting with software packages from the Fedora project helps Yellow Dog Linux avoid compatibility problems suffered by some Linux distributions. Users can also rely on well-known RPM packaging tools for adding, removing, and managing software.

✦ **Anaconda installer.** Yellow Dog takes advantage of the well-tested Anaconda installer for easy installation.

✦ **Kudzu hardware detection.** By starting with the Fedora Core kudzu facility for detecting and configuring hardware, Yellow Dog has a stable foundation for probing equipment that has been extended to work with Mac hardware.

Refer to Chapter 8 for more information on the Fedora Core project and some of the specifics regarding its implementation.

Installing Yellow Dog Linux

Before you can install Yellow Dog Linux, you need to get a copy of it from some of the many resources available. The first and most recommended avenue is to purchase it from the vendor. This has the dual effect of your acquiring the distribution from the source as well as supporting the company that creates Yellow Dog Linux so it can continue development for the PowerPC platform.

To purchase Yellow Dog Linux from Terra Soft Solutions, visit the Terra Soft Solutions Web store at `http://terrasoftsolutions.com/store/`. When purchasing from Terra Soft Solutions, you receive the following in a box set:

✦ Four install CDs and four source CDs.

✦ *Getting Started with Yellow Dog Linux,* a book that covers all the information a beginning Linux user would need to know to get a fully operational Yellow Dog Linux system running.

✦ Optional 60 days of installation support (you can purchase the box set with or without support, depending on your needs and skill level with Linux).

✦ Other goodies (sticker, flexible flier depending on package purchased).

✦ The knowledge that you are supporting the company that created the product, allowing further development.

Alternatives to purchasing the Yellow Dog Linux box set include:

✦ **Purchasing a subscription to YDL.net.** This is Terra Soft Solutions online resource for Yellow Dog Linux users. You can get e-mail accounts and Web space as well as prerelease access to the latest version of Yellow Dog Linux before it is available for general release. The costs vary depending on which version you choose. More information is available at `http://www.ydl.net/`.

✦ **Downloading and creating your own ISO.** You can download the distribution from one of the many Linux mirrors as identified at `http://yellowdoglinux.com/resources/ftp_mirrors.shtml` and burn your own ISO.

✦ **Purchasing online.** If you have a slow Internet connection and want to try Yellow Dog, you can purchase burned CDs from various Linux stores on the Internet. Use your favorite search engine to locate one near you.

Hardware Support

Hardware support with the Linux operating system was a major issue in the past, but as Linux's popularity has grown, many device makers have provided access to their hardware drivers or in some cases have created hardware drives for Linux. While this is still an issue with hardware that is brand new in the X86 community, the effects are lessened with the PowerPC platform because all hardware is generally created to Apple's exacting standards. Terra Soft Solutions' focus on Apple hardware and generally fewer variations in hardware add up to support being much faster for the PowerPC platform.

One of the great things about Yellow Dog Linux is that as you dig into it (no pun intended), you discover that some of the hardware compatibility issues faced by the X86 Linux crowd (such as with Winmodems, the plethora of hardware configuration options, and so forth) are minimized or eliminated. With Terra Soft Solutions, a fully authorized Apple Value Added Reseller, you are assured that the hardware you are using will be supported. There are some notable hardware support differences with the release of YDL 4.0, but the fully capable 3.0.1 version covers any gaps of the 4.0 product.

In addition to being able to install Yellow Dog Linux on your own Apple hardware, you can purchase Apple hardware from Terra Soft Solutions with Yellow Dog Linux preinstalled.

Terra Soft Solutions has developed official lists of hardware configurations that have been specifically tested with Yellow Dog Linux (`http://yellowdoglinux.com/support/hardware/breakdown/index.php`). The Yellow Dog 4.0 list includes:

✦ Power Mac G3 (Yosemite Blue and White 300–450 MHz G3)

✦ Power Mac G4 (Power Mac G4 PCI 350–400 MHz G4 and above)

✦ Power Mac G5 (1.6 GHz G5 and above)

✦ iMac (Rev A,B 233 MHz G3)

✦ PowerBook (Lombard 333–400 MHz G3, Pismo 400–500 MHz FW G3, Titanium 400 MHz–1 GHz G4, Powerbook 12" 867 MHz–1.33 GHz, and Powerbook 15–17" 1.0–1.5 GHz G4)

✦ iBook (300–366 MHz G3 — 800 MHz 1.2 GHz G4)

✦ HPC (Xserver Cluster Node 1.33 MHz G4, Single/Dual 1.33 GHz G4, Cluster Node 2.0 GHz G5, and Single/Dual 2.0 GHz G5)

Most notably missing from Yellow Dog Linux 4.0 supported hardware is Old World ROM or beige G3 and below hardware such as 8500s, 7200s, and Performa PowerPCs. YDL 3.0.1 supports this hardware and most of the hardware currently supported by Yellow Dog Linux 4.0. The hardware supported and tested for Yellow Dog Linux 3.0.1 includes:

✦ Power Mac 4400–9600

✦ Power Mac beige G3 models and blue-and-white G3 models

✦ Most hardware supported by Yellow Dog Linux 4.0

If you have older hardware that isn't officially supported, you should still be able to use Yellow Dog Linux 4.0, but you'll be running in an unsupported configuration, so caveat emptor. The reason for the dropping of older hardware is so that Terra Soft Solutions could focus on the most likely configurations, instead of trying to support every possible system, of which the Old World ROM systems were particularly troublesome.

Planning Your Installation

Before starting installation, back up any data you want to retain on external media (CD, hard drive, and so on). This is a precautionary measure in case your system overwrites data that is important to you. The next step is to determine if you are going to multiboot Mac OS with Yellow Dog Linux or if you are going to install Yellow Dog Linux as a standalone product. If you choose to multiboot, you must decide if you will use two hard drives or partition (or logically divide) a single hard drive to house both Linux and Mac OS.

Installing Mac OS X and Yellow Dog Linux on One Hard Drive

If you choose to use one hard drive to house both Mac OS and Yellow Dog Linux, you need to load Mac OS (X or 9) first and then create a partition for Yellow Dog Linux as the first partition. In Mac OS X do the following:

1. Boot off the Mac OS X CD by holding down the C key with the Mac OS X CD-ROM inserted (to boot off the CD-ROM).

2. From the Install menu, select Open Disk Utility.

3. Select your hard drive and then click the partition tab on the right side.

4. Choose how many partitions you want (2 partitions is a good selection for both Mac OS X and Yellow Dog Linux, or if you want to install Mac OS 9 or below and Mac OS X, you can choose the number of partitions needed.)

5. Choose the first gray partition that is untitled (it should be the top one).

6. In the Format menu, select Free Space for your Yellow Dog Linux partition. Note that you can change the size of the partition if you don't want to use the defaults by entering the size you want or by using the slider. You can also name the partition if you like.

Note

Be sure to create a partition large enough for your Linux installation. The default sizes for some of the types of installations (discussed later in this chapter) are:

> Personal Desktop — 2GB
>
> Workstation — 2.5GB
>
> Server — 1GB
>
> Everything — 6GB

These are size estimations, and you will need more room for any other applications you want as well as for personal files, etc.

7. Choose the second gray partition and leave it as the default (Mac OS Extended) for your Mac OS X partition. You can name this as well if you like and adjust the size according to your needs.

8. Click the Partition button and then quit the partition tool.

Resume your installation of Mac OS X as normal.

Installing Mac OS 9 or Below and Yellow Dog Linux on One Hard Drive

If you want to install Mac OS 9 or below in addition to Yellow Dog Linux on one hard drive, you can perform the following for a dual-booted machine:

1. Boot off the Mac OS CD by holding down the C key with the Mac OS CD-ROM inserted (to boot off the CD-ROM).

2. Double-click the Utilities or Disk Tools folder. Double-click the Drive Setup application.

3. Select your hard drive in the List of Drives in the Drive Setup window.

4. Click the Initialize button, and then click the Custom Setup button.

5. Choose how many partitions you want in the Custom Setup pop-up window (2 partitions is a good selection for both Mac OS and Yellow Dog Linux, or 3 partitions for Mac OS, Mac OS X, and Yellow Dog Linux). You can use the slider bar to change the size of the partitions here.

6. Choose the top partition and select Unallocated in the menu that by default displays Mac OS Extended. The second partition should be Mac OS Standard for Mac OS, and if you are loading Mac OS X as well, the third partition should be Mac OS Extended (only available if you chose 3 partitions). Make sure to label the partitions appropriately.

7. Select OK and then Initialize.

Resume your installation of Mac OS as normal.

Installing Mac OS 9 or Below, Mac OS X, and Yellow Dog Linux on Multiple Hard Drives

Because of the way the system boots, you should have the drive to which you plan to install Yellow Dog Linux as the first hard drive in the IDE chain, set as Master. Mac OS or Mac OS X should be placed as the second drive in the chain and have the jumper set to Slave.

Then install the other versions of Mac OS (9 or below or X) onto the other hard drives. You only need to select a drive other than the first one during the install procedure. You must install Yellow Dog Linux as the last operating system and on the first drive.

Yellow Dog Linux 3.0.1 Special Considerations

All the planning noted previously applies to Yellow Dog Linux 3.0.1, but there is one special consideration to take into account. Yellow Dog Linux 4.0 supports only New World ROM systems, which are the blue-and-white G3 and above systems.

Note   There are two versions of the G3, one that has a beige case and another that has the blue-and-white case.

If you are installing Yellow Dog on a New World ROM system, go right to the next section, "Beginning the Installation."

If you are using an Old World ROM system, which are beige G3 systems and below, refer to the Yellow Dog Linux Web site (http://www.yellowdoglinux.com) for more information.

Beginning the Installation

After you have determined how you will boot your system (multiboot or single Yellow Dog Linux boot) and have loaded Mac OS X or Mac OS 9 or below as appropriate, you can begin installing Yellow Dog Linux. This procedure focuses on Yellow Dog Linux 4.0, but special notes on aspects of the 3.0.1 install are included where appropriate.

1. Insert Yellow Dog Linux CD 1 into your CD-ROM drive and press C to boot off the CD-ROM.

2. If you downloaded Yellow Dog or have a burned CD-R, you may want to check your media by appending mediacheck to the end of any of the install types (see step 3 for install types). For example:

   install-safe mediacheck

   This goes through all your media to determine if it is suitable for loading the operating system. This can save you a lot of time by determining that all of your CDs are good before you invest your time in the installation procedure.

Note   Although it doesn't show up in the Yellow Dog 3.0.1 text menu, you can still type **mediacheck** after install or install-text to check your CD-ROMs.

3. After some cursory probing messages, you are prompted with a menu asking how you want to boot the CD-ROM. If you are using a New World ROM G3 or G4 (blue-and-white G3 and above machine), type **install** at the prompt to use the graphical user interface method of installation. If you are using a G5 machine, type **install-g5** at the prompt to install using the graphical user interface. If you can't get either of these methods to work, type **install-safe** for G3 or G4 machines or **install-g5-safe** for G5 machines to use a generic video mode for installation. If neither of these methods works, you can type **install text** for G3 or G4 machines or **install-g5 text** for G5 machines to install with the text installation method if you find that the graphical version doesn't work for you.

Note Yellow Dog Linux 3.0.1 only has `install` and `install-text` options available. Choose `install` first, and if that doesn't work, choose `install-text` after rebooting.

4. The system will have been probed prior to this point to determine the hardware configuration. After the text messages, you are presented with a welcome screen. (You can choose to review the release notes by clicking the Release Notes button at the bottom-left side.) When you're ready to move on, click the Next button on the bottom-right side.

5. Select the language with which you are most comfortable. All future information presented by the installer will be in the language you select.

6. Choose the keyboard type that matches your current configuration.

7. Choose the type of installation you want. The options are:

   - **Personal Desktop** — Most home users will want this installation because it contains the most appropriate software set for home or office users (including laptops). Games, word processors, Internet tools, and other useful packages are included.

   - **Workstation** — Similar to the personal desktop type but includes tools for system administration as well as software development.

   - **Server** — Installs software needed for providing external services, including file and print, Web, and mail services. This is an advanced installation type and should be used only if you need it because you could misconfigure your system and create a security vulnerability. You can choose to install a graphical user interface as well, so if you don't want the extra overhead of a GUI, you can go without one on this type.

   - **Custom** — Provides the most flexibility because you can configure the partitions and software packages you want (everything!). This is your choice if you want to have more control over the installation. If you want to experience a large set of applications, you can choose this instead of installing applications one by one. You can also choose a more specific set of packages if this is to be a server used for external services, providing a higher level of security.

   For this chapter, the Custom installation type is used and assumed.

8. Decide how you want to partition your hard drive. You have two choices:

   - **Automatically partition** — If you choose this method, click Next and you are presented with three options:

   Remove all Linux partitions. Deletes all previous Linux partitions and replaces only previously identified Linux partitions.

   Remove all partitions. Use this only on New World ROM systems or on a single-drive Yellow Dog installation. If you use this option on a multiboot system, it removes *all* previous installations, including any Mac OS or MAC OS X installation. If you use this on an Old World ROM system, regardless of the installation type, it destroys the installation and requires a reformat and reload of Mac OS.

Caution   Be extremely careful using the Remove All Partitions option, and if at all possible, avoid using it at all because you can accidentally destroy your Mac OS installation!

Keep all partitions and use existing free space. The one you want to use in most cases, because it won't alter your Mac OS or Mac OS X installations and uses only the identified free space (as created previously). This is the option you should select if you are using Automatically partition.

- **Manually Partition with Disk Druid** — This is the more advanced option that allows you to create your partitions to your preference. Here is the sequence for creating new Linux partitions:

Choose the drive on which you want to install Yellow Dog Linux.

Choose New to create a new partition. You must create three partitions. First, choose Filesystem Type⇨Apple BootStrap. No mount point is needed. It should be 1MB and fixed size. This partition is for booting and should be the very first partition. Second, choose Filesystem Type ⇨ Swap. No mount point required. It should be a minimum 256MB (256MB is generally enough, although some say this should be set to twice the size of your physical RAM. More won't degrade system performance, though, and it doesn't hurt to be safe) and fixed size. This partition is the swap space that Linux uses for processes when the RAM is full. Third, create your root partition by selecting / as the mount point. This is where the file system is mounted. The root partition is absolutely critical because your other file systems will mount from this. You generally want to have your root partition consume the rest of the hard drive unless you are creating more partitions. Additional partitions are optional.

9. Identify your network settings, including DHCP. You use your network configuration for LAN (local area network) connections, such as when you are using a router between your cable or DSL connection and the local, internal network. You should know these settings ahead of time, so be sure to check them out before you start.

Cross-Reference   Refer to Chapter 5 for descriptions of IP addresses, netmasks, and other information you need to set up your LAN.

Select eth0 (your first network interface card) and click Edit. You have the following options:

- **Configure using DHCP** — Enables you to automatically obtain a DHCP address from your LAN if there is a DHCP server (such as Linksys or D-Link Routers). If you check here, you do not need to fill out anything else in this section.

- **Activate on boot** — Enables you to turn on your network connection during boot. Under most circumstances you will want to do so if you are using a LAN.

- **IP Address** — A four-octet number that uniquely identifies your computer address. Your system will have a unique IP on your LAN or WAN (wide area network) connection.

- **Netmask** — Identifies the Host and network portions of the IP address. A class A network is 255.0.0.0, a class B is 255.255.0.0, and a class C is 255.255.255.0 by default (if no subnet masking is in place).

Click OK and, if you aren't using DHCP, set your hostname by selecting Hostname ➪ Manually. This can be any name you want to represent your computer. If this is a server, follow your company's naming convention. If you prefer to have DHCP set your hostname, select the Automatically via DHCP radio button.

The last options are grayed out if you have selected DHCP. If you chose to manually configure your network options, enter the following:

- **Gateway IP address** — The IP address of the machine that is the gateway or router between your network and the outside networks. For instance, 192.168.1.1 might be your gateway if you have a Linksys or D-Link router between your computer and your cable or DSL connection.

- **Primary, secondary, and tertiary DNS** — The server that your system uses for address name translation (converting a hostname into an IP address). Your ISP usually gives you this information.

10. Configure the firewall. A firewall acts as a conduit between your computer and other computers that request access to the services it is providing. If you are connected to the Internet or other networks, enable your firewall. Even if you are not connected to an untrusted network, you should enable the firewall in case you connect at a later date. Two choices are available in this section:

- **No firewall** — Don't choose this option because it does not check against requests for services. Even if your system is not currently providing services, it's best to not select this option (things can change as the system grows).

- **Enable firewall** — The preferred selection. It provides a modicum of security against malicious entities that may want to attack your systems. Only the default services are allowed at this level, and you can configure access for more services as needed. Some of the defaults are:

  Remote login (SSH). An encrypted protocol that replaces the vulnerable telnet protocol. With SSH you can log in to the system with an interactive shell, as well as securely transfer files interactively (SFTP) or noninteractively (SCP). For more information on this, type **man ssh** at the command line after installation.

Note

When SSH is unchecked, you can still use these utilities on outgoing connections. This only controls incoming requests from outside your computer. If you need to access your system remotely, you can choose this, but it is best to leave it unchecked for security reasons. The same applies to the other options presented.

Web Server (HTTP, HTTPS). Allows your system to serve regular (HTTP) Web pages or encrypted (HTTPS) Web pages. Unless you need to run a Web server, it is recommended that you do not check this.

File Transfer (FTP). Allows users to interactively log in to your system and transfer files. This protocol is unencrypted and not needed by most users. If you must allow file transfers, SFTP (provided with SSH) is the preferred method because the password and username are sent encrypted.

Mail Server (SMTP). Allows your system to accept mail requests or mail relay requests. You can still send and receive mail if you do not check this; it just allows your machine to act as a mail server. If you install and improperly configure SMTP, your system can become a spam relay, so only more experienced users should check this.

Note   These settings can be reconfigured later using `iptables`. See the man page for iptables for more information.

11. If you need additional language support, select it here. Your default language (chosen during install language selection) should already be selected. Click Next to continue.

12. Select the time zone in which you reside or the time zone you want to use for your server. If your hardware uses UTC (Greenwich Mean Time — GMT), select the check box at the bottom. Click next to continue.

13. Set your root password. This password provides the keys to the kingdom; with the root account, a user can do *anything*, including destroy the entire file system. You must set to a strong password (not any personally identifiable information such as identification number, phone number, pet's name, family member's birthday, etc.). Enter your password twice (to ensure it is the same), and then press Enter.

Caution   The importance of a good root or any other account password should not be minimized. This is crucially important to the security of your system. See `http://securityfocus.com/infocus/1537` for more information on choosing good passwords.

14. Select the different packages you want to install on the system. Choose Everything (for all software packages) or Minimal (only the basics to run the system). Selecting the package groups enables you to see the individual packages included in each group (you can select or deselect from that list for more granularity). Note that KDE is chosen by default; if you prefer to use GNOME or want to use both, check GNOME. When you're finished, click Next.

Note   *Red Hat Fedora Linux 3 Bible* includes descriptions of the software included with each of the packages for Fedora Core Linux. The packages described in Appendix B of that book are similar to Yellow Dog Linux selections because Yellow Dog is based on the Fedora Core distribution. That entire book can also be used as a reference guide to Yellow Dog Linux.

15. You've reached the About to Install phase. You're warned that the system will begin writing to the disk. You can back out of anything at this point with no damage to the system, so if you made a mistake or are not sure about installing, you can simply reboot. If you are ready to commit your configuration to the system, click Next. Your system begins writing the software to the hard drive. This can take from 10 minutes to an hour or more depending on the speed of your system and the amount of software you decided to load. You are shown a list of the CDs that your system needs to load the software. Be sure to have those CDs ready to load into the system. After each CD is completed, you are prompted to insert another CD until the installation is complete.

16. After the installation finishes, the congratulations screen appears. Click Reboot when you are ready.

17. The system reboots and goes through system initialization. Afterward, a welcome screen appears.

18. The initial setup begins here. Click Next to move forward.

19. The license agreement appears in a text box. Read it and then click No if you do not agree to the terms, and the process stops. Click Yes if you agree to the terms.

20. Set the date and time for the system. If you want to use Network Time Protocol (NTP) to synchronize your system date and time with a remote network system for maximum assurance of correct date and time, check the Enable Network Time Protocol box, and then select one of the two NTP servers provided.

21. Set the display resolution and color depth to your preference. (You can change this in the system after installation.)

22. Create your nonroot daily user account. Enter a username (the name you use to log in with) and the full name of the user (for administrative purposes), and then enter the password twice. If you need to use network login, you can configure that here as well (your system administrator can provide this information if needed).

Caution   Do not log in with the root account for normal day-to-day activities. That can be very dangerous in that you could accidentally damage the system with an errant command, but it also means that you might surf the Web using root or install software with root without thinking twice about it, possibly introducing malicious software. Use the nonroot account for all nonadministrative purposes and regular interaction with the system.

23. Configure your sound card. If everything seems to be configured properly, try to play a test sound. A pop-up window asks if you heard the sound. Answer appropriately, and click Next when you're ready to move on.

24. If you have any additional CDs from which to install software, insert them into the CD-ROM and select them here (the CD you insert will show on the list). Click Next to continue.

25. At this point you are done installing and configuring your system, and you are booted up into the graphical user interface with a prompt for the username and password.

Updating Yellow Dog Linux

Yellow Dog Updated, Modified (yum) is included with Yellow Dog and ships with Fedora, Mandrake, and other Linux distributions as well. It's a utility that enables you to update your system packages to the latest available version. Because new security vulnerabilities are released on all operating systems frequently, updating your system packages regularly is essential. Updating your packages also gives you the newest features available for the applications you are using. Here are some of the most widely used options available with yum (replace *package* with name of package):

Option	Description
yum list	Shows all the packages available to be installed (but not installed).
yum list installed	Shows installed packages.
yum list updates	Shows all installed packages that have updates (patches) available.
yum install *package*	Installs the package you identify in *package*.
yum update *package*	Updates the package you identify in *package*. The great thing about this is it installs all package dependencies, which used to be a major headache when administering patches.
yum update	Updates all packages on the system. (Same as preceding option but does not specify package name.)
yum remove *package*	Removes the package identified in *package*.
yum info *package*	Provides detailed information on the package identified in *package*.

Using this information, assume that you want to run gimp—GNU Image Manipulation Project (GIMP) is a very popular graphics editing program—and you haven't installed it previously. If you want to get more information on it, you'd run:

```
yum info gimp
```

If you decide you want to install it:

```
yum install gimp
```

If an update becomes available a week later and you want to patch it:

```
yum update gimp
```

If it had been a month and you decided you no longer needed gimp, you could remove it with

```
yum remove gimp
```

Yum makes updating packages very easy and should be used regularly to keep your system updated with the latest patches (you can even run it from a cron job for true automation).

Running Mac Applications with Mac-on-Linux

Mac-on-Linux is a very interesting project that enables Mac users to have the best of both Linux and Mac. With this software, you can run Linux as the primary operating system and still access your Mac OS or Mac OS X operating systems (or even another Linux operating system) via a window within your operating Linux session.

Mac-on-Linux presents a virtual machine that provides a real environment to the Mac OS or Mac OS X installation. Because there is no emulation, Mac-on-Linux is very fast and capable. Mac-on-Linux is very stable and works with minimal configuration. For more information on what Mac-on-Linux provides and on instructions for its use visit http://maconlinux.org/.

Support Options

If you run into problems using or installing Yellow Dog Linux, you can obtain support in many ways. The Linux community at large is very supportive, proffering numerous Web pages available to assist the newcomer. If you encounter problems with hardware, try one of the following options:

✦ **Yellow Dog Mailing List Archive Search** — A free service that enables you to search some of the more common problems encountered by users. Use the Search Lists box at the top right side of the http://yellowdoglinux.com/support/installation/ page.

✦ **Yellow Dog Community Board** — Another free support option that is run by Yellow Dog Linux enthusiasts. It is available at http://yellowdog-board.com/.

✦ **Yellow Dog Mail Lists** — If your questions didn't get answered through the preceding sites, you could subscribe to some of the numerous Yellow Dog mailing lists where you can ask your questions. Directions for use are at http://lists.terrasoftsolutions.com/mailman/listinfo.

✦ **Yellow Dog Linux User Channel** — If you are comfortable with IRC (Internet Relay Chat), you can use `irc.freenode.net` and join #yellowdog for interactive support that is community driven.

✦ **Yellow Dog Official Support** — If you can't find the information you need from the previous sources or `http://yellowdoglinux.com/support/installation/`, you can purchase support from Terra Soft Solutions through `http://terrasoftsolutions.com/tss_contact.shtml`. If you purchased Yellow Dog Linux through Terra Soft Solutions with 60 days of support, you can contact the company through `http://terrasoftsolutions.com/support/`.

If you need software support after your installation, use some of the other more generic support options available from the Linux community. These options include using a search engine to search for the problem and visiting community-driven Web sites such as the following:

✦ **The Linux Documentation Project** (`http://tldp.org/`) — The premier Web site for how-to guides for using the Linux operating system.

✦ **Linux Journal Help Desk** (`http://linuxjournal.com/helpdesk.php`) — Offers guidance on using Linux.

✦ **Just Linux** (`http://justlinux.com/`) — Offers some basic guides on Linux use.

✦ **Linux.com Tips** (`http://tips.linux.com/`) — Offers some great tips.

You can use your favorite search engine to find more of the many, many helpful Linux Web sites out there.

The Linux community is generally very supportive of new users, and you can find help from local Linux User Groups (LUGs) or via many places on the Internet.

Summary

Yellow Dog Linux is a very stable, fully functioning version of Fedora Core available on the PowerPC platform. It has the capability to extend the life of your Mac hardware and to run Mac OS 9 or below or even Mac OS X on your running Linux installation using Mac-on-Linux. Linux is not the sole domain of the X86 community, and now PowerPC users can use Linux while still enjoying their Mac OS or Mac OS X environment through multibooting or using the innovative Mac-on-Linux software.

✦   ✦   ✦

Running Gentoo Linux

Gentoo is a rising star of Linux distributions among Linux enthusiasts. Of all the popular distributions, this is the first one I'd recommend to a technically oriented friend who wanted to learn Linux and the last one I'd recommend to my wife ("Just show me what button to click for my e-mail"). That's because to install and maintain Gentoo effectively, you have to care (to an almost unnatural extent) about what is going on with your computer.

This chapter describes why you might want to use Gentoo, what the Gentoo community is like, and how to get and install Gentoo Linux.

 The Gentoo universal install CD image is included on the DVD that comes with this book. You can copy and burn the Gentoo image to CD as described in Appendix A. Because this CD does not contain a complete Gentoo install, you will need an Internet connection or some medium containing the needed Gentoo packages (CD, DVD, or hard disk) to get the software you need to complete the Gentoo installation.

Understanding Gentoo

Performance and efficiency were the critical goals that led to the creation of the Gentoo Linux distribution. A dedication to the spirit of open source software (and to those drawn to it) has been a key to its incredible growth.

In the few years it has been in existence, Gentoo has grown from having one maintainer — its creator, Daniel Robbins — to having more than 250 active developers. It boasts perhaps the strongest user community among all Linux distributions. Gentoo users seem willing to contribute so freely because they feel that they get back what they give to Gentoo.

The Portage software distribution management system is the key technology that separates Gentoo from other Linux distributions. Based on the BSD Ports system, Portage can be used to build almost the entire Gentoo distribution from source codes, and manage and upgrade that software as well.

Gentoo's Open Source Spirit

Although Gentoo could someday produce a commercial Linux distribution, Robbins and the Gentoo project are committed to the goals of open source software, while still allowing those who use the software to make money. Ways that those goals are reflected in Gentoo — and not in other distributions — include:

✦ **Passing bug fixes upstream.** Software bugs in open source projects are often shaken out when actual Linux distributions are put together. When a distribution finds a bug, it is considered good practice to pass the fix to that bug upstream, to the project maintaining the original software.

Not passing bug fixes upstream could potentially give a commercial Linux distribution an advantage over other distributions that don't have the fix. There have been many cases where fixes in early Red Hat Linux and other commercial distributions have not made it to the upstream projects. Gentoo, on the other hand, has a reputation for sharing bug fixes with the open source community.

✦ **Transparent development process.** Not only is the open source software made available to everyone, but the tools for building that software are also freely distributed. Gentoo users can see exactly what their software contains, along with all the decisions made to build that software. It is also a fairly simple procedure to change any of those build decisions in the process of users building their own Gentoo software.

✦ **Choices for creating Gentoo.** You can build your own Gentoo Linux from the source code pages (as described in this chapter) or start from prebuilt binary packages provided by the Gentoo project. Freedom, in the Gentoo philosophy, means to let users create the kind of Linux system the users want. So, if users don't want to make decisions about how their packages are built, they can simply take ready-made packages from the Gentoo project.

✦ **Not-for-profit organization.** When the Linux distribution is dedicated to the community and not beholden to stockholders, open source enthusiasts often feel better about freely contributing to improving that distribution. Gentoo is a not-for-profit organization.

This open source spirit has also helped Gentoo gain a community that is extraordinarily active and helpful to its members.

The Gentoo Community

The open source spirit of Gentoo pervades its community. The size and activity of that community is best reflected in its forums (http://forums.gentoo.org), in which there are literally hundreds (and sometimes thousands) of new posts per day. If there's something about Gentoo you can't find using Google, try searching the Gentoo forums.

To get a sense of the activity levels on the forums, check out the board statistics (http://forums.gentoo.org/statistics.php). You can see how many posts, topics, and users there are in the forums per day. You can also see, and visit, the most active topics in the forums.

Many Gentoo enthusiasts seem to live on the forums. Although most of the posts stick closely to Linux, nobody seems to blink an eye when someone posts questions about the existence of God or what to do when a guy's wife has left him. The forums verge on the feel of a coffeehouse at times.

It never hurts to start with the Frequently Asked Questions (FAQs) forums. However, I think most will want to start with the Installing Gentoo forum (because you are likely to get hung up on installation when you first try installing it). If you are interested in live communications about Gentoo, try the Gentoo IRC #gentoo channel at irc.freenote.net (you can use xchat in most Linux systems to access IRC channels). Another good starting forum is the Documentation, Tips, & Tricks forum, where you can find cool little tricks to tweak your system.

Building, Tuning, and Tweaking Linux

Gentoo is sometimes referred to as the build-from-source Linux system. Most other Linux distributions give you a set of prebuilt packages to install and never expect you to build the whole system yourself. While you can get Gentoo with packages prebuilt for you, the distribution was made for you to be able to build the Linux kernel and all packages right on the machine where you will install it.

When you install from prebuilt binary software packages, which is expected with Gentoo and most other Linux distributions, many decisions have already been made for you about what each package includes and what it is tuned for. By building a Gentoo distribution from source code, you can create a distribution that specifically takes into account the following about your situation:

✦ **What processor you are running on.** Most distributions choose a particular architecture (such as x86, PowerPC, or Sparc) and a generic selection of settings for using the processor. With Gentoo, however, you can choose the exact type of processor you're using and compile all software to take advantage of features from that processor (while not including features specific to other processors).

✦ **What hardware you might have.** Most distributions install tons of modules to support hardware that you might someday add (it will load them as you need them into the kernel). It will also build a kernel for you that includes support for features that it believes you do need (for example, some distributions include ext3 file system report, expecting that to be your basic file system type). With Gentoo, you can choose exactly what features are in the kernel to support only the hardware you know you have. Likewise, you can get and install drivers for hardware if you decide to install that hardware later.

✦ **What services you want.** Some Linux distributions suffer some performance problems by having processes taking up memory for services that you don't necessarily want (such as daemons for Web, file, print, and other server types). With Gentoo, you can be selective to a fine detail about the services that are installed and running on Gentoo (including the order in which they are started).

✦ **What software is available.** Linux distributions such as Red Hat Enterprise Linux offer a preset selection of software packages that are well-tested and integrated into a set of CDs or DVDs. Gentoo has a massive repository of software packages from which you can choose the exact packages you need. Each package carries its own set of dependencies with it as well, so you don't have to add every library or utility to your system to support software you might want someday. With an Internet connection and the `emerge` tool, you can always add more software you need, when you need it.

✦ **What features are available.** Because in Gentoo you are making decisions about what software you use at compile time, you can select to turn on or off optional features within each software component. For example, if you are building Mozilla mail, you can choose whether the package you build will include support for LDAP address books. In theory, removing support for unneeded features makes the software you end up with run faster and use less memory.

The features just described help characterize the type of person who is attracted to Gentoo. Gentoo enthusiasts like to configure, tune, tweak, and update their Linux systems continuously, and Gentoo users generally end up with systems that run faster, take up less disk space, and run in less memory than would be the case with any other Linux that you just get off a shelf.

Where Gentoo Is Used

As you may have guessed by now, Gentoo is most popular with Linux enthusiasts as their personal Linux systems. Among Gentoo users you find those who like to tinker with desktops and run servers where performance is critical (such as game servers). Because Gentoo can be so easily configured and tuned, users can make very efficient Linux desktop and server systems that include only the software needed for the particular job.

With the slant toward personal use, there is a lot of interest in Gentoo forums for configuring desktops, configuring multimedia applications, and getting popular games running. There are also significant discussions about securing Gentoo because most of its security tools don't come with friendly, graphical interfaces and require a lot of manual setup.

Despite that fact that you can use Gentoo to create an extraordinarily efficient, finely tuned Linux desktop or server, the distribution is not yet widely accepted in business or educational institutions. There are probably several reasons for that:

✦ **Stability.** To stay on the bleeding edge of the latest Linux software, Gentoo sacrifices the extreme level of stability demanded by most businesses.

Note   People I know who use Gentoo on their personal computers tend to use Debian or Fedora Core for small Web, file, or print servers when they do consulting work, and Red Hat Enterprise Linux or SUSE Linux for larger enterprise installations.

✦ **Support.** There are no official support packages offered with Gentoo, so if something goes wrong, there is no official help available (although the forums can be quite helpful).

✦ **Training.** If you are supporting a lot of machines, the people who support those machines will need training. Unlike Red Hat or SUSE Linux, you can't get training from the creators of Gentoo.

So far, the factors just mentioned have kept Gentoo from making any significant inroads into enterprise computing. However, as a learning tool and a personal Linux distribution, Gentoo is hard to beat.

What's in Gentoo

No two Gentoo systems are alike because you can select and build only the pieces of Linux you want to use. Coming into 2005, there were more than 7,000 software packages available for the project, and the list was growing.

Unlike distributions such as Red Hat and SUSE Linux, Gentoo tends to not force its own look-and-feel on the projects it includes. Each software package ported to a Gentoo system gives the user a view of the included open source software packages as they were intended from the individual projects. For example, a KDE desktop looks like a KDE desktop as it was delivered from the KDE project itself; there are no Gentoo menus and icons or graphical administration tools to alter it.

Gentoo's focus on tools for managing and building source code has helped make Gentoo extraordinarily portable. Besides the common x86 (PC) version of Gentoo, there are Gentoo ports for AMD64, PowerPC, UltraSparc, ALpha, and MIPS processors. There are also optimized Linux kernels available with Gentoo for different specific processors within each architecture. Some of the ports are still a work in progress, so at the moment you will probably get the best experience using an x86 platform to run Gentoo.

To explore Gentoo, it's more appropriate to start with the tools for getting what you want than it is to talk about what you end up with. If you build Gentoo turned to your hardware and include just the software that you need, your system isn't going to look like any other Gentoo system.

Managing Software with Portage

At the heart of Gentoo is the Portage software management system. Based on the FreeBSD Ports system, Portage enables you to find, download, configure, build, and install the exact software you choose.

Using the portage system can give you some excellent insights into how Linux is created. As Daniel Robbins says, ". . .we are documenting how to build a Linux system at the same time we are moving Gentoo Linux development forward."

Those developing software are encouraged not only to contribute their software to the Gentoo project but also to contribute the scripts they use to build that software. Portage tools and build scripts open up Linux technology beginning at the source-code level.

Key components of the Portage package management system include the `emerge` command and the package build scripts (contained in the `/usr/portage` directory). You can use these tools to build the entire Gentoo distribution from scratch or rely on some prebuilt binaries to save some compile time. In most cases, you won't have to modify any configuration files to get a solid Gentoo installation.

Following are some examples of the `emerge` command that you can use with Gentoo. To use some of the examples, you need to either have a connection to the Internet or have downloaded all package updates to your local computer. When the `emerge` command is run to install software or to get updated software packages, it looks on a Gentoo mirror site if it can't find the packages it needs locally. The first example lets you search (`-s`) the `/usr/portage` directory tree for packages that interest you (substitute the package name you want for *package*):

```
# emerge -s package
```

To build and install a package you choose, simply type **emerge** with the package name:

```
# emerge package
```

To update your Portage directory tree so that it contains the latest information to install software packages, type the following:

```
# emerge sync
```

To get your Gentoo system up-to-date, use the `-u world` option. The following command checks all the software packages you have installed on your computer and then goes to a Gentoo mirror site to download and install the latest versions of each of those packages:

```
# emerge -u world
```

To view the many other options available with `emerge`, type **man emerge** or run `emerge` with the help option:

```
# emerge -h | less
```

You can use `emerge` to install packages that are contained on your local computer or have the packages downloaded automatically from Gentoo software mirror sites. During the build process, `emerge` handles getting all the dependencies that the software you choose requires.

Finding Software Packages

Part of the Gentoo installation process includes installing the Portage directory tree in the `/usr/portage` directory. You can step around that directory to see the packages that are available. As I mentioned earlier, there are several thousand to choose from.

Software packages fall into the following categories:

- ✦ **app** — Applications software packages, such as editors, anti-virus software, administrative tools, accessibility tools, CD writing applications, and many other packages.
- ✦ **dev** — A wide variety of development tools.
- ✦ **games** — Dozens of board, arcade, first-person-shooter, puzzle, and strategy games, and games servers.
- ✦ **media** — A variety of audio, video, and other multimedia tools.
- ✦ **net** — Communications, server, firewall, and other network tools.
- ✦ **sys** — System configuration tools.
- ✦ **www** — Web communications servers and related software packages.
- ✦ **x11** — Miscellaneous tools for the X Window System graphical interface, along with related themes and window managers.

Simply step through the `/usr/portage` directory structure to see the software packages you can install, information about how each is built, and patches that are available.

Installing Gentoo

A Gentoo installation is more like building your own Linux than it is like typical Linux installs. While many Linux installations start you with a precompiled set of software and nice screens to lead you through, Gentoo boots you to a shell and expects you to set up the computer by hand. In the example installation, you'll even build your own binaries from source code.

To someone who has never used Linux (or other UNIX systems), Gentoo installs can appear daunting. If you can tough through it, however, you will learn what goes into setting up and making a Linux system in a way that you won't find in any other Linux distribution.

The advantages to your installing Gentoo are that, as mentioned earlier, there is excellent documentation available and an extraordinary community supporting Gentoo. If you make it through the install, you will have:

✦ **A tuned system.** Because you are making decisions about your software before the binaries are produced, you can tune your system to be built specifically for the hardware you are using. You can tell Gentoo the exact processor, file system types, sound cards, or other features you want built into the kernel or loadable modules.

✦ **The software you want.** Gentoo enables you to select the software you want to install, and because you are compiling it yourself, you can even tell Gentoo what features to include with it. For example, if you are adding the Evolution e-mail client, you can choose to include (or not include) LDAP support for shared address books on your network.

✦ **Fewer dependency issues.** When you build software yourself, dependency issues are taken care of at compile time, so you don't have to worry about getting a software package that was created for a different architecture or kernel. Your applications will be built for your operating system because you build them that way.

Getting Gentoo

The Gentoo Linux distribution is available in several different forms. To provide the full feel of installing Gentoo, this chapter illustrates a Gentoo install that is done from a minimal disk image. You will download and compile most of the software you need (including the kernel itself). To do this procedure, you need a broadband Internet connection (no dial-up).

Begin with the following CD image: install-x86-minimal-2004.2.iso. This bootable minimal install CD image (only about 78MB) includes just enough software to begin the install procedure. This CD image is included on the CD that comes with this book, so you can copy and burn that image to CD to start this installation procedure. You can also find this image in any Gentoo mirror site (in the releases/x86/2004.2/livecd directory).

If you have a slow computer or no broadband Internet connection, I recommend that you get the universal CD instead, as well as the packages CD before you begin installing. Those two CDs will enable you to do a complete Gentoo install without needing to get on the Internet. You can download the disk images from Gentoo mirror sites (refer to www.gentoo.org/main/en/mirrors.xml for the locations of Gentoo mirror sites). Here's where you can find the universal and packages CD images:

✦ install-x86-universal-2004.2.iso. This bootable install CD image contains enough software to enable you to have a working Gentoo system without going on the Internet. It is located in releases/x86/2004.2/livecd directories on a mirror site.

✦ packages-x86-2004.2.iso. This nonbootable CD image contains many popular packages you might want with Gentoo. The contents include popular, precompiled packages that you can add after the basic Gentoo system is installed. While this CD saves you download and compile time, it does not let you do the optimization for your particular machine on the packages it includes. Its image is located in releases/x86/2004.2/packagecd/x86 on a mirror site.

 Note   By the time you read this, there will certainly be a later version of Gentoo available. If you decide to use a later version, you should find the associated install procedure from the Gentoo site. Version numbers include the year and release number. For example, 2004.2 represents the second release in 2004.

For a more detailed description of the Gentoo install process, refer to the Gentoo Linux/x86 Handbook (www.gentoo.org/doc/en/handbook/handbook-x86.xml).

Starting Gentoo Installation

Here are the minimum computer requirements for a Gentoo installation using the x86 procedure described in this chapter:

✦ 1GB of hard disk space

✦ 64MB of RAM

✦ A 486 processor (or better)

✦ 300MB of total memory (combined RAM and swap)

If you have a slow processor, consider getting precompiled packages because the full compilation process can take a long time.

Note   If you need further information about any of the steps described in this procedure, refer to the Gentoo Handbook: www.gentoo.org/doc/en/handbook/index.xml.

With the install CD in hand, here's how to install Gentoo on your computer:

1. Insert the CD (minimal or universal) into your computer's CD or DVD drive.

2. Reboot your computer.

3. **Boot CD.** From the boot prompt, press Enter. (If you are not able to boot the install medium, press F1 or F2 to see other install options that might help you get going.)

   Gentoo should detect your computer hardware, start the install process, and display a boot prompt.

4. **Set date.** Type the date command to make sure the date and time are set correctly. If they need to be changed, use the date command (with options) to change them. For example, to set the date to 8:15 a.m., June 15, 2005, you would type:

   `# date 061508152005`

5. **Load modules.** If some piece of hardware was not auto-detected, you may have to load the module you need to access that hardware. Use the modprobe command with the name of the module you want to load. For example, to load the module for an Orinico wireless LAN card, you could type:

   `# modprobe orinoco`

Tip   Search the Web for the term "Linux" and the name of the hardware that is not being detected to find out what module to load.

6. **Configure network.** Type ifconfig eth0 to see if the Internet connection to your first Ethernet card is up and running. Then try to ping a computer on the Internet to make sure you can get out (for example, ping www.gentoo.org). If you are not able to pick up a DHCP server to automatically connect to the Internet, you can set up your Internet connection manually, by typing:

   `# net-setup eth0`

   Refer to the network configuration information in the installation procedure in Chapter 8 to help you answer questions about setting up your Internet connection manually.

7. **Partition hard disk.** Partition your hard disk to prepare it to receive your Gentoo installation. You can use the fdisk utility to do this. Gentoo recommends a 64MB boot volume (ext2 file system), a swap partition that's double the size of your RAM, and a large root (/) partition (ReiserFS file system). Start fdisk by following the command with the name of your first hard disk (such

as `/dev/hda` or `/dev/sda` for your first IDE or SCSI hard disk, respectively). Then type **h** to display a list of commands. (See Chapter 7 for information about using `fdisk` to partition your hard disk.)

Caution

Repartitioning your disk will destroy existing data on your hard disk. Back up any data you value before starting this procedure. Be sure not to delete or change any partitions that have data on them that you want to keep.

```
# fdisk /dev/hda
```

8. **Make file systems.** To create the appropriate file systems on your disk partitions, use the `mk2fs` and `mkswap` commands. For example, with an IDE hard drive that has the first partition as the boot partition (`/dev/hda1`), the second as swap (`/dev/hda2`), and the third as the root (`/`) partition (`/dev/hda3`), you could type the following:

```
# mke2fs /dev/hda1
# mkswap /dev/hda2
# mkreiserfs /dev/hda3
```

9. **Turn on swap.** Use the `swapon` command to turn on your swap partition. For our example (with hda2 being the swap partition), you would type:

```
# swapon /dev/hda2
```

10. **Mount root (/) partition.** You need to mount the root (`/`) partition temporarily to begin installing Gentoo to it. In this example (with the root file system on `/dev/hda3`), you would type:

```
# mount /dev/hda3 /mnt/gentoo
```

11. **Mount the /boot partition.** Next, mount the boot partition to install to it:

```
# mkdir /mnt/gentoo/boot
# mount /dev/hda1 /mnt/gentoo/boot
```

12. **Get the stage1 tarball.** Assuming that you have the minimal Gentoo installation CD, you need to download the stage1 tarball. Find a mirror site near where you are (as described earlier). Then make a directory on your hard disk to copy it to and download the tarball using a tool such as wget. Here is an example:

Note

If you are using the universal CD, the stage1 tarball is available there. Instead of downloading it, jump to the next step and extract the tarball from `/mnt/cdrom/stages/stage1*.tar.bz2`.

```
# mkdir /mnt/gentoo/tmp2
# cd /mnt/gentoo/tmp2
# wget -c http://gentoo.osuosl.org/releases/x86/2004.2/
stages/x86/stage1-x86-2004.2.tar.bz2
```

Note

The `wget` command, which appears on two lines here, should all be typed on one line. (There's no space between the slash at the end of the first line and the word "stages" at the beginning of the next.) If the download should stop in the middle, you can restart it by running the same command again in the same directory.

13. Extract the stage 1 tarball.

```
# cd /mnt/gentoo
# tar -xvjpf /mnt/gentoo/tmp2/stage1-*.tar.bz2
```

You can remove the stage1 tarball once you have untarred it.

14. Select mirror site. Use the `mirrorselect` command to search for a Gentoo mirror site from which you can efficiently download the files you need to do the install. Run the following command to select an efficient mirror and add it to your `make.conf` file (it will take awhile to test download speed from more than 150 servers):

```
# mirrorselect -a -s4 -o |grep GENTOO_MIRRORS >> /mnt/gentoo/etc/make.conf
```

Note If, when you run `emerge` commands later in this procedure, you see messages that files are not found from any of the download sites, you might need to add other mirror sites to the `make.conf` file.

15. Mount file systems. Mount the `/proc` and `/devfs` directories as follows:

```
# mkdir /mnt/gentoo/devfs
# mount -t devfs devfs /mnt/gentoo/devfs
# mkdir /mnt/gentoo/proc
# mount -t proc none /mnt/gentoo/proc
```

16. Change root directory. Use the `chroot` command to change `/mnt/gentoo` to be your root directory, but first copy the `resolve.conf` file so it can be used from there:

```
# cp /etc/resolv.conf /mnt/gentoo/etc/resolv.conf
# chroot /mnt/gentoo /bin/bash
```

17. Update environment. Read in environment variables as follows:

```
# env-update; source /etc/profile
```

18. Update Portage tree. Type the following command to have the latest package information installed to your `/usr/portage` directory:

```
# emerge sync
```

19. Modify `make.conf`. Use the nano text editor to change the `make.conf` file that is used to build your Gentoo system. Here's how:

```
# nano -w /etc/make.conf
```

If you don't know what to change, refer to the `/etc/make.conf.example` file for information about the settings you may want to change before continuing. If you don't know what processor your computer has, type `cat /proc/cpuinfo`.

20. Bootstrap Gentoo:

```
# cd /usr/portage/ ; scripts/bootstrap.sh
```

21. Install Gentoo:

```
# emerge system
```

 It will take a long time for the `emerge system` command to complete. If it fails before it is finished, check that the settings in your `make.conf` file are correct.

22. Set the time zone:

```
# ln -sf /usr/share/zoneinfo/path /etc/localtime
```

You need to substitute *path* with the path to the file that represents the time zone your computer is in. For example, the entire path for Central time in the United States would be `/usr/share/zoneinfo/US/Central`.

23. Create file system table. Add the file systems you want to mount automatically at boot time to your `/etc/fstab` file. Here's an example:

```
# nano -w /etc/fstab
```

Here's what the `/etc/fstab` might look like (given the partitions created earlier in this example procedure):

```
# <fs>                <mountpoint> <type>  <opts>         <dump/pass>
/dev/hda1             /boot        ext2    noauto,noatime    1 2
/dev/hda2             none         swap    sw                0 0
/dev/hda3             /            reiserfs noatime          0 1
/dev/cdroms/cdrom0    /mnt/cdrom   auto    noauto,user       0 0
none                  /proc        proc    defaults          0 0
none                  /dev/shm     tmpfs   defaults          0 0
```

24. Build kernel. Either install a prebuilt kernel or build one yourself. To build one, you need a kernel sources package (gentoo-sources is recommended). Type the `emerge` command as follows to get the gentoo-sources package:

```
# emerge gentoo-sources
```

Next, use the following command to get the genkernel package and configure a kernel using `menuconfig`:

```
# emerge genkernel
# genkernel --menuconfig all
```

After you have made any changes you want to your kernel configuration, select Exit, and then choose Yes to save it. At this point, `genkernel` makes your new kernel. This will take awhile.

 Configuring your own kernel can be quite tricky at first. If you run into problems, refer to the Gentoo Linux Handbook (`www.gentoo.org/doc/en/handbook/handbook-x86.xml`). Select Section 7, "Configuring the Kernel," for further information.

25. Configure system services. Install your system services: system logger, cron service, hotplug, and reiserfs service, and set the domain name. Then turn on each of those services, as follows:

```
# emerge syslog-ng
# rc-update add syslog-ng default
# emerge vixie-cron
# rc-update add vixie-cron default
# emerge hotplug
# rc-update add hotplug default
# emerge reiserfsprogs
# rc-update add domainname default
```

26. Add special driver support. There may be particular kernel modules required by your computer at this point. For example, if you have a special Ethernet adapter or a special type of video card, use the emerge command to install kernel modules now. You may not need any of them. Here are a few examples:

```
# emerge nvidia-kernel
# emerge nforce-audio
# emerge e100
# emerge e1000
# emerge emu10k1
# emerge ati-drivers
```

These emerge command lines are only used if you have special hardware associated with the kernel drivers. Respectively, those commands load drivers for accelerated Nvidia video cards, audio for Nvidia NForce motherboards, Intel e100 Fast Ethernet cards, Intel e1000 Gigabit Ethernet card, Sound Blaster Live!/Audigy support for 2.4 kernel, and ATI Radeon+/FireGL graphics acceleration video cards.

27. Add user and machine information. Add a password for the root user, a regular user account name of your choosing (chris in this example), a machine name, and a domain name. If you like, you can also edit the /etc/hosts and /etc/rc.conf files to add IP addresses and hostname or change the basic system startup script.

```
# passwd
# useradd chris -m -G users,wheel,audio -s /bin/bash
# passwd chris
# echo mymachine > /etc/hostname
# echo mydomain.com > /etc/dnsdomainname
# nano -w /etc/hosts
# nano -w /etc/rc.conf
```

28. Set up networking. Edit the net file, and then run rc-update to add the eth0 interface as the default. (Uncomment the line iface eth0="dhcp" to have the network use DHCP to start up automatically.)

```
# nano -w /etc/conf.d/net
# rc-update add net.eth0 default
```

29. **Add kernel modules.** Add any extra kernel modules that you need to add a boot time. You usually only need to do this if some piece of hardware isn't detected and the module needed to use it isn't automatically loaded. Use either kernel-2.4 or kernel-2.6, depending on which kernel you are using.

```
# nano -w /etc/modules.autoload.d/kernel-<version>
```

You can type `uname -a` to see what your current kernel version is.

30. **Configure the boot loader.** You need to install a boot loader (grub in this example) and configure it. The example makes the following assumptions about your setup:

   • Gentoo is installed on your first IDE hard disk (`/dev/hda`).

   • You have a separate `/boot` partition on `/dev/hda1`.

   • Your initrd file in the `/boot` directory is `initrd-2.4.26-gentoo-r9`.

   • Your kernel file in the `/boot` directory is `kernel-2.4.26-gentoo-r9`.

If any of that information is different for your setup, you will need to adapt the following step appropriately. To configure grub, install it with `emerge`, run the `grub` command, and then create the `grub.conf` file as follows:

```
# emerge grub
# grub
grub> root (hd0,0)
grub> setup (hd0)
grub> quit
# nano -w /boot/grub/grub.conf
default 0
timeout 15
splashimage=(hd0,0)/grub/splash.xpm.gz

title=Gentoo Linux
   root (hd0,0)
   kernel /kernel-2.4.26-gentoo-r9 root=/dev/hda0
   initrd /initrd-2.4.26-gentoo-r9
```

31. **Reboot.** Exit from your chroot partition by running `umount` to unmount all partitions and then rebooting as follows:

```
# exit; cd /
# umount /mnt/gentoo/devfs /mnt/gentoo/proc /mnt/gentoo
# reboot
```

Remove the installation CD and allow the computer to boot from hard disk. After a few moments, you should see the GRUB boot screen. Select Gentoo Linux (press Enter).

Note

From here on, you will be booting from the hard disk and working directly from the operating system you installed. If you see error messages, such as missing kernel drivers, I recommend that you go to `http://forums.gentoo.com` and search for the driver that's causing problems. Chances are that someone else has had the same problem and can offer you a solution.

32. **Install a Desktop.** For most of us, it's not much fun just working from the command line. The following command installs a basic set of desktop packages, including the X Window System (xfree), KDE desktop (kde), Mozilla browser (mozilla), and Openoffice.org office suite (openoffice-bin). This will take a long time to install over the network!

```
# emerge xfree kde mozilla openoffice-bin
```

As an alternative, if you have these packages available on CD-ROM, you can type the following commands to identify the location of the packages and install them from that location:

```
# export PKGDIR="/mnt/cdrom/packages"
# emerge -k xfree gnome kde mozilla openoffice-bin
```

You could also consider saving some time by installing only gnome or kde (not both). If you don't plan to create documents or spreadsheets, you probably don't need to install openoffice-bin either.

33. **Configure the X server.** Now that your desktop software is installed, you need to configure the X Window System to work properly with your video card and monitor. Type the following to configure your video card and monitor:

```
# /usr/X11R6/bin/xf86config
```

At this point, you should have a working Gentoo system. For further documentation, check out www.gentoo.org/doc/en/index.xml.

Summary

In just a few years, Gentoo has distinguished itself as a premier distribution for Linux enthusiasts who are interested in complete control of the components and settings of their Linux systems.

The jewel of the Gentoo system is the Portage package management system. Using the Portage emerge command, you can install any of thousands of Gentoo software packages. Those packages can be downloaded and built from scratch, using settings you choose to tune them for how you use your Linux system.

If you don't want to learn about the inner workings of a Linux system (and spend lots of time getting it to work), Gentoo may not be for you. An experienced Linux person usually takes several tries to get Gentoo going, while someone new to Linux may not get it installed and running at all without lots of help. However, if you like to tune and tweak your operating system, Gentoo is a great way to go.

✦   ✦   ✦

Running Slackware Linux

Ask old-time Linux users what the first Linux distribution they used was and many will tell you it was Slackware. Slackware is the oldest Linux distribution that is still actively developed today. Although it does not have a fancy graphical installer or specialized GUI tools, Slackware still has a loyal following and is a good way to get a basic Linux system that is both secure and stable.

This chapter explores the Slackware distribution, discusses its strengths and weaknesses, and introduces those who use it. It also explains how to install Slackware.

On the DVD-ROM

The first Slackware 10 CD image is on the DVD that comes with this book. You can copy and burn that image to CD as described in Appendix A. The first CD lets you install a good, basic set of features. If you want to install a GNOME or KDE desktop, you can install those features from the second CD, (which you can obtain from www.slackware.com/getslack).

Getting into Slackware

Although full graphical installs and GUI administration tools can make installing and configuring Linux easy, those tools carry with them some overhead. They also hide some of the details of how Linux is being configured.

Ask Slackware devotees the value of Slackware, and they might recite their mantra, the "4S Rule": Stable, Solid, Simple, and Sensible. By keeping things basic, Slackware offers the following advantages:

✦ **Better comprehension.** Because you use commands and configuration files with Slackware, you learn more about how Linux works on the inside. Most graphical installers and GUI tools hide the actual configuration that is going on and often limit the features you can use. If something goes wrong, it can be hard to debug a problem with most graphical interfaces. The Slackware installer is menu-based, very flexible, and quite intuitive.

✦ **Less bloat.** In general, graphical interfaces consume far more resources than their command-line counterparts. GUIs require more room on the distribution medium, plus more hard disk space and more RAM. Slackware relies primarily on basic Linux commands, text-based configuration files, and some simple menu-driven administration tools. With a Slackware 4.0 system, you can install a command-line version on a 100MB hard disk.

✦ **Better for low-end computers.** Slackware is the first distribution I recommend to run on low-end machines. A special ZipSlack distribution (`www.slackware.com/zipslack`) can be installed from a 100MB Zip drive or floppy disks. ZipSlack can install on a 386 PC with as little as 4MB of RAM. Even with the latest Slackware distribution, if you want a GUI, the installation procedure for Slackware lets you choose small, efficient window managers, Web browsers, mail clients, and other graphical tools.

✦ **Packages as projects intended.** Slackware doesn't mold the software it includes into one look-and-feel. The Apache Web server, KDE desktop, or Samba file/printer sharing projects work pretty much as they are delivered from those projects. So, again, the knowledge you gain from using those projects will transfer fairly easily to those same projects on other Linux systems.

Instead of providing a unified look-and-feel, Slackware allows the desktop environment or window manager you choose to dictate the desktop presentation. You can change your desktop as you like, using the menus or preference windows that come with those environments. Full KDE or GNOME desktops are available with Slackware (contained mostly on the second of two Slackware installation CDs). Or you can opt for a lighter, more efficient window manager, such as xfce, fvwm2, or twm.

For system administration, Slackware offers some tools that are based on the ncurses library. Ncurses allows an application to provide a screen-oriented interface from a character terminal, so you can use forms, menus, and sometimes even a mouse to configure some basic Linux features from any shell (no GUI required).

Anything you can do with other Linux distributions, you can do with Slackware. It might just take a bit more manual work to get there. Slackware doesn't yet officially use a package management system, such as the Red Hat RPM or Debian deb files. (Although there are some software management tools you can use, which are described later.) In general, however, most Slackware users become adept at building and installing their own applications (using tar, make, and similar tools).

Note Slackware comes with a good set of libraries that will take care of the dependency needs of most Linux applications. However, for video, audio, and some other types of applications, you may find yourself hunting around for libraries. Tools for satisfying package dependencies (such as yum and apt) can save you that trouble in other distributions.

Characterizing the Slackware Community

Like many other successful Linux distributions, Slackware was started by a strong-minded individual who created the kind of Linux system that suited himself. Slackware users are people who pretty much agree with him.

The Slackware Creator

Patrick Volkerding started Slackware in 1993 as a Linux distribution to use for himself and his friends. He was kind enough to answer some questions I had about Slackware, and I want to share his answers with you here:

Patrick originally used a Linux distribution called SLS Linux (named after Soft Landing Linux, the company that made it). Why didn't he just contribute to SLS instead of starting his own distribution?

> **Patrick:** I tried. By April of 1993 I had collected a huge list of bugs in SLS, along with the fixes for most of them. Plenty of people tried to get these to Peter MacDonald (SLS's author/maintainer), but the bugs in SLS (many of which were quite obvious) never seemed to get fixed.
>
> Of course, I'd started work on my patched version of SLS with no plan to try to launch a lasting distribution. I figured I'd get it online and SLS would fix the issues, and that might just be that. SLS was a great distribution and isn't given enough credit for all the ideas that started there. Unfortunately, it was while Peter was busy working on inventing kernel modules that SLS sat online for a few months, full of bugs and not getting any updates.

Patrick decided to take the leap to separate Slackware from SLS after MacDonald suggested that Slackware was infringing on his copyrights (despite the only license on the SLS code saying "Distribute freely; do not restrict."):

> **Patrick:** So, I promised Peter that I would write a new installer for Slackware instead of using a modified SLS one, and that the new installer would be the next change made to Slackware online.

Did the great success of Slackware from the get-go surprise him?

> **Patrick:** Absolutely. I knew it worked better than the other distributions that were out at the time, but I didn't expect the kind of mass exodus from SLS that occurred.

What kind of person would choose Slackware over other Linux distros?

> **Patrick:** It seems to attract the kind of users who want to configure software the old-fashioned way (using a text editor), and who don't want a lot of unnecessary things running in the background. I try to compile software with as few of my own changes as possible, which also makes it pretty easy to update things from source if you decide to go that route.
>
> In the early days of Linux I think most of the users were like this, and as time has moved on and various distributions focused on different markets, the profile of the average Linux user has changed quite a lot. Most of today's commercial Linux distributions seem to target a user who wants to administer his machine with a point-and-click interface much like Windows. Slackware and other lower-level distributions serve a different niche — users who don't mind a learning curve if it means the operating system will stay out of their way.

Today, Patrick is still the Project Lead and maintains complete control over Slackware's features and release schedule. In this arrangement, Patrick can choose the features to include, and he doesn't add features that don't suit him (even popular ones). This is how Patrick characterizes the Slackware development process:

> **Patrick:** Most of what I do is research(trying to figure out where Linux is going so I can make (hopefully) sane choices about what to implement. There's not really a core development team (which really streamlines the development process by sidestepping the usual time-wasting squabbles that usually happen in any official development hierarchy). But I get a ton of help from people who e-mail me with problems or suggestions, that lead to an upgrade or fix somewhere in the system.

The best way to keep up with Slackware development issues is to read the Change Logs (available from the Slackware home page). Slackware aficionados expect releases on an "it's ready when it's ready" schedule, as the Slackware FAQ notes: "As things are built for the upcoming release, they'll be uploaded into the -current tree. If the -current does not exist, it probably means we have just released a new version of Slackware."

Slackware Users

From a purely subjective perspective, my friends who use Slackware tend to be technically oriented but not the extreme overclockers and tweakers who might be drawn to Gentoo, for example. They like Slackware because it works so simply and so well that they believe it gives them more time to slack.

Slackware users often think of themselves as loners, despite the fact that they all hang out together at LAN parties and Internet cafes. They like the more purist, less commercial approach of Slackware. For their personal desktop, gaming box, or small-office server, they see no need for the graphical tools that you get with Red Hat or SUSE Linux systems. They are comfortable with commands and man pages.

I've often heard users refer to Slackware as being easier to use than other Linux distributions. To someone coming from a UNIX or BSD background, this is probably true. You don't have to wait for graphical tools to pop up, and almost everything is covered on a man page.

Note   Man pages are the traditional means of documenting commands, file formats, devices, system calls, and most any other component of a UNIX or Linux system. Man pages date back to the very first UNIX systems. You can read man pages using the `man` command, followed by a component name, from any shell. To learn about how the man page system itself works, type **man man.**

Slackware Internet Sites

The Slackware home page (`www.slackware.com`) is a good place to start for information about Slackware. There are two main mailing lists plus an IRC channel available through the Web site, as well as links to download sites, some documentation, and the Slackware Store (`store.slackware.com`).

There's a Slackware Linux Essentials online book (`slackware.com/book`) and four FAQs (`slackware.com/faq`) available from the Slackware site. There's also no "news" to speak of at the Slackware site, so the best way to keep up on what's happening with the project is to read the change logs (`slackware.com/changelog`).

Outside the official Slackware site, a lot of new sites have been popping up recently that provide information about Slackware. A good place to bring questions about Slackware is `http://linuxquestions.org` (follow the links: Linux Forums ➪ Linux Distributions ➪ Slackware). The Linux Packages site (`www.linuxpackages.net`) offers some active forums on different aspects of Slackware.

Challenges of Using Slackware

There is no commercial organization behind Slackware and no official support, so if something goes wrong with your Slackware system, you are on your own to solve the problem. The Slackware project, however, does maintain a list of third-party organizations that provide technical support at `www.slackware.com/support`.

Although functionally Slackware can be used in most any computing environment, in places where you feel the need to have a company behind the computer systems you install (such as a large enterprise), you would do better to look toward a Red Hat or SUSE system.

The lack of official package management tools poses another challenge to Slackware users. Slackware doesn't do dependency checks when you install software, but because Slackware includes libraries that nearly all applications would require, most applications work just fine. However, at some point you will probably find yourself needing to track down some library that Slackware didn't include.

When a software package made to add to Slackware requires a library that is not in the standard Slackware distribution, the developers often build the needed library into the package. If the software fails, however, indicating a missing library, there are a couple of things you can try:

✦ Look in the software package's readme file for descriptions of the libraries it needs.

✦ Search the Web for the terms "Slackware" and the name of the missing library.

Tools that do some level of package management have begun appearing for Slackware. Swaret (www.swaret.org), slapt-get (http://software.jaos.org), and SlackUpdate (freshmeat.net/projects/slup) are available packages. Patrick told me that he resists putting these or other package management tools into Slackware because:

✦ Some package management tools add unnecessary files (including adding extra directories to /etc/ld.so.conf).

✦ Package updates sometimes don't properly handle the way someone has changed a package's configuration files. Getting configuration files right after an update may require manually editing the files.

✦ Package management tools may overwrite changes a person has made to configuration files, causing important information to be lost completely.

As someone comfortable with UNIX and Linux, I find the text-based tools that come with Slackware helpful and fairly intuitive to use. If you are coming from a Windows environment, however, you may find the lack of GUI-based tools and cohesive end-to-end procedures for setting up features a bit disconcerting.

Because Slackware is not backed up by a big support organization, it has not made much headway into the corporate enterprise arena. The fact that most commercial applications are created specifically for Red Hat Linux distributions and won't just run out of the box on Slackware makes Slackware an even harder sell for corporate environments.

Using Slackware as a Development Platform

Slackware has long been a preferred platform for developing open source software. It contains a large set of libraries and includes nearly every tool you could want for developing applications.

Because Slackware is a clean, basic Linux system, applications that run in Slackware will run on most other Linux systems as well. In other words, you won't be encouraged to add a lot of special Slackware hooks that would prevent software from being portable across a wide range of Linux, UNIX, and BSD systems. Also, every Linux system will be able to work with Slackware packages, which are in tar/gzip format (.tgz).

Slackware can easily provide an efficient development workstation environment for technical people because the distribution doesn't get in the way of its powerful features. It's easy to configure a simple window manager and not incur the overhead of background processes that try to "help" you when you insert a CD or need software updates. You simply have an efficient desktop that lets you do what you need to do.

If you become interested in building and submitting packages for Slackware, there are some good descriptions of how to do so at the Linux Packages site (www.linux packages.net). Look for links to building and submitting packages on the site's home page in the Information box.

Installing Slackware

Slackware is freely available from several different sources. It installs and runs well on low-end computers. Some Linux or UNIX expertise would be useful, especially if something goes wrong.

Getting Slackware

Slackware comes on four CDs: two installation CDs and two source code CDs. The first Slackware CD (which you can burn to a CD from a disk image on this book's DVD) can be used for a good, basic install. If you want to add a full KDE or GNOME desktop, you will need the second installation CD as well. The full Slackware CD set is available from a few dozen mirror sites on the Web (see www.slackware.com/getslack).

 Note For many years, Slackware was available on one install CD, but adding KDE and GNOME to the distribution made a second CD necessary.

To help support the project, you can purchase the boxed set of Slackware from http://store.slackware.com. At the store, you also can get a subscription to Slackware, so that the Slackware Store sends you a new version each time one is released (every six to eight months). The store will just ship it when it's available and charge your credit card. People who like Slackware often pay the subscription fee just to show their support.

Hardware Requirements

While some older versions of Slackware will run on a 386, the Slackware site recommends 486 as a minimum processor. Without a graphical interface (X Window System), the minimum amount of RAM required is 16MB. With the GUI, at least 128MB of RAM is recommended. (With the KDE desktop, the more RAM, the better.)

The Zipslack distribution (a small Slackware distribution that you can install from a Zip drive or floppy disks) can install on a hard disk with as little as 100MB space. You can find Zipslack on any Slackware mirror site (`ftp://distro.ibiblio.org/pub/Linux/distributions/slackware/slackware-10.0/zipslack`, for example).

If you are installing Slackware 10.0, 500MB is the minimum amount of disk space you should have available on your Linux partition. The recommended amount of hard disk space is at least 2GB for a full desktop install.

All IDE and SCSI controllers supported by the Linux kernel are also supported by Slackware.

Starting Installation

Although the Slackware installer has evolved over the years, its basic look-and-feel hasn't changed much. There are some things you still need to do manually, such as setting up RAID or doing partitioning.

The following steps describe how to install Slackware from the first installation CD. For more detailed information (or if something goes wrong during the installation that isn't covered here), refer to the Slackware-HOWTO, which is on the first Slackware CD.

1. **Obtain the first CD in the two-CD Slackware 10.0 installation set.** (As mentioned earlier, you can copy the CD from the DVD that comes with this book as described in Appendix A or download it from a Slackware mirror site and burn it to CD. If you want to do a full Slackware install, you'll need to get the second Slackware CD, which is not on the DVD.)

2. **Insert the Slackware CD** into the drive and reboot your computer.

3. **From the boot prompt, simply press Enter** to start the default boot process, or press F2 for help on choosing a kernel to boot or F3 to see what kernel images are available, to best suit your hardware.

   If Slackware installation boots properly, you are prompted to enter a keyboard map.

Note   If your Slackware medium won't boot, refer to the `BOOTING.TXT` file on the Slackware CD for information on things you can try to get around the problem. (If you can't access the CD at all, you can get this file from any Slackware mirror site.)

4. **If you are using a U.S. keyboard map, press Enter;** to use a keyboard map for a different language/country, type **1**, press Enter, and then select the one you want. The Slackware login prompt appears.

5. Type **root** and press Enter. A shell prompt appears.

6. **Partition your hard disk.** Chapter 7 discussed partitioning your hard disk. Slackware doesn't have a graphical partitioning tool, such as Disk Druid, so you have to use the fdisk or cfdisk command to partition your hard disk (again, refer to Chapter 7, or see the Slackware-HOWTO for details).

To install Slackware, you should have at least one swap partition (up to twice the size of your RAM, with a maximum of about 500MB) and one Linux partition (such as ext3). You should have at least 500MB of hard disk space, with a recommended 2GB of disk space available for a full install of Slackware 10.0.

7. **Type the following command** to enter setup mode:

```
# setup
```

The Slackware Linux Setup screen appears, with the following options:

```
HELP      Read the Slackware Setup Help file
KEYMAP    Remap your keyboard if you're not using a US one
ADDSWAP   Set up your swap partition(s)
TARGET    Set up your target partitions
SOURCE    Select source media
SELECT    Select categories of software to install
INSTALL   Install selected software
CONFIGURE Reconfigure your Linux system
EXIT      Exit Slackware Linux Setup
```

Type the first letter in the option name (or use the arrow keys) to highlight the option you want, and then press Enter. The following steps describe options you need to configure Slackware.

8. **Select ADDSWAP.** The Swap Space Detected menu appears, listing the swap partitions you have available. Select the one you want (there will usually be just one) and select Yes to install it as your swap partition. (If you don't have a swap partition, exit the setup screen and run fdisk to create one.)

The swap partition will be checked for bad blocks, formatted, and activated. Select OK to continue. The Select Linux Installation Partition menu appears.

9. **Select root partition.** From the Linux partition that is displayed, highlight the one that you want to use as your root (/) partition and choose Select. The / partition is where Linux and all your data will go by default. (Other partitions can be added later.)

Choose to do a quick format (Format) or a slow format that includes bad block checking (Check). Or you can select No to not format the partition.

Note   Normally, you would overwrite your / partition, although you might keep data from another partition. I often maintain a separate data partition that I will attach to the file system in a location such as /mnt/data. With that technique, I can keep my data and still install a whole new operating system.

Choose the file system type for the root file system. These days, most people select either the ext3 or reiserfs file systems as their Linux root partition. Both of those file system types do journaling, so they can recover quickly if the system is shut down improperly (such as someone kicking out the power cord).

Choose the Inode Density. Select 4096 (the default, which is fine in most cases), 2048, or 1024 bytes. (A smaller number allows more inodes on the file system, which is useful only if you have many small files, as you might on a news server.)

10. **Select other partitions.** If you created other Linux partitions, you can assign file system types and format them as well. Identify where in the file system the other partitions are connected. (Again, check Chapter 7 for information on where you might want to attach a partition to your Linux file system.)

11. **Choose your source media.** Select 1, usually, so that Slackware is installed from the CD. You can also install Slackware from a partition on your hard drive, from an NFS shared file system, or from a premounted directory.

    You can have Setup scan for your Slackware CD or tell it a particular device to use (if you have multiple drives and you want to tell it which to use).

12. **Select the different packages series that you want to install and press OK.** General package series include:

    - Base Linux system (the core of the operating system and basic utilities)
    - Various Applications that do not need X (nongraphical commands)
    - Program Development (C, C++, Lisp, Perl, and so on)
    - GNU Emacs (a text editor)
    - FAQ lists, HOWTO documentation
    - GNOME desktop
    - Linux kernel source

    The K Desktop Environment (including QT)

    - International support for KDE
    - System libraries (needed by X, KDE, GNOME, and others)
    - Networking (TCP/IP, UUCP, mail, news, and so on)
    - TeX typesetting
    - Tcl/tk scripting languages
    - X Window System
    - X Applications
    - Games

    If you are installing from the single CD image, deselect GNOME, KDE, and KDEI because they come on the second CD. (Later in this procedure, you have an opportunity to select a simple window manager such as xfce, blackbox, fluxbox, or fvwm, as many Slackware users like to do.)

Note While it's safest just to install everything with the two install CDs so that you're sure to have everything you want and won't miss a dependent package, with the single Slackware CD I had no dependency problems simply deselecting GNOME and KDE package groups. Remember, the second CD is not on this book's DVD, so you need to obtain it separately.

13. **Choose how you are prompted to select packages.** Here are your choices:

   - **Full**—If you have both Slackware install CDs, this installs everything. Do not choose option if you have only the first install CD.

   - **Expert**—Lets you choose individual packages interactively.

   - **Menu**—Enables you to choose groups of packages interactively.

   - **Newbie**—Shows you a lot about what is being installed on your Slackware system and lets you choose whether to install optional packages. You just have to sit there for a long time and keep pressing Enter.

14. **Choose a Linux kernel.** In most cases where you have an IDE controller, you can choose the default `bare.i` kernel. If you have a SCSI controller, choose one of the kernels with a `.s` at the end. If your computer has very little RAM, try the `lowmem.i` kernel. Other specialized kernels are described in the Slackware-HOWTO document.

15. **Make a boot disk.** If you have a floppy drive, make a boot disk. It will enable you to reboot your computer if your hard disk ever becomes unbootable. (If you don't have a floppy drive, you can use the Slackware install CD as a boot disk in an emergency.)

16. **Configure a modem.** Select No Modem if you don't plan to use a modem with your computer. If you have an external, serial modem, choose the COM port it is connected to (represented by `/dev/tty?`; with COM1 associated with `ttyS0`). For PCI modems (slots directly in the motherboard), device names usually begin at `/dev/ttyS4`.

17. **Enable hotplug subsystem.** Select Yes to enable the hotplug subsystem at boot time. This lets Slackware try to activate devices that are plugged into the computer while it is running (such as Cardbus and USB devices). By enabling the system at boot time, it can also can detect other hardware, including PCI cards.

18. **Install the LILO boot loader.** Choose Simple to have the setup process try to automatically install the LILO boot loader, or choose Expert if you want to configure the boot loader to do something special. (You can add kernel parameters and set frame buffer console features in either mode.) Special things to do in Expert mode include:

   - Add other bootable Linux partitions

   - Add a bootable Windows partition

   - Install an existing `lilo.conf` file instead of creating a new one

   You can have graphics appear on the boot screen by enabling the frame buffer console. Choose the resolution and number of colors (such as 1024×768×256) to use with the frame buffer console.

When prompted, add any parameters you want fed to the kernel when you boot. In particular, you might add kernel parameters if you want to turn off autoprobing on certain devices (for example, nousb) or turn off power management features (noacpi). (Chapter 11 describes some kernel parameters that might be useful to you.)

LILO is usually placed in the root of the Linux partition or in the master boot record for the entire hard disk. It's safest to put LILO in the superblock (Root) of the Linux partition or on a formatted floppy disk. For the former, you need to indicate that the Linux partition is bootable (using the `fdisk` command when you return to a shell prompt). It can be unsafe to put LILO in the master boot record. However, for a system where only one operating system is installed (in this case, Slackware), the master boot record is a common place to put LILO.

19. **Configure the network.** Select Yes to configure your network (for example, your LAN connection from your Ethernet card). Refer to Chapter 7 for information on configuring your network connection.

20. **Select startup services.** For server software that you installed, you need to tell Slackware whether to start that service at boot time. In general, you should turn on only services you want to have on (you can always turn any others on later). Among the services that will be on by default (assuming you installed the packages) are the sshd service, to enable remote login using ssh; system logging (rc.syslog), to log system activity; and sendmail, to receive e-mail. To share your printer, you may want to enable CUPS; to be a Web server, you should turn on Apache (rc.httpd).

21. **Configure console fonts.** You can try some custom screen fonts. If you find one you particularly like, you can choose to use it instead of the default.

22. **Set hardware clock.** The clock on your computer can be set to local time or to UTC time (Greenwich mean time). Most often you will set it to local time.

23. **Choose a time zone.** Select your current time zone from the list.

24. **Select a default window manager.** Choices include KDE desktop, GNOME desktop, or any of a number of simple window managers, such as xfce, blackbox, fluxbox, fvwm (selections look like Windows systems), and TWM (too lightweight for most people). If you installed only from the first Slackware CD, KDE and GNOME will not be among your choices.

25. **Set root password.** Select a root password when you are prompted to do so.

At this point you can return to the Slackware Linux Setup menu.

26. **Select EXIT** to leave the setup screen. The install CD should eject.

27. **Press Ctrl+Alt+Delete** to reboot your computer.

Starting with Slackware

The LILO Boot menu appears when you first boot Slackware. It should contain at least a listing for your Linux partition and possibly for a Windows partition (if there is one on your computer).

Press Enter at the boot prompt to start Slackware. Log in as the root user when you see the login prompt. You are going to be at a Linux command line prompt; if you don't know what that is, refer to Chapter 2.

Here are a few things you might want to do to get started with Slackware:

✦ **Get mail.** Type `mail` at the command line prompt. You should have a couple of mail messages there for the root user, including one from Patrick Volkerding. Type the number of that message and page through it (using the Enter key) to read some additional setup steps that may interest you. (Type **q** to exit the message and **x** to exit mail.)

✦ **Add another user.** Because most people don't use the root user account for their daily use of Linux, you should add a regular user account and give it a password. Here's what you would run to add a user named robby:

```
# useradd -m robby
# passwd robby
Changing password for robby
New password: ********
Re-enter new password: ********
```

✦ **Start the desktop.** If you installed X and either a window manager or whole desktop environment (KDE or GNOME), you can start it by typing:

```
# startx
```

If X and your chosen desktop don't start properly (the screen may be unreadable or X may simply crash), press Ctrl+Alt+Backspace to exit X and return to the shell. Instructions for solving X problems, choosing different window managers, and configuring X are included in Chapter 3's "Configuring Your Own Desktop" section.

✦ **Configure sound.** When you first boot Slackware, the ALSA sound system should be set up to work, but the volume is muted. To configure ALSA and check that your sound card is ready to go, run the `alsaconf` command. It will search for installed sound cards, and when it finds one, it adds any modules needed to use the card, raises the volume, and tests the card.

Once your sound card is configured, use the `alsamixer` command to adjust volume levels for your sound card.

✦ **Add modules.** If any of your computer hardware was not properly detected and configured, you can add the modules you need after Slackware is running. In addition to the standard /etc/modules.conf file, Slackware provides its own file where you can load extra drivers: /etc/rc.d/rc.modules.

The rc.modules file is useful because it contains the command lines to load many useful modules. The lines are commented out, so you simply have to remove the comment character to have the modules load on the next reboot.

Note If some of your computer hardware is not being detected properly and you don't know what module is required for it to work, try booting KNOPPIX (from the DVD included with this book). If the hardware works in KNOPPIX, run the lsmod command to see what modules are loaded. From that list, you should be able to add the necessary modules as just described.

✦ **Configure a printer.** While you can start your print service in several different ways, Patrick recommends using the Apsfilter package. Connect your printer to a parallel port, make sure that TCP/IP is configured, and be sure that the printing software (LPRng package) is installed. Then run the following command:

/usr/share/apsfilter/SETUP

Using Apsfilter, you can select your printer driver, choose how the printer is connected, select the paper format, and set several other options. The result should be a working /etc/printcap and /etc/apsfilter files.

✦ **Configure networking.** If you didn't configure your Ethernet cards at installation time, you can do it now. Type the following command:

netconfig

The menu system enables you to configure your network interface using the same screens as at install time.

✦ **Install additional software packages.** You can use the pkgtool command to install Slackware packages. Download any packages you want to install to a directory. Then change to that directory and run the pkgtool command. Choose Current to install packages from the current directory. A screen appears, describing the first software package available for you to install. Select Yes to install the package.

Note One place to find Slackware packages is LinuxPackages.net. Likewise, you can install software packages from any open source project (such as sourceforge.net) that are either identified as being created for Slackware or simply tar.gz packages that you can build from scratch.

The pkgtool utility also enables you to list the contents of installed packages and to remove packages.

If you are used to other Linux systems, you should familiarize yourself with a few things you might find different in Slackware. For example, system startup scripts are contained in /etc/rc.d, rather than a whole series of links to various /etc/rc?.d directories.

Summary

Slackware is the oldest active Linux distribution. It is run by Patrick Volkerding, as it has been for more than a decade, and keeps as its goals stability and security. Slackware has a loyal following, but the project is not geared for wide deployment in enterprise computing situations. Slackware is a great distribution to learn Linux on because it keeps its configuration simple and near to the command line and configuration files.

Look for Slackware to continue to be among the most efficient Linux distributions. There are currently no plans to add a graphical installer or fancy software package management system. You can expect Slackware to remain trim and true to its roots, making it one of the best Linux distributions to run on older computer hardware.

✦   ✦   ✦

Running Linspire

The brief history of Linspire is colorful and has been portrayed as a "David and Goliath" story, at least in some of the news media. In this case, Linspire is David and a PC desktop market share is Goliath. How this "battle" will turn out is anybody's guess.

Linspire began as Lindows, founded by Michael Robertson in 2001, after his tenure with MP3.com. His goal was to bring Linux to the desktop once and for all.

The general concept was to develop an operating system that would be inexpensive, easy to install and use, and a competitive alternative to Microsoft Windows on the desktop PC. To accomplish that, Lindows needed to be simple enough for a nontechnical user (even someone who has never really used a PC before) to install, configure, and use. While this is, indeed, a laudable goal, most of this product's press has come as the result of its tension with Microsoft Corporation.

The main point of contention with Microsoft was the name Lindows. In several legal proceedings, Microsoft claimed that the Lindows name infringed on the term Windows, which Microsoft claimed was a trademark. Lindows and many others contended that the term *windows* was generic before Microsoft began using the term.

Microsoft's attempts to get U.S. courts to protect the Windows trademark were not initially successful, but in other venues, the issue was not as litigious. It was one of those victories that forced the Lindows name change to Linspire. Basically, Microsoft won a favorable ruling in one of the countries where Lindows was sold, and Lindows stated that it could not remedy the situation without changing its name.

The ruling said there was a trademark issue and that Lindows could not allow citizens of that country to access the Lindows Web site or access their product under the Lindows name. Because keeping one country's residents off a particular Web site would have proved very difficult, Lindows had to make some drastic changes, most notable being the alteration of its name.

Microsoft was still pursuing an injunction or summary judgment and would soon see its Windows trademark challenged in court. To avoid a costly court battle, Microsoft offered a reported $20 million and some other items including some technology licensing to settle the case. Linspire accepted, and that was the end of the dispute.

Linspire is a commercial product and is not included on this book's DVD. You can download its installation CD from www.linspire.com/lindows_storefront. php. You will need to create a user account and have payment information ready. Burn the CDs using instructions in Appendix A, and then install Linspire as described later in this chapter.

There are several Linspire packages available for purchase and download. Each package is based on the same core software and is really defined by the kinds of supplementary software that are included with it. The packages are:

✦ **Linspire 4.5** — The bare-bones package, for someone who is just interested in installing Linspire 4.5 without all the bells and whistles. It includes Linspire 4.5, LinspireLive!, and Linspire Español.

✦ **LinspireLive!** — Includes the core Linspire 4.5 operating system and some productivity software. The real appeal of this installation is that it is CD-based. The user inserts the CD into any PC with compatible hardware and can boot into Linspire. This package is primarily marketed as a tool for persuading Microsoft Windows users to give desktop Linux a try.

✦ **Linspire 4.5 Value Bundle** — The most general product package. It includes the basic operating system and multimedia, productivity, and entertainment software. It also includes LinspireLive! and Linspire Español, as well as a year's subscription to the Click-N-Run (CNR) Warehouse, which provides more than 1,800 easy-to-install applications.

✦ **Linspire 4.5 Developers Edition** — Similar to the Value Bundle, except that this package includes more than 100 development utilities.

✦ **Desktop Linux Enterprise Assessment Kit** — Includes nearly every Linspire option, with all the available 4.5 configurations and a hardware assessment tool to evaluate existing systems for potential migration to Linspire.

The value package makes the most sense for the general user. It offers the best balance between cost and value of software included and adds in access to the Click-N-Run Warehouse. CNR is a feature that provides much of Linspire's value.

Getting into Linspire

Linspire is a Debian-based Linux distribution that is being developed with a focus on ease of use. The key features of Linspire include:

✦ An almost entirely automated installation process that enables the beginning user to install Linspire without becoming involved or intimidated by lengthy screens of output.

✦ Easy software management using the Click-N-Run utility.

✦ Support that incorporate online and offline resources designed to be accessible to novice users.

✦ An intuitive user interface based on the KDE environment.

Installing Software with Click-N-Run

One of the bigger complaints from acolyte Linux users is the difficulty in installing additional software. It has become very clear that to make serious inroads onto the desktop PCs of Joe and Jane Q. Public, Linux needs to keep improving ease of use. Continuing with the "it's so easy" theme, Linspire has developed one of the most trouble-free software installation processes in use on a desktop Linux system: Click-N-Run (CNR). This process connects users with tons of applications and requires almost no effort at all to install.

Click-N-Run has been described, accurately, as apt-get taken to new, graphical heights. Apt-get is a tool used to manage software packages. The beginnings of apt-get are most closely associated with Debian and .DEB packages, yet it has been adapted to handle RPMs and is widely available for platforms other than Debian. Apt-get is complemented by detailed man pages, although it lacks a graphical interface. The CNR process enables you to select the desired application, click a little green button, and wait while the package downloads and installs. You only need an existing Linspire installation and to click the green globe with a running man in the middle to get started. Here are some of the CNR tool's features:

✦ **Logon/Logout** — Use this button to configure your login information for CNR. To use the CNR Warehouse, you need a valid user account.

✦ **Configure Click-N-Run** — This option enables you to specify where CNR will look for files when you are installing new applications. If you do not have your own repository, leave this setting alone. The capability to select your source location is relevant only if you choose to install packages not in the CNR Warehouse, such as an application your network administrator has made available for installation by users on the local network. For most users, this is not a real selling point because the real return for buying Linspire comes from accessing applications in the CNR Warehouse.

✦ **Install** — After you've selected a software package to install from your source location (local files, CD-based, on the network, or from the CNR Warehouse), you can initiate the installation process. Items in the warehouse can be installed by clicking the green globe icon next to the product name in lieu of using the CNR's Install button.

✦ **Update** — Select an application and then use the Update feature to check for newer versions of the software.

✦ **Run** — After you have installed an application, you can use this option to run the program immediately. You can also run the program from the launch menu or a desktop shortcut.

✦ **Pause** — You can pause your download of online installation files. This makes working with large installation files over slower or shared network connections easier.

✦ **Add to Desktop** — Creates a desktop shortcut to any of your applications in addition to the launch menu icons.

✦ **Uninstall** — When you run the uninstall option on a selected application, all of the program files, icons, and folders for that application are automatically removed.

CNR is a great tool for getting software from the warehouse, and Click-N-Run Express is a CNR version that can be used to install applications from any location. It enables you to designate local or remote repositories and then install the products. If you configure the download option, CNR Express stores a local copy of the installed applications for later use, enabling you to install, remove, and reinstall when you want without having to download the installation package all over again. When your installation is complete, the application waits for you to use it by browsing to the application title in your K menu.

Tip   One of the truly handy, proprietary applications available in the CNR Warehouse is Win4Lin, which can be used to get many Win32 applications up and running on your Linspire system.

Other Installation Options

While the Click-N-Run application is the quickest means of managing software on your Linspire installation, it may not meet every user's needs. With this in mind, there are a couple of other options for managing software on your install:

✦ .DEB packages can be used to manually install software. Open a Terminal window and run the command `'dpkg - i filename.deb'`.

Tip   For more information about using the dpkg installation utility, check out the related Debian FAQ at `http://debian.org/doc/FAQ/ch-pkgtools.en.html`.

✦ RPM packages can be used if you make use of an installation package converter such as Alien (`www.kitenet.net/programs/alien/`). This method should be employed only if you have no more convenient options. Package conversion is not a sure thing, and unexpected consequences could arise from using converted packages.

✦ Apt-get, a tool for managing software packages, can be used as can its graphical derivative, Synaptic. They offer the same functionality as CNR, but without the ease of use.

Note A fairly thorough description of apt-get and related management tools can be found in Chapter 9.

✦ Installer scripts (`.sh`) and compiling source from tarball enable you to do things the "old way" if needed and to exert granular control of unpackaged software. This functionality helps keep Linspire a flexible platform for running a variety of software. (A tarball is a compressed archive of files created with a special utility. Source code distributions are often packaged as tarballs.)

Linspire Support and Software

Support is one of the really nice benefits of being a Linspire consumer. The level of support available from Linspire is not particularly expansive, especially when compared to other product communities. It is, however, very easy to find information on the support site and make contact with users willing to help you out should you have any questions or need help with using Linspire or most of the Click-N-Run applications (although most application support is unofficial).

Linspire Forums and Information

If you should encounter any problems or simply want to ask some questions about Linspire, you can start by checking out the Linspire support pages. By taking your Web browser to `http://support.linspire.com`, you can access user forums, FAQs, and (if you have a product logon) access to personalized support (and phone support when it becomes available).

While the FAQs and personalized support are very useful at times, you will get the most mileage out of the user forums. Most of the forums allow posts by registered users only, but there are guest areas as well. (Not that this is a big deal because most Linspire packages include access to all the support options.) These forums are frequented by other users and product developers and are a great resource for getting future product information and providing your feedback on how Lindows works for you.

Audio Assistant

What good would new software be without a product tour peppered with a touch of product evangelism? Linspire offers both with the Audio Assistant. This animated tour of the Linspire OS runs after your initial installation. The Assistant will walk you through using Click-N-Run, configuring your desktop, and a lot more.

Note   You can check out the online version of the Audio Assistant at `http://media.linspire.com/howto/kiosk.swf`.

Should you install Linspire and bypass the Audio Assistant tutorial, have no fear. You can relaunch the tutorials by clicking the life jacket icon in the lower-left corner of your desktop (in the toolbar).

Installing Linspire 4.5

If you plan ahead, a Linspire installation is one of the most straightforward software installations. This includes Apple and Microsoft as well as other Linux distributions. There are very few configuration options and no disk partitioning options other than either selecting an installation partition or wiping the entire hard disk. For maximum joy, make sure you have no data on the computer/partition/drive where Linspire will be installed. The target location for the installation will be wiped out.

Also make sure that you check the supported hardware list (`www.linspire.com/lindows_hwsw_compatibility.php`) before you begin your installation to make sure there are no surprises there.

Linspire Hardware Requirements

While Linspire is top-notch when it comes to ease of use, it won't be very easy if your hardware doesn't work with the software. Linspire system requirements follow the product's "keep it simple" theme, and there is no discussion of RAID controllers or other such arcane items. Like any version of Linux, the minimum requirements are pretty sparse, but you need to make sure your PC meets them:

✦ **800 MHz or faster processor** — Any processor that crosses this performance threshold will work.

✦ **128MB of RAM** — This will get you by, but Linspire recommends you splurge and install 256MB or more of RAM for optimum performance.

✦ **Hard disk** — Linspire does not specify any particular disk size requirements. This is fine because any hard drive purchased in the same time frame as qualifying hardware is probably over 1GB, and that's plenty.

✦ **Video** — You need a color monitor capable of supporting a screen resolution of 1024×768. Some of the games included with various packages or available from the CNR Warehouse require some kind of 3D graphics accelerator hardware.

✦ **Sound** — You need a Linspire-compatible soundcard with speakers and/or headphones. Check your sound card at `www.linspire.com/lindows_hwsw_compatibility.php` before beginning your install.

✦ **Modem** — Your 56K, cable, or DSL modem also needs to be Linspire-compatible. Before beginning your install, check your equipment at `www.linspire.com/lindows_hwsw_compatibility.php`.

✦ **Network card** — Any Ethernet card is acceptable. While Linspire does not specifically recommend it, you would be wise to check the hardware compatibility list to make sure your Ethernet adapter is supported.

Like most flavors of Linux, the range of hardware supported is pretty wide. If you find that your hardware is not on the supported devices list, check the hardware vendor's Web site for Debian drivers for your device. It is entirely possible that you can install the driver manually (if Linspire cannot configure it).

Tip   To make sure that your hardware will work, or confirm that it will not, select the diagnostics option when booting from the Linspire CD. Running diagnostics shows you any errors relating to the configuration or detection of your hardware.

Installing Linspire

The Linspire installer is simple and effective. You select the appropriate option from the boot screen of the installation CD, and from that point on you pretty much follow the prompts. The entire installation usually takes 15 to 20 minutes to complete. This walk-through takes you through the installation and the initial startup process:

Caution   Both basic and advanced installations wipe out all data on the target drive/partition. Back up anything you think you might want to keep before proceeding.

1. Start the computer and boot the install CD. You'll see two options. The first is to install, and the second is for running diagnostics. Select option 1 and press Enter, or simply wait, and the installation will proceed after a few moments.

2. On the Install Type screen, you can select a basic or advanced installation. A basic installation is useful when you have only one hard disk and partition. An advanced installation enables you to select the hard disk and/or partition to which you want to install. Make your selection, and then click Next.

3. The Select Computer Name and Password screen appears. You need to name the PC and provide an admin (root) password if you opt to provide one. For a home configuration replacing a Windows installation, for example, leaving the password blank might be acceptable. In any working environment or if the PC is not going to be shielded from the Internet, providing a strong root password is essential. When you have made your selection, click the Next button.

4. You're asked to confirm your computer name and the installation method you selected. If you are happy with your selections, click Next.

5. A Warning window asks you to make absolutely certain that you want to proceed. You are again warned that all data on the target drive/partition will be lost. You are given the options "Yes, I am sure" and "Let me make changes." Select "Yes, I am sure" and you go to the next step. Select "Let me make changes" and you return to the installation type screen.

Tip At any point up to and including step 5, you can use the Back button to review and/or change your previous configuration decisions.

6. The next screen indicates the progress of the installation process. Scrolling messages fill the space, and in a few minutes you see the following message:

```
Linspire setup complete
press OK to restart your computer.
```

Click OK.

7. A final message appears, instructing you to remove your CD and press any key. Your CD tray opens. Grab the CD and press any key. Your installation is complete.

8. When Linspire starts up, you can specify which startup path you would like to take. The startup options are called *boot options*, and there are three boot options in your startup screen (called the Linux Loader or LILO): Linspire, Redetect, and Diagnostics.

   Linspire, the default option, boots into the Linspire operating system; you can select it or just wait for Linspire to load. Unless you have hardware installed since the last time you started Linspire or you are having some serious startup issues, always select the default option to launch Linspire.

   Redetect identifies installed hardware, which is useful if you've added new items since your last installation. This is roughly equivalent to the plug-and-play functionality most Windows users enjoy.

   Diagnostics is an option used when you are experiencing some kind of server system issues, such as failed or improperly configured hardware. A series of applications runs, and the results of their detection and diagnosis are displayed. This screen can be very intimidating and difficult to interpret if you are not familiar with the Linux startup process.

   Select Linspire, and the operating system finishes loading.

9. The First Time Setup window provides a button for setting the system time, a check box for agreeing to the Linspire license agreement, and an Advanced button that enables you to set or change the administrator (root) password; set the desktop (display) resolution that you prefer and that your hardware supports; and invoke the Linspire user tool User Manager, with which you can create new users, assign them capabilities, and delete them as needed. You also get one opportunity to rename your PC. You set the computer name and administrator password during startup, so there is not likely to be a reason to change them here, but you can if you like.

Summary

Linspire may not excite the battle-hardened Linux-using community, but it serves as a positive example of a user-oriented desktop Linux system. Linspire is by far the most accessible version of Linux for new users. With a computer that has supported hardware, literally anyone can install Linspire and get up and running with new applications, surfing the Web and sending e-mail in a couple of hours.

The Click-N-Run application takes ease of installation to a new level, making Linspire hopeful proof of the concept that a desktop version Linux can succeed in the home and office. The installation walk-through at the end of the chapter demonstrates that there are some trade-offs for this ease of use. Because the existing partitioning options are very limited, integrating Linspire onto systems where a less-skilled user wants it to coexist with Windows might be tricky. It is likely that with some additional partitioning options (such as the Mandrakelinux implementation of the user-friendly NTFS resizing utility), Linspire could prove valuable to a huge range of users. While Linspire does support a wide range of both Windows and Linux applications, it is still difficult to run some of the more popular games and applications on it without having to go well beyond the graphical tools offered with the distribution.

✦ ✦ ✦

Running Mandrakelinux

Mandrakelinux has a moderately split personality. Under the umbrella of Mandrakesoft (www.mandrake soft.com), a collection of commercial products is produced and supported. If you're more interested in the core product and willing to go without support, there is a "generalist" build of Mandrakelinux (http://www.mandrakelinux.com/en-us/) on the downloads page. This separation is not like the RHEL and Fedora division except superficially. Mandrakelinux distributions appear to make use of a mostly unified development group. That is, no marked divisions exist between the development efforts that produce the core of either the "free" product or the retail version. It is the extras added to the retail products that really differentiate retail and nonretail versions.

On the DVD-ROM

Mandrakelinux is not on the DVD that comes with this book. To get a copy of the Mandrakelinux, visit the Mandrakelinuxclub site (http://www.mandrakeclub .com/), where you are asked to join the Mandrakelinux Users Club before you download the distribution. You do not have to join the club to download, but the folks at Mandrakelinux strongly encourage your financial participation. Alternatively, you can go to the Mandrakelinux store (http://store.mandrakesoft.com) and purchase boxed sets or pre-installed versions of Mandrakelinux.

As of the Mandrakelinux 10 release, basically four versions of the product are available for public, retail consumption. Three are retail products in the same competitive space with other retail versions of Linux, and the fourth is the freely available Mandrakelinux 10 distribution. The real difference is in the kinds of tools, utilities, and applications distributed with each product. Here is a brief overview of what you can expect from each retail package:

 ✦ **Mandrakelinux Discovery 10** — Designed with the entry-level desktop user in mind. The package includes basic productivity software such as OpenOffice, Kdeprintfax, and planning/finance software. Also included are the requisite networking tools for e-mail, FTP, and Web browsing. Several multimedia components are also installed enabling audio and video playback, image editing, and scanning documents as well as CD recording.

✦ **Mandrake Powerpack 10**—Includes all the features that Discovery 10 has and adds a set of development tools that includes the Kdevelop integrated development environment, GCC GNU compiler collection, GDB GNU debugger, J2RE, and others.

✦ **Mandrakelinux Powerpack + 10**—Includes everything in Powerpack 10, plus a number of server applications. Some of the included applications are Samba, MySQL, Postfix (e-mail), and ProFTPd, which are ready to use after the default installation, making this product well-suited to a network environment where a cost-effective, multipurpose server is needed.

Note   MandrakeMove is a fifth package that is distributed alongside Discovery 10. It runs Mandrakelinux from a CD, can store configuration data on a USB key, and requires no installation. This product offers a simple method of using Mandrakelinux without any kind of commitment. A download version is available as well at `http://www.mandrakelinux.com/en-us`.

Exploring Mandrakelinux 10

Mandrakelinux has long hung its hat on the concept of "ease of use," the idea being that its distributions should be readily accessible to a large pool of users. Mandrakelinux was heralded early on for its exceptional use of a graphical installer and configuration tools. Its quality support for hardware, video acceleration, and audio playback (especially MP3 playback) also tends to be top-notch. When coupled with the fact that the Mandrakelinux installer frequently detected and configured hardware that left other distributions' installation routines mystified, you can see why Mandrakelinux has been, and will probably continue to be, a popular distribution. Mandrakelinux 10 comes with a number of attractive features, including:

✦ Largely automated installation process that has new features such as the capability to resize NTFS partitions.

✦ Hardware detection and configuration has been improved over previous Mandrakelinux releases. In particular the security, printing, and user configuration tools have been completely overhauled to provide additional functionality and ease of use.

✦ Updated versions of the RPM Package Manager and the Internet update software have improved the ease of installing new software as well as system patches.

✦ Security maintenance is comprehensive. The Mandrakelinux 10 distribution includes easy-to-use configuration tools for setting general system security and setting up a firewall. Mandrakelinux 10 also supports a range of security protocols such as SSH, SSL, LDAP, and NIS.

✦ User interface is consistent across desktop environments.

In addition, there are a few tools that make a particularly big impact on the usability and consistency of Mandrakelinux. These features utilities are DrakX, RPMDrake, and Control Center.

Mandrakelinux Installer (DrakX)

DrakX is a highly acclaimed and user-friendly installer that has been one of Mandrakelinux's key differentiators against other Linux builds. Included in Mandrakelinux since version Mandrakelinux 7.0, this installer was one of the first successful attempts at automated installers that most novice Linux users could successfully use.

Although the installer is almost "newbie"-proof, it's still possible to invoke advanced installation options enabling detailed control of the install at any point during the installation process. As with most versions of Linux, you can install from a boot CD, another drive, or a network. Here are the key features of the DrakX installer included in the current version of Mandrakelinux:

✦ Package installation options enable convenient configuration using predefined packages, rather than attempting to choose individual packages from the wide selection that is available. You can select individual packages if you do not want to use one of the predefined package options. Workstation and Server Package groups are available for various roles and needs, for example.

✦ The ability to format, configure RAID, and resize partitions of many types, including NTFS, FAT32, EXT3, ReiserFS, and XFS.

✦ Support for a wide range of network file systems.

✦ Improved upgrade support.

✦ Automated installation tools.

✦ Rescue mode for failed/problematic installation.

In addition to the straightforward boot CD, the DrakX installer supports a number of other installation methods, including:

✦ **Network installs** — If needed, you can start the DrakX installation process and connect to a variety of network servers to access the installation files. This includes NFS, HTTP, SBM, SSH, Web Proxy, and FTP servers.

✦ **Kickstart installs** — In environments such as customer support call centers, school computer labs, and large offices, you might find yourself needing to install and configure large numbers of computers in a short period of time. Kickstart installations use an answer file to automate most of the installation process. Mandrakelinux's installation routine enables you to create floppies to use when performing your kickstart installations. Mandrakelinux enables you to make semi-interactive or completely automated setup floppies.

✦ **Upgrades** — The only constant thing is change. Very cliché, but in the world of software development, it is very true. The DrakX installer supports an upgrade path to bring older installs up to snuff with the newest release.

You can try out the DrakX installer in the walk-through included in this chapter.

RPM Package Management with RPMDrake

Adding software to and removing software from your Linux installation should not be a time-consuming chore. RPMDrake provides an intuitive graphical interface for managing installed software. You can easily see what is installed and add or remove packages as needed. Once you open RPMDrake, there are a few things you should know:

✦ You can configure your list of sources by invoking the Define Sources feature. This enables you to specify the location of installable packages, which could be local network locations, CD-ROM media, or HTTP/FTP archives of installation packages. There is a List of Mirrors option that you can refresh to make sure you're ready to get access to the latest security and system updates.

✦ Using the Mandrake Update button is probably the easiest way to maintain your system because it automatically downloads and installs updates for your system when you initiate the updates.

✦ You need the root password when installing packages. RPMDrake prompts you for it as needed.

✦ RPMDrake offers improved upgrade support. You can use it to scan for software updates, download them, and offer them in the list of installable programs for the user to select.

RPMDrake supports a search feature that enables you to use a variety of criteria to search for desired software within configured sources. You can search by package name, or you can search based on a description. Either way, once you find the package you want, all you need to do is select the target package and use the Install/Remove button to get going.

But what if you just want to remove software? This is a very straightforward process as well. Locate the package you want to remove under the Installed Applications tab. Select it, click the Install/Remove button, and the package and any that depend on it are removed from the system.

Mandrakelinux Control Center (MCC)

The Mandrakelinux Control Center (MCC), which is also called DrakConf, provides an intuitive and accessible means of configuring various system resources. You can use this tool to add new hardware, configure installed applications, add or remove applications (by invoking RPMDrake), and change the configuration of your existing hardware.

You can also use it adjust your default system security levels, change your display options, schedule events, manage user accounts, and even change the system time/date setting. The MCC uses a number of installation and configuration wizards to help you get rolling. For example, a wizard for Apache Web server setup enables you to get your HTTP server online in just a few minutes. Some of the key improvements and features of MCC in Mandrakelinux 10 are

✦ Secure, remote system configuration from any network.

✦ Automatic detection of hot swappable devices without restarting the system.

✦ Large icons that are easy to see and appropriately related to the functions they invoke.

The Mandrakelinux Community

Like many distributions of Linux, Mandrakelinux has developed a split personality of sorts. Mandrakesoft distributes value-added versions of Mandrakelinux complete with numerous utilities, applications, and support. The core Mandrake development effort produces an unsupported, but just as useful, version of the core Mandrakelinux build. With this "free" copy, you get the OS and the basic utilities and applications but no access to the Mandrakeclub.

Mandrakeclub allows folks with a paid membership to access early builds, the full suite of downloadable one-click applications, forums, support, and downloads of current releases using its club-member-only bit torrent system. For someone trying to make Linux a desktop system for use by folks coming from Apple and Microsoft GUI operating systems, these added features are extremely useful.

RPM Repository on Mandrakeclub

The Mandrakeclub Web site (www.mandrakeclub.com) has a massive collection of software that is tested for use with Mandrakelinux and is directly accessible to members. (A nonmember can view the available packages, but he will not be able to access the files until he provides a valid Mandrakeclub membership.) A search tool and various precompiled lists by category, creation date, product name, maintaining organization/user, and distributor are features of this site.

 Note   If you don't have access to the RPM files on Mandrakeclub, you can find volumes of RPM packaged applications at www.rpmfind.net/linux/RPM/. This site uses the same indexing technology as Mandrakeclub, including support for searching and indexes.

Mandrakelinux Forums and News

If you have any interest in tracking product development and maybe getting a little help if you need it, you'll want to keep on top of Mandrakelinux news, forums, and Linux User Groups (LUGs). For Mandrakelinux product news, it's hard to beat the Mandrakelinux news Web site at `http://mandrakelinux.com/en/fnews.php3`. This site contains regular updates on Mandrakelinux development and the activities of Mandrakesoft.

Note   If you cannot live without your Mandrakelinux news on your Handspring or Palm, check out `www.mandrakelinux.com/en/pda/`, the PDA-friendly version of the Mandrakelinux news site.

User forums are a priceless tool for finding solutions to problems, getting involved in software-related projects, or just connecting with other Mandrakelinux users. The Mandrakelinux users' forum (`www.mandrakeusers.org`) is a great one with especially in-depth information on installation and configuration. The Mandrakeclub forums (`www.mandrakeclub.com`) are also popular. You get temporary free access to Mandrakeclub when you purchase any retail Mandrakelinux product, or you can separately enroll in the club and make use of its services. If you find you like Mandrakelinux and will be using it long term, it's probably a good idea to join the Mandrakeclub because you'll have access to official support and your funds will help the development of the product.

Another critical resource for information on all things Linux is your (hopefully) local Linux user group (LUG). Each LUG is different, but you are apt to find a number of like-minded users with whom to interact in a variety of situations. If you have no idea how to find the nearest LUG, you can try a directory such as GLUE (Groups of Linux Users Everywhere), located at `www.ssc.com:8080/glue/groups`. Search for your location or one nearby and make contact.

Installing Mandrakelinux 10

To get up to your elbows as quickly as possible, you need to snag the CD images for the Mandrakelinux installation CDs. Downloading these is not for the weak of heart — the three images top 2GB! To get the installation images, head to the Mandrakelinux Web site (`www.mandrakelinux.com/en-us`) and click the Download link. Although the project encourages contributions, you are not required to make one. When you get to the download page, scroll to the bottom. You can either join the Mandrake Linux Users Club (costs money, takes time) or you can opt to join at some future time and move on to the FTP/HTTP mirror list for the various distributions. Alternatively, you can scroll back to the top of the download page and click the Download link one or two more times. That will take you directly to the FTP/HTTP mirrors list without agreeing to anything. Check back often because the list seems to change regularly and is considerably smaller than it once was.

The process you'll go through later in this chapter uses the boot CD installation method alongside an existing Microsoft Windows installation that is using the NTFS file system.

Note   Appendix A explains how to burn the installation CDs from the CD images.

The Right Hardware for Mandrakelinux 10

As with software packages, look before you leap. It is important to make sure your hardware is up to the task before you install Mandrakelinux. Fear not, users of less-than-stellar hardware; the hardware requirements are far from onerous. To use Mandrakelinux you need (or you can use):

- ✦ **x586 class processor or above** — The Intel Pentium I-IV, AMD K6/II/III, Duron, or Athlon/XP/MP.

- ✦ **RAM** — For the text installation, you will need 32MB of memory. If you plan to use the GUI, the minimum is 64MB, but 128MB is recommended.

- ✦ **Hard disk** — 500MB of SCSI, IDE, or Serial ATA hard disk space is the bare minimum required. 1GB is recommended, and if you decide to install additional packages, you should have at lease 2GB of free disk space available.

- ✦ **RAID controllers** — There is wide support for SCSI RAID controllers. In addition, 3Ware IDE and Serial ATA controllers are also supported.

- ✦ **DVD or CD drive** — To run the installation from a CD/DVD source disk, you need the appropriate drive. This drive will need to support bootable CD/DVD media.

- ✦ **Input/Output** — Of course, if you want to interact with your Mandrakelinux install, you'll at least need a keyboard and a monitor. A mouse is not needed for the installation, but it is handy and recommended.

Note   For those who live life on the bleeding edge, there is a separate distribution of Mandrakelinux that supports the AMD Athlon64 processor. This distribution is available currently only as a commercial product from the retail side of Mandrakelinux, http://www.mandrakesoft.com.

As you can see from the system specifications, you can use a wide range of hardware to run your Mandrakelinux installation. Do you have an old P233 with 64MB of RAM, a CD-ROM, and a blank 540MB hard disk? No problem. How about a "gaming war machine" sporting a 3.2 GHz P4, Gig of RAM, DVD-R, and an ocean of hard disk space? Bring it on! The vast assortment of hardware supported includes popular video cards such as NVIDIA FX series and ATI Radeon video adapters. Large numbers of Ethernet and Wi-Fi network adapters, USB 2.0, and other hardware make your chances of installation and configuration success very high.

Note If you want to make sure your hardware is supported by Mandrakelinux 10, go to www.mandrakelinux.com/en/hardware.php3 and use the search tool to see if your hardware is on the list. The Web site also includes suggestions for what to do if your hardware is not on the supported/tested devices list. Hardware is sorted into four categories: Not Supported, Known (reported working), Tested, and Certified.

This installation requires no special hard disk configuration. As mentioned, this install assumes a preexisting Microsoft Windows operating system using the NTFS file system. You will "make room" on the existing partition and install Mandrakelinux there. In addition to using a boot disk (as you will here) you can also take advantage of the installation options such as FTP and NFS as outlined briefly in this chapter and in more detail in Chapter 7.

Caution Do not make your first installation attempt on a mission-critical system. Resizing an NTFS partition can have unintended effects. Back up any information you cannot live without, especially if you resize existing partitions as the following instructions show.

Begin the DrakX Installation

You have a PC that can handle Mandrakelinux, and you have your installation CDs; it's time to begin. Depending how fast your hardware is and how big a partition you choose to resize, installation time will vary. On a system with a PIII800, 512MB of RAM, 30GB IDE hard disk, 40X CD-ROM, and an existing NTFS partition with Microsoft Windows (2000 Server SP4) on, the installation takes approximately 30 to 40 minutes. Here's what to do:

1. Back up all your vital information.

2. With all three CDs ready to go (from the retail box set or your downloaded images), insert CD 1 and start your computer. If the BIOS didn't catch the CD and boot from it, just press Ctrl+Alt+Delete to restart. If it does not boot to the DrakX installer, make sure that your BIOS is configured to boot the CD first, and then restart.

Tip If you don't see the installation screen, your CD-ROM drive may not be bootable. You may be able to make the drive bootable, though. Here's how: Restart the computer. Immediately, you should see a message telling you how to go into setup, such as by pressing the F1, F2, or Del key. Enter setup and look for an option such as Boot Options or Boot From. If the value is A: First, Then C:, change it to CD-ROM First, Then C: or something similar. Save the changes and try to install again.

3. The main boot screen appears, prompting you to either press the F1 key for more options or press the Enter key to set up Mandrakelinux. Press the Enter key.

Note

If you hit F1 during the initial setup screen, you expose yourself to a wide range of installation options that are not explored in detail here. After pressing F1 you receive a prompt (boot:) and you can enter a variety of commands to begin different installation routines. You can run a low-resolution, GUI-based, text-based installation, go back to the standard DrakX install, or enter an expert graphical installation. In the expert mode of installation you can configure the most mundane details of your system. It is generally wise to invoke F1 and use the expert graphical installation if you are building a server because it enables you to configure a static IP on your network card. It is also in this F1 menu that you can access the rescue feature to attempt recovering failed installations of Mandrakelinux.

4. In the next screen, select the appropriate language for your Mandrakelinux installation. (If you need support for multiple languages, you can opt to install multiple language packages by using the Advanced button on this screen.) When you're finished, click Next.

5. The license agreement appears. To continue with your installation, agree to the software's licensing conditions by selecting the Accept bullet. Click Next to move on.

6. Setting your security level is critical if you plan to use your installation to provide services to other computers. This screen presents four security configuration options from which you can choose a security level:

   - **Standard**—Designed for a typical desktop client that will connect to the Internet.

   - **High**—Implements some access restrictions and performs daily checks of the system for signs of unwanted activity.

   - **Higher**—Enough security to reasonably allow inbound server services (Web, FTP, and such) on your server.

   - **Paranoid**—Basically "lock down." The maximum local security available, this level enables you to tighten up everything and open ports and access as you see fit. Not for the faint of heart.

Tip

Keep on top of current Mandrakelinux security-related patches and updates by regularly checking the Mandrakesoft security advisories page, `www.mandrakesoft.com/security/advisories`.

After you select your security level, click Next.

7. The next screen begins the disk partitioning portion of the Mandrakelinux installation. (General guidance regarding the size and types of partitions you'll need is included in Chapter 7.) The DrakX partition program gives you three general configuration options:

- **Erase** — Wipes the existing hard disk in preparation for your install. This is a great option for critical server systems or if there is no data on the disk you need.

- **Use free space on Microsoft Windows partition** — Exactly what it sounds like. You can use free disk space on the FAT, FAT32, or NTFS partition that houses your Windows installation to house your Mandrakelinux install. Pretty nifty if you want both operating systems to be able to access all of the files on the system.

- **Custom** — Here's where the real magic happens: You can create custom volumes, resize existing volumes, and in general torture your hard drives as much as you like.

Selecting the Custom option opens a new window that shows all the existing hard drives and configured partitions. If your system only has an existing Windows installation on an NTFS partition, all that will be visible are the blue markers indicating a Windows partition. Once you click on the partition that you want to use for your Mandrakelinux installation, a new option appears in the left portion of the disk configuration window. By clicking the Resize button, you can change the size (within limitations) of the existing NTFS partition.

Give it a shot if you have the opportunity. Click the Resize button, and a new window appears. It has a slider that's all the way to the right by default. As you slide the indicator to the left, the corresponding value displayed gets smaller. This number reflects the size (in MB) that the NTFS partition will be after you've completed the resizing operation. For example, if you have a 30GB NTFS partition and you want to free up 10GB of space for the creation of a set of native Linux partitions, simply slide the indicator from the maximum value of 30000MB to 20000MB, and you will have freed the required 10000MB. The amount of space you can create depends on the size of the disk, how much data is stored, and whether the partition has been defragmented. To find out the degree to which you can resize the partition, move the slider all the way to the left. That displays the smallest size you can make the existing Windows partition.

Caution

There is a catch to resizing NTFS partitions. The 2.6 Linux kernel misreports hard disk geometries, and the incorrect information can cause a flawed partition table to be written to the disk at the end of the resize. See `www.mlf.linux.rulez. org/mlf/ezaz/ntfsresize.html#troubleshoot` for more details.

When you've selected the size you want, click the Next button. You are shown a warning to make sure you have backed up any information you depend on before performing the partition resizing. If you're ready to commit, click the OK button. It is foolish to tinker with partitions and volumes if you have important information on them and no backup. Resizing is a pretty predictable process, but the process is not perfect, and you could end up with a working Mandrakelinux install and a sizeable, useless Windows partition.

If all went well, you now have an unformatted partition available. Click the empty partition and create the native Linux partitions you need or want. After you've sorted all your partitions in the manner you would like, click the Done button. A warning message asks if you're sure you want to do this. Click OK and the deed is done.

8. The next screen gives you the option of selecting packages to install on your Linux system. Mandrakelinux offers a set of general package groups that you can use to meet general configuration goals. These four prefab package groups are:

Caution

Make sure that you have selected the Higher or Paranoid security level if you plan to expose this server to inbound connections from the Internet or other public network. If you fail to do so, you increase your risk of unauthorized intrusion to your server and any other devices to which it has access.

- **Workstation options** — You can choose to install productivity, multimedia, and some more advanced user tools. Each subgroup is individually selectable. Productivity software (in the Office Workstation group) is comprised of OpenOffice.org and a collection of time, financial, and document management tools. Your entertainment options (in the Game Station and Multimedia Station groups) include multimedia playback applications and a set of arcade-style games. A number of network-related package groups (Network Computer and Internet Station groups) are available for Web browsers, e-mail clients, news readers, and network client (NFS) utilities. For configuring your system you have the option of installing console tools (Console Tools group) and graphical configuration (Configuration group) utilities. Should you plan to use the computer for scientific analysis and study, you can install some useful applications by selecting the Scientific Workstation package group. The Office Workstation, Multimedia Station, Internet Station, Configuration, and Console Tool package groups are selected by default.

- **Server options** — Package groups for server services fall into Web/FTP, Mail, Database, Firewall/Router, and Network Computer Server groups. If you want to experiment with these services, feel free to check all the server boxes, and install all of them. If you already know which package group you want to use (mail service, for example), install only the package group you need.

- **Other options** — In addition to the server/workstation options you can select the interfaces that you would like installed (KDE, GNOME, Other). You can also elect to install comprehensive documentation and development applications. Also, if you need them for a development effort or testing, you can install the Linux Standard Base (LSB group) files, which will install Kernel version 2.4 instead of Kernel 2.6. Unless you know you need the LSB group, leave it unchecked.

- **Individual package selection** — If one-size-fits-all package groups just don't cut it for you, you can elect to install individual packages. To do this, check the Individual Package Selection box at the bottom of the Package Group Selection window and then click Next. If later you find a need to add or remove packages, just invoke the RPMDrake utility described earlier in this chapter.

When you've selected the packages you want, click Next. If you have gone into the individual package selection window, you need to click the Install button when you finish making your selection. Alternatively, you can click Previous if you want to return to the simplified package selection window.

9. The installation process copies files and sets your configuration options. All you need to do is watch the progress bar move from left to right, swap CDs when prompted, and read the informative space filler that is displayed.

10. In the next screen, you're prompted to set the root password. Make it a good one! Click the Next button when you're done.

11. Create the user accounts that you need. You can select the icon each user will click to log on. (I am partial to the ostrich, but after much consideration I picked the palm trees and white sand.) When you are done creating any users, click Next.

12. In the next window you are given a choice about using automatic user logon. By default, the auto logon check box is checked. This is a lifesaver for users who are moving from a nonauthenticating operating system such as many versions of Windows and some Apple operating systems to Linux. For the casual home user, this option is just fine. For situations where access control to the computer (locally) is important, clear this box and have the users log on individually. Without the automatic logon feature enabled, users will be prompted for a username and password each time they need to access the computer. Leave the box checked or uncheck it, and click Next.

13. Next up is the DrakX installer's device configuration screen. Here you can see the hardware that has been detected, and you can configure the devices if you choose. You can also attempt to configure devices not properly detected earlier in the installation process. For example, if your sound card is not set up, click the corresponding Configure button. You are asked a series of questions

(depending on the device), and then DrakX attempts to detect and configure the device. If this still fails, you get a message recommending that after Mandrakelinux is installed, you use HardDrake to configure your device. This is a good time to configure your desktop settings and test them. Locate the desktop configuration options and set your resolution, color depth, and refresh rate. When you are finished exploring the options of DrakX, click Next.

14. If you have a working Internet connection, you can take advantage of the Web update feature of the installation process. It looks for patches and updated installation packages to make sure your current install is as up-to-date as possible. Make your selection and click Next.

15. In the final installer screen are two very important buttons: Advanced and Reboot. The Advanced button enables you to create automated installation floppies. These are very handy if you need to install a large number of Mandrakelinux systems or if you plan to reinstall your existing system often, as you might in a testing environment. There are two options for the installation floppies. The first is the Fully Automated Install method, which allows no user interaction and results in installations that are 100% identical. The second is the Replay Installation method. Most of it is automated, but you can interact at critical junctures and change the configuration settings. This is useful if your hardware is identical, but each system requires some customization. After you've created your installation floppies, click the Reboot button to complete your installation. If you elect to not create installation floppies, click Reboot as well.

16. Before jumping into Mandrakelinux, you need to check the status of your coexisting Windows installation. Select the Windows entry from the Linux boot loader and launch Windows. Windows NT, 2000, XP, and 2003 Server should launch CHKDSK to examine the integrity of the partition and then reboot.

17. After you've verified that Windows has survived, you are ready to dive into Mandrakelinux 10. From Windows, perform a restart. When the computer boots back to the Linux boot loader, either select the Linux option from the boot loader, or just let it load itself (Linux is the default option).

Summary

Although Mandrakelinux may not be as widely known as other Linux distributions, it is arguably the most accessible version for novice desktop users. It is especially useful to those who want their Linux installations to exist alongside Windows installations that may not have free partitions for a dedicated Mandrakelinux installation.

This chapter explored some of the defining features of Mandrakelinux, including the installer, which incorporates the capability to resize existing Windows partitions nondestructively; an RPM package management (RPMDrake); and system configuration tools. In addition to enabling you to wedge a Linux installation onto a 100% Windows partition, the Mandrakelinux installer reliably detects your hardware and provides you with the option of simplified or very granular package selection. The RPM package management enables you to install, uninstall, and update software from a consistent and user-friendly graphical interface. If you need to add or trouble-shoot hardware, Mandrakelinux provides graphical configuration tools (HardDrake) to make the task easier after the initial installation, and DrakX for detection during the installation. If you join the Mandrakeclub, there's a wealth of support and application downloads available.

Finally, in this chapter you went through the installation of a desktop configuration that involved resizing an existing NTFS partition without destroying the Windows 2000 Server installation that used the partition.

✦   ✦   ✦

Running a Linux Firewall/Router

CHAPTER

17

In This Chapter

Understanding
firewalls

Protecting desktops
with firewalls

Managing firewalls
with iptables

Making a Coyote
Linux bootable
firewall floppy

Getting other
bootable firewalls

A firewall can protect your computer or private network
from outside intruders. Placing a firewall on the route
between your local network and the Internet gives you tremendous power and flexibility to manage your network traffic. You
can react to every packet coming in or going out of your network based on where it's from, where it's going, and what it is
requesting to do.

Linux is often used as a firewall. In fact, there are several Linux
distributions configured to act exclusively as a firewall (running
on media as small as a floppy disk). Because firewall tools can
also be used for protecting personal desktop systems, several
Linux distributions include graphical tools for managing firewalls in an appropriate way for desktops. So, in effect, almost
any Linux distribution can be used as a dedicated firewall or
can simply be configured to use firewall features to protect
itself from unwanted outside access.

In this chapter, you explore the features that are used in nearly
every Linux system today for creating firewalls (iptables) and
how to use graphical firewall tools in Red Hat Linux (Fedora
Core and Red Hat Enterprise Linux) and Mandrakelinux. To
comprehend how a lot of firewall features can fit in a very
small space, you look at how to use the Coyote Linux Floppy
Firewall distribution (that comes with this book).

On the
CD-ROM

The CD that comes with this book contains what you need
to create a bootable floppy-disk firewall with Coyote Linux.
The iptables firewall feature is included with every Linux distribution that comes with this book.

Understanding Firewalls

Every recent Linux system has firewall features available because they are built into the Linux kernel in a facility called *iptables*. But firewalls in Linux can be used differently, depending on what you are doing with your Linux system:

✦ **Desktop system** — A Linux system used just to run applications and browse the Web may simply use its firewall to block all (or nearly all) incoming requests for services. By doing so, the only data that can come into the desktop system is in responses to requests initiated by that computer itself. When that desktop itself is behind a corporate firewall, firewall rules can often be relaxed to allow various kinds of file and printer sharing to take place behind that firewall.

✦ **Server system** — On a Linux server, a firewall can be used to block requests to all incoming ports except those used to provide the specific services offered by that server. It can also be used to block any requests from addresses known to be particularly abusive or to allow more services to computers known to be friendly.

✦ **Firewall/router system** — Linux is often used as a dedicated firewall, providing a buffer between a private network and a public network (such as the Internet). Using Linux in this scenario, you can make best use of the full range of firewall features in iptables. Any packet trying to pass through the firewall can be filtered and then allowed to pass, be dropped, or be redirected in some way. The firewall can even hide (masquerade) the identity of private computers coming through the firewall to use the Internet.

Firewalls don't require fancy graphical interfaces (in fact, dedicated firewalls usually don't have X running at all, although they often serve up Web content to others). In fact, a Linux firewall in a home or small-office environment might run on a discarded 486 computer. Its footprint can be so small that it doesn't even need a hard disk — just a bootable floppy or CD that includes (or can access) the needed configuration information.

Firewalls are a prime example of an opportunity to use a special-purpose Linux distribution (later in this chapter you'll see how to build and run your own Coyote Linux firewall distribution, which fits on a floppy disk). Linux firewall distributions typically:

✦ Are tuned to include primarily those components that are needed to be a firewall.

✦ Contain scripts for easily configuring firewall settings.

✦ Don't include X, requiring that you use the command line or a Web browser from another machine on the network, allowing the distribution to fit in a much smaller space.

✦ Include a few other tools for diagnosing network problems.

For the average desktop user, however, there are graphical tools available with Linux to set up a basic, secure firewall without understanding the syntax of iptables. Let's examine some of those tools.

Protecting Desktops with Firewalls

If you are using a desktop Linux system, a simplified GUI firewall tool is a good way to begin protecting your computer. At the very least, you can use your firewall to explicitly allow others to use selected services from your computer, while blocking requests for other services.

Tools that come with Mandrakelinux, Fedora Core, and Red Hat Enterprise Linux (RHEL) can illustrate a few GUI ways to configure a firewall. During installation of Fedora or RHEL, Red Hat offers a screen for selecting your level of firewall protection. Mandrakelinux offers a firewall tool with its Control Center.

Starting Your Firewall in Red Hat Linux

During the process of installing Fedora or RHEL systems, the Firewall Configuration screen (see Figure 17-1) enables you to put a basic firewall in place.

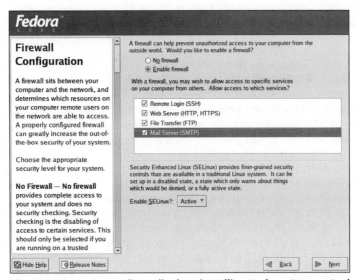

Figure 17-1: Set up a firewall when installing Fedora Core or Red Hat Enterprise Linux.

The Firewall Configuration screen handles almost everything the average desktop user would need in a firewall. Here is what you can do with the settings on that page:

✦ **No firewall** — Although this option is not generally recommended, some people choose No Firewall if they are directly connected to a router firewall or feel no threat from their network connection. This allows connection requests through to all ports. Requests to configured services are allowed, while requests for other services are ignored. The firewall just passes these requests through without question.

✦ **Enable firewall** — Select this option to set up a basic set of iptables firewall rules for you, without your having to figure out how iptables works. If you are offering services to share Web pages (WWW/HTTP), FTP server (FTP), remote copy and login services (SSH), or a mail server (SMTP), you can simply click boxes to begin those services.

✦ **Other ports** — Although not in Fedora Core 3, earlier versions of Red Hat Linux systems allowed you to add the port numbers associated with other services in an "Other ports" field. If the Red Hat distribution you are installing has that field available, you can simply add a port number or associate a particular port with a protocol, using the port name or number followed by a colon and the protocol name. Here's the example Red Hat gives:

```
imap:tcp
```

This enables requests from your network for IMAP services (port 143) from TCP protocols. You can also add multiple ports by separating them by commas. For example:

```
53, 110
```

would enable the computer to be a domain name system server or serve up mailboxes using POP3.

Note Open your IMAP and POP3 ports only if your computer is a mail server. If you're just downloading and reading mail from your computer, you can get your mail just fine from an IMAP or POP3 server without opening those ports.

✦ **Select network devices** — Another feature in Red Hat Linux, before Fedora Core 3, is a select network devices box that displayed interfaces associated with network cards on your computer. For Ethernet cards, you would see eth0, eth1, and so on (one for each card found). If you want to accept all requests made from one of those interfaces, click the check box next to it. For example, if you plan to dial out (ppp0) to get to the Internet but have a connection to people on your LAN (eth0) that you plan to use to share your Internet connection with, you can click on eth0.

Note Once Fedora or RHEL is installed, run the `system-config-securitylevel` command to open the Security Level Configuration window. That window provides a way to select trusted network devices and add accessible ports (by name or number) to your `iptables` firewall.

The firewall you set up will start after your Red Hat Linux distribution is installed and rebooted. When your system is up and running, examine the /etc/sysconfig/iptables file to see the firewall rules you created from your selections on the Firewall Configuration window. Those rules are loaded into the kernel from the /etc/init.d/iptables script (which is automatically set to run when you start Red Hat). See the "Using Firewalls with Iptables" section for details how to work with your firewall manually.

Note

I like to check a few services just to see the rules that the Firewall Configuration screen creates. Later, if I want to add access to other services on my computer, I can simply copy one of the lines that allows a service and then change the service number or name to the one I want to allow. Service numbers and names are included in the /etc/services file. A common service that a desktop system might want to use and offer is Windows file and printer sharing (using Samba in Linux). To share files with Samba, you might need to open ports 137, 138, and 139 in your firewall. (Open Samba ports to local, trusted networks and never to the Internet.)

Creating a Firewall in Mandrakelinux

Mandrakelinux offers a way of configuring your firewall after Mandrakelinux is installed:

1. From the main menu, select System ➪ Configuration ➪ Configure your computer. You are prompted to enter the root password.

2. Type the root password and click OK. The Mandrake Control Center appears.

3. Select Security ➪ Firewall. The Firewall service appears in the window.

4. Select particular services you would like to have available from your desktop system and click OK.

   The default settings shown might be appropriate for many desktop systems. With SSH, FTP, and Echo request on, someone could log into your system over the network (with appropriate login and password), get files you offer through your own FTP service, and ping your computer to see if it is up and running on the network. Of course, opening your firewall to allow SSH and FTP service assumes you have those two services turned on and configured as you like.

   If you want to add other ports, click the Advanced button. The Mandrake tool uses a different syntax for adding ports than does Red Hat. You need to separate port numbers and protocols with a slash (for example, 123/udp 123/tcp to open network time protocol for those two protocols). Open a range of ports for a protocol by separating them with a colon (for example, 137:139/tcp 137:139/udp to allow Windows file and printer sharing from your computer). Separate multiple entries with spaces instead of commas.

5. Click the down arrow next to the Net Device pane and select the interface that is connected to the Internet. For a dial-out connection, choose ppp+. For a wired Ethernet connection (to your LAN, cable modem, or DSL), choose eth0, eth1, or similar. Click OK.

Mandrake uses a facility called Shorewall to set up and manage its iptables rules. So, instead of looking in /etc/sysconfig/iptables for the changes you just made, look in the /etc/shorewall directory for files such as rules, policy, and interfaces. You can have those rules take effect immediately by restarting the Shorewall service (as root user, from a Terminal window):

```
service shorewall restart
```

When Shorewall restarts, look for any messages that are displayed. The output can give you information about any problems with the rules you have set up.

To find out more about how Shorewall works to configure your iptables firewalls, refer to the Shorewall Web site (www.shorewall.net). You can still use iptables commands to view the current firewall (iptables -L) or temporarily flush your firewall (iptables -F). However, other changes you might make with iptables will be temporary because the next time you reboot, Shorewall will take over again.

Using Firewalls with Iptables

Understanding how iptables works will help you with any firewall you have configured in a Linux system. Previous firewall features — ipchains and ipfwadm — are no longer included in the Linux kernel. Unless you are using a Linux with an older kernel (which only a few floppy firewall distributions still do), iptables is your primary tool for firewall configuration in Linux.

The commands used to configure iptables are not very intuitive. Using the iptables command, you can add rules (one by one) to your running Linux kernel. When you have a set of rules you like, save those rules to a file using iptables-save. Then, when you are ready to use them again, you read them back in using iptables-restore.

Although most Linux systems offer some sort of interface to automatically manage and load your iptables firewall, very few offer the full range of features you might want. So you will need to understand iptables to do some configuration by hand. Just understanding iptables will help you go from one Linux to another, regardless of the interface an individual distribution will put on top of it.

Starting with Iptables

If you have a running Linux system in front of you, there are ways that you can immediately get a feel for how your firewall is working. To go beyond just listing the current firewall rules, however, I recommend that you try the procedure I describe in the next section on a Linux system that is set up for you to play with. Booting KNOPPIX is a great way to try that procedure without doing any harm (because everything disappears at your next reboot). Otherwise, just read along.

Setting Some Rules

Studying the following steps will help you understand the syntax of firewall rules and the types of information you can set with them. This procedure is made to run from beginning to end on a computer that you have complete control over. In the process of setting up your firewall rules, you will temporarily cut off all communications to and from the machine, so do not try this on a machine that must stay connected to the network.

This example procedure illustrates a case where you have two Ethernet interfaces on a computer (as is typical with a dedicated firewall). The interface defined as eth0 is connected to the Internet, and the interface defined as eth1 is connected to a private network of computers that the firewall is protecting. Presumably, the private computers are a bunch of desktop computers that need to go through the firewall to browse the Internet.

Iptables lets you set up tables containing rules for how to handle Internet Protocol (IP) packets that enter the computer. The filtering table is the table you use by default (`-t filter`) if none is specified on the iptables command line. Other firewall tables you can configure include NAT (`-t nat`) and mangle (`-t mangle`). Special uses of NAT and mangle tables will be explained later. It's the filter table that's used in this example.

Rules for what to do with packets that enter and leave the firewall are defined within the context of what are called *chains*. Available chains for filter tables are `INPUT` (packets received by the firewall), `FORWARD` (packets to be routed through the firewall), and `OUTPUT` (packets created on the local firewall itself). Filtering is done on those chains based on the set of rules you set up.

When a packet comes to the firewall, it steps through the rules in the chain until it finds a rule that matches. A match might depend on where a packet came from or where it is going, for example. When a match is made, the chain jumps to the action (also called a *target*) for that rule, which might define that the packet should be accepted or dropped, or have some other action done on it.

Caution   Setting up a firewall can be serious business. A misconfigured firewall can reject legitimate requests, forward packets to the wrong places, or even make your computer completely inaccessible from the network. Be very cautious if you are trying the following procedure on a computer that you rely on to be safe and accessible from a network.

1. From a Terminal window, become root user:

```
$ su -
Password: ********
#
```

2. Type the following to see what filtering firewall rules are set on your system:

```
# iptables -L
Chain INPUT (policy ACCEPT)
target      prot opt source                    destination

Chain FORWARD (policy ACCEPT)
target      prot opt source                    destination

Chain OUTPUT (policy ACCEPT)
target      prot opt source                    destination
```

The example output shows that no filtering rules are currently set for this Linux system, meaning that all packets are accepted (policy ACCEPT) by default. (If you see a complex set of firewall rules, you might consider using a different machine to try this.)

3. These three commands change the default behavior for how packets are filtered for your computer:

```
# iptables -P INPUT DROP
# iptables -P OUTPUT DROP
# iptables -P FORWARD DROP
```

In this example, the default behavior is changed such that all packets that come into your network interfaces (INPUT), go out of your network interfaces (OUTPUT), or request to travel through them (FORWARD) are dropped. At this point, no packets should be able to come in or go out of any network interfaces. You can run iptables -L again to see that all policies have changed from ACCEPT to DROP. (If this concerns you, don't worry. You can run the commands again, changing DROP to ACCEPT, to make your firewall wide open once more. Likewise, a reboot gets you back to your original state.)

4. This step is for configuring how your firewall will accept or reject ICMP packets. Internet Control Message Protocol (ICMP) messages are for reporting error conditions and controlling connections to your server. Your server receives ICMP packets from computers that want to find out the state of your machine, such as if the machine is currently accessible.

Packets from the Internet that are accepted for ICMP protocol requests in the following example are those for ICMP types 8 and 11. Type 8 service allows your computer to accept echo reply messages, making it possible for people to ping your computer to see if it is available. Type 11 service relates to packets with a time to live (TTL) that was exceeded in transit, and for which you are accepting a Time Exceeded message that is being returned to you. (You need to accept Type 11 messages to use the traceroute command to find broken routes to hosts you want to reach.)

```
# iptables -A INPUT -p ICMP -i eth0 -s 0/0 --icmp-type 8 -j ACCEPT
# iptables -A INPUT -p ICMP -i eth0 -s 0/0 --icmp-type 11 -j ACCEPT
```

These two lines define rules for ICMP packets that come into the computer on the first Ethernet interface (eth0) from any source (-s 0/0). The first lines says to ACCEPT type 8 service, and the second says to ACCEPT type 11 service.

5. The following are examples of commands that define the packets that will be allowed to come into and go out of the computer from the local computer or the private LAN that the firewall is protecting:

```
# iptables -A INPUT -p ALL -i lo -s 127.0.0.1 -j ACCEPT
# iptables -A INPUT -p ALL -i lo -s 10.0.0.1 -j ACCEPT
# iptables -A INPUT -p ALL -i lo -s 323.45.67.89 -j ACCEPT
# iptables -A INPUT -p ALL -i eth1 -s 10.0.0.0/24 -j ACCEPT
# iptables -A INPUT -p ALL -i eth1 -d 10.0.0.255 -j ACCEPT
```

The result of these commands is that any packets sent from the local host (lo) are accepted, whether the source of those packets is the local host itself (-s 127.0.0.1), an interface to the local LAN (-s 10.0.0.1), or the Internet (-s 323.45.67.89). The IP addresses 10.0.0.1 and 123.45.67.89 are examples of local interfaces to those networks (your addresses will probably be different). The last two lines indicate that the firewall should accept input of packets that are from the private LAN (-s 10.0.0/24) or destined for any address on that LAN (-d 10.0.0.255) network, respectively.

Note The 323.45.67.89 address is not a real IP address. You will replace that with the IP address assigned from your ISP for your external Internet interface. No valid IP address can include a part higher than 255.

The following commands define acceptable outgoing packets from the firewall computer:

```
# iptables -A OUTPUT -p ALL -s 127.0.0.1 -j ACCEPT
# iptables -A OUTPUT -p ALL -s 10.0.0.1 -j ACCEPT
# iptables -A OUTPUT -p ALL -s 323.45.67.89 -j ACCEPT
# iptables -A OUTPUT -p ALL -s 10.0.0.0/24 -j ACCEPT
# iptables -A OUTPUT -p ALL -d 10.0.0.255 -j ACCEPT
```

As with the input commands, the firewall will accept outgoing packets that come from any of the local firewall interfaces (127.0.0.1, 10.0.0.1, and 323.45.67.89). It will also accept outgoing packets associated with destinations on the private LAN (10.0.0.0/24 and 10.0.0.255).

6. This last set of commands defines what packets that originated from the Internet are allowed into the firewall. For packets attempting to enter your computer from the Internet, you want to be more restrictive, allowing in packets only for services you want to provide. Here are some examples of specific rules you might set to allow requests for services from a server:

```
# iptables -A INPUT -p TCP -i eth0 -s 0/0 --destination-port 21 -j ACCEPT
# iptables -A INPUT -p TCP -i eth0 -s 0/0 --destination-port 22 -j ACCEPT
# iptables -A INPUT -p TCP -i eth0 -s 0/0 --destination-port 80 -j ACCEPT
# iptables -A INPUT -p TCP -i eth0 -s 0/0 --destination-port 113 -j ACCEPT
# iptables -A INPUT -p UDP -i eth0 -s 0/0 --destination-port 53 -j ACCEPT
# iptables -A INPUT -p UDP -i eth0 -s 0/0 --destination-port 2074 -j ACCEPT
# iptables -A INPUT -p UDP -i eth0 -s 0/0 --destination-port 4000 -j ACCEPT
```

The first four lines open up the ports for the TCP services you want to provide to anyone from the Internet: for FTP service (`--destination-port 21`), secure shell service (22), Web service (80), and `IDENTD` authentication (113), the last of which might be necessary for protocols such as IRC.

Caution You want to ensure that the services on the ports to which you are allowing access are properly configured before you allow packets to be accepted. In other words, don't open port 80 until you have a Web server configured or port 53 before you have a DNS server configured.

The last three lines define the ports where connection packets are accepted from the Internet for UDP services. This example assumes that DNS service (`--destination-port 53`) is configured on the computer. It also illustrates lines that accept requests for two other optional ports: Port 2074 is needed by some multimedia applications the users on your LAN might want to use, and port 4000 is used by the ICQ protocol (for online chats).

At this point you can run `iptables -L` again to see your new set of rules. If you have a connection to the computer from your LAN, as we illustrated with some options above, you can try to ping the computer from the LAN. You can also try configuring different services and accessing them from your network interfaces.

With this part of the procedure completed, your new firewall rules are built into the Linux kernel but do not exist anywhere in a configuration file. Unless you save those rules, they will be gone the next time you reboot your computer. The following section discusses saving your firewall settings so you can use them permanently.

Saving Firewall Settings

If you think you have a good set of rules in your current kernel, you can save them using the `iptables-save` command so they can be reloaded later using the `iptables-restore` command. Here's an example of how to use the `iptables-save` command:

```
# iptables-save > /root/iptables
```

In this example, the current firewall rules are stored in the `/root/iptables` file (you can put them anywhere you like for the time being). These rules can be copied to where they can be loaded automatically on some Linux systems. For example, in Red Hat Linux systems, copy this file to `/etc/sysconfig/iptables`, and the rules are installed when the computer reboots. If they don't load automatically, you can restore them yourself as follows:

```
# iptables-restore < /root/iptables
```

The previously saved rules are now restored to the currently running kernel.

Checking Your Firewall

Now that your firewall is configured, you should check it to make sure that it appears to the outside world (in our example, to the Internet on eth0 and your local LAN on eth1) as you would like it to. A popular tool for checking what services are available on a network interface is called nmap.

 Caution

> While nmap is an excellent tool for checking network interfaces on your own computer or private LAN, it should not be used to check for available services on computers that are not yours. Using nmap on someone else's computer is like checking all the doors and windows on a person's house to see if you can get in. It is considered to be an intrusive act. Use nmap only to make sure your own "doors and windows" are secure.

Following is an example of using nmap to scan a large number of ports on the firewall system you just configured to see what services appear to be available from the two network interfaces on the firewall (eth0 and eth1). To do this effectively, you need to run the nmap command from a computer outside your local firewall. That's because you don't want to see what is going on inside your firewall; you want to see the outside world's view of your firewall.

From the firewall computer, you'd first get the IP address of the external Internet interface on eth0 by running ifconfig eth0. For this example, that IP address is 323.45.67.89. (Remember that is not a real IP address; it's used so you don't nmap a real computer on the Internet.)

Then, from another Linux machine on the Internet, type the following:

```
# nmap 323.45.67.89
Starting nmap 3.50 ( http://www.insecure.org/nmap/) at 2004-10-22 14:56 CDT
Interesting ports on 323.45.67.89:
(The 1653 ports scanned but not shown below are in state: filtered)
PORT      STATE  SERVICE
21/tcp    closed ftp
22/tcp    open   ssh
53/tcp    closed domain
80/tcp    closed http
113/tcp   closed auth
4000/tcp  closed remoteanything

Nmap run completed -- 1 IP address (1 host up) scanned in 72.951 seconds
```

The output shows that 1653 ports scanned on this address were filtered (blocked from access) and 6 were not blocked. Services not filtered include TCP ports 21, 22, 53, 80, 113, and 4000 (which you made available when you set up the firewall earlier). Notice that only ssh has a server listening (providing service) at the moment. The other services are open from the firewall (not filtered), but the servers are not running yet.

It's possible that you won't have access to a Linux machine on the Internet to test outside access to your computer. If you have another computer on your LAN, try running nmap from that computer. If you have only Windows machines, you can always run a bootable Linux and try nmap from that.

Using Iptables to Do NAT or IP Masquerading

You can use Source Network Address Translation (SNAT) or IP Masquerading (MASQUERADE) to allow computers on your LAN with private IP addresses to access the Internet through your iptables firewall. Choose SNAT if you have a static IP address for your Internet connection, and use MASQUERADE if the IP address is assigned dynamically.

When you create the MASQUERADE or SNAT rule, it is added to the NAT table and the POSTROUTING chain. For MASQUERADE you must provide the name of the interface (such as eth0, ppp0, or slip0) to identify the route to the Internet or other outside network. For SNAT you must also identify the actual IP address of the interface.

The following examples assume that the connection to the Internet is provided through the first Ethernet card (eth0). Here's an example of a MASQUERADE rule:

```
# iptables -t nat -A POSTROUTING -o eth0 -j MASQUERADE
```

And here's an example of a SNAT rule:

```
# iptables -t nat -A POSTROUTING -o eth0 -j SNAT --to-source 12.12.12.12
```

You can add several source addresses if you have multiple addresses that provide a route to the Internet (for example, --to-source 12.12.12.12.1-12.12.12.12.254). Although MASQUERADE uses some additional overhead, you probably need to use it instead of SNAT if you have a dial-up connection to the Internet for which the IP address changes on each connection.

Make sure that IP forwarding is turned on in the kernel. (It is off by default.) To turn it on temporarily, do the following:

```
# echo 1 > /proc/sys/net/ipv4/ip_forward
```

To turn on IP forwarding permanently, add the following line to the /etc/sysctl.conf file:

```
net.ipv4.ip_forward = 1
```

If you require it, here's how to turn on dynamic IP addressing:

```
# echo 1 > /proc/sys/net/ipv4/ip_dynaddr
```

Adding Modules with Iptables

Some firewall features require that modules be added to the kernel. For example, if a client behind your firewall needs to access an FTP server using passive FTP, special modules are required. With passive FTP, the FTP client sends its IP address and the port number on which it will listen for data to the server. If that client is on a computer that is behind your firewall, for which you are doing NAT, that information must be translated as well or the FTP server will not be able to communicate with the client.

The iptables facility uses modules to track connections, looking inside the FTP data themselves (that is, not in the IP packet header) to get the information it needs to do NAT (remember that computers from the Internet can't talk directly to your private IP addresses). For FTP connection tracking, you need to have the following modules loaded:

```
ip_conntrack
ip_conntrack_ftp
ip_nat_ftp
```

For client computers to use some chat servers from behind the firewall, you need to add connection tracking and NAT as well. In those cases, addresses and port numbers are stored within the IRC protocol packets, so those packets must be translated, too. To allow clients on your LAN to use IRC services, you need to load the following modules:

```
ip_conntrack_irc
ip_nat_irc
```

The default port for IRC connections is 6667. If you don't want to use the default, you can add different port numbers when you load the connection-tracking modules:

```
insmod ip_conntrack_irc.o ports=6668,6669
```

Using Iptables as a Transparent Proxy

You can use REDIRECT to cause traffic for a specific port on the firewall computer to be directed to a different port. This feature enables you to direct host computers on your local LAN to a proxy service on your firewall computer without those hosts knowing it.

Here's an example of a command line that causes a request for Web service (port 80) to be directed to a proxy service (port 3128):

```
# iptables -t nat -A PREROUTING -p tcp --dport 80 \
        -j REDIRECT --to-ports 3128
```

In this example, any packet destined for port 80 (`--dport 80`) is redirected to port 3128 (`--to-ports 3128`). Note that the packet is changed before it is routed (`-A PREROUTING`).

You can only use `REDIRECT` targets in `PREROUTING` and `OUTPUT` chains within a `nat` table. You can also give a range of port numbers to spread the redirection across multiple port numbers.

Using Iptables for Port Forwarding

What if you have only one public IP address but you want to use a computer other than your firewall computer to provide Web, FTP, DNS, or some other service? You can use the Dynamic Network Address Translation (DNAT) feature to direct traffic for a particular port on your firewall to another computer.

For example, if you want all requests for Web service (port 80) that are directed to the firewall computer (`-d 15.15.15.15`) to be directed to another computer on your LAN (such as 10.0.0.25), you could use the following `iptables` command:

```
# iptables -t nat -A PREROUTING -p tcp -d 15.15.15.15 --dport 80 \
          -j DNAT --to-destination 10.0.0.25
```

(This example should actually appear on one line. The backslash indicates continuation on the next line.)

You can also spread the load for the service you are forwarding by providing a range of IP addresses (for example, `--to-destination 10.0.0.1-10.0.0.25`). Likewise, you can direct the request to a range of ports as well.

Getting Iptables Scripts

Rather than type in all your firewall rules by hand, there are many scripts available on the Internet (licensed under the GPL) that you can modify to suit your needs. Many of these scripts contain sections in the front where you can add IP addresses, port numbers, and other information that is specific to your firewall setup.

A nice set of scripts that illustrate how to use iptables comes from Oskar Andreasson, the author of the iptables tutorial. The set can be found at `http://iptables-tutorial.frozentux.net/scripts/`. In particular, the `rc.firewall.txt` is a good file to step through.

Finding Out More about Iptables

So far, you've seen an overview of many of the features in iptables and gotten a basic understanding of what it can do. Creating complex firewalls, especially in situations where there are a lot of people trying to break in, requires a much deeper knowledge of iptables. I suggest that, from here, you refer to the following:

✦ **The Iptables Tutorial** (http:// iptables-tutorial.frozentux.net) — This tutorial by Oskar Andreasson is the standard by which other iptables information is measured.

✦ **Netfilter project** (www.netfilter.org) — Get the latest information about iptables development, patches, security issues, mailing lists, and news.

✦ **Linux Gurus** (www.linuxguruz.com/iptables) — Provides a nice range of links to iptables FAQs, scripts, chat locations, HOWTOs, tutorials, tools, security sites, and mailing lists.

Making a Coyote Linux Bootable Floppy Firewall

In as little as a 1.4MB floppy disk, you can have a firewall that does a good job protecting your LAN against unwanted access from the Internet. With a CD-ROM, you can add literally hundreds of tools for managing your firewall and keeping your network running smoothly.

There are a handful of bootable Linux firewall distributions available today. The rest of this chapter steps you through the setup of Coyote Linux and then describes a few others that might interest you.

Creating a Coyote Linux Firewall

Using a single, simple script, Coyote Linux lets you create a bootable Linux firewall that fits on a floppy disk. Once you install and boot Coyote Linux, you can manage it from another computer on your LAN. You can use a Web interface or log into it using ssh and manage Coyote Linux from a Linux shell.

Coyote Linux contains an amazing set of features for such a small space. After booting the Coyote Linux boot floppy you create, you have a firewall with which you can:

✦ Route packets between your LAN and the Internet.

✦ Provide network interfaces to Ethernet LAN (TCP or PPPoE) or Dial-up (PPP) network connections.

✦ Create firewall rules supported by iptables. (It starts with a few basic rules, but you can add your own rules to include IP Masquerading and NAT, port forwarding, transparent proxies, or many other iptables features.)

✦ Enable DHCP. Coyote Linux can act as a DHCP server, providing IP addresses and other information to the computers on your LAN.

✦ Log activities. In addition to creating logs of activities on the firewall, Coyote can be set to pass those log files to another computer on your LAN.

✦ Monitor network activities. There are a few basic administrative tools in Coyote Linux to check out your network a bit. Those tools include `traceroute` and `nslookup`.

✦ Log in remotely (ssh) and get around the shell. The sshd daemon in Coyote Linux lets you log in from another computer on your LAN. The busybox utility (`www.buysbox.net`) provides a good set of basic shell tools.

✦ Open a Web interface to Coyote Linux. From any Web browser on your LAN, you can open the Coyote Linux Web Administrator interface by typing your firewall's IP address and port 8180 (for example, `http://192.168.0.1:8180`).

The following section shows you how to create a Coyote Linux boot floppy firewall/router. Once you have your Coyote Linux firewall up and running, you can change settings for that firewall from another computer on your LAN using the Web browser or shell (ssh) interface to the computer. If you are familiar with the shell and firewall features (described earlier in the chapter), there are a lot of things such as routing, demand dialing, and DHCP service that you can do with this nice little distribution.

Note   For more information, refer to the Web site of Vortech Consulting, LLC (`www.vortech.net`), which created the Coyote Linux project. Like many companies that support open source software, it offers commercial products that relate to its open source project. If you want more advanced products and support, you can consider purchasing its corporate and small-office firewall products.

Building the Coyote Linux Floppy

To get just what you want in your Coyote Linux firewall floppy, you need to build it yourself. That entails:

✦ **Creating the floppy.** You'll need a computer with a floppy drive to which you can write raw data. That machine should be running Linux (KNOPPIX should work fine if you don't have a Linux already installed).

✦ **Running the firewall.** For this, you want a computer that can boot from a floppy disk and have two network interfaces. That computer can be as low as a discarded 486 machine. In the example, the firewall computer will have a dial-up modem to connect to the Internet and an Ethernet card to connect it to your LAN (although a better and simpler way is to have an Ethernet connection to the Internet that can basically turn on automatically in most cases).

And, of course, you need a floppy disk.

The computer with which you create the floppy disk and the computer on which you run it may be the same computer.

Caution You need to know the Linux driver name for your Ethernet cards before you run the procedure to create your firewall floppy. If you don't know what it is, I recommend starting KNOPPIX on your machine and then using the `lsmod` and `lspci` commands to determine the driver names for your Ethernet cards (they should have been autodetected). Use `modinfo` if you are not sure if the driver name is the right one (for example, `modinfo 8139too`).

If possible, it's better to use a broadband or other Ethernet interface to connect to the Internet because dial-up modems can require extra configuration to work, provide slower connections, and make you deal with issues of using a phone line and bringing connections up and down all the time. Because, however, this section is meant to illustrate how to use minimal hardware with an extraordinarily compact Linux, it shows how to use an inexpensive connection type as well.

Figure 17-2 shows an example of the firewall configuration you'll create in the following Coyote Linux procedure.

Figure 17-2: A Coyote Linux firewall runs from a floppy disk, managing traffic between your network and the Internet.

Here's what you do to create a firewall with Coyote Linux:

1. On a computer that has a CD drive and a floppy drive, copy the Coyote Linux directory from the CD that comes with this book to your computer's hard drive. Then open a Terminal window (or other shell) and change to that directory. (See Appendix A for the location of Coyote Linux on the CD.)

2. Unzip and untar the Coyote Linux file by typing the following:

```
# tar xvfz coyote*tar.gz
```

3. Change to the `coyote` directory that was just created and start the
`makefloppy.sh` batch script to build the Coyote Linux floppy disk, as follows:

```
# ./makefloppy.sh

Coyote floppy builder script v2.9

Please choose the desired capacity for the created floppy:
1) 1.44Mb (Safest and most reliable but may lack space needed
   for some options)
2) 1.68Mb (Good reliability with extra space) - recommended
3) 1.72Mb (Most space but may not work on all systems or with
   all diskettes)
```

4. Choose the capacity of your floppy disk. I used 3 (1.72Mb) and it worked fine.
With an older floppy drive, you may have to use a lower capacity, which will
include fewer features.

```
Enter selection: 3
Please select the type of Internet connection that your
system uses.

1) Standard Ethernet Connection
2) PPP over Ethernet Connection
3) PPP Dialup Connection
```

5. This example uses a PPP Dial-up Connection here, so type **3**:

> **Note**
>
> If you have a broadband (DSL, cable modem, or other Ethernet connection) to the
> Internet, you would typically select 1 here. Select 2 if your ISP said you have a PPPoE
> connection. Configuring an Ethernet connection is actually simpler than configur-
> ing dial-up. Instead of defining the dialer, you typically just select to connect to the
> Internet via DHCP and enter a hostname (when prompted).

```
Enter Selection: 3
       .
       .
       .
By default, Coyote uses the following settings for the
local network interface:

IP Address: 192.168.0.1
Netmask:    255.255.255.0
Broadcast:  192.168.0.255
Network:    192.168.0.0
```

6. You can simply accept the default IP address (and related Netmask, Broadcast,
and Network numbers) by typing **N**. If you are creating a new set of addresses
for your LAN, this is a common set of IP addresses for you to use (192.168.0.1,
192.168.0.2, etc.). Reasons to consider changing the IP address are if it conflicts
with your current network numbering or if that set of IP addresses is being
used on your interface to the Internet.

```
Would you like to change these settings? [Y/N]: N

OPTIONS CONFIGURATION
Demand Dial:
Initiate the link only on demand, i.e. when data
traffic is present.
```

7. Here's where you set up your dial-up features (providing you are using dial-up to get to the Internet, as this example does). The first question is whether to allow demand dialing. Type **y** if you want the Internet connection to start up every time someone tries to open a connection to that interface (say, for trying to browse the Web or sending e-mail from the local system or any computer on your LAN using this as a route to the Internet):

```
Do you want to enable the demand dial option [y/n]: y
```

8. Type the number of seconds of idle time (time when no data is sent over the network connection) after which the dial-up connection to the Internet is dropped. The default is 180 (three minutes). I changed it to 600 (10 minutes).

```
Enter number of seconds for idle disconnect [180]: 600
```

9. To come up on the Internet with a particular IP address (assigned from the ISP), type **y** then add the IP address as requested. In most cases, however, you will just have the ISP assign you an IP address by typing **n** here.

```
Did your ISP assign you a static IP ADDRESS? [y/n]: n
Setting up for dynamic PPP Address

Set the local PPP interface IP address. Should not be the
same as 192.168.0.1, but on the same subnet.
```

10. You need an initial IP address to start the PPP interface. As noted, you should use an IP address that is on the same network as your LAN.

```
Press enter for [192.168.0.3]: 192.168.0.3
```

11. The next several questions relate to setting up your dial-out connection. The tty device is the serial port where your modem is connected (ttyS0 for COM1, ttyS1 for COM2, and so forth). The port speed is how fast your computer can talk to the modem (the default, 115200, is fine). ATZ is the normal script for initializing a modem (check your modem manual if you need something else). Type any name representing your ISP (no spaces). Enter the phone number to dial to get your Internet connection. Finally, enter the username and then the password that was provided to you by the ISP for this Internet account.

```
Enter tty device name for modem (ttyS0, etc)[ttyS0]: ttyS0
Enter ttyS0's port speed (115200, 57600, etc)[115200]: 115200
Enter modem init string (Enter = ATZ): ATZ
Enter name of ISP (no whitespace)[isp]: att
Enter phone number to dial: 5551212
Enter username: jsmith
Enter password: tkNOstf
```

12. Type **n** to not send clear-text passwords during login. You may need to change this to **y** if your ISP requires CHAP or PAP authentication.

    ```
    If you enable this, your password will be sent in clear
    text over the line. Say yes here only if despite having
    verified everything, you still cannot connect to your ISP.
    Login during chat? [y/n]: n
    ```

13. Because this example firewall will provide IP addresses to the other computers on the LAN, it needs to be enabled as a DHCP server (**y**). Then list the range of addresses it can assign to those computers. If you plan to have 100 or fewer computers on your LAN, the address range in this example should work fine for you:

    ```
    Do you want to enable the coyote DHCP server? [y/n]: y
    Enter DHCP range starting IP [192.168.0.100]: 192.168.0.100
    Enter DHCP range ending IP [192.168.0.200]: 192.168.0.200
    ```

14. A DMZ is a way of further shielding your local network from the outside world if you want to have a Web server protected by the same firewall. In this case, you could add another Ethernet card to the firewall, connect that to the Web server, and then allow incoming requests for Web services to go through to the Web server. This enables you to still block all incoming traffic to the desktop systems on your LAN. For this example, I just chose N.

    ```
    If you don't know what a DMZ is, just answer NO
    Would you like to configure a De-Militarized Zone? [Y/N]: N
    ```

15. Set the domain name with which this firewall is associated, and enter the IP address(es) of the DNS server(s) it will use to resolve addresses (probably provided by your ISP, unless you are running your own DNS server):

    ```
    Enter Domain Name: example.com
    Enter DNS Server 1: 123.45.68.799
    Enter DNS Server 2 (optional): 123.45.68.800

    If you have a syslog server on your LAN you want Coyote to
    send its syslog data to, you can specify the address here.
    If unsure or you do not have a syslog server, leave this
    entry blank.
    ```

16. You can have Coyote log its activities to another server on your network. This can be very handy, in that it removes logs from the firewall (so someone can't tamper with them) and enables you to centrally administer logs on your network. Before you can use this feature, you need to configure support for remote logging on your logging computer. To do this, I recommend reading the syslog daemon man page (man syslogd) on most Linux systems. Look for the "Support for Remote Logging" section. To disable the feature, as in this example, just press Enter to continue.

    ```
    Syslog server address:
    ```

17. Coyote Linux supports a nice range of Ethernet cards. You must know the name of the Ethernet driver module for each Ethernet card on your firewall and enter it here. (You should already have this information if you followed the Caution at the beginning of this section.) For ISA cards, which you probably

don't have unless it's a much older machine, you need to add IO and IRQ information.

```
Enter the module name for your local network card: 8139too
Enter IO address (Leave blank for PCI cards):
Enter IRQ (Leave blank for PCI cards):

Checking module dependencies...
8139too deps = mii

Building package: etc
Building package: local
Building package: modules
Building package: root
Building package: dhcpd
Building package: webadmin
```

18. Insert a blank floppy into the floppy drive and press Enter to build your floppy-disk Coyote Linux distribution:

```
Make sure that you have a floppy in the first floppy drive
in this system and press enter to continue...

Formatting /dev/fd0u1440
Double-sided, 80 tracks, 18 sec/track. Total capacity 1440
kB.
Formatting ... done
Verifying ... done
bin/mkdosfs 2.2 (06 Jul 1999)
Installing boot loader...
Copying files...
cp: omitting directory `floppy/config'
`floppy/dhcpd.tgz' -> `mnt/dhcpd.tgz'
`floppy/etc.tgz' -> `mnt/etc.tgz'
`floppy/linux' -> `mnt/linux'
`floppy/local.tgz' -> `mnt/local.tgz'
`floppy/modules.tgz' -> `mnt/modules.tgz'
`floppy/root.tgz' -> `mnt/root.tgz'
`floppy/syslinux.cfg' -> `mnt/syslinux.cfg'
`floppy/SYSLINUX.DPY' -> `mnt/SYSLINUX.DPY'
`floppy/webadmin.tgz' -> `mnt/webadmin.tgz'
`floppy/config/coyote.cfg' -> `mnt/config/coyote.cfg'
`floppy/config/fireloc.cfg' -> `mnt/config/fireloc.cfg'
`floppy/config/firewall.cfg' -> `mnt/config/firewall.cfg'
`floppy/config/hosts.dns' -> `mnt/config/hosts.dns'
`floppy/config/portfw.cfg' -> `mnt/config/portfw.cfg'
`floppy/config/qosfilt.cfg' -> `mnt/config/qosfilt.cfg'
`floppy/config/reserve.cfg' -> `mnt/config/reserve.cfg'
```

19. After the floppy is created, you are asked if you want to create another floppy disk. Type **y** if you want another floppy disk and insert another floppy disk to create it. Otherwise, just type **n** and you are done:

```
Would you like to create another copy of this disk [y/n]? n
```

Now you're ready to try out your Coyote Linux floppy disk firewall.

Running the Coyote Linux Floppy Firewall

To start up your firewall, simply insert the floppy disk into your firewall computer and reboot. The firewall should come up as you configured it to run. There is no direct shell interface from the firewall's console once it's up and running. In fact, you don't even have to have a monitor on the firewall because you won't see a login prompt anyway. Any administration of the firewall should be done over your LAN.

If you configured it as just described, your firewall is now:

✦ Offering addresses to the computers on your LAN using DHCP.

✦ Launching a dial-up connection from your firewall to your ISP as soon anyone from your LAN or the firewall itself tries to access the Internet.

✦ Allowing traffic from your LAN to the Internet.

✦ Offering login (`sshd`) and Web administration service to you from your LAN.

If the firewall is not behaving as you would like it to, go to the next section to further tune it.

Managing the Coyote Linux Floppy Firewall

With the firewall up and running, you almost surely will want to manage it further. There are a couple of ways to access your running firewall so that you can change its configuration, with a Web interface or a remote login. Before you can use the remote login, however, you must change the system (root user) password, and that can only be done through the Web interface.

Using a Web Interface

The Coyote Linux Web Administrator can be run from any browser on your LAN to view and change your firewall configuration. It is available from that machine on port 8180. To access the site you configured in the preceding example, you'd type the following in the location box on your browser: `http://192.168.0.1:8108`.

The first thing you want to do is click the System Password button in the main menu and add a password for the root user. Figure 17-3 shows the Internet configuration that was set up to dial out to the Internet in the previous section.

Using a Remote Login

The firewall floppy was configured to run the sshd daemon, enabling you to log in over your LAN (using the ssh command) to access your Coyote Linux firewall from the shell. In the example, you could type:

```
# ssh -l root 192.168.0.1
root@192.168.0.1's password: *******
```

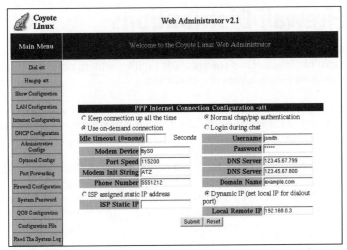

Figure 17-3: Administer Coyote Linux from your Web browser.

Enter the password (that you added from your Web interface as just described) and you are taken to the following Configuration menu:

```
Coyote Linux Gateway -- Configuration Menu
   1) Edit main configuration file    2) Change system password
   3) Edit rc.local script file       4) Custom firewall rules file
   5) Edit firewall configuration     6) Edit port forward configuration

   c) Show running configuration      f) Reload firewall
   r) Reboot system                   w) Write configuration to disk
   d) Dial PPP connection             h) Hangup PPP connection

   q) Exit Menu                       l) Logout
-----------------------------------------------------------------------
   Selection:
```

Select the letter of the configuration item you want to change. Type **q** when you are done and you are left at a regular Linux shell prompt. At that point, you can use Coyote Linux as you would any (somewhat limited) Linux system from a shell. (Type **menu** if you want to return to the menu interface.)

As previously noted, the first time you open the browser interface to Coyote Linux, change the root password. As for basic administrative tasks, you want to read the system log on occasion and back up your configuration changes (which you have made in RAM) so they are copied back to the floppy.

Note

To use ssh from a Windows machine to get to your firewall, or to get to any other Linux system for that matter, many people use the putty utility. You can get putty from its development home page: http://chiark.greenend.org.uk/~sgtatham/putty/.

Using Other Firewall Distributions

Coyote Linux was chosen for this book to illustrate how small, yet still really useful a Linux distribution can be. It also uses the iptables facility, which, once you learn how to use it, is useful in all recent Linux distributions.

There are, however, many other bootable firewalls available today. I strongly recommend that you check some of these other distributions if you want more or different features than those offered by Coyote Linux.

The Sentry Firewall CD is a very nice bootable CD firewall. Sentry Firewall CD takes advantage of the extra space on its CD to provide many extra tools for managing and watching your network. You can create a virtual private network connection using FreeS/WAN, manage SNMP services with net-snmp, and set up a variety of servers (using Apache, sendmail, bind, and others).

Sentry Firewall supports many different types of IDE and SCSI hardware (so you are not limited to PCI Ethernet cards and modems). It offers both a shell and Web interface for managing your firewall.

For a list of some additional firewall/router distributions, see the DistroWatch.com site: `www.distrowatch.com/dwres.php?resource=firewalls`.

Summary

No computer should be connected to the Internet or any public network without either being behind a firewall or being configured as a firewall itself. All of the latest Linux systems have iptables built right into the kernel to offer excellent firewall features (earlier Linux systems included ipchains or ipfwadm).

Desktop Linux systems often offer simplified, graphical tools for configuring a firewall. Every Linux system, however, enables you to use the iptables command directly to change the rules in your running Linux system. There are also tools to save and restore your firewall rules.

Coyote Linux illustrates how a Linux distribution with many valuable features can fit on a medium as small as a floppy disk. You stepped through creating the firewall floppy, booting it, and configuring the running firewall.

✦   ✦   ✦

Running Bootable Linux Distributions

There are now dozens, and probably will soon be hundreds, of bootable Linux distributions (also called *live CDs*). By stuffing removable media (CDs, DVDs, floppies, and even USB pen drives) with a select mix of open source software, bootable Linuxes enable you to bypass the hard disk completely and have a special Linux distribution running on almost any computer within minutes.

If you are willing to build your own bootable distribution, the concept of bootable Linux distributions can be extended any way you like. Your bootable business card or CD can carry all the applications you are used to having, so you can use them anywhere from a handy PC. But it can also hold your presentations, documents, mail-server settings, address books, favorite backgrounds and screen savers, personal photos, and any other kinds of data you want as well.

This chapter describes a variety of available bootable Linux distributions.

Exploring Bootable Linuxes

Although the most popular bootable Linux (KNOPPIX) and a cool example of a firewall Linux on a floppy disk (Coyote Linux) have already been covered in this book, I'd like to spark your imagination about more ways of using a bootable Linux. Here's a list of some ideas that others have had:

 ✦ **Rescue CD** — Rescuing broken systems and diagnosing network problems are among the most popular uses of bootable Linuxes. At a point where your hard disk might be inaccessible, bootable rescue CDs or DVDs can literally save damaged or infected computers. Rescue CDs often come with a wide range of tools for monitoring Linux or Windows systems, scanning for viruses, and debugging networks.

✦ **Multimedia** — Some bootable Linuxes are tailored specifically to let you play movies, music, and images. Most let you play whatever content you have on your hard disk or can point to from the Internet. Many run in a small enough amount of memory to let you remove the bootable DVD or CD containing Linux and insert your own content (like a music CD or movie DVD) to play.

✦ **Tiny desktops** — A small CD, shaped in the form of a business card, can fit in your wallet. A USB pen drive can hang from your keychain. There are whole bootable Linux distributions that let you boot up a desktop with which you can connect to the Internet, browse the Web, play music, send and receive e-mail, do instant messaging, write documents, and work with spreadsheets. And they can do all that in about 50MB of space on a removable medium.

Note   CD business cards are really just regular CDs that have been cut into the shape of a business card. Depending on the one you choose, it can hold from 40MB to 52MB of data. A mini-CD can hold about 180MB of data. You can purchase these CDs in bulk from many locations that sell regular CDs, and you can play them in any CD drive. (However, it's best to use these CDs in trays that have a mini-CD inset, because have been known to fly loose and break CD drives.)

There are also some neat bootable special-use Linux servers that are designed to serve up particular types of content or provide special services. For example, there are distributions that serve up photo albums or Web pages, as well as dedicated file- and print-servers that can serve the content on your Windows computers while completely bypassing the Windows operating system.

Many bootable Linuxes these days are either based on KNOPPIX or the Bootable Business Card project (www.lnx-bbc.org). I know of several Linux Users Groups that have tailored their own bootable business card projects from the lnx-bbc.org BBC project to hand out to represent their groups. Many bootable Linux distributions for media larger than business-card-size tend to be based on KNOPPIX.

There are several places you can look for bootable Linux distributions:

✦ **Knoppix Customizations** — The Knoppix Customizations page (www.knoppix. net/docs/index.php/KnoppixCustomizations) lists several distributions based on KNOPPIX.

✦ **LinuxLinks.com** — This site has a list of minidistributions, many of which are bootable Linux systems. The page that contains this list is www.linuxlinks. com/Distributions/Mini_Distributions.

✦ **DistroWatch.com** — DistroWatch keeps a list of CD-based Linux distributions and live Linux CDs (`distrowatch.com/dwres.php?resource=cd`). Its site also contains information and links to hundreds of distributions.

Because these distributions are based on open source technology, they rely on many of the same components in their basic technology. The SYSLINUX Project (`http://syslinux.zytor.com`) is responsible for the boot-loader technology used in most Linux distributions. Hardware detection is often based on Kudzu libraries created by Red Hat Inc. and enhanced by the KNOPPIX project. If a graphical interface is included, all but the most compact distributions use the X Window system (`www.x.org`), with space requirements dictating the exact window manager used with it.

If you have trouble running any bootable Linux distributions, try adding options to the boot prompt. Because so many of the distributions are based on KNOPPIX, refer to the KNOPPIX boot options (also called *cheat codes*) described in Chapter 11 to help get your Linux distribution to start up the way you would like. View these codes online at `www.knoppix.net/docs/index.php/CheatCodes`.

This book comes with several bootable Linux distributions, and these are noted as you read through the descriptions later in this chapter. You can get more recent versions of distributions that interest you (some are updated quite often) by following links from sites that were just mentioned.

Caution Most bootable Linux distributions are created by individuals and should still be considered as experimental in nature. The quality can vary widely and sometimes the controls are not as stringent as they would be for commercial Linux systems, such as Red Hat or SUSE. You can limit your risks by doing such things as mounting all hard disk partitions read-only (as is usually done by default), but remember that this software is distributed with no warranty.

Booting Rescue Distributions

Rescue CDs are not a new concept. Nearly every commercial operating system comes with a CD that lets you boot your computer if the hard disk fails. But the availability of a wide range of high-quality open source software for diagnosing and fixing problems on a computer or network have made Linux-based rescue CDs the choice of many professional IT troubleshooters.

Popular Linux rescue CDs that illustrate very well how many tools you can get on a single CD include the Knoppix-STD and the Inside Security Rescue Toolkit (INSERT) rescue CDs.

Caution   When you use a rescue CD to change a master boot record, fix partition tables, or clean viruses from a system, you risk doing irreparable damage to your computer system. Remember that GPL software comes with no warranty, so you use that software at your own risk.

KNOPPIX Security Tools Distribution

The Knoppix-STD goes lightweight on the window manager to go heavyweight on the diagnostic tools. The distribution contains hundreds of security tools that can be used for repairing and assessing computer and network security (see `http://knoppix-std.org/tools.html`).

Instead of a full GNOME desktop, Knoppix-STD uses Fluxbox window manager. It will run on lesser machines, but you'll get a usable GUI on almost any Pentium-class machine with at least 64MB of RAM. With at least 640MB of RAM, you can run the entire distribution from RAM (type **knoppix toram** to boot it to run entirely from RAM). With Knoppix-STD running in RAM, the system operates faster and your CD or DVD drive is available for other purposes.

Ways of using Knoppix-STD tools include (but aren't limited to):

✦ **Assessing vulnerability**—Knoppix-STD has literally dozens of tools for assessing vulnerabilities. There are tools to let you scan shared Windows SMB folders (nbtscan), NetWare servers, CGI scripts (nikto and screamingCobra), the computer's ports (nmap), as well as scan for viruses (clamAV). You can also check if someone has used a rootkit to replace critical system files (chkrootkit) or use a scanner dispatch (warscan) to test any exploit you like across lots of machines.

✦ **Running forensics on Windows machines**—If you believe a Windows system has been compromised, there are many tools you can use to find problems and correct them. You can recover Internet Explorer cookies (galleta), convert Outlook Express dbx files to mbox format (readdbx and readoe), check system integrity with (ftimes), and check the Windows recycle bin (rifiuti).

✦ **Recovering data**—If a Windows or other operating system won't boot or is otherwise impaired, you can get data off that computer. You can copy files over the network (using rsync, scp, or others) or back up to local CD or tape (cpio, tar, or others). You can selectively recover file types from disk images (foremost) or check and recover lost partitions (testdisk).

✦ **Dealing with intruders**—Tools like Snort (`www.snort.org`) let you analyze network traffic in real time, as well as log and analyze data as attacks are happening. Honeypots let you watch intruders' moves as it leads them to believe they've compromised your system. Honeypots in Knoppix-STD include honeyd (`http://honeyd.org`), thp (`www.alpinista.org/thp`). Kill zombies from DDoS attacks with `zz`.

✦ **Using and analyzing encryption techniques** — Many tools enable you to use encryption techniques to protect your data and find when others have tried to compromise it. GNP privacy guard (gpg) is used for verifying the authenticity of computers and people. For setting up virtual private networks, there are stunnel and super-freeSWAN VPNs. You can find images (giffshuffle, stegbreak and stegdetect) and music (mp3stego) that contain hidden messages from a technique called *steganography*.

✦ **Managing a firewall** — Bring a firewall up quickly or assess what's happening on a running firewall. The `blockall` script can block all inbound TCP traffic, `flushall` flushes your firewall rules, and `fwlogwatch` can monitor firewall logs. The `firestarter` and `floppyfw` utilities offer quick ways to start up a firewall. Tools for managing iptables firewalls include `gtk-iptables` and `shorewall`.

These tools only touch the surface of what you can do with Knoppix-STD. Go to the project's Tools page (`www.knoppix-std.org/tools.html`) to find out about more feature in the project. Or, go to the download page (`www.knoppix-std.org/download.html`) to download and try it yourself.

The Inside Security Rescue Toolkit

INSERT (Inside Security Rescue Toolkit) is another KNOPPIX derivative that includes features from Damn Small Linux as well. It bills itself as a disaster recovery and network analysis system. It contains a more compact set of tools to fit on a bootable business card (about 50MB). Check it out at `www.freshmeat.net/projects/INSERT/`.

On the CD-ROM

The INSERT CD image is included on the CD that comes with this book. Refer to Appendix A for information on copying and burning INSERT to CD.

The Fluxbox window manager offers some docked system monitors for monitoring CPU, network traffic, memory and swap use, and battery (if you are on a laptop). Another applet displays the Matrix screen saver (double-click it to launch a Terminal window). The mount applet lets you step through the CD, floppy, and hard-disk partitions on your computer. Click the key button on that applet (so it turns green), and you can double-click it to mount and open that device or partition.

Right-click the desktop to see a menu that lets you select from a handful of graphical tools for troubleshooting your computer and network, most of which will run from the shell. Figure 18-1 shows the INSERT desktop.

You can find what's in INSERT from the List of Applications page on the Inside Security site (`www.inside-security.de/applicationlist.html`).

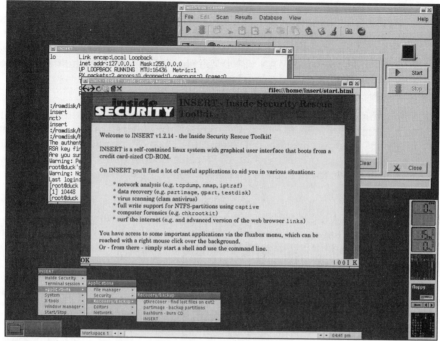

Figure 18-1: Use INSERT to troubleshoot computers and networks.

Booting Multimedia Distributions

Because one of the things people like to do best with a home desktop system is play music and video, it's no surprise that there are several bootable Linux distributions that do just that. Using these Linuxes, you can immediately turn any PC into a dedicated multimedia player.

Two examples of bootable multimedia distributions are MoviX and GeeXboX.

MoviX

With MoviX (http://movix.sourceforge.net), you run a multimedia player that disregards the operating systems (Windows, Linux, or otherwise) installed on your system. Because MoviX is small enough to run in your system memory, after it has booted you can remove it and insert the CD or DVD. With MoviX, you can play:

✦ **Videos**—You can play video from many different formats, including DivX/XVID, MPEG 1 and 2, and MPEG 4. So that MoviX can be freely distributed, it does not include the capability to play most DVD movies.

Caution The libdvdcss library, needed to decrypt DVD movies (even if only for playback), has been the subject of legal suits. Although this library is available on the Internet, no legitimate Linux systems in the U.S. distribute this library, and using it could be illegal. You should research this issue yourself if you plan to add libdvdcss to MoviX or any other Linux distribution that includes MPlayer or xine media players.

✦ **Music** — Audio files in AVI, MP3, Ogg Vorbis, and other formats can be played.

✦ **Images** — You can run a slide show using the Linux Frame Buffer Image (fbi) viewer that displays images in JPEG, PNG, and a variety of other image formats.

Because the MoviX player itself doesn't include any video, music, or images for you to play, it gives you choices on where you can load those items from. Here are the possibilities, depending on what is available from your computer:

✦ **DVDs** — If you have a DVD drive on your computer, you can play supported content from there. (As previously stated, that doesn't include most commercial movies, by default.)

✦ **VCDs and SVCD** — These are video formats that can be put on standard CDs.

✦ **Audio CDs** — Standard music CDs (including AVI, MP3, and other formats) can be played.

✦ **Hard disk files** — Any supported content that is on the local hard disk can also be played from MoviX. Like KNOPPIX, MoviX detects hard disk partitions and then mounts them as you request files from those partitions. The mounts are done read-only, by default, so you can play your content without any risk of deleting or otherwise damaging it.

✦ **Network** — MoviX boots onto the network if a DHCP server is detected. Although the friendly user interface doesn't appear to support it yet, software in MoviX should enable you to get content from your LAN or Internet to playback using an NFS (UNIX file sharing) or FTP (standard Internet file sharing facility) file server.

MoviX boots right up to MPlayer, so you can eject the MoviX disk, insert a CD, DVD, or VCD into your drive and play any supported content. Right-click the desktop to see your choices for selecting content.

If you are comfortable moving around in Linux, you can go to different virtual terminals while you are using MoviX. Press Ctrl+Alt+F2 to view a sound mixer or Ctrl+Alt+F3 to go to a Linux shell. Then press Ctrl+Alt+F4 to get back to the main screen (with MPlayer). Select Switch to MoviX from the menu, and you can choose to run your audio player, slide show, or TV viewer (the latter if you have a television card installed).

If you think MoviX is cool, you'll really like the idea of the eMoviX project. With eMoviX, you put a mini-MoviX distribution on a CD or DVD with your video, so that your video content comes with its own bootable player! (See `http://movix.sourceforge.net/Docs/eMoviX` for details.)

At the time of this writing, MoviX hadn't reached a 1.0 release number yet. That implies that there are probably more features and bug fixes to come before the developers feel comfortable calling it a real release. While there are still some rough edges to it, MoviX is fun to play with.

GeeXboX

GeeXboX (`www.geexbox.org`) is another bootable multimedia player distribution. From the screen that appears after GeeXboX boots, you can use your cursor to select the location of the content you want to choose. Like MoviX, you can play a variety of audio and video content. It also boots up on your network, so you can get audio and video content from it.

Because GeeXboX is so small (just a few megabytes), you can fit it easily on a mini-CD, bootable business card, or even a pen drive (provided your computer can be booted from those media). There is no graphical interface; you just use the keyboard to select content and simple controls from menus.

Use arrow keys to move among the few GeeXboX selections (Open, Controls, Options, Help, and Quit). Press Enter to make a selection. You can open a file from hard disk, a music playlist, directory of images, or removable media (DVD, VCD/XCD, or audio CD) containing video content. Press M to show or hide menus and use P to pause.

Booting Tiny Desktop Distributions

If you want to take Linux on the road so you can read your e-mail and browse the Web, there are a bunch of mini-desktop distributions that fit in 64MB or less. Because most of these distributions are based on KNOPPIX, you get many of the great features of hardware detection, network connections, and software installation built in.

The distributions, however, focus on getting the most important applications available to you in a small space. For that reason, they may not have drivers for every piece of hardware on your computer or include your favorite software. However, once you are up and running, because these distributions are capable of booting up on the network, they often let you download the software you want to use right into your running system.

Two examples of tiny desktop Linux distributions are Damn Small Linux and Feather Linux.

Damn Small Linux

If you want your desktop Linux distribution to fit in your wallet, Damn Small Linux is one of your best choices. Damn Small is one of the first distributions based on KNOPPIX to fit on a bootable business card (about 48MB currently).

On the CD-ROM

Damn Small Linux is included on the CD that comes with this book. Insert that CD into the CD drive on your computer, reboot, and press Enter from the Linux Bible boot screen to start Damn Small Linux. There is also an ISO image of Damn Small Linux on the CD, so you can burn it to a CD or bootable business card CD.

With KNOPPIX inside, you have many of the features you get with KNOPPIX: excellent hardware detection and boot-up to a desktop with network connectivity (provided you have an Ethernet connection with DHCP). Many features specific to Damn Small, however, are there to let you get a workable desktop system in a small medium (mini-CD) and low RAM.

Damn Small's default desktop is pretty simple. Right-click the desktop to see a menu of features you can select. Here are a few things you want to do when you first boot up Damn Small:

✦ **Enhance your desktop** — Right-click to see the Damn Small menu, then select Desktop⇨Full Enhanced Desktop. This adds some icons to your desktop to launch applications, some applets in the lower-right corner to display system information, and a workspace editor. Select Desktop again if you want to change the Styles (colors and window borders) or Configuration to change desktop behavior.

✦ **Get a network connection** — If you don't automatically get on the Internet at boot time, select System⇨Net Setup from the Damn Small menu. Then you can choose to configure your Ethernet card, DSL connection, dial-up modem, or wireless card.

✦ **Browse the Web** — Damn Small comes with the Dillo Web browser. Select Apps⇨Net⇨Dillo to start browsing. The browser is small, fast, and can run on any X window manager because it doesn't require GNOME libraries.

✦ **Configure and read e-mail** — The Sylpheed e-mail client is also very compact and runs fast. Select Apps⇨Net⇨Sylpheed to open it. Configure it and you can be up and reading your e-mail within a few minutes.

✦ **Try out other applications** — Right-click and look through the menu for applications that interest you. To see descriptions of those applications, visit http://damnsmalllinux.org/applications.html.

✦ **Get other applications** — Even though it is not included on the Damn Small CD, you can download the Firefox Web browser from Mozilla to use live with your Damn Small Linux. Select Apps⇨Net⇨Got, the bandwidth, and then chooseFirefox.

Note You can get other DSL files that will let you download other applications from your desktop as well. Visit `www.damnsmalllinux.org` and select the link to the myDSL repository.

More information about using Damn Small Linux is available at the project FAQ page, `www.damnsmall.org/faq.html`.

Feather Linux

Because it is fashioned to run in 64MB, the Feather Linux distribution fits on a mini-CD or 64MB bootable USB pen drive. The developer took technology from KNOPPIX and scaled it back to what you absolutely need in a desktop system.

The Feather Linux CD image is included on the CD that comes with this book. Refer to Appendix A for more information on copying and burning Feather Linux to CD.

The way Feather Linux presents its applications on the desktop makes it easy to find them. The icons are attractive and go well with the available themes. Figure 18-2 shows an example of the Feather Linux desktop.

Figure 18-2: Feather Linux provides key desktop features while fitting in 64MB.

Boot Feather Linux and it comes up with a simple Fluxbox window manager. With an Ethernet card and DHCP server, you are automatically connected to the network. To use that network, you have Sylpheed as your e-mail client and Dillo as your Web browser. Play music with xmms and view PDF files with XPDF.

If the computer you are using has enough memory, you can install more applications. Right-click the desktop and select Enhancements and Extras⇨Install. Then choose the application you want from menus such as games, multimedia, office, and other categories.

You might want different Web and mail clients (such as Mozilla Thunderbird and Firefox) or a different window manager (like ICEwm or XFCE). (I chose AbiWord from the office menu. Feather Linux downloaded it and added the Abiword icon right to the desktop.)

Summary

Dozens of bootable Linux distributions have appeared in the past few years. Those distributions can contain anywhere from 1.4MB of data on a firewall bootable Linux to many gigabytes of data on a bootable DVD. Without needing to touch the computer's hard disk, these distributions can offer full-featured systems that are tailored to be desktop systems, multimedia players, rescue systems, or many other types of systems.

Many bootable Linuxes are based on KNOPPIX (described in Chapter 11), so they feature very fine hardware detection and strong network connectivity. Nearly all offer ways to access data from the hard disks of the computers on which they are running. While many bootable Linuxes are still experimental in nature, you can have lots of fun playing with them — just be sure to handle with a bit of care.

✦   ✦   ✦

Running Applications

Playing Music and Video

One of the most popular and enjoyable activities on a computer is playing audio and video. With improved multimedia players and tools for storing and managing content, Linux has become a great platform for storing, playing, and managing your music and video files.

In this chapter, you learn to use the sound, video, digital imaging, and other multimedia tools available for Linux. You explore the process of configuring audio and select video devices and examine the kinds of media formats available for Linux platform, how they work, and how to make the most of them by using the right applications.

Linux is an excellent platform for taking advantage of widely used formats such as MPEG, AVI, OGG, QuickTime, and RealMedia. There are several players available for the various formats, and this chapter discusses several of them to help you determine which might be the right one (or combination) for your interests and/or needs.

Probably still the most widely used piece of multimedia technology remains the CD-ROM, so this chapter takes a detailed look at setting up and burning your own CDs. Regardless of your need to store data or create audio and software CDs, you will find there are many tools to help you get the job done.

Playing Digital Media and Obeying the Law

What an end user can legally do with digital media is a hot topic right now. What exactly can you do as far as making copies of your CDs, DVDs, and other media? Unfortunately, there is no real good answer. This issue affects just about every computer user, either directly or indirectly.

How you are allowed to use the audio, video, and other media you keep on your computers is increasingly dictated by law (U.S. and international). There was a time when you could essentially disregard this issue, but in the era where individual computer users have been successfully sued by corporations and industry groups, a little more caution is required.

Copyright Protection Issues

The biggest factor in the new world of digital media policy is the 1998 Digital Millennium Copyright Act (DMCA). This law ostensibly establishes a framework for implementing several international treaties concerning copyright protection.

The DMCA has been widely criticized because it potentially intrudes on the free-speech provisions of the U.S. Constitution. Many people view computer code as a protected form of speech. A conflict arises because the DMCA forbids the development of applications that are designed to intentionally circumvent content security. For example, Dmitry Skarlov is a Russian cryptographer who was arrested by the FBI while attending a conference in Las Vegas because he demonstrated an application that could decrypt Adobe eBooks.

If nothing else this event demonstrated that the DMCA had teeth. Unfortunately these teeth have been used not only to protect legitimate commerce, but to pursue computer scientists at academic institutions researching content protection schemes, encryption, and a range of other technologies. Because the DMCA makes it a crime to manufacture and transport technology used to circumvent copyright protection schemes, many researchers have abandoned valuable research that could yield better (stronger and more useful) protection schemes or reveal critical flaws in existing ones.

While DCMA has provided some clout for content providers to legitimately protect their material, such as persuading search engines to drop information about links to illegally posted and copyrighted information, there are times when that clout has been abused. Some copyright holders, it seems, are more than willing to use the DMCA to curtail three "rights" allowed under pre-DMCA copyright law. Copyright law stipulates:

✦ Users can make a copy of any copyrighted work for academic purposes, reporting or critique. This includes a wide range of uses, from students/instructors copying materials for research to someone creating a parody of published materials. But what about a student making a copy of some DVD materials for a multimedia presentation? The student has fair-use access to the material on the DVD, but the DMCA makes it illegal for the student to break the DVD encryption that would allow the student to actually copy the material.

Note　　The fair-use rule is a privilege in others than the owner of the copyright to use the copyrighted material in a reasonable manner without his consent.

✦ Users can sell copyrighted works that they own. You can sell your books, DVDs, audio CDs, and other materials as long as you are not retaining a copy for yourself, or (of course) selling copies of the work without permission from the copyright holder. Some people arguing in favor of file trading with copyrighted materials claim that the DMCA infringes on their ability to "share" content they "own." In fact under existing copyright law they do not "own" much at all and certainly do not possess the rights to redistribute the content unless they are reselling them in an allowed manner.

✦ Copyrights will expire at some time in the future and fall into the public domain. Basically, you run into the same issue as with the first item. So your DVD movie falls into the public domain (eventually), but to freely copy the content you must again circumvent the protection inherent on the DVD and by doing so, you run afoul of the DMCA.

It is important to realize the DMCA is very vague about how it defines many of the acts that are illegal. What is a protection scheme? Some argue that it could be nearly anything. Many pundits fear that the DMCA can be used to curtail the use of nondigital copyrighted works such as books because the law is so vague in defining its own borders.

While the courts are trying to clarify where the legal line is in any particular situation, there's a problem in that often the company suing to protect its copyrights is a large corporation or group and the defendant is either a new company or even an individual user. Court battles are expensive, and the broad scope of the DMCA essentially prevents "the little" guy from ever making his case because he cannot afford to fight.

Note

In 1998 a law known as the Sonny Bono Copyright Term Extension Act, or CTEA , was passed. This act took the already lengthy copyright protection period (generally 70 years) and extended it by another 20 years, preventing several valuable properties, including film and images of Steamboat Willie (the first Mickey Mouse), from entering the public domain.

The question of practicality is very important when examining copyright issues. In other words what does all of this mean to you as a Linux user? Well, it means that if you have to use any trickery to copy MP3s off your CD collection, you could be breaking the law.

Several CD protection schemes used by record companies are designed to prevent digital piracy, but they are very easy to circumvent in most cases. But should you get caught making MP3s off a protected CD, you could be sued and or arrested (hypothetically speaking). It is quite possible that some of the security on CDs is intentionally weak. It saves development costs and allows the copyright holder to pursue anyone who has ripped the CD because there is no legal means of doing so. But that is just speculation.

Relatively few audio CDs come with protection of any kind, particularly those CDs already owned by the world's audiophiles. If you make fair-use copies of materials you own for your own use, you're not likely to have to worry about anything. If you should decide to transport copyrighted works in a public forum (peer-to-peer networks for example), you are rolling the dice. The RIAA (Recording Industry Association of America) and MPAA (Motion Picture Association of America) have both successfully located and sued users — including children — distributing content illegally online.

Exploring Codecs

If you want to play a video or audio file you need the appropriate codec installed and ready for use by your media player. There are many codecs available, so making sure you have the ones you need is not usually an issue. Advances in codecs have continued to increase the quality of the encoded content, while reducing file size. Fortunately most widely distributed videos and audio files (from news sites, for example) are created using a few commonly used codecs.

Note   A codec is a *compressor-de*compressor that is generally used to take existing digital audio/video data and reduce the size of the content while retaining the quality of the output. If you encounter a media file that you know is a working (i.e., playable) file and you cannot play the file, you may need to identify and install the proper codec. This often involves installing the proper playback application such as the DivX 5.0.5 for Linux, which will install the MPEG4 codec for video and audio playback.

While there are some commonly used encoding standards, there are also a slew of proprietary codecs in use today as well. This is really a battleground of sorts with each vendor/developer trying to produce the superior standard and hopefully the spoils of market share that could follow. For the end user this means you may have to spend time chasing a variety of playback utilities to handle multiple video and audio formats.

Another debate continues: Can digital media match the quality of analog formats? Not really much of question anymore because DVD has shown the potential for high-quality digital video, and MPEG codecs have made huge strides in digital audio fidelity. The quality of digital media files is very high and getting better all the time. Some of the key technologies that have made this the case and are still improving include:

✦ **Ogg Vorbis** — This audio codec has been developed as a freely available tool — no patents or licensing needed. Ogg is the "data container" portion of the codec, and Vorbis is the audio compression scheme. There are other compression schemes that can be used with Ogg such as Ogg FLAC, which is used for archiving audio in a lossless format, and Ogg Speex, which is used to specifically handle encoding speech.

✦ **Real Networks** — Real has developed a set of audio and video codecs that have an amazing ability to serve up streaming content. This protocol is not widely supported by anyone but Real. The Helix project produces a player for Linux that enables playback of Real media encoded files.

✦ **WMA** — Windows Media Audio is used to create high-quality digital audio. WMA is considered a lossless codec, and among its other benefits is that it's one of the first widely used codecs to support digital surround sound.

✦ **WMV** — Windows Media Video is used, not surprisingly, to encode and decode video. This is also a very high-quality encoder and is billed to produce a video that is half the size of a MPEG-4 encoded video at a comparable quality level.

✦ **DivX** — This video codec has revolutionized digital video. Extremely high-quality video can be stored with amazingly small file sizes when using this codec. DivX (Digital Video Express) is based on the MPEG-4 video standard and can produce 640×480 video that is about 15 percent of the size of the source DVD material.

Some of these codecs are integral parts of Digital Rights Management (DRM) scenarios. For example, WMA, WMV, and DivX have elements that support DRM. DRM is basically proprietary copy protection. The term "DRM" applies to a wide range of technologies that use server-based activation, encryption, and other elements to control who can access content and what they can then do with the content once it has been accessed. While it is very attractive to distributors of audio and video, who are trying to prevent unchecked digital piracy of their content, it can be a real stumbling block for the consumer.

Many DRM solutions require proprietary software and even hardware to work with the protected content. A prime example is the recent production of some DRM-protected audio CDs, particularly in Europe. Some of these disks will not play in older standalone CD players, some will play only on a computer that supports the DRM application on the CD itself, and (especially frustrating) some will not play on a computer at all.

Just to make things clear, the codecs just discussed do not use DRM inherently, but some are specifically designed to integrate with DRM solutions. In other words, all of these codecs can theoretically be used to play encoded content on a Linux system. If the content is protected by a DRM solution, the likelihood that the content is playable on a Linux system is fairly remote. Despite this fact, however, Linus Torvalds has not excluded the possibility of including support for DRM in Linux. Likewise, there are several open source projects working on Linux DRM solutions.

Playing Music

With an understanding of the challenges and advances in digital media under your belt, let's move on to actually putting digital media to use. This section shows you how to set up your Linux installation for audio playback. It examines the process for getting the hardware up and running and then explores available software options for audio playback.

Setting Up Audio Cards

To start your "quadraphonic wall of sound," you need to have a sound card in your PC. A sound card can be an add-in PCI (or even ISA) card, or it can be integrated on your motherboard. Your card will have a ton of uses — from gaming to audio/video playback, having a multimedia system just isn't the same without sound.

Troubleshooting Your CD-ROM

If you are unable to play CDs on your CD-ROM drive, here are a few things you can check to correct the problem:

✦ Verify that your sound card is installed and working properly.

✦ Verify that the CD-ROM drive was detected when you booted Linux. If your CD-ROM drive is an IDE drive, type **dmesg | grep ^hd**. You should see messages about your CD-ROM that look like this: `hdc: CD-ROM CDU701, ATAPI CDROM drive` or this: `hdc: ATAPI 14X CD-ROM drive, 128kB Cache`.

✦ If you see no indication of a CD-ROM drive, verify that the power supply and cables to the CD-ROM are connected. To make sure that the hardware is working, you can also boot to DOS and try to access the CD.

✦ Try inserting a software CD-ROM. If you are running the GNOME or KDE desktop, a desktop icon should appear indicating that the CD mounted by itself. If no such icon appears, go to a Terminal window and type **mount /dev/cdrom**. Then change to the `/mnt/cdrom` or `/dev/media` directory and list the contents using the command `cd /mnt/cdrom; ls`. This tells you if the CD-ROM is accessible.

✦ If you get the CD-ROM working but it fails with the message "CDROM device: Permission denied" when you try to play music as a non–root user, the problem may be that `/dev/cdrom` (which is typically a link to the actual hardware device) is not readable by anyone but root. Type **ls -l /dev/cdrom** to see what the device is linked to. Then (as the root user), if, for example, the CD device were `/dev/hdc`, type **chmod 644 /dev/hdc** to enable all users to read your CD-ROM and to enable the root user to write to it. One warning: If others use your computer, they will be able to read any CD you place in this drive.

Fortunately most modern PCs include a sound card, often of the integrated variety. In the rare case that one isn't included (or the slightly more common case where it isn't supported in Linux), you can add a supported sound card starting for only a few dollars. If you're really pinched, check out eBay, where you probably can get a decent SoundBlaster (still *the* standard) compatible card for next to nothing.

Note　If you try the procedures in this book but still don't have a working sound card, visit the Advanced Linux Sound Architecture at www.alsa-project.org, home of the ALSA sound architecture. ALSA is the preferred sound software for Linux and is built into the Linux kernel itself (beginning with the 2.6 kernel). The ALSA site offers support, information, and help.

The following list summarizes the basic features that are included in the popular SoundBlaster family of sound cards:

✦ **Sound recording and playback** — The card can convert analog sound into 8-bit or 16-bit digital numbers. To convert the sound, the board samples the sound in waves from 5 KHz to 48 KHz, or 5,000 to 48,100 times per second. (Of course, the higher the sampling, the better the sound and larger the output.)

✦ **Full-duplex support** — This allows for recording and playback to occur at the same time. This is particularly useful for bidirectional Internet communication or simultaneous recording and playback.

✦ **Input/output ports** — Several different ports on the board enable you to connect other input/output devices. These ports include:

Line-In — Connects an external CD player, cassette deck, synthesizer, MiniDisc, or other device for recording or playback. If you have a television card, you might also patch that card's line out to your sound card's line in.

Microphone — Connects a microphone for audio recording or communications.

Line-Out (Speaker Out) — Connects nonpowered speakers, headphones, or a stereo amplifier.

Joystick/MIDI — Connects a joystick for gaming or MIDI device.

Internal CD Audio — Connects the sound card to your computer's internal CD-ROM board (this port isn't exposed when the board is installed).

Sound drivers provided in Linux come from many sources, including a project that no longer exists: Open Sound System/Free (OSS/Free). However, as previously mentioned, Advanced Linux Sound Architecture (ALSA) is the sound system that is integrated into the 2.6 kernel. The older OSS drivers are useful if ALSA does not support your sound card.

Caution　Before you install a separate sound driver distribution, check to see if your current distribution already has a recent driver. Using the driver that came with the kernel is always a safe play if you are not experiencing a specific driver-related issue.

The devices that the audio programs use to access audio hardware in most Linux distributions include:

✦ **/dev/audio, /dev/audio1** — Compatible with Sun workstation audio implementations (audio files with the `.au` extension). These devices are not recommended for new sound applications.

✦ **/dev/cdrom** — Represents your first CD-ROM drive. (Additional CD-ROM drives are located at `/dev/cdrom1`, `/dev/cdrom2`, and so on.)

✦ **/dev/dsp, /dev/dsp1** — Digital sampling devices, which many audio applications identify to access your sound card.

✦ **/dev/mixer, /dev/mixer1** — Sound-mixing devices.

✦ **/dev/sequencer** — Provides a low-level interface to MIDI, FM, and GUS.

✦ **/dev/midi00** — Provides raw access to midi ports.

✦ **/dev/sndstat** — Displays the status of sound drivers.

For general information about sound in Linux, see the Sound-HOWTO (for tips about sound cards and general sound issues) and the Sound-Playing-HOWTO (for tips on software for playing different types of audio files). You can find Linux HOWTOs at `www.tldp.org`.

Choosing an Audio CD Player

The GNOME CD player (gnome-cd) pops up automatically on the GNOME desktop when you insert a CD. It's the default CD player for the GNOME desktop. It has standard play buttons and lets you get track information automatically from a CD database, such as `freedb.org`. (If your CD isn't listed in the database, you can enter your own track information manually.)

However, there are a variety of CD players that come with Linux distributions or that may be downloaded and installed. Here is a cross-section of your other choices for playing CDs with Linux:

✦ **Rhythmbox** (`rhythmbox`) — Import and manage your CD collection with Rhythmbox music management and playback software for GNOME. It uses Gstreamer on the audio backend and compresses music using Ogg Vorbis audio format. In addition to enabling you to create playlists of your music library, Rhythmbox also has features for playing Internet radio stations.

✦ **KsCD player** (`kscd`) — The KsCD player comes with the KDE desktop. To use it, the kdemultimedia package must be installed. From the main menu on the KDE desktop, select Multimedia⇨KsCD (or type **kscd** from a Terminal window). Like gnome-cd, this player lets you get title, track, and artist information from the CD database. KsCD, however, also lets you submit information to a CD database (if your CD isn't found there).

✦ **Grip** (grip) — While the Grip window is primarily used as a CD ripper, it can also play CDs. Select Multimedia ➪ Grip (or type **grip** from a Terminal window). It includes tools for gathering data from and submitting data to CD databases. It also includes tools for copying (ripping) CD tracks and converting them to different formats (encoding). (The grip package must be installed to use this command.)

✦ **CDPlay** (cdp) — If you don't have access to the desktop, you can use the text-based cdp command. This player lets you use keyboard keys to play your CD, select tracks, go forward or back, or eject. (The cdp or cdplay package, depending on your Linux distribution, must be installed to use this command.)

✦ **X Multimedia System** (xmms) — The XMMS player plays a variety of audio formats but can also play directly from a CD.

 If you try some of these CD players and your CD-ROM drive is not working, see the sidebar "Troubleshooting Your CD-ROM" for further information.

Automatically Playing CDs

When you put an audio CD into your CD-ROM drive, a CD player automatically pops up on your desktop. If you are using the GNOME desktop, you can probably thank magicdev, which monitor your CD-ROM drives and opens a CD player when it sees an audio CD.

 While most Linux distributions still use magicdev to launch a CD player on your desktop, the GNOME 2.8 desktop (included with Fedora Core 3 on this book's DVD) relies on the new GNOME volume manager. This volume manager monitors CDs, DVDs, USB drives, digital cameras, and other removable media and offers a range of options about how to manage those devices. If you are running Fedora Core 3, select Preferences ➪ Removable Storage to see how your system is configured to handle removable media.

The fact that inserting a CD starts a player automatically is nice to some people and annoying to others. If you just want the CD to play, this behavior is a good thing. However, if you want to choose your own CD player or not play the CD until you choose, you may find autoplaying a bother. If you insert a data CD or a blank CD, magicdev exhibits different behavior. Here is what magicdev does by default with the GNOME desktop:

✦ **Audio CD** — When the music CD is inserted, magicdev starts gnome-cd and begins playing the first track of the CD.

✦ **Data CD** — When a data CD is inserted, the CD is mounted on your file system, any autorun program that may be on the CD is launched, and a CD icon appears on the desktop. The first CD drive's mount point (/dev/cdrom) is /mnt/cdrom. If you have two drives, the second (/dev/cdrom1) is mounted on /mnt/cdrom1 (and so on).

✦ **Blank CD** — When a blank CD is inserted, a nautilus window opens with burn:/// as the location.

You can change the behavior of magicdev for the GNOME desktop in the CD and DVD preferences window. To do so:

1. On the main menu, choose Preferences ➪ CD and DVD. The CD and DVD preferences window appears.

2. For data CDs, select from the following options:

   • **Mount discs when inserted** — If this is selected, an inserted data CD is automatically mounted in a subdirectory of /mnt. This option is on by default.

   • **Start autorun program on newly mounted discs** — If this is selected, after a data CD is mounted, the user is asked to choose whether to run an autorun program from the CD. This option is on by default if the first option is checked.

3. For Audio CDs, you can select the Run Command When Audio CD Is Inserted check box to have the CD start playing automatically after it's inserted. The command shown in the box labeled Command is used to play the CD. By default, the option is on, and the gnome-cd player is chosen for you.

4. For blank CDs, the nautilus window opens with burn:/// as the location. With this feature enabled, you can drag-and-drop files on the nautilus window to gather the files you want to write to CD. Click Write to CD to burn the selected files to the CD.

5. For DVDs, click the check box next to Run Command When DVD (Video) Is Inserted to have the DVD play automatically (using the vlc command) when you insert a DVD.

6. Click Close.

Playing CDs with gnome-cd

Like most graphical CD players, the gnome-cd player has controls that look similar to what you would see on a physical CD player. If you are using the GNOME desktop, from the main menu select Sound & Video ➪ CD Player, or from a Terminal window, type:

```
$ gnome-cd &
```

If your computer is connected to the Internet, then for most CDs you'll see the title and artist information. Even obscure artists are represented in the free online databases. If the information isn't available, you can enter it yourself.

The interface for adding information about the CD and its tracks is very nice. Click the Open Track Editor button. You can add Artist and Title information about the CD. Then you can select each track to type in the track name. To add the name of the artist and the disk title, click in the appropriate text box, and type in that information. Figure 19-1 shows the CD Player and the CDDB Track Editor.

Figure 19-1: Play CDs and store artist, title, and track information with gnome-cd.

Playing CDs with Cdp

If you are working from a dumb terminal or just don't have your X desktop running, you can run the cdp utility to play CDs. Cdp is available in most Linux distributions but is a "free to distribute and copyrighted" piece of software and may not show up in all distributions. I don't suggest running this utility from a Terminal window; it doesn't display properly.

Insert the music CD you want to play, and then at a shell prompt type:

```
$ cdp
```

You should see a blue screen containing the cdp display. To start the CD on a track other than 1, include the track number with the play command. Here's an example of starting a CD on track 5:

```
$ cdp play 5
```

When cdp starts, you can see all the tracks, how long each track plays, and total play time. To control the play of the CD, use the following controls (turn on Num Lock to use these numbers from the numeric keypad):

> **9**—Play
>
> **8**—Pause/Resume
>
> **7**—Stop
>
> **6**—Next Track

5—Replay Current Track

4—Previous Track

3—Forward 15 Seconds

2—Quit (Stop Music, Exit, and Eject)

1—Back 15 Seconds

0—Exit (Continue Music and Exit)

.—Help (Press the period key)

The cdp display also lets you enter the names of the artist, CD, and each song. Because this information is saved, you can see it each time you play the CD. Type these commands while the cdp display is showing to edit information about the CD currently playing:

a—Edit the Artist Name and press Enter.

c—Edit the CD Name and press Enter.

Enter—Edit the title of the current song and press Enter again.

Caution

If you try to edit a song name and cdp crashes, type **eject** to stop the CD from playing. Editing the song name seems to work better if you pause the song first.

The arrow keys are also pretty handy for controlling CDs in cdp. The up arrow is for pause/play, and the left arrow is to go back a track. The right arrow is to go forward a track, and the down arrow is to eject.

Playing Music with Rhythmbox Audio Player

Rhythmbox provides the GNOME music player that lets you do everything, at least according to the Rhythmbox documentation. You can play music files, import music from CDs, and play Internet radio stations, all from one interface.

The first time you run Rhythmbox, the program displays a setup wizard (see Figure 19-2). You can tell Rhythmbox where you store your music files, and Rhythmbox will index, sort, and help you maintain a music library.

After you've gone through the setup wizard, you'll see the main music library interface (see Figure 19-3). Rhythmbox makes it easy to organize even large collections of music files.

Note

If your distribution does not include support for MP3 playback with Rhythmbox, fear not—there is hope! You can download updates for Rhythmbox at www.gstreamer.net. **You want the package** gstreamer-plugins-mp3.

Figure 19-2: Defining where you store your music.

Figure 19-3: Viewing a music library with Rhythmbox.

In addition to playing music files, Rhythmbox can launch Sound Juicer to rip CDs (see the "Ripping CDs with Grip" section later in the chapter for more on ripping CD audio). Rhythmbox can also play Internet radio stations. The easiest way to do this is to find a streaming radio station (you want to look for Shoutcast PLS files, usually with a .pls extension). Save the PLS file, and then double-click the file in the Nautilus file browser. Nautilus comes configured to launch Rhythmbox for playing audio. Figure 19-4 shows Rhythmbox with three Internet radio stations.

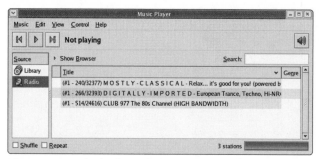

Figure 19-4: Rhythmbox playing Internet radio.

Tip

The site www.di.fm lists a number of free Internet radio channels.

Playing Music with XMMS Multimedia Player

The XMMS (X Multimedia System) multimedia player provides a graphical interface for playing music files in MP3, Ogg Vorbis, WAV, and other audio formats. XMMS has some nice extras too, including an equalizer, a playlist editor, and the capability to add more audio plug-ins. One of its greatest attributes is that XMMS is easy to use. If the player looks familiar to you, that's because it is styled after the Windows Winamp program.

Note

Red Hat removed all software that does MP3 encoding or decoding because of patent concerns related to MP3 format. Although the XMMS player was designed to play MP3 files, the XMMS plug-in required to actually decode MP3 is not included. To add MP3 support back into your Red Hat/Fedora Core distribution, you can get and install an MP3 plug-in. One place to get RPM packages that support MP3 decoding is http://rpm.livna.org. They are also available from other sources, including www.xmms.org and www.gurulabs.com/downloads.html. This issue does not necessarily apply to other Red Hat–derived distributions, such as Mandrake 10.0.

Start the XMMS audio player by selecting Sound & Video ➪ Audio Player or by typing **xmms** from a Terminal window. Figure 19-5 shows the XMMS audio player with the associated equalizer (below) and the Playlist Editor (to the right).

As noted earlier, you can play several audio file formats. Supported formats include:

✦ MP3 (with added plug-in)

✦ Ogg Vorbis

✦ WAV

✦ AU

✦ CD Audio

✦ CIN Movies

Figure 19-5: Play Ogg Vorbis and other audio files from the XMMS playlist.

> **Note** If XMMS is not able to find a configured sound card, it redirects its output to the Disk Writer plug-in. This causes the files you play to be written to hard disk as WAV files.

You can get many more audio plug-ins from `www.xmms.org`. The XMMS audio player can be used in the following way:

1. Obtain music files by ripping songs from a CD or copying them from the Web so that they are in an accessible directory, or by inserting a music CD in your CD-ROM drive. (XMMS expects the CD to be accessible from `/dev/cdrom`.)

2. From the red hat menu, select Sound & Video ⇨ Audio Player. The X Multimedia System player appears.

3. Click the Eject button. The Load files window appears.

4. If you have inserted a CD, the contents of `/mnt/cdrom` appear in the Files pane. Select the files you want to add to your Playlist and click the Add Selected Files or the Add All Files in Directory button to add all songs from the current directory. To add audio files from your file system, browse your files and directories and click the same buttons to add the audio files you want. Select Close.

5. Click the Play List button (the tiny button marked PL) on the console. A Playlist Editor window appears.

6. Double-click the music file, and it starts to play.

7. With a file selected and playing, here are a few actions you can take:

   • **Control play**—Buttons for controlling play are what you would expect to see on a standalone CD player. From left to right, the buttons let you go to a previous track, play, pause, stop, go to the next track, and eject the CD. The eject button opens a window, enabling you to load the next file.

   • **Adjust sound**—Use the left slider bar to adjust the volume. Use the right slider bar to change the right-to-left balance.

   • **Display time**—Click in the elapsed time area to toggle between elapsed time and time remaining.

- **View file information** — Click the button in the upper-left corner of the screen to see the XMMS menu. Then select View File Info. You can often find out a lot of information about the file: title, artist, album, comments, and genre. For an Ogg file, you can see specific information about the file itself, such as the format, bit rate, sample rate, frames, file size, and more. You can change or add to the tag information and click Save to keep it.

8. When you are done playing music, click the Stop button to stop the current song. Then click the X in the upper-right corner of the display to close the window.

Special features of the XMMS audio player let you adjust frequencies using a graphic equalizer and gather and play songs using a Playlist Editor. Click the button marked EQ next to the balance bar on the player to open the Equalizer.

Using the Equalizer

The Equalizer lets you use slider bars to set different levels to different frequencies played. Bars on the left adjust lower frequencies, and those on the right adjust higher frequencies. Click the EQ button to open the Equalizer. Here are tasks you can perform with the Equalizer:

✦ If you like the settings you have for a particular song, you can save them as a Preset. Set each frequency as you like it and click the Preset button. Then choose Save ➪ Preset. Type a name for the preset and click OK.

✦ To reload a preset you created earlier, click the Preset button and select Load ➪ Preset. Select the preset you want and click OK.

The small window in the center/top of the Equalizer shows the sound wave formed by your settings. You can adjust the Preamp bar on the left to boost different levels in the set range.

Using the Playlist Editor

The Playlist Editor lets you put together a list of audio files that you want to play. You can add and delete files from this list, save them to a file, and use them again later. Click the PL button in the XMMS window to open the Playlist Editor.

The Playlist Editor enables you to:

✦ **Add files to the playlist** — Click the Add button. The Load Files window appears. Select the directory containing your audio files (it's useful to keep them all in one place) from the left column. Then either select a file from the right column and click Add Selected Files or click Add All Files in the Directory. Click OK. The selected file or files appear(s) in the playlist. You can also add music files by dragging them from the Nautilus file manager onto the playlist window.

✦ **Select files to play** — To select from the files in the playlist, use the previous track and next track buttons in the main XMMS window. The selected file is highlighted. Click the Play button to play that file. Alternatively, you can double-click any file in the playlist to start it playing.

✦ **Delete files from the playlist** — To remove files from the playlist, select the file or files you want to remove (use the next track and previous track buttons), right-click the playlist window, and click Remove ⇨ Selected. The selected files are removed.

✦ **Save the playlist** — To save the current playlist, hold the right mouse button down on the List button and then select Playlist ⇨ Save List from the pop-up menu. Browse to the directory you want, and then type the name you want to assign to the playlist and click OK. The filename should end with a `.m3u` extension, such as `monkees_hits.m3u`.

✦ **Load the playlist** — To reload a saved playlist, click the List button. Select a playlist from the directory in which you saved it and click OK.

There is also a tiny set of buttons on the bottom of the Playlist Editor screen. These are the same buttons as those on the main screen used for selecting different tracks or playing, pausing, stopping, or ejecting the current track.

Using MIDI Audio Players

MIDI (Musical Instrument Digital Interface) files are created from synthesizers and other electronic music devices. They tend to be smaller than other kinds of audio files because instead of storing the complete sounds, they contain information about the notes played, tempo and articulation. You can think of a MIDI file as electronic sheet music. The MIDI player reproduces the notes to sound like a huge variety of MIDI instruments.

There are lots of sites on the Internet for downloading MIDI files. Try the Ifni MIDI Music site (`www.ifni.com`), for example, which contains songs by the Beatles, Led Zeppelin, Nirvana, and others organized by album. Most of the MIDI music is pretty simple, but you can have some fun playing with it.

Linux distributions that include the KDE desktop (such as Fedora Core) often come with the kmid MIDI player. Kmid provides a GUI interface for midi music, including the capability to display karaoke lyrics in real time. To start kmid in Fedora, select Sound & Video ⇨ KMid (or type **kmid &** from a Terminal window).

Performing Audio File Conversion and Compression

There are many different formats for storing and compressing speech and music files. Because music files can be large, they are usually stored in a compressed format. While MP3 has been the compression format of choice, Ogg Vorbis is quickly becoming a favorite for compressing music in the open source community. Ogg Vorbis has the added benefit of not being encumbered by patents as MP3 is.

Tools that come with Fedora Core for converting and compressing audio files include:

- ✦ sox **(SoX)** — A general-purpose tool for converting audio files among a variety of formats.
- ✦ oggenc — A tool for specifically converting music files to Ogg Vorbis format.

Converting Audio Files with SoX

If you have a sound file in one format, but you want it to be in another format, Linux offers some conversion tools. The SoX utility can translate to and from any of the audio formats listed in Table 19-1.

 Tip Type **sox -h** to see the supported audio types, as well as supported options and effects.

Table 19-1
Sound Formats Supported by SoX Utility

File Extension or Pseudonym	Description	File Extension or Pseudonym	Description
.8svx	8SVX Amiga musical instrument description format.	.aiff	Apple IIc/IIgs and SGI AIFF files. May require a separate archiver to work with these files.
.au, .snd	Sun Microsystems AU audio files. This was once a popular format. The .snd extension is ambiguous because it's also been used on NeXT format and headerless Mac/PC format.)	.avr	Audio Visual Research format, used on the Mac.
.cdr	CD-R files used to master compact disks.	.cvs	Continuously variable slope delta modulation, which is used for voice mail and other speech compression.
.dat	Text data files, which contain a text representation of sound data.	.gsm	Lossy Speech Compression (GSM 06.10), used to shrink audio data in voice mail and similar applications.

File Extension or Pseudonym	Description	File Extension or Pseudonym	Description
.hcom	Macintosh HCOM files.	.maud	Amiga format used to produce sound that is 8-bit linear, 16-bit linear, A-law, and u-law in mono or stereo.
.ogg	Ogg Vorbis compressed audio, which is best used for compressing music and streaming audio.	.ossdsp	Pseudo file, used to open the OSS /dev/dsp file and configure it to use the data type passed to SoX. Used to either play or record.
.prc	Psion record.app format, newer than the WVE format.	.sf	IRCAM sound files, used by CSound package and MixView sample editor.
.sph	Speech audio SPHERE (Speech Header Resources) format from NIST (National Institute of Standards and Technology).	.smp	SampleVision files from Turtle Beach, used to communicate with different MIDI samplers.
.sunau	Pseudo file, used to open a /dev/audio file and set it to use the data type being passed to SoX.	.txw	Yamaha TX-16W from a Yamaha sampling keyboard.
.vms	Used to compress speech audio for voice mail and similar applications.	.voc	Sound Blaster VOC file.
.wav	Microsoft WAV RIFF files. This is the native Microsoft Windows sound format.	.wve	8-bit, a-law, 8 KHz sound files used with Psion Palmtop computers.
.raw	Raw files (contain no header information, so sample rate, size, and style must be given).	.ub, .sb, .uw, .sw, .ul, .al, .lu, .la, .sl	Raw files with set characteristics. ub is unsigned byte; sb is signed byte; uw is unsigned word; sw is signed word; and ul is u-law.

If you are not sure about the format of an audio file, you can add the .auto extension to the filename. This triggers SoX to guess what kind of audio format is contained in the file. The .auto extension can only be used for the input file. If SoX can figure out the content of the input file, it translates the contents to the sound type for the output file you request.

In its most basic form, you can convert one file format (such as a WAV file) to another format (such as an AU file) as follows:

```
$ sox file1.wav file1.au
```

To see what SoX is doing, use the -V option. For example:

```
$ sox -V file1.wav file1.voc

sox: Reading Wave file: Microsoft PCM format, 2 channel, 44100 samp/sec
sox: 176400 byte/sec, 4 block align, 16 bits/samp, 50266944 data bytes
sox: Input file: using sample rate 11025
        size bytes, style unsigned, 1 channel
sox: Input file1.wav: comment "file1.wav"

sox: Output file1.voc: using sample rate 44100
        size shorts, encoding signed (2's complement), 2 channels
sox: Output file: comment "file1.wav"
```

You can apply sound effects during the SoX conversion process. The following example shows how to change the sample rate (using the -r option) from 10,000 KHz to 5,000 KHz:

```
$ sox -r 10000 file1.wav -r 5000 file1.voc
```

To reduce the noise, you can send the file through a low-pass filter. Here's an example:

```
$ sox file1.voc file2.voc lowp 2200
```

For more information on SoX and to get the latest download, go to the SoX — Sound eXchange — home page (www.sourceforge.net/projects/sox/).

Compressing Music Files with oggenc

The oggenc command takes music or other audio data and converts it from uncompressed formats (such as WAV, RAW, or AIFF) to the compressed Ogg Vorbis format. Using Ogg Vorbis, audio files can be significantly reduced in size without a noticeable loss of sound quality. (I used the default settings in oggenc and reduced a 48MB WAV music file to 4MB.)

In its most basic form, you can use oggenc with one or more WAV or AIFF files following it. For example:

```
$ oggenc *.wav
```

This command would result in all files ending with .wav in the current directory to be converted to Ogg Vorbis format. An OGG file is produced for each WAV file, with oggenc substituting .ogg for .wav as the file suffix for the compressed file. Ogg Vorbis files can be played in many different audio players in Linux, including the XMMS player (described earlier).

Tip

If you want to rip music files from a CD and compress them, you can use the Grip window (described later in this chapter). Grip enables you to select oggenc as the tool to do the file compression.

If you're are interested in making a CD jukebox that rips, records, and compresses music CDs using oggenc and other open source software, check out the book *Linux Toys* by Christopher Negus and Chuck Wolber from Wiley Publishing.

Recording and Ripping Music

Writable CD-ROM drives are a standard device on computers. Where once you had to settle for a floppy disk (1.44MB) or a Zip disk (100MB) to store personal data, a CD-ROM burner lets you store more than 600MB of data in a format that can be exchanged with most computers. On top of that, you can create CD music disks!

Both graphical and command-line tools exist for creating CDs on Linux. The cdrecord command enables you to create audio and data CDs from the command line, writing to CD-recordable (CD-R) and CD-rewritable (CD-RW) drives. This command is discussed in the following section.

Creating an Audio CD with cdrecord

You can use the cdrecord command to create either data or music CDs. You can create a data CD by setting up a separate file system and copying the whole image of that file system to CD. Creating an audio CD consists of selecting the audio tracks you want to copy and copying them all at once to the CD.

This section focuses on using cdrecord to create audio CDs. cdrecord can use audio files in .au, .wav, and .cdr formats, automatically translating them when necessary. If you have audio files in other formats, you can convert them to one of the supported formats by using the sox command (described previously in this chapter).

One way to create an audio CD is to use cdda2wav to extract (copy) the music tracks to a directory and then use cdrecord to write them from the directory to the CD. Here's an example:

Note

If you prefer a graphical tool for copying and burning CDs and DVDs, refer to Appendix A, which describes how to use the K3B CD Kreator for burning CD images. That tool can also be used for copying audio CDs.

1. Create a directory to hold the audio files, and change to that directory. (Make sure the directory can hold up to 660MB of data—less if you are burning fewer songs.) For example:

```
# mkdir /tmp/cd
# cd /tmp/cd
```

2. Insert the music CD into your CD-ROM drive. (If a CD player opens on the desktop, close it.)

3. Extract the music tracks you want by using the cdda2wav command. For example:

```
# cdda2wav -D /dev/cdrom -B
```

This reads all of the music tracks from the CD-ROM drive. The -B option says to output each track to a separate file. By default, the cdda2wav command outputs the files to the WAV audio format.

Instead of extracting all songs, you can choose a single track or a range of tracks to extract. For example, to extract tracks 3 through 5, add the -t3+5 option. To extract just track 9, add -t9+9. To extract track 7 through the end of the CD, add -t7.

Note If you have a low-quality CD drive or an imperfect CD, cdda2wav might not be the best ripping tool. You might try cdparanoia -B to extract songs from the CD to hard disk instead.

4. When cdda2wav is done, insert a blank CD into your writable CD drive.

5. Use the cdrecord command to write the music tracks to the CD. For example:

```
# cdrecord -v dev=/dev/cdrom -audio *.wav
```

The options to cdrecord tell the command to create an audio CD (-audio) on the writable CD device located at /dev/cdrom. cdrecord writes all .wav files from the current directory. The -v option causes verbose output.

6. If you want to change the order of the tracks, you can type their names in the order you want them written (instead of using *.wav). If your CD writer supports higher speeds, you can use the speed option to double (speed=2) or to quadruple (speed=4) the writing speed.

After you have created the music CD, indicate the contents of the CD on its label side. It's now ready to play on any standard music CD player.

Ripping CDs with Grip

For GNOME users, the Grip window provides a more graphical method of copying music from CDs to your hard disk so that you can play the songs directly from your hard disk or burn them back onto a blank CD. Besides just ripping music, you can also compress each song as you extract it from the CD.

You can open Grip from the red hat menu by selecting Sound & Video ➪ Grip (or by typing **grip** from a Terminal window). Figure 19-6 shows an example of the Grip window.

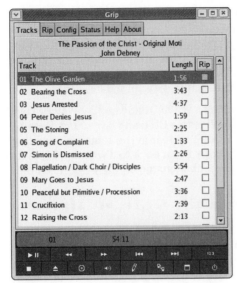

Figure 19-6: Rip and play songs from the Grip window.

To rip audio tracks from a CD with `grip`, do the following:

1. With the Grip window open, insert a music CD into your CD drive. If you have an active connection to the Internet and the CD is known to the CD database, the title, artist, and track information appear in the window.

2. Click each track that you want to rip (that is, copy to your hard disk). A check mark appears in that track's Rip column.

3. Click the Config tab at the top of the page, and then select Encode.

4. You can choose the type of encoder used to compress the music by clicking the Encoder box and selecting an encoder (by default, `oggenc` compresses files in Ogg Vorbis, assuming that Ogg Vorbis was installed on your Linux distribution).

5. Click the Rip tab at the top of the page.

6. Click one of the following:

   • **Rip+Encode** — This rips the selected songs and (if you left in the default oggenc compression in step 4) compresses them in Ogg Vorbis format. You need an Ogg Vorbis player to play the songs after they have been ripped in this format (there are many Ogg Vorbis players for Linux).

   • **Rip only** — This rips the selected songs in WAV format. You can use a standard CD player to play these songs. (When I tried this, the same song ripped in WAV was 12 times larger than the Ogg Vorbis file.)

Songs are copied to the hard disk in the format you selected. By default, the files are copied into a subdirectory of $HOME/ogg (such as /home/jake/ogg). The subdirectory is named for the artist and CD. For example, if the user jake were ripping the song called "High Life" by the artist Mumbo, the directory containing ripped songs would be /home/jake/ogg/mumbo/high_life. Each song file is named for the song (for example, fly_fly_fly.wav).

7. Now you can play any of the files using a player that can play WAV or Ogg files, such as XMMS. Or you can copy the files to a CD using cdrecord. Because the filenames are the song names, they don't appear in the same order as they appear on the CD, so if you want to copy them back to a writable CD in their original order, you may have to type each filename on the cdrecord command line. For example:

```
# cdrecord -v dev=/dev/cdrom -audio fly_fly.wav big_news.wav
about_time.wav
```

The Grip window can also be used to play CDs. Use the buttons on the bottom of the display to play or pause, skip ahead or back, stop, and eject the CD. The toggle track display button lets you shrink the size of the display so it takes up less space on the desktop. Click toggle disc editor to see and change title, artist, and track information.

Creating CD Labels with cdlabelgen

The cdlabelgen command can be used to create tray cards and front cards to fit in CD jewel cases. You gather information about the CD and cdlabelgen produces a PostScript output file that you can send to the printer. The cdlabelgen package also comes with graphics (in /usr/share/cdlabelgen) that you can incorporate into your labels.

Here's an example of a cdlabelgen command line that will generate a CD label file in PostScript format (type it all on one line or use backslashes, as shown, to put it on multiple lines):

```
cdlabelgen -c "Grunge is Gone" -s "Yep HipHop" \
-i "If You Feed Me%Sockin Years%City Road%Platinum and Copper%Fly Fly \
Fly%Best Man Spins%What A Headache%Stayin Put Feelin%Dreams Do Go \
Blue%Us%Mildest Schemes" -o yep.ps
```

In this example, the title of the CD is indicated by -c "Grunge is Gone" and the artist by the -s "Yep HipHop" option. The tracks are entered after the -i option, with each line separated by a % sign. The output file is sent to the file yep.ps with the -o option. To view and print the results, use the ggv command like this:

```
$ ggv yep.ps
```

The results of this example are shown in Figure 19-7.

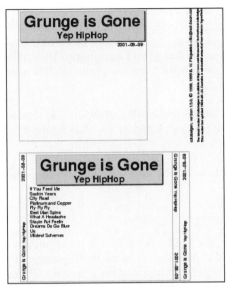

Figure 19-7: Generate CD jewel case labels with cdlabelgen and print them with ggv.

You'll want to edit the cdlabelgen command line to include the title and song names for the CD label and rerun ggv a few times to get the label correct. When you are ready to print the label, click Print All to print the label.

Working with TV, Video, and Digital Imaging

Getting TV cards, Webcams, and other video devices to play in Linux is still a bit of an adventure. Most manufacturers of TV cards and Webcams are not losing sleep to produce Linux drivers. As a result, most of the drivers that bring video to your Linux desktop have been reverse-engineered (that is, they were created by software engineers who watched what the video device sent and received, rather than seeing the actual code that runs the device).

The first and probably biggest trick is to get a TV card or Webcam that is supported in Linux. Once you are getting video output from that device (typically available from /dev/video0), you can try out a couple of applications to begin using it.

This section explores the tvtime program for watching television and the GnomeMeeting program for video conferencing.

Watching TV with Tvtime

The tvtime program (`tvtime` command) enables you to display video output—television channels, in particular—on your desktop. You can change the channels, adjust volume, and fine-tune your picture. In addition, tvtime sports a slick onscreen display and support for a widescreen display.

Note   Tvtime will not display output from some low-quality Webcams. To use your Webcam, consider obtaining the xawtv package, which is available for most Linux distributions.

The following sections describe how to choose a TV capture card and use tvtime to watch television on your desktop.

Getting a Supported TV Card

Video4Linux (V4l/V4l2) is the video interface available for Linux. It supports a variety of TV capture cards and cameras, and is included in some distributions. If your distribution does not include V4l or V4L2, you can install it on your own, although it is not the easiest task to accomplish. For more information about obtaining and installing V4l and the appropriate driver, visit `http://linux.bytesex.org/v4l2/index.html`.

To see a list of supported TV cards that you can use with tvtime, refer to the `CARDLIST` and `Cards` files of your V4l installation. To view these files, you need to have the kernel-source package installed. You'll find the `Cards` file in `/usr/src/linux*/Documentation/video4linux/bttv/Cards` on your Linux system. The `Cards` file applies to the Video4Linux bttv driver. In addition, look at all files starting with `CARDLIST` in `/usr/src/linux*/Documentation/video4linux/CARDLIST*`.

Video4Linux is designed to autodetect your TV capture card and load the proper modules to activate it. Install the TV-card hardware (with the appropriate connection to your TV reception), boot Linux, and run the `tvtime` command as described in the next section. You should see video displayed on your tvtime window.

If your card doesn't appear to be working, here are a few things you can try:

✦ Check that your TV card was properly seated in its slot and detected by Linux, by typing:

```
$ /sbin/lspci
```

This shows you a list of all valid PCI cards on your computer. If your card doesn't show up, you probably have a hardware problem.

✦ It is possible that the card is there but that the right card type is not being detected. Improper detection is most likely if you have a card for which there are several revisions, with each requiring a different driver. If you think your card is not being properly detected, find your card in the CARDLIST files. Then add the appropriate line to the /etc/modprobe.conf file. For example, to add a Prolink PV-BT878P, revision 9B card, add the following line to the file:

```
options   bttv   card=72
```

✦ You can also add other options listed in the Insmod-options file for the bttv driver. If you are still having problems getting your card to work, a mailing list is available on which you can ask questions about Video4Linux issues: http://listman.redhat.com/mailman/listinfo/video4linux-list. While this list is for Red Hat specifically, the information is germane to most distributions.

One possible reason that you don't see any video when you try to run tvtime or other video applications is that some other person or video application already has the video driver open. Only one application can use the video driver at a time. Another quirk of video4linux is that the first person to open the device on your system becomes the owner. So you might need to open the permissions of the driver to allow people other than the first person to use it to access the video4linux driver.

Running Tvtime

To start up the tvtime viewer, simply select TVtime Televison Viewer from the Sound & Video or Multimedia menu (depending on your Linux distribution), or type the following from a Terminal window on your desktop:

```
$ tvtime &
```

A video screen should appear in a window on the desktop. Click on the window to see a list of stations. Right-click to see the onscreen Setup menu.

Here are a few things you can now do with your tvtime onscreen display:

✦ **Configure input** — Change the video source, choose the television standard (which defaults to NTSC for the U.S.), and change the resolution of the input.

✦ **Set up the picture** — Adjust the brightness, contrast, color, and hue.

✦ **Adjust the video processing** — Control the attempted frame rate, configure the deinterlacer, or add an input filter.

✦ **Adjust output** — Control the aspect ratio (for 16:9 output, for example), apply a matte, or set the overscan mode.

Videoconferencing with GnomeMeeting

The GnomeMeeting window lets you communicate with other people over a network through video, audio, and typed messages. Because GnomeMeeting supports the H323 protocol (a standard for multimedia communications), you can use it to communicate with people using other popular videoconferencing clients, such as Microsoft NetMeeting, Cu-SeeMe, and Intel VideoPhone.

Note   GnomeMeeting does not support the NetMeeting shared whiteboard functions, just videoconferencing.

To be able to send video, you need a Webcam that is supported in Linux—you'll find a few dozen models from which to choose. The following sections show you how to set up your Webcam and use GnomeMeeting for videoconferencing.

Getting a Supported Webcam

As with support for TV capture cards, Webcam support is provided through the video4linux interface. To see if your Webcam is supported, check the /usr/src/linux*/Documentation directory. A few parallel-port video cameras are described in the video4linux subdirectory; however, the bulk of the supported cameras are listed in the usb directory.

Tip   After doing some research, I purchased a Logitech QuickCam Pro 3000. The driver for this Webcam was made for a Philips USB Webcam, but it also works for Webcams from Logitech, Samsung, Creative Labs, and Askey. Before making the purchase, I checked out the driver's description at www.smcc.demon.nl/webcam.

Supported USB cameras should be autodetected, so that when you plug them in, the necessary modules are loaded automatically. Just start up GnomeMeeting (gnomemeeting command), and you should see video from your Webcam on your Linux desktop.

You can check to see that your Webcam is working properly by typing the following:

```
# lsmod
pwc                43392      1
videodev            5120      2  [pwc]
usbcore            59072      1  [audio pwc usb-uhci]
```

The output from lsmod shows that the pwc driver is loaded and associated with the videodev module and usbcore module.

Opening Your Firewall for GnomeMeeting

You need to open a variety of ports in your firewall to use GnomeMeeting. In particular, you need to open TCP port 1720 and TCP port range 30000 to 30010. For UDP ports, you must open ports 5000 through 5007 and ports 5010 through 5013. Examples of exact iptables settings you can use to open these ports are contained in the GnomeMeeting FAQ (www.gnomemeeting.org/index.php?rub=3).

Running GnomeMeeting

To start GnomeMeeting from a Terminal window, type **gnomemeeting &.** If it is not installed, you can get the package for your Linux distribution when you install the GNOME desktop. The first time you run GnomeMeeting, the GnomeMeeting Configuration Assistant starts, enabling you to enter the following information:

✦ **Personal Data**—Your first name, last name, e-mail address, comment, and location. You can also choose whether you want to be listed in the GnomeMeeting ILS directory.

✦ **Connection Type**—Indicate the speed of your Internet connection (56K modem, ISDN, DSL/Cable, T1/LAN, or Custom).

Once you have entered the data, the GnomeMeeting window opens.

Figure 19-8 shows the GnomeMeeting window with the call log to the right. Select Tools ⇨ Calls History to open that log. It shows a history of the calls you make during this session. To open the Address book, select the address book icon from the left side of the GnomeMeeting window. Add ILS servers and friends to that window, and then select the user or server you want to contact and click Contact ⇨ Call Contact.

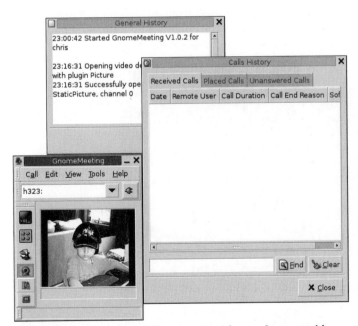

Figure 19-8: Connect to ILS servers to videoconference with GnomeMeeting.

Use the tabs beneath the video window to adjust your audio levels and video appearance. The History tab shows a log of your activities.

Watching Movies and Video

Although several fairly high quality video players are available for Linux, it is rare to see the players included in formal distributions because of legal complications. The issues surrounding the playing of encoded DVD movies in Linux might be responsible for keeping players such as the MPlayer (`freshmeat.net/mplayer`), Ogle (`http://.dtek.chalmers.se/groups/dvd`), and xine (`xine.source forge.net`) video players out of common distributions.

By most accounts, however, you can get and use these video players to play a variety of video content for personal use as long as you don't download and use the DeCCS (software for decrypting DVD movies). The following sections provide descriptions of some commonly used video players.

Watching Video with Xine

The xine player is an excellent application for playing a variety of video and audio formats. You can get xine from `xine.sourceforge.net` or from software repositories associated with your Linux distribution.

You can start the xine player by typing **xine&** from a Terminal window. Figure 19-9 shows an example of the xine video player window and controls.

Figure 19-9: Play video CDs, MP3s, QuickTime, and other video formats with xine.

Note   When you try to install xine, it tells you if you need any additional packages. If your xine player fails to start, see the "Xine Tips" section later in this chapter.

Xine supports a bunch of video and audio formats, including:

✦ MPEG (1, 2, and 4)

✦ QuickTime (see "Xine Tips" if your QuickTime content won't play)

✦ WMV

✦ DVDs, CDs, and VCDs

✦ Motion JPEG

✦ MPEG audio (MP3)

✦ AC3 and Dolby Digital audio

✦ DTS audio

✦ Ogg Vorbis audio

Xine understands different file formats that represent a combination of audio and video, including `.mpg` (MPEG program streams), `.ts` (MPEG transport streams), `.mpv` (raw MPEG audio/video streams), `.avi` (MS AVI format), and `.asf` (Advanced Streaming format). While xine can play Video CDs and DVDs, it can't play encrypted DVDs or the Video-on-CD hybrid format (because of legal issues mentioned earlier related to decrypting DVDs).

Using Xine

With xine started, right-click in the xine window to see the controls. The quickest way to play video is to click one of the following buttons, and then press the Play button (right arrow or Play, depending on the skin you are using):

✦ VCD (for a video CD)

✦ DVD (for a DVD in `/dev/dvd`)

✦ CDA (for a music CD in `/dev/cdaudio`)

Next, you can use the Pause/Resume, Stop, Play, Fast Motion, Slow Motion, or Eject buttons to work with video. You can also use the Previous and Next buttons to step to different tracks. The controls are very similar to what you would expect on a physical CD or DVD player.

To select individual files, or to put together your own list of content to play, use the Playlist feature.

Creating Playlists with Xine

Click the Playlist button on the left side of the xine control window. A Playlist Editor appears, showing the files on your current playlist. You can add and delete content and then save the list to call on later.

Xine content is identified as media resource locators (MRLs). Each MRL is identified as a file, DVD, or VCD. Files are in the regular file path (`/path/file`) or preceded by `file:/`, `fifo:/`, or `stdin:/`. DVDs and VCDs are preceded by `dvd` and `vcd`, respectively (for example, `vcd://01`).

Here's what the xine Playlist Editor buttons do:

Button	Description
CDA, DVD, or VCD	All content from that CD or DVD is added to the playlist.
Add	See the MRL Browser window. From that window, click File to choose a file from your Linux file system, and then click Select to add that file to the Playlist Editor. (MRL stands for Media Resource Locator, which defines the form in which remote and local content are identified.)
Move Up Selected MRL Move Down Selected MRL	Move up and down the playlist.
Play	Play the contents of the playlist.
Delete Selected MRL	Remove the current selection.
Delete All Entries	Clear the whole playlist.
Save	Save the playlist to your home directory (`$HOME/.xine/playlist`).
Load	Read in your (saved) playlist.

Xine Tips

Getting video and audio to work properly can sometimes be a tricky business. Here are a few quick tips if you are having trouble getting xine to work correctly (or at all):

✦ **Xine won't start** — To work best, xine needs an X driver that supports xvid. If there is no xvid support for your video card in X, xine shuts down immediately when it tries to open the default Xv driver. If this happens to you, try starting xine with the X11 video driver (which is slower, but should work) as follows:

```
$ xine -VXSHM
```

✦ **Xine playback is choppy** — If playback of files from your hard disk is choppy, there are a couple of settings you can check: 32-bit IO and DMA, features that, if supported by your hard disk, generally improve hard disk performance. Here's how to check:

 Caution

Improper disk settings can result in destroyed data on your hard disk. Perform this procedure at your own risk. This procedure is only for IDE hard drives (no SCSI)! Also, be sure to have a current backup and no activity on your hard disk if you change DMA or IO settings as described in this section.

1. First, test the speed of hard disk reads. To test the first IDE drive (/dev/hda), type:

```
# hdparm -t /dev/hda
Timing buffered disk reads: 64 MB in 19.31 seconds = 3.31
MB/sec
```

2. To see your current DMA and IO settings, as root user type:

```
# hdparm -c -d /dev/hda
/dev/hda:
 I/O support = 0 (default 16-bit)
 using_dma   = 0 (off)
```

3. This result shows that both 32-bit IO and DMA are off. To turn them on, type:

```
# hdparm -c 1 -d 1 /dev/hda
/dev/hda:
 I/O support = 1 (32-bit)
 using_dma   = 1 (on)
```

4. With both settings on, test the disk again:

```
# hdparm -t /dev/hda
Timing buffered disk reads: 64 MB in 2.2 seconds = 28.83
MB/sec
```

In this example, buffered disk reads of 64MB went from 19.31 seconds to 2.2 seconds after changing the parameters described. Playback would be much better now.

✦ **Xine won't play particular media** — Messages such as no input plug-in mean that either the file format you are trying to play is not supported or it requires an additional plug-in (as is the case with playing DVDs). If the message is maybe xyx is a broken file, the file may be a proprietary version of an otherwise supported format. For example, I had a QuickTime video fail that required an SVQ3 codec (which is currently not supported under Linux), although other QuickTime files played fine.

Using Helix Player and RealPlayer 10

A tremendous amount of content is available on the Internet in the RealMedia and RealAudio formats. You can see and hear video clips of popular musicians and comics; view live events, such as conferences, news stories, and concerts; and listen to your favorite radio stations when you are out of town.

To play RealMedia and RealAudio content you need, as you may have guessed, RealPlayer. Real Networks (www.real.com) is a leader in streaming media on the Internet. More than 50 million unique users have registered with Real Networks and its Web site, downloading more than 175,000 files per day. And that's not even the good news. The good news is that RealPlayer is available to run in Fedora Core.

RealPlayer 10 for Linux is available via the Linux area of www.download.com and www.tucows.com and at http://proforma.real.com/real/player/unix/unix.html. This player is not supported by Real Networks directly. In addition, Real has opened up the source code to the RealPlayer under the name Helix Player. Fedora Core 3 (on the DVD included with this book) includes a prereleased version of the Helix Player that you can try out.

The instructions for configuring RealPlayer are delivered in HTML format, so you can read it in Mozilla or some other Web browser. If any patches or workarounds are required, you can find them by querying for the word "Linux" in the Real Networks Knowledge Base. To get there, click Support (from most Real Networks pages), and then click Knowledge Base.

When you install RealPlayer, you are asked if you want to configure it to be used as a Netscape plug-in (which I recommend so that you can play real content in Mozilla). After that, when you open any Real content in your browser, RealPlayer opens to handle it. Alternatively, you can start RealPlayer from a Terminal window on your desktop by typing the following:

```
$ realplay &
```

Real Networks has gone to a subscription model for its content (you sign up and pay a monthly fee). To see what's available, and to decide if it is worth signing up, I suggest starting at the RealGuide site (www.realguide.real.com), which includes a few clips you can try out.

Using a Digital Camera with Gtkam and gPhoto2

With the gtkam window, you can download and work with images from digital cameras. The gtkam window is a front end to gPhoto2, which provides support for dozens of digital cameras in Linux. The gtkam window works by attaching a supported digital camera to a serial or USB port on your computer. You can view thumbnails of the digital images from the camera, view full-size images, and download the ones you select from the camera to your hard disk.

Note   If you have a camera that saves images to a floppy disk, just insert that disk into your disk drive and the contents of the disk should open automatically on your desktop. In addition, if your camera saves images to SD or CF cards, you can purchase a USB card reader and view these files from Linux.

Check the gPhoto2 Web site (`www.gphoto.org/proj/libgphoto2/support.php`) for information on supported cameras as well as other topics related to gPhoto. Including experimental units and cameras under testing, there are 433 supported cameras. Here is a list of currently supported digital cameras.

Brand	Supported Model(s)
AEG	Snap 300
Agfa ePhoto	307, 780, 780C, 1280, 1680, and CL18
Aiptek	PalmCam Trio and PenCam Trio
Apple QuickTake	200
Argus	DC-100, DC-1500, DC-1510, DC-2000, and DC-2200
Barbie	
Canon	IXY Digital, IXY Digital 300, MV630i, MVX2i, Optura 10, Optura 20, Optura 200 MC, and ZR70MC
Canon Digital	IXUS, IXUS 2, IXUS 300, IXUS 330, IXUS 400, IXUS i, IXUS II, IXUS v, IXUS v2, and IXUS v3
Canon EOS	10D, 300D, D30, Digital Rebel, and Kiss Digital
Canon PowerShot	A5, A5 Zoom, A10, A20, A50, A60, A70, A80, A100, A200, A300, G1, G2, G3, G5, Pro70, Pro90 IS, S10, S20, S30, S40, S45, S50, S100, S110, S200, S210, S300, S400, and SD100
Casio QV	10, 10A, 11, 30, 70, 100, 200, 700, and 5000SX
Chinon	ES-1000
CoolCam	CP086
Digitaldream	200, l'elegante, l'elite, l'espion, l'esprit, and la ronde
Dynatron	Dynacam 800
Epson PhotoPC	300z, 500, 550, 600, 700, 800, and 850z
Fuji	ix-100, DS-7, DX-5, DX-10, IX-1, MX-500, MX-600, MX-700, MX-1200, MX-1700, MX-2700, and MX-2900

Continued

Brand	Supported Model(s)
Generic Soundvision	Clarity2
Hawking	DC120
Hot Wheels	
Hewlett-Packard PhotoSmart	618, 912, C20, C30, C200, C500, 120, 318, 320, 43x, 612, 620, 715, 720, 812, 850, and 935
IOMagic	400 and 420
Jentoptik	JD11 and JD12 800ff
KBGear	JamCam
Kodak DC	CX4200, CX4210, CX4230, CX4300, CX6200, CX6230, CX6330, DC120, DC220, DC240, DC260, DC265, DC280, DC290, DC3200, DC3400, DC4800, DC5000, DX3215, DX3500, DX3600, DX3700, DX3900, DX4330, DX4530, DX4900, DX6340, DX6440, DX6490, LS420, LS443, LS663, and MC3
Konica	e-mini, Q-EZ, Q-M100, Q-M100V, and Q-M200
Leica	Digilux Zoom
Media-Tech	mt-406
Minolta	Dimage V
Mustek	VDC-3500
Nicon CoolPix	100, 300, 600, 700, 800, 880, 900, 900S, 910, 950, 950S, 990, 995, 2000, 2100, 2500, 3100, 3500, 4300, 4500, 5000, 5400, 5700, and SQ
Olympus	D-100Z, D-200L, D-220L, D-300L, D-320L, D-330R, D-340L, D-340R, D-360L, D-400L Zoom, D-450Z, D-460Z, D-500L, D-560Z, D-600L, D-600XL, D-620L, C-350Z, C-400, C-400L, C-410, C-410L, C-420, C-420L, C-800, C-800L, C-820, C-820L, C-830L, C-840L, C-860L, C-900 Zoom, C-900L Zoom, C-1000L, C-1400L, C-1400XL, C-2000Z, C-2020Z, C-2040Z, C-21000UZ, C-2500L, C-3000Z, C-3020Z, C-3030Z, C-3040Z, and X-250
Oregon Scientific	DShot II and DShot III
Panasonic	Coolshot KXL-600A and KXL-601A, and NV-DCF5E, DC1000, DC1580, PV-L691, and PV-L859
Pencam	Tevion MD 9456
Philips	ESP2, ESP50, ESP60, ESP70, ESP80, and ESP80SXG
Polaroid	PDC 640, PDC 2300Z, and DC700
Ricoh RDC	300, 300Z, 4200, 4300, and 5000

Brand	Supported Model(s)
Samsung	Kenox SSC-350N and Digimax 800K
Sanyo	DSC-X300, DSC-X350, VPC-G200, VPC-G210, VPC-G200EX, and VPC-G250
Sony	DSC-F1, DSC-F55, DSC-F707V, DSC-P30, DSC-P31, DSC-P32, DSC-P5, DSC-P50, DSC-P52, DSC-P72, DSC-P92, DSC-S75, DSC-S85, DSC-U20, DSC-V1, Memory Stick Adapter, MSAC-SR1, and DCR-PC100
Toshiba	PDR-M1

New cameras are added frequently, so check the support page if you do not see your camera listed.

Downloading Digital Photos with Gtkam

The following procedure describes how to download images from your digital camera.

1. Using a cable provided with your digital camera, connect your camera to the USB or COM port on your computer (I had better luck with the USB port).

2. Set your camera to Send and Receive mode.

3. From the main menu on your desktop, choose Graphics ⇨ Digital Camera Tool. The gtkam window appears.

4. Click Camera ⇨ Add Camera. The Select Camera window appears.

5. Click the down arrow next to the Model box, select your camera, and click Detect.

6. Click Apply, and then click OK. Your camera model should be listed in the gtkam window.

7. To begin downloading images from your digital camera, click the camera name that appears in the left column, and then select the folder containing the images from that camera. After the images download (which can take a while), thumbnails appear in the main gtkam.

8. Select the images that interest you, and click the Save Selected Photos button to save the selected images. The Save Photos window that appears lets you choose a directory to save them to. You can rename the images or just use the names assigned by the camera.

9. Choose images you want to delete, and click the Delete button.

Using Your Camera as a Storage Device

Some digital cameras let you treat them like a storage device to manage pictures. By mounting a digital camera as a USB mass storage device, you can view, copy, delete, and move the pictures on your camera as you would files on a hard disk or CD (just at a lower speed).

The following list is a partial summary of digital cameras that can be used as a USB storage device:

Brand	Supported Models
Casio	Supported modelsQV-2400UX, QV-2x00, QV-3x00, QV-4000 and QV-8000
Fuji	FinePix 1300, 1400Zoom, 2300Zoom, 2400Zoom, 2800Zoom, 4200Z, 4500, 4700 Zoom, 4900 Zoom, 6800 Zoom, A101, A201, and S1 Pro
HP	PhotoSmart 315, 318xi, 618, and C912
Konica	KD200Z, KD400Z, and Revio KD300Z
Kyocera	Finecam s3
Leica	Digilux 4.3
Minolta	Dimage 5, Dimage 7, and Dimage X
Nikon	CoolPix 2500, 885, 5000, 775, and 995
Olympus	Brio Zoom D-15, C-100, C-200Z, C-2040, C-220Z, C-2Z, C-3020Z, C-3040Z, C-4040Zoom, C-700, C-700UZ, C-860L, D-510, D-520Z, E-10, and E-20
Pentax	EI2000, Optio 330, and Optio 430
Sony	DSC-F505, DSC-F505V, DSC-F707, DSC-P1, DSC-P20, DSC-P5, DSC-P71, DSC-S30, DSC-S70, DSC-S75, DSC-S85, MVC-CD300, and MVC-FD92
Vivitar	Vivicam 3550
Yashica	Finecam s3

To Linux, the USB mass storage camera appears as a SCSI drive containing a VFAT file system with image files on it. Here's a procedure for using your digital camera as a USB storage device:

1. Use the cable provided with your digital camera to connect your camera to a USB port on your computer, and turn the camera on so it is ready to send and receive data.

2. Boot your computer.

3. Open the /etc/fstab file as root user and see if an entry was created for your digital camera. If you have no other SCSI devices on your computer, the camera is probably detected as /dev/sda1 device. Here's what the entry might look like:

```
/dev/sda1    /mnt/camera    auto    defaults, user,noauto    0 0
```

If no such entry appears, create the entry. Create the mount point directory (as root user, type **mkdir /mnt/camera**).

4. As root user, type the command to mount the camera: **mount /mnt/camera**.

5. Open the /mnt/camera directory as you would any other directory from the shell or from a file manager. Copy, delete, move, and rename files as you would any files on your hard disk.

6. When you are done, unmount the camera (as root user from a Terminal window):

```
# umount /mnt/camera
```

Caution   If you unplug your camera without unmounting the file system, it could damage the files on your camera.

You can follow this procedure to use other USB mass storage devices (CD drives, keychains, and so on) in Linux. Use different mount directories (such as /mnt/keychain) and check which SCSI device is being assigned to the USB storage device.

To see if your USB storage device can be seen by Linux, check the /var/log/dmesg file or run the usbview command. Either will tell you if the device is being detected properly by Linux.

Summary

Getting up and running with digital media can take some doing, but once it's set up, you can play most audio and video content that is available today. This chapter takes you through the steps of setting up and troubleshooting your sound card and explains how to find software to play music through that card.

Every desktop Linux distribution comes with one or more ways of playing music from files or CDs. Popular music players include XMMS and Rhythmbox. Tools for ripping and recording CDs include grip and command-line utilities such as cdda2wav and cdrecord.

Also explained was playing live video from TV cards and Webcams in the sections on tvtime and GnomeMeeting, respectively. Finally, you saw how the xine player could be used to play a variety of video formats and explored the gtkam window for downloading images from a digital camera. If your computer has a CD burner, use the descriptions in this chapter to create your own music CDs and CD labels.

✦   ✦   ✦

Working with Words and Images

Computers are great for collecting and recording music, playing games, and communicating with far-off lands. While these functions are popular and exciting, there is one tool that has been considered essential since the earliest days of personal computers: document-creating applications. From ultrasimple text-only editors to feature-rich groupware systems, you'll be hard-pressed to find a PC without this basic functionality. This software is so important that Microsoft has made billions of dollars each year selling productivity tools for the Windows OS.

Linux users are, on most levels, no different than any other PC user. They need to write letters, make presentations, write books, and sort information in spreadsheets. For the Linux user, a copy of Microsoft Office is simply not in the cards yet, but there are many powerful tools from which to choose. OpenOffice.org, for example, is a powerful open source office suite available as a download and as part of many Linux distributions. Based on the Sun Microsystem's StarOffice productivity suite, OpenOffice.org includes a word processor, spreadsheet program, presentation manager, and other personal productivity tools. In most cases, OpenOffice.org can be a drop-in replacement for Microsoft Office.

The first document and graphics tools for Linux were mostly built on older, text-based tools. Recently, more sophisticated tools for writing, formatting pages, and integrating graphics have been added. Despite their age, many of the older publishing tools (such as Groff and LaTeX) are still used by people in the technical community.

This chapter examines both text-based and GUI-based document preparation software for Linux, and discusses tools for printing and displaying documents, as well as software for working with images.

Using OpenOffice.org

Some have called OpenOffice.org a significant threat to Microsoft's dominance of the desktop market. If a need to work with documents in Microsoft Word format has kept you from using Linux as your desktop computer, OpenOffice.org is a big step toward removing that obstacle. You can use a program such as WINE that (among other things) allows you to run older versions of Microsoft Office directly on your Linux PC, but for the vast majority of users there is no reason to bother doing so. In this section we'll take a high-level overview of the suite and spend a little time examining one of the more commonly used elements, Writer, in some detail.

Many distributions of Linux include the entire OpenOffice.org suite of desktop applications. Some include the StarOffice suite in addition to or in lieu of OpenOffice.org. If neither is present, you can always download and install OpenOffice.org from its Web site, www.openoffice.org. StarOffice is commercial software and can be purchased from www.sun.com.

OpenOffice.org, which shares its source code with StarOffice, consists of the following office-productivity applications:

✦ **Writer**—A word-processing application that can work with documents in file formats from Microsoft Word, StarOffice, and several others. Writer also has a full set of features for using templates, working with fonts, navigating your documents, including images and effects, and generating tables of contents.

✦ **Calc**—A spreadsheet application that lets you incorporate data from Microsoft Excel, StarOffice, Dbase, and several other spreadsheet formats. Some nice features in Calc enable you to create charts, set up database ranges (to easily sort data in an area of a spreadsheet), and use the data pilot tool to arrange data in different points of view.

✦ **Draw**—A drawing application that enables you to create, edit, and align objects; include textures and colors; and work with layers of objects. It lets you incorporate images, vector graphics, AutoCAD, and a variety of other file formats into your drawings. Then, you can save your drawing in the OpenOffice.org Drawing or StarDraw formats.

✦ **Math**—A calculation program that lets you create mathematical formulas.

✦ **Impress**—A presentation application that includes a variety of slide effects. You can use Impress to create and save presentations in the Microsoft PowerPoint, StarDraw, and StarImpress formats.

Unlike other applications that were created to work with Microsoft document and data formats, OpenOffice.org (although not perfect) does a very good job of opening and saving those files with fewer problems. Very basic styles and formatting that open in OpenOffice.org often don't look noticeably different from the way they appear in Microsoft Office. In other cases, such things as bullets, alignment, and indentation can appear quite different in Writer than they do in Word. Also, some Word features, such as macros and scripting features, may not work at all in Writer.

To open OpenOffice.org applications, select the relevant menu item (such as the OpenOffice Writer icon) from the system menu (K-Menu, for example). In most distributions, there's a folder called Office (or something very similar) located on the system menu as well. Figure 20-1 shows a Microsoft Word document open for editing in OpenOffice.org Writer.

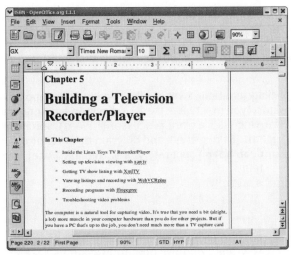

Figure 20-1: Work with Microsoft Word documents in OpenOffice.org Writer.

The controls in Writer are similar to the ones you find in Word. Toolbars include boxes for changing styles, font types, and font sizes. Buttons let you save and print the file; change the text alignment; and cut, copy, and paste text. In other words, Writer includes almost everything you expect in an advanced word processor. In addition, Writer includes a handy PDF button to output a file directly to the PDF format, which is very useful for exchanging documents or placing data on the Internet.

Note Although this book cannot cover all the OpenOffice.org applications, you can download the productivity suite from www.OpenOffice.org and try them all out for yourself. (Incidentally, the name of the suite is "OpenOffice.org" for copyright reasons associated with simply calling it "OpenOffice.")

Other Word Processors

If your distribution does not include the OpenOffice.org suite, or you just want to try something else, you have some other choices:

✦ **StarOffice** — The StarOffice productivity suite contains applications for word processing, spreadsheets, presentation graphics, e-mail, news, charting, and graphics. It was created to run on Linux systems, but it runs in other environments as well. It can import and export a variety of Microsoft file formats. StarOffice is owned by Sun Microsystems, which sells it as a commercial product.

✦ **AbiWord** — The AbiWord word processor (`abiword` command), is noncommercial software and is the first application produced by the AbiSource project (`www.abisource.com`). In addition to working with files in its own format (`.abw` and `.zabw`), AbiWord can import files in Microsoft Word and several other formats.

✦ **KOffice** — The KOffice package contains a set of office productivity applications designed for the KDE desktop (you must have the KDE desktop environment). The noncommercial software includes a word processor (KWord), spreadsheet (KSpread), presentation creator (KPresenter), and diagram-drawing program (KChart). These applications can be run separately or within a KOffice Workspace.

Using StarOffice

The StarOffice suite from Sun Microsystems Inc. (`www.sun.com/staroffice`) is a product that runs on Linux, UNIX, and Windows operating systems. Like OpenOffice.org, StarOffice contains many features that make it compatible with Microsoft Office applications. In particular, it includes the capability to import Microsoft Word and Excel files.

StarOffice is probably the most complete integrated office suite for Linux. It includes:

✦ **Writer** — StarOffice's word-processing application. It can import documents from a variety of formats, with special emphasis on Word documents.

✦ **Calc** — The StarOffice spreadsheet program. You can import spreadsheets from Microsoft Excel and other popular programs.

✦ **Impress** — Create presentations with this application.

✦ **Draw** — A vector-oriented drawing program that includes the capability to create 3D objects and to use texturing.

✦ **Base** — Manage your data sources. You can access a variety of database interfaces.

Other tools in StarOffice enable you to create business graphics, edit raster images, and edit mathematical formulas.

You can download StarOffice 7 for Linux or purchase a boxed set from the StarOffice Web site at `www.sun.com/staroffice`. Although StarOffice was once available free for download, the current price to download the software for home users is $75.95.

One reason for paying for StarOffice when you can get OpenOffice.org software for free is that you get a bunch of extras with StarOffice. The extras include a spell-checker, clip art, many more file converters (although the best ones are for converting Microsoft formats), a database module, and technical support.

Note

OpenOffice.org is an open source project sponsored by Sun Microsystems. Sun takes the shared source code used to create OpenOffice.org and combines it with other modules to produce the StarOffice suite. This is very similar to Mozilla, an open source Web browser, and Netscape, a commercial product built from the Mozilla sources.

Using AbiWord

The AbiWord word processor is a very nice, free word processor from the AbiSource project (`www.abisource.com`). If you are starting documents from scratch, AbiWord includes many of the basic functions you need to create good-quality documents.

With AbiWord, you can select the type of document the file contains, and select to read the file in the following formats:

AbiWord (`.abw`)

GZipped AbiWord (`.zabw`)

Rich Text Format (`.rtf`)

Microsoft Word (`.doc`)

UTF8 (`.utf8`)

Text (`.txt`)

AbiWord doesn't yet import all these file types cleanly. Although the recent version supports Word styles, sometimes tables, graphics, and other features don't translate perfectly. If you want to work with a Word document in AbiWord, open it as AbiWord, correct any font problems, and save the document in AbiWord format. AbiWord has vastly improved in the past few releases, but you may still experience problems if you need to exchange files with others who are using Word. (If you want to keep files in the Word format, you'll find that OpenOffice.org and StarOffice work much better, but not perfectly.)

AbiWord is a great first try as a usable word processor. Recently added features, such as styles and bullets, continue to make it a more useful word-processing tool. It's not yet competitive with comparable commercial products, but its developers continue to improve it.

Using KOffice

There is now a KDE office suite of applications that goes with the KDE desktop. The KOffice package has the basic applications you would expect in an integrated office suite: a word processor (KWord), spreadsheet (KSpread) program, a presentation creator (KPresenter), and a diagram-drawing program (KChart).

Start by opening the KOffice Workspace (usually from a KDE panel menu). In the workspace window that opens, you can select from the different office applications presented in the left column. Open multiple documents in any of the applications, and then click on Documents in the left column to choose which one to display at the moment.

Figure 20-2 shows the KOffice workspace, displaying a KWord document.

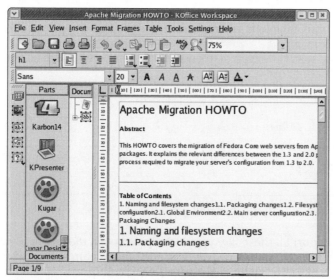

Figure 20-2: The KOffice Workspace lets you work with multiple KDE office applications at once.

You can work with a variety of document, spreadsheet, and image types. Not many commercial document types are supported yet, so you may need to import documents using other tools before you can read them into KWord. KSpread, however, can open several different spreadsheet styles, including Microsoft Excel and GNUmeric spreadsheets.

Getting Away from Windows

For casual home users, small-office workers, and large corporation personnel alike, moving away from Microsoft Office to another Office suite is an experience that can range from simple to harrowing. In general, it is useful to examine this migration in terms of "home use" versus "work use." Home users typically have to concern themselves with maintaining access to their own documents. In a personal context, it may be rare for friends and relatives to send Excel spreadsheets, Word documents, and PowerPoint presentations. But over the years you may have accumulated untold numbers for term papers, recipes, letters to the editor, and other such documents that you'd like to be able to read and print. Because many of these formats are easily read by OpenOffice.org or can be readily saved in Microsoft Office to another, more interoperable format, your issues should be few.

At work, in addition to accumulation of documents over time, there is a more pressing issue; other people will be sending you Microsoft Office documents. So while home users need to concern themselves mostly with access to historical documents, in the workplace you will probably need to accommodate new documents as well as your historical information. Because you can also convert your documents, there are no real challenges to migrating simple documents. However, if your Microsoft Office documents include extensive macro, scripting, or embedded object usage, you may find the conversion is not a very clean one. Make sure you attempt conversions using the following options before moving on to the last resort of using multiple applications or re-creating documents.

Using Microsoft Office to convert documents enables you to save your files in an alternative format. For example, Word 2002 allows you to save your .doc files (the Word versions anyway) to a variety of formats, including:

✦ HTML (.htm/.html)—HTML is a great format for your information if it is basically text and you need only a few formatting options and some embedded images and links. The resulting HTML document will be smaller than the corresponding .doc file.

✦ Rich Text Format (.rtf)—Another wonderful minimalist format that will preserve some formatting and graphics, but any scripting or macro usage will be lost.

✦ Plain Text (.txt)—Works if all you need to save is the text of the file. Everything else will be lost.

✦ Word 6.0/95 (.doc)—An alternative format that may save some of the elements you want yet make it more accessible to OpenOffice.org. Using this format may not resolve all of the issues you have with converting those hard-to-change documents, but it just might do the trick.

Other Microsoft office applications offer similar functionality. PowerPoint can convert presentations to HTML and general image formats such as JPEG and TIFF. Excel can save tab- and comma-delimited files that are easily importable into a large number of applications. If you make use of Access to save data, you may want to move your .mdb-stored data into a SQL database. SQL is more scalable, powerful, and virtually platform-independent. Migrating to SQL will preserve your data, but if your .mdb file will not open in OpenOffice.org, you will need to re-create any forms for accessing the data that you would like to continue using.

If you are likely to continue to receive Microsoft Office files and you are concerned about interoperation, here are some options to consider:

✦ Keep a copy of Microsoft Office installed using WINE and the CodeWeavers plug-in.

✦ Ask individuals sending you documentation to use a less-vendor-specific format, such as Adobe PDF. Document formatting can be exquisitely preserved and will be viewable by anyone capable of installing a PDF viewer, which supports virtually every operating system in widespread use today.

✦ For forms that have user-editable fields, scripting, or complex embedded information, use HTML documents instead. Anyone with a compliant Web browser will be able to interact with the document, and Microsoft Office applications universally support saving files into this format.

Caution   Before making any wholesale conversion away from Microsoft Office, make sure the files you need to use will work as expected with the new office suite you have selected or that you construct suitable replacements if needed. Testing things ahead of time enables you to make necessary adjustments without later having to endure the frustration of finding some important document inaccessible or unusable.

Using Traditional Linux Publishing Tools

With old-school text processors such as Groff and TeX, you can ignore document appearance while writing. Plain-text macros instruct postprocessors how to lay out a document for printing after writing is done. With word processors such as OpenOffice.org Word and StarOffice Writer, you mark up text and see the basic layout of the document as you write.

Some attributes of the traditional Linux document preparation tools make them particularly well suited for certain types of projects. TeX and Groff (which is based on TeX) are a pair of these "classic" tools and have been popular among technical people because:

✦ You can manipulate files in plain text. Using tools such as sed and grep, you can scan and change one document or hundreds with a single command or script.

✦ Scientific notation is supported. With geqn, you can create complex equations. LaTeX and TeX are suited for technical notation, and some math publications require LaTeX.

✦ Editing can be faster because traditional Linux documents are created with a text editor. You usually get better performance out of a text editor than a word processor.

Simple page layouts work well with Linux documentation tools. For example, a technical book with a few flow charts and images can be easily produced and maintained using Groff or TeX documentation tools. Letters and memos are also easy to do with these tools. And, of course, Linux man pages are created with text-based tools.

Additionally, Linux likes PostScript. Although people think of PostScript as a printing language, it is really more of a programming language (you could write PostScript code directly). Most Linux document-processing software includes print drivers for PostScript. Some documents on the Web are distributed in PostScript (.ps).

The drawback to the traditional Linux document tools is that they are not intuitive. Although there are some easier front ends to LaTeX (see the description of LyX later in this chapter), if you are creating documents in a text editor, you need to learn what macros to type into your documents and which formatting and print commands to use.

Note   For many years, the UNIX system documentation distributed by AT&T was created in troff/nroff formats, which predate Groff. The documents used separate macro packages for man pages and guide material. Using a source code control system (SCCS), thousands of pages of documentation were ported to different UNIX systems.

Creating Documents in Groff or LaTeX

You can use any text editor to create documents for both Linux's Groff (troff/nroff) and LaTeX (TeX) styles of publishing. Most Linux distributions come with several text editors. You always have the option to download others from the Internet. (See the "Choosing a Text Editor" sidebar for more information.)

Here are the general steps for creating documents in Groff or LaTeX:

1. Create a document with any text editor. The document will contain text and markup.

2. Format the document using a formatting command that matches the style of the document that you created (for example, with groff or latex). During this step, you may need to indicate that the document contains special content, such as equations (eqn command), tables (tbl command), or line drawings (pic command).

Choosing a Text Editor

Hardcore UNIX or Linux users tend to edit files with either the vi or emacs text editor. These editors have been around a long time and are hard to learn but efficient to use. (Your fingers never leave the keyboard.) The emacs editor has some GUI support, although it runs fine in a Terminal window. There are also GUI versions of vi and emacs that add menu and mouse features to the editors. These are GVim (`gvim` command in the vim-X11 package) and Xemacs (`xemacs` command) editors.

The following are some of the other, simpler text editors that can run on your graphical desktop:

Text Editor	Command	Description
gedit	`gedit`	Lightweight text editor that comes with the GNOME desktop environment. It has simple edit functions (cut, copy, paste, and select all), and you can set indentations and word wrap. Special functions, such as a spell-checker and a diff feature, are included. Start by typing **gedit** from a Terminal window. Go to `http://gedit.sourceforge.net` for more information.
Advanced Editor	`kwrite`	Includes a menu bar to create, open, and save files, and simple edit functions (cut, copy, paste, undo, and help). Other features enable you to set indents, find and replace text, and select all. This tool comes with the KDE desktop; access it by selecting Accessories ⇨ More Accessories ⇨ Kwrite.
Text Editor	`kedit`	A simple text editor that comes with the KDE desktop. Features let you open files from your file system or from a URL. It also includes a convenient toolbar and a spell-checker. Access it by selecting Accessories ⇨ More Accessories ⇨ Text Editor.
nedit	`nedit`	A rather plain-looking, but very advanced, X-based text editor. It provides all the usual editing functions, syntax-highlighting modes for a plethora of programming languages, and an advanced macro system. Despite its advanced features, it's easy for beginners to use.
joe	`joe`	A text-mode editor that's much simpler than either vi or emacs and has the capability to mimic other text editors, such as vi, emacs, pico, and even the late, lamented WordStar. In addition to standard features like search and replace, arrow key movements for the cursor, and so on, it offers macros, code-editing features, and the capability to move or format large chunks of text easily.

3. Send the document to an output device (a printer or a display program).

If you are accustomed to a word processor with a GUI, you may find these publishing tools difficult to learn at first. In general, Groff is useful for creating man pages for Linux. LaTeX is useful if you need to produce mathematical documents, perhaps for publication in a technical journal.

Text Processing with Groff

The `nroff` and `troff` text formatting commands were the first interfaces available for producing typeset-quality documents with the UNIX system. They aren't editors, but commands through which you send your text, with the result being formatted pages. `nroff` produces formatted plain text and includes the capability to do pagination, indents, and text justification, as well as other features. `troff` produces typeset text, including everything `nroff` can do, plus the capability to produce different fonts and spacing. The `troff` command also supports kerning.

The `groff` command is the front end for producing nroff/troff documentation. Because Linux man pages are formatted and output in Groff, most of the examples here help you create and print man pages with Groff.

People rarely use primitive `nroff`/`troff` markup. Instead, there are common macro packages that simplify creating `nroff`/`troff` formatted documents, which include:

- ✦ **man** — These macros are used to create Linux man pages. You can format a man page using the `-man` option to the `groff` command.

- ✦ **mm** — The mm macros (memorandum macros) were created to produce memos, letters, and technical white papers. This package includes macros for creating tables of contents, lists of figures, references, and other technical-document-style features. You can format an mm document using the `-mm` option to the `groff` command.

- ✦ **me** — These macros are popular for producing memos and technical papers on Berkeley UNIX systems. Format an me document using the `groff` command option `-me`.

Groff macro packages are stored in `/usr/share/groff/*/tmac`. The man macros are called from the `an.tmac` file, mm macros are from `m.tmac`, and me macros are from `e.tmac`. The naming convention for each macro package is *xxx*`.tmac`, where *xxx* is replaced by one or more letters representing the macro package. In each case, you can understand the name of the macro package by adding an m to the beginning of the file suffix.

Tip   Instead of noting a specific macro package, you can use `-mandoc` to choose one.

When you run the `groff` formatting command, you can indicate on the command line which macro packages you are using. You can also indicate that the document should be run through any of the following commands that preprocess text for special formats:

- ✦ `eqn`—Formats macros that produce equations in `groff`.
- ✦ `pic`—Formats macros that create simple line drawings in `groff`.
- ✦ `tbl`—Formats macros that produce tables within `groff`.

The formatted Groff document is output for a particular device type. The device can be a printer, a window, or (for plain text) your shell. Here are output forms supported by Groff:

Form	Produces
ps	PostScript output for PostScript printer or a PostScript previewer
lj4	Output for an HP LaserJet4 printer or other PCL5-compatible printer
ascii	Plain-text output that can be viewed from a Terminal window
dvi	Output in TeX dvi, to output to a variety of devices described later
X75	Output for an X11 75 dots/inch previewer
X100	Output for an X11 100 dots/inch previewer
latin1	Typewriter-like output using the ISO Latin-1 character set

Formatting and printing documents with Groff

Try formatting and printing an existing Groff document using any man pages on your system. You'll find some in `/usr/share/man/*`; they're compressed, so copy them to a temporary directory and unzip them to try out Groff.

The following commands copy the chown man page to the `/tmp` directory, unzip it, and format it in plain text so you can page through it on your screen:

```
$ cp /usr/share/man/man1/chown.1.gz /tmp
$ gunzip /tmp/chown.1.gz
$ groff -Tascii -man /tmp/chown.1 | less
```

In this example, the chown man page (`chown.1.gz`) is copied to the `/tmp` directory, unzipped (using `gunzip`), and output in plain text (`-Tascii`) using the man macros (`-man`). The output is piped to `less`, to page through it on your screen. Instead of piping to `less` (`| less`), you could direct the output to a file (`> /tmp/chown.txt`).

To format a man page for typesetting, you could specify PostScript or HP LaserJet output. Direct the output to a file or to a printer. Here are a couple of examples:

```
$ groff -Tps -man /tmp/chown.1 > /tmp/chown.ps
$ groff -Tlj4 -man -l /tmp/chown.1
```

The first example creates PostScript output (-Tps) and directs it to a file called /tmp/chown.ps. That file can be read by a PostScript previewer (such as Ghostscript) or sent to a printer (lpr /tmp/chown.ps). The next example creates HP LaserJet output (-Tlj4) and directs it to the default printer (-l option).

Creating a Man Page with Groff

Before HOWTOs and info files, man pages were the foundation for information about UNIX and UNIX-like systems. Each command, file format, device, or other component either had its own man page or was grouped on a man page with similar components. To create your own man page requires that you learn a few macros (in particular, man macros). Figure 20-3 shows the source for a fictitious man page for a command called waycool.

```
.\"
.\" waycool.1 - the *roff document processor source for the waycool command
.\"
.TH waycool 1 "May 12, 2002" GNU "Linux Programmer's Manual"
.SH NAME
waycool \- my cool command
.SH SYNTAX
\fBwaycool\fR [ \fB-abcv\fR ] [ \fI file ... \fR ]
.SH VERSION
This man page documents the GNU waycool version X.XX
.SH DESCRIPTION
\fBwaycool\fR is a way cool command.
.SP
This version of \fBwaycool\fR is better than the last one.
.SH OPTIONS
.IP -a
Run all options with it.
.IP -b
Run some options.
.IP -c
affect symbolic links instead of any referenced file
(available only on systems that can change the
ownership of a symlink)
.IP -v
Print the version number with the command.
.SH COMMENTS
If you don't like the command, don't tell me. It will just hurt my feelings.
.SH ENVIRONMENT VARIABLES
These environment variables are used by  \fBwaycool\fR:
.IP "DISPLAY"
This sets the X Display variable.
.IP "WAYCOOL"
This contains the location of the waycool database.
.SH FILES
/usr/local/waycool - Directory containing waycool stuff.
.SH AUTHOR
Chris Craft <chris@handsonhistory.com>
.SH "REPORTING BUGS"
Report bugs to <bug-fileutils@gnu.org>.
.SH COPYRIGHT
Copyright \(co 2001 Free Software Foundation, Inc.
.br
This is free software; see the source for copying conditions.  There is NO
warranty; not even for MERCHANTABILITY or FITNESS FOR A PARTICULAR PURPOSE.
.SH ACKNOWLEDGEMENTS
I'd like to thank all my friends.
```

Figure 20-3: Simple markup is required to create man pages.

Tip

Most man pages are stored in subdirectories of /usr/share/man. Before you create a man page, refer to similar man pages to see the markup and the headings they include. Man1 has commands; man2 has system calls; man3 has library functions; man4 has special device files (/dev/*); man5 has file formats; man6 has games; man7 has miscellaneous components; and man8 has administrative commands.

A few other kinds of macros are used in the man page. The .IP macros format indented paragraphs for things such as options. The man page also contains some lower-level font requests; for example, \fB says to change the current font to bold, \fI changes the font to italic, and \fR changes it back to regular font. (This markup is better than asking for a particular font type because it just changes to bold, italic, or regular for the current font.) Figure 20-4 shows what the waycool man page looks like after it is formatted with groff:

```
$ groff -man -Tps -l waycool.1
```

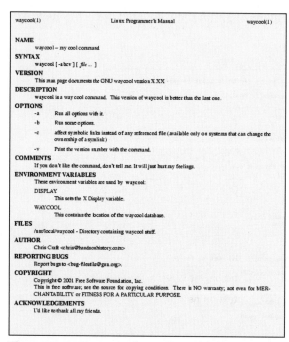

Figure 20-4: Man page formatting adds headers and lays out the page of text.

Table 20-1 lists the macros that you can use on your man pages. These macros are described on the man(7) manual page (type **man 7 man** to view that page).

Table 20-1
Man Macros

Macro	Description
.B	Bold
.BI	Bold, then italics (alternating)
.BR	Bold, then roman (alternating)
.DT	Set default tabs
.HP	Begin a hanging indent
.I	Italics
.IB	Italics, then bold (alternating)
.IP	Begin hanging tag. For options. Long tags use .TP.
.IR	Italics, then roman (alternating)
.LP	Begin paragraph
.PD	Set distance between paragraphs
.PP	Begin paragraph
.RB	Roman, then bold (alternating)
.RE	End relative indent (after .RS)
.RI	Roman, then italics (alternating)
.RS	Begin relative indent (use .RE to end indent)
.SB	Small text, then bold (alternating)
.SM	Small text. Used to show words in all caps.
.SH	Section head
.SS	Subheading within a .SH heading.
.TH	Title heading. Used once at the beginning of the man page.
.TP	Begin a hanging tag. Begins text on next line, not same line as tag.

Creating a Letter, Memo, or White Paper with Groff

Memorandum macros (which are used with the -mm option of Groff) were once popular among UNIX users for producing technical documents, letters, and memos. Although more modern word processors with a variety of WYSIWYG templates have made the mm macros outdated, in a pinch they are still a quick way to create a typeset-style document in a text environment.

To format and print (to a PostScript printer) a document with mm macros, use the following:

```
$ groff -mm -Tps -l letter.mm
```

Here's a simple example of how to use mm macros to produce a letter:

```
.WA "Christopher T. Craft"
999 Anyway Way
Anytown, UT 84111 USA
.WE
.IA
John W. Doe
111 Notown Blvd.
Notown, UT 84111
.IE
.LO RN "Our telephone conversation"
.LO SA "Dear Mr. Doe:"
.LT
In reference to our telephone conversation on the 4th, I am
calling to confirm our upcoming appointment on the 18th. I look
forward to discussing the merger. I believe we have a win-win
situation here.
.FC "Yours Truly,"
.SG
```

Use the command line $ groff -mm -Tps -l letter.mm, and the output will look like Figure 20-5.

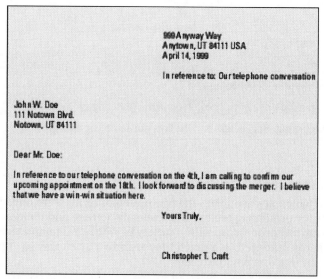

Figure 20-5: Create a simple letter using mm macros.

The mm macros were often used to produce technical memos. The following is an example of a sign-off sheet that might go at the front of a larger technical memo:

```
.TL
Merger Technical Specifications
.AF "ABC Corporation"
.AU "Christopher Craft"
.AT "President"
.AS
This memo details the specifications for the planned merger.
.AE
.MT "Merger Description and Marching Orders"
As a result of our talks with XYZ corporation, we plan to go
forward with the merger. This document contains the following:
.BL
.LI
Schedule and time tables.
.LI
Financial statements.
.LI
Asset allocations.
.LE
.SP
Please add any corrections you have, then sign the approval
line indicated at the bottom of this sheet.
.FC
.SG
.AV "John W. Doe, XYZ Corporation President"
.AV "Sylvia Q. Public, XYZ Corporation CFO"
.NS
Everyone in the corporation.
.NE
```

Figure 20-6 shows the output of this memo.

Note For a complete listing of mm macros, see the groff_mm man page. More than 100 mm macros exist. Also, dozens of defined strings let you set and recall information such as figure names, tables, table of contents information, and text that is automatically printed with different headings.

Figure 20-6: Add headings and approval lines automatically to memos.

Adding Equations, Tables, and Pictures

To interpret special macros for equations, tables, and line drawings, you can run separate commands (eqn, tbl, and pic commands) on the file before you run the groff command. Alternatively, you can add options to the groff command line to have the file preprocessed automatically by any of the commands (-e for eqn, -t for tbl, and -p for pic).

Here are some examples of EQN, TBL, and PIC markup included in a Groff document. The first example shows an equation that can be processed by eqn:

```
.EQ
a ~ mark = ~ 30
.EN
.sp
.EQ
a sup 2 ~ + ~ b sup 2~lineup = ~ 1000
```

```
.EN
.sp
.EQ
x sup 3 ~ + ~ y sup 3 ~ + ~ z sup 3~lineup = ~ 1400
.EN
```

If this appeared in a memo called `memoeqn.mm`, the memo would be preprocessed by eqn and then sent to the printer using the following command:

```
$ groff -Tps -l -mm -e memoeqn.mm
```

All data between the .EQ and .EN macros are interpreted as equations. The resulting output from the equation would appear as shown in Figure 20-7.

$$a = 30$$

$$a^2 + b^2 = 1000$$

$$x^3 + y^3 + z^3 = 1400$$

Figure 20-7: Produce equations in documents with the use of the eqn command's .EQ and .EN macros.

To create a table in a Groff document, use the .TS and .TE macros of the tbl preprocessor. The following is an example of the markup used to produce a simple table:

```
.TS
center, box, tab(:);
c s s
c | c | c
l | l | l.
Mergers and Acquisitions Team
=
Employee:Title:Location
=_
Jones, James:Marketing Manager:New York Office
Smith, Charles:Sales Manager:Los Angeles Office
Taylor, Sarah:R&D Manager:New York Office
Walters, Mark:Information Systems Manager:Salt Lake City Office
Zur, Mike:Distribution Manager:Portland Office
.TE
```

The .TS macro starts the table, and the next line indicates that the table should be centered on the page (center) and surrounded by a line box and that a colon will be used to separate the data into cells (tab(:)). The third line shows that the heading should be centered in the box (c) and should span across the next two cells (s s). The fourth line says that the heading of each cell should be centered (c | c | c) and the fifth line indicates that the data cells that follow should be left justified (l | l | l).

Caution   There must be a period at the end of the table definition line. In this example, it is after the l | l | l. line. If the period is not there, tbl will try to interpret the text as part of the table definition, fail, and stop processing the table; the table will not print.

The rest of the information in the table is the data. Note that the tab separators are colon characters (:). End the table with a .TE macro. If the table were in a memo called memotbl.mm, tbl could preprocess the memo and then send it to the printer using the following command:

```
$ groff -Tps -l -mm -t memotbl.mm
```

Data between .TS and .TE macros are interpreted as tables. Figure 20-8 displays the output from this example.

Employee	Title	Location
Jones, James	Marketing Manager	Jones, James
Smith, Charles	Sales Manager	Smith, Charles
Taylor, Sarah	R&D Manager	Taylor, Sarah
Walters, Mark	Information Systems Manager	Walters, Mark
Zur, Mike	Distribution Manager	Zur, Mike

Figure 20-8: Set how text is justified and put in columns with the use of the tbl command's .TS and .TE macros.

The PIC macros (.PS and .PE) let you create simple diagrams and flow charts to use in Groff. PIC is really only qualified to create simple boxes, circles, ellipses, lines, arcs, splines, and some text. The following is some PIC code that could be in a Groff document:

```
.PS
box invis "Start" "Here"; arrow
box "Step 1"; arrow
circle "Step 2"; arrow
ellipse "Step 3"; arrow
box "Step 4"; arrow
box invis "End"
.PE
```

The first line after the .PS indicates an invisible box (invis) that contains the words Start Here, followed by an arrow. That arrow connects to the next box, containing the words Step 1. The next elements (connected by arrows) are a circle (Step 2), an ellipse (Step 3), another box (Step 4), and another invisible box (End). The .PE indicates the end of the pic drawing.

If these lines appeared in a document called `memopic.mm`, you could preprocess the PIC code and print the file using the following command:

```
$ groff -Tps -l -mm -p memopic.mm
```

Figure 20-9 shows an example of this drawing.

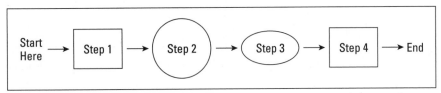

Figure 20-9: Create simple flow diagrams with the `pic` command's .PS and .PE macros.

Text Processing with TeX/LaTeX

TeX (pronounced *tech*) is a collection of commands used primarily to produce scientific and mathematical typeset documents. The most common way to use TeX is by calling a macro package. The most popular macro package for Tex is LaTeX, which takes a higher-level approach to formatting TeX documents. TeX and LaTeX tools are contained in the tetex-latex package.

TeX interprets the LaTeX macros from the latex format file (`latex.fmt`). By default, the `latex.fmt` and `plain.fmt` format files are the only ones that are automatically built when the TeX package is installed. Other macro files that you can use with TeX include:

✦ **amstex** — Mathematical publications, including the American Mathematical Society, use this as their official typesetting system.

✦ **eplain** — Includes macros for indexing and table of contents.

✦ **texinfo** — Macros used by the Free Software Foundation to produce software manuals. Text output from these macros can be used with the Linux `info` command.

You can create a TeX/LaTeX file using any text editor. After the text and macros are created, you can run the `tex` command (or one of several other related utilities) to format the file. The input file is in the form `filename.tex`. The output is generally three different files:

File	Description
`filename.dvi`	Device-independent output file that can be translated for use by several different types of output devices (such as PostScript).
`filename.log`	A log file that contains diagnostic messages.
`filename.aux`	An auxiliary file used by LaTeX.

The `.dvi` file produced can be formatted for a particular device. For example, you could use the `dvips` command to output the resulting `.dvi` file to your PostScript printer (`dvips filename.dvi`). Or you could use the `xdvi` command to preview the `.dvi` file in X.

Creating and Formatting a LaTeX Document

Because LaTeX is the most common way of using TeX, this section describes how to create and format a LaTeX document. A LaTeX macro (often referred to as a command) appears in a document in one of the two following forms:

> `\string{option}[required]` — A backslash (\) followed by a command. (Replace `string` with the name of the command.) Optional arguments are contained in braces ({ }), and required arguments are in brackets ([ ]).

> `\?{option}[required]` — A backslash (\) followed by a single character (not a letter) command. (Replace `?` with the command character.) Optional arguments are contained in braces ({ }), and required arguments are in brackets ([ ]).

Each command defines some action to be taken. The action can control page layout, the font used, spacing, paragraph layout, or a variety of other actions on the document. The minimum amount of formatting that a LaTeX document can contain is the following:

```
\documentclass{name}
\begin{document}
   TEXT GOES HERE!
\end{document}
```

Replace `{name}` with the name of the class of document you are creating. The text for the file, along with your formatting commands, goes between the `begin` and `end` document commands.

The best way to get started with LaTeX is to use the LyX editor, which provides a GUI for creating LaTeX documents. It also contains a variety of templates you can use instead of just creating a document from scratch. Figure 20-10 shows an example of the LyX editor.

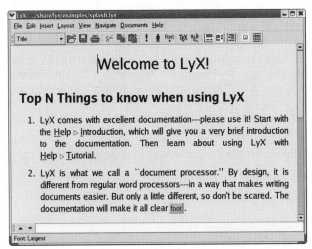

Figure 20-10: Create LaTeX documents graphically with the LyX editor.

If you want to edit LaTeX in a regular text editor, you must be familiar with the LaTeX commands. For a complete listing of the LaTeX commands, type **info latex** and then go to the "Commands within a LaTeX Document" section.

Using the LyX LaTeX Editor

Start the LyX LaTeX editor with the lyx command. LyX comes with a lot of supporting documentation. Click Help to select a tutorial, user's guide, or other information.

To start your first document, I recommend that you select one of the templates provided with LyX. Templates are located in /usr/share/lyx/templates. To open a template, click File ⇨ New from Template. A list of available templates appears. You can use them to create letters, slides, and articles, for example.

Besides offering standard editing functions, such as cut, copy, and paste, you can perform a variety of markup functions from the Layout menu. As for mathematical functions, the Math menu enables you to insert fractions, square root, exponent, sum, and integral functions into your document. When you are done, you can:

- ✦ **Print** the file to a PostScript printer or output a PostScript (.ps) file. (Click File ⇨ Print, select the printing method, and then click OK.)

- ✦ **Export** the file to LaTeX, DVI, PostScript, or ASCII Text. (Click File ⇨ Export and choose from the list of file formats.)

LyX calls itself a WYSIWYM editor — What You Say Is What You Mean. As a result, what you see on the screen as you edit is not exactly what the printed document will look like. For example, no extra white space will appear between lines by pressing Enter multiple times.

Because LyX supports style files, it enables you to create documents that meet several different standards. For example, LyX supports typesetting for the American Mathematics Society (AMS) journals using the article text class. Other text classes supported include:

✦ **article** — One-sided paper with no chapters.

✦ **report** — Two-sided report, tending to be longer than an article.

✦ **book** — Same as report, with additional front and back matter.

✦ **slides** — For producing transparencies.

✦ **letter** — Includes special environments for addresses, signatures, and other elements.

Printing LaTeX Files

Whether you create your own LaTeX file, export one from the LyX LaTeX editor, or download one from the Internet, several utilities are available to format, print, or display the output. Here are some of your choices:

✦ To format a LaTeX file (*filename*.tex), run the following command:

```
$ latex filename.tex
```

✦ To print a DVI file (*filename*.dvi), send it to your default PostScript printer, and type the following:

```
$ dvips filename.dvi
```

✦ To display a DVI file in an X window, type the following:

```
$ xdvi filename.dvi
```

To print a DVI file to a PCL printer, such as an HP LaserJet, type the following:

```
$ dvicopy filename.dvi
$ dvilj filename.dvi
```

The dvilj command doesn't support virtual fonts directly. The dvicopy command converts the fonts so that the PCL printer can handle them.

Converting Documents

Documents can come to you in many different formats. Search just some of the Linux FTP sites on the Interne,t and you will find files in PostScript, DVI, man, PDF, HTML, and TeX. There are also a variety of graphics formats. The following is a list of common document and graphics conversion utilities:

Utility	Converts	To
dos2unix	DOS text file	UNIX (Linux) text file
fax2ps	TIFF facsimile image files	Compressed PostScript format (The PostScript output is optimized to send to a printer on a low-speed line. This format is less efficient for images with a lot of black or continuous tones, for which tiff2ps might be more effective.)
fax2tiff	Fax data (Group 3 or Group 4)	TIFF format (The output is either low-resolution or medium-resolution TIFF format.)
g32pbm	Group 3 fax file (either digifax or raw)	Portable bitmap
gif2tiff	GIF (87) file	TIFF format
man2html	Man page	HTML format
pal2rgb	TIFF image (palette color)	Full-color RGB image
pbm2g3	Portable bitmap image	Fax file (Group 3)
pdf2dsc	PDF file	PostScript document dsc file (The PostScript file conforms to Adobe Document Structuring Conventions. The output enables PostScript readers such as Ghostview to read the PDF file a page at a time.)
pdf2ps	PDF file	PostScript file (level 2)
pfb2pfa	Type 1 PostScript font (binary MS-DOS)	ASCII-readable
pk2bm	TeX pkfont font file	Bitmap (ASCII file)
ppm2tiff	PPM image file	TIFF format
ps2ascii	PostScript or PDF file	ASCII text
ps2epsi	PostScript file	Encapsulated PostScript (EPSI) (Some word-processing and graphic programs can read EPSI. Output is often low quality.)
ps2pdf	PostScript file	Portable Document Format (PDF)
ps2pk	Type 1 PostScript font	TeX pkfont
pstotext	PostScript file	ASCII text (pstotext is similar to ps2ascii but handles font encoding and kerning better. It doesn't convert PDFs.)
ras2tiff	Sun raster file	TIFF format
texi2html	Texinfo file	HTML

Continued

Utility	Converts	To
tiff2bw	RGB or Palette color TIFF image	Grayscale TIFF image
tiff2ps	TIFF image	PostScript
unix2dos	UNIX (Linux) text file	DOS text file

Many graphical applications, such as the GIMP, will also enable you to save images into several different formats (BMP, JPEG, PNG, TIFF, and so on), using the Save As feature.

Building Structured Documents

Documentation projects often need to produce documents that are output in a variety of formats. For example, the same text that describes how to use a software program may need to be output as a printed manual, an HTML page, and a PostScript file. The standards that have been embraced most recently by the Linux community for creating what are referred to as structured documents are SGML, XML, and DocBook.

Understanding SGML and XML

Standard Generalized Markup Language (SGML) was created to provide a standard way of marking text so that it could be output later in a variety of formats. Because SGML markup is done with text tags, you can create SGML documents using any plain-text editor. Documents consist of the text of your document and tags that identify each type of information in the text.

Unlike markup languages such as Groff and HTML, SGML markup is not intended to enforce a particular look when you are creating the document. So, for example, instead of marking a piece of text as being bold or italic, you would identify it as an address, a paragraph, or a name. Later, a style sheet would be applied to the document to assign a look and presentation to the tagged text.

Because SGML consists of many tags, other projects have cropped up to simplify producing documents based on SGML and to better focus the ways in which SGML is used. In particular, the Extensible Markup Language (XML) was created to offer a manageable subset of SGML that would be specifically tailored to work well with Web-based publishing.

So far in describing SGML and XML, only the frameworks that are used to produce structured documents have been discussed. Specific documentation projects need to create and, to some extent, enforce specific markup definitions for the type of documents they need to produce. These definitions are referred to as Data Type Definitions (DTDs). For documentation of Linux itself and other open source projects, DocBook has become the DTD of choice.

Understanding DocBook

DocBook is a DTD that is well-suited for producing computer software documents in a variety of formats. It was originally created by the OASIS Consortium (`www.oasis-open.org`) and is now supported by many different commercial and open source tools.

DocBook's focus is on marking content, instead of indicating a particular look (that is, font type, size, position, and so on.). It includes markup that lets you automate the process of creating indices, figure lists, and tables of contents, to name a few.

DocBook is important to the Linux community because many open source projects use it to produce documentation. For example, the following is a list of organizations that use DocBook to create the documents that describe their software:

✦ Linux Documentation Project (`www.tldp.org/LDP/LDP-Author-Guide`)

✦ GNOME Documentation (`developer.gnome.org/projects/gdp/handbook/gdp-handbook`)

✦ KDE Documentation Project (`www.kde.org/documentation`)

✦ FreeBSD Documentation Project (`www.freebsd.org/docproj`)

If you want to contribute to any of these documentation projects, refer to the Web sites for each organization. In all cases, they publish writers' guides or style guides that describe the DocBook tags that they support.

Creating DocBook Documents

You can create the documents in any text editor, using tags that are similar in appearance to HTML tags (with beginning and end tags appearing between less-than and greater-than signs). Certain word-processing programs also allow you to create DocBook markup.

The following steps show an example of a simple DocBook document produced with a plain-text editor and output into HTML using tools that are available in many Linux systems.

1. Create a directory in your home directory to work in and go to that directory. For example, you could type the following from a Terminal window:

```
$ mkdir $HOME/doctest
$ cd $HOME/doctest
```

2. Open a text editor to hold your DocBook document. For example, you could type:

```
$ gedit cardoc.sgml
```

(A text editor such as jedit, which you can get at www.jedit.org, can also be useful for dealing with the long tag names used in DocBook.)

3. Enter the tags and text that you want to appear in your document. Most DocBook documents are either <book> type (large, multichapter documents) or <article> type (single-chapter documents). To try out a DocBook document, type the following:

```
<xml version="1.0">
<article>
  <title>Choosing a new car</title>
  <artheader>
     <abstract>
       In this article, you will learn how to price,
       negotiate for, and purchase an automobile.
     </abstract>
  </artheader>
  <section>
    <title>Getting Started</title>
    <para>
      The first thing you will learn is how to figure out
      what you can afford.
    </para>
  </section>
  <section>
      <title>The Next Step</title>
      <para>
      After you know what you can afford, you can begin
      your search.
      </para>
    </section>
</article>
```

You should notice a few things about this document. The entire document is wrapped in article tags (<article> </article>). The article title is in title tags (<title> </title>). The section tags (<section> </section>) indicate sections of text that each have a title and paragraph. These sections can later be treated separately in the TOC.

4. Save the file and exit from the text editor.

5. Next, you can try translating the document you just created into several different formats. For example, to create HTML output, you could type the following:

```
$ db2html cardoc.sgml
```

The result is a new directory called `cardoc`. The result from `db2html` in the `cardoc` directory is the creation of a stylesheet-images directory, a `t2.html` file, and an `x12.html` file.

To view the HTML file just created, I typed the following:

```
$ epiphany $HOME/doctest/cardoc/t2.html
```

Figure 20-11 shows an example of the output created from the `db2html` command. The screen on the left shows the first page. Click the Next link at the top of the page. The second page that you see is shown on the right. During conversion to HTML, the `db2html` command adds Next/Previous buttons to each page. It also puts the title of each section in a Table of Contents on page one and in the browser's title bar.

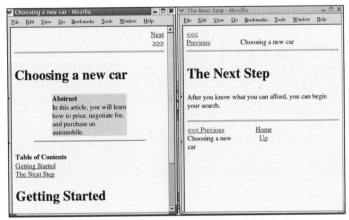

Figure 20-11: The DocBook file is output in HTML with the `db2html` command.

From this point, you can continue to add content and different types of tags. If you are writing documents for a particular project (such as the Linux projects mentioned earlier), you should get information on the particular tags and other style issues they require.

Converting DocBook Documents

The previous example shows how to create a simple DocBook document and convert it to HTML output. The following utilities convert DocBook to other formats:

Utility	Converts DocBook File To
docbook2dvi	Device Independent file format
docbook2html	HTML format
docbook2man	man page format
docbook2pdf	Portable Document Format (PDF)
docbook2ps	PostScript format
docbook2rtf	Rich Text Format (RTF)
docbook2tex	TeX format
docbook2texi	GNU TeXinfo format
docbook2txt	bare text format

Printing Documents in Linux

Printing in most Linux systems these days is provided by the Common UNIX Printing System (CUPS) service. As a nonadministrative user, you don't have a lot of control over how the printers are configured. You can, however, check which printers are available to print to, check the status of print queues (documents waiting to print), and remove any of your own queued print jobs.

 Cross-Reference   Refer to Chapter 25 for information on configuring a printer using the CUPS service.

Printing to the Default Printer

When your system administrator (or you) configured printers for your computer, one of those printers was defined as the default printer. If you are not sure which printer is your default in a Fedora Core or other Red Hat Linux distribution, type **system-config-printer** and look for the printer with the check by it. For other Linux distributions, check the CUPS Web-based interface to see how your printers are configured.

Most graphical word processors, such as StarOffice Writer and OpenOffice.org Writer, let you choose a printer from those available. Some of the less sophisticated Linux utilities that run from the command line, however, use only the default printer. For example, dvips (to print a PostScript file) and groff -l (to print a troff/nroff file) automatically send the output to the default printer.

As a regular user, you can override the default printer using the PRINTER environment variable. If the default printer on your computer is lp0, for example, and you want to print regularly to lp1, change your default printer by setting the PRINTER variable as follows:

```
$ export PRINTER=lp1
```

To have this take effect all the time, you could add this line to one of your shell configuration files (such as $HOME/.bashrc, if you use the bash shell).

Printing from the Shell

The lpr command is used to print files from the shell. You can use lpr to print whether the LPRng or CUPS print service is being used. If you have a file already formatted, use lpr to print it. For example, if you have a PostScript output file (file.ps) and you want to print it to your PostScript printer, use the following command line:

```
$ lpr file.ps
```

If you want to specify a particular printer (other than the default), add the -P*printer* option. For example, to print to the lp0 printer, you would type the following:

```
$ lpr -Plp0 file.ps
```

If you want to print more than one copy of a document, use the -#*num* option, where *num* is replaced by the number of copies you want. For example, to print five copies of a file, use:

```
$ lpr -#5 file.ps
```

The lpr command can also accept standard output for printing. For example, you could print the output of a groff command by piping that output to lpr as follows:

```
$ groff -Tps -man /tmp/chown.1 | lpr -Plp0
```

Tip The enscript command (in the enscript package) is another useful tool for printing plain-text files. It converts the files to PostScript and sends them to a printer or to a specified file.

Checking the Print Queues

To check the status of print jobs that have been queued, you can use the lpq command. By itself, lpq prints a listing of jobs that are in the queue for the default printer. For example:

```
$ lpq
hp is ready and printing
Rank      Owner      Job   Files         Total Size
active    root       3     hosts         1024 bytes
1st       root       7     (stdin)       625 bytes
2nd       root       8     memo1.ps      12273 bytes
3rd       chuck      9     bikes.ps      10880 bytes
```

The output from `lpq` shows the printer status and the files waiting to be printed. `Rank` lists the order in which they are in the queue. `Owner` is the user who queued the job. `Job` shows the job number. The `Files` column shows the name of the file or standard output (if the file was piped or directed to `lpr`). `Total Size` shows how large each file is in bytes.

You can add options to `lpq` to print different kinds of information. By adding `-Pprinter`, you can see the queue for any available printer. You can also add the job number (to see the status of a particular print job) or a user name (to see all queued jobs for a user).

Removing Print Jobs

If you have ever printed a large document by mistake, you understand the value of being able to remove a print job from the queue. Likewise, if a printer is going to be down for a while and everyone has already printed their jobs to another printer, it's sometimes nice to be able to clear all the print jobs when the printer comes back online.

Remove print jobs using `lprm`. For example, to remove all jobs for the user named bill (assuming you are either bill or the root user), type the following:

```
$ lprm bill
```

The root user can remove all print jobs from the queue. To do this, you add a dash (-) to the `lprm` command line, as follows:

```
$ lprm -
```

You can also remove queued print jobs for a particular printer (`-Pprinter`) or for a particular job number by just adding the job number to the `lprm` command line.

Checking Printer Status

Sometimes nothing comes out of a printer, and you have no idea why. `lpc` is a printer status command that might give you a clue about what's going on with your printer. It is intended for administrators, so it may not be in your default PATH. To start the `lpc` command, type the following:

```
# /usr/sbin/lpc
```

When the command returns the `lpc>` prompt, type the word **status**:

```
lpc> status
hp:
                printer is on device 'lpd' speed -1
                queueing is enabled
                printing is enabled
                no entries
                daemon present
lpc>
```

This example shows the status of printer hp: queuing and printing are enabled, the printer shows no problems, and no print jobs are waiting. To quit the `lpc` command, type **exit** at the `lpc>` prompt.

Displaying Documents with Ghostscript and Acrobat

Document publishing can be very paper-intensive if you send a Groff or LaTeX document to the printer each time you want to make a change to the document's content or formatting. To save paper and time spent running around, use a print preview program to display your document on the screen as it will appear on the printed page. The following sections describe the `ghostscript` command for displaying PostScript files and the Adobe Acrobat Reader for displaying Portable Document Format (PDF) files.

Using the ghostscript and gv Commands

To display PostScript or PDF documents in Linux, you can use the `ghostscript` command. It is a fairly crude interface, intended to let you step through documents and interpret them one line at a time.

You can display any PS or PDF file you happen to have on your computer. For example, if the samba package is installed, you could type the following to display a PDF file (otherwise, you could find your own PDF file to try it):

```
$ ghostscript /usr/share/doc/samba-*/docs/Samba-HOWTO-Collection.pdf
>>showpage, press <return> to continue<<
```

At the prompt, press Enter (or Return) to go through the file one page at a time. When you have reached the end of the document, you can type the name of another PostScript or PDF file and page through that file. When you are done, type **quit**.

The ggv command (GNOME ghostview) is another, more friendly way of viewing PostScript files. To use ggv to open a file called rbash.ps, you would type the following:

```
$ ggv /usr/share/doc/bash-doc-*/bashref.ps
```

When the ghostview window opens, you can see the document. Left-click on the page and move the mouse up and down to scroll the document. Use the Page Up and Page Down keys to page through the document. You can click a page number in the left column to jump to a particular page or click the Print All button to print the entire document.

Using Adobe Acrobat Reader

The Portable Document Format (PDF) provides a way of storing documents as they would appear in print. With Adobe Acrobat Reader, you can view PDF files in a very friendly way. Adobe Acrobat makes it easy to move around within a PDF file. A PDF file may include hyperlinks, a table of contents, graphics, and a variety of type fonts.

You can get Adobe Acrobat Reader for Linux from the Adobe Web site (www.adobe. com/products/acrobat/readstep2.html). Select Linux as the platform from that site. A recent version of the Adobe Acrobat Reader is available in RPM format for Fedora from Guru Labs (www.gurulabs.com/downloads.html).

After you install Adobe Acrobat Reader, type the following command to start the program:

```
$ acroread
```

Click File ➪ Open, and then select the name of a PDF file you want to display. Figure 20-12 shows an example of a PDF file viewed in Adobe Acrobat.

Adobe Acrobat has a lot of nice features. For example, you can display a list of bookmarks alongside the document and click on a bookmark to take you to a particular page. You can also display thumbnails of the pages to quickly scroll through and select a page.

Using the menu bar or buttons, you can page through the PDF document, zoom in and out, go to the beginning or end of the document, and display different views of the document (as well as display bookmarks and page thumbnails). To print a copy, click File ➪ Print.

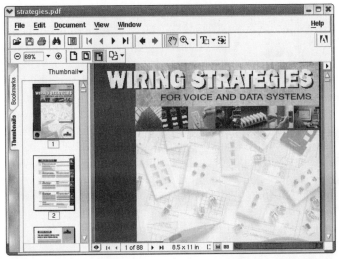

Figure 20-12: Display PDF files in the Adobe Acrobat Reader.

Working with Graphics

Tools for creating and manipulating graphics are becoming both more plentiful and more powerful in Linux systems as a whole. Leading the list is the GNU Image Manipulation Program (GIMP). GIMP lets you compose and author images as well as retouch photographs. Other tools for creating graphics include ksnapshot (a program for taking screen captures) and kpaint (for working with bitmap images).

Manipulating Images with GIMP

The GIMP is a free software program for manipulating photographs and graphical images. To create images with GIMP, you can either import a drawing, photograph, or 3D image, or you can create one from scratch. You can start GIMP from the system menu by selecting Graphics ➪ The GIMP or by typing **gimp&** from a Terminal window.

Figure 20-13 shows an example of GIMP.

In many ways, GIMP is similar to Adobe Photoshop. Some people feel that GIMP's scripting features are comparable to or even better than Actions in Adobe Photoshop. One capability that GIMP lacks, however, is support for CMYK (cyan-magenta-yellow-black) separations. If CMYK is not critical for your graphics needs, you will probably find GIMP to be just as powerful and flexible as Photoshop in many ways.

Figure 20-13: GIMP is a powerful tool for graphic manipulation.

One of the easiest ways to become familiar with GIMP is to crop, or trim, an image file already on your computer. To crop a file, follow these steps:

1. Start GIMP and open an image file.

2. Right-click on the image. From the contextual menu that appears, select Tools ⇨ Transform Tools ⇨ Crop and Resize. The crop cursor appears (two overlapping L shapes), as does the Crop and Resize Information window.

3. Position the crop cursor at the upper-left corner of the area of the image that you want to crop. Click and drag the cursor to the lower-right corner of the area to be cropped. A selection rectangle appears around the selected area as you do so.

4. Release the mouse button. Four selection handles appear in the corners of the border around the selected area. Click and drag the handles to resize the border.

5. When the border is in the right place, click the Crop button in the Information window. The image is cropped to the border.

Tip

If you make a mistake, select Edit ⇨ Undo from the GIMP menu, or press the Ctrl+Z key combination.

Acquiring Screen Captures

If you want to show examples of the work via screenshot, use the Screen Capture program.

To open Screen Capture, select Graphics ⇨ Ksnapshot from most Linux KDE menus, or type **ksnapshot**. Figure 20-14 shows an example of the Screen Capture program.

Figure 20-14: Grab a picture of your desktop or selected window with Screen Capture.

When Screen Capture first opens, it takes a snapshot of the full desktop. To take a new snapshot, choose the Capture Mode (Full Screen, Window Under Cursor, or Region) and click the New Snapshot button. Use the Save As button to save the snapshot to a file in X bitmap, MS Windows icons, PNG, portable pixmap, JPEG, X pixmap, Encapsulated PostScript, or Windows BMP formats. Click the Print button to send the snapshot to your printer.

Modifying Images with KPaint

Using the KPaint window, a utility that comes with KDE, you can work with and convert images in several formats. Figure 20-15 shows an example of KPaint.

Start KPaint from either the desktop (from most KDE desktops, click Graphics ⇨ Paint Program) or from a Terminal window (/usr/bin/kpaint&). Start with either a blank canvas or by opening an image in one of the supported formats (File ⇨ Open, browse for a file, and then click OK). Look in the /usr/share/backgrounds directory for graphics to try.

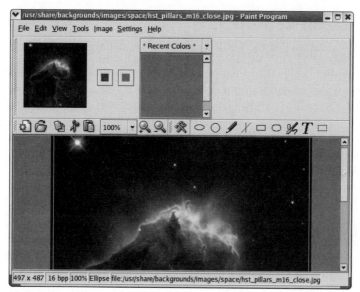

Figure 20-15: Edit bitmap images with KPaint.

The painting tools let you draw ovals, boxes, lines, and other shapes. You can save the file to several different formats, including MS Windows PCX format, Encapsulated PostScript image, MS Windows icons, JPEG, PNG, PNM, TIFF, X bitmap, and X Window pixmap.

Using Scanners Driven by SANE

Software for using a scanner with Linux is being driven by an effort called *Scanner Access Now Easy (SANE)*. This effort hopes to standardize how device drivers for equipment such as scanners, digital still cameras, and digital video cameras are created, as well as help simplify the interfaces for applications that use those devices. SANE is now included with a variety of Linux distributions.

Someone wanting to use Linux as a publishing platform is generally interested in two issues about scanners: which scanners are supported and which applications are available to use the scanners. In general, more SCSI scanners are supported than parallel scanners.

Because of the ongoing development effort, new scanners are being supported all the time. You can find a current list of supported scanners at `www.sane-project.org/sane-supported-devices.html`, with USB scanners listed at `www.buzzard.me.uk/jonathan/scanners-usb.html`. As for applications, some of the more widely used tools available today include:

✦ **xsane** — An X-based graphical front end for SANE scanners, xsane can work as a GIMP plug-in or as a separate application (from most KDE desktops, select Graphics ⇨ Scanning). It supports 8-bit output in JPG, TIFF, PNG, PostScript, and PNM formats. There is experimental 16-bit support for PNM (ASCII), PNG, and raw formats.

✦ **scanimage** — Use this command-line interface to obtain scanned images. The command acquires the scanned image, and then directs the data to standard output (so you can send it to a file or pipe it to another program). It supports the same formats as xscanimage.

In addition to these applications, the OpenOffice.org suite supports SANE.

Because of the architecture of SANE scanner drivers, it is possible to separate scanner drivers from scanner applications. This makes it possible to share scanners across a network.

Summary

In recent times, modern GUI-based publishing tools have augmented the text-based publishing tools that have always been available with Linux. Powerful open source publishing tools such as OpenOffice.org are becoming competitive with commercial office suites. Traditional publishing tools such as Groff (which implements traditional troff/nroff text processing) and LaTeX (a TeX macro interface that is particularly suited for scientific and mathematical publishing) are still available with Fedora.

✦　　✦　　✦

E-Mailing and Web Browsing

Web browsers and e-mail clients available with Linux have made incredible improvements over the past few years. Their features rival those you can get on the most popular Windows clients. Security issues with Outlook mail clients and Internet Explorer browsers have many people taking a fresh look at Linux and open source software for accessing the Internet.

This chapter describes some of the best Web, e-mail, chat, and related tools for accessing the Internet that you can get with the Linux distributions described in this book. If you have never worked with the Internet from Linux, or haven't for a few years, you might be blown away by what's available today.

Using E-Mail

Most friendly Linux desktop systems will have at least one or two applications for sending, receiving, and managing your e-mail just a click away. Some feel that superior tools for managing spam (junk e-mail) and generally better security mechanisms make Linux a great desktop platform for managing your e-mail.

Choosing an E-Mail Client

Choices of e-mail clients range from those that look like clones of popular Windows e-mail programs to those that run in plain text from the shell, and interfaces vary widely with the e-mail clients that are available with Linux. Here are some different ways in which e-mail clients are integrated into Linux:

✦ **With a Web browser** — Many popular Web browsers include an integrated e-mail client. By configuring the e-mail client that comes with your browser, you are ready to launch a new e-mail message by clicking on a mailto link from a browser window. You can also easily open the e-mail client from your Web browser's toolbar.

Feature-rich Mozilla mail (`www.mozilla.org`) is probably the most popular e-mail client for Linux to come with a Web browser. Netscape Communicator (`www.netscape.com`) is another Web browser that has its own mail client (although it has been dropped from many Linux distributions because of licensing issues).

The Opera (`www.opera.com`) Web browser also includes an integrated e-mail client. It is perhaps the most elegant of the e-mail clients that comes with a Web browser. Opera is available for personal use without cost if you agree to allow ads to be displayed. (Pay for Opera, and you get it without the ads.)

✦ **With groupware** — Some e-mail clients have been bundled with other personal productivity applications to form integrated groupware applications. The most popular of these in Linux is Ximian Evolution, which is bundled as the default e-mail client with several different Linux distributions. Besides e-mail, Evolution includes a calendar, task list, and contacts directory. (Ximian was purchased by Novell, Inc. and is transitioning the name of this product to Novell Evolution.)

✦ **From the shell** — Many old-school UNIX and Linux power users prefer to use an e-mail client that runs without a graphical desktop. Although not always intuitive to use, text-based e-mail readers can run much faster than their graphical counterparts. The `mail` command dates back to the earliest UNIX systems (where there was no GUI). The mutt e-mail client is popular among power users because of its capability to manage large mailboxes and attachments efficiently.

Features inside each e-mail client can help you distinguish between them. Although most e-mail clients let you get, compose, send, and manage e-mail messages, here are a few extra features you might look for:

✦ **Filters and spam catchers** — Mozilla, Evolution, and other mail clients offer message filters and junk-mail detectors. You use filters to set up rules to sort incoming mail into different folders, delete certain messages, or otherwise respond to incoming mail. Some e-mail clients also have features that try to automatically detect when junk mail has arrived. If you get a lot of e-mail, these can be invaluable tools for managing your e-mail. (Select the Tools menu from your e-mail client, and then look for a Filters or Junk Mail selection.)

✦ **Security features** — E-mail clients such as Thunderbird (`www.mozilla.com`) enable you to use message encryption, digital signatures, and other security features to keep your e-mail private.

✦ **Sorting, searching, marking, and displaying** — Again, if you are managing lots of e-mail messages at once (some people manage thousands of messages), the capability to refer to the one you want can be critical. Some clients let you sort by date, sender, priority, subject, and other items. You might be able to search message contents for text or choose how to display the messages (such as without showing attachments or with source code shown).

✦ **Mail composition tools** — Some mail composers let you include HTML in your messages, which enables you to add images, links, tables, colors, font changes, and other visual enhancements to your messages. (One warning: Some mailing lists don't like you to send messages in HTML because some people still use plain-text readers.)

✦ **Multiple accounts** — Many e-mail clients let you configure multiple e-mail accounts to be served by your e-mail reader. Early plain-text e-mail clients only pointed to one mailbox at a time.

✦ **Performance** — Some lightweight graphical e-mail clients give you much better performance than others. In particular, the Sylpheed e-mail client (that comes with Damn Small Linux) was created to use a minimal amount of memory and processing power yet still provide a graphical interface. E-mail clients that run from the keyboard, in particular the mutt e-mail client, will run much faster than, say, most full-blown graphical e-mail clients such as Ximian Evolution.

For most home and small-business users, Ximian Evolution or Mozilla mail are often available from a Linux desktop and will give you much the same experience you would expect from Windows mail clients, such as Outlook Express. If you are using the KDE desktop, you almost always have the KMail e-mail client available. Lately, Thunderbird has been added to many Linux distributions.

Even though the Linux distribution you are using may have only one or two of the e-mail clients described in this section, you can always add a client that interests you.

Getting Here from Windows

To understand how to transition your e-mail client from Windows to Linux, you need to know a bit about your current e-mail setup. Whether you are using Outlook, Outlook Express, or any other e-mail client running in Windows, here are some things you should know:

✦ **Server type** — Is your e-mail server a POP3 or IMAP server? If it is an IMAP server, all your messages are being stored on the server. Transitioning to a different e-mail server might simply mean pointing the new e-mail client at your server and continuing to use e-mail as you always have. If it is a POP3 server, your messages have probably been downloaded to your local client. To keep your old messages, you need to somehow bring your current mail folders over to your new client. (This is a bit tricky.)

✦ **Address book** — You need to export your current address book to a format that can be read by your new e-mail client and import it to your new e-mail client.

To transition to Linux, you may want to add a cross-platform e-mail client such as Mozilla Mail or Thunderbird to your Windows systems so that you can get at your resources (addresses, stored mail messages, and so on) during the transition to your new mail client. When you eventually move off Windows altogether, Mozilla Mail or Thunderbird for Linux will work almost exactly as it does in Windows.

If your current e-mail server is a Microsoft Exchange 2000 server, you need to get a Ximian Connector for Microsoft Exchange license to allow Evolution to access information from that server. The license, which once needed to be purchased, can now be obtained from Novell (which owns SUSE). Check here for availability: `www.novell.com/products/connector/download.html`.

Getting Started with E-Mail

Most Linux systems include an e-mail client that you can select on a panel or by left-clicking on the desktop to bring up a menu. Look for an envelope icon on a panel or a submenu labeled something like Internet. If you want a graphical e-mail reader, you can start by looking for one of these clients: Evolution, Mozilla Mail, Thunderbird, and KMail.

After you have launched your chosen e-mail client, you need some information to use it. When you first start most graphical e-mail clients, a configuration screen of some sort asks you to set up an account. Here's how to begin setting up a mail account for the e-mail clients described in this chapter:

✦ **Evolution** — The Evolution Setup Assistant starts the first time each user opens Evolution. After that, select Tools⇨Settings from the main Evolution window. Then choose Mail Accounts and double-click the mail account you want to modify.

✦ **Mozilla Mail** — An account wizard starts the first time you open Mozilla Mail. After that, you can set up or modify accounts from the Mozilla Mail window by clicking Edit ⇨ Mail & Newsgroups Account Settings.

✦ **Thunderbird** — This is a next-generation mail client from the people who bring you Mozilla (`Mozilla.org`). The fact that as of this writing, it is not yet at version 1 (it's at 0.7) implies that it is not ready for prime time yet. With its more advanced security features, you might consider Thunderbird, if you don't mind a glitch here and there. Thunderbird is meant to be a complement to Mozilla's Firefox.

✦ **KMail** — From the KMail window, select Settings⇨Configure KMail. From the Configure KMail window that appears, select the Network icon. From there, you can click on Sending or Receiving tabs to configure your outgoing and incoming e-mail settings.

Initial configuration for text-based e-mail clients is described later in this chapter.

Information you will need to configure your e-mail accounts is much the same for the different graphical e-mail clients covered in this chapter:

✦ **Name** — Enter your name as you want it to appear on outgoing messages.

✦ **Email Address** — Enter the e-mail address from which you are sending. You may also be offered the opportunity to supply a different reply-to address, if you want replies to go to an address other than the one you sent from.

✦ **Mail server type** — Most mail servers are POP3 or IMAP type servers. (Configuring those types of servers is discussed in Chapter 24.)

✦ **Server names** — Enter the names of the servers you will use to send outgoing e-mail and receive incoming e-mail. The names can be fully qualified domain names (such as `mail.linuxtoys.net`) or IP addresses. In many cases, the incoming and outgoing mail servers are the same.

✦ **User name** — Enter the name by which the mail server knows you. For example, if your e-mail address were `chris@linuxtoys.net`, your username to the mail.linuxtoys.net server might simply be chris. However, it's possible that your username on the mail server might be different, so you should find that out from the administrator of your mail server.

✦ **Account title** — Enter the name that you want to call this mail account so you can refer to it later in your list of mail and news group accounts.

✦ **Authentication type** — Indicate the type of authentication to use when you get your mail (sometimes authentication is needed to send your mail as well). Password authentication is normal. Usually you can have your e-mail client remember your password if you want. Typically, you are prompted for the password the first time you connect to get your mail.

This is most of the basic information you need to start getting and sending e-mail. However, you may want to further tune how your e-mail client interacts when it gets and sends e-mail.

Tuning Up E-Mail

With your basic settings done, you should be ready to start sending and receiving your e-mail. Before you do, however, you should consider some of the other settings that can affect how you use mail:

✦ **Automatically check messages** — You can set your e-mail client to automatically check and download your messages from the mail server every few minutes.

✦ **Leave messages on server** — If you turn this feature on for a POP server, your e-mail messages remain on the server after you have downloaded them to your e-mail client. People sometimes turn this feature on if they want to check their mail messages while they are on the road and want to download their messages from their permanent desktop computer later.

✦ **Certificates** — Your e-mail client may provide a way of using certificates to sign your outgoing messages. For example, Evolution and Mozilla Mail each have Security tabs for your mail settings that let you enter information about your certificates and indicate that your e-mail be signed. You can also choose to use the certificates for encryption.

Step through your mail account settings because they are slightly different for each e-mail client.

Reading E-Mail with Mozilla Mail

The Mozilla Mail client program is a full-featured mail and newsgroup reader that usually comes with the Mozilla Web browser on many Linux systems. Mozilla Mail includes features for

✦ Sending, receiving, reading, and managing e-mail.

✦ Managing multiple mail and newsgroup accounts.

✦ Composing HTML e-mail messages.

✦ Controlling junk e-mail.

✦ Message encryption and signing.

After launching the Mozilla Web browser, you can start Mozilla Mail from the Window menu. For example, in Fedora Core you can open Mozilla Mail from your Mozilla browser window by choosing Window ➪ Mail & Newsgroups. Figure 21-1 shows an example of the Mozilla Mail window that is ready to use mail and news.

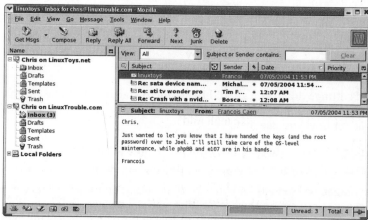

Figure 21-1: Handle multiple mail accounts in Mozilla Mail.

Tip

A new Junk Mail feature was recently added to Mozilla Mail. With it, Mozilla Mail automatically tags any message it believes to be junk mail with a blue recycle-bin icon. Using the Junk Toolbar, you train the Junk Mail feature by telling it when a message is or isn't junk mail. After you have identified which messages are junk mail, you can automatically move incoming junk mail to the Junk folder.

Connecting to the Mail Server

After you have set up your mail accounts in Mozilla Mail, you can explicitly ask to download any available mail messages from the server (for POP accounts). To do that, click the Get Msgs button.

You are prompted for the password for your account on the mail server. Using that password, Mozilla Mail downloads all your messages from the mail server. It downloads messages again every 10 minutes, or you can click the Get Msgs button at any time.

If you want to change how often mail is downloaded, or other features of your account, choose Edit ➪ Mail & Newsgroup Account Settings. Under the e-mail account you added are categories to change the setup and behavior of the account. (Click Server Settings to change how often, if at all, new messages are automatically downloaded from the mail server.)

Managing Incoming Mail

Various ways exist to store and manage the e-mail messages in Mozilla Mail. Here's a quick rundown of how to manage incoming mail:

✦ **Mail folders**—Mail messages are stored in folders in the left column. There should be a separate heading for each mail account you have. For each mail account, incoming messages are stored (by default) in your Inbox folder. You can create additional folders to better keep track of your mail (right-click Inbox and select New Folder to add a folder). Other folders contain drafts of messages set aside for a time (Drafts), templates for creating messages (Templates), messages you have sent (Sent), and messages that you have discarded (Trash).

✦ **Sort messages**—Messages are sorted by date for the folder you select, in the upper-right corner of the display. Click the headings over the messages to sort by subject, sender, or priority.

✦ **Read messages**—When you select a message, it appears in the lower-right corner of the display. Click the e-mail address from the sender and a menu enables you to add that address to your address book, compose mail to that address, copy mail to that address, or create a filter from that message.

✦ **Filter mail**—When Mozilla Mail grabs your e-mail from the mail server, it drops it into the Inbox associated with your mail account by default. Mozilla Mail 1.7, however, has some nice features for checking each message for information you choose, and then acting on that message to move it to another folder, label it, or change its priority. See the "Filtering Mail and Catching Spam" section later in this chapter for details.

✦ **Search messages** — You can use the search feature to retrieve messages that are in one of your mail folders. With the folder you want to search being the current folder, type a word to search on into the Subject or Sender Contains box. Messages with sender names or subject lines that don't contain that string will disappear from the list of messages. To do more detailed searches, choose Tools⇨Search Messages.

Composing and Sending Mail

To compose e-mail messages, you can either start from scratch or respond to an existing e-mail message. The following are some quick descriptions of how to create outgoing mail:

✦ **New Messages** — To create a new message, choose Message⇨New Message (or click Compose on the toolbar).

✦ **Reply to Messages** — To reply to a mail message, click on the message on the right side of your screen and then choose Message⇨Reply (to reply only to the author of the message) or Message⇨Reply to All (to reply to everyone listed as a recipient of the message).

✦ **Forward Messages** — To forward a mail message, click on the message on the right side of your screen and then choose Message⇨Forward. You can also forward a message and have it appear in the text (Message⇨Forward As⇨Inline) or as an attachment (Message⇨Forward As⇨Attachment).

In each case, a mail Compose window appears, in which you compose your e-mail message. As you compose your message in the Compose window, you can use:

✦ **Address book** — Add e-mail addresses from your personal address book (or from one of several different directory servers) by selecting Options⇨Select Addresses. A list of your stored addresses appears for you to choose from. Click Collected Addresses to see a list of addresses that have been collected from e-mail messages you have received.

✦ **Attachments** — Add attachments such as a word-processing file, image, or executable program by choosing File⇨Attach File and then selecting a file from your file system to attach. (You can also choose File⇨Attach Web Page to choose the URL of a Web page that you want to attach.)

✦ **Certificates** — Add certificates or view security information about your mail message by selecting View⇨Message Security Info.

When you are finished composing the message, click Send to send the message. If you prefer, queue the message to be sent later by choosing File⇨Send Later. (Send Later is useful if you have a dial-up connection to the network and you are not currently online.)

Tip   If you want to quit and finish the e-mail message later, choose File⇨Save As⇨Draft, and then click the X in the upper-right corner to close the window. When you are ready to resume work on the message, open the Draft folder in the Mozilla Mail window and double-click the message.

Filtering Mail and Catching Spam

Mozilla Mail can do more with incoming messages than just place them in your Inbox. You can set up filters to check each message first and then have Mozilla Mail take an action you define when a message matches the rule you set up.

For example, your filter can contain a rule that checks the subject, sender, text body, date, priority, status, recipients, or age in days of the message for a particular word, name, or date, as appropriate. If there is a match, you can have Mozilla Mail put that message in a particular folder, label it with a selected phrase, change its priority, or set its junk-mail status. You can add as many rules as you like. For example, you can

✦ Have all messages sent from a particular address sorted into a separate mail folder. For example, I do this so that important mail doesn't get lost when there's a lot of activity on the mailing lists to which I subscribe.

✦ Mark incoming messages from important clients as having highest priority.

✦ Have messages from particular people or places that are being mistakenly marked as spam change their junk status to Not Junk.

To set up filter rules in Mozilla Mail, choose Tools⇨Message Filters. The Message Filters' pop-up appears. If you have multiple mail accounts, select the account you want to filter. Then click New. From the Filter Rules pop-up window, choose the following:

✦ **For incoming messages that** — Create what to match on. You can check parts of a message in different ways. For example, you can check whether the Sender is in the address book. You can check what the Priority is: low, medium, or high. You can create multiple rules for a filter (click More to add another rule), and then choose if you want to match all or any of the rules to continue to the action.

✦ **Perform these actions** — The information in this section describes what to do with a message that matches the rules you've set. You can have the message moved to any existing folder, or label the message. With labels, the message appears in a different color depending on the label: important (red), work (orange), personal (green), to do (blue), or later (purple). You can also change the message priority.

Figure 21-2 shows a rule I created to highlight mail from my friend Tweeks in red (Important) when it comes in.

Figure 21-2: Create filter rules to sort or highlight your e-mail messages.

A nice feature of Mozilla's filtering rules is that you can apply the rules after the fact as well. If you decide you want to move all messages in your Inbox from a particular person to a different folder, for example, you can open the Message Filters window, create a rule to move the selected messages, select Inbox, and click Run Now.

For junk mail, with a mail message selected, click the Junk button in the toolbar. The message is marked as junk. Your selection helps teach Mozilla what you think is junk mail. Choose Tools⇨Run Junk Mail Controls on Folder and Mozilla Mail will look for other messages that look like junk mail. (You can take the junk marker off of any message you think is not junk.) Then select Tools⇨Delete Mail Marked as Junk in Folder, and the junk mail is deleted. To open a window to configure how you handle junk mail, select Tools⇨Junk Mail Controls.

Managing E-Mail in Evolution

If you are using Fedora Core, Evolution is the e-mail client that you can start right from the desktop (look for the envelope icon on the panel). After you launch Evolution for the first time and run the Startup Assistant, the Evolution window appears, showing the different types of operations you can perform. Figure 21-3 shows an example of the Evolution window.

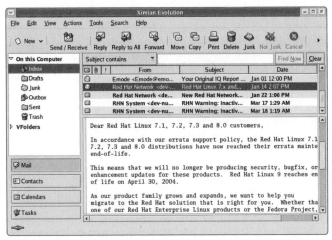

Figure 21-3: Evolution can be used to manage your mail, appointments, and tasks.

Evolution is a groupware application, combining several types of applications that help groups of people communicate and work together. The features of Evolution include the following:

✦ **E-mail** — A complete set of features for getting, reading, managing, composing, and sending e-mail on one or more e-mail accounts.

✦ **Contacts** — Create contact information such as names, addresses, and telephone numbers for friends and associates. A Categories feature helps you remember who gets birthday and anniversary gifts.

✦ **Calendar** — Create and manage appointments on your personal calendar. You can e-mail appointment information to others and do keyword searches of your calendar.

✦ **Tasks** — Organize ongoing tasks into folders.

Features recently added to Evolution include improved junk-mail handling and vfolders (for managing multiple physical folders as one folder).

Receiving, Composing, and Sending E-Mail

Evolution offers a full set of features for sending, receiving, and managing your e-mail. Here's a quick rundown on these tasks:

✦ **Read e-mail** — Click Inbox in the left column. Your messages appear to the right. Message headers are in the upper right; the current message is displayed in the lower pane. Double-click a message header to display it in a separate window.

✦ **Delete e-mail** — After you have read a message, select it and press the Delete key. Choose View⇨Hide Deleted Messages to toggle whether you can see deleted messages. Choose Actions⇨Expunge to permanently remove all messages marked for deletion in the current folder.

✦ **Send and receive** — Click the Send/Receive button to send any e-mail queued to be sent and receive any e-mail waiting for you at your mail server. (You may not need to do this if Evolution is configured to download your messages every few minutes. Click Tools⇨Settings, and then double-click on your mail account. The Receiving Options tab indicates if automatic mail checking is being done.)

✦ **Compose e-mail** — Choose New⇨Mail Message. A Compose a Message window appears. Type your recipient's e-mail address, enter a subject line, and fill in the body of the message. Click Send when you are finished. Buttons on the Compose window enable you to add attachments, cut and paste text, choose a format (HTML or plain text), and sign the message (if you have set up appropriate keys).

✦ **Use address books** — Click the Contacts button to see a list of names, addresses, and other contact information for the people in your address book. When you compose a message, click the To or CC buttons to select addresses from the book to add as recipients for your message.

✦ **Create folders** — If you like to keep old messages, you may want to save them outside your Inbox (so it won't get too junked up). To create a folder in which to keep them, right-click the Inbox and select New Folder. You can choose to store the new folder as a subfolder to any existing folder. Type a folder name and click OK.

✦ **Move messages** — With new folders created, you can easily move messages from your Inbox to another folder. The easiest way is to simply drag-and-drop each message (or a set of selected messages) from the message pane to the new folder.

✦ **Search messages** — Type a keyword in the search box over your e-mail message pane and select whether to search your message by subject line, sender, recipient, or message body. Click Find Now to search for the keyword. After viewing the messages, click Clear to have the other messages reappear.

Managing E-Mail with Virtual Folders

Managing large amounts of e-mail can become difficult when the messages you want to refer span several folders, dates, or senders. With virtual folders (vfolders), you can identify criteria to group together messages from all your mail folders so you can deal with them in one vfolder. Here's a procedure for creating a vfolder:

1. With Evolution open to read mail (click Inbox to get there), select File⇨New⇨Folder. A Create New Folder pop-up appears.

2. Select VFolders, type a folder name (like FromJohn), and click OK. A New VFolder pop-up appears.

3. Click Add and select criteria for including a message in your vfolder. You can search to see if the sender, recipient, subject, message body, or other part of the message contains or doesn't contain the string you type in the next box. Click Add again if you want to add more criteria.

4. If you want to search only specific folders, click Add in the vFolder Sources box and select the folder you want to search. You can repeat the Add to choose more than one. Otherwise, you can select to search all local folders, all active remote folders, or all local and active remote folders. Then click OK.

5. Make sure the folder bar is visible (View⇨Folder Bar). The folder you just created is listed under the VFolders heading. Click on that folder to see the messages you gathered with this action.

At this point, you can work with the messages you gathered in the vfolder. Although it appears that there are multiple versions of each message across your mail folders, there is really only one copy of each, so deleting or moving the message from a vfolder actually causes it to be deleted or moved from the original folder in which the real message resides.

Filtering E-Mail Messages

You can take action on an e-mail message before it even lands in your Inbox. Choose Tools⇨Filters, and a Filters window opens to let you add filters to deal with incoming or outgoing messages. Click Add to create criteria and set actions.

For example, you could have all messages from a particular sender, subject, date, status, or size sorted to a selected folder. Or you could have messages matching your criteria deleted, assigned a color, or play a sound clip.

Evolution also supports many common features, such as printing, saving, and viewing e-mail messages in various ways. The help system that comes with Evolution (click the Help button) includes a good manual, FAQ, and service for reporting bugs.

Getting Thunderbird

One open source e-mail client has gotten a lot of attention before it's even reached version 1 status. Thunderbird, from Mozilla.org, is being touted as Mozilla's next-generation e-mail client.

Note   Projects listed with versions of less than 1, such as .5 or .7, are considered to not be fully completed and tested.

Thunderbird is included with Fedora Core 3, which is on the DVD that comes with this book. However, because Thunderbird is not being delivered with every Linux distribution yet, you may need to download it to try it out — go to www.mozilla .org/products/thunderbird. Or, you can find out if there is a package available for your distribution (for example, there's a Thunderbird package for Fedora at http://download.fedora.us).

After Thunderbird is installed, look for a Thunderbird menu entry on your panel menu (usually under an Internet submenu). As an alternative, you can just run the `thunderbird` command from a Terminal window. Figure 21-4 shows an example of the Mozilla Thunderbird e-mail client.

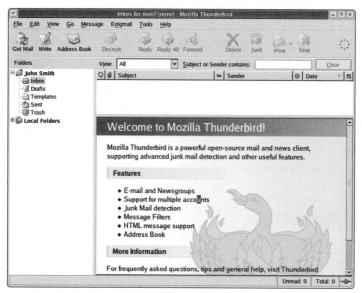

Figure 21-4: Mozilla Thunderbird was designed to be a fast, efficient e-mail client.

Find out the latest on the Thunderbird project at `http://texturizer.net/thunderbird`.

Working with Text-Based E-Mail Readers

The first text-based mail clients could be configured quite simply. Mail clients such as mutt, mail, or pine were often run with the user logged into the computer that's acting as the mail server. So instead of downloading the messages, using POP3 or IMAP, the mail client would simply open the mailbox (often under the user's name in `/var/spool/mail`) and begin working with mail.

Many text-based mail programs are available for reading, sending, and working with your mail. Many of these programs have been around for a long time, so they are full of features and have been well debugged. As a group, however, they are not very intuitive.

Tip   Most of these programs use the value of your $MAIL environment variable as your local mailbox. Usually, that location is /var/spool/mail/*user*, where *user* is your username. To set your $MAIL so that it points to your Mozilla mailbox (so you can use either Mozilla Mail or a text-based mail program), add the following line to one of your startup files:

```
export MAIL=$HOME/.mozilla/default/*/Mail/hostname/Inbox
```

If you usually use Mozilla for mail, set this variable temporarily to try out some of these mail programs.

Mail readers described in the following sections are text based and use the entire Terminal window (or other shell display). Although some features are different, menu bars show available options right on the screen.

Mutt Mail Reader

The mutt command is a text-based, full-screen mail user agent for reading and sending e-mail. The interface is quick and efficient. Type **mutt** to start the program. Move arrow keys up and down to select from your listed messages. Press Enter to see a mail message and type **i** to return to the Main menu.

The menu bar indicates how to mark messages for deletion, undelete them, save messages to a directory, and reply to a message. Type **m** to compose a new message, and it opens your default editor (vi, for example) to create the message. Type **y** to send the message. If you want to read mail without having your fingers leave your keyboard, mutt is a nice choice. (It even handles attachments!)

Pine Mail Reader

The pine mail reader is another full-screen mail reader, but it offers many more features than does mutt. With pine, you can manage multiple mail folders and newsgroup messages as well as mail messages. As text-based applications go, pine is quite easy to use. It was developed by a group at the University of Washington for use by students on campus but has become widely used in UNIX and Linux environments.

Start this mail program by typing **pine**. The following menu is displayed, from which you can select items by typing the associated letter or using up and down arrows and pressing Enter:

```
?   HELP               - Get help using Pine
C   COMPOSE MESSAGE    - Compose and send a message
I   MESSAGE INDEX      - View messages in current folder
L   FOLDER LIST        - Select a folder to view
A   ADDRESS BOOK       - Update address book
S   SETUP              - Configure Pine Options
Q   QUIT               - Leave the Pine program
```

To read your e-mail, select either I or L. Commands are listed along the bottom of the screen and change to suit the content you are viewing. Left (←) and right (⇨) arrow keys let you step backward and forward among the pine screens.

Mail Reader

The mail command was the first mail reader for UNIX. It is text-based, but not screen-oriented. Type **mail,** and you will see the messages in your mailbox. You get just a prompt after message headings are displayed — you are expected to know what to do next. (You can use the Enter key to step through messages.) Type **?** to see which commands are available.

While in mail, type **h** to see mail headings again. Simply type a message number to see the message. Type **d#** (replacing # with a message number) to delete a message. To create a new message, type **m**. To respond to a message, type **r#** (replacing # with the message number).

Choosing a Web Browser

Many Web browsers available in Linux are based on the Mozilla Web browser. Web browsers that might come with your Linux distribution include the following:

✦ **Mozilla Navigator** — Based on the former industry-leading Netscape Navigator browser, Mozilla Navigator has been the most popular open source Web browser for the past few years.

✦ **Konqueror** — Comes as the default browser with many KDE desktop environments. Konqueror is a file manager as well as a Web browser. It includes Gecko, which is the Mozilla browser engine that renders the Web page you see on your screen.

✦ **Firefox** — Being touted as Mozilla's next-generation browser, Firefox is designed to be fast, efficient, and safe for Web browsing.

✦ **links, lynx, and w3m** — If you are in a text-based environment (operating from the shell), these are among several text-based Web browsers you can try out.

The following sections describe Mozilla, Firefox, and some text-based Web browsers that are available with many Linux systems.

Web Browsing with Mozilla

During the early 1990s, Netscape Navigator was the most popular Web browser. When it became apparent that Netscape was losing its lead to Microsoft Internet Explorer, its source code was released to the world as open source code.

Mozilla.org (www.mozilla.org) was formed to coordinate the development of a new browser from that code. The result was the Mozilla browser that is now available with many computing platforms, including many Linux distributions. The availability on multiple platforms is great, especially if you must switch between Linux and Windows; for example, using Windows at work and Linux at home. Mozilla looks and acts the same on many platforms.

At the center of Mozilla, of course, is the Navigator Web browser. Mozilla also includes the following features:

✦ **Mail and Newsgroups**—A full-featured program for sending, receiving, and managing e-mail, as well as for using newsgroups. (The mozilla-mail RPM must be installed.)

✦ **IRC Chat**—An Internet Relay Chat (IRC) window, called ChatZilla, for participating in online, typed conversations. (The mozilla-chat package must be installed.)

✦ **Composer**—A Web page (HTML) composer application.

✦ **Address Book**—A feature to manage names, addresses, telephone numbers, and other contact information.

In Linux distributions such as Fedora Core, you start the Mozilla Web browser by clicking its icon on the desktop panel or by simply typing **mozilla** from a Terminal window.

In Linux distributions such as Fedora Core, you start the Mozilla Web browser by clicking its icon on the desktop panel or by simply typing **mozilla** from a Terminal window. Figure 21-5 shows the Mozilla home page (www.mozilla.org) as displayed by the browser.

Figure 21-5: Mozilla is the open source Web browser based on Netscape source code.

Mozilla has all the basic features you need in a Web browser plus a few special features. The following sections describe how to get the most out of your Mozilla Navigator Web browser.

Setting Up Mozilla Navigator

You can do many things to configure Mozilla to run like a champ. The following sections describe some ways to customize your browsing experience in Mozilla Navigator.

Setting Navigator Preferences

You can set your Mozilla Navigator preferences in the Preferences window (see Figure 21-6). To open Mozilla preferences, select Edit➪Preferences.

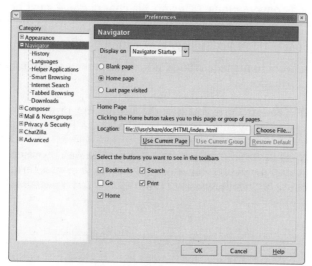

Figure 21-6: Change settings for navigating the Web from Mozilla's Preferences window.

The following are some Navigator preferences that you might want to change:

✦ **Navigator**—Select the location to use as your home page, and choose which buttons you see on the toolbar.

✦ **History**—Choose how long to store addresses of the sites you have typed in your location bar. (These addresses appear in the History tab on the Mozilla sidebar.)

✦ **Languages**—For Web pages that can appear in multiple languages, this sets the order in which you would prefer languages to be displayed. (For example, you might choose English/United States, English, French, and German. Then Mozilla will try to display a Web page you open in each of those languages successively, until one is matched.

✦ **Helper Applications**—Set up applications for handling different types of data that may be encountered while browsing the Web. You can select the Plug-in Finder Service box to have the Netscape Plug-in Finder Service used to look for plug-ins (small applications that run within the browser) to handle the type of data you encounter.

✦ **Smart Browsing**—Choose to do keyword searches when you type partial addresses in the Location box. Smart browsing is off by default, so typing **netscape** would cause Mozilla to look for `www.netscape.com` instead of searching for Netscape links.

✦ **Internet Search**—Select which search engine to use for Internet searches. You can also change how the Search tab is used with searches.

✦ **Tabbed Browsing**—Use these selections to have search results appear in tabs on the Mozilla Navigator window instead of appearing in the full screen.

✦ **Download**—Choose what you see during downloads from the Internet (a download manager, a progress dialog, or nothing).

Set Advanced Preferences to fine-tune your Web browsing experience. That includes choosing how data are cached on your computer and whether proxies are used. On the main Advanced preferences panel you can choose whether to enable Java content to be displayed in your browser. Here are some preferences that might interest you:

✦ **Scripts & Plug-ins**—The Web content you choose can try to open, move, resize, raise, and lower windows. It can request to change your images, status bar text, or bits of information stored in what are called *cookies*. These preferences let you restrict what the content you request can do.

✦ **Cache**—By default, the most recent 4MB of Web pages you visit are stored in RAM, and the most recent 50MB of pages you visit are stored on your hard disk. If a page is not out-of-date, caching makes it possible to return to a page quickly, without needing to reload from the original Web server. Cache preferences let you change how much information is cached, and where the hard-disk cache is located. Other preferences let you clear all memory and disk cache immediately.

✦ **Proxies**—If you have direct access to the Internet, you don't need to change any proxy settings. However, if you need to access the Internet via a proxy server, you can identify the location of that server (or servers) here. To access the Web via proxy servers, you must explicitly identify the proxy server to use for each type of content you request (HTTP, SSL, FTP, Gopher, and SOCKS).

✦ **HTTP Networking** — If you are using a proxy server, that proxy server may require that you make HTTP requests using either HTTP/1.0 or HTTP/1.1 standards (1.1 is the default). You can set which version of HTTP requests you should use.

✦ **Software Installation** — Choose to allow or disallow requested Web content attempts to install software, such as updates, on your computer.

✦ **Mouse Wheel** — Change how Mozilla behaves when you use a mouse wheel. By default, the wheel scrolls a line at a time. You can also assign each keyboard modifier key (Alt, Control, and Shift) to a different function.

✦ **DOM Inspector** — Turn this on to check the structure of a Web page (for debugging). This is very useful if you need to create Web pages, especially dynamic Web pages.

Adding Helper Apps

Although the main type of content provided by Web pages is HTML, many other content types can be displayed, played, or presented by a Web browser. Most additional data encountered by Mozilla is handled in one of two ways: plug-ins or helper apps.

Plug-ins are self-contained programs that allow data to play within the Mozilla window. A helper app can be any program that is available on your Linux system. It is up to you to identify the plug-in or helper app to have Mozilla launch when a certain type of data is encountered.

At the time you open a Web page and data of a specific type is encountered, Mozilla evaluates the data based on the following criteria and then launches the appropriate plug-in or helper app:

✦ **Suffixes** — If the browser is reading a file that has a particular extension (such as .exe for an application or .gz for a compressed zip file), it can use that suffix to determine the file's contents. When a file's extension matches a suffix configured for a particular helper app or plug-in, the helper app or plug-in is used to play or display the data.

✦ **MIME type** — Because data may come to the browser in a stream or have no suffix, Mozilla can use the MIME type attached to the data to determine which plug-in or helper app to use. (MIME stands for Multipurpose Internet Mail Extensions.)

You can add your own helper app to automatically handle a particular type of data in your browser. Here's how:

1. Choose Edit➪Preferences. The Mozilla Preferences window appears.

2. Click the plus next to the Navigator category, and select Helper Applications.

3. Click New Type. A dialog box appears that enables you to add information about the helper app and the data that it can handle. Type in a description of the data, the MIME type, and the file suffixes (if any) on files that contain that type of data.

Note   When you add the suffix, don't include the dot.

Choose an application to handle the data type. If the application needs a Terminal window to run, type **xterm -e**, followed by the command line you need to enter. This executes the command in an xterm window, reading in data as needed.

4. Click OK when you are done.

The next time you open data in Mozilla of the type you just added, a pop-up window asks you if you want to use the application you just entered to open the data.

Adding Plug-Ins

Few plug-ins are available for use in most Linux versions of Mozilla. To see a list of plug-ins associated with the browser, choose Help⇨About Plug-ins.

Check PluginDoc (`http://plugindoc.mozdev.org/linux.html`) for a list of plug-ins available for Mozilla. Here are descriptions of a few of those plug-ins:

✦ **Adobe Acrobat Plug-in** (`www.adobe.com/support/downloads`) — Displays files in Adobe Systems' PDF (Portable Document Format) format.

✦ **Cult3D Plug-in** (`www.cult3d.com`) — Displays high-quality, interactive real-time 3D images on the Web. This plug-in is part of the Cult3D product line from Cycore Inc. (Click Download from the Cult3D home page to find the plug-in. A cult3d RPM is available that requires tailoring to work in Mozilla.)

✦ **DjVu Plug-in** (`djvu.sourceforge.net`) — Displays images in DjVu image compression technology. This plug-in is from AT&T.

✦ **RealOne Player** (`www.real.com`) — Plays Real Audio and Video content. (Real Networks and its open source Helix community have recently made RealVideo 9 codecs available to the Linux community.)

✦ **Macromedia Flash Player** (`www.macromedia.com`) — Displays multimedia vector graphics and animation. This plug-in is from Macromedia, Inc. Flash Player is available for Mozilla, but Macromedia's Shockwave plug-in is not yet available for Linux.

Follow the installation instructions that come with the plug-in you downloaded. If the plug-in comes in an RPM file, install it as you would any other software package if you are using an RPM-based Linux distribution (`rpm -Uvh package` command).

Otherwise, probably just copy the plug-in file (a `.so` file) to the system plug-in directory (such as `/usr/lib/mozilla/plugins`) or your personal plug-ins directory (probably `$HOME/.mozilla/plugins`), if you are not otherwise instructed. When you restart Mozilla, the plug-ins will automatically be picked up from those locations.

> **Note**   The CrossOver Plug-in is a commercial product that lets you use many Windows plug-ins in Mozilla. See the section "Adding a CrossOver Plug-In," later in this chapter for details.

Using Mozilla Navigator Controls

If you have used a Web browser before, the Mozilla Navigator controls are probably as you might expect: location box, forward and back buttons, file and edit menus, and so on. A few controls come with Mozilla, though, that you might not be used to seeing, such as these:

✦ **Display Sidebar**—Press the F9 function key to toggle the sidebar on and off. The sidebar is a left column on your Mozilla screen for allowing quick access to Searches, Bookmarks, and History. Use the Search tab to search for Web content, the Bookmarks tab to add your own bookmarks, and the History tab to return to pages on your history list. The What's Related tab shows a list of links available from the current Web page.

✦ **Send Web Content**—You can send an e-mail containing either the current Web page (File⇨Send Page) or the URL of the current Web page (File⇨Send Link) to selected recipients.

✦ **Search the Internet**—You can search the Internet for a keyword phrase in many different ways. Choose Tools⇨Search the Web to open a Netscape Web site that lets you search the Internet, or type one or more keywords in the Location box and then click Search. And of course you can use the sidebar's Search tab described earlier.

✦ **View Web Page Info**—You can view information about the location of a Web page, the location of each of its components, the dates the page was modified, and other information by choosing View⇨Page Info. On the Page Info window, click the Links tab to see links on that page to other content on the Web. Click the Security tab to see information about verification and encryption used on the page.

Improving Mozilla Browsing

Every Web site you visit with Mozilla is not going to play well. Some sites don't follow standards, use unreadable fonts, choose colors that make it hard to see, or demand that you use a particular type of browser to view their content. To improve your browsing experience, there are several things you can add to Mozilla.

Note If you encounter a problem with Mozilla that you can't overcome, I recommend that your refer to the Mozilla Bugzilla database (`https://bugizilla.mozilla.org`). This site is an excellent place to search for bugs others have found (many times you can get workarounds to your problems) or enter a bug report yourself.

Adding a CrossOver Plug-In

QuickTime 5 movies, Shockwave Director multimedia content, and various Microsoft movie, file, and data formats simply do not play natively in Mozilla Navigator. Using software built on WINE for Linux on x86-based processors, CodeWeavers (`www.codeweavers.com`) created the CrossOver Plug-in. Although it costs a few dollars ($24.95 U.S. for a one-user-at-a-time license), the plug-in lets you play some content that you simply could not otherwise use in Linux.

After you install the plug-in, you see a nice setup window that lets you selectively install plug-ins for QuickTime 6, Windows Media Player 6.4, Shockwave 8.5, Flash 6, and Microsoft Word, Excel, and PowerPoint viewers. (Support for later versions of these content formats may be available by the time you read this.) You can also install other multimedia plug-ins, as well as a variety of fonts to use with those plug-ins.

Adding a Preferences Toolbar

Did you ever run into a Web page that required you to use a particular type or version of a browser or had fonts or colors that made a page unreadable? The Mozilla preferences toolbar called PrefBar2 lets you try to spoof Web sites into thinking you are running a different browser. It also lets you choose settings that might improve colors, fonts, and other attributes on difficult-to-read pages.

You can install the neat little toolbar from the Mozdev.org site (`http://prefbar.mozdev.org`). Click the Install link, and then after it is installed, restart Mozilla.

Tip You must have write permissions to `/usr/lib/mozilla-1.6` for the Install link to work. This may require you to log in as root, start Mozilla, install PrefBar, and then log out as root.

Figure 21-7 shows an example of PrefBar2 that has been installed in Mozilla.

Figure 21-7: Change colors, fonts, and browser types on-the-fly with the Mozdev.org preferences toolbar.

The default set of buttons lets you do the following:

- ✦ **Colors**—Change between default colors and those set on the Web page.
- ✦ **Images**—Toggle between having images loaded or not loaded on pages you display.
- ✦ **JavaScript**—Allow or disallow JavaScript content to play in Mozilla Navigator.
- ✦ **Clear Cache**—Delete all cached content from memory and disk.
- ✦ **Kill Flash**—Kill all embedded Flash content on the current page.
- ✦ **Real UA**—Choose to have your browser identified as itself (current version of Mozilla) or any of the following: Mozilla 1.0 (in Windows 98), Netscape Navigator 4.7 (in Macintosh), Netscape 6.2 (in Linux), Internet Explorer 5.0 (in Macintosh), or Internet Explorer 6.0 (in Windows XP).

The user agent (UA) setting is very useful when dealing with Web sites that require Internet Explorer (IE) (and usually IE on Windows, not MacOS). The IE 6.0 WinXP setting is good enough to allow Mozilla to log onto the Microsoft Exchange webmail service, which is usually set up to require IE. If you want to run Linux in a mostly Windows organization, install the preferences toolbar.

Click the Customize button to add other buttons to the toolbar. You can add buttons to clear your History or Location bar entries. You can even add a Popups button to prevent a page from opening a pop-up window from Mozilla.

Many of the preferences take effect immediately. Others may require you to restart Mozilla.

Adding Java Support

If you want to display some Java content, but you only see a broken puzzle piece and a failure message that says you need a plug-in to view application/x-java-whatever content, you can install the software you need from the Sun Microsystems Web site (www.sun.com). Look for the Java 2 Runtime Environment package from java.sun.com/download. (It should say something like Java 2 Platform, Standard Edition that runs on Linux.)

Doing Cool Things with Mozilla

Some neat bells and whistles are built into Mozilla that can make your browsing more pleasant. The following sections explore a few of those features.

Blocking Pop-Ups

You can block annoying pop-up windows using the Mozilla Preferences window. Here's how:

1. Choose Edit⇨Preferences. The Preferences window appears.

2. Click Popup Windows under the Privacy & Security category.

3. Click the Block Unrequested Popup Windows box.

4. Click OK. You won't get any more pop-up windows from this point on.

As the Preferences window notes, by blocking all pop-ups you might keep some Web sites from working properly. Click the Allowed Sites button to allow pop-ups on certain sites that you choose.

Using Tabbed Browsing

If you switch back and forth among several Web pages, you can use the tabbed browsing feature to hold multiple pages in your browser window at once. You can open a new tab for browsing by simply selecting File⇨New⇨Navigator Tab or by pressing Ctrl+T. You can also tailor how tabbed browsing works from a Web page or from the Location box. Here's how:

1. Choose Edit⇨Preferences. The Preferences window appears.

2. Click Tabbed Browsing under the Navigator category.

3. Click one or both of these boxes, depending on how you want to use tabbed browsing:

   • **Middle-click, Control+click, or Control+Enter on links in a Web page** — Selecting this box lets you open a link to another Web page in a new tab. For this to work, click the middle mouse button on a link, hold the Ctrl key while you click the left mouse button on a link, or (with the link highlighted) hold the Ctrl key and press Enter.

   • **Control+Enter in the Location bar** — After you type a Web address (URL) into the Location box, hold the Ctrl key and press Enter to open the new page in a tab.

4. Click OK. You can begin using the tabbed browser feature.

A tab for each tabbed page appears at the top of the Navigator pane. To close a tab, create a new tab, bookmark a group of tabs, or reload tabs, right-click one of the tabs and choose the function you want from the drop-down menu.

One of the easiest ways to open a link in a tab is to right-click over a link on an HTML page. Select the Open Link in New Tab choice.

Using the DOM Inspector

If you are debugging a Web page that you are creating, the Document Object Model (DOM) Inspector can be useful for checking out the structure of your page and dynamically updating the DOM you are traversing. To open the DOM inspector, from the Mozilla window choose Tools⇨Web Development⇨DOM Inspector.

In the DOM Inspector window, type the URL to the Web page you want to check out. The nodes representing the head, body, tables, fonts, and so on appear in the left column. Values for each node appear in the right column. Click a node name and the selected area is highlighted on the page below, with the node value appearing to the right. You can also use DOM Inspector to inspect a window.

Resizing the Web Page

There is a nice keyboard shortcut that lets you quickly resize the text on most Web pages in Mozilla. Hold the Ctrl key and press the plus (+) or minus (-) keys. In most cases, the text on the Web page gets larger or smaller, respectively. That page with the insanely small type font is suddenly readable.

Using Text-Based Web Browsers

If you become a Linux administrator or power user, over time you will inevitably find yourself working on a computer from a remote login or where there is no desktop GUI available. At some point while you are in that state, you will want to check an HTML file or a Web page. To solve the problem, many Linux distributions include several text-based Web browsers.

With text-based Web browsers, any HTML file available from the Web, your local file system, or a computer where you're remotely logged in can be accessed from your shell. There's no need to fire up your GUI or read pages of HTML markup if you just want to take a peek at the contents of a Web page. In addition to enabling you to call up Web pages, move around within those pages, and follow links to other pages, some browsers even display graphics right in a Terminal window!

Which browser you use is a matter of which you are more comfortable with. Browsers that are available include the following:

✦ **links** — You can open a file or a URL and then traverse links from the pages you open. Use search forward (*/string*) and back (*?string*) features to find text strings in pages. Use up and down arrows to go forward and back among links. Press Enter to go to the current link. Use the right and left arrow keys to go forward and back among pages you have visited. Press Esc to see a menu bar of features from which to select.

✦ **lynx** — The lynx browser has a good set of help files (press the ? key). Step through pages using the spacebar. Although lynx can display pages containing frames, it cannot display them in the intended positioning. Use the arrow keys to display the selected link (right arrow), go back to the previous document (left arrow), select the previous link (up arrow), and select the next link (down arrow).

✦ **w3m** — This browser can display HTML pages containing text, links, frames, and tables. It even tries to display images (although it is a bit shaky). Both English and Japanese help files are available (press H with w3m running). You can also use w3m to page through an HTML document in plain text (for example, `cat index.html | w3m -T text/html`). Use the Page Up and Page Down keys to page through a document. Press Enter on a link to go to that link. Press B to go back to the previous link. Search forward and back for text using the / (slash) and ? (question mark) keys, respectively.

The w3m seems the most sophisticated of these browsers. It features a nice default font selection, seems to handle frames neatly, and its use of colors also makes it easy to use. The links browser lets you use the mouse to cut and paste text.

You can start any of these text-based Web browsers by giving it a filename, or if you have an active connection to the network, a Web address. For example, to read the w3m documentation (which is in HTML format) with a w3m browser, type the following from a Terminal window or other shell interface:

```
$ w3m /usr/share/doc/w3m-0*/doc/MANUAL.html
```

An HTML version of the W3M Manual is displayed. Or you can give w3m a URL to a Web page, such as the following:

```
$ w3m www.handsonhistory.com
```

After a page is open, you can begin viewing the page and moving around to links included in it. Start by using the arrow keys to move around and select links. Use the Page Up and Page Down keys to page through text.

Running Firefox Web Browser

A final Web browser that deserves a mention is called Firefox. This is the latest Web browser from Mozilla.org and is intended to set a new direction and standard for Web browsers.

Firefox contains the same rendering engine (Gecko) that comes in Mozilla Navigator, but the user interface and many security features are brand new. Firefox also features faster performance and can run in less memory. Because it doesn't include all the mail, news, IRC, and similar clients (those are available separately from Mozilla), it should load and launch faster than Mozilla Navigator. If you are using applications other than Mozilla to provide those features, Firebird might be for you.

Firefox is delivered with Fedora Core 3 (which is included on the DVD that comes with this book). If your Linux distribution doesn't include Firefox, you can read about and download Firefox at `www.mozilla.org/products/firefox`. (A nice feature of the Damn Small Linux distribution is that it offers a menu selection for downloading and starting Firefox from a bootable Linux environment. Right-click the desktop, and then look for how to download Firefox on the Network menu.)

Summary

You have a lot of high-quality applications available to fulfill your needs for a Web browser and e-mail client in Linux. Most Web browsers are based on the Mozilla Gecko engine (which came originally from Netscape Navigator). Firefox is being slated as the next-generation replacement for Mozilla Navigator.

Graphical and text-based e-mail clients include Ximian Evolution, Mozilla Mail, and KMail. Thunderbird is set to become the next-generation e-mail client to replace Mozilla Mail.

✦   ✦   ✦

Gaming Alone and Online

As Linux has grown in popularity, the need and availability of Linux-based entertainment options has naturally increased. From simple parlor games to fast-paced OpenGL First Person Shooters (FPS), there have been great strides recently in Linux gaming opportunities. In fact, the advance of processor-devouring 3D games has helped drive improvements in computer technology in general.

Gaming software that you can use with Linux is a mixed bag of sorts. A lot of the old software is still around (and is free), while newer software is available in demo form but costs money to get a full version. Some experts predict that gaming will be the software category that brings Linux into homes. The unfortunate truth is that many of the current "hot" titles still need to be coaxed onto Linux with some kind of Win32 emulation, although even this is getting easier and more dependable. While the number of commercial game applications created specifically for Linux is fairly limited at the moment, like everything else in Linux, more are becoming available each day.

This chapter examines the current state of gaming in Linux, including the basics on getting your gaming environment going, and hardware considerations for gaming. It describes the free games (mostly fairly simple X Window games) that come with various Linux distributions or that can be easily downloaded. For running games that were created for other platforms, this chapter describes game emulators such as Cedega.

It also explores some popular commercial games that have demo versions available for Linux. If you like the demos, you can purchase these games, which run natively in Linux.

Basic Linux Gaming Information

There isn't much you need to know to run basic X Window–based games that come with Linux. The following sections describe basic information about Linux gaming.

Where to Get Information About Linux Gaming

There are many Web sites that provide information about the latest games available for Linux, as well as links to download sites. If you're looking for information about Linux gaming, start with your distribution's home page (www.redhat.com for example), the home page of your desktop environment (www.kde.org or www.gnome.com, for example) or simply search for "Linux Games" or your favorite game title and "Linux" in any search engine. Here are several to get you started:

✦ **TransGaming Technologies** (www.transgaming.com)—This company's mission is to bring games from other platforms to Linux. It is the provider of Cedega, formerly known as WineX, a powerful tool that enables you to play hundreds of PC games on your Linux system.

✦ **The Linux Game Tome** (http://happypenguin.org)—Features a database of descriptions and reviews of tons of games that run in Linux. You can do keyword searches for games listed at this site. There are also links to where you can get the different games and to other gaming sites.

✦ **Linuxgames.com** (http://linuxgames.com)—This site can give you some very good insight into the state of Linux gaming. There are links to HOWTOs and Frequently Asked Questions (FAQs), as well as forums for discussing Linux games. There are also links to Web sites that have information about specific games.

✦ **id Software** (www.idsoftware.com)—Go to the id Software site for information on Linux demo versions for Quake and Return to Castle Wolfenstein.

✦ **Linuxgamepublishing.com** (www.linuxgamepublishing.com)—A new entrant into the Linux gaming world, linuxgamepublishing.com aims to be a one-stop shopping portal for native Linux games, as well as for ports of games from other platforms. At the time of writing, it offered 15 games. To purchase games from this site, you must create a user account.

✦ **Loki Entertainment Software** (www.lokigames.com)—Loki provided ports of best-selling games to Linux but went out of business in 2001. Its products included Linux versions of Civilization: Call to Power, Myth II: Soulblighter, SimCity 3000, Railroad Tycoon II, and Quake III Arena. The Loki Demo Launcher is still available to see demo versions of these games, and some boxed sets are available for very little money.

✦ **Tux Games** (www.tuxgames.com)—If you are ready to purchase a game, the Tux Games Web site is dedicated to the sale of Linux games. Besides offering

Linux gaming news and products, the site lists its top-selling games and includes notices of games that are soon to be released.

✦ **Linux Gamers' FAQ** (http://icculus.org/lgfaq) — Contains a wealth of information about free and commercial Linux games. It lists gaming companies that have ported their games to Linux, tells where to get Linux games, and answers queries related to common Linux gaming problems. For a list of Linux games without additional information, see http://icculus.org/lgfaq/gamelist.php.

If the idea of developing your own games interests you, try the Linux Game Development Center (http://lgdc.sunsite.dk).

Getting Started with Linux Gaming

How you get started with Linux gaming depends on how serious you are about it. If all you want to do is play a few games to pass the time, you can find plenty of diverting X Window games that come with Linux. If you want to play more powerful commercial games, you can choose from:

✦ **Games for Microsoft Windows (Cedega 4.0.1)** — Many of the most popular commercial games created to run on Microsoft operating systems will run in Linux using Cedega. To get RPM versions of Cedega, you must sign up for a Cedega subscription at www.transgaming.com. Make sure to check in with www.linuxgames.com to see if there is a relevant HOW-TO for working with the particular game you have in mind. Many games are covered there including Half-Life and Unreal Tournament.

✦ **Games for Linux (id Software and others)** — Certain popular games have Linux versions available. Most notably, id Software offers its DOOM and Return to Castle Wolfenstein in Linux versions.

Games are still available from the now defunct company Loki Software, Inc. While you cannot purchase the titles directly from Loki, you can go online to one of Loki's resellers at www.lokigames.com/orders/resellers.php3. For example, Amazon.com (one of the listed resellers) shows 16 titles including Quake III, Myth II: Soulblighter, and Heretic II for Linux.

Choosing a Video Card for Gaming

Because high-end games place extraordinary demands on your video hardware, choosing a good video card and configuring it properly is one of the keys to ensuring a good gaming experience. For advanced gaming, you will need to go beyond what a basic 64-bit card can do for you.

One feature that many games may require of your video card is Direct Rendering Infrastructure (DRI). Whether you are running the games using Cedega or natively in Linux, to play demanding games in Linux you need a card that supports DRI to do hardware acceleration. Following is a list of manufacturers whose video cards support DRI. The list is from the DRI project site (http://dri.sourceforge.net/).

✦ **ATI Technologies** — Chipsets from ATI Technologies that support DRI include the Mach64 (Rage Pro), Radeon 7X00 (R100), Radeon 2 / 8500 (R200), and Rage 128 (Standard, Pro, Mobility). Cards based on these chipsets include All-in-Wonder 128, Rage Fury, Rage Magnum, Xpert 99, Xpert 128, and Xpert 2000.

✦ **3dfx** — If you can find a used unit on eBay, there are several 3dfx cards that support DRI. In particular, the Voodoo (3, 4, and 5) and Banshee chipsets have drivers that support DRI. Voodoo 5 cards support 16 and 24 bpp. Scan Line Interleaving (SLI), where two or more 3D processors work in parallel (to result in higher frame rates), is not supported for 3dfx cards.

✦ **3Dlabs** — Graphics cards containing the MX/Gamma chipset from 3Dlabs have drivers available that support DRI in Linux.

✦ **Intel** — Supported video chipsets from Intel include the i810 (e, e2, and -dc100), i815, and i815e.

✦ **Matrox** — The Matrox chipsets that have drivers that support DRI include the G200, G400, and G450. Cards that use these chips include the Millennium G450, Millennium G400, Millennium G200, and Mystique G200.

✦ **NVIDIA** — Cards from NVIDIA are not supported by DRI because NVIDIA has not released hardware specifications to DRI developers. However, NVIDIA cards work for most Linux games. To get NVIDIA drivers, which are produced by NVIDIA but are not open source drivers, you must download them from the NVIDIA Web site (www.nvidia.com). On the NVIDIA home page, click the download button and follow the instructions for downloading and installing the correct drivers for your card. RPM packages are available.

To find out whether DRI is working on your current video card, type the following:

```
$ glxinfo | grep rendering
direct rendering: Yes
```

This example shows that direct rendering is enabled. If it were not supported, the output would say No instead of Yes. Even if DRI is not supported, you may experience the best game play with a high-end card from either ATI or NVIDIA. While DRI can be important, many games implement OpenGL rendering, which is a feature supported by both NVIDIA and ATI video cards. Both companies have specific driver requirements, so make sure you research the cards, driver requirements, and any game-specific issue before you plop down big money on a top-tier 3D video card.

X Window Games

The X Window System created a great opportunity for games in Linux/Unix systems to become graphic-based rather than character-based, so that instead of having little character symbols representing robots and arrows, the games could actually show pictures of little robots and arrows.

A lot of entertaining games run in X. Unless otherwise noted, all of the X games described in this section are free. Also, the GNOME and KDE environments that come with most desktop Linux distributions (described in Chapter 3) each have a set of games associated with it.

GNOME Games

GNOME games consist of some old card games and a bunch of games that look suspiciously like ones you would find on Windows systems. If you are afraid of losing your favorite desktop diversion (such as Solitaire, FreeCell, and Minesweeper) when you leave Windows, have no fear. You can find many of them under GNOME games.

Table 22-1 lists the GNOME games available with most GNOME desktop systems from the panel menu, including Fedora Core 3. See the GNOME Games site (`www.gnome.org/projects/gnome-games`) for further details. Many KDE games (see Table 22-2) are available if you have a KDE desktop installed.

Table 22-1 GNOME Games	
Game	**Description**
AisleRiot (solitaire)	Lets you select from among 28 different solitaire card games.
Chess	Gnuchess game in X. (Runs the `xboard` and `gnuchess` commands.)
Chromium Configuration	Set options such as skill level, screen size, and sound for Chromium.
Chromium	Deliver supplies to troops in battle in this action game.
FreeCell	A popular solitaire card game.
Freeciv (Isometric tileset)	In this strategy game, you try to lead your civilization to extinguish all others. (Uses Isometric tile set to represent cities, oceans, and other terrain.)
Freeciv Server (new game)	Server program needed to play Freeciv.

Continued

	Table 22-1 *(continued)*
Game	**Description**
Ataxx	Board game where you flip over circles to consume enemy pieces.
Lines	Match five colored balls in a row to score points.
Four-In-A-Row	Drop balls to beat the game at making four in a row.
Nibbles	Steer a worm around the screen while avoiding walls.
Robots	Later version of Gnobots, which includes movable junk heaps.
Mines	Minesweeper clone. Click on safe spaces and avoid the bombs.
Stones	Move around a cave, collect diamonds, and avoid rocks.
Tetravex	A clone of Tetravex from the GNOME project. Move blocks so that numbers on each side align.
Klotski	Move pieces around to allow one piece to escape.
Tali	Yahtzee clone. Roll dice to fill in categories.
Iagno	Flip black and white chips to maneuver past the opponent.
Maelstrom	Navigate a spaceship through an asteroid field.
Mahjongg	Classic Asian tile game.
Same GNOME	Eliminate clusters of balls for high score.
Tux Racer	Steer a penguin as he races down a hill on his belly.

KDE Games

There are a bunch of games available for the KDE desktop environment. (In Fedora Core 3, these games come in the kdegames package.) Table 22-2 contains a list of KDE games that come with Fedora Core 3. There may be a different set of games included with your Linux distribution.

	Table 22-2 **Games for the KDE Desktop**
Game	**Description**
Arcade Games	
Kasteroids	Destroy asteroids in the classic arcade game.
Kbounce	Add walls to block in bouncing balls.

Game	Description
KFoul Eggs	Squish eggs in this Tetris-like game.
Klickety	Click color groups to erase blocks in this adaptation of Clickomania.
Kolf	Play a round of virtual golf.
Ksirtet	Tetris clone. Try to fill in lines of blocks as they drop down.
KsmileTris	Tetris with smiley faces.
KsnakeRace	Race your snake around a maze.
KspaceDuel	Fire at another spaceship as you spin around a planet.
Ktron	Snake-style race game.
Boardgames	
Atlantik	Play this Monopoly-like game against other players on the network.
KBackgammon	Online version of backgammon.
Kbattleship	Sink the opponent's battleship in this online version of the board game.
KblackBox	Find hidden balls by shooting rays.
Kenolaba	Move game pieces to push opponents' pieces off the board.
Kmahjongg	Classic oriental tile game.
Kreversi	Flip game pieces to outmaneuver the opponent.
Shisen-Sho	Tile game similar to Mahjongg. Very addicting.
Kwin4	Drop colored pieces to get four pieces in a row.
Cardgames	
Patience	Choose from nine different solitaire card games.
Kpoker	Video poker clone. Play five-card draw, choosing which cards to hold and which to throw.
Lieutenant Skat	Play the card game Skat.
Megami	Play four blackjack hands against a dealer.
Tactics and Strategy	
KJumping Cube	Click squares to increase numbers and take over adjacent squares.
Katomic	Move pieces to create different chemical compounds.
Konquest	Expand your interstellar empire in this multiplayer game.
Kolor Lines	Move marbles to form five-in-a-row and score points.
Kmines	Minesweeper clone. Click safe spaces and avoid the bombs.
Ksokoban	The Japanese warehouse keeper game.
SameGame	Erase game pieces to score points.

The games on the KDE menu range from amusing to quite challenging. If you are used to playing games in Windows, KMines and Patience will seem like old favorites. KAsteroids and KPoker are good for the mindless game category. For a mental challenge (it's harder than it looks), try KSokoban. For a challenging multiuser game on the GNOME menu, try Freeciv. And of course there is Chess (XBoard version of gnuchess).

Note Boson is a fun real-time strategy that runs on KDE desktops. Although the game is still in its early stages of development (0.10 release), it's a good way to try out the capabilities of your gaming hardware in Linux. You can download it from `http://boson.eu.org/download.php`.

The following sections describe a couple of the more interesting games that are distributed with common Linux distributions.

Chess Games

Chess was one of the first games played on computer systems. While the game hasn't changed over the years, the way it's played on computers has. Most chess programs that come with Linux let you play against the computer (in text or graphical modes), have the computer play against itself, or replay stored chess games. You can even play chess against other users on the Internet using Internet Chess Servers (ICS).

The XBoard program is an X-based chess game that provides a graphical interface for gnuchess. GNU Chess (represented by the gnuchess package) describes itself as a communal chess program. It has had many contributors, and it seeks to advance a "more open and friendly environment of sharing" in the chess community. With XBoard, you can move graphical pieces with your mouse. To play against the computer, click Games⇨Chess from the Red Hat menu, then start by just moving a piece with your mouse. While in the XBoard window, select Mode⇨Two Machines to have the computer play itself. Select File⇨Load Game to load a game in Portable Game Notation (PGN). Figure 22-1 shows the XBoard window with a "Two Machines" game in progress.

You can use XBoard to play online against others by connecting an XBoard session to an Internet Chess Server (ICS). To start XBoard as an interface to an ICS, type the following command line:

```
$ xboard -ics -icshost name
```

In this example, *name* should be replaced by the name of the ICS host. In ICS mode, you can watch games, play against other users, or replay games that have finished. The ICS host is a gathering place for enthusiasts who want to play chess against others on the Internet, watch games, participate in tournaments, or just meet chess people. Here's an example of starting an ICS session at chess.net from a Terminal window:

```
$ xboard -ics -icshost chess.net
Please wait.
Press return to enter chess.net as "guest 141":
chess% <Enter>
```

After you press Enter, you're logged into the chess server as a guest. The XBoard window opens on your screen. Keep an eye on the Terminal window where you started the session. Someone will probably challenge you to a game within a few moments. For example, if a challenge ended with "Type '/accept 102' to accept the sought challenge," you'd respond:

```
chess%  /accept 102
```

You can begin playing. To learn more about how to play, visit http://chess.net/ help. Select the Beginners Manual to start. Other chess servers you can try include the Internet Chess Club (ICC) at www.chessclub.com or Free Internet Chess Server at www.freechess.org.

Figure 22-1: In the XBoard window, you can set xgame to either play against the computer or to replay saved games.

Freeciv

Freeciv is a free clone of the popular Civilization game series from Atari. A commercial port of Civilization Call to Power to Linux was created a few years ago by Loki Games (described later in this chapter). With Freeciv, you create a civilization that challenges competing civilizations for world dominance.

The commonly distributed version of Freeciv contains both client software (to play the game) and server software (to connect players together). You can connect to your server and try the game yourself or (with a network connection) play against up to 14 other players on the Internet. To install Freeciv, check out the download page on the www.freeciv.org Web site. Choose your language, start downloading, install, and have fun.

You can start Freeciv from a Terminal window by typing:

```
$ civ &
```

Figure 22-2 shows the two windows that appear when you start Freeciv. The Connect to Freeciv Server window contains your username, host name, and port number. The Freeciv window is where you play the game.

Note　If Freeciv won't start, you may be logged in as root. You must be logged in as a regular user to run the civ command.

Figure 22-2: Play Freeciv to build civilizations and compete against others.

Starting Freeciv

You can play a few games by yourself, if you like, to get to know the game before you play against others on the network. The following procedure describes how to start your first practice Freeciv game:

1. Start Freeciv:

   ```
   $ civ &
   ```

2. From a Terminal window, start the Freeciv server by typing:

   ```
   $ civserver
   This is the server for Freeciv version 1.13.0
   You can learn a lot about Freeciv at http://www.freeciv.org/
   2: Now accepting new client connections.

   For introductory help, type 'help'.
   >
   ```

3. Click Connect in the Connect to Freeciv Server window.

4. At the server prompt in the Terminal window, type the following:

   ```
   > start
   Starting game.
   2: Loading rulesets
   >
   ```

5. A What Nation Will You Be? window (see Figure 22-3) appears on the client. Choose a nation, name a leader, select your gender, choose the style of the city, and then click OK.

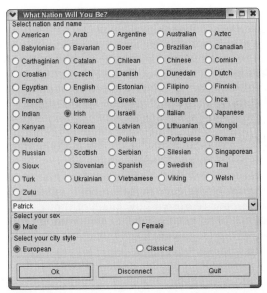

Figure 22-3: Choose a nation to begin Freeciv.

6. At this point, you should have a Terminal window (running the server) and the Freeciv window (running the client) open on your desktop. Click the Freeciv window title bar to return to that window to start the game.

Beginning with Freeciv

Check out the Freeciv window before you start playing the game:

✦ Click the Help button for topical information on many different subjects that will be useful to you as you play. (You can find more help at the Freeciv site.)

✦ The world (by default) is 80 x 50 squares, with 11 x 8 squares visible at a time.

✦ The active square contains an icon of the active unit (flashing alternatively with the square's terrain).

✦ Some squares contain special resources. Press and hold the middle mouse button for information on what special resources a square contains. (With a two-button mouse, hold the Ctrl key and click the right mouse button.) Try this a few times to get a feel for the land around you. This action also identifies any units on the terrain, as well as statistics for the unit.

✦ To see the world outside your 11 x 8 viewing area, click the scroll bars outside the map. At first, the part of the world you haven't explored yet will be black. As units are added, areas closer to those units will be visible. (Press C to return to the active part of your map.)

✦ An overview map is in the upper-left corner of the Freeciv window. As the world becomes more civilized, this provides a good way to get an overview of what is going on. Right-click a spot on the overview map to have your view-port centered there.

✦ The menu bar contains buttons you can use to play the game. The Game menu lets you change settings and options, view player data, view messages, and clear your log. The Kingdom menu lets you change tax rates, find cities, and start revolutions. The View menu lets you place a grid on the map or center the view. The Orders menu is where you choose the items you build and the actions you take. The Reports menu lets you display reports related to cities, military, trade, and science, as well as other special reports.

✦ A summary of the economy of your civilization appears under the overview map. Information includes number of people, current year, and money in the treasury.

✦ Ten icons below the overview information represent how money is divided among luxuries (an entertainer), science (a researcher), and taxes (a tax collector). Essentially, these icons represent how much of your resources are placed into improving each of those attributes of your community.

✦ When you have made all your moves for a turn, click Turn Done. Next to that, a light bulb indicates the progress of your research (increasing at each turn). A sun icon starts clear, but becomes brighter from pollution to warn of possible global warming. A government symbol indicates that you begin with a despotic government. The last icon tells you how much time is left in a turn.

✦ The Unit box shows information about your current unit. You begin with two Settlers units (covered wagon icons) and one Explorer (a man icon) unit. Click on a Settler, Explorer, city, or other unit to use it or learn about it.

Building Your Civilization

Start building your civilization. The Freeciv manual makes these suggestions:

✦ To change the distribution of money, choose Kingdom⇨Tax Rates. Move the slider bars to redistribute the percentage of assets assigned to luxury, science, and taxes. Try increasing science and reducing taxes to start off.

✦ Change the current unit to be a settler as follows: Click the stack of units on the map and click one of the Settlers from the menu that appears.

✦ Begin building a city by clicking on Orders⇨Build City. When prompted, type a name for the city and click OK. The window that appears shows information about the city. It starts with one happy citizen, represented by a single icon (more citizens will appear as the game progresses).

✦ The Food, Prod, and Trade lines reflect the raw productivity statistics for the city. The first number shows how much is being produced; the second (in parentheses) shows the surplus above what is needed to support the units. The Gold, Luxury, and Science lines indicate the city's trade output. Granary numbers show how much food is stored and the size of the food store. The pollution level begins at zero.

✦ Close the city window by clicking Close.

Exploring Your World

To begin exploring, move the Settlers and the Explorer:

1. Using the numeric keypad, press the 9 key three times to begin exploring. You can move the Explorer up to three times per turn. You begin to see more of the world.

2. When the next unit (a Settler) begins blinking, move it one square in another direction. When you have made all the moves you want to make (or all that the game allows), the Turn Done button is highlighted. Click Turn Done to start your next turn. Information for the city is updated (the city changes and grows, simply through the passage of time reflected in the turns).

3. Click the City to see the city window. Notice that information about the city has been updated. In particular, you should see food storage increase. Close the city window.

4. Continue exploring and build a road. With the Explorer flashing, use the numeric keypad to move it another three sections. When the Settler begins blinking, press R to build a road. A small R appears on the square to remind you that the Settler is busy building a road. Click Turn Done.

Using More Controls and Actions

Now that you have some understanding of the controls and actions, the game can begin taking a lot of different directions. Here are a few things that might happen next and things you can do:

✦ After you take a turn, the computer gets a chance to play. As it plays, its actions are reported to you. You can make decisions on what to do about those actions. Choose Game⇨Message Options. The Message Options window appears, containing a listing of different kinds of messages that can come from the server and how they will be presented to you.

✦ As you explore, you will run into other explorers and eventually other civilizations. Continue exploring by selecting different directions on your numeric keypad.

✦ Continue to move the Settler one square at a time, after it has finished creating the road. (The Settler will blink again when it is available.) Click Turn Done.

✦ At this point, you should see a message that your city has finished building Warriors. When buildings and units are complete, you should usually check out what has happened. Click the message associated with the city, and then click Popup City. The city window appears, showing you that it has additional population. The food storage may appear empty, but the new citizens are working to increase the food and trade. You may see an additional warrior unit.

✦ A science advisory may also appear to let you choose your city's research goals. Click Change and select Writing as your new research goal. You can then select a different long-term goal as well. Click Close when you are done.

✦ If your new Warrior is now blinking, press the S key to assign sentry mode to the Warrior.

✦ Select Reports from time to time to keep track of statistics about your Cities, Units, Economy, Science, and other attributes of your world.

Those moves provided familiarity with some of the actions of Freeciv. To learn some basic strategies for playing the game, choose Help⇨Help Playing.

Commercial Linux Games

When Loki Software, Inc. closed its doors a few years ago, the landscape of commercial gaming in Linux changed. Loki produced Linux ports of popular games, including Myth II and Civilization: Call to Power, to name a couple. Since then, no other company has stepped up to port that wide a range of best-selling games to Linux. Today, commercial games that run natively are led by several popular games from id Software (described in the next section) and a few gaming companies that have ported individual titles to Linux.

Some Loki games are still available for purchase on the Web. They sell for a fraction of their original price, but you are on your own if they don't work because Loki Software is no longer there to support them. The Loki Games Demo is still around, if you want to get a feel for a particular Loki game before it disappears completely (I describe how to find demo and packaged Loki Games later in this chapter).

In the wake of Loki's demise, TransGaming Technologies has been working on an approach to bringing popular games to Linux that relies on a version of WINE called Cedega. In most cases, instead of having different ports of popular games (as Loki did), TransGaming lets users run existing Windows games in Linux by adapting Cedega to each game that needs a tweak here and there.

While the state of Linux gaming has improved somewhat in the last few years, Linux leaves much to be desired as a gaming platform. Linux has some of the technology needed to support advanced games, but the technology and developer support have not yet really come together. Most serious gamers still maintain a Windows partition to support their gaming habits. According to top game developers, there are significant hurdles — both technological and economic — that hinder development of games for Linux. Issues with video and audio hardware, as well as problems with GNU/Linux development itself (in particular, glibc), have made new games difficult to produce. In addition, the relatively small size of the Linux gaming market means that incentives to overcome these issues are not particularly strong. However, these limitations are not overwhelming. As you'll see later in this chapter, even the hardcore game nut can successfully use Linux.

id Software Games

Among the most popular games running natively in Linux are Quake III Arena and Return to Castle Wolfenstein from id Software, Inc. You can purchase Linux versions of these games or download demos of each game before you buy.

Note   If you have trouble getting any id Software games running in Linux, refer to the Linux FAQs available from id Software at: `http://zerowing.idsoftware.com/linux`.

Quake III Arena

Quake III Arena is a first-person, shooter-type game where you can choose from lots of weapons (lightning guns, shotguns, grenade launchers, and so on) and pass through scenes with highly detailed 3D surfaces. You can play alone or against your friends. There are multiplayer death-match and capture-the-flag competitions. Standalone play allows you to advance through a tournament structure of skilled AI opponents. This version of the game has a selectable difficulty level, from fairly easy to beat to downright impossible.

A demo version of Quake III Arena for Linux is available from the id Software Web site (click the demo link at `www.idsoftware.com/games/quake/quake3-gold/` and then look for the Linux demo). Figure 22-4 shows a screenshot from Quake III Arena.

Figure 22-4: Quake III Arena is a popular first-person shooter game that runs in Linux.

Return to Castle Wolfenstein

You battle with the Allies to destroy the Third Reich in Return to Castle Wolfenstein, which mixes World War II action with creatures conjured up by Nazi scientists. It's based on the Quake III Arena engine and offers single-player mode as well as team-based multiplayer mode.

If you purchase Return to Castle Wolfenstein for Linux, you actually get the Windows version with an extra Linux installer. If you already have the Windows version, you can download the Linux installer and follow some instructions to get it going.

I downloaded the installer called `wolf-linux-1.31.x86.run` from `www.id software.com/games/wolfenstein/rtcw/index.php?game_section=updates`. The `INSTALL` file (in `/usr/local/games/wolfenstein`) describes what files you need to copy from the Windows CD.

To get a demo of Return to Castle Wolfenstein, go to `www.idsoftware.com/games/ wolfenstein/rtcw/index.php?game_section=overview`. Both single-player and multiplayer demos are available.

Caution You need an NVIDIA card to run Return to Castle Wolfenstein.

Figure 22-5 is a screenshot from Return to Castle Wolfenstein running in Linux.

Figure 22-5: Return to Castle Wolfenstein combines strange creatures and WW II battles.

TransGaming and Cedega Gaming

TransGaming Technologies brings to Linux some of the most popular games that currently run on the Windows platforms. Working with WINE developers, TransGaming is developing Cedega, which enables you to run many different games on Linux that were originally developed for Windows. Although TransGaming is producing a few games that are packaged separately and tuned for Linux, in most cases it sells you a subscription service to Cedega instead of the games. That subscription service lets you stay up-to-date on the continuing development of Cedega so you can run more and more Windows games.

Note Depending on your distribution, you may need to get the vanilla kernel from `kernel.org` and boot that on your system before running games with Cedega.

To get Windows games to run in Linux, Cedega particularly needs to develop Microsoft DirectX features that are required by many of today's games. There are also issues relating to CD keys and hooks into the Windows operating system that must be overcome (such as requiring Microsoft Active Desktop). In fact, a Cedega subscription has value, in part, because it lets you vote on which games you'd like to see TransGaming work on next.

A full list of games supported by TransGaming, as well as indications of how popular they are and how well they work, is available from the TransGaming site (search for the games that interest you by going to www.transgaming.com and clicking on Games). More than 100 games are currently listed with a rating of 4 out of 5 (meaning that the game will run well, if not flawlessly). Eight games are rated a 5 (meaning that they run flawlessly).

Note   You can use TransGaming's Cedega software to run Doom 3 right out of the box. For news about other product milestones, check out the "Hot off the Press" link on the TransGaming home page.

Support or major enhancements for the following games were recently added to Cedega 4.0.1:

Doom 3	City of Heros
Morrowwind	Steam

Here is a list of some of the new and popular games that are being used by the TransGaming community and that are said to run well in Cedega (rated a 4 or 5):

James Bond 007: NightFire	Everquest 2
Tron 2.0	Jagged Alliance 2: Wildfire
Doom 3	Star Craft: Brood War
Warlords Battlecry III	Far Cry
Hitman Contracts	World of Warcraft

Check the TransGaming list yourself for additions and changes.

With Cedega 4.0.1, TransGaming added several new Point2Play features. Point2Play provides a graphical window for installing, configuring, and testing Cedega on your computer. This OpenGL-dependent application also lets you install and organize your games so you can launch them graphically. Figure 22-6 shows an example of the TransGaming Point2Play window:

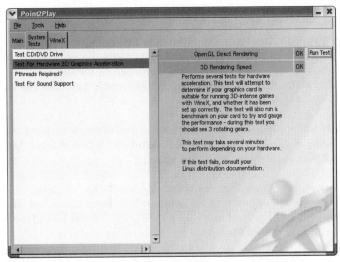

Figure 22-6: Use the Point2Play window to check computer hardware for Cedega gaming.

Other features in the new Point2Play window include the ability to select among different installed versions of Cedega for running applications and tools for individually configuring how each game runs under Cedega. (If a game won't run from the GUI, try launching it from a Terminal window.)

To get binary copies (ones that are already compiled to run) of Cedega and Point2Play, you need to subscribe to TransGaming. For details on how to become a "TransGamer," click the Subscribe Here link on the TransGaming home page (www.transgaming.com). Benefits currently include:

✦ Downloads of the latest version of Cedega

✦ Access to Cedega support forums

✦ Ability to vote on which games you want TransGaming to support next

✦ Subscription to the Cedega newsletter

Cedega used to be known as WineX. The source code for WineX may become available in the near future if you want to build your own WineX/Cedega package. To check availability, try the SourceForge.net project site for WineX (sourceforge. net/projects/winex).

Loki Software Game Demos

To encourage people to get to know its games, the now-defunct Loki Software, Inc. offered a demo program that let you choose from among more than a dozen of its games to download and try. You can still find some of its games for sale. For example, a recent search for Loki at Amazon.com turned up 16 different Loki games (including the ones described here), many selling for $9.99.

 Caution If you try to download any of the demos described in the following sections, make sure you have plenty of disk space available. It is common for one of these demos to require several hundred megabytes of disk space.

The Loki Demo Launcher page (`www.lokigames.com/products/demos.php3`) still offers links to FTP sites from which you can download the Demo Launcher. The file that you want to save is `loki_demos-full-1.0e-x86.run`. Save it to a directory (such as `/tmp/loki`) and do the following:

1. Change to the directory to which you downloaded the demo. For example:

   ```
   # cd /tmp/loki
   ```

 Note You may not need to be root user to install these games. However, the paths where the Demo Launcher tries to write by default are accessible only to the root user.

2. As root user, run the following command (the program may have a different name if it has been updated):

   ```
   # sh loki_demos-full-1.0e.x86.run
   ```

3. If you have not used the Demo Launcher before, a screen appears asking you to identify the paths used to place the Install Tool. If the default locations shown are okay with you, click Begin Install.

4. Assuming that there was no problem writing to the install directories, you should see an Install Complete message. Click Exit.

5. The Uninstall Tool window displays. If the paths for holding the Uninstall Tool are okay, click Begin Install. The Install Complete message appears. Click Exit.

6. The next window enables you to set the locations for installing the Demo Pack. If the paths are okay, click Begin Install.

7. A box shows the different demo games that are available. As you move the cursor over each game, the disk space need for the game is displayed. Click the games you want to install and then click Continue.

8. A window displays the progress of each download. You may need to click an Update button to complete the update and then click Finish to finish it.

9. The demo should now be ready to start. Either click Play or type `loki_demos` from a Terminal window to start the program.

10. Select to start the game, and you're ready to go.

The following sections describe a few games that may still be available. Again, these games may not be available for long.

Civilization: Call to Power

You can build online civilizations with Civilization: Call to Power (CCP). Like earlier versions and public spinoffs (such as the Freeciv described earlier in this chapter), Civilization: Call to Power for Linux lets you explore the world, build cities, and manage your empire. The last version offered by Loki Games includes multiplayer network competition and extensions that let you extend cities into outer space and under the sea.

If you like Freeciv, you will love CCP. Engaging game play is improved with enhanced graphics, sound, and animation. English, French, German, Italian, and Spanish versions are available.

> **Note**   Freeciv is dependent on the Open Sound System for audio support. The Open Sound home page (`www.opensound.com/osshw.html`) has a list of supported sound cards, mostly older devices. If you do not have a card that's on the list, you may be unable to enjoy the audio.

The CCP demo comes with an excellent tutorial to start you out. If you have never played a civilization game before, the tutorial is a great way to start. Figure 22-7 shows an example scene from the Civilization: Call to Power for Linux demo.

Figure 22-7: Civilization: Call to Power features excellent graphics and network play.

Myth II: Soulblighter

If you like knights and dwarves and storming castles, Myth II: Soulblighter for Linux might be for you. In Myth II, you are given a mission and some troops with various skills. From there, you need strategy and the desire to shed lots of virtual blood to meet your goal.

Myth II was created by Bungie Software (www.bungie.com) and ported to Linux by Loki Entertainment Software (www.lokigames.com). The Loki port of the popular Myth game includes improved graphics and new scenarios. A demo version is available that runs well in most distributions (particularly Fedora/Red Hat). You can get it via the Demo Launcher described earlier. You need at least a modest Pentium 133 MHz, 32MB RAM, 80MB swap space, and 100MB of free disk space. You also need network hardware for multiuser network play (network card or dial-up), and a sound card if you want audio. Figure 22-8 shows a screen in Myth II.

Figure 22-8: Use warriors, archers, and dwarves to battle in Myth II.

Heretic II

Based on the Quake Engine, Heretic II sets you on a path to rid the world of a deadly, magical plague. As the main character, Corvus, you explore dungeons, swamps, and cities to uncover and stop the plague. The graphics are rich, and the game play is quite engaging.

You will experience some crashing problems with Heretic II out of the box. Be sure to check for the update to Heretic II at www.updates.lokigames.com, which should fix most of the problems.

Neverwinter Nights

BioWare (www.bioware.com) dipped its foot into Linux gaming waters with a Linux client for its wildly popular Neverwinter Nights game. Neverwinter Nights is a classic role-playing game in the swords-and-sorcery mold. You can develop your character and go adventuring or play online with others via a LAN or over the Internet. You can even build your own worlds and host adventures as the Dungeon Master. Neverwinter Nights is licensed by Wizards of the Coast to use Dungeons & Dragons rules and material.

Of course, to use the Neverwinter Nights Linux client, you must purchase the game from BioWare. You must also have access to certain files from a Windows installation of the game. Keep in mind that getting Neverwinter Nights running is not a simple process. Important installation instructions and downloadable files are located at `http://nwn.bioware.com/downloads/linuxclient.html`. This site includes additional information about expansion packs and updates. If you want the Neverwinter Nights experience on your Linux system to be pleasant, I highly recommend reading the instructions thoroughly. And you will need patience in addition to a high-bandwidth Internet connection. Depending on the version of Neverwinter Nights to which you have access, you may need to download up to 1.2GB of files.

Summary

With the addition of hot titles such as Doom 3, Far Cry, and EverQuest 2 to the list of playable titles, Linux continues to grow as a gaming platform. You can spend plenty of late nights gaming on Linux. Old UNIX games that have made their way to Linux include a variety of X Window–based games. There are card games, strategy games, and some action games for those less inclined to spend 36 hours playing Doom 3.

On the commercial front, Civilization: Call to Power for Linux and Myth II are available to use on your Linux system. Unfortunately, these will probably disappear because Loki Software (which ported those applications to Linux) went out of business. Fortunately, the future of high-end Linux gaming seems to be in the hands of TransGaming Technologies, which has created Cedega from previous WINE technology to allow Windows games to run in Linux.

Commercial games that run natively in Linux are also available. These include games from id Software, such as Quake III Arena and Return to Castle Wolfenstein.

✦ ✦ ✦

Running Servers

✦ ✦ ✦ ✦

✦ ✦ ✦ ✦

Running a Linux, Apache, MySQL, and PHP (LAMP) Server

With the growing availability of broadband Internet connections and a popular desire to run personal Web sites and Web logs (blogs), an increasing number of people are setting up Web application servers on their home Internet connections. Web applications are also finding more popularity in business environments because Web applications reduce the number of programs that need to be maintained on workstations.

One popular variety of Web application server is what has recently come to be known as a *LAMP server* because it brings together Linux, Apache, MySQL, and PHP. LAMP servers combine components from several open source projects to form a fast, reliable, and economical platform for other readily available applications.

This chapter will help you install and configure your own LAMP server, starting with an introduction to the various components, guiding you through the installation and configuration, and finishing with the installation of a sample Web application.

The examples in this chapter are based on a system running Debian GNU/Linux but conceptually should work on other distributions, taking into account that other Linux systems use different ways to install the software and start and stop services. Descriptions of how to set up LAMP configuration files, however, should work across multiple Linux distributions with only slight modifications. More information about Debian can be found in Chapter 9.

Components of a LAMP Server

You're probably familiar with Linux by this point, so this section focuses on the other three components — Apache, MySQL, and PHP — and the functions they serve within a LAMP system.

Apache

Within a LAMP server, Apache HTTPD provides the service with which the client Web browsers communicate. The daemon runs in the background on your server and waits for requests from clients. Web browsers connect to the HTTP daemon and send requests, which the daemon interprets, sending back the appropriate data. Apache HTTPD includes an interface that allows modules to tie into the process to handle specific portions of a request. Among other things, modules are available to handle the processing of scripting languages such as Perl or PHP within Web documents and to add encryption to connections between clients and the server.

Apache began as a collection of patches and improvements from the National Center for Supercomputing Applications (NCSA), University of Illinois, Urbana-Champaign, to the HTTP daemon. The NCSA HTTP daemon was the most popular HTTP server at the time, but had started to show its age after its author, Rob McCool, left NCSA in mid-1994.

Note   Another project that came from NCSA is Mosaic. Most modern Web browsers can trace their origins to Mosaic.

In early 1995, a group of developers formed the Apache Group and began making extensive modifications to the NCSA HTTPD code base. Apache soon replaced NCSA HTTPD as the most popular Web server, a title it still holds today.

Note   The name "Apache" refers to the nation of Native Americans having the same name and does not refer to "a patchy" Web server.

The Apache Group later formed the Apache Software Foundation (ASF) to promote the development of Apache and other free software. With the start of new projects at ASF, the Apache server became known as Apache HTTPD, although the two terms are still used interchangeably. Current ASF projects include Jakarta (open source Java solutions), mod_perl (an Apache-embedded Perl interpreter), and SpamAssassin (an e-mail filtering program).

MySQL

MySQL is an open source DBMS (database management system) that has become popular among Web masters because of its speed, stability, and features. MySQL consists of a server that handles storage and access to data and clients to handle interfacing with and managing the server. Client libraries are also included, and they can be used by third-party programs, such as PHP, to connect to the server.

In a LAMP server, MySQL is used for storing data appropriate to the Web applications that are being used. Common uses include data such as usernames and passwords, entries in a journal, and data files.

> **Note** Data within a database are stored in tables; each table contains columns and rows. You could compare a table to a spreadsheet, in which each column contains a specific data field and each row contains a record. Instead of a graphical representation of the data, individual rows are accessed using a query that returns only the rows desired.

MySQL was originally developed by Michael (Monty) Widenius of TcX (Sweden). In 1994, TcX needed a backend database for Web applications and decided to use one supporting SQL, a standardized and widely recognized language for interacting with databases.

TcX investigated the free databases that were available at the time, plus some commercial databases, but could not find a system that supported the features it needed and could handle its large databases at the same time. Because it already had experience writing database programs, TcX decided that the best way to get what it wanted was to develop a new system that supported SQL.

In 1995, TcX released the source code for MySQL on the Internet. MySQL was not an open source program at that time (due to some of the restrictions in its license), but it still began to see widespread use. MySQL was later released under the GNU General Public License (GPL).

PHP

PHP is a programming language that was developed specifically for use in Web scripts. It is preferred by many developers because it's designed to be embedded within HTML documents, making it simpler to manage Web content and scripts within a single file.

PHP originated as a set of Perl scripts by Rasmus Lerdorf called *PHP/FI (Personal Home Page/Forms Interpreter)*. Over time, more features were implemented, and Rasmus rewrote PHP/FI in C.

In late 1997, Andi Gutmans and Zeev Suraski began working on a complete rewrite of PHP/FI. As the language evolved and more features were implemented, Gutmans and Suraski decided that it would be appropriate to rename the project to more accurately reflect these features. The name "PHP Hypertext Preprocessor (PHP)" was chosen, with Lerdorf's approval, to maintain familiarity for users of PHP/FI.

The core features of PHP are included within the PHP code itself, and additional features are implemented in the form of extensions. On Debian, PHP is contained in the php4 package, and the extensions are stored in separate packages that can be installed at any time. Some of the most popular packages include:

✦ **php4-curl** — This extension interfaces with the CURL library, which contains interfaces for several types of servers, including LDAP, HTTP, and FTP.

✦ **php4-domxml** — Functions related to processing XML.

✦ **php4-gd** — The GD library is used for creating images. It is most popular for its graph generation functions.

✦ **php4-ldap** — Functions for communicating with LDAP servers.

✦ **php4-mysql** — Functions for communicating with a MySQL database server.

✦ **php4-pear** — Functions and support programs for using the PHP Extension and Application Repository (PEAR). PEAR is similar to the CPAN archive for Perl programs and contains a large number of useful modules. (More information about PEAR modules can be found at `http://pear.php.net`.)

✦ **php4-pgsql** — Functions for communicating with a PostgreSQL database server.

✦ **php4-snmp** — Functions for performing network management using the SNMP protocol.

Setting Up Your LAMP Server

Before proceeding through the examples in this section, be sure that your Debian operating system is configured. You may also choose to set up a server on a system that has been configured using the layout and software packages intended for a workstation, but that's not recommended unless you will only be providing services for a very small number of users whom you know well and trust.

Installing Apache

The next step toward a functioning LAMP server is to install the Apache HTTP server, which can be found in the apache package. Use APT to retrieve and install the package:

```
# apt-get install apache
```

During the configuration process, you will be asked whether you want to enable the suexec mechanism. The suexec feature increases the security of CGI applications and is generally recommended. You can change your selection later using `debconf` to reconfigure the apache package. More information about `debconf` can be found in Chapter 9.

Note This installation process installs Apache version 1.3, and all the configuration examples here have been tested against it. If you would rather install Apache 2.0, it is available in the apache2-mpm-prefork package and uses libapache2-mod-php4 instead of the php4 package mentioned later in this chapter.

The server should automatically start once the installation is finished, which means that you're now ready to install PHP.

Installing PHP

Now you're ready to install and test the PHP module in Apache. This is the most common method for installing PHP but introduces some security concerns on multi-user systems because all PHP scripts will be run as the same user as the Apache daemon. Be sure to read the Security section of the PHP manual at http://php.net/ manual/en/security.php before granting other users access to manipulate PHP files on your server.

The PHP Apache module is contained in the php4 package, which is installed using APT. The following lines download and install the module and the mysql extensions, configure Apache to load the module automatically, and instruct Apache to reload its configuration:

```
# apt-get install php4 php4-mysql
# apache-modconf apache enable mod_php4
Replacing config file /etc/apache/modules.conf with new version
# apachectl restart
```

Don't worry if the second line does not print out a message as this example shows. That simply means that the module has already been configured.

At this point, Apache should be ready to process HTTP requests, complete with processing of PHP files. To test it, create a file named /var/www/info.php containing a call to the phpinfo() function:

```
# cat > /var/www/info.php
<?php
    phpinfo();
?>
^D
# chmod 644 /var/www/info.php
```

The ^D means that you should press Ctrl+D on your keyboard. This tells the cat command that you are at the end of the input. Now try opening the page by going to http://your server's address/info.php. You should see a page full of information about your Apache and PHP installation, as shown in Figure 23-1.

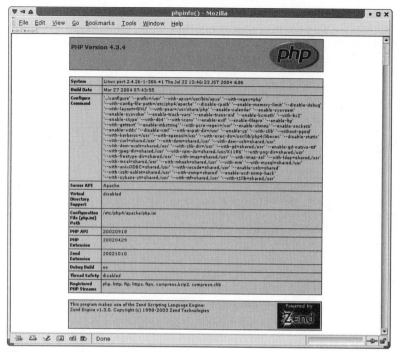

Figure 23-1: The PHP information page.

If, instead of an information page, you are prompted to download the file, check the appropriate PHP installation section (earlier in the chapter) to verify that all the steps were completed successfully.

After everything is tested and working, it's safe to remove the info.php file that you created:

```
# rm -f /var/www/info.php
```

Installing MySQL

The MySQL database system is divided into three main packages: the server, clients, and client libraries. The server is contained within the mysql-server package and requires the other two to function. APT is aware of this, which means the packages will be installed automatically when you install mysql-server:

Note

Make sure the hostname settings have been configured as described in Chapter 9 before installing the mysql-server package. Failure to do so could result in an error that will cause the installation to fail.

```
# apt-get install mysql-server
```

The installation scripts in the mysql-server package provide you with a couple of notices and ask whether you want to remove databases when purging the mysql-server package. "No" is the safest option because it reduces the chance of accidentally losing your data. You also are asked whether you want the MySQL server to start on boot. You should probably say "Yes" here.

Access to databases within MySQL is managed based on account information stored within the mysql database. As with UNIX systems, the superuser account is named root. The default installation does not set a password on this account, and it creates an anonymous account and a test database that should be removed unless you are certain that you need them:

```
# mysql -u root mysql
Welcome to the MySQL monitor.  Commands end with ; or \g.
Your MySQL connection id is 3 to server version: 4.0.18-log

Type 'help;' or '\h' for help.  Type '\c' to clear the buffer.

mysql> UPDATE user SET Password=PASSWORD('newpassword')
    -> WHERE User='root';
Query OK, 2 rows affected (0.00 sec)
Rows matched: 2  Changed: 2  Warnings: 0

mysql> DELETE FROM user WHERE User = '';
Query OK, 2 rows affected (0.00 sec)

mysql> FLUSH PRIVILEGES;
Query OK, 0 rows affected (0.00 sec)

mysql> DROP DATABASE test;
Query OK, 0 rows affected (0.00 sec)

mysql> \q
Bye
```

The UPDATE command changes the password for the MySQL root account (replace *newpassword* with the password you want to use), the DELETE command removes the anonymous user, and the FLUSH command tells the running MySQL server to reload the list of user accounts from the database. Finally, the DROP command removes the test database.

Operating Your LAMP Server

With the components of your LAMP server installed and running, you are ready to configure Apache and try it out. For this example, Apache is set up to serve content for your own domain using a feature called *virtual hosting*, after which you'll see how to install the Gallery application (http://gallery.menalto.com), which enables you to create an online photo gallery on your LAMP server.

Editing Your Apache Configuration Files

The configuration files for Apache HTTPD are incredibly flexible, meaning that you can configure the server to behave in almost any manner you want. This flexibility comes at the cost of increased complexity in the form of a large number of configuration options (called *directives*), but in practice there are only a few directives with which you'll need to be familiar.

Note   See `http://httpd.apache.org/docs/` for a complete list of directives supported by Apache.

The Apache configuration is stored in text files that are read by the Apache server, beginning with `/etc/apache/httpd.conf`. Configuration is read from start to finish, with most directives being processed in the order in which they are read.

Additional files may also be read based on the `AccessConfig`, `ResourceConfig`, and `Include` directives. On modern installations, the `AccessConfig` and `ResourceConfig` options point to empty files, and the traditional contents of those files have been moved to the main `httpd.conf` file.

The `Include` directive is distinct from `AccessConfig` and `ResourceConfig` in that it can appear more than once and can include more than one file at a time. Files referenced by `Include` directives are processed as if their contents appeared at the location of the relevant `Include` statement. `Include` can point to a single file, to a directory in which all files are read, or to a wildcard that specifies a specific set of files within a directory.

Note   Subdirectories are also processed when `Include` points to a directory.

The scope of many configuration directives can be altered based on context. In other words, some parameters may be set on a global level and then changed for a specific file, directory, or virtual host. Other directives are always global in nature, such as those specifying which IP addresses the server listens on, and some are valid only when applied to a specific location.

Locations are configured in the form of a start tag containing the location type and a resource location, followed by the configuration options for that location, and finishing with an end tag. This form is often called a *configuration block,* and looks very similar to HTML. A special type of configuration block, known as a *location block,* is used to override settings for specific files or directories. These blocks take the following form:

```
<locationtag specifier>
(options specific to objects matching the specifier go within this block)
</locationtag>
```

Different types of location tags exist, and are selected based on the type of resource location that is being specified. The specifier that is included in the start tag will be handled based on the type of location tag. The ones you will generally use and encounter are Directory, Files, and Location.

> **Note** In this chapter, Location refers specifically to the third type of tag, and location refers generically to any of the three.

✦ **Directory** tags are used to specify a path based on the location on the file system. For instance, `<Directory />` refers to the root directory on the computer. Directories inherit settings from directories above them, with the most specific Directory block overriding less specific ones, regardless of the order in which they appear in the configuration files.

✦ **Files** tags are used to specify files by name. Files tags can be contained within Directory blocks to limit them to files under that directory. Settings within a Files block will override the ones in Directory blocks.

✦ **Location** tags are used to specify the URI that is used to access a file or directory. This is different from Directory in that it relates to the address contained within the request and not to the real location of the file on the drive. Location tags are processed last and will override the settings in Directory and Files blocks.

Match versions of these tags — DirectoryMatch, FilesMatch, and LocationMatch — have the same function but can contain regular expressions in the resource specification. FilesMatch and LocationMatch blocks are processed at the same time as Files and Location, respectively. DirectoryMatch blocks are processed after Directory blocks.

Apache can also be configured to process configuration options contained within files with the name specified in the `AccessFileName` directive (which is generally set to `.htaccess`). Directives in access configuration files are applied to all objects under the directory they contain, including subdirectories and their contents. Access configuration files are processed at the same time as Directory blocks, using a similar "most specific match" order.

> **Note** Access control files are useful for allowing users to change specific settings without having access to the server configuration files. The configuration directives permitted within an access configuration file are determined by the `AllowOverride` setting on the directory in which they are contained. Some directives do not make sense at that level and will generally result in a "server internal error" message when trying to access the URI. The `AllowOverride` option is covered in detail at `http://httpd.apache.org/docs/mod/core.html#allowoverride`.

Three directives commonly found in location blocks and access control files are `DirectoryIndex`, `Options`, and `ErrorDocument`:

✦ `DirectoryIndex` tells Apache which file to load when the URI contains a directory but not a filename. This directive doesn't work in Files blocks.

✦ `Options` is used to adjust how Apache handles files within a directory. The `ExecCGI` option tells Apache that files in that directory can be run as CGI scripts, and the `Includes` option tells Apache that server-side includes (SSI) are permitted. Also commonly used is the `Indexes` option, which tells Apache to generate a list of files if one of the filenames found in the `DirectoryIndex` setting is missing. An absolute list of options can be specified, or the list of options can be modified by adding + or - in front of an option name. See `http://httpd.apache.org/docs/mod/core.html#options` for more information.

✦ `ErrorDocument` directives can be used to specify which file to send in the result of an error. The directive must specify an error code and the full URI for the error document. Possible error codes include 403 (access denied), 404 (file not found), and 500 (server internal error). More information about the `ErrorDocument` directive can be found at `http://httpd.apache.org/docs/mod/core.html#errordocument`.

Another common use for location blocks and access control files is to limit access to a resource. The `Allow` directive can be used to permit access to matching hosts, and the `Deny` directive can be used to forbid it. Both of these options can occur more than once within a block and are handled based on the `Order` setting. Setting `Order` to `Deny,Allow` permits access to any host that is not listed in a `Deny` directive. A setting of `Allow,Deny` denies access to any host not allowed in an `Allow` directive. Like most other options, the most specific `Allow` or `Deny` option for a host is used, meaning that you can `Deny` access to a range and `Allow` access to subsets of that range. By adding the `Satisfy` option and some additional parameters, you can add password authentication. For more information about access control, see `http://httpd.apache.org/docs/mod/mod_access.html`.

Location blocks (in the generic sense) can be enclosed within a `VirtualHost` block. Virtual hosts, which are described in greater detail in the next section, are a convenient (and almost essential) tool for altering server behavior based on the server address or name that a request is directed to. Most global configuration options are applied to virtual hosts but can be overridden by directives within the `VirtualHost` block.

Adding a Virtual Host to Apache

Apache supports the creation of separate Web sites within a single server to keep content separate. Individual sites are configured in the form of virtual hosts, which also are useful when only a single site will be used. Here's how to configure a virtual host:

Create a file named `/etc/apache/conf.d/vhosts.conf` using this template:

```
NameVirtualHost *:80
<VirtualHost *:80>
     ServerName       www.example.org
     ServerAlias      web.example.org
     DocumentRoot     /home/username/public_html/
     User             username
     Group            groupname
     DirectoryIndex   index.php index.html index.htm
</VirtualHost>
```

The NameVirtualHost line tells Apache to determine which virtual host to serve documents from based on the hostname provided by the HTTP client. The *:80 means that requests to port 80 on any IP address will be treated in this manner.

Similarly, the *:80 specification in the VirtualHost block indicates what address and port this virtual host applies to. The port is optional for both the NameVirtualHost and VirtualHost specifications but should always be used to prevent interference with SSL virtual hosts.

The ServerName and ServerAlias lines tell Apache which names this virtual host should be recognized as, so replace them with names appropriate to your site. You can leave out the ServerAlias line if you do not have any alternate names for the server, and you can specify more than one name per ServerAlias line or have multiple ServerAlias lines if you have several alternate names.

The DocumentRoot specifies where the Web documents for this site are stored. If you plan to have more than one site per user, you will need to modify this layout appropriately. Replace username with the name of the account that is administrating the Web site. For this example, each Web site is required to be administered by a different user account.

The User and Group lines are used by suexec to determine which account to run scripts as. The groupname parameter should be changed to username's primary group. In most modern installations, this is the same as the username. These two lines must be left out if you aren't using suexec.

When you are done, use apachectl to check the configuration and then do a graceful restart:

```
# apachectl configtest
Syntax OK
# apachectl graceful
```

Note   Unless you have already created it, you will receive a warning about the public_ html not existing. Run mkdir ~/public_html as the user that owns the Web site in order to create it.

Additional virtual hosts can be added by repeating the VirtualHost block and repeating the configuration test (configtest) and reload (graceful) steps.

Note You may want to place individual virtual hosts in separate files for convenience. However, you should be careful to keep your primary virtual host in a file that will be read before the others because the first virtual host receives requests for site names that don't match any in your configuration. In a commercial Web-hosting environment, it is common to make a special default virtual host that contains an error message indicating that no site by that name has been configured.

Installing a Web Application: Gallery

Gallery is a Web-based photo gallery management system written in PHP. Through its Web interface, you can upload pictures to your own photo galleries, which will then be available on the Web through your LAMP server.

Note Gallery stores its information in data files in your Web directory and does not require that MySQL be installed on your server.

Despite its many advanced features, such as support for multiple photo albums and automatic generation of thumbnails, Gallery only takes a few minutes to install once your LAMP server has been configured. Before proceeding with this section, you will need to add a virtual host for Gallery. Then you'll be ready to install Gallery, as shown here:

1. There are several programs that Gallery uses in order to perform image manipulation. You can install these using APT:

   ```
   # apt-get install netpbm libjpeg-progs jhead unzip
   ```

2. Configure your virtual host so that the security features needed by Gallery are permitted by Apache by adding this to the `<VirtualHost>` block in `/etc/apache/conf.d/vhosts.conf`:

   ```
   <Directory /home/username/public_html>
           AllowOverride   Limit Options FileInfo
   </Directory>
   ```

Note Be sure to replace *username* with the name of the user account that owns the Web documents.

3. Test and reload the Apache HTTP server configuration:

   ```
   # apachectl configtest
   Syntax OK
   # apachectl graceful
   ```

4. Log out of your root account and log in as the user who owns the Web document folder.

5. Download the latest Gallery version 1.x package from `http://gallery.menalto.com/index.php` and extract it to the location where you want to have it installed. A `gallery` directory under your `public_html` folder is an ideal location:

```
$ cd ~/public_html
$ wget http://dl.sourceforge.net/sourceforge/gallery/gallery-1.4.4-p12.tar.gz
$ tar xzf gallery-1.4.4-p12.tar.gz
```

The second code line (starting $ `wget http:`) is too long to fit on one line in this book. Just keep typing on one line until you finish `.tar.gz`, and then press Enter.

Note   The `wget` and `tar` command lines may be different from this example if you use different versions of Gallery.

6. Run the Gallery preconfigure script to set up the necessary file permissions, and create an albums directory that the Web scripts will be able to write to:

```
$ cd ~/public_html/gallery
$ sh configure.sh
$ mkdir -m 777 ../albums
```

7. Go through the setup process at the Gallery setup page, `http://yourserver name/gallery/setup/`. A screenshot of the Gallery configuration page can be seen in Figure 23-2. The first page tests for all of the necessary programs, which are available if you installed the prerequisites in step 1. It indicates the installation status. There will be one warning about the `composite` program not being found and another indicating that no additional languages were downloaded.

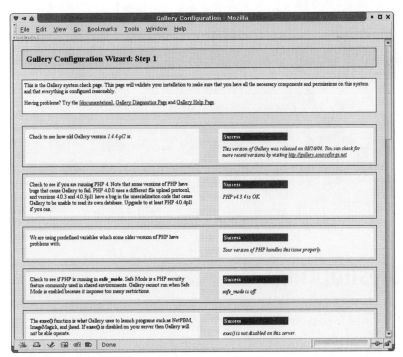

Figure 23-2: The Gallery setup page.

8. In the General settings, make sure you set an admin password. Under Locations and URLs, set the temporary directory to /tmp. The other default settings should work, but you can change the look and feel or gallery name to suit your tastes.

9. Tighten the permissions on gallery/.htaccess and gallery/config.php:

```
$ cd ~/public_html/gallery
$ sh secure.sh
```

10. You're now ready to start administrating your photo gallery through the Web interface at http://*yourservername*/gallery/.

Figure 23-3 shows an example photo gallery.

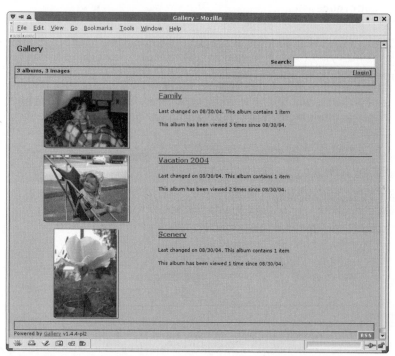

Figure 23-3: A sample Gallery installation, with photos.

Troubleshooting

In any complex environment, you will occasionally run into problems. This section includes tips for isolating and resolving the most common errors that you may encounter.

Note This section refers to the Apache HTTPD binary as `apache`, which is what it is named on Debian systems. However, in most other distributions, the binary is named `httpd`. On different systems, you may need to substitute *httpd* for *apache* when it appears by itself, although not for commands such as `apachectl`.

Configuration Errors

You may occasionally run into configuration errors or script problems that prevent Apache from starting or that prevent specific files from being accessible. Most of these problems can be isolated and resolved using two Apache-provided tools: the `apachectl` program and the system error log.

When encountering a problem, first use the `apachectl` program with the `configtest` parameter to test the configuration. In fact, it's a good idea to develop the habit of running this every time you make a configuration change:

```
# apachectl configtest
Syntax OK
# apachectl graceful
/usr/sbin/apachectl graceful: httpd gracefully restarted
```

In the event of a syntax error, `apachectl` indicates where the error occurs and also does its best to give a hint about the nature of the problem. You can then use the `graceful` restart option (`apachectl graceful`) to instruct Apache to reload its configuration without disconnecting any active clients.

Note The `graceful` restart option in `apachectl` automatically tests the configuration before sending the reload signal to `apache`, but it is still a good idea to get in the habit of running the manual configuration test after making any configuration changes.

Some configuration problems pass the syntax tests performed by `apachectl`, but then result in the HTTP daemon exiting immediately after reloading its configuration. If this happens, use the `tail` command to check Apache's error log for useful information. On Debian systems, the error log is in `/var/log/apache/error.log`. On other systems, the location can be found by looking for the `ErrorLog` directive in your Apache configuration.

One of the more commonly encountered errors looks something like this:

```
[crit] (98)Address already in use: make_sock: could not bind to port 80
```

This error often indicates that something else is bound to port 80 (not very common unless you have attempted to install another Web server), that another Apache process is already running (`apachectl` usually catches this), or that you have told Apache to bind the same IP address and port combination in more than one place.

You can use the `netstat` command to view the list of programs (including Apache) with TCP ports in the `LISTEN` state:

```
# netstat -nltp
Active Internet connections (only servers)
Proto  Local Address   Foreign Address   State     PID/Program name
tcp    0.0.0.0:80      0.0.0.0:*         LISTEN    2105/apache
```

The output from `netstat` (which was shortened to fit here) indicates that an instance of the `apache` process with a process ID of 2105 is listening (as indicated by the `LISTEN` state) for connections to any local IP address (indicated by `0.0.0.0`) on port 80 (the standard HTTP port). If a different program is listening to port 80, it will be shown there. You can use the `kill` command to terminate the process, but if it is something other than `apache` (or `httpd`), you should also find out why it is running.

If you don't see any other processes listening on port 80, it could be that you have accidentally told Apache to listen on the same IP address and port combination in more than one place. There are three configuration directives that can be used for this: `BindAddress`, `Port`, and `Listen`:

✦ `BindAddress` enables you to specify a single IP address to listen on, or you can specify all IP addresses using the `*` wildcard. You should never have more than one `BindAddress` statement in your configuration file.

✦ `Port` specifies which TCP port to listen on but does not enable you to specify the IP address. Port is generally not used more than once in the configuration.

✦ `Listen` enables you to specify both an IP address and a port to bind to. The IP address can be in the form of a wildcard, and you can have multiple `Listen` statements in your configuration file.

Generally, it is a good idea to use only one type of these directives to avoid confusion. Of the three, `Listen` is the most flexible, so it is probably the one you'll want to use the most. A common error when using `Listen` is to specify a port on all IP addresses (`*:80`) as well as that same port on a specific IP address (`1.2.3.4:80`), which will result in the error from `make_sock`.

Configuration errors relating to SSL (discussed later in this chapter) will commonly result in Apache not starting properly. Make sure all key and certificate files exist and that they are in the proper format (use `openssl` to examine them, as shown later in this chapter).

For other error messages, try doing a Web search to see if somebody else has encountered the problem. In most cases, you can find a solution within the first few matches.

If you aren't getting enough information in the `ErrorLog`, you can configure it to log more information using the `LogLevel` directive. The options available for this directive, in increasing order of verbosity, are `emerg`, `alert`, `crit`, `error`, `warn`, `notice`, `info`, and `debug`. Select only one of these. Any message that is at least as important as the `LogLevel` you select will be stored in the `ErrorLog`. On a typical server, this is set to `warn`. You should not set it to any lower than `crit` and should avoid leaving it set to `debug` because that can slow down the server and result in a very large `ErrorLog`.

As a last resort, you can also try running `apache` manually to check for crashes or other error messages:

```
# /usr/sbin/apache -d /etc/apache -F ; echo $?
```

The `-d` flag tells `apache` where to look for its configuration file, and the `-F` flag tells it to run in the foreground. The semicolon separates this command from the `echo` command, which will display the return code (`$?`) from Apache after it exits. In the event that `apache` crashes during this step, you can use tools such as `gdb` and `strace` to trace the problem.

Access Forbidden and Server Internal Errors

There are two common types of errors that you may encounter when attempting to view specific pages on your server: permission errors and server internal errors. Both types of errors can usually be isolated using the information in the error log. After making any of the changes below to attempt to solve one of these problems, try the request again and then check the error log to see if the message has changed (for example, to show that the operation completed successfully).

> **Note**
>
> "File not found" errors can be checked in the same way as access forbidden and server internal errors. You may sometimes find that Apache is not looking where you think it is for a specific file. Generally, the entire path to the file shows up in the error log. Make sure you are accessing the correct virtual host, and check for any `Alias` settings that might be directing your location to a place you don't expect.

A "file permissions prevent access" error indicates that the `apache` process is running as a user that is unable to open the requested file. Make sure that the account has execute permissions on the directory and every directory above it, as well as read permissions on the files themselves. Read permissions on a directory are also necessary if you want Apache to generate an index of files. See the manual page for `chmod` for more information about how to view and change permissions.

Note   Read permissions are not necessary for compiled binaries, such as those written in C or C++, but can be safely added unless there is a need to keep the contents of the program secret.

A "client denied by server configuration" error indicates that Apache was configured to deny access to the object. Check the configuration files for `<Location>` and `<Directory>` sections that might affect the file you are trying to access, remembering that settings applied to a path are also applied to any paths below it. You can override these by changing the permissions only for the more specific path to which you want to allow access.

The "Directory index forbidden by rule" error indicates that Apache could not find an index file with a name specified in the `DirectoryIndex` directive and was configured to not create an index containing a list of files in a directory. Make sure your index page, if you have one, has one of the names specified in the relevant `DirectoryIndex` directive, or add an `Options Indexes` line to the appropriate `<Directory>` or `<Location>` section for that object.

"Premature end of script headers" errors can indicate that a script is crashing before it finishes. Sometimes, the errors that caused this also show up in the error log. When using `suexec` or `suPHP`, this error may also be caused by a file ownership or permissions error. These errors are indicated in `/var/log/apache/suexec.log` or `/var/log/apache/suphp.log`.

Securing Your Web Traffic with SSL/TLS

You'll want to add security for your server, including your own certificates. Your data is important, and so is your capability to pass it along your network or the Internet to others. Networks just aren't secure enough by themselves to protect your communications. This section examines ways you can help guard them.

Electronic commerce applications such as online shopping and banking are generally encrypted using either the Secure Socket Layer (SSL) or Transport Layer Security (TLS) specifications. TLS is based on version 3.0 of the SSL specifications, so they are very similar in nature. This similarity, combined with the fact that SSL is older, results in the SSL acronym often being used to refer to either variety. For Web connections, the SSL connection is established first, and then normal HTTP communication is "tunneled" through it.

Note   Because SSL negotiation takes place before any HTTP communication, name-based virtual hosting (which occurs at the HTTP layer) does not work with SSL. As a consequence, every SSL virtual host you configure will need to have a unique IP address.

During connection establishment between an SSL client and an SSL server, asymmetric (public key) cryptography is used to verify identities and establish the session parameters and the session key. A symmetric encryption algorithm, such as DES or RC4, is then used with the negotiated key to encrypt the data that are transmitted during the session. The use of asymmetric encryption during the handshaking phase allows safe communication without the use of a preshared key, and the symmetric encryption is faster and more practical for use on the session data.

In order for the client to verify the identity of the server, the server must have a previously generated private key, as well as a certificate containing the public key and information about the server. This certificate must be verifiable using a public key that is known to the client.

Note   In some cases, the server also requires the client to present a certificate that it can verify. However, this is not commonly found on Web servers, except in high-security environments with smaller numbers of clients, where the management of certificates is more practical. More information about the SSL protocol can be found at `http://developer.netscape.com/docs/manuals/security/sslin/contents.htm`.

Certificates are generally digitally signed by a third-party certificate authority (CA) that has verified the identity of the requester and the validity of the request to have the certificate signed. In most cases, the CA is a company that has made arrangements with the Web browser vendor to have its own certificate installed and trusted by default client installations. The CA then charges the server operator for its services.

Commercial certificate authorities vary in price, features, and browser support, but remember that price is not always an indication of quality. Some common ones include InstantSSL (`www.instantssl.com`), Thawte (`www.thawte.com`), and VeriSign (`www.verisign.com`).

You also have the option of creating self-signed certificates, although these should only be used for testing or when a very small number of people will be accessing your server and you do not plan to have certificates on multiple machines. Directions for generating a self-signed certificate are included in the following section.

The last option is to run your own certificate authority. This is probably only practical if you have a small number of expected users and the means to distribute your CA certificate to them (including assisting them with installing it in their browsers). The process for creating a CA is too elaborate to cover in this book but is a worthwhile alternative to generating self-signed certificates. Guides on running your own CA can be found at these sites:

✦ `http://pseudonym.org/ssl/ssl_cook.html`

✦ `http://sial.org/howto/openssl/ca/`

The following procedure describes how to generate and use SSL keys with the LAMP server (running on a Debian GNU/Linux system) configured in this chapter. For a general discussion of SSL keys and procedures specific to Fedora and other Red Hat Linux systems, refer to Chapter 6.

Generating Your Keys

To begin setting up SSL, use the `openssl` command, which is part of the OpenSSL package, to generate your public and private key:

1. Use APT to verify that OpenSSL is installed. If it is not present, APT will download and install it automatically:

   ```
   # apt-get install openssl
   ```

2. Generate a 1024-bit RSA private key and save it to a file:

   ```
   # cd /etc/apache/ssl.key/
   # openssl genrsa -out server.key 1024
   # chmod 600 server.key
   ```

Note

You can use a filename other than `server.key` and should do so if you plan to have more than one SSL host on your machine (which requires more than one IP address). Just make sure you specify the correct filename in the Apache configuration later.

In higher-security environments, it is a good idea to encrypt the key by adding the `-des3` argument after the `genrsa` argument on the `openssl` command line:

```
# openssl genrsa -des3 -out server.key 1024
```

3. You are asked for a passphrase, which will be needed every time you start Apache. Do not lose this passphrase because it cannot be easily recovered.

4. If you plan to have your certificate signed by a CA (including one that you run yourself), generate a public key and a certificate signing request (CSR):

   ```
   # cd ../ssl.csr/
   # openssl req -new -key ../ssl.key/server.key -out server.csr
   Country Name (2 letter code) [AU]:US
   State or Province Name (full name) [Some-State]:Washington
   Locality Name (eg, city) []:Bellingham
   Organization Name (eg, company) [Internet Widgits Pty
   Ltd]:Example Company, LTD.
   Organizational Unit Name (eg, section) []:Network Operations
   Common Name (eg, YOUR name) []:secure.example.org
   Email Address []:dom@example.org

   Please enter the following 'extra' attributes
   to be sent with your certificate request
   A challenge password []:
   An optional company name []:
   ```

The Common Name should match the name that clients will use to access your server. Be sure to get the other details right if you plan to have the CSR signed by a third-party CA.

5. When using a third-party CA, submit the CSR to it and then place the certificate it provides you into `/etc/apache/ssl.crt/server.crt` (or a different file, as desired).

6. If you don't plan to have your certificate signed, or if you want to test your configuration, generate a self-signed certificate and save it in a file named `server.crt`:

```
# cd ../ssl.crt/
# openssl req new -x509 -nodes -sha1 -days 365 -key
../ssl.key/server.key -out server.crt
Country Name (2 letter code) [AU]:.
State or Province Name (full name) [Some-State]:.
Locality Name (eg, city) []:.
Organization Name (eg, company) [Internet Widgits Pty
Ltd]:TEST USE ONLY
Organizational Unit Name (eg, section) []:TEST USE ONLY
Common Name (eg, YOUR name) []:secure.example.org
Email Address []:dom@example.org
```

Configuring Apache to Support SSL/TLS

Once your keys have been generated, you will need to install the mod_ssl Apache module, which adds SSL/TLS support to Apache and then configure it using the appropriate configuration directives. Here's how:

1. SSL and TLS support can be added to Apache by installing the mod_ssl package:

```
# apt-get install libapache-mod-ssl
# apache-modconf apache enable mod_ssl
Replacing config file /etc/apache/modules.conf with new
version
```

2. Add an SSL-enabled virtual host to your Apache configuration files. Using the earlier virtual host as an example, your configuration will look something like this:

```
Listen *:443
<VirtualHost *:443>
    ServerName       secure.example.org
    DocumentRoot     /home/username/public_html/
    User             username
    Group            groupname
    DirectoryIndex   index.php index.html index.htm
    SSLEngine        On
    SSLCertificateKeyFile /etc/apache/ssl.key/server.key
    SSLCertificateFile /etc/apache/ssl.crt/server.crt
    SSLCACertificateFile /etc/apache/ssl.crt/ca.crt
</VirtualHost>
```

This example uses a wildcard for the IP address in the VirtualHost declaration, which saves you from having to modify your configuration file in the event that your IP address changes but will also prevent you from having multiple SSL virtual hosts. In the event that you do need to support more than one SSL virtual host, replace * with the specific IP address that you assign to that host.

Note See the "Troubleshooting" section earlier in the chapter for more information about the Listen directive.

A CA generally provides you with a certificate file to place in ca.crt and sometimes also provides you with a separate file that you will need to reference using a SSLCertificateChainFile directive. The mod_ssl package also includes an /etc/apache/ssl.crt/ca-bundle.crt, which contains the certificates from most of the well-known certificate authorities and can be referenced as long as the appropriate CA certificate is included. When running your own CA, point this directive to a file containing the public key from that CA. Omit this line when using a self-signed certificate.

3. Test the Apache configuration and then perform a full restart:

```
# apachectl configtest
Syntax OK.
# apachectl stop
# apachectl start
```

4. Browse to https://servername/ and verify the SSL configuration. When using a self-signed certificate, or one signed by a CA, you will be asked whether you want to accept the certificate.

Summary

Combining Linux with an Apache Web server, MySQL database, and PHP scripting content (referred to as a LAMP server) makes it possible for everyone to configure their own full-featured Web server. By following the instructions in this chapter, you learned how to set up Apache to do virtual hosting, add content to a MySQL database, and allow PHP scripting in the content on your server. For added security, this chapter described how to add your own certificates and troubleshoot problems that might arise with your server.

✦   ✦   ✦

Running a Mail Server

Electronic mail hardly requires introduction. Communications made through the original forms of e-mail helped shape the Internet. Widespread availability of access to e-mail and modern enhancements such as MIME (Multipurpose Internet Mail Extensions, which allow for inclusion of attachments and alternate message formats) have helped to make e-mail the most popular application on the Internet.

With a Linux system and a suitable Internet connection, you can easily set up your own mail server for personal or business use. This chapter presents two mail-system configurations, compares their features so that you can select the one that best suits your needs, and then guides you through the installation processes.

In the final section, you learn how to secure network communications between clients and a Postfix-based server through the use of SSL/TLS (Secure Sockets Layer and Transport Layer Security protocols).

The examples in this chapter are based on a Debian GNU/Linux system. (See Chapter 9 for more information about Debian.) However, much of the knowledge you gain from setting up a mail server in Debian (such as the way you would configure a `sendmail.mc` file) applies to other Linux systems as well.

Internet E-Mail's Inner Workings

E-mail messages are generated either by an automated process, such as a form processor on a Web page or an automated notification system, or by an MUA (Mail User Agent) controlled by an end user. Messages are delivered through one of two methods to the software performing the MTA (Mail Transfer Agent) function on a server:

✦ **SMTP** — The Simple Mail Transfer Protocol is a network-based protocol that allows for transmission of messages between systems.

✦ **Local IPC** — Interprocess communications are often used instead of SMTP when transferring a message between programs within a system.

Upon receiving a message, the MTA places it in a queue to be processed by an MDA (Mail Delivery Agent). Mail Delivery Agents come in two varieties:

✦ **Local** MDAs, which deliver messages to mailboxes on the local server. Simple versions (such as sendmail's `mail.local`) copy messages directly to a specified mailbox, while complex implementations (such as procmail and maildrop) can alter messages or delivery parameters based on user-specified rules.

✦ **Remote** MDAs, which deliver messages over the network to remote servers. Full remote MDAs use DNS (the Domain Name System) to determine the mail exchanger hosts for recipient addresses and deliver to the best one available for each. Simple remote MDAs (sometimes also called "null clients") forward messages to a central server to continue the delivery process. Most remote MDAs are capable of either method and will act as configured by the administrator that performed the configuration.

Note You will often see the term MTA used in reference to the software that performs both MTA and MDA functions. This is a carry-over from older designs that did not separate the functions and is still fairly accurate given the fact that most mail server implementations include a minimum of an MTA, remote MDA, and basic local MDA.

When a message reaches its destination server, it is written to the user's mailbox by the local MDA. From that point, the message may be viewed by the user using one of three methods:

✦ **Direct access to the mailbox** — An MUA (Mail User Agent) with access to the mailbox file, directly or through a network file system, can read messages from the disk and display them for the user. This is generally a console or webmail application running on the server.

✦ **Downloaded to a workstation for local viewing** — Most mail users use POP3 (Post Office Protocol, version 3) to download messages to their local computers and view them in applications such as Evolution or Balsa. By default, messages are removed from the server during this process (similar to when you get your "snail mail" from the mailbox).

✦ **Accessed interactively over the network** — Most clients also support viewing messages while they are still on the server, through IMAP (Internet Message Access Protocol). Unlike POP3, this protocol enables users to access multiple folders on their servers and also allows them to access their messages from anywhere. However, this also creates a heavier burden on the server because it must process (and store) everything that the user decides to keep. Most webmail applications use IMAP as their backend protocol for accessing mailboxes; this eliminates the need for direct access to the mail files and makes it easier to split functions between systems.

Server Configuration Options

This section examines two different server configurations. Both configurations provide the same basic features (mail delivery, complete with spam and virus filters) but do so in very different ways. Read the descriptions, decide which configuration is right for you, and then proceed to the "Preparing Your System" section for information about how your system should be configured before you begin the mail system installation.

> **Note** The features available in these two configurations are a result of how they're being configured and not a result of a lack of features in either sendmail or Postfix. Both programs support nearly the same set of features. The choice of which to configure in what manner was completely arbitrary for the examples in this chapter, and the diversity is intended to help broaden your experience with mail systems.

The first configuration demonstrated is based on sendmail, which provides the MTA and MDA functions. Mail retrieval is provided by Qpopper using the POP3 protocol. Direct access to mailboxes is also available using Mutt. All content filtering (spam and virus) takes place before messages are accepted by the server. With the exception of the spam and virus filtering, this is a configuration that you will find on most traditional mail servers. This configuration is suitable for situations in which the following apply:

✦ Users will be downloading messages directly to their systems for viewing. Optionally, Mutt can be installed to allow users to check new messages through SSH (secure shell) connections when they are not at their workstation.

✦ Conditions (business or otherwise) require that the server administrator have the capability to control acceptable message content.

The second configuration is based on Postfix, which provides the MTA and remote MDA functions. Local MDA functions, including calls to the content filters and sorting, are provided by maildrop. Mail access is provided through the IMAP facilities in courier-imap. This configuration is suitable for situations in which the following apply:

✦ Messages may be left on the server to allow central backups.

✦ The capability to access all messages remotely is desirable.

✦ Individualized content filter settings are desirable.

> **Note** This second option is great for home systems on broadband connections. As long as your Internet service provider will permit it, you can use your own mail server and get to your mail whether you're at home or away. If you do not have an always-on connection, you can still use this method to run a mail server that is accessible to machines within your own network.

Preparing Your System

You will need a few common items for either configuration, starting with the proper hardware. A personal mail server can easily run on a Pentium-class computer, although you may notice occasional slowdowns while incoming messages are being scanned. Disk space requirements depend mostly on how much mail you want to have room for, so plan on having a few gigabytes for the operating system (which will leave you plenty of extra, just in case), plus the amount of mail you want to store.

The operating system should be installed with only the basic set of packages before you begin these examples. Some general information about the installation is provided in Chapter 9. Although the software described in this chapter works even if you aren't running Debian, the installation methods will not. If you don't have a spare system to act as a dedicated mail server, you can still use it as your workstation, although this is obviously recommended only for personal use.

Network Configuration

Your network settings should also be properly configured before you begin installing the mail software. The exact requirements depend on the method by which mail will be delivered to your server:

✦ **Direct delivery** is the method used by most traditional mail servers. DNS records tell remote servers that any mail addressed to your domain should be sent to your server via SMTP.

✦ **Retrieval from a mail host** is also possible using an MRA (Mail Retrieval Agent) such as Fetchmail. This option can be used when you have a mailbox under a shared domain but want to access the mail on your own server. This can also be done in combination with direct delivery if you have both your own domain and mailboxes under shared domains.

Note   Configuration of Fetchmail is explained in the "Configuring Mail Clients" section of this chapter.

Configuring for Direct Delivery

For direct delivery to function, the SMTP service (TCP port 25) must always be accessible to the outside world through a fixed name in DNS. This name will be in the form of an A (Address) record. A records allow DNS resolver processes to determine the IP address associated with a specific name and are used by most of the common protocols on the Internet. A typical DNS A record looks something like this:

```
bigserver.example.org    IN    A    1.2.18.12
```

The first parameter, bigserver.example.org, is the label, and the second parameter is the class (IN for Internet, which is where most DNS records are found). The A indicates the type, and the final parameter is the IP address associated with the label.

Once you have your A record, you can direct mail to your server using an MX (Mail eXchanger) record. The domain for the A and MX records do not need to be part of the same domain, which allows for much greater flexibility. Here is a sample MX record:

```
widgets.test.      IN    MX   0   bigserver.example.org.
```

This MX record indicates that mail for (any address)@widgets.test should be sent through the server bigserver.example.org. The 0 indicates the numeric priority for this MX record. When more than one MX record exists for a given label, the MX with the lowest priority is tried first. If a temporary error is encountered, the next highest priority mail server is tried, and so on until the list is exhausted. At that point the sending server will keep trying periodically until the message times out (generally five days). If multiple MX records exist with the same priority, they are tried in a random order.

Note Most mail servers will also fall back on the IP address listed in the A record for a label in the event that no MX records exist. However, it is considered bad practice to rely on this.

In some cases, it may be complicated to establish an A record because your IP address frequently changes. Obviously, this is not suitable for commercial purposes, but there is a workaround that is acceptably reliable for personal use. This is achieved through dynamic DNS services that are available (often at no charge) through a number of different companies. A list of these companies is maintained at `http://dmoz.org/Computers/Software/Internet/Servers/Address_Management/Dynamic_DNS_Services/`. Three of the most popular (in no particular order) are:

✦ DynDNS.org (`http://dyndns.org/`), supported by the ddclient or ipcheck packages

✦ ZoneEdit (`http://zonedit.com/`), supported by the ez-ipupdate package

✦ No-IP (`http://no-ip.com/`), supported by the no-ip package

Note The ez-ipupdate package supports all three of these, plus a number of others. View the package description (`apt-cache search ez-ipupdate`) for more information.

Most of these services will provide you with a hostname under a shared domain at no charge and can also provide a similar service for your own domain for a reasonable fee.

Configuring for Retrieval from a Mail Host

The configuration requirements when retrieving mail from a mail host are pretty limited. Your server should be ready to accept mail addressed to localhost and should generally have a name that is unique to it. In the event that a message sent to one of your mailboxes is rejected, the server will need to have a valid host name by which to identify itself when sending out the DSN (Delivery Status Notification).

You must be able to access the server from clients, although you may only need to do so from clients within your network. In either case, you should read over the information about DNS and A records in the previous section.

Common Packages

Two software packages will be used by both system configurations. You'll install these programs first so that they are (mostly) ready when the system is ready to use them.

 ✦ **SpamAssassin** (http://spamassassin.apache.org/) is a spam filtering program written in Perl. It uses a large set of rules to help determine how "spammy" a message looks and assigns a score based on the total of the rule values. For performance reasons, SpamAssassin uses a background daemon called spamd to perform message analysis. Access to this daemon is performed through the spamc client. A spamassassin command that performs the analysis without using spamd is also installed but is not used by either of the example configurations in this chapter.

 ✦ **ClamAV** (http://www.clamav.net) is an open source virus scanner that detects more than 20,000 viruses, worms, and Trojans. It uses a virus pattern database to identify viruses and includes a program named freshclam that handles updating the database automatically. Like SpamAssassin, ClamAV includes a daemon (clamd), a client (clamdscan), and a second command-line tool that does not use the daemon (clamscan). The daemon is used in the sendmail setup but is not used by the Postfix setup for logistical reasons.

You'll use APT to install these two programs, which are contained in the clamav and spamassassin packages:

```
# apt-get install clamav spamassassin
```

Debconf will ask you several questions about the configuration for ClamAV:

 ✦ For the virus update method, select either Daemon or Cron. The former is best for most situations.

 ✦ Select the appropriate source for the virus database. The second part of the server name is the country code, so U.S. residents will want to select db.us.clamav.net.

 ✦ You may be prompted for HTTP proxy information. If you have a direct connection to the Internet, you probably don't need to enter anything here. If you're uncertain, you can ask your network administrator or the technical support at your ISP whether you need a proxy server to access Web pages.

Now that the system is prepared, you can proceed to the section containing the configuration that you have selected.

Installing and Running sendmail

Sendmail (`http://www.sendmail.org/`) is the granddaddy of SMTP mail systems. It is still the default MTA on most systems, and a recent survey showed that 41% of active mail servers were running sendmail.

A fairly recent addition to sendmail is the Milter API. This API allows for the writing of mail filters that can filter messages at the SMTP level, allowing for careful control over what messages are accepted by the server.

A standard milter consists of a daemon that runs in the background and waits for a connection from the sendmail daemon. Almost every line that is sent from an SMTP client to the server is passed to the milter, which can accept, temporarily reject, or permanently reject the message at any point in the process. Milters also have the capability to modify message content. This capability is most commonly used to add headers to messages indicating status information.

A number of milters have been written to perform various tasks. Two such milters are Spamass-Milter (`http://savannah.nongnu.org/projects/spamass-milt/`) and ClamAV-Milter (`http://clamav.net/`). As you would expect, these milters use SpamAssassin and ClamAV to perform content identification.

> **Note** You can find general information about milters at `http://milter.org/`.

The final component is Qpopper (`http://qpopper.sourceforge.net`), which is the most widely used POP3 daemon. You can find configuration options for Qpopper in `/etc/qpopper.conf`, although you won't need to change any of the defaults for this server.

Follow these steps to install and configure the needed software:

1. Use APT to install the sendmail packages:

   ```
   # apt-get install sendmail sendmail-bin sendmail-doc
   ```

   APT will download the packages, remove Exim (the default MTA on Debian systems), and install sendmail. During the configuration process, you will see warnings about databases not existing. It is safe to ignore these warnings.

2. Configure SpamAssassin's startup parameters. Start by editing the file `/etc/default/spamassassin` and changing the `ENABLED` and `OPTIONS` parameters. The file should look something like this when you are done:

   ```
   # /etc/default/spamd.conf

   # Change to one to enable spamd
   ENABLED=1

   # Options
   # See man spamd for possible options. The -d option is
   # automatically added.
   OPTIONS="-m 25 -H"
   ```

3. Configure SpamAssassin to not modify message bodies by adding the following line to the end of /etc/spamassassin/local.conf:

```
report_safe 0
```

4. Start SpamAssassin:

```
# invoke-rc.d spamassassin start
```

5. Install the ClamAV virus scanning daemon:

```
# apt-get install daemon clamav-daemon
```

6. Install the milter programs that sendmail will use to perform the content filtering:

```
# apt-get install spamass-milter clamav-milter
```

7. Edit the spamass-milter startup parameters in /etc/default/spamass-milter. The configuration settings shown here instruct spamass-milter to not modify the message body (which can result in significant performance decreases) and to reject messages with a spam score higher than 20.

```
# spamass-milt startup defaults
# OPTIONS are passed directly to spamass-milter.
# man spamass-milter for details
OPTIONS="-m -r 20"
```

Note the last line in this example. If you have several options to specify, you include them in a single OPTIONS line as shown.

8. The master sendmail configuration file is /etc/mail/sendmail.cf. Its format is very complicated, which is why the preferred method is to edit /etc/mail/sendmail.mc. /etc/mail/sendmail.mc contains macros that are translated and copied to the sendmail.cf when you run sendmailconfig or when you run make from the /etc/mail directory. Open sendmail.mc in your text editor and make the following changes:

```
DAEMON_OPTIONS(`Family=inet, Name=MTA-v4, Port=smtp, Addr=127.0.0.1')dnl
```

This line tells sendmail to only listen for connections on the loopback interface. If you plan to receive messages directly via SMTP, replace 127.0.0.1 with 0.0.0.0.

Add the following line after the DAEMON_OPTIONS lines if you do not have control over all hosts within the domains that you are relaying for (doing so will help prevent other machines within those domains from relaying mail through your server without authorization):

```
FEATURE(`relay_hosts_only')dnl
```

Insert this line if you have to send all outgoing mail through a specific server:

```
define(`SMART_HOST', `mail.example.org')dnl
```

If you are going to allow client machines to relay messages through your server (see step 12 and the associated Caution), find this line:

```
FEATURE(`access_db', , `skip')dnl
```

and replace skip with /etc/mail/access.

The following lines cause sendmail to rewrite the domain in the return path of all outgoing messages:

```
FEATURE(`always_add_domain')dnl
MASQUERADE_AS(`mail.example.com')dnl
FEATURE(`allmasquerade')dnl
FEATURE(`masquerade_envelope')dnl
```

This is often not desirable, so comment out these lines by adding dnl (including the space after dnl) to the front of each line:

```
dnl FEATURE(`always_add_domain')dnl
dnl MASQUERADE_AS(`mail.example.com')dnl
dnl FEATURE(`allmasquerade')dnl
dnl FEATURE(`masquerade_envelope')dnl
```

The next two lines tell sendmail what forms of mail delivery it should handle. They may be missing from your configuration by default, so make sure they are added toward the end of the file.

```
MAILER(local)dnl
MAILER(smtp)dnl
```

The following lines tell sendmail how to communicate with the milter processes. The INPUT_MAIL_FILTER ones define the connection parameters for the individual milters, and the define statement specifies the order in which they will be processed.

```
INPUT_MAIL_FILTER(`spamassassin',
                `S=local:/var/run/sendmail/spamass.sock,
                F=, T=S:4m;R:4m;E:10m')dnl
INPUT_MAIL_FILTER(`clamav',
                `S=local:/var/run/clamav/clamav-milter.ctl,
                F=, T=S:4m;R:4m')dnl
define(`confINPUT_MAIL_FILTERS', `spamassassin,clamav')dnl
```

Note The F= option tells sendmail to continue message processing even if it is unable to communicate with the milter. Replace it with F=T if you need to have messages temporarily fail in such an event (but make sure you watch your mail logs closely when doing so).

9. Make sure that any domains for which your server will be accepting mail are listed, one per line, in /etc/mail/local-host-names.

10. Regenerate the sendmail configuration file:

```
# sendmailconfig
Configure sendmail with the existing /etc/mail/sendmail.conf?
[Y]y
[...]
Configure sendmail with the existing /etc/mail/sendmail.mc?
[Y]y
[...]
Reload the running sendmail now with the new configuration?
[Y]y
```

11. Install and start Qpopper if you want to provide POP3 access:

```
# apt-get install qpopper
```

Note   If desired, you can also enable IMAP support by installing uw-imapd package.

12. If any client machines are going to be relaying messages through your server, add their IP addresses to /etc/mail/access and run make in the /etc/mail directory to update the database. This change does not require that you reload the sendmail configuration.

Caution   The default /etc/mail/access file contains REJECT settings for a number of IP address blocks. These addresses are not assigned to any networks right now but are sometimes abused by spammers. From time to time, one of these address blocks is assigned to a regional IP address registry and then further divided among networks. When this happens, your server will continue to reject mail from those addresses. You can find a list of these networks at http://cymru.com/Bogons/index.html. If you don't have time to check the list regularly for removals, then you may want to remove the entries now.

You now have a fully functioning mail server that you can access from any standard mail client.

Installing and Running Postfix

Postfix (http://postfix.org/) was created by Wietse Venema as a replacement for sendmail. It was designed to be fast, easy to administer, and secure. It was also designed to behave similarly enough to sendmail that existing users would be able to switch without needing to make any major changes to other programs.

Maildrop (http://flounder.net/~mrsam/maildrop/) is the local MDA for the Courier mail system and is also available as a standalone package. It can be configured to sort messages based on rules that are specified on a system-wide or per-user level and is used in this example configuration to run messages through SpamAssassin and ClamAV and then move them to a Trash folder if either filter identifies them as undesirable.

Courier-IMAP (http://courier-mta.org/imap/), like maildrop, is a part of the Courier mail system and is also available as a separate package.

Follow these steps to install and configure the needed software:

1. Install the Postfix and maildrop packages:

```
# apt-get install postfix postfix-doc maildrop
```

2. Debconf asks several questions about how to configure Postfix:

- Select Internet Site as the configuration type, unless you have to send outgoing mail through a specific server, in which case you should select Internet With Smarthost.

- Direct all mail to the appropriate account on your system. Generally this is the account that you created while installing Debian.

- Enter the name of the primary domain for which you will be accepting mail.

- Answer **no** to the question about adding your domain to simple addresses.

- If you selected the smarthost option, enter the name of that server when prompted.

- Enter the entire list of hosts for which you plan to accept mail. This is generally your main domain, localhost, and localhost.localdomain.

- Do not force synchronous writes for mail unless you expect your server to have frequent unexpected reboots and are ready to take the performance decrease.

3. Configure Postfix to use `maildrop` as its local MDA by editing the `mailbox_command` line in `/etc/postfix/main.cf`:

```
mailbox_command = /usr/bin/maildrop -d ${USER}
```

If you will be relaying mail for any clients, add their IP addresses to the mynetworks line.

4. The only filter mechanism supported by maildrop requires that the external filter program read the original message on its input and then write the entire message to its output. ClamAV does not include this feature, so an intermediate program will be needed to perform some of the filtering steps. Create a file named `/usr/local/sbin/clam-mailscan` that contains the following:

Note By the time this book goes to press, this script should be available online at `http://www.tuckerlabs.com/wayne/projects/clam-mailscan/`.

```python
#!/usr/bin/env python

from sys import stdin, stdout
from os import execv, popen, umask, unlink
from tempfile import mktemp

CLAMSCAN='/usr/bin/clamscan'

umask(0077)

errors = []
```

```
tmpfn = mktemp()
tmpfh = open(tmpfn, 'w+b')

while True:
    rbuf = stdin.read(1024)
    if rbuf == '':
        break
    tmpfh.write(rbuf)

tmpfh.close()

vscan = popen("%s --no-summary --stdout --infected --mbox %s" % \
            (CLAMSCAN, tmpfn), 'r')

while True:
    rbuf = vscan.readline()
    if rbuf == '':
        break
    if rbuf.find("FOUND"):
        errors.append(rbuf[rbuf.find(':')+2:-1])

vscan.close()

tmpfh = open(tmpfn, 'r')
if len(errors) > 0:
    while True:
        rbuf = tmpfh.readline()
        if rbuf == '\n':
            break
        stdout.write(rbuf)
    for e in errors:
        stdout.write('X-Virus-Alert: %s in message\n' % e)
stdout.write('\n')

while True:
    rbuf = tmpfh.read(1024)
    if rbuf == '':
        break
    stdout.write(rbuf)

tmpfh.close()
unlink(tmpfn)
```

When called from `maildrop` to process a message, this program will save the message to a temporary file that it scans using `clamscan` (which is part of the ClamAV package). It then processes the output from `clamscan` to determine whether any viruses were found. Finally, it passes the message back to `maildrop`, including a `X-Virus-Alert` header (as appropriate), and removes the temporary file.

5. Set the permissions on `clam-mailscan` so that it can be executed by any user:

```
# chmod 0755 /usr/local/sbin/clam-mailscan
```

6. Configure maildrop to filter messages through SpamAssassin and ClamAV by changing your `/etc/maildroprc` file to look like this:

```
# Global maildrop filter file
DEFAULT="$HOME/Maildir"

if ( $SIZE < 60000 )
{
    xfilter "/usr/bin/spamc -f"
}

xfilter "/usr/local/sbin/clam-mailscan"

if (/^X-Spam-Flag: YES/ || /^X-Virus-Alert:/ )
{
    exception {
        to "$DEFAULT/.Trash/"
    }
}
```

The line starting with `DEFAULT` tells `maildrop` which location messages should be stored to. This causes maildrop to save the messages to a directory named `Maildir` under the recipient's home directory (which is automatically substituted for the `$HOME` variable by `maildrop`). The IMAP server is expecting to find messages in this directory.

The first `if` block filters messages that are less than 60,000 bytes through `spamc`, and the line after that runs the message through the `clam-mailscan` program.

The final `if` block checks for the presence of `X-Spam-Flag` and `X-Virus-Alert` headers. If either of these headers are found, maildrop attempts to deliver the message to a Trash folder located under the default folder. By enclosing this step within an `exception` block, `maildrop` is instructed to take the default action instead of aborting delivery in the event that this step fails. This allows you to safely prevent mail sorting for an individual account by simply removing its Trash folder.

Note You can find more information about the features and syntax of the `/etc/mail droprc` file by running `man maildropfilter` and `man maildropex`.

7. Create `Maildir` mail directories for every user already on the system. This step needs to be performed for every user that is already on the system and needs to be run as the user because executing it as root results in `maildrop` being unable to write to the new directories:

```
$ maildirmake.maildrop $HOME/Maildir
$ maildirmake.maildrop -f Trash $HOME/Maildir
```

8. Create mail directories under `/etc/skel`. The contents of `/etc/skel` will be copied to the home directories of any new accounts:

```
# maildirmake.maildrop /etc/skel/Maildir
# maildirmake.maildrop -f Trash /etc/skel/Maildir
```

9. Signal Postfix to reload its configuration so that it starts using maildrop instead of its own built-in MDA:

```
# invoke-rc.d postfix reload
```

10. Install the Courier-IMAP daemon:

```
# apt-get install courier-imap
```

Note   If you want to allow POP3 access, you can also install the courier-pop package at this step. Keep in mind, however, that POP3 clients will be unable to access the Trash folders under their accounts.

11. Debconf asks whether you want to create directories for Web-based administration. This interface has limited features, so I recommend that you not enable it.

You now have a fully functioning mail server that you can access from any standard mail client.

Testing and Troubleshooting

The best way to test your mail system is to try sending a message to your new address. Messages can be sent using your mail client or from the command line using the mail program. Messages with attachments can be sent from the command line using mpack.

To verify that your virus scanner is scanning messages properly, try sending yourself a test file. Test files containing fake viruses that should be detected by ClamAV can be found in the clamav-testfiles package. Use mpack to send one of the files, such as test.zip, in /usr/share/clamav-testfiles/ to an address on your server and verify that it was handled properly:

```
# mpack -s "test message" /usr/share/clamav-testfiles/test.zip
e-mail address of recipient
```

Note   The mpack program is part of the mpack package, which may not be installed by default. You can use apt-get to install it very easily.

To test SpamAssassin, try sending yourself a message that looks a lot like spam. Usually, a message containing a lot of capital letters and ! and $ symbols will receive a high spam score from SpamAssassin.

If something is not working properly, you should first check the mail logs in /var/log/mail.log. If you don't recognize an error message that you find in there, try doing a Web search. More often than not, you'll find a solution within a few search hits.

You should also check that all of the daemons are running. Both configurations require that spamd be running in the background. The sendmail configuration also requires that clamd, clamav-milter, and spamass-milter be running normally.

Any errors relating to clamav-milter and spamass-milter not running will be in the `mail.log` file and will look something like this:

```
[...] Milter (clamav): to error state
```

Configuring Mail Clients

Any mail client with support for the appropriate protocol for your configuration (POP3 for the first configuration, IMAP for the second) should be able to access mail from your server. Just use the name of your server in the mail server settings, and follow the troubleshooting steps in the previous section if something doesn't work.

Cross-Reference You can find more information about mail clients for Linux in Chapter 21.

Configuring Fetchmail

Fetchmail is an MRA (Mail Retrieval Agent) that you can use to pull mail from a remote account to your new server. It is configured in the `$HOME/.fetchmailrc` file, and is very easy to set up. To pull mail to your server, log in as the user that the mail should go, then configure and run it from there.

Note Run Fetchmail as the user for whom the mail is being retrieved. You should never run it as root. If you're doing a complex setup in which you retrieve mail from a single mailbox that needs to be sorted out for multiple users, see the `fetchmail` man page for information about multidrop mailboxes.

A `.fetchmailrc` file can be as simple as this:

```
poll mailserver.yourisp.example protocol pop3 username "foo"
```

If you have more than one mail server, you can add it as an additional line. If the server from which you are pulling mail supports IMAP, you can use `imap` instead of `pop3`. Other options that you can have are `password=your password>` and `ssl`. Storing the password in the file enables you to run Fetchmail without entering a password, and the `ssl` option tells Fetchmail to use an SSL/TLS connection to the server.

Note Your `.fetchmailrc` file should not be readable by others, and Fetchmail will generally complain if it is. To set the permissions so that only you can read it, run `chmod 0600 $HOME/.fetchmailrc/`.

Running Fetchmail is as simple as typing

```
$ fetchmail
```

If you want to have Fetchmail run in the background, you can use the `--daemon` (or `-d`) flags with a parameter telling it how often (in seconds) to poll the servers:

```
$ fetchmail --daemon 300
```

To have Fetchmail automatically start when the system boots, add this to your `crontab` file:

```
@reboot    /usr/bin/fetchmail --daemon 300
```

Note Fetchmail cannot prompt for passwords when run in this manner, which means that you must store the passwords in `.fetchmailrc` for this to work.

If you haven't configured a crontab file before, setting it up can be as easy as performing the following steps:

```
$ cat > mycron
@reboot    /usr/bin/fetchmail --daemon 300
(hit Ctrl-D here)
$ crontab mycron
```

Configuring Web-Based Mail

If you're running an IMAP server, you can offer Web-based access by installing IMP (`http://horde.org/imp/`, also in the imp3 package) or SquirrelMail (`http://squirrelmail.org/`, also found in the squirrelmail package). Start by configuring your system as a LAMP server (Chapter 23), and then install and configure the appropriate package.

Note IMP is considerably more complex to configure than SquirrelMail and may be more difficult to install. If you aren't sure which one is right for you, try the online demos for both and see which one you like best.

Securing Communications with SSL/TLS

Because communication between mail clients and the server often contains sensitive information such as passwords, it is usually desirable to enable SSL/TLS encryption. Here's how to enable SSL/TLS in Postfix and Courier-IMAP:

1. SSL/TLS for Postfix and Courier-IMAP are provided in the postfix-tls and courier-imap-tls packages, respectively. Use APT to install them:

   ```
   # apt-get install postfix-tls courier-imap-ssl
   ```

2. Third-party CA certificates are provided in the ca-certificates package. This will be referenced in the configuration, so install it too:

   ```
   # apt-get install ca-certificates
   ```

Debconf will ask you whether you want to trust the CA certificates by default. In most cases, you will want to select Yes.

3. If you are going to be using a certificate from a CA that is not already recognized (this is generally only true if you are running your own CA), place the CA public certificate in its own file in /etc/ssl/certs/ and update the certificate database:

```
# update-ca-certificates
```

4. Generate the private key and certificate signing request, as described in Chapter 23. The best location for these files is /etc/ssl/private/. Here's an example:

```
# cd /etc/ssl/private
# umask 0077
# openssl genrsa -out mail.key 1024
# openssl req -new -key mail.key -out mail.csr
```

5. Get your CSR (Certificate Signing Request) signed and place the certificate in /etc/mail/private/mail.crt. Or, to do a self-signed certificate, do the following:

```
# openssl req -new -x509 -nodes -sha1 -days 365 -key mail.key -out mail.crt
```

Caution

Many mail programs will refuse to connect to the server if they do not recognize the certificate. If you are running your own CA, you can overcome this by distributing the CA public key to all clients.

6. Concatenate the private key and certificate into a single file:

```
# cd /etc/ssl/private
# umask 0077
# cat mail.key mail.crt >> mail.pem
```

7. Tell Postfix where to find certificates and keys by adding the following lines to the end of /etc/postfix/main.cf:

```
smtpd_tls_cert_file = /etc/ssl/private/mail.pem
smtpd_tls_key_file = $smtpd_tls_cert_file
smtpd_tls_CAfile = /etc/ssl/certs/ca-certificates.crt
```

8. Configure the Postfix daemons to support SSL/TLS by adding -o smtpd_use_tls=yes to the line in /etc/postfix/master.cf that starts with smtpd. There will also be three commented-out lines at the end of the file that start with tlsmgr, smtps, and 587. Uncomment them and remove the -o smtpd_sasl_auth_enable=yes parameters. When finished, the lines will look something like this:

```
smtp    inet n - - -    - smtpd -o smtpd_use_tls=yes
(there will be quite a few lines in between)
# only used by postfix-tls
tlsmgr fifo - - n 300 1 tlsmgr
smtps   inet n - n -    - smtpd -o smtpd_tls_wrappermode=yes
587     inet n - n -    - smtpd -o smtpd_enforce_tls=yes
```

Caution

Some remote mail servers may refuse to send messages to you if you are using a certificate that is not signed by a CA that they recognize. If this happens, then you may need to remove the `-o smtpd_use_tls=yes` option from the `smtp` line.

Replace `smtpd_enforce_tls` with `smtpd_enable_tls` on the port 587 line if you need to maintain support for non-TLS clients on that port due to packet filters.

9. Enable SSL/TLS in the Courier-IMAP daemon by editing `/etc/courier/imapd-ssl` and replacing the values for `TLS_CERTFILE` and `TLS_TRUSTCERTS` with the following:

```
TLS_CERTFILE=/etc/ssl/private/mail.pem
TLS_TRUSTCERTS=/etc/ssl/certs/ca-certificates.pem
```

10. Restart Postfix and the Courier-IMAP daemons:

```
# invoke-rc.d postfix restart
# invoke-rc.d courier-imap restart
# invoke-rc.d courier-imap-ssl restart
```

11. Configure your mail clients to use SSL. All SSL-enabled clients should support SSL/TLS when sending to port 465 and when receiving on port 993. Newer clients that support the STARTTLS extension should also be able to use SSL/TLS when sending to port 25 or 587, and when receiving from port 143.

Summary

Using Linux and a good Internet connection, you can set up and maintain your own mail server. Preparing your computer to become a mail server includes configuring your network connection, setting up delivery and retrieval methods, and adding required software packages.

This chapter describes how to install, configure, and troubleshoot two of the most popular open source server packages: sendmail and Postfix. Those packages can be used in tandem with spam filtering software (such as SpamAssassin) and virus scanning software (such as ClamAV). Methods for securing your mail server include configuring support for SSL/TLS encryption.

✦   ✦   ✦

Running a Print Server

Sharing printers is a good way to save money and make your printing more efficient. Very few people need to print all the time, but when they do want to print something, they usually need it quickly. Setting up a print server can save money by eliminating the need for a printer at every workstation. Some of those savings can be used to buy printers that can output more pages per minute or have higher-quality output.

You can attach printers to your Linux system to make them available to users of that system (standalone printing) or to other computers on the network as a shared printer. You can also configure your Linux printer as a remote CUPS or Samba printer. With Samba, you are emulating Windows printing services, which is pretty useful given the abundance of Windows client systems.

This chapter describes configuring and using printers on Linux systems with various desktop environments in use. Some of the details may vary from one distribution to another, but the information included here should work well for the more commonly used distributions. This chapter focuses on Common UNIX Printing Service (CUPS), which is the recommended print service for the majority of Linux installations. Examples in this chapter use the Printer Configuration options in the GNOME and K Desktop environments.

Once a local printer is configured, print commands such as lpr are available for carrying out the actual printing. Commands also exist for querying print queues (lpq), manipulating print queues (lpc), and removing print queues (lprm). A local printer can also be shared as a print server for users on other computers on your network.

Common UNIX Printing Service (CUPS)

CUPS has become the standard for printing from Linux and other UNIX-like operating systems. It was designed to meet today's needs for standardized printer definitions and sharing on IP-based networks (as most computer networks are today). Nearly every Linux distribution today comes with CUPS as its printing service. Here are some of the service's features:

✦ **IPP** — At its heart, CUPS is based on the Internet Printing Protocol (www.pwg. org/ipp), a standard that was created to simplify how printers can be shared over IP networks. In the IPP model, printer servers and clients who want to print can exchange information about the model and features of a printer using HTTP (that is, Web content) protocol. A server could also broadcast the availability of a printer so a printing client could easily find a list of locally available printers.

✦ **Drivers** — CUPS also standardized how printer drivers are created. The idea was to have a common format that could be used by printer manufacturers so that a driver could work across all different types of UNIX systems. That way, a manufacturer only had to create the driver once to work for Linux, Mac OS X, and a variety of UNIX derivatives.

✦ **Printer classes** — You can use printer classes to create multiple print server entries that point to the same printer or one print server entry that points to multiple printers. In the first case, multiple entries could each allow different options (such as pointing to a particular paper tray or printing with certain character sizes or margins). In the second case, you could have a pool of printers so that printing is distributed, decreasing the occurrence of congested print queues often caused by a malfunctioning printer or a printer that is dealing with very large documents.

✦ **UNIX print commands** — To integrate into Linux and other UNIX environments, CUPS offers versions of standard commands for printing and managing printers that have been traditionally offered with UNIX systems.

Many Linux distributions come with simplified methods of configuring CUPS printers. Here are two examples:

✦ In Fedora and other Red Hat Linux systems, the Printer Configuration window (system-config-printer command) enables you to configure printers that use the CUPS facility.

✦ In SUSE, the YaST facility includes a printer configuration module. From the YaST Control Center select Hardware ➪ Printer.

For distributions that don't have their own printer configuration tools, there are several ways to configure CUPS using tools that aren't specific to a Linux distribution. Here are a couple of them:

✦ CUPS offers a Web-based interface for adding and managing printers. You can access this service by typing **localhost:631** from a Web browser on the computer running the CUPS service. (See the section titled "Using Web-Based CUPS Administration," later in this chapter.) The KDE desktop comes with a tool for managing CUPS server features. To launch the KDE CUPS Server Configuration window, type **/usr/bin/cupsdconf** from a Terminal window.

✦ You also can configure CUPS manually (that is, edit the configuration files and start the cupsd daemon manually). Configuration files for CUPS are contained in the /etc/cups directory. In particular, you might be interested in the cupsd.conf file, which identifies permission, authentication, and other information for the printer daemon, and printers.conf, which identifies addresses and options for configured printers. Use the classes.conf file to define local printer classes.

Note   You can print to CUPS from non-UNIX systems as well. For example, you can use a PostScript printer driver to print directly from Windows XP to your CUPS server. You can use CUPS without modification by configuring the XP computer with a PostScript driver that uses http://printservername:631printers/target Printer as its printing port.

To use CUPS, you need to have it installed. Most Linux distributions let you choose to add CUPS during the initial system install or will simply add CUPS by default. If CUPS was not added when you first installed your Linux distribution, check your original installation medium (DVD or CD) to see if it is there for you to install now. Fedora, Slackware, SUSE, and other Linux distributions all have CUPS on the first CD or DVD of their installation sets.

Setting Up Printers

While it is usually best to use the printer administration tools that are specifically built for your distribution, many Linux systems simply rely on the tools that come with the CUPS software package. This section explores how to use CUPS Web-based administration tools that come with every Linux distribution and then examines the printer configuration tool system-config-printer that comes with Fedora and Red Hat Enterprise Linux systems for setting up printers.

Using Web-Based CUPS Administration

CUPS offers its own Web-based administrative tool for adding, deleting, and modifying printer configurations on your computer. The CUPS print service (using the cupsd daemon) listens on port 631 to provide access to the CUPS Web-based administrative interface.

If CUPS is already running on your computer, you can immediately use CUPS Web-based administration from your Web browser. To see if CUPS is running and start setting up your printers, open a Web browser on the local computer and type the following into its location box:

```
http://localhost:631/admin
```

You are prompted for a valid login name and password. Type the root login name and the root user's password, and then click OK. A screen similar to the one shown in Figure 25-1 appears.

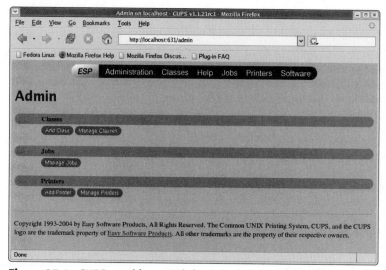

Figure 25-1: CUPS provides a Web-based administration tool.

By default, Web-based CUPS administration is available only from the local host. To access Web-based CUPS administration from another computer, you must change the /admin section in the /etc/cups/cupsd.conf file. As recommended in the text of this file, you should limit access to CUPS administration from the Web. The following example includes an Allow line to permit access from a host from IP address 10.0.0.5 (you must also change the Listen 127.0.0.1:631 line to listen outside your local host, as described a bit later).

```
<Location /admin>
AuthType Basic
AuthClass System
Order Deny, Allow
Deny from All
Allow From 127.0.0.1
Allow From 10.0.0.5
</Location>
```

From the computer at address `10.0.0.5`, you would type:

`http://localhost:631/admin`

(substituting the CUPS server's name or IP address for `localhost`), and when prompted, enter the root username and password.

Now, with the Admin screen displayed, here's how to set up a printer:

1. Click the Add Printer button. The Add New Printer screen appears.

2. Type a name, location, and description for the printer and click Continue.

3. Select the device to which the printer is connected. The printer can be connected locally to a parallel, SCSI, serial, or USB port directly on the computer. Alternatively, you can select a network connection type for Apple printers (appSocket/HP JetDirect), Internet Printing Protocol (http or ipp), or a Windows printer (using SAMBA or SMB).

4. If prompted for more information, you may need to further describe the connection to the printer. For example, you may need to enter the baud rate and parity for a serial port, or you might be asked for the network address for an IPP or Samba printer.

5. Select the make of the print driver (if you don't see the manufacturer of your printer listed, choose PostScript for a PostScript printer or HP for a PCL printer). For the make you choose, you will be able to select a specific model.

6. If the printer is added successfully, the next page you see shows a link to the description of that printer. Click on that link. From the new printer page, you can print a test page or modify the printer configuration.

After you are able to print from CUPS, you can return to the CUPS Web-based administration page and do further work with your printers. Here are a few examples of what you can do:

✦ **List print jobs.** Click Jobs to see what print jobs are currently active from any of the printers configured for this server. Click Show Completed Jobs to see information about jobs that are already printed.

✦ **Create a printer class.** Click Classes; then click Add Class and identify a name and location for a printer class. Click Continue. Then, from the list of Printers configured on your server, select the ones to go into this class.

✦ **View printers.** You can click the Printers link from the top of any of the CUPS Web-based administration pages to view the printers you have configured. For each printer that appears, you can click Stop Printer (to stop the printer from printing but still accept print jobs for the queue), Reject Jobs (to not accept any further print jobs for the moment), or Print Test Page (to print a page). Figure 25-2 shows the Printers page.

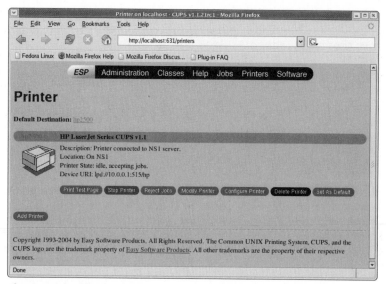

Figure 25-2: Print test pages or temporarily stop printing from the Printers page.

Using the Red Hat Printer Configuration Window

If you are using Fedora, RHEL or other Red Hat Linux systems, you can use the Printer Configuration window to set up your printers. In fact, it's recommended that you use it instead of CUPS Web administration because the resulting printer configuration files are tailored to work with Red Hat systems.

To install a printer from your GNOME desktop in Fedora, start the Printer Configuration window by selecting System Setting ⇨ Printing (or as root user by typing **system-config-printer**). This tool lets you add and delete printers and edit printer properties. It also lets you send test pages to those printers to make sure they are working properly.

The key here is that you are configuring printers that are managed by your print daemon (cupsd for the CUPS service). After a printer is configured, users on your local system can use it. Subsequently, you can refer to the "Configuring Print Servers" section to learn how to make the server available to users from other computers on your network.

The printers that you set up can be connected directly to your computer (as on a parallel port) or to another computer on the network (for example, from another UNIX system or Windows system).

Choosing a Printer

The PostScript language is the preferred format for Linux and UNIX printing and has been for many years. Every major word-processing product that runs on Fedora, Red Hat Linux, SUSE, Debian, and UNIX systems supports PostScript printing, so a printer that natively supports PostScript printing is sure to work in Linux.

If you get a PostScript printer and it is not explicitly shown in the list of supported printers, simply select the PostScript filter when you install the printer locally. No special drivers are needed. Your next best option is to choose a printer that supports PCL. In either case, make sure that the PostScript or PCL is implemented in the printer hardware and not in the Windows driver.

Avoid printers that are referred to as *Winprinters*. These printers use nonstandard printing interfaces (those other than PostScript or PCL). Support for these low-end printers is hit or miss. For example, some low-end HP DeskJet printers use the pnm2ppa driver to print documents in Printing Performance Architecture (PPA) format. Some Lexmark printers use the pbm217k driver to print. Although drivers are available for many of these Winprinters, many of them are not fully supported.

Ghostscript may also support your printer; if it does, you can use that tool to do your printing. Ghostscript (found at `www.ghostscript.com`) is a free PostScript-interpreter program. It can convert PostScript content to output that can be interpreted by a variety of printers. There are both GNU and Aladdin Ghostscript drivers available. Although the latest Aladdin drivers are not immediately released under the GPL, you can use older Aladdin drivers that are licensed under the GNU.

You'll find an excellent list of printers supported in Linux at `www.linuxprinting.org` (select the Printer Listing link). I strongly recommend that you visit that site before you purchase a printer to work with Linux. In addition to showing supported printers, the site also has a page describing how to choose a printer for use with Linux (`www.linuxprinting.org/suggested.html`).

Configuring Local Printers in Red Hat

Add a local printer (in other words, a printer connected directly to your computer) with the Printer Configuration window using the following procedure. (See the "Choosing a Printer" sidebar if you don't yet have a printer.)

 Tip Connect your printer before starting this procedure. This enables the printer software to autodetect the printer's location and to immediately test the printer when you have finished adding it.

Adding a Local Printer in Red Hat

To add a local printer from Fedora or other Red Hat Linux systems, follow these steps:

1. Select System Settings ⇨ Printing from the main menu or type the following as root user from a Terminal window:

   ```
   # system-config-printer &
   ```

   The Printer Configuration window appears.

2. Click New. An Add a New Print Queue window appears.

3. Click Forward. The Queue Name window (Figure 25-3) opens.

Figure 25-3: Add printers connected locally or remotely with the Printer Configuration window.

4. Add the following information:

   Name — Add the name you want to give to identify the printer. The name must begin with a letter, but after the initial letter, it can contain a combination of letters, numbers, dashes (-), and underscores (_). For example, an HP printer on a computer named maple could be named hp-maple.

   Description — Add a few words describing the printer, such as its features (an HP LaserJet 2100M with PCL and PS support) or its location (in Room 205 under the coffeepot).

5. Click Forward. The Queue Type window appears.

6. Select Locally-connected, choose the device to which the printer is connected (/dev/lp0, /dev/usb/lp0, and /dev/ttyS0 are the first parallel, usb, and serial ports, respectively), and click Forward. (Type **lpinfo -v | less** to see all available ports.) Alternatively, you could do one of the following:

- If your printer is not on the list because you have not yet connected it, connect it now and select Rescan Devices to have your computer try again to detect the printer.

- If you intend to connect your printer later, or for some reason it's not being scanned, click Custom Device and specify the device name where the printer will be found.

7. Click Forward. The Printer Model window opens.

8. Click the arrow on the Select Manufacturer box, and then choose the manufacturer of your printer. From the list that appears, select your printer model.

 Tip

If your printer doesn't appear on the list but supports PCL (HP's Printer Control Language), try selecting one of the HP printers (such as HP LaserJet). If your printer supports PostScript, select PostScript printer from the list. Selecting Raw Print Queue enables you to send to the printer documents that are already formatted for that printer type.

9. Click the Notes button. In many cases, you'll see good information from the Linux Printing Database about how your printer is configured and how to tune it further. (Close the information window when you are done.) Click OK to continue.

10. If the information looks correct, click Finish to create the entry for your printer.

11. A pop-up window asks if you want to print a test page. Click Yes, and click Yes again when told the test page has printed. The test page tells you interesting information about your printer, the resolution, and the type of interpreter used (such as PostScript), for example.

    The printer appears in the main Printer Configuration window. If it is the only printer configured, a check mark appears next to it, identifying it as the default printer. As you add other printers, you can change the default printer by selecting the one you want and clicking the Default button.

12. From the Printer Configuration window, choose Apply to save the changes (if necessary). If you have no other printers to add, you can close the Printer Configuration window at this point (select Action ⇨ Quit), or you can try more tests.

If you would like to try other test pages, click Test and select one of the following:

- **US Letter PostScript test page** — Sends a letter-sized (8.5 x 11) page to the printer in PostScript format. If you have a color printer, the page appears in color.

- **A4 PostScript test page** — Sends an A4 PostScript-formatted page to the printer.

- **ASCII text test page** — Sends plain text to the named printer.

- **Duplex test** — Sends a test page to see if the printer is in half or full duplex.

- **JPEG test** — Sends a JPEG image to the printer.

Printing should be working at this point. (If you want to share this printer with other computers on your network, refer to the "Configuring Print Servers" section of this chapter.)

> **Note**   Adding a printer in the K Desktop Environment (KDE) is very similar to the GNOME process. Select System Menu ➡ Printing System ➡ Add Printer; the New Printer Wizard opens. Check out `http://docs.kde.org/en/HEAD/kdebase/kdeprint/` for more details on using the New Printer Wizard (and printing in general) with KDE.

Editing a Local Printer in Red Hat

After you have created a printer queue, you can edit the printer queue definitions to change how the printer behaves. From the Printer Configuration window, do the following:

1. Select your printer, and click Edit. The Edit a Print Queue page appears. The following steps describe how to change options besides those you added originally.

2. Click the Queue Options tab. From this tab, you can:

   - **Add banner pages at the beginning and/or end of a job.** This is good practice for a printer that is shared by many people. The banner page helps you sort who gets which print job. The standard banner page shows the ID of the print job, the title of the file, the user who requested the print job, and any billing information associated with it.

   - **Change the image area by setting all four side margins.** The default is 36 points (one inch) on all four margins. You can adjust any of the four margins.

   - **Add or remove filter options.** These options define attributes of printing to the selected printer. Click the Add button to see queue options you can add. Options are stored in the `/etc/cups/lpoptions` file for each printer. Options that you might want to change include cpi (print text documents 10, 12, or 17 characters per inch) or lpi (print text documents 6 or 8 lines per inch). For descriptions of other options, check out the CUPS Internet Printing Protocol page (`/usr/share/doc/cups-*/ipp.html`).

3. Click Driver Options to set defaults for options related to the printer driver. Many of these options can be overridden when someone prints a document. Here are a few of the options you might want to set:

   Media Source — For multitray printers, you can select which tray to use by default.

   Page Size — The default is U.S. letter size, but you can also ask the printer to print legal size, envelopes, or ISO A4 and A3 standard pages.

Resolution — Select the default printing resolution (such as 300, 600, or 1,200 dots per inch). Higher resolutions result in better quality but take longer to print.

Printing Mode — Choose to print in grayscale or color.

4. Click OK when you are satisfied with the changes you made to the local printer.

Configuring Remote Printers in Red Hat

To use a printer that is available on your network, you must identify that printer to your Linux system. Supported remote printer connections include Networked CUPS (IPP) printers, Networked UNIX (LPD) printers, Networked Windows (SMB) printers, NetWare printers, and JetDirect printers. (Of course, both CUPS and UNIX print servers can be run from Linux systems as well as other UNIX systems.)

In each case, you need a network connection from your Linux system to the servers to which those printers are connected. To use a remote printer requires that someone set up that printer on the remote server computer. See the section titled "Configuring Print Servers" later in this chapter for information on how to do that on your Linux server.

Use the Printer Configuration window to configure each of the remote printer types:

1. From the GNOME menu in Fedora, select System Settings ⇨ Printing. The comparable step in the K Desktop Environment is to select Printer System ⇨ Print Manager.

2. Click New. The Add a New Printer Queue window appears.

3. Click Forward. The Queue Name window appears.

4. Type a short name and description of the printer and click Forward.

5. Click the Select a Queue Type box and select one of the following:

   • Networked CUPS (IPP)

   • Networked UNIX (LPD)

   • Networked Windows (SMB)

   • Networked Novell (NCP)

   • Networked JetDirect

6. Click Forward.

Continue following the steps in whichever of the following sections is appropriate.

Adding a Remote CUPS Printer

If you chose to add a CUPS printer from the Printer Configuration window, you must add the following information to the window that appears:

✦ **Server**—Host name of the computer to which the printer is attached (or otherwise accessible). This can be an IP address or TCP/IP host name for the computer (the TCP/IP name is accessible from your /etc/hosts file or through a DNS name server).

✦ **Path**—Printer name on the remote CUPS print server. CUPS supports the concept of printer instances, which allows each printer to have several sets of options. If the remote CUPS printer is configured this way, you will be able to choose a particular path to a printer, such as hp/300dpi or hp/1200dpi. A slash character separates the print queue name from the printer instance.

Complete the rest of the procedure as you would for a local printer (see the "Adding a Local Printer in Red Hat" section earlier in this chapter).

Adding a Remote UNIX Printer

If you chose to add a UNIX printer from the Printer Configuration window, you must add the following information to the window that appears:

✦ **Server**—Host name of the computer to which the printer is attached (or otherwise accessible). This is the IP address or TCP/IP name for the computer (the TCP/IP name is accessible from your /etc/hosts file or through a DNS name server).

✦ **Queue**—Printer name on the remote UNIX computer.

Complete the rest of the procedure as you would for a local printer (see the "Adding a Local Printer in Red Hat" section earlier in this chapter).

Tip   If the print job you send to test the printer is rejected, the print server computer may not have allowed you access to the printer. Ask the remote computer's administrator to add your host name to the /etc/lpd.perms file. (Type **lpq -P***printer* to see the status of your print job.)

Adding a Windows (SMB) Printer

Enabling your computer to access an SMB printer (the Windows printing service) involves adding an entry for the printer in the Printer Configuration window.

When you choose to add a Windows printer to the Printer Configuration window (described previously), you are presented with a list of computers on your network that have been detected as offering SMB services (file and/or printing service). You:

1. Select the server (click the arrow next to its name so that it points down).

2. Select the printer from the list of available printers shown.

3. When prompted, fill in the username and password needed to access the SMB printer. (You may also fill in the Workgroup information, if required.) Click OK to continue.

Alternatively, you could identify a server that does not appear on the list of servers. Click the Specify button and enter the following information in the appropriate fields:

✦ **Workgroup**—The workgroup name assigned to the SMB server. Filling in the workgroup name isn't necessary in all cases.

✦ **Server**—NetBIOS name or IP address for the computer, which may or may not be the same as its TCP/IP name. To translate this name into the address needed to reach the SMB host, Samba checks several places where the name may be assigned to an IP address. Samba checks the following (in the order shown) until it finds a match: the local /etc/hosts file, the local /etc/lmhosts file, a WINS server on the network, and responses to broadcasts on each local network interface to resolve the name.

✦ **Share**—Name under which the printer is shared with the remote computer. It may be different from the name by which local users of the SMB printer know the printer.

✦ **User**—Username is required by the SMB server system to give you access to the SMB printer. A username is not necessary if you are authenticating the printer based on share-level rather than user-level access control. With share-level access, you can add a password for each shared printer or file system.

✦ **Password**—Password associated with the SMB username or the shared resource, depending on the kind of access control being used.

Caution

When you enter a User and Password for SMB, that information is stored unencrypted in the /etc/cups/printers.conf file. Be sure that the file remains readable only by root.

Complete the rest of the procedure as you would for a local printer (see the "Adding a Local Printer in Red Hat" section earlier in this chapter).

The result is new entries in the /etc/cups/cupsd.conf and printers.conf files. This /etc/cups/printers.conf entry shows the printer entry just created:

```
<Printer NS1-PS>
Info Created by redhat-config-Eprinter 0.6.x
DeviceURI smb://jjones:my9passswd@FSTREET/NS1/hp
Location HP on ns1
State Idle
Accepting Yes
JobSheets none none
QuotaPeriod 0
PageLimit 0
KLimit 0
</Printer>
```

The DeviceURI line is packed with the key information. It identifies the location (an smb object), username (jjones), user's password (my9passswd), workgroup (FSTREET), server (NS1), and printer queue name (hp).

The contents of the cupsd.conf file define who you will allow to use this printer.

```
<Location /printers/NS1-PS>
Order Deny,Allow
Deny From All
Allow From 127.0.0.1
AuthType None
</Location>
```

Based on this example information, only users from the local host (127.0.0.1) are allowed to use the printer, and no authentication is necessary for them to use it.

If everything is set up properly, you can use the standard lpr command to print the file to the printer. Using this example, employ the following form for printing:

```
$ cat file1.ps | lpr -P NS1-PS
```

Tip   If you are receiving failure messages, make sure that the computer to which you are printing is accessible. For the Printer NSI-PS example, you could type **smbclient -L NS1 -U jjones**. Then type the password (my9passswd, in this case). If you get a positive name query response after you enter a password, you should see a list of shared printers and files from that server. Check the names, and try printing again.

Adding a NetWare Printer

To set up your Linux system to use a printer that is connected to (or otherwise managed by) a NetWare file and print server, you must gather the information about the server, queue, user, and password.

Select to add a Novell printer (Novell created NetWare) from the Printer Configuration window (described previously), and then fill in the following information:

✦ **Server**—Host name of the computer to which the printer is attached (or otherwise accessible). This is the NetWare Server name for the computer.

✦ **Queue**—Name of the print queue on the NetWare server.

✦ **User**—Username required by the NetWare server system to enable access to the NetWare printer.

✦ **Password**—Password associated with the username.

Complete the rest of the procedure as you would for a local printer (see the "Adding a Local Printer in Red Hat" section earlier in this chapter).

Working with CUPS Printing

Tools like CUPS Web-based Administration and Red Hat's Printer Configuration window effectively hide the underlying CUPS facility. There may be times, however, when you want to work directly with the tools and configuration files that come with CUPS. The following sections describe how to use some special CUPS features.

Configuring the CUPS Server (cupsd.conf)

The cupsd daemon process listens for requests to your CUPS print server and responds to those requests based on settings in the /etc/cups/cupsd.conf file. The configuration variables in cupsd.conf file are in the same form as those in the Apache configuration file (httpd.conf).

Red Hat's Printer Configuration window adds access information to the cupsd.conf file. For other Linux systems, you may need to configure the cupsd.conf file manually. You can step through the cupsd.conf file to further tune your CUPS server. Let's take a look at some of the settings in the cupsd.conf file.

No classification is set by default. With the classification set to topsecret, you can have Top Secret displayed on all pages that go through the print server:

```
Classification topsecret
```

Other classifications you can substitute for topsecret include: classified, confidential, secret, and unclassified.

The ServerCertificate and ServerKey lines (commented out by default) can be set up to indicate where the certificate and key are stored, respectively:

```
ServerCertificate /etc/cups/ssl/server.crt
ServerKey /etc/cups/ssl/server.key
```

Activate these two lines if you want to do encrypted connections. Then add your certificate and key to the files noted.

Browsing is the feature whereby you broadcast information about your printer on your local network and listen for other print servers' information. Browsing is on by default only for the local host (@LOCAL). You can allow CUPS browser information (BrowseAllow) for additional selected addresses. Browsing information is broadcast, by default, on address 255.255.255.255. Here's how these defaults appear in the cupsd.conf file:

```
Browsing On
BrowseProtocols cups
BrowseOrder Deny,Allow
BrowseAllow from @LOCAL
BrowseAddress 255.255.255.255
Listen *:631
```

To enable Web-based CUPS administration, the cupsd daemon listens on port 631 for all network interfaces to your computer based on this entry: Listen *:631.

By turning on BrowseRelay (it's off by default), you can allow CUPS browse information to be passed among two or more networks. The source-address and destination-address can be individual IP addresses or can represent network numbers:

```
BrowseRelay source-address destination-address
```

This is a good way to enable users on several connected LANs to discover and use printers on other nearby LANs.

You can allow or deny access to different features of the CUPS server. An access definition for a CUPS printer (created from the Printer Configuration window) might appear as follows:

```
<Location /printers/ns1-hp1>
Order Deny,Allow
Deny From All
Allow From 127.0.0.1
AuthType None
</Location>
```

Here, printing to the ns1-hp1 printer is allowed only for users on the local host (127. 0.0.1). No password is needed (AuthType None). To allow access to the administration tool, the CUPS must be configured to prompt for a password (AuthType Basic).

Starting the CUPS Server

For Linux systems that use SystemV-style startup scripts (such as Fedora, RHEL, and SUSE), starting and shutting down the CUPS print service is pretty easy. Use the chkconfig command to turn on CUPS so it starts at each reboot. Run the cups startup script to have the CUPS service start immediately. Type the following as root user:

```
# chkconfig cupsd on
# /etc/init.d/cups start
```

If the CUPS service was already running, you should use restart instead of start. Using the restart option is also a good way to reread any configuration options you may have changed in the cupsd.conf file.

Other Linux systems vary in how they start up the CUPS service. For example, in Slackware, you can turn on CUPS printing permanently by simply making the rc.cups script executable and then turn it on immediately by executing it (typing the following as root user):

```
# chmod 755 /etc/rc.d/rc.cups
# /etc/rc.d/rc.cups start
```

In Gentoo Linux, you'd use the `rc-update` command to add the CUPS service to start at each reboot and run the `cupsd` runlevel script to start it immediately. For example, type the following as root user:

```
# rc-update add cupsd default
# /etc/init.d/cupsd start
```

Most Linux systems have similar ways of starting the CUPS service. You may need to poke around to see how CUPS starts on the distribution you are using.

Configuring CUPS Printer Options Manually

If your Linux distribution doesn't have a graphical means of configuring CUPS, you can edit configuration files directly. For example, when a new printer is created from the Printer Configuration window, it is defined in the `/etc/cups/printers.conf` file. Here is what a printer entry looks like:

```
</Printer hp>
<DefaultPrinter printer>
Info Created by system-config-printer 0.6.x
DeviceURI parallel:/dev/lp0
Location HP LaserJet 2100M in hall closet
State Idle
Accepting Yes
JobSheets none none
QuotaPeriod 0
PageLimit 0
KLimit 0
</Printer>
```

This is an example of a local printer that serves as the default printer for the local system. The most interesting information relates to `DeviceURI`, which shows that the printer is connected to parallel port `/dev/lp0`. The state is `Idle` (ready to accept printer jobs), and the `Accepting` value is `Yes` (the printer is accepting print jobs by default).

The DeviceURI has several ways to identify the device name of a printer, reflecting where the printer is connected. Here are some examples listed in the `printers.conf` file:

```
DeviceURI parallel:/dev/plp
DeviceURI serial:/dev/ttyd1?baud=38400+size=8+parity=none+flow=soft
DeviceURI scsi:/dev/scsi/sc1d610
DeviceURI socket://hostname:port
DeviceURI tftp://hostname/path
DeviceURI ftp://hostname/path
DeviceURI http://hostname[:port]/path
DeviceURI ipp://hostname/path
DeviceURI smb://hostname/printer
```

The first three examples show the form for local printers (parallel, serial, and scsi). The other examples are for remote hosts. In each case, *hostname* can be the host's name or IP address. Port numbers or paths identify the locations of each printer on the host.

> **Tip**
>
> If you find that you are not able to print because a particular printer driver is not supported in CUPS, you can set up your printer to accept jobs in raw mode. This can work well if you are printing from Windows clients that have the correct print drivers installed. To enable raw printing in CUPS, uncomment the following line in the /etc/cups/mime.types file in Linux:
>
> ```
> application/octet-stream
> ```
>
> And uncomment the following line in the /etc/cups/mime.convs file:
>
> ```
> application/octet-stream application/vnd.cups-raw 0 -
> ```
>
> After that, you can print files as raw data to your printers without using the -oraw option to print commands.

Using Printing Commands

To remain backward compatible with older UNIX and Linux printing facilities, CUPS supports many of the old commands for working with printing. Most command-line printing with CUPS can be performed with the lpr command. Word-processing applications such as StarOffice, OpenOffice, and AbiWord are set up to use this facility for printing.

You can use the Printer Configuration window to define the filters needed for each printer so that the text can be formatted properly. Options to the lpr command can add filters to properly process the text. Other commands for managing printed documents include lpq (for viewing the contents of print queues), lprm (for removing print jobs from the queue), and lpc (for controlling printers).

Printing with lpr

You can use the lpr command to print documents to both local and remote printers. Document files can be either added to the end of the lpr command line or directed to the lpr command using a pipe (|). Here's an example of a simple lpr command:

```
$ lpr doc1.ps
```

When you specify just a document file with lpr, output is directed to the default printer. As an individual user, you can change the default printer by setting the value of the PRINTER variable. Typically, you would add the PRINTER variable to one of your startup files, such as $HOME/.bashrc. Adding the following line to your .bashrc file, for example, would set your default printer to lp3:

```
export PRINTER=lp3
```

To override the default printer, specify a particular printer on the `lpr` command line. The following example uses the `-P` option to select a different printer:

```
$ lpr -P canyonps doc1.ps
```

The `lpr` command has a variety of options that enable `lpr` to interpret and format several different types of documents. These include `-# num`, where *num* is replaced by the number of copies to print (from 1 to 100) and `-l` (which causes a document to be sent in raw mode, presuming that the document has already been formatted). To learn more options to lpr, type **man lpr**.

Listing Status with lpc

Use the `lpc` command to list the status of your printers. Here is an example:

```
$ lpc status
hp:
                        printer is on device 'parallel' speed -1
                        queuing is enabled
                        printing is disabled
                        no entries
                        daemon present
deskjet_5550:
                        printer is on device '/dev/null' speed -1
                        queuing is enabled
                        printing is disabled
                        no entries
                        daemon present
```

This output shows two active printers. The first (hp) is connected to your parallel port. The second (deskjet_5550) is a network printer (shown as /dev/null). The hp printer is currently disabled (offline), although the queue is enabled so people can continue to send jobs to the printer.

Removing Print Jobs with lprm

Users can remove their own print jobs from the queue with the `lprm` command. Used alone on the command line, `lprm` removes all the user's print jobs from the default printer. To remove jobs from a specific printer, use the `-P` option, as follows:

```
$ lprm -P lp0
```

To remove all print jobs for the current user, type the following:

```
$ lprm -
```

The root user can remove all the print jobs for a specific user by indicating that user on the lprm command line. For example, to remove all print jobs for the user named mike, the root user would type the following:

```
$ lprm mike
```

To remove an individual print job from the queue, indicate its job number on the lprm command line. To find the job number, type the lpq command. Here's what the output of that command may look like:

```
$ lpq
printer is ready and printing
Rank    Owner           Job Files               Total Size Time
active  root            133 /home/jake/pr1          467
2       root            197 /home/jake/mydoc      23948
```

The output shows two printable jobs waiting in the queue. (The printer is ready and printing the job listed as active.) Under the Job column, you can see the job number associated with each document. To remove the first print job, type the following:

```
# lprm 133
```

Configuring Print Servers

You've configured a printer so that you and the other users on your computer can print to it. Now you want to share that printer with other people in your home, school, or office. Basically, that means configuring the printer as a print server.

The printers that are configured on your Linux system can be shared in different ways with other computers on your network. Not only can your computer act as a Linux print server (by configuring CUPS), it can also look to client computers such as an SMB print server. After a local printer is attached to your Linux system and your computer is connected to your local network, you can use the procedures in this section to share it with client computers using a Linux (UNIX) or SMB interface.

Configuring a Shared CUPS Printer

Making the local printer added to your Linux computer available to other computers on your network is fairly easy. If a TCP/IP network connection exists between the computers sharing the printer, you simply grant permission to all hosts, individual hosts, or users from remote hosts to access your computer's printing service.

To manually configure a printer entry in the /etc/cups/cupsd.conf file to accept print jobs from all other computers, add an Allow from All line. Using an example from a cupsd.conf entry earlier in this chapter, here's what the new entry would look like:

```
<Location /printers/ns1-hp1>
Order Deny,Allow
Deny From All
Allow From 127.0.0.1
AuthType None
Allow from All
</Location>
```

Instead of `Allow from All`, you could allow a particular network (for example, `10.0.0.0/255.255.255.0`), network interface (`Allow from @IF(eth0)`), or individual IP address (`Allow from 10.0.0.1`).

On Fedora and other Red Hat Linux systems, it's best to set up your printer as a shared printer using the Printer Configuration window. Here's how:

1. From the main red hat menu, select System Settings ⇨ Printing. The Printer Configuration window appears.

2. Click the name of the printer you want to share. (If the printer is not yet configured, refer to the "Setting Up Printers" section earlier in this chapter.)

3. Select Action ⇨ Sharing. The Sharing Properties window appears.

4. On the Queue tab, click the check box next to This Queue Is Available to Other Computers. The words "All hosts" should appear in the Allowed Hosts box, indicating that all computers that can access your computer from the network can access the selected printer.

   If you don't want the printer accessible to everyone, you can always click Edit and change the configuration to share your printer in one of the following ways:

   • **All hosts** — The default, where any computer can print on the printer.

   • **Network devices** — If you have a LAN connection, you can select Network Devices and click the interface (such as eth0) to allow computers on the LAN to access your printer. This is a good choice if, for example, your computer is acting as a router. You could allow computers on your LAN to access your printer but not allow computers from the Internet to use the printer.

   • **Network address** — You can restrict access to your printer to a select set of network addresses. The address pool can be indicated with a CIDR address (for example, a CIDR equivalent for a class C netmask of `255.255.255.0` is `/24`).

   • **Single IP address** — You can indicate that a particular IP address can access your printer. Repeat this step to add more than a single IP address.

5. If you want only selected hosts to access your printer, click Remove (to remove the All Hosts line), and then click Add.

6. Click OK to continue.

7. In the Sharing Properties window, click OK.

8. From the Printer Configuration window, click Apply to apply the changes.

Now you can configure other computers to use your printer, as described in the "Setting Up Printers" section of this chapter. If you try to print from another computer and it doesn't work, here are a few troubleshooting tips:

✦ **Open your firewall.** If you have a restrictive firewall, it may not permit printing. You must enable access to port 513 (UDP and TCP) to allow access to printing on your computer. See Chapter 17 for information on configuring your firewall.

✦ **Enable LPD-style printing.** Certain applications may require an older LPD-style printing service to print on your shared printer. To enable LPD-style printing on your CUPS server, you must turn on the cups-lpd service. Most Linux distributions that include CUPS should also include cups-lpd. In Fedora and other Red Hat systems, type **chkconfig cups-lpd on** as root user. Then restart the xinetd daemon (`service xinetd restart`).

✦ **Check names and addresses.** Make sure that you entered your computer's name and print queue properly when you configured it on the other computer. Try using the IP address instead of the host name (if that works, it indicates a DNS name resolution problem). Running a tool such as ethereal enables you to see where the transaction fails.

Access changes to your shared printer are made in the `/etc/cups/cupsd.conf` file.

Configuring a Shared Samba Printer

Your Linux printers can be configured as shared SMB printers. To share your printer as though it were a Samba (SMB) printer, all you need to do is configure basic Samba server settings as described in Chapter 26. All your printers should be shared on your local network by default. The next section shows what the resulting settings look like and how you might want to change them.

Understanding smb.conf for Printing

When you configure Samba, the `/etc/samba/smb.conf` file is constructed to enable all of your configured printers to be shared. Here are a few lines from the `smb.conf` file that relate to printer sharing:

```
printcap name = /etc/printcap
load printers = yes
printing = cups
encrypt passwords = yes
smb passwd file = /etc/samba/smbpasswd
unix password sync = Yes
[printers]
        comment = All Printers
        path = /var/spool/samba
        browseable = yes
        writeable = no
        printable = yes
```

These example settings are the result of configuring Samba from the Samba Server Configuration window in Fedora Linux. The lines show that printers from /etc/printcap were loaded and that the CUPS service is being used. Password encryption is on, and the /etc/samba/smbpasswd file stores the encrypted passwords. Because password sync is on, each user's Samba password is synchronized with the user's local UNIX password.

The last few lines are the actual printers' definition. It shows that users can print to all printers (printable = yes).

Setting Up SMB Clients

Chances are good that if you're configuring a Samba printer on your Linux computer, you will want to share it with Windows clients. If Samba is set up properly on your computer and the client computers can reach you over the network, their finding and using your printer should be fairly straightforward.

The first place a client computer looks for your shared Samba printer is in Network Neighborhood (or My Network Places, for Windows 2000). From the Windows 9*x* desktop, double-click the Network Neighborhood icon. (From Windows 2000 or XP, double-click the My Network Places icon.) The name of your host computer (the NetBIOS name, which is probably also your TCP/IP name) appears on the screen or within a workgroup folder on the screen. Open the icon that represents your computer. The window that opens shows your shared printers and folders.

If your computer's icon doesn't appear in Network Neighborhood or My Network Places, try using the Search window. From Windows XP, choose Start ➪ Search ➪ Computer or People ➪ A Computer on the Network. Type your computer's name into the Computer Name box and click Search. Double-click your computer in the Search window results panel. A window displaying the shared printers and folders from your computer appears (see Figure 25-4).

Figure 25-4: You can search for your computer's printers.

After your shared printer appears in the window, configure a pointer to that printer by opening (double-clicking) the printer icon. A message tells you that you must set up the printer before you can use it. Click Yes to proceed to configure the printer for local use. The Add Printer Wizard appears. Answer the questions that ask you how you intend to use the printer, and add the appropriate drivers. When you are done, the printer will appear in your printer window.

Another way to configure an SMB printer from a Windows XP operating system is to go to Start ⇨ Printers and Faxes. In the Printers and Faxes window that appears, click the Add a Printer icon in the upper-left portion of the window, and then select Network Printer from the first window. From there you can browse and/or configure your SMB printer.

Summary

Providing network printing services is an essential efficiency on today's business network. With the use of a few network attached devices, you can focus your printer spending on a few high-quality devices that multiple users can share instead of numerous lower-cost devices. In addition, a centrally located printer can make it easier to maintain the printer, while still enabling everyone to get his or her printing jobs done.

The default printing service in Linux is the Common UNIX Printing Service (CUPS). Any Linux system that includes CUPS offers the CUPS Web-based administrative interface for configuring CUPS printing. It also offers configuration files in the /etc/cups directory for configuring printers and the CUPS service (cupsd daemon).

In Fedora and other Red Hat Linux systems, you can configure your printer with the Printer Configuration windows available in both K Desktop and GNOME environments under the systems menu. A variety of filters make it possible to print to different kinds of printers, as well as to printers that are connected to computers on the network.

You can set up your computer as a Linux print server, and you can also have your computer emulate an SMB (Windows) print server. After your network is configured properly and a local printer is installed, sharing that printer over the network as a UNIX or SMB print server is not very complicated.

✦   ✦   ✦

Running a File Server

Most networked computers are on the network in the
first place so that users can share information. Some
users need to collectively edit documents for a project, share
access to spreadsheets and forms used in the daily operation
of a company, or perform any number of similar file-sharing
activities. It also can be efficient for groups of people on a
computer network to share common applications and directories of information needed to do their jobs. By far the best
way to accomplish the centralized sharing of data is through a
file server.

A centralized file server can be backed up, preserving all
stored data in one fell swoop. It can focus on the tasks of getting files to end users, rather than running user applications
that can use client resources. And a centralized file server can
be used to control access to information — security settings
can dictate who can access what.

Linux systems include support for each of the most common
file server protocols in use today. Among the most common file
server types in use today are the Network File System (NFS),
which has always been the file-sharing protocol of choice for
Linux and other UNIX systems and Samba (SMB protocol),
which is often used by networks with many Windows and
OS/2 computers.

This chapter describes how to set up file servers and clients
associated with NFS and Samba and how to set up NetWare
file servers set up in Linux.

Tip
> When selecting file services to provide, keep in mind that
> less is more. If your clients and servers support multiple-file
> access capabilities (NFS, SMB, and AppleTalk, for example),
> pick the service that lends itself to making the task less
> complicated. In many cases NFS is supported by clients and
> servers regardless of the operating system that they use.
> It's rare that you would need to enable more than one of
> the file services discussed in this chapter.

Setting Up an NFS File Server

Instead of representing storage devices as drive letters (A, B, C, and so on), as they are in Microsoft operating systems, Linux systems connect file systems from multiple hard disks, floppy disks, CD-ROMs, and other local devices invisibly to form a single Linux file system. The Network File System (NFS) facility enables you to extend your Linux file system in the same way, to connect file systems on other computers to your local directory structure.

An NFS file server provides an easy way to share large amounts of data among the users and computers in an organization. An administrator of a Linux system that is configured to share its file systems using NFS has to perform the following tasks to set up NFS:

1. **Set up the network.** If a LAN or other network link is already connecting the computers on which you want to use NFS, you already have the network you need.

2. **Choose what to share on the server.** Decide which file systems on your Linux NFS server to make available to other computers. You can choose any point in the file system to make all files and directories below that point accessible to other computers.

3. **Set up security on the server.** You can use several different security features to suit the level of security with which you are comfortable. Mount-level security lets you restrict the computers that can mount a resource and, for those allowed to mount it, lets you specify whether it can be mounted read/write or read-only. With user-level security, you map users from the client systems to users on the NFS server so that they can rely on standard Linux read/write/ execute permissions, file ownership, and group permissions to access and protect files.

4. **Mount the file system on the client.** Each client computer that is allowed access to the server's NFS shared file system can mount it anywhere the client chooses. For example, you may mount a file system from a computer called maple on the /mnt/maple directory in your local file system. After it is mounted, you can view the contents of that directory by typing **ls /mnt/maple**. Then you can use the cd command below the /mnt/maple mount point to see the files and directories it contains.

Figure 26-1 illustrates a Linux file server using NFS to share (export) a file system and a client computer mounting the file system to make it available to its local users.

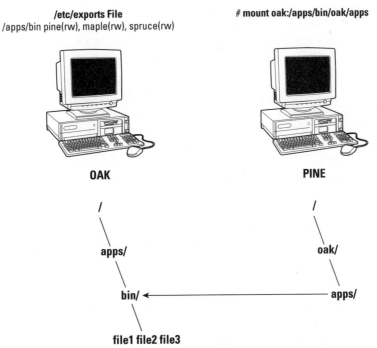

Figure 26-1: NFS can make selected file systems available to other computers.

In this example, a computer named oak makes its `/apps/bin` directory available to clients on the network (pine, maple, and spruce) by adding an entry to the `/etc/exports` file. The client computer (pine) sees that the resource is available and mounts the resource on its local file system at the mount point `/oak/apps`, after which any files, directories, or subdirectories from `/apps/bin` on oak are available to users on pine (given proper permissions).

Although it is often used as a file server (or other type of server), Linux is a general-purpose operating system, so any Linux system can share file systems (export) as a server or use another computer's file systems (mount) as a client. Contrast this with dedicated file servers, such as NetWare, which can only share files with client computers (such as Windows workstations) and never act as a client.

Note A file system is usually a structure of files and directories that exists on a single device (such as a hard disk partition or CD-ROM). A Linux file system refers to the entire directory structure (which may include file systems from several disks or NFS resources), beginning from root (/) on a single computer. A shared directory in NFS may represent all or part of a computer's file system, which can be attached (from the shared directory down the directory tree) to another computer's file system.

Getting NFS

While nearly every Linux system supports NFS client and server features, NFS is not always installed by default. You'll need different packages for different Linux systems to install NFS; here are some examples:

✦ **Fedora Core and other Red Hat Linux systems** — You need to install the nfs-utils package to use Fedora as an NFS server. There is also a graphical NFS Configuration tool that requires you to install the system-config-nfs package. NFS client features are in the base operating system. To turn on the nfs service, type the following:

```
# service nfs start
# chkconfig nfs on
```

✦ **Debian** — To act as an NFS client, the nfs-common and portmap packages are required; for an NFS server, the nfs-kernel-server package must be added. The following apt-get command line (if you are connected to the Internet) installs them all. Then, after you add an exported file system to the /etc/exports file (as described later), you can start the nfs-common and nfs-kernel-server scripts, as shown here:

```
# apt-get install nfs-common portmap nfs-kernel-server
# /etc/init.d/nfs-kernel-server start
# /etc/init.d/nfs-common start
```

✦ **Gentoo** — With Gentoo, NFS file system and NFS server support must be configured into the kernel to use NFS server features. Installing the nfs-utils package (emerge nfs-utils) should get the required packages. To start the service, run rc-update and start the service immediately:

```
# emerge nfs-utils
# rc-update add portmap default
# rc-update add nfs default
# /etc/init.d/nfs start
```

The commands (mount, exportfs, and so on) and files (/etc/exports, /etc/fstab, and so on) for actually configuring NFS are the same on every Linux system I've encountered. So once you have NFS installed and running, just follow the instructions in this chapter to start using NFS.

Sharing NFS File Systems

To share an NFS file system from your Linux system, you need to export it from the server system. Exporting is done in Linux by adding entries into the /etc/exports file. Each entry identifies a directory in your local file system that you want to share with other computers. The entry also identifies the other computers that can share the resource (or opens it to all computers) and includes other options that reflect permissions associated with the directory.

Remember that when you share a directory, you are sharing all files and subdirectories below that directory as well (by default). So, you need to be sure that you want to share everything in that directory structure. There are still ways to restrict access within that directory structure, and those are discussed later in this chapter.

Configuring the /etc/exports File

To make a directory from your Linux system available to other systems, you need to export that directory. Exporting is done, on a permanent basis, by adding information about an exported directory to the /etc/exports file. As root user, you can use any text editor to configure /etc/exports to modify shared directory entries or add new ones. Here's an example of an /etc/exports file:

```
/cal    *.linuxtoys.net(rw)              # Company events
/pub    (ro,insecure,all_squash)         # Public dir
/home   maple(rw,squash uids=0-99) spruce(rw,squash uids=0-99)
```

The /cal entry represents a directory that contains information about events related to the company. It is made accessible to everyone with accounts to any computers in the company's domain (*.linuxtoys.net). Users can write files to the directory as well as read them (indicated by the rw option). The comment (# Company events) simply serves to remind you of what the directory contains.

The /pub entry represents a public directory. It allows any computer and user to read files from the directory (indicated by the ro option) but not to write files. The insecure option enables any computer, even one that doesn't use a secure NFS port, to access the directory. The all_squash option causes all users (UIDs) and groups (GIDs) to be mapped to the nfsnobody user, giving them minimal permission to files and directories.

The /home entry enables a set of users to have the same /home directory on different computers. Say, for example, that you are sharing /home from a computer named oak. The computers named maple and spruce could each mount that directory on their own /home directories. If you gave all users the same username/UIDs on all machines, you could have the same /home/user directory available for each user, regardless of which computer they logged into. The uids=0-99 is used to exclude any administrative login from another computer from changing any files in the shared directory.

These are just examples; you can share any directories that you choose, including the entire file system (/). Of course, there are security implications of sharing the whole file system or sensitive parts of it (such as /etc). Security options that you can add to your /etc/exports file are described throughout the sections that follow.

The format of the /etc/exports file is

```
Directory   Host(Options)   # Comments
```

where *Directory* is the name of the directory that you want to share, and *Host* indicates the host computer to which the sharing of this directory is restricted. *Options* can include a variety of options to define the security measures attached to the shared directory for the host. (You can repeat Host/Option pairs.) *Comments* are any optional comments you want to add (following the # sign).

Host Names in /etc/exports

You can indicate in the /etc/exports file which host computers can have access to your shared directory. If you want to associate multiple host names or IP addresses with a particular shared directory, be sure to have a space between each host name. However, add no spaces between a host name and its options. For example:

```
/usr/local maple(rw) spruce(ro,root_squash)
```

Notice that there is a space after (rw) but none after maple. Here are ways to identify hosts:

✦ **Individual host** — Enter one or more TCP/IP host names or IP addresses. If the host is in your local domain, you can simply indicate the host name. Otherwise, use the full host.domain format. These are valid ways to indicate individual host computers:

```
maple
maple.handsonhistory.com
10.0.0.11
```

✦ **IP network** — Allow access to all hosts from a particular network address by indicating a network number and its netmask, separated by a slash (/). Here are valid ways to designate network numbers:

```
10.0.0.0/255.0.0.0
172.16.0.0/255.255.0.0
192.168.18.0/255.255.255.0
```

✦ **TCP/IP domain** — Using wildcards, you can include all or some host computers from a particular domain level. Here are some valid uses of the asterisk and question mark wildcards:

```
*.handsonhistory.com
*craft.handsonhistory.com
???.handsonhistory.com
```

The first example matches all hosts in the handsonhistory.com domain. The second example matches woodcraft, basketcraft, or any other host names ending in craft in the handsonhistory.com domain. The final example matches any three-letter host names in the domain.

Note Using an asterisk doesn't match subdomains. For example, `*.handsonhistory.com` would *not* cause the host name `mallard.duck.handsonhistory.com` to be included in the access list. Also, separate multiple host names with spaces, but if you add options after each host name, leave no spaces between the host name and the parentheses. For example:

```
*.handsonhistory.com(rw) *.example.net(ro)
```

✦ **NIS groups** — You can allow access to hosts contained in an NIS group. To indicate an NIS group, precede the group name with an at (@) sign (for example, `@group`).

Access Options in /etc/exports

You don't have to just give away your files and directories when you export a directory with NFS. In the options part of each entry in `/etc/exports`, you can add options that allow or limit access by setting read/write permission. These options, which are passed to NFS, are as follows:

✦ **ro** — Client can mount this exported file system read-only. The default is to mount the file system read/write.

✦ **rw** — Explicitly asks that a shared directory be shared with read/write permissions. (If the client chooses, it can still mount the directory read-only.)

User Mapping Options in /etc/exports

In addition to options that define how permissions are handled generally, you can use options to set the permissions that specific users have to NFS shared file systems.

One method that simplifies this process is to have each user with multiple user accounts have the same username and UID on each machine. This makes it easier to map users so that they have the same permissions on a mounted file system that they do on files stored on their local hard disks. If that method is not convenient, user IDs can be mapped in many other ways. Here are some methods of setting user permissions and the `/etc/exports` option that you use for each method:

✦ **root user** — The client's root user is generally mapped into the `nfsnobody` username (UID 65534). This prevents a client computer's root user from being able to change all files and directories in the shared file system. If you want the client's root user to have root permission on the server, use the `no_root_squash` option.

Tip There may be other administrative users, in addition to root, that you want to squash. I recommend squashing UIDs 0–99 as follows: `squash_uids=0-99`.

✦ **nfsnobody user/group** — By using nfsnobody username and group name, you essentially create a user/group with permissions that do not allow access to files that belong to any real users on the server, unless those users open permission to everyone. However, files created by the nfsnobody user or group are available to anyone assigned as the nfsnobody user or group. To set all remote users to the nfsnobody user/group, use the all_squash option.

The nfsnobody user is assigned to UIDs and GIDs of 65534 to prevent the ID from running into a valid user or group ID. Using anonuid or anongid options, you can change the nfsnobody user or group, respectively. For example, anonuid=175 sets all anonymous users to UID 175, and anongid=300 sets the GID to 300. (Only the number is displayed when you list file permission unless you add entries with names to /etc/password and /etc/group for the new UIDs and GIDs.)

✦ **User mapping** — If a user has login accounts for a set of computers (and has the same ID), NFS, by default, maps that ID. This means that if the user named mike (UID 110) on maple has an account on pine (mike, UID 110), he could use his own remotely mounted files on either computer from either computer.

If a client user who is not set up on the server creates a file on the mounted NFS directory, the file is assigned to the remote client's UID and GID. (An ls -l on the server shows the UID of the owner.) Use the map_static option to identify a file that contains user mappings.

The exports main page describes the map_static option, which enables you to create a file that contains new ID mappings so that you can remap client IDs into different IDs on the server.

Exporting the Shared File Systems

After you have added entries to your /etc/exports file, run the exportfs command to have those directories exported (made available to other computers on the network). Reboot your computer or restart the NFS service, and the exportfs command runs automatically to export your directories. If you want to export them immediately, run exportfs from the command line (as root).

It's a good idea to run the exportfs command after you change the exports file. If any errors are in the file, exportfs will identify them for you.

Here's an example of the exportfs command:

```
# /usr/sbin/exportfs -a -v
exporting maple:/pub
exporting spruce:/pub
exporting maple:/home
exporting spruce:/home
exporting *:/mnt/win
```

The -a option indicates that all directories listed in /etc/exports should be exported. The -v option says to print verbose output. In this example, the /pub and /home directories from the local server are immediately available for mounting by those client computers that are named (maple and spruce). The /mnt/win directory is available to all client computers.

Running the exportfs command temporarily makes your exported NFS directories available. To have your NFS directories available on an ongoing basis (that is, every time your system reboots), you need to set your nfs startup scripts to run at boot time. This is described in the next section.

Starting the nfs Daemons

If for some reason NFS has been disabled on your system (or is not active by default), you need to start the service. Different Linux distributions have different ways of turning on the NFS service, as you saw in the "Getting NFS" section earlier in the chapter. This section explores how the service is turned on in Fedora Core and other Red Hat Linux systems.

In Fedora, you can use the chkconfig command to turn on the NFS service so that your files are exported and the nfsd daemons are running when your system boots. There are two startup scripts you want to turn on for the service to work properly. The NFS service exports file systems (from /etc/exports) and starts the nfsd daemon that listens for service requests. The nfslock service starts the lockd daemon, which helps allow file locking to prevent multiple simultaneous use of critical files over the network.

To turn on the NFS service, type the following as root user:

```
# chkconfig nfs on
# chkconfig nfslock on
```

The next time you start your computer, the NFS service will start automatically, and your exported directories will be available. If you want to start the service immediately, without waiting for a reboot, type the following:

```
# /etc/init.d/nfs start
# /etc/init.d/nfslock start
```

The NFS service should now be running and ready to share directories with other computers on your network.

Using NFS File Systems

After a server exports a directory over the network using NFS, a client computer connects that directory to its own file system using the mount command. That's the same command used to mount file systems from local hard disks, CDs, and floppies, but with slightly different options.

`mount` can automatically mount NFS directories that are added to the `/etc/fstab` file, just as it does with local disks. NFS directories can also be added to the `/etc/fstab` file in such a way that they are not automatically mounted (so you can mount them manually when you choose). With a `noauto` option, an NFS directory listed in `/etc/fstab` is inactive until the `mount` command is used, after the system is up and running, to mount the file system.

Manually Mounting an NFS File System

If you know that the directory from a computer on your network has been exported (that is, made available for mounting), you can mount that directory manually using the `mount` command. This is a good way to make sure that it is available and working before you set it up to mount permanently. Here is an example of mounting the `/tmp` directory from a computer named maple on your local computer:

```
# mkdir /mnt/maple
# mount maple:/tmp /mnt/maple
```

The first command (`mkdir`) creates the mount point directory (`/mnt` is a common place to put temporarily mounted disks and NFS file systems). The `mount` command identifies the remote computer and shared file system separated by a colon (`maple:/tmp`), and the local mount point directory (`/mnt/maple`) follows.

Note   If the mount fails, make sure the NFS service is running on the server and that the server's firewall rules don't deny access to the service. From the server, type **ps ax | nfsd** to see a list of `nfsd` server processes. If you don't see the list, try to start your NFS daemons as described in the previous section. To view your firewall rules, type **iptables -L** (see Chapter 17 for a description of firewalls). By default, the nfsd daemon listens for NFS requests on port number 2049. Your firewall must accept udp requests on ports 2049 (nfs) and 111 (rpc).

To ensure that the mount occurred, type **mount**. This command lists all mounted disks and NFS file systems. Here is an example of the `mount` command and its output (with file systems not pertinent to this discussion edited out):

```
# mount
/dev/hda3 on / type ext3 (rw)
. . .
. . .
. . .
maple:/tmp on /mnt/maple type nfs (rw,addr=10.0.0.11)
```

The output from the `mount` command shows the mounted disk partitions, special file systems, and NFS file systems. The first output line shows the hard disk (`/dev/hda3`), mounted on the root file system (`/`), with read/write permission (`rw`), with a file system type of ext3 (the standard Linux file system type. The just-mounted NFS file system is the `/tmp` directory from maple (`maple:/tmp`). It is mounted on `/mnt/maple` and its mount type is `nfs`. The file system was mounted read/write (`rw`), and the IP address of maple is `10.0.0.11` (`addr=10.0.0.11`).

This is a simple example of using mount with NFS. The mount is temporary and is not remounted when you reboot your computer. You can also add options for NFS mounts:

✦ -a — Mount all file systems in /etc/fstab (except those indicated as noauto).

✦ -f — This goes through the motions of (fakes) mounting the file systems on the command line (or in /etc/fstab). Used with the -v option, -f is useful for seeing what mount would do before it actually does it.

✦ -r — Mounts the file system as read-only.

✦ -w — Mounts the file system as read/write. (For this to work, the shared file system must have been exported with read/write permission.)

The next section describes how to make the mount more permanent (using the /etc/fstab file) and how to select various options for NFS mounts.

Automatically Mounting an NFS File System

To set up an NFS file system to mount automatically each time you start your Linux system, you need to add an entry for that NFS file system to the /etc/fstab file. That file contains information about all different kinds of mounted (and available to be mounted) file systems for your system.

Here's the format for adding an NFS file system to your local system:

```
host:directory     mountpoint     nfs     options     0     0
```

The first item (host:directory) identifies the NFS server computer and shared directory. mountpoint is the local mount point on which the NFS directory is mounted. It's followed by the file system type (nfs). Any options related to the mount appear next in a comma-separated list. (The last two zeros configure the system to not dump the contents of the file system and not to run fsck on the file system.)

The following are examples of NFS entries in /etc/fstab:

```
maple:/tmp    /mnt/maple nfs    rsize=8192,wsize=8192  0 0
oak:/apps     /oak/apps  nfs    noauto,ro              0 0
```

In the first example, the remote directory /tmp from the computer named maple (maple:/tmp) is mounted on the local directory /mnt/maple (the local directory must already exist). The file system type is nfs, and read (rsize) and write (wsize) buffer sizes (discussed in the "Using mount Options" section later in this chapter) are set at 8192 to speed data transfer associated with this connection. In the second example, the remote directory is /apps on the computer named oak. It is set up as an NFS file system (nfs) that can be mounted on the /oak/apps directory locally. This file system is not mounted automatically (noauto), however, and can be mounted only as read-only (ro) using the mount command after the system is already running.

Tip   The default is to mount an NFS file system as read/write. However, the default for exporting a file system is read-only. If you are unable to write to an NFS file system, check that it was exported as read/write from the server.

Mounting noauto File Systems

Your /etc/fstab file contains devices for other file systems that are not mounted automatically (probably /dev/cdrom and /dev/fd0, for your CD-ROM and floppy disk devices, respectively). The noauto option for these devices is what prevents them from being mounted at boot time. A noauto file system can be mounted manually when you need it. The advantage is that when you type the mount command, you can type less information and have the rest filled in by the contents of the /etc/fstab file. For example, you could type:

```
# mount /oak/apps
```

With this command, mount knows to check the /etc/fstab file to get the file system to mount (oak:/apps), the file system type (nfs), and the options to use with the mount (in this case ro for read-only). Instead of typing the local mount point (/oak/apps), you could have typed the remote file system name (oak:/apps) and had other information filled in.

Tip   When naming mount points, including the name of the remote NFS server in that name can help you remember where the files are actually being stored. This may not be possible if you are sharing home directories (/home) or mail directories (/var/spool/mail). For example, you might mount a file system from a machine called duck on the directory /mnt/duck.

Using mount Options

You can add several mount options to the /etc/fstab file (or to a mount command line itself) to influence how the file system is mounted. When you add options to /etc/fstab, they must be separated by commas. The following are some options that are valuable for mounting NFS file systems:

✦ hard—If this option is on and the NFS server disconnects or goes down while a process is waiting to access it, the process will hang until the server comes back up. This is helpful if it is critical that the data you are working with not get out of sync with the programs that are accessing it. (This is the default behavior.)

✦ soft—If the NFS server disconnects or goes down, a process trying to access data from the server will time out after a set period of time when this is on. An input/output error is delivered to the process trying to access the NFS server.

✦ rsize—The number of bytes of data read at a time from an NFS server. The default is 1024. Using a larger number (such as 8192) will get you better performance on a network that is fast (such as a LAN) and is relatively error-free (that is, one that doesn't have a lot of noise or collisions).

✦ wsize—The number of bytes of data written at a time to an NFS server. The default is 1024. Performance issues are the same as with the rsize option.

✦ `timeo=#`—Sets the time after an RPC timeout occurs that a second transmission is made, where # represents a number in tenths of a second. The default value is seven-tenths of a second. Each successive timeout causes the timeout value to be doubled (up to 60 seconds maximum). Increase this value if you believe that timeouts are occurring because of slow response from the server or a slow network.

✦ `retrans=#`—Sets the number of minor timeouts and retransmissions that need to happen before a major timeout occurs.

✦ `retry=#`—Sets how many minutes to continue to retry failed mount requests, where # is replaced by the number of minutes to retry. The default is 10,000 minutes (which is about one week).

✦ `bg`—If the first mount attempt times out, try all subsequent mounts in the background. This option is very valuable if you are mounting a slow or sporadically available NFS file system. By placing mount requests in the background, your system can continue to mount other file systems instead of waiting for the current one to complete.

Note

If a nested mount point is missing, a timeout to allow for the needed mount point to be added occurs. For example, if you mount `/usr/trip` and `/usr/trip/extra` as NFS file systems and `/usr/trip` is not yet mounted when `/usr/trip/extra` tries to mount, `/usr/trip/extra` will time out. Hopefully, `/usr/trip` comes up and `/usr/trip/extra` mounts on the next retry.

✦ `fg`—If the first mount attempt times out, try subsequent mounts in the foreground. This is the default behavior. Use this option if it is imperative that the mount be successful before continuing (for example, if you were mounting `/usr`).

Any of the values that don't require a value can have `no` appended to it to have the opposite effect. For example, `nobg` indicates that the mount should not be done in the background.

Using autofs to Mount NFS File Systems on Demand

With the autofs facility configured and turned on, you can cause any NFS shared directories to mount on demand. If you know the host name and directory being shared by another host computer, simply change (`cd`) to the autofs mount directory (`/net` by default) and have the shared resource automatically mount and be accessible to you.

The following steps explain how to turn on the autofs facility:

1. As root user from a Terminal window, open the `/etc/auto.master` file and uncomment the last line, so it appears as follows:

```
/net    /etc/auto.net
```

This causes the `/net` directory to act as the mount point for the NFS shared directories you want to access on the network.

2. Start the autofs service by typing the following as root user:

```
# service autofs start
```

3. Set up the autofs service to restart every time you boot your system:

```
# chkconfig autofs on
```

Believe it or not, that's all you have to do. If you have a network connection to the NFS servers from which you want to share directories, try to access a shared NFS directory. For example, if you know that the /usr/local/share directory is being shared from the computer on your network named shuttle, you could do the following:

```
$ cd /net/shuttle
```

If that computer has any shared directories that are available to you, you can successfully change to that directory.

You also could type the following:

```
$ ls
usr
```

You should be able to see that the usr directory is part of the path to a shared directory. If there were shared directories from other top-level directories (such as /var or /tmp), you would see those as well. Of course, seeing any of those directories depends on how security is set up on the server.

Try going straight to the shared directory as well. For example:

```
$ cd /net/shuttle/usr/local/share
$ ls
info man music television
```

At this point, the ls should reveal the contents of the /usr/local/share directory on the computer named shuttle. What you can do with that content depends on how that it was configured for sharing by the server.

Unmounting NFS File Systems

After an NFS file system is mounted, unmounting it is simple. You use the umount command with either the local mount point or the remote file system name. For example, here are two ways you could unmount maple:/tmp from the local directory /mnt/maple.

```
# umount maple:/tmp
```

```
# umount /mnt/maple
```

Either form works. If `maple:/tmp` is mounted automatically (from a listing in `/etc/fstab`), the directory will be remounted the next time you boot Linux. If it was a temporary mount (or listed as `noauto` in `/etc/fstab`), it won't be remounted at boot time.

Tip   The command is `umount`, not `unmount`. This is easy to get wrong.

If you get the message "device is busy" when you try to unmount a file system, it means the unmount failed because the file system is being accessed. Most likely, one of the directories in the NFS file system is the current directory for your shell (or the shell of someone else on your system). The other possibility is that a command is holding a file open in the NFS file system (such as a text editor). Check your Terminal windows and other shells, and `cd` out of the directory if you are in it, or just close the Terminal windows.

If an NFS file system won't unmount, you can force it (`umount -f /mnt/maple`) or unmount and clean up later (`umount -l /mnt/maple`). The `-l` option is usually the better choice because a forced unmount can disrupt a file modification that is in progress.

Other Cool Things to Do with NFS

You can share some directories to make it consistent for a user to work from any of several different Linux computers on your network. Some examples of useful directories to share are:

✦ `/var/spool/mail` — By sharing this directory from your mail server and mounting it on the same directory on other computers on your network, users can access their mail from any of those other computers. This saves users from having to download messages to their current computers or from having to log in to the server just to get mail. There is only one mailbox for each user, no matter from where it is accessed.

✦ `/home` — This is a similar concept to sharing mail, except that all users have access to their home directories from any of the NFS clients. Again, you would mount `/home` on the same mount point on each client computer. When the user logs in, she has access to all of the startup files and data files contained in her `/home/user` directory.

Tip   If your users rely on a shared `/home` directory, you should make sure that the NFS server that exports the directory is fairly reliable. If `/home` isn't available, the user may not have the startup files to log in correctly, or any of the data files needed to get work done. One workaround is to have a minimal set of startup files (`.bashrc`, `.Xdefaults`, and so on) available in the user's home directory when the NFS directory is not mounted. This enables the user to log in properly at those times.

✦ /project—Although you don't have to use this name, a common practice among users on a project is to share a directory structure containing files that people on the project need to share so that everyone can work on original files and keep copies of the latest versions in one place. (Of course, a better way to manage a project is with CVS or some other version control-type software, but this is a poor person's way to do it.)

✦ /var/log—An administrator can keep track of log files from several different computers by mounting the /var/log file on the administrator's computer. (Each server may need to export the directory to enable root to be mapped between the computers for this to work.) If there are problems with a computer, the administrator can then easily view the shared log files live.

If you are working exclusively with Linux and other UNIX systems, NFS is probably your best choice for sharing file systems. If your network consists primarily of Microsoft Windows computers or a combination of systems, you may want to look into using Samba for file sharing.

Setting Up a Samba File Server

Samba is a software package that enables you to share file systems and printers on a network with computers that use the Session Message Block (SMB) protocol. This package is distributed with most Linux flavors but can be obtained from www.samba.org if you do not find it on your distribution. SMB is the protocol that is delivered with Windows operating systems for sharing files and printers. Although you can't always count on NFS being installed on Windows clients (unless you install it yourself), SMB is always available (with a bit of setup).

Note   In Windows file and printer sharing, SMB is sometimes referred to as CIFS (Common Internet File System), which is an Internet standard network file system definition based on SMB, or NetBIOS, which was the original SMB communication protocol.

The Samba software package contains a variety of daemon processes, administrative tools, user tools, and configuration files. To do basic Samba configuration, start with the Samba Server Configuration window, which provides a graphical interface for configuring the server and setting directories to share.

Most of the Samba configuration you do ends up in the /etc/samba/smb.conf file. If you need to access features that are not available through the Samba Server Configuration window, you can edit /etc/samba/smb.conf by hand or use SWAT, a Web-based interface, to configure Samba.

Daemon processes consist of smbd (the SMB daemon) and nmbd (the NetBIOS name server). The smbd daemon makes the file-sharing and printing services you add to your Linux system available to Windows client computers. The Samba package supports the following client computers:

Windows 9*x*	Windows for Workgroups
Windows NT	MS Client 3.0 for DOS
Windows ME	OS/2
Windows 2000	Dave for Macintosh Computers
Windows XP	Samba for Linux

As for administrative tools for Samba, you have several shell commands at your disposal: `testparm` and `testprns`, with which you can check your configuration files; `smbstatus`, which tells you what computers are currently connected to your shared resources; and `nmblookup` command, with which you can query computers.

Samba uses the NetBIOS service to share resources with SMB clients, but the underlying network must be configured for TCP/IP. Although other SMB hosts can use TCP/IP, NetBEUI, and IPX/SPX to transport data, Samba for Linux supports only TCP/IP. Messages are carried between host computers with TCP/IP and are then handled by NetBIOS.

Getting and Installing Samba

You can get Samba software in different ways, depending on your Linux distribution. Here are a few examples:

✦ **Debian** — To use Samba in Debian, you must install the samba and smbclient packages using `apt-get`. Then start the Samba service by running the appropriate scripts from the `/etc/init.d` directory, as follows:

```
# apt-get install samba samba-common smbclient swat
# /etc/init.d/samba start
# /etc/init.d/smb-client start
```

✦ **Gentoo** — With Gentoo, you need to have configured NFS file system and NFS server support into the kernel to use NFS server features. Installing the nfs-utils package (`emerge nfs-utils`) should get the required packages. To start the service, run rc-update and start the service immediately:

```
# emerge samba
# rc-update add samba default
# /etc/init.d/samba start
```

✦ **Fedora Core and other Red Hat Linux systems** — You need to install the samba, samba-client, samba-common, and optionally, the system-config-samba and samba-swat packages to use Samba in Fedora. You can then start Samba using the `service` and `chkconfig` commands as follows:

```
# service smb start
# chkconfig smb on
```

The commands and configuration files are the same on most Linux systems using Samba. The Samba project itself comes with a Web-based interface for administering Samba called Samba Web Administration Tool (SWAT). For someone setting up Samba for the first time, SWAT is a good way to get it up and running.

Note   If your Linux installation does not have help documents for Samba available, consult the documentation on the Samba project home page. Also, check the extensive help information that comes with SWAT.

Configuring Samba with SWAT

In addition to offering an extensive interface to Samba options, SWAT (Samba Web Administration Tool) also comes with an excellent help facility. And if you need to administer Samba from another computer, SWAT can be configured to be remotely accessible and secured by requiring an administrative login and password.

Turning on the SWAT Service

Before you can use SWAT, you must do some configuration. The first thing you must do is turn on the SWAT service, which is done differently in different Linux distributions.

Here's how to set up SWAT in Fedora Core and other Red Hat Linux systems:

1. Turn on the SWAT service by typing the following, as root user, from a Terminal window:

   ```
   # chkconfig swat on
   ```

2. Pick up the change to the service by restarting the xinetd startup script as follows:

   ```
   # service xinetd restart
   ```

Linux distributions such as Debian, Slackware, and Gentoo turn on the SWAT service from the inetd superserver daemon. After SWAT is installed, you simply remove the comment character from in front of the swat line in the /etc/inetd.conf file (as root user, using any text editor) and restart the daemon. Here's an example of what the swat line looks like in Debian:

```
swat    stream    tcp    nowait.400    root    /usr/sbin/tcpd    /usr/sbin/swat
```

With the SWAT service ready to be activated, restart the inetd daemon so it rereads the inetd.conf file. To do that in Debian, type the following as root user:

```
# /etc/init.d/inetd restart
```

The init.d script and xinetd services are the two ways that SWAT services are generally started in Linux. So if you are using a Linux distribution other than Fedora or Debian, look in the /etc/inetd.conf file or /etc/xinetd.d directory (which is used automatically in Fedora), for the location of your SWAT service.

When you have finished this procedure, a daemon process will be listening on your network interfaces for requests to connect to your SWAT service. You can now use the SWAT program, described in the next section, to configure Samba.

Starting with SWAT

You can run the SWAT program by typing the following URL in your local browser:

```
http://localhost:901/
```

Enter the root username and password when the browser prompts you. The SWAT window (Figure 26-2) appears.

Figure 26-2: Use SWAT from your browser to manage your Samba configuration.

Tip Instead of running SWAT from your local browser, you can run it from another computer on the network by substituting the server computer's name for localhost. (To allow computers besides localhost to access the swat service on Fedora systems, you must change or remove the only_from = 127.0.0.1 line from the /etc/xinetd.d/swat file and restart the xinetd service.)

Continue reading to learn how to use SWAT to create your configuration entries (in /etc/samba/smb.conf) and to work with that configuration.

Caution

Anytime you use a GUI to change a plain-text configuration file (as you do with SWAT), you may lose some of the information that you put in by hand. In this case, SWAT deletes comment lines and rearranges other entries. To protect changes you have made manually, make a backup copy of your /etc/samba/smb.conf file before you edit it with SWAT.

Creating Global Samba Settings in SWAT

A group of global settings affects how file and print sharing are generally accomplished on a Samba server. These settings appear under the [global] heading in the /etc/samba/smb.conf file. To view and edit global variables, click the GLOBALS button on the SWAT window.

Seven types of options are available: base, security, logging, tuning, printing, browse, and WINs.

Note

Each option relates to the exact parameters used in the /etc/samba/smb.conf file. You can refer to the smb.conf man page (type **man smb.conf**) to get more information on these parameters.

Base Options

The following options relate to basic information associated with your Samba server:

✦ **Workgroup** — The name of the workgroup associated with the group of SMB hosts. By default, the value for this field is WORKGROUP.

✦ **Realm** — If you are using kerberos authentication, this value indicates the kerberos realm to use. Typically, that is reflected by the host name of the server providing the service.

✦ **NetBIOS name** — The name assigned to this Samba server. You can use the same name as your DNS host name or make it blank, in which case the DNS host name is used automatically. Your DNS host name is filled in for you by default.

✦ **NetBIOS alias** — Enables you to set a way of referring to a host computer (an alias) that is different from the host's TCP/IP DNS name.

✦ **Server string** — A string of text identifying the server. This name appears in places such as the printer comment box. By default, it says Samba and the version number.

✦ **Interfaces** — Enables you to set up more than one network interface and let Samba browse several different subnetworks. The form of this field can be IP Address/Subnetwork Mask. Or, you could identify a network interface (such as eth0 for the first Ethernet card on your computer). For example, a Class C network address may appear as:

192.168.24.11/255.255.255.0

Security Options

Of the security options settings, the first (security) is the most important one to get right. It defines the type of security used to give access to the shared file systems and printers to the client computers. (To see some of the fields described here, you need to click the Advanced view.)

✦ **Security** — Sets how password and user information is transferred to the Samba server from the client computer. As noted earlier, it's important to get this value right. Samba 2.0 and later has a different default value for security (security=user) than the earlier versions of Samba do (security=share). If you are coming from an earlier version of Samba and clients are failing to access your server, this setting is a good place to start. Here are your options:

- **user** — The most common type of security used to share files and printers to Windows 95/98/2000/NT/XP clients. It is the default set with Samba in the current release. This setting is appropriate if users are doing a lot of file sharing (as opposed to a Samba server used mostly as a print server). It requires that a user provide a username/password before using the server. The easiest way to get this method working is to give a Linux user account to every client user who will use the Samba server, therefore providing basically the same file permissions to a user account through Samba as the same user would get if he or she were logged in directly to Linux.

- **share** — The share value for security works best for just print sharing or for providing file access that is more public (guest sharing). A client doesn't need to provide a valid username and password to access the server. However, the user typically has a guest level of permission to access and change files. See the "Assigning Guest Accounts" sidebar in this chapter for further information.

- **server** — From the client's point of view, this is the same as user security in that the client still has to provide a valid username/password combination to use the Samba server at all. The difference is on the server side. With server security, the username/password is sent to another SMB server for validation. If that fails, Samba tries to validate the client using user security.

- **domain** — From the client's point of view, this also looks the same as user security. This setting is used only if the Samba server has been added to a Windows NT domain (using the smbpasswd command). When a client tries to connect to the Samba server in this mode, its username and password are sent to a Windows NT Primary or Backup Domain controller. This is accomplished the same way that a Windows NT server would perform validation. Valid Linux user accounts must still be set up.

✦ **Encrypt passwords** — Controls whether encrypted passwords can be negotiated with the client. This is on (Yes) by default. For domain security, this value must be Yes. Later versions of Windows NT (4.0 SP3 or later) and Windows 98 and Windows 2000 expect encrypted passwords to be on.

✦ **Update encrypted** — Allows users who log in with a plain-text password to automatically have their passwords updated to encrypted passwords when they log in. Normally, this option is off. Turn it on when you want an installation using plain-text passwords to have everyone updated to encrypted password authentication. It saves users the trouble of running the smbpasswd command directly from the server. After everyone is updated, this feature can be turned off. When this option is on, the encrypt passwords option should be set to No.

✦ **Obey PAM restrictions** — Turn this on (Yes) if you want to use PAM for account and session management. Even if activated, PAM is not used if the encrypted passwords feature is turned on (encrypt passwords = yes). (PAM stands for *Pluggable Authentication Modules* and is used for authenticating host computers and users.)

✦ **PAM password change** — Indicates to use the PAM password change control flag for Samba. If this is on (Yes), SMB clients will use PAM instead of the program listed in the Password Program value for changing SMB passwords.

✦ **Passwd program** — Indicates which password program to use to change Linux user passwords. By default, /usr/bin/passwd is used, with the current username (%u) inserted.

✦ **Passwd chat** — Sets the chat that goes on between the Samba daemon (smbd) and the Linux password program (/usr/bin/passwd by default) when smbd tries to synchronize SMB passwords with Linux user passwords.

✦ **Username map** — Sets the file used to map Samba usernames. By default, this file is /etc/samba/smbusers.

✦ **UNIX password sync** — With this on (Yes), Samba tries to update a user's Linux user password with his or her SMB password when the SMB password is changed. To do this, SMB runs the passwd command as the root user. This is on by default.

✦ **Guest account** — Specifies the username for the guest account. When a service is specified as Guest OK, the name entered here is used to access that service. The account is usually the nobody username.

Tip

Make sure that the guest account is a valid user. (The default of nobody should already be set up to work.) With an invalid user as the guest account, the IPC$ connection that lists the shared resources fails.

✦ **Hosts allow** — Contains a list of one or more hosts that are allowed to use your computer's Samba services. By default, users from any computer can connect to the Samba server (of course, they still have to provide valid usernames and passwords). Generally, you use this option to allow connections from specific computers (such as 10.0.0.1) or computer networks (such as 10.0.0.) that are excluded by the hosts deny option.

✦ **Hosts deny** — Contains a list of one or more hosts from which users are not allowed to use your computer's Samba services. You can make this option fairly restrictive, and then add the specific hosts and networks you want to use the Samba server. By default, no hosts are denied.

Assigning Guest Accounts

Samba always assigns the permissions level of a valid user on the Linux system to clients who use the server. In the case of share security, the user is assigned a guest account (the nobody user account by default).

If the guest account value isn't set, Samba goes through a fairly complex set of rules to determine which user account to use. The result is that it can be hard to ensure which user permissions will be assigned in each case. That's why user security is recommended if you want to provide more specific user access to your Samba server.

Logging Options

The following options help define how logging is done on your Samba server:

✦ **Log level** — Sets the debug level used when logging Samba activity. Raise the level from the default (0) to log more Samba activity.

✦ **Log file** — Defines the location of the Samba `smb` log file. By default, Samba log files are contained in `/var/log/samba` (with file names `log.nmbd`, `log.smbd`, and `smb.log`). In this option, the %m is replaced by `smb` to set the smb log file as `/var/log/samba/smb.log`.

✦ **Max log size** — Sets the maximum amount of space, in kilobytes, that the log files can consume. By default, the value is set to 0 (no limit).

Performance Options

The Socket Options option lets you pass options to the protocols Samba uses to communicate. The following options are set by default: `TCP_NODELAY`, `SO_RCVBUF=8192`, and `SO_SNDBUF=8192`. The first option disables Nagle's algorithm, which is used to manage the transmission of TCP/IP packets. The other two options set the maximum size of the sockets receive buffer and send buffer to 8192, respectively. These options are set to improve performance (reportedly up to 10 times faster than without setting these options). In general, you shouldn't change these options.

Printing Options

The printing options are used to define how printer status information is presented. For the overwhelming majority of Linux systems, the `printing` value is set to `cups`. You can use printing styles from other types of operating systems, such as UNIX System V (`sysv`), AIX (`aix`), HP UNIX (`hpux`), and Berkeley UNIX (`bsd`), to name a few. LPRng (`lprng`), offered by many UNIX systems, is also included. Other printing options enable you to redefine the location of basic printing commands (`lpq`, `lprm`, and so on) and printing files (such as the name of the printcap file).

Browse Options

A browse list is a list of computers that are available on the network to SMB services. Clients use this list to find computers that are on their own LAN and also computers in their workgroups that may be on other reachable networks.

In Samba, browsing is configured by options described later in this section and implemented by the nmbd daemon. If you are using Samba for a workgroup within a single LAN, you probably don't need to concern yourself with the browsing options. However, if you are using Samba to provide services across several physical subnetworks, you might want to consider configuring Samba as a domain master browser. Here are some points to think about:

✦ Samba can be configured as a master browser, which allows it to gather lists of computers from local browse masters to form a wide-area server list. (Browse masters keep track of available shared directories and printers on the network of Samba systems and broadcast information about those resources as necessary.)

✦ If Samba is acting as a domain master browser, Samba should use a WINS server to help browse clients resolve the names from this list.

✦ Samba can be used as a WINS server, although it can also rely on other types of operating systems to provide that service.

✦ There should be only one domain master browser for each workgroup. Don't use Samba as a domain master for a workgroup with the same name as an NT domain.

If you are working in an environment that has a mix of Samba and Windows NT servers, use an NT server as your WINS server. If Samba is your only file server, choose a single Samba server (nmbd daemon) to supply the WINS services.

Note A WINS server is basically a name server for NetBIOS names. It provides the same service that a DNS server does with TCP/IP domain names: It can translate names into addresses. A WINS server is particularly useful for allowing computers to communicate with SMB across multiple subnetworks where information is not being broadcast across the subnetworks' boundaries.

To configure the browsing feature in Samba, you must have the workgroup named properly (described earlier in this section). Here are the global options related to SMB browsing:

✦ **Os level**—Set a value to control whether your Samba server (nmbd daemon) may become the local master browser for your workgroup. Raising this setting increases the Samba server's chance to control the browser list for the workgroup in the local broadcast area.

If the value is 0, a Windows machine will probably be selected. A value of 60 ensures that the Samba server is chosen over an NT server. The default is 20.

✦ **Preferred master**—Set this to Yes if you want to force selection of a master browser and give the Samba server a better chance of being selected. (Setting Domain Master to Yes along with this option ensures that the Samba server will be selected.) This is set to Auto by default, which causes Samba to try to detect the current master browser before taking that responsibility.

✦ **Local master** — Set this to Yes if you want the Samba server to become the local browser master. (This is not a guarantee, but gives it a chance.) Set the value to No if you do not want your Samba server selected as the local master. Local Master is Auto by default.

✦ **Domain master** — Set this to Yes if you want the Samba server (nmbd daemon) to identify itself as the domain master browser for its workgroup. This list will then allow client computers assigned to the workgroup to use SMB-shared files and printers from subnetworks that are outside their own subnetwork. This is set to No by default.

Note If browsing isn't working, check the nmbd log file (/var/log/samba/log.nmbd). To get more detail, increase the debug information level to 2 or 3 (described earlier in this section) and restart Samba. The log can tell you if your Samba server is the master browser and, if so, which computers are on its list.

WINS Options

Use the WINS options if you want to have a particular WINS server provide the name-to-address translation of NetBIOS names used by SMB clients:

✦ **Wins server** — If there is a WINS server on your network that you want to use to resolve the NetBIOS names for your workgroup, enter that server's IP address here. Again, you probably want to use a WINS server if your workgroup extends outside the local subnetwork.

✦ **Wins support** — Set this value to Yes if you want your Samba server to act as a WINS server. (It's No by default.) Again, this is not needed if all the computers in your workgroup are on the same subnetwork. Only one computer on your network should be assigned as the WINS server.

In addition to the values described here, you can access dozens more options by clicking the Advanced View button. When you have filled in all the fields you need, click Commit Changes on the screen to have the changes written to the /etc/samba/smb.conf file.

Configuring Shared Directories with SWAT

To make your shared directory available to others, add an entry to the SWAT window. To use SWAT to set up Samba to share directories, do the following:

Note You may see one or more security warnings during the course of this procedure. These messages warn you that someone can potentially view the data you are sending to SWAT. If you are working on your local host or on a private LAN, the risk is minimal.

1. From the main SWAT window, click the SHARES button.

2. Type the name of the directory that you want to share in the Create Share box, and then click Create Share.

3. Add any of these options:

Comment — A few words to describe the shared directory (optional).

Path — The path name of the directory you are sharing.

Guest account — If Guest OK is selected, the username that is defined here is assigned to users accessing the file system. No password will be required to access the share. The nobody user account (used only by users who access your computer remotely) is the default name used. (The FTP user is also a recommended value.)

Read only — If Yes, files can only be read from this file system, but no remote user can save or modify files on the file system. Select No if you want users to be allowed to save files to this directory over the network.

Guest ok — Select Yes to enable anyone access to this directory without requiring a password.

Hosts allow — Add the names of the computers that will be allowed to access this file system. Separate host names by commas, spaces, or tabs. Here are some valid ways of entering host names:

> **localhost** — Allows access to the local host.

> **192.168.12.125** — IP address. Enter an individual IP address.

> **192.168.12** — Enter a network address to include all hosts on a network. (Be sure to put a dot at the end of the network number or it won't work!)

> **pcren, pcstimpy** — Enables access to individual hosts by name.

> **EXCEPT** *host* — If you are allowing access to a group of hosts (such as by entering a network address), use EXCEPT to specifically deny access from one host from that group.

Hosts deny — Denies access to specific computers by placing their names here. By default, no particular computers are excluded. Enter host names in the same forms you used for Hosts Allow.

Browseable — Indicates whether you can view this directory on the list of shared directories. This is on (Yes) by default.

Available — Enables you to leave this entry intact but turns off the service. This is useful if you want to close access to a directory temporarily. This is on (Yes) by default. Select No to turn it off.

4. Select Commit Changes.

At this point, the shared file systems should be available to the Samba client computers (Windows 9*x*, Windows NT, Windows 2000, OS/2, Linux, and so on) that have access to your Linux Samba server. Before you try that, however, you can check your Samba configuration.

Checking Your Samba Setup with SWAT

From the SWAT window, select the STATUS button. From this window, you can restart your smbd and nmbd processes. Likewise, you can see lists of active connections, active shares, and open files. (The preferred way to start the smbd and nmbd daemons is to set up the smb service to start automatically. Type **chkconfig smb on** to set the service to start at boot time.)

Working with Samba Files and Commands

Although you can set up Samba through the Samba Server Configuration window or SWAT, many administrators prefer to edit the /etc/samba/smb.conf directly. As root user, you can view the contents of this file and make needed changes. If you selected User security (as recommended), you will also be interested in the smbusers and smbpasswd files (in the /etc/samba directory). These files, as well as commands such as testparm and smbstatus, are described in the following sections.

Editing the smb.conf File

Changes you make using the Samba Server Configuration window or SWAT Web interface are reflected in your /etc/samba/smb.conf file. Here's an example of a smb.conf file (with comments removed):

```
[global]
workgroup = ESTREET
server string = Samba Server on Maple
hosts allow = 192.168.0.
printcap name = /etc/printcap
load printers = yes
printing = cups
log file = /var/log/samba/%m.log
max log size = 0
smb passwd file = /etc/samba/smbpasswd
security = user
encrypt passwords = Yes
unix password sync = Yes
passwd program = /usr/bin/passwd %u
passwd chat = *New*password* %n\n *Retype*new*password* %n\n *passwd:
        *all*authentication*tokens*updated*successfully*
pam password change = yes
obey pam restrictions = yes
socket options = TCP_NODELAY SO_RCVBUF=8192 SO_SNDBUF=8192
username map = /etc/samba/smbusers
dns proxy = no
```

```
[homes]
comment = Home Directories
browseable = no
writable = yes
valid users = %S
create mode = 0664
directory mode = 0775

[printers]
comment = All Printers
path = /var/spool/samba
browseable = no
guest ok = no
writable = no
printable = yes
```

We won't go through every line of this example, but here are some observations. In the [global] section, the workgroup is set to ESTREET, the server is identified as the Samba Server on Maple, and only computers that are on the local network (192.168.0.) are allowed access to the Samba service. You must change the local network to match your network.

Definitions for the local printers that will be shared are taken from the /etc/printcap file, the printers are loaded (yes), and the CUPS printing service is used.

Separate log files for each host trying to use the service are created in /var/log/samba/%m.log (with %m automatically replaced with each host name). There is no limit to log file size (0).

This example uses the user-level security (security = user), which allows a user to log in once and then easily access the printers and the user's home directory on the Linux system. Password encryption is on (encrypt passwords = yes) because most Windows systems have password encryption on by default. Passwords are stored in the /etc/samba/smbpasswd file on your Linux system.

The dns proxy = no option prevents Linux from looking up system names on the DNS server (used for TCP/IP lookups).

The [homes] section enables each user to access his or her Linux home directory from a Windows system on the LAN. The user will be able to write to the home directory. However, other users will not be able see or share this directory. The [printers] section enables all users to print to any printer that is configured on the local Linux system.

Adding Samba Users

Performing user-style Samba security means assigning a Linux user account to each person using the Linux file systems and printers from his or her Windows worksta-tion. (You could assign users to a guest account instead, but in this example, all users have their own accounts.) Then you need to add SMB passwords for each user. For example, here is how you would add a user whose Windows workstation login is chuckp:

1. Type the following as root user from a Terminal window to add a Linux user account:

   ```
   # useradd -m chuckp
   ```

2. Add a Linux password for the new user as follows:

   ```
   # passwd chuckp
   Changing password for user chuckp
   New UNIX password: ********
   Retype new UNIX password: ********
   ```

3. Repeat the previous steps to add user accounts for all users from Windows workstations on your LAN that you want to give access to your Linux system to.

4. Type the following command to create the Samba password file (smbpasswd) on Fedora Linux systems:

   ```
   # cat /etc/passwd | /usr/bin/mksmbpasswd.sh >
   /etc/samba/smbpasswd
   ```

   (In Debian systems, use the /usr/sbin/mksmbpasswd command instead of mksmbpasswd.sh.)

5. Add an SMB password for the user as follows:

   ```
   # smbpasswd chuckp
   New SMB password: **********
   Retype new SMB password: **********
   ```

6. Repeat this step for each user. Later, each user can log into Linux and rerun the passwd and smbpasswd commands to set private passwords.

Note   In the most recent version of Samba, there are options available in the smb.conf file that cause SMB and Linux passwords to be synchronized automatically. See descriptions of the passwd program, passwd chat, and UNIX password sync options in the SWAT section of this chapter.

Starting the Samba Service

When you have your Samba configuration the way you would like it, restart the Samba server as described earlier in the "Getting and Installing Samba" section. You can now check SMB clients on the network to see if they can access your Samba server.

Testing Your Samba Permissions

You can run several commands from a shell to work with Samba. One is the testparm command, which you can use to check the access permissions you have set up. It lists global parameters that are set, along with any shared directories or printers.

Checking the Status of Shared Directories

The `smbstatus` command can view who is currently using Samba shared resources offered from your Linux system. The following is an example of the output from `smbstatus`:

```
Samba version 3.0.3-4
PID     Username     Group          Machine
-----------------------------------------------------------------------

Service     pid     machine      Connected at
--------------------------------------------------------------
IPC$        10865   shuttle      Wed Aug 25 07:22:13 2004
tmp         10866   shuttle      Wed Aug 25 07:29:14 2004
tmp         10874   10.0.0.177   Wed Aug 25 07:33:01 2004

Locked files:
Pid   DenyMode   Access R/W   Oplock Name
--------------------------------------------------------------
10874 DENY_FCB   0x3    RDWR NONE   /tmp/.m.swp Wed Aug 25 07:22:21 2004
10874 DENY_NONE  0x1    RDWR NONE   /tmp/m      Wed Aug 25 08:12:33 2004
```

This output shows that from the Linux Samba server, the `tmp` service (which is a share of the `/tmp` directory) is currently open by the computer named `shuttle`. PID 10874 is the process number of the smbd daemon on the Linux server that is handling the service. The files open are the `/tmp/m` and `/tmp/.m.swap`, which happen to be opened by a `vi` command. Both have read/write access.

Using Samba Shared Directories

Once you have configured your Samba server, you can try using the shared directories from a client computer on your network. The following sections describe how to use your Samba server from another Linux system or from various Windows systems.

Using Samba from Nautilus

To connect to a Samba share from a Nautilus file manager, use the Open Location box by clicking File➪Open Location. Then type **smb:** into your Nautilus file manager Location box.

A list of SMB workgroups on your network appears in the window. You can select a workgroup, choose a server, and then select a resource to use. This should work for shares requiring no password.

The Nautilus interface seems to be a bit buggy when you need to enter passwords. It also requires you to either send clear-text passwords or type the username and password into your location box. For example, to get to my home directory (`/home/chris`) through Nautilus, I can type my username, password, server name, and share name as follows:

```
smb://chris:my72mgb@arc/chris
```

Mounting Samba Directories in Linux

Linux can view your Samba shared directories as it does any other medium (hard disk, NFS shares, CD-ROM, and so on). Use mount to mount a Samba shared file system so that it is permanently connected to your Linux file system.

Here's an example of the mount command in which a home directory (/home/chris) from a computer named toys on a local directory (/mnt/toys) is mounted. The command is typed, as root user, from a Terminal window:

```
# mkdir /mnt/toys
# mount -t smbfs -o username=chris,password=a72mg //arc/chris /mnt/toys
```

The file system type for a Samba share is smbfs (-t smbfs). The username (chris) and password (a72mg) are passed as options (-o). The remote share of the home directory on toys is //toys/chris. The local mount point is /mnt/toys. At this point, you can access the contents of /home/chris on toys as you would any file or directory locally. You will have the same permission to access and change the contents of that directory (and its subdirectories) as you would if you were the user chris using those contents directly from toys.

To mount the Samba shared directory permanently, add an entry to your /etc/fstab file. For the example just described, you'd add the following line (as root user):

```
//toys/chris    /mnt/toys    smbfs    username=chris,password=a72mg
```

Troubleshooting Your Samba Server

A lot can go wrong with a Samba server. If your Samba server isn't working properly, the descriptions in this section should help you pinpoint the problem.

Basic Networking in Place?

You can't share anything with other computers without a network. Before computers can share directories and printers from Samba, they must be able to communicate on your LAN.

Your Samba server can use the TCP/IP name as the NetBIOS name (used by Window networks for file and printer sharing), or a separate NetBIOS name can be set in the smb.conf file. It is critical, however, that the broadcast address be the same as the broadcast address for all clients communicating with your Samba server. To see your broadcast address, type the following (as root user):

```
# ifconfig -a
eth0      Link encap:Ethernet  HWadd 00:D1:B3:75:A5:1B
          inet addr:10.0.0.1  Bcast:10.0.0.255  Mask:255.255.255.0
```

The important information is the broadcast address (Bcast: 10.0.0.255), which is determined by the netmask (Mask:255.255.255.0). If the broadcast address isn't the same for the Samba server and the clients on the LAN, the clients cannot see that the Samba server has directories or printers to share.

Samba Service Running?

A basic troubleshooting check is to see if the service is running. Try the smbclient command from your Linux system to see that everything is running and being shared as you expect it to be. The smbclient command is a great tool for getting information about a Samba server and even accessing shared directories from both Linux and Windows computers. While logged in as root or any user who has access to your Samba server, type the following:

```
$ smbclient -L localhost
Password: **********
Domain=[ESTREET] OS=[Unix] Server=[Samba 3.0.3-4]

    Sharename      Type      Comment
    ---------      ----      -------
    homes          Disk      Home Directories
    IPC$           IPC       IPC Service (Samba Server)
    ADMIN$         Disk      IPC Service (Samba Server)
    hp-ns1         Printer
Domain=[ESTREET] OS=[Unix] Server=[Samba 3.0.8-4]

    Server                   Comment
    ---------                -------
    PINE                     Samba Server
    MAPLE                    Windows XP
    NS1                      Samba Server

    Workgroup                Master
    ---------                -------
    ESTREET                  PINE
```

The Samba server is running on the local computer in this example. Shared directories and printers, as well as servers in the workgroup, appear here. If the Samba server is not running, you see "Connection refused" messages, and you need to start the Samba service as described earlier in this chapter.

Firewall Open?

If the Samba server is running, it should begin broadcasting its availability on your LAN. If you try to access the server from a Windows or Linux client on your LAN but get a "Connection refused" error, the problem may be that the firewall on your Linux Samba server is denying access to the NetBIOS service. If you have a secure LAN, you can type the following (as root user) to flush your firewall filtering rules temporarily:

```
# iptables -F
```

Try to connect to the Samba Server from a Windows or Linux client. If you find that you can connect to the server, turn the firewall back on:

```
# /etc/init.d/iptables restart
```

You then need to open access to ports 137, 138, and 139 in your firewall so that the Samba server can accept connections for services. (See Chapter 17 for information about modifying your firewalls.)

User Passwords Working?

Try accessing a shared Samba directory as a particular user (from the local host or other Linux system on your LAN). You can use the smbclient command to do this. Here is an example:

```
# smbclient //localhost/tmp -U chris
added interface ip=10.0.0.1 bcast=10.0.0.255
nmask=255.255.255.0
Password: *******
Domain=[ESTREET] OS=[Unix] Server=[Samba 2.2.7a]
smb: \>
```

In this example, smbclient connects to the directory share named tmp as the Samba user named chris. If the password is accepted, you should see information about the server and a smb:\> prompt. If you cannot access the same shared directory from a Windows client, it's quite possible that the client is passing an improper username and password. Part of the problem may be that the Windows client is not providing encrypted passwords.

For certain Windows clients, using encrypted passwords requires that you change a Windows registry for the machine. One way to change the registry is with the Windows regedit command. Registry changes required for different Windows systems are contained within the /usr/share/doc/samba-*/docs/Registry directory.

Tip
The smbclient command, used here to list server information and test passwords, can also be used to browse the shared directory and copy files after you are connected. After you see the smb:\> prompt, type **help** to see the available commands. The interface is similar to any ftp client, such as sftp.

If your particular problem has not been addressed in this troubleshooting section, please refer to the user documentation that accompanies the Samba project. On Fedora systems, look in the /usr/share/doc/samba-*/htmldocs directory for some excellent documentation you can read from your Web browser. In particular, refer to the Samba-HOWTO-Collection/diagnosis.html file for help with troubleshooting.

Summary

By providing centralized file servers, an organization can efficiently share information and applications with people within the organization, with customers, or with anyone around the world. Several different technologies are available for making your Linux computer into a file-serving powerhouse.

The Network File System (NFS) protocol was one of the first file server technologies available. It is particularly well suited for sharing file systems among Linux and other UNIX systems. NFS uses standard `mount` and `umount` commands to connect file systems to the directory structures of client computers.

The Samba software package that comes with many Linux distributions (or can be easily installed if it doesn't) contains protocols and utilities for sharing files and printers among Windows and OS/2 operating systems. It uses SMB protocols that are included with all Microsoft Windows systems and therefore provides a convenient method of sharing resources on LANs containing many Windows systems.

✦   ✦   ✦

Programming
in Linux

Programming Environments and Interfaces

You can slice and dice the topic of Linux programming environments and interfaces in a variety of ways. For example, a list of the programming languages known to have compilers that target or run on Linux easily runs to three single-spaced, typewritten pages. You could also examine the literally hundreds of programming libraries that exist for Linux. Alternatively, you can organize the discussion by dividing everything into three categories: graphically oriented interfaces, command-line interfaces, and neither.

To some readers, a "programming environment" means a graphical, point-and-click integrated development environment (IDE) like that provided by Borland's Kylix or IBM's Visual Age. Yet another way to approach the subject is to look at Linux's development support for certain academic and computing subjects, such as graphics, databases, mathematics, engineering, chemistry, text processing, physics, biology, astronomy, networking, and parallel computing.

Unfortunately, there's no one definitive taxonomic organization that will work for everyone, so this chapter takes the easy way out and divides things into environments and interfaces. For the purposes of this chapter, a *programming environment* refers to the setting in which programming takes place and the accoutrement with which someone performs programming tasks.

Conventionally understood, a programming environment is either graphically- or command-line-oriented. However, the Linux programming environment also consists of the services and capabilities provided by the system itself, that is, by the kernel and the core system components. Whether you use a mouse-driven IDE or a text editor and make, Linux imposes certain requirements and provides a number of capabilities that determine what the code you write in an IDE or text editor must do and can do.

A *programming interface,* as this chapter uses the phrase, refers to the rules or methods followed to accomplish a particular task. As with programming environments, programming interfaces are usually thought of as graphical or command-line. A graphical interface uses the X Window system to receive and process user input and display information. A command-line interface is a strictly text-based affair that does not require a windowing system to run. For example, Firefox, a Web browser, has a graphical interface; it won't work if X isn't running. Pine, a popular e-mail client, has a command-line interface; it works whether X is running or not.

There is a third type of interface, however, an application programming interface, or API. An API provides a structured method to write a program that performs a certain task. For example, to write a program that plays sounds, you use the sound API; to write a program that communicates over a TCP/IP network, you use the socket API. Neither playing a sound nor communicating over a TCP/IP network necessarily requires a graphical or command-line interface; both graphical and command-line programs can play sounds or use TCP/IP, provided they use the proper API.

Linux Programming Environments

Linux boasts arguably the richest programming environment of any operating system currently available. As remarked earlier, this chapter uses the term *programming environment* to describe the tools used to write computer programs on a Linux system and to refer to underlying services that make programming on a Linux system possible (or, perhaps, worthwhile).

This section looks first at the fundamental services and capabilities that inform and constrain programming on a Linux system. Next, you'll examine a few of the most popular graphical IDEs for creating programs on a Linux system. The section closes with a look at some of the command-line tools used for writing programs. As you will discover, some of the graphical IDEs provide comfortable editors for writing code, drawing dialog boxes, and navigating the file system, but use the command-line tools to do the work of compiling the code, hiding the command-line tools beneath an attractive interface.

The Linux Development Environment

The Linux development environment consists of the services and capabilities provided by the kernel and core system components. These services and capabilities both define and limit how to write programs that run on a Linux system. Consider files and the file system. Linux, like the UNIX systems on which it is modeled, is built on the key idiom that "everything is file." This is a powerful metaphor and model that dramatically simplifies writing application programs to communicate with all sorts of devices. How? You can use the same function, the `write()` system call, to write data to a text file, to send data to a printer, to send keystrokes to an application, and, if you had one, to tell your network-connected coffeepot to brew another pot of coffee.

The file metaphor works this way because Linux treats all devices, such as modems, monitors, CD-ROM drives, disk drives, keyboards, mice, and printers as if they were files. Device drivers, which are part of the kernel, sit between a device and the user, and applications trying to access it translate an application's write() call into a form that the device the driver operates can understand. So, if you write data to a text file on an ext3 file system, the ext3 driver writes the necessary bytes to a file on the disk, but if you write that same data to a printer, the printer driver transmits that data out the parallel port (or across the network) and to the printer in a manner that the printer can understand and interpret. This is one way in which the Linux development environment informs, or defines, writing programs on a Linux system.

The catch? If the device you want to use doesn't have a driver, you can't use the write() call to do anything with that device. You simply do not have a way to communicate with the device. This is how the Linux development environment constrains programming on a Linux system.

What, then, in addition to the file idiom already discussed, are the key features of Linux that characterize its development environment? In no particular order:

✦ The process model

✦ CPU and memory protection

✦ The security model

✦ Preemptive multitasking

✦ Its multiuser design

✦ Interprocess communication

✦ The building blocks approach

Let's take a closer look at each of these features.

The Process Model

The process model is the way that Linux creates and manages running processes. Provided that a process has the necessary privileges, it can create (or spawn) other processes, referred to as *child processes*. The parent process can also exchange data with child processes. Of course, the capability to create child processes is not unique to Linux, but the particular way in which Linux does so is characteristic of all UNIX-like systems.

> **Note** Actually, the child process created when a process fork()s, isn't an exact duplicate of the parent. The process ID (PID) of the child process is different, as is the parent PID (PPID); any file locks held by the parent are reset; and any signals pending for the parent are cleared in the child.

When process calls the fork() system call, it creates an exact copy of itself. After being created by the fork() call, the child process typically calls one of a family of functions collectively known as exec(), providing a program to execute and any options or arguments to that program. Listing 27-1 illustrates the fork()/exec() process.

Listing 27-1: **Simple fork() and exec() Sequence**

```
/*
 * forkexec.c - illustrate simple fork/exec usage
 */
#include <stdio.h>
#include <unistd.h>
#include <sys/types.h>
#include <sys/wait.h>

int main(int argc, char *argv[])
{
        pid_t child;
        int status;

        child = fork();
        if (child == 0) {
                printf("in child\n");
                execl("/bin/ls", "/bin/ls", NULL);
        } else {
                printf("in parent\n");
                waitpid(child, &status, 0);
        }

        return 0;
}
```

Don't worry about what all the code means. The key points to understand are:

✦ The child - fork() statement creates a new (child) process.

✦ The code between if (child -- 0) and the else statements is executed in the child process. In particular, the child uses the execl() function call to execute the /bin/ls program, which creates a directory listing of the current directory.

✦ The waitpid() statement is executed in the parent process, which means that the parent process will wait for the child process to terminate before continuing execution.

You can compile this program with the following command (if you have the GCC compiler installed):

```
$ gcc forkexec.c -o forkexec
```

And then execute it like this:

```
$ ./forkexec
in parent
in child
28.doc  a.out  forkexec  forkexec.c
```

Your output might be slightly different. The point to take away from this example is that Linux makes it very easy to create new processes programmatically. Because it is so easy, it is a common and powerful programming technique and a characteristic of the Linux programming model. Linux is hardly alone in providing a mechanism by which one program can start another, but the fork()/exec() technique is unique to Linux (and the UNIX systems on which it is based).

CPU and Memory Protection

Another fundamental component of programming on Linux systems is that the operating system itself, which consists of the Linux kernel, is almost entirely insulated from all application programs. The kernel runs in a protected CPU mode known variously as ring 0, kernel mode, or, more prosaically, kernel space. User programs, such as Web browsers, e-mail clients, graphics programs, and games run outside kernel mode in what is colloquially referred to as *user space.* The distinction between kernel space and user space is important. The kernel has raw, uncontrolled access to system resources such as the CPU, RAM, and attached peripherals. The kernel mediates all access from user space programs to system resources, funneling it through the system call, or syscall, interface. The syscall interface carefully checks the data passed in from user programs before passing that data on to other parts of the kernel. As a result of this careful gatekeeping, it is extremely rare for even the most poorly written user space program to crash the kernel. The strict division between kernel and user space code is what contributes to Linux's reliability and stability and why you hardly ever see the familiar Windows "Blue Screen of Death" on a Linux system (except in a screensaver).

In addition to the distinction between kernel and user mode code, the kernel and user programs also have their own distinct memory regions. Each process, each instance of a running program, has a virtual memory space, known more formally as the process address space, of 4GB. Under most circumstances, the kernel gets 1GB of this space, while user space gets the other 3GB. User space programs are not permitted to access kernel memory directly. As with CPU and peripheral protection, the motivation for strict memory partitioning is to prevent ill-behaved (or even deliberately malicious) programs from modifying kernel data structures, which can create system instability or even crash the system.

The distinction between kernel and user space is another fundamental feature of the Linux development environment that gives developers considerable flexibility to write almost any code they want with reasonable assurance that if their program crashes, it won't also crash the system. At the same time, the syscall interface that serves as the gateway between user mode and kernel mode code enables user mode programs to access kernel features and services in a safe, controlled manner. Moreover, the kernel can perform tasks that ordinarily might be executed by user space programs without needing a different programming model. For example, if you implement some sort of user space functionality, such as providing a basic HTTP server, in the kernel, the same syscall interface makes it possible to interact with the HTTP server; there is no need to use a new or different programming interface.

On the downside, the sharp delineation between kernel and user space creates some disadvantages for normal users. For example, unlike Microsoft Windows, user space programs do not have direct access to hardware devices. For user space programs to access a sound card, for example, the system administrator must take steps to permit this sort of access. However, this is a small inconvenience compared to the increased stability for which Linux systems are known.

The Security Model

As you learned earlier in this book, all users are not created equal. Some users, like the root user, are effectively omnipotent and can do anything on a system. Most users have more limited access. The user (and group) IDs of these less privileged users control what programs they can execute and the files they can access. The same restrictions apply to the development environment. For example, if you write a program, you might not be able to access a certain feature, such as locking memory with the mmap() system call, unless your program runs with root permissions.

If your program creates files, the default file permissions are controlled by the umask of the user executing the program and/or a umask that you might specifically set at runtime using the umask() system call. Naturally, your program cannot create, delete, or modify files or directories if it doesn't have the necessary privileges. The Linux development environment also makes it possible for a program to drop or add privileges at runtime by calling functions that change its UID or GID.

The impact of the Linux security model on programming is twofold. First, the same rules and restrictions that affect running programs and other elements of normal system usage also affect the process of creating programs and what those programs can do. This effect is no more than the logical consequence of the Linux security model itself. Programmatically, however, you have more ways, or perhaps more finely-grained ways, to interact with the security subsystem than you do as a normal user of the system.

The second effect of the Linux security model for programmers is that writing a program imposes significant burdens on programmers to program securely. An e-mail program, for example, that stores usernames and passwords in a text file that is unencrypted and/or world-readable is just as insecure as a program that fails to check user input for buffer overflow. To use a subtler example, when faced with a problem that seems to require root privileges, such as access to a sound card, the initial impulse is usually to run the program as root. However, there are often user space solutions that can accomplish the same goal and that do not require root access. In the case of writing programs that access a sound card, for example, the ALSA (Advanced Linux Sound Architecture) libraries give application programmers access to a rich interface for emitting squeaks and squawks without needing to rely on running a program as the root user.

Preemptive Multitasking

Perhaps the easiest way to express the preemptive multitasking characteristic of programming in a Linux environment is simply to write "You don't own the CPU; it only seems like you do." In imprecise terms, the CPU (actually, the CPU scheduler, which is part of the kernel) allocates a quantum of time (on the order of 50 milliseconds) to execute your program , then preempts it (interrupts or suspends it) to spend another 50 millisecond quantum executing another program, then preempts the second program to execute a third, and so on until the scheduler returns to your program, when (under normal circumstances) the round robin starts again. The context switch between programs happens so rapidly that you have the illusion that your program is running all the time.

Task preemption happens automatically and unavoidably; very few processes escape preemption. What you might not realize, however, is that a process can voluntarily yield its quantum of CPU time. That is, while a process cannot request additional CPU time, it can voluntarily give it up. The implication of this for a developer is that you can delay executing certain blocks of code if they are either noncritical or rely on input from other processes that are still running. The function that makes this possible is named sched_yield().

Multitasking, while a boon for computer users, poses (at least) three potential problems for programmers: deadlocks, livelocks, and races. A *deadlock* occurs when two or more processes are unable to proceed because each is waiting for one of the others to do something. Deadlocks can happen in several ways. For example, suppose an e-mail client is communicating with a mail server, waiting on the server to send a message. A deadlock occurs if the mail server is waiting for input from the e-mail client before sending the message. This type of deadlock is sometimes referred to as a *deadly embrace*. A *starvation deadlock* occurs when one or more low-priority processes never get time on the CPU because they are crowded out by higher-priority processes. A third common type of deadlock occurs when two processes are trying to send data to each other but can't because each process's input buffers are full because they are so busy trying to send data that they never read any data sent by the other process. This type of deadlock is colorfully referred to as *constipation*.

Livelocks occur when a task or process, usually a server process, is unable to finish because its clients continue to create more work for it to do before the server can clear its queue. The difference between a livelock and a deadlock is that a deadlocked process doesn't have any work queued; it is blocked or waiting for something to happen. A livelocked process, on the other hand, has too much work to do and never empties its work queue.

Races occur when the result of a computation depends on the order in which two events occur. Say, for example, that two processes are accessing a file. The first process writes data to the file, and the second process reads data from the file to calculate and display a summary value. If the reader process reads the file after the writer completes, the reader calculates and returns the correct value. If the reader process reads the file before the writer completes, the reader will calculate and return an incorrect summary value.

The likelihood of deadlocks, livelocks, or races occurring increases dramatically on multitasking (and multiuser) systems because the number of processes that are potentially competing for access to a finite number of resources is greater. Good design, careful analysis, and the judicious use of locks, semaphores, and other mutual exclusion (or mutex) mechanisms, which mediate access to shared resources, can prevent or reduce their occurrence.

Multiuser by Design

Linux is multiuser by design, an element of the Linux development model that has far-reaching consequences for developers. A program cannot assume, for example, that it has sole access to any resource such as a file, memory, peripheral devices, or CPU time; multiple programs might be attempting to print simultaneously or try-ing to allocate memory. Similarly, a program cannot be written with the assumption that only one copy of the program is running at a time. So, if you are writing a pro-gram that creates temporary working files in /tmp, you need to ensure sure that the temporary files created by Bubba's copy of the program are distinct from the tem-porary files created by Mary Beth's instance of the program, or hilarity will ensue (if not hilarity, at least confusion and consternation). Another common need is for programs to honor per-user configurations. At startup time, a program might apply reasonable global defaults and then read a user's configuration file to apply, say, a custom color scheme.

There are also a number of per-user settings, such as environment variables, that programs need to know how to accommodate. For example, the MAIL environment variable identifies where the user's mail spool file is kept; the VISUAL environment variable defines the user's preferred full screen editor (which all true Linux users know is vi); the PRINTER environment variable stores the name of the user's default printer; and, of course, HOME identifies the user's home directory.

In a system such as Linux that is pervasively multiuser, programs and programmers must always take into account that most resources a program might want to use are usually shared resources and that most real-world usage scenarios (more formally known as *use cases*) assume that multiple instances of the program are running at the same time.

Interprocess Communication

Interprocess communication (IPC) enables programs to share data and resources with a minimum amount of overhead and is used extensively on all Linux systems. It is especially common with daemons and server process that spawn child pro-cesses to handle client connections. IPC comes in three varieties:, shared memory, semaphores, and message queues. *Shared memory* is just what the name suggests, a region or segment of memory specifically set aside for use by multiple processes. Because shared memory is never paged out to disk, it is an extremely fast way for two processes to exchange data.

Semaphores, briefly mentioned in the "Preemptive Multitasking" section, serve as flags that indicate a condition controlling the behavior of processes. For example, one process can set a semaphore to indicate a specific file is in use. Before other processes attempt to access that file, they check the semaphore's status and don't (or shouldn't) attempt to access the file if the flag is set.

Message queues are first-in, first-out (FIFO) data structures that make it possible for processes to exchange short messages in a structured, orderly manner.

Note   Message queues are not necessarily accessed in FIFO data structures. System V UNIX-style message queues are, but POSIX message queues enable readers to pull messages off a queue in an arbitrary order.

Shared memory, semaphores, and message queues are idiomatic in the Linux development environment. They solve three distinct domains of problems that arise when multiple processes need to exchange data or share resources without having to resort to slow disk files. All of which is to say that you don't always need IPC, but it sure is nice to have when you do need it.

The Building Blocks Philosophy

The building blocks philosophy that characterizes the Linux development is best expressed as a short series of rules or principles:

- ✦ Do one thing very well.
- ✦ Whenever possible, accept input data from standard input and send output data to standard output.
- ✦ Keep individual programs as self-contained as possible.
- ✦ Remember that someone will use your program in ways you didn't intend and for purposes that you never imagined.

The first rule simply means that programs should not try to be all things to all people: a text editor doesn't need to be able to send e-mail messages, and a drawing program doesn't also need to be able to function as a Web browser. Although it is less true today than it used to be, the best Linux programs don't have every imaginable feature (also known as *featuritis*). Rather, developers spend time perfecting the program's intended purpose and making it possible for programs to interoperate.

The second rule allows you to create chains of commands, each of which uses the output of the previous command as its input. A typical use of this behavior is a command pipeline, such as the following rather contrived example:

```
$ cat /etc/passwd | cut -f 5 -d: | tr [:lower:] [:upper:] | sort | head -5
```

The first part of the command pipeline, `cat /etc/passwd`, writes the contents of the `/etc/passwd` file to standard output. The second part, `cut -f 5 -d:`, cuts out the fifth field of its standard input (the contents of `/etc/passwd`), using the colon character, `:`, as the field delimiter (the fifth field of `/etc/passwd` is the GECOS or name field). The third part, `tr [:lower:] [:upper:]`, translates all lowercase characters in the standard input to uppercase characters. The next element, `sort`, performs an alphabetic sort on the first letter of its input before sending the sorted list to standard output. The final component, `head -5`, displays only the first five lines of its standard input to standard out. The output of this pipeline might resemble:

```
ADM
BIN
DAEMON
GAMES
LP
```

The following command pipeline should prove more useful: it e-mails the current uptime and load average to the root user:

```
uptime | mailx -s "System Usage" root
```

The third rule, keeping programs self-contained, is related to the second. The concept behind it is that programs intended for use in command pipelines should make no assumptions about what their input might look like or do any massaging of the output. Consider the `cut` command shown in the first command pipeline. It takes arbitrarily formatted input and allows the user to specify on what piece of data to operate (the fifth field in the example, where fields are colon-delimited) and then just displays the requested data on standard output. `cut` doesn't do any postprocessing of the output, allowing the user to do with it as she pleases, probably using another tool.

The fourth rule is really more a philosophical observation that you can't really predict all the ways in which your program might be put to use. Indeed, as S.C. Johnson once noted, "A successful [software] tool is one that was used to do something undreamed of by its author."

The point is that the Linux toolkit, for both developers and end users, is full of small tools and utilities that are building block programs routinely used to create larger programs and tools that, together, perform complex tasks that no single program can do, or can do efficiently. Another element of the building blocks approach is that it enables tasks to be performed in batch mode, without active user intervention or participation. This building block philosophy is another characteristic feature of the Linux development environment, one that can make your life a lot simpler once you grok the idea.

Graphical Programming Environments

If you are sitting in front of a Linux system, chances are pretty good it is running some version of the X Window System, that there are several xterms (terminal emulators) running on top of X's graphical interface, and that there are one or more natively graphical programs also running, such as a Web browser. Linux programming environments can be divided into two broad categories: graphical IDEs and discrete collections of command-line-based tools. Developers and users coming from a predominantly Windows background will be familiar with IDEs; the 800-pound gorilla in the Windows world is Microsoft's Visual Studio project. This section looks at some of the full-featured graphical IDEs that collect and merge all the constituent components necessary for the development task, such as an editor, compiler, linker, debugger, class browser, and project manager, in a single, unified interface. The examples discussed include the open source Eclipse environment;

Eclipse: The Universal Tool Platform

Eclipse is a large, Java-based development platform. In principle and in practice, Eclipse is a universal IDE that is used for applications as diverse as Web sites, C, C++, and Java programs, and even plug-ins that extend Eclipse itself. Eclipse is amply capable of handling every aspect of Linux development in an astonishing variety of languages. Figure 27-1 shows Eclipse with the "Hello, World" example program, written in Java, on the screen.

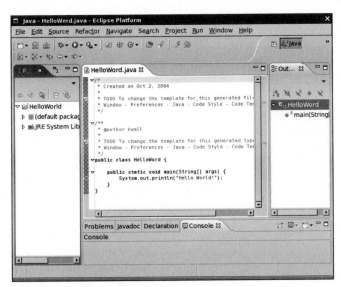

Figure 27-1: The Eclipse IDE.

Figure 27-1 illustrates a number of characteristics typical of IDEs. The project view on the left side of the screen provides a project file browser that enables you to see at a glance the contents of the programming project. You can see the primary project folder, HelloWorld, and some of the associated files necessary to support Java projects, such as the default package for Java projects and a folder containing the necessary JRE (Java Runtime Environment) files. The code editor view in the center of the screen shows the code for the HelloWorld.java program. Although it isn't visible in the black-and-white figure produced for this book, the code editor performs on-the-fly syntax highlight using color and font-style changes. Java keywords are purple; plain comments appear in green; javadoc-style comments appear in a pale blue; strings are colored blue; and normal code is black.

The right side of Eclipse displays another feature common among IDEs, a class browser. Class browsers enable developers to see the structure of their programs from the point of view of the code modules that make up the program rather than as mere files in a directory. This feature is not terribly useful for a small program such as HelloWorld.java, but larger programs that consist of dozens of classes or code modules are much easier to navigate using a code or class browser.

The bottom of the screen shows various information and status windows. For example, the Problems view shows problems that might have occurred while compiling the program. Eclipse, like many other IDEs, enables you to double-click on an error in the Problems view to jump right to the error in the associated code file (see Figure 27-2).

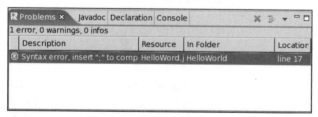

Figure 27-2: Eclipse's Problems view.

The Javadoc view, which is unique to the Eclipse Java development plug-in, enables you to view the output of Javadoc, a tool that creates documentation from specially formatted Java source code comments. The Declaration view works in combination with the class browser to show you the complete declaration of methods and data types. The Console view shows the actual output of the Java program.

Note   For more information about Eclipse, including download information, visit the Eclipse home page at www.eclipse.org/.

KDevelop: KDE's IDE

KDevelop, another open source IDE licensed under the GPL, was originally created to provide an IDE that interoperated seamlessly with KDE and the Qt framework (a large C++ application framework) on which KDE is based. Over the years, however, KDevelop has evolved into an attractive, feature-rich development environment supporting a number of languages other than C++. Today, KDevelop is a general-purpose IDE, although it works best when used to create Qt-based applications written in C++. Figure 27-3 shows a representative screenshot of Kdevelop.

Figure 27-3: The KDevelop IDE.

If you compare KDevelop's appearance to Eclipse's appearance, you will see that both have the same type of components. In Figure 27-3, the class browser is located on the left side of the screen, the project window is located in the upper-right portion of the screen, and KDevelop's version of the Declaration view is displayed in the lower-right portion of the screen. The log view that occupies the bottom of the KDevelop interface in Figure 27-3 shows the compilation process. As with Eclipse, KDevelop's toolbars and menus are stuffed with buttons and menu items that cater to the needs of developers, just as a word processor is customized with buttons and menu items specific to the task of writing and formatting documents.

Note   For more information about KDevelop, including download information, visit the KDevelop home page at `http://kdevelop.kde.org/`. The language status support page (`www.kdevelop.org/HEAD/doc/api/html/LangSupportStatus.html`) shows the current list of supported programming languages.

Code Crusader

Code Crusader is a commercially available and supported IDE written in C++ and specifically targeted at the Linux developer; it is not available for Windows. You can use Code Crusader to write Java, FORTAN, C++, and, of course, C programs. Unlike the IDEs discussed so far, Code Crusader does not include a built-in debugger. Rather, New Planet Software, developers of Code Crusader, makes its debugger application, Code Medic, available separately (although you can buy the two together as an IDE bundle). Figure 27-4 shows Code Crusader with the forkexec.c program from Listing 27-1 open in an editor window.

Figure 27-4: The Code Crusader IDE.

As you can see in Figure 27-4, Code Crusader has a much simpler, cleaner interface than the other IDEs mentioned so far. Another significant difference between Code Crusader and the larger IDEs like Eclipse and KDevelop is that each IDE component, such as the project browser, the class browser, editor windows, and the log viewer, open in their own, independent windows rather than being part of a single-document interface (SDI). Having multiple windows is more consistent with traditional Linux and UNIX windowing conventions, but developers coming from a Windows background might find Code Crusader's multiple-document interface (MDI) a little jarring at first. On the other hand, programmers who prefer a leaner, cleaner interface might prefer Code Crusader to the rather overstuffed-looking interfaces that Eclipse and KDevelop offer.

Note   For more information about Code Crusader, including download information, visit the Code Crusader home page at www.newplanetsoftware.com/jcc/.

There are many more IDEs than the three discussed in this section. Some are less mature or still in beta stage. Others are special-purpose IDEs, such as the Quanta HTML editor, the GLADE interface designer for GNOME. If Eclipse, KDevelop, and Code Crusader don't appeal to you, a quick search at Freshmeat (use URL `http://freshmeat/net/browse/65/` to get right to the IDE category) or SourceForge (`http://sourceforge.net/softwaremap/trove_list.php?form_cat=65` takes you straight to the IDE category) should turn up many options from which to choose. When this paragraph was written in September 2004, the Freshmeat IDE category had 151 entries and the SourceForge IDE category had 453 entries; there's something available for everyone. This is Linux, after all, so you are free to choose the IDE that appeals to you the most. As you'll learn in the next subsection, though, not everyone wants (or needs) a GUI IDE.

The Command-Line Programming Environment

The Linux command-line programming environment or CLI (command-line interface) stands in sharp contrast to the GUI IDEs described in the previous section. It often shocks developers who have only a Windows development background and who aren't accustomed to using a CLI.

To be fair, it must be intimidating to find yourself in front of a command prompt without anything to double-click to start and not the faintest clue how to proceed. That said, while a CLI might seem Spartan to the newcomer, programming at the command line is surprisingly powerful and allows you to mix and match best-of-breed tools in a way that most IDEs cannot begin to approach. The CLI programming environment can match the environment provided by GUIs feature for feature, with the single exception of the graphical interface itself.

The inconvenience, if inconvenience it is, arises from the fact that the CLI programming environment relies on separate tools. For example, assuming you are working in the X Window System, you might be running one or more text editors, such as vi, pico, nano, joe, or emacs, each in its own xterms You might use another xterm for compiling your program, either by invoking the compiler gcc (the GNU compiler collection) directly, or by using the make utility. In still another window you might be running a debugger such as gdb (the GNU debugger). If you are unfamiliar with the library you are using, you might have a Web browser open to view some sort of online documentation, or you might be using a program such as xman, that displays Linux manual (man) pages in a graphical format.

It is not a given, however, that graphical IDEs are better than using discrete tools. Rather, it is a matter of with what model developers feel most comfortable, what method makes developers the most productive, and what approach best fits each developer's personal working style. Even though I work for a company that develops and sells an Eclipse-based set of development tools for embedded Linux, I personally feel more comfortable with and work more productively using the tools I have been using since 1993: vi or emacs for writing and editing code, `gcc` and `make` for compilation, and `gdb` and `kgdb` for debugging.

In any event, the lines are not so sharply drawn. Emacs, for example, has the facility to invoke both compilation and debugging facilities, has an extremely rich code editing interface (syntax highlighting and automatic indentation, for example), and also supports other code development features such as source code control, symbol and class browsing, and built-in support for at least three different online help facilities. If you prefer vi, it also can be configured to support symbol and class browsing using the ctags program, has basic syntax highlighting (depending on the implementation), and can also work with the error messages produced by failed compilation.

Perhaps the GUI versus CLI debate boils down to this distinction: CLI-oriented programming environments give developers direct access to the tools and utilities they need, don't consume system resources to draw an attractive GUI, and don't provide so-called point-and-click programming. GUI-oriented programming environments hide the tools and utilities underneath a consistent, unified interface; provide a convenient dashboard or instrument panel for access to the necessary programming tools; and let developers take advantage of some of the conveniences associated with graphical environments.

Linux Programming Interfaces

As defined at the beginning of this chapter, a programming interface refers to the rules or methods followed to accomplish a particular task. Programming interfaces are usually thought of as graphical or command-line. Graphical interfaces use the X Window System to receive and process user input and display information. Command-line interfaces, sometimes referred to as text-mode user interfaces (TUIs), are strictly text-based and do not require a windowing system to run but, thanks to the X Window System, you can also execute CLI-based programs in terminal emulators running on top of X. There is a third type of interface, however: an application programming interface or API. This section of the chapter looks at the ncurses library used to create text-mode user interfaces, examines some of the popular graphical interfaces in use today, and describes a small set of the most popular APIs used by Linux programmers.

Creating Command-Line Interfaces

There are three primary means of creating programs that interact with users at the command line. Two use libraries of screen manipulation routines, S-Lang and ncurses, to create TUIs, and the third just uses standard input and standard output, conventionally known as stdin and stdout, respectively. Using stdin and stdout is trivially simple. Input and output occur one line at a time; users type input using the keyboard or pipe input in from a file, and output is displayed to the screen or redirected to a file. Listing 27-2, `readkey.c`, shows such a program.

Listing 27-2: **Reading and Writing to stdin and stdout**

```c
/*
 * readkey.c - reads characters from stdin
 */
#include <stdio.h>

int main(int argc, char *argv[])
{
        int c, i = 0;

        /* read characters until newline read */
        printf("INPUT: ");
        while ((c = getchar()) != '\n') {
                ++i;
                putchar(c);
        }
        printf("\ncharacters read: %d\n", i + 1);

        return 0;
}
```

To compile this program, use the following command:

```
$ gcc readkey.c -o readkey
```

readkey.c reads input from stdin until it encounters a newline (such as pressing the Enter key). Then it displays the text entered and the number of characters read (the count includes the newline) and exits.

Here's how it works:

```
$ ./readkey
INPUT: There are three primary means of creating programs that interact with
users at the command line
There are three primary means of creating programs that interact with users at
the command line
characters read: 96
```

The text wraps oddly because of this book's formatting constraints. You can also feed readkey.c input from stdin using the cat command:

```
$ cat /etc/passwd | ./readkey
INPUT: root:x:0:0::/root:/bin/bash
characters read: 28
```

In this case, you only see the first line of /etc/passwd because each line of the file ends with a newline. It should be clear that programmatically interacting with the command line is simple, but not terribly user-friendly or attractive.

Creating TUIs with Ncurses

Screen manipulation libraries such as S-Lang and ncurses create more attractive programs, but, as you might expect, the trade-off for a nicer looking interface is more complicated code. Ncurses, which stands for new curses, is free re-implementation of the classic curses UNIX screen-handling library. The term *curses* derives from the phrase "cursor optimization," which succinctly describes what the curses library does: computes the fastest way to redraw a text-mode screen and places the cursor in the proper location.

Ncurses provides a simple, high-level interface for screen control and manipulation. It also contains powerful routines for handling keyboard and mouse input, creating and managing multiple windows, and using menus, forms, and panels. Ncurses works by generalizing the interface between an application program and the screen or terminal on which it is running. Given the literally hundreds of varieties of terminals, screens, and terminal emulation programs available, and the different features they possess (not to mention the different commands to use these features and capabilities), UNIX programmers quickly developed a way to abstract screen manipulation. Rather than write a lot of extra code to take into account the different terminal types, ncurses provides a uniform and generalized interface for the programmer. The ncurses API insulates the programmer from the underlying hardware.

Ncurses gives to character-based applications many of the same features found in graphical X Window applications — multiple windows, forms, menus, and panels. ncurses windows can be managed independently, may contain the same or different text, scroll or not scroll, be visible or hidden. Forms enable the programmer to create easy-to-use data entry and display windows, simplifying what is usually a difficult and application-specific coding task. Panels extend ncurses' capability to deal with overlapping and stacked windows. Menus provide, well, menus, again with a simpler, generalized programming interface.

To give you an idea of how ncurses works and what is involved in writing code to use it, Listing 27-3 shows the readkey.c program introduced in Listing 27-2 adapted to work with ncurses (now named nreadkey.c).

Listing 27-3: **Reading Input and Writing Output with Ncurses**

```
/*
 * readkey.c - reads characters from stdin
 */
#include <stdio.h>
#include <curses.h>

int main(int argc, char *argv[])
{
        int c, i = 0;
        int maxx, maxy;
        int y, x;
```

```
/* start ncurses */
initscr();

/* draw a purty border */
box(stdscr, ACS_VLINE, ACS_HLINE);
mvwaddstr(stdscr, 1, 1, "INPUT: ");
refresh();

/* read characters until newline read */
noecho();
while ((c = getch()) != '\n') {
        ++i;
        getyx(stdscr, y, x);
        /* at the right margin */
        if (x == 79) {
                mvaddch(y + 1, 1, c);
        } else {
                waddch(stdscr, c);
        }
        waddch(stdscr, c);
        refresh();
}
echo();
refresh();

/* print the character count */
getmaxyx(stdscr, maxy, maxx);
mvwprintw(stdscr, maxy - 2, 1, "characters read: %d\n", i + 1);
curs_set(0);
refresh();

/* time to look at the screen */
sleep(3);

/* shutdown ncurses */
endwin();

return 0;
}
```

One of the first things you notice is that nreadkey.c is about twice as long as readkey.c. The additional code is due entirely to the need to make sure the screen is set up, the cursor positioned appropriately, and so forth. To see if the additional code is worth it, compile nreadkey.c using the following command:

```
$ gcc nreadkey.c -lncurses -o nreadkey
```

To run the program, type **./nreadkey**. Figure 27-5 shows the result after typing the same text as typed for **readkey.c** earlier.

Figure 27-5: An ncurses-based TUI.

Ncurses-based programs can also read input piped from stdin. Figure 27-6 shows the results of the command `cat /etc/passwd | ./nreadkey`.

Figure 27-6: Displaying input piped to an ncurses-based program.

As you saw with the command pipeline used with the readkey.c program (shown in Listing 27-2, the input is truncated at the end of the first line because each line in `/etc/passwd` ends with the newline character, and readkey.c uses the newline character to signal the end of input.

Note   For more information about ncurses, including download information, visit the ncurses Web page at `http://dickey.his.com/ncurses/ncurses.html`.

Creating TUIs with S-Lang

S-Lang, created by John Davis, is an alternative to ncurses for creating TUIs. In addition to providing screen manipulation and cursor control routines, S-Lang also consists of an embeddable S-Lang interpreter, a large library of built-in (intrinsic) routines that simplify certain parts of programming, and a variety of predefined data types and data structures. Listing 27-4 shows the same program as Listing 27-3, with appropriate updates to reflect use of S-Lang instead of ncurses.

Listing 27-4: **Reading Input and Writing Output with S-Lang**

```c
/*
 * sreadkey.c - simple S-Lang-based UI
 */
#include <stdio.h>
#include <string.h>
#include <slang/slang.h>

int main(int argc, char *argv[])
{
        int i = 0;
        unsigned int ch;

        /* start s-lang */
        SLtt_get_terminfo();
        SLang_init_tty(-1, 0, 1);
        SLsmg_init_smg();

        /* draw a purty border */
        SLsmg_draw_box(0, 0, 24, 80);
        SLsmg_gotorc(1, 1);
        SLsmg_write_nchars("INPUT: ", 7);
        SLsmg_refresh();

        /* read characters until newline read */
        while(1) {
                ++i;
                ch = SLang_getkey();
                if (ch == 13)
                        break;
                if (SLsmg_get_column() == 79)
                        SLsmg_gotorc(2, 1);
                SLsmg_write_char(ch);
                SLsmg_refresh();
        }

/* print the character count */
        SLsmg_gotorc(22, 1);
        SLsmg_write_nchars("characters read: ", 17);
        SLsmg_printf("%d", i);
        SLsmg_refresh();

        /* time to look at the screen */
        sleep(3);
```

Continued

Listing 27-4 *(continued)*

```
/* shutdown s-lang */
SLsmg_reset_smg();
SLang_reset_tty();

return 0;
}
```

To compile this program using the following command:

```
$ gcc sreadkey.c -lslang -o sreadkey
```

To run the program, type **./sreadkey**. Figure 27-7 shows the result after typing the same text as typed for readkey.c earlier.

Figure 27-7: An S-Lang-based TUI.

As you can see from Figure 27-7, the basic appearance and functionality of sreadkey.c is the same as nreadkey.c. What has changed, the TUI framework used to create sreadkey.c, is invisible to the user. S-Lang-based programs can also read input piped from stdin.

From a developer's perspective, there are significant differences between ncurses and S-Lang in program structure and the actual library usage, but the output is almost identical.

Note   For more information about S-Lang, including download information, visit the S-Lang Web page at www.s-lang.org.

Creating Graphical Interfaces

When it comes to creating GUIs, Linux programmers have more options available to them than they do for creating TUIs. Probably the most popular and certainly the best known toolkits used to create graphical applications are Qt and GTK+. Qt is the C++ application framework that powers KDE, the K Desktop Environment. GTK+ is the toolkit underneath GNOME, the GNU Network Object Model Environment. GTK+ is written largely in C, but it has language bindings available for many other programming languages, such as Perl, C++, and Python, so you can use GTK+ features in many programming environments. Due to the limited space available, this chapter does not show examples of Qt and GTK+ applications.

Note For more information about GTK+, visit the GTK+ Web site at `www.gtk.org`. Information about the Qt framework can be seen at `www.trolltech.no`.

Although Qt and GTK+ are the big hammers of Linux graphical development, there are many other toolkits, frameworks, and libraries that you can use to develop GUI-based applications for Linux. The following list, arranged alphabetically, describes some of the most common ones. Most of these toolkits and frameworks describe widget sets, which are implemented in one or more programming libraries. Widget is the term applied to a user interface abstraction, such as a scroll bar or a button, created using the toolkit.

✦ **Athena** — The Athena library was one of the earliest widget libraries available for the X Window System. It was a thin layer of abstraction on top of raw Xlib calls that made it slightly less painful to create scroll bars, text entry boxes, and other typical GUI elements. It is part of the standard X11 distribution.

✦ **3-D Athena Toolkit** — The 3-D Athena Toolkit was a 3-D version of the original Athena toolkit. It gave Athena a 3-D look and was a considerable visual improvement over plain vanilla Athena. The 3-D Athena Toolkit, although no longer widely used, is still available on the Web at `www.visi.com/~hawkeyd/xaw3d.html`.

✦ **FLTK** — FLTK, which is pronounced "full tick," is an acronym for the Fast Light Toolkit. FLTK is a GUI for X, MacOS X, and Microsoft Windows. Written in C++, FLTK makes it possible to write GUIs that look almost identical regardless of the platform on which the GUI runs. FLTK also supports OpenGL graphics. You can find more information about FLTK on the Web at `www.fltk.org`.

✦ **XForms** — XForms is a GUI toolkit based on Xlib. It isn't highly configurable like the other GUI toolkits discussed in this section, but its simplicity makes XForms easier to use than the other graphical toolkits. It comes with a GUI builder that makes it fast and easy to get working application up and running. More information about XForms can be found on the Web at `http://world.std.com/~xforms/`.

✦ **OpenGL** — OpenGL is the industry-standard 3-D graphics toolkit. It provides the most realistic and lifelike graphics currently available for the X Window System. It is generally available as part of XFree86. More information about OpenGL is available on the Web at `www.opengl.org`.

✦ **Motif** — Motif was one of the first widget or interface toolkits available for the X Window System that combined both an interface toolkit and a window manager. Originally available only as a commercial product, it is now available in an open source version at `www.openmotif.org`.

✦ **Xlib** — Xlib is shorthand for the X library, a low-level, C-based interface to the raw X Window System protocol . If you want to write as close to the X graphics core as possible, you write Xlib-based programs. Indeed, most window managers, widget libraries, and GUI toolkits are written using Xlib function. While using straight Xlib gives you the best performance, it is extremely code intensive. Xlib is an essential ingredient of the standard X distribution. You can learn more about Xlib from the HTML manual page, available on the Web at `www.the-labs.com/X11/XLib-Manual`.

✦ **Xt** — The Xt Intrinsics are a very thin layer of functions and data structures on top of Xlib. Xt Intrinsics create an object-oriented interface that C programs can use to create graphical elements. Without other widget sets, the Intrinsics are not especially useful. Xt, like Xlib, is a part of the standard X distribution and is not available separately.

Application Programming Interfaces

Application programming interfaces, or APIs, provide programmers with libraries of code for performing certain tasks. There are many APIs, probably as many as there are types of programming problems that need to be solved. The ncurses library, for example, provides an API that you can use to create text-mode user interfaces. In turn, ncurses works by using either the terminfo or termcap API to perform the actual screen updates in a manner consistent with the underlying type of display device in use. If developers keep having to perform a specific type of programming task, such as updating a database, communicating over a network, getting sound out of a sound card, or performing complicated mathematical calculations, there is at least one database API, socket API, sound API, or mathematical API already in existence that they can use to simplify the task.

APIs consist of three components:

✦ **Header file** — Declares the interface (the function calls, macros, and data structures) the developers can use in their own programs.

✦ **One or more library files** — Implement the interfaces declared in the header files and against which programs must be linked.

✦ **API documentation** — Describes how to use the API and often provides example code. The documentation might be provided in manual pages, text files, HTML files, GNU TeXinfo files, or some combination of all of these formats.

Table 27-1 describes many popular or widely used APIs, but the list provided here is far from complete.

<table>
<tr><td colspan="3" align="center">Table 27-1
Common Linux APIs</td></tr>
</table>

API	Category	Description
Aalib	ASCII art	AA-lib is an ASCII art graphics library output as ASCII art.
Arts	Sound	The analog real-time synthesizer (aRts) is KDE's core sound system, designed to create and process sound using small, specialized modules. These modules might create a waveform, play samples, filter data, add signals, perform effects (like delay, flanger, or chorus), or output the data to the sound card.
Atk	Accessibility	atk is a library of accessibility functions used by GNOME.
Audiofile	Audio	audiofile, used by the esound daemon (Enlightened Sound Daemon), is a library for processing various audio file formats. You can also use it to develop your own audio-file-based applications.
db4	Database	The Berkeley Database (Berkeley DB) library enables developers to create applications with database support.
Expat	XML	Expat is a stream-oriented C library for parsing XML. It is used by Python, GNOME, Xft2, and other applications.
Gdbm	Database	The GNU Database Manager (GDBM) is a set of database routines that work similar to the standard UNIX dbm routines.
gdk-pixbuf	2-D Graphics	GdkPixbuf is an API for loading, scaling, compositing, and animating images. GdkPixBuf is required by many GTK+ programs.
Glib	General	GLib is a general purpose API of C language routines. The library includes support for features such as lists, trees, hashes, memory allocation, and many other things. GLib is required by almost every GTK+ application.
Glut	3-D Graphics	The GL Utility Toolkit (GLUT) is a 3-D graphics library based on the OpenGL API. It provides a higher-level interface for creation OpenGL-based graphics.
Gmp	Mathematics	The GNU Multiple Precision (GMP) API implements a library for arbitrary precision arithmetic, such as operations on signed integers, rational numbers, and floating-point numbers.
Gnet	Network	GNet is an object-oriented library of network routines. Written in C and based on the GLib library, GNet is used by gnomeicu and Pan.

Continued

Table 27-1 *(continued)*

API	Category	Description
Imlib	Graphics	ImLib (image library) is an image loading and rendering API designed to simplify and speed up the process of loading images and obtaining X Window System.
Libao	Audio	libao is a cross-platform audio library used by other libraries and programs that use audio, including ogg123, GAIM, and the Ogg Vorbis libraries.
libart_lgpl	2-D Graphics	Libart is a library for high-performance 2-D graphics used by KDE and GNOME.
Libexif	Graphics	This library provides an API allowing programs to read, parse, edit, and save Exchangeable Image File Format (EXIF) data in image files. EXIF is a format used to store extra information in images, such as the JPEG files produced by digital cameras.
Libglade	Graphics	The GLADE library, used heavily in GNOME programs, allows programs to load user interfaces from definitions stored in external files. This allows the interface to be changed without recompiling the program.
libid3tag	Audio	libid3tag is a library for reading ID3 tags. ID3 tags allow extra information to be embedded in audio files.
libieee1284	Hardware	libieee1284 enables applications that need to communicate with (or at least identify) devices that are attached via IEEE1284-compliant parallel ports, such as scanners.
Libjpeg	Graphics	The JPEG library provides a rich API for manipulating JPEG-format images, including reading, writing, converting, compressing, and decompressing images.
Libmad	Audio	libmad provides a high-quality MPEG audio decoder API. libmad provides full 24-bit PCM output, so applications using this API can produce high-quality audio.
Libmng	Graphics	libmng implements the Multiple-image Network Graphics (*MNG*) API. MNG provides multi-image animation capabilities similar to animated GIFs, but free of patent encumbrances.
Libogg	Audio	libogg is a library for reading and writing ogg format bitstreams. libogg is needed to use the Ogg Vorbis audio format.
Libpng	Graphics	The Portable Network Graphics (PNG) standard is an extensible file format for the lossless, portable, well-compressed storage of images. PNG provides a patent-free replacement for GIF.
Libtermcap	Hardware	libtermcap implements the GNU termcap library API, a library of C functions that enable programs to send control strings to terminals in a way independent of the terminal type.

API	*Category*	*Description*
Libtiff	2-D Graphics	The TIFF library provides an API for working with images stored in the Tag Image File Format (TIFF), a widely used format for storing high-quality, high-resolution images.
Libungif	2-D Graphics	libungif provides an API unencumbered by patents for loading and saving images in GIF format.
Libusb	Hardware	libusb allows user space application access to USB devices.
Libvorbis	Audio	This library supports the Vorbis General Audio Compression Codec, commonly known as Ogg Vorbis. Ogg Vorbis is an open, patent-and-royalty-free, general-purpose compressed audio format for audio and music.
Libwmf	Graphics	libwmf provides an API for interpreting, displaying, and converting metafile images to standard image formats such as PNG, JPEG, PS, EPS and SVG.
libxml2	XML	libxml2 is the XML parser library used by GNOME and KDE.
Libxslt	XML	libxslt provides XSLT support for libxml2. XSLT is a language used to transform XML documents into other formats.
Orbit	CORBA	ORBit is a high-performance Common Object Request Broker Architecture (CORBA) object request broker (ORB). ORBit allows programs to send requests and receive replies from other programs, regardless of the locations of the two programs. GNOME uses ORBit heavily.
Pango	Text layout	Pango is a library for layout and rendering of text, with an emphasis on internationalization. Pango forms the core of text and font handling in GTK+-2.0.
Pcre	Regular expressions	The Perl-compatible regular expression (PCRE) library implements an API for regular expression pattern matching that uses the same syntax and semantics as Perl 5. The PCRE library is used by many programs.
pilot-link	PalmOS	pilot-link implements a library for communicating with Palm handheld devices and with other devices that adhere to the PalmOS interface standard. gnome-pilot and KPilot.use pilot-link.
Popt	General	popt is a C library for parsing command-line parameters. popt was heavily influenced by the `getopt()` and `getopt_long()` functions, but improves on them by allowing more powerful argument expansion and allows command-line arguments to be aliased via configuration files.
Sdl	Multimedia	The Simple DirectMedia Layer (SDL) provides a generic, cross-platform API for low-level access to audio, keyboards, mice, joysticks, 3-D hardware via OpenGL, and 2-D framebuffers.

Continued

	Table 27-1 *(continued)*	
API	**Category**	**Description**
t1lib	Graphics	t1lib provides an API for generating character and string glyphs from Adobe Type 1 fonts.
Taglib	Audio	TagLib is a library for reading and editing the meta-data stored in ID3v1 and ID3v2 (MP3 files) and Ogg Vorbis comments and ID3 tags Ogg Vorbis.
Zlib	Data Compression	zlib provides a general-purpose, thread-safe data compression library that implements the data formats defined by RFC1950, RFC1951, and RFC1952 (see `ftp://ds.internic.net/rfc/rfc1950.txt`, `ftp://ds.internic.net/rfc/rfc1951.txt`, and `ftp://ds.internic.net/rfc/rfc1952.txt`).

As you can see, a wide variety of APIs exist for performing an equally wide variety of programming tasks. Chances are pretty good that if you need to perform some sort of programming task, someone has written a library that you can use to do it.

Summary

The phrase "Linux programming environments and interfaces" is a shorthand term that masks a rich set of features which, taken together, only partially characterize the activity of programming on a Linux system. This chapter looked at both graphical programming IDEs and the less visually attractive but just as powerful command-line or text-mode programming environments. You also learned some of the characteristics of Linux and of Linux systems that define and shape programming and programs on and for Linux. The second part of the chapter looked at the variety of programming interfaces, the methods available for getting particular programming tasks done. You learned that you can create text-mode or command-line interfaces and that you could choose from a variety of graphical interfaces for structuring user interaction with your program. Finally, you took a fast-paced look at some of the many APIs that make it possible to do a variety of things, such as manipulate or create images or interact with a database.

✦   ✦   ✦

Programming Tools and Utilities

The preceding chapter provided a high-level view of Linux programming, focusing on overall development environment and the introducing the idioms that give programming on a Linux system its distinctive character. This chapter goes into greater detail and describes some of the tools and toys found on a typical Linux development system. The goal is not to turn you into a developer in 30 pages or less, but simply to explore some of the variety of tools developers use so you will at least know what they are and what they do. You'll also learn how to use some of the programs and utilities.

The Well-Stocked Toolkit

Whether you prefer a graphical development environment or the classic command-line environment, you need a good set of tools if you want to write, compile, and debug programs for Linux. The good news is that Linux has plenty of editors, compilers, and debuggers from which to choose. The bad news is that Linux has plenty of editors, compilers, and debuggers from which to choose. The range of options is good news for developers because they can pick the best and most appropriate tools for the development task at hand. The proliferation of choices is bad news for system administrators who need to install and maintain the tools and for people who evaluate the tools. Too many choices make choosing the right one a difficult task. This chapter discusses the most popular programs and utilities of their types. In most cases, alternatives (and sometimes multiple alternatives), exist, but I only cover one to keep the discussion simple (I try to mention the others just so you'll be familiar with their names).

What constitutes a well-stocked Linux development toolkit? The basics include an editor to write the code, one or more compilers to turn source code into binaries, and a debugger to track down the inevitable bugs. Most people have a favorite editor, and you'd have a difficult time trying to persuade them to try a new one. Most editors support some set of programming-related functionality (some more than others, to be sure). There are too many to cover in this space, so suffice it to say, "You'll need an editor."

Perhaps the most popular editors are vi and emacs. Vi is a commercial editor, being part of the commercial UNIX offerings, so what you can actually get is usually a clone such as vim, elvis, or (my own personal favorite) nvi (*new* vi). I prefer nvi because it is a port of vi from BSD UNIX to Linux. Other popular editors include pico (the Pine mail client editor made available as a separate program), jed, joe, jove, and nano. If you prefer graphical editors, gedit in GNOME and kedit in KDE also provide basic programming support.

When it comes to compilers, GCC is the compiler of choice, or, if you will, the choice of the GNU generation, so this chapter only discusses GCC. Other compilers are available for Linux, such as Intel's C and C++ compiler and a very powerful (and expensive) offering from the Portland Compiler Group. Similarly, GDB, the GNU debugger, is the only debugger described in this chapter.

In Chapter 27 you examined the role that programming interfaces play in simplifying the development task. Interfaces almost always include one or more libraries that implement the functionality that interfaces define. Because you need to be able to work with programming libraries, utilities for creating, examining, and manipulating libraries also occupy the well-stocked programming toolkit.

To this list, most developers would add a build automation tool, such as make, because most nontrivial projects need some sort of utility that handles building and rebuilding complicated, multifile projects with a minimum of effort and time.

Another challenge for large projects is tracking changes in source code and maintaining a record of what code changed, when it changed, how it changed, and who changed it. This task is the province of source code control systems, and this chapter looks at two: RCS and CVS.

Using the GCC Compiler

The GNU Compiler Collection (GCC) is by far the most dominant compiler (rather, the most dominant collection of compilers) used on Linux systems. It compiles programs written in C, C++, or Objective-C. GCC also compiles Fortran (under the auspices of g77) and Java (using gcj). This chapter focuses on the C compiler. GCC gives programmers extensive control over the compilation process. That process includes up to four stages: preprocessing, compilation, assembly, and linking. You can stop the process after any of these stages to examine the compiler's output at that stage. GCC can also handle the various C dialects, such as ANSI C or traditional

(Kernighan and Ritchie) C. You can control the amount and type of debugging information, if any, to embed in the resulting binary. And like most compilers, GCC can also perform code optimization.

The gcc command invokes the C compiler. To use it, provide it the name of a C source file and use its -o option to specify the name of the output file. gcc will preprocess, compile, assemble, and link the program, generating an executable, often called a binary. Here's the simplest syntax :

```
gcc infile.c [-o outfile]
```

infile.c is a C source code file and -o says to name the output file outfile. The [] characters indicate optional arguments throughout this book. If the name of the output file is not specified, gcc names the output file a.out by default.

The following example uses gcc to create the hello program from the source file hello.c. First, the source code:

```
/*
 * hello.c - canonical hello world program
 */
#include

int main(int argc, char *argv[])
{
        printf("Hello, Linux programming world!\n");
        return 0;
}
```

Now, to compile and run this program, type

```
$ gcc hello.c -o hello
```

If all goes well, gcc does its job silently and returns to the shell prompt. It compiles and link the source file hello.c (gcc hello.c), creating a binary named hello, as specified using the -o hello argument.

If you run the program, here's the output you get:

```
$ ./hello
Hello, Linux programming world!
```

Caution The command that executed the hello program specifically included the current directory, denoted with a ., because having the current directory in your path is a security risk. That is, instead of a $PATH environment variable that resembles /bin:/usr/bin:/usr/local/bin:., it should be /bin:/usr/bin:/usr/local/bin so that a cracker cannot put a dangerous command in your current directory that happens to match the name of the more benign command you really want to execute.

GCC relies on file extensions to determine what kind of source code file it is, that is, in which programming language the source code is written. Table 28-1 lists the most common extensions and how GCC interprets them.

	Table 28-1 **GCC's File Naming Conventions**	
Extension	**Type**
.a, .so	Compiled library code
.c	C language source code
.C, .cc	C++ language source code
.i	Preprocessed C source code
.ii	Preprocessed C++ source code
.m	Objective-C source code
.o	Compiled object code
.S, .s	Assembly language source code

Compiling Multiple Source Code Files

Most nontrivial programs consist of multiple source files, and each source file must be compiled to object code before the final link step. To do so, provide gcc the name of each source code file it has to compile. GCC handles the rest. The gcc invocation might resemble:

```
$ gcc file1.c file2.c file3.c -o progname
```

gcc would create *file1.o*, *file2.o*, and *file3.o* and then link them all together to create *progname*. As an alternative, you can use gcc's -c option on each file individually, which creates object files from each file. Then in a second step, you link the object files together to create an executable. Thus, the single command just shown becomes:

```
$ gcc -c file1.c
$ gcc -c file2.c
$ gcc -c file3.c
$ gcc file1.o file2.o file3.o -o progname
```

One reason to do this is to avoid recompiling files that haven't changed. If you only change the source code in file3.c, for example, you wouldn't need to recompile file1.c and file2.c to recreate progname. Another reason to compile source code files individually before linking them to create the executable is to avoid long-running compilation. Compiling multiple files in a single gcc invocation can take awhile if one of the source code modules is really lengthy.

Let's take a look at an example that creates a single binary executable from multiple source code files. The example program named newhello is comprised of a C source code file, showit.c (Listing 28-1); a header file, msg.h (Listing 28-2); and another C source code file, msg.c (Listing 28-3).

Listing 28-1: **Main Program for newhello**

```
/*
 * showit.c _ driver
 */
#include
#include "msg.h"

int main(int argc, char *argv[])
{
        char msg_hi[] = { "Hi there, programmer!" };
        char msg_bye[] = { "Goodbye, programmer!" };

        printf("%s\n", msg_hi);
        prmsg(msg_bye);
        return 0;
}
```

Listing 28-2: **Header file for newhello Helper Function**

```
/*
 * msg.h - header for msg.c
 */

#ifndef MSG_H_
#define MSG_H_

void prmsg(char *msg);

#endif /* MSG_H_ */
```

> **Listing 28-3: Definitions for newhello Helper Function**
>
> ```
> /*
>  * msg.c - function declared in msg.h
>  */
> #include
> #include "msg.h"
>
> void prmsg(char *msg)
> {
>         printf("%s\n", msg);
> }
> ```

The command to compile these programs to create `newhello` is

```
$ gcc msg.c showit.c -o newhello
```

To create the object files individually, you might use the following commands:

```
$ gcc -c msg.c
$ gcc -c showit.c
```

Then, to create `newhello` from the object files, use the following command:

```
$ gcc msg.o showit.o -o newhello
```

Running this program, the output is:

```
$ ./newhello
Hi there, programmer!
Goodbye, programmer!
```

Before it creates the `newhello` binary, `gcc` creates object files for each source file. Typing long commands like this does become tedious, however. The section titled "Automating Builds with Make" later in this chapter shows you how to avoid having to type long, involved command lines.

GCC Command-Line Options

The list of command-line options GCC accepts runs to several pages, so Table 28-2 describes only the most common ones.

Table 28-2
GCC Command-Line Options

Option	Description
`-ansi`	Supports the ANSI/ISO C standard, turning off GNU extensions that conflict with the standard.
`-c`	Compiles without linking, resulting in an object file but not an executable binary.
`-Dfoo=bar`	Defines a preprocessor macro *foo* with a value of *bar* on the command line.
`-g`	Includes standard debugging information in the binary.
`-ggdb`	Includes lots of debugging information in the binary that only the GNU debugger (GDB) can understand.
`-Idirname`	Prepends *dirname* to the list of directories searched for include files.
`-Ldirname`	Prepends *dirname* to the list of directories searched for library files. By default, gcc links against shared libraries.
`-lfoo`	Links against lib*foo*.
`-MM`	Outputs a make-compatible dependency list.
`-o file`	Creates the output file *file* (not necessary when compiling object code). If *file* not specified, the default is a.out.
`-O`	Optimizes the compiled code.
`-On`	Specifies an optimization level *n*, 0<=n<=3.
`-pedantic`	Emits all warnings required by the ANSI/ISO C standard.
`-pedantic-errors`	Emits all errors required by the ANSI/ISO C standard.
`-static`	Links against static libraries.
`-traditional`	Supports the Kernighan and Ritchie C syntax (if you don't understand what this means, don't worry about it).
`-v`	Shows the commands used in each step of compilation.
`-W`	Suppresses all warning messages.
`-Wall`	Emits all generally useful warnings that gcc can provide. Specific warnings can also be flagged using `-Wwarning`.
`-werror`	Converts all warnings into errors, stopping the compilation.

As mentioned earlier, -o *file* tells GCC to place output in the file *file* regardless of the output being produced. If you do not specify -o, for an input file named *file.* *suffix*, the defaults are to name the executable a.out, the object file *file*.o, and the assembly language file *file*.s. Preprocessor output goes to stdout.

Automating Builds with Make

The make utility is a tool to control the process of building and rebuilding software. Make automates what software gets built, how it gets built, and when it gets built, freeing programmers to concentrate on writing code. It also saves a lot of typing because it contains logic that invokes GCC compiler-appropriate options and arguments. Use this section to familiarize yourself with the look and layout of a makefile.

For all but the simplest software projects, make is essential. In the first place, projects composed of multiple source files require long, complex compiler invocations. Make simplifies this by storing these difficult command lines in the makefile, a text file that contains all of the commands required to build software projects.

Make is convenient for both the developer and the user who want to build a program. As developers make changes to a program, whether to add new features or incorporate bug fixes, make makes it possible to rebuild the program with a single, short command. Make is convenient for users because they don't have to read reams of documentation explaining in excruciating, mind-numbing detail how to build a program. Rather, they can simply be told to type **make** followed by **make test** followed by **make install**. Most users appreciate the convenience of simple build instructions.

Finally, make speeds up the edit-compile-debug process. It minimizes rebuild times because it is smart enough to determine which files have changed, and only recompiles files that have changed.

So, how does make accomplish its magical feats? By using a makefile, which contains rules that tell make what to build and how to build it. A rule consists of the following:

✦ A target, the "thing" make ultimately tries to create

✦ A list of one or more dependencies (usually files) required to build the target

✦ A list of commands to execute to create the target from the specified dependencies

Makefiles constitute a database of dependency information for the programs they build and automatically verify that all of the files necessary for building a program are available.

When invoked, GNU make looks for a file named GNUmakefile, makefile, or Makefile, in that order. For some reason, most Linux programmers use the last form, Makefile. Makefile rules have the general form

```
target : dependency dependency [...]
        command
        command
        [...]
```

target is usually the file, such as a binary or object file, to create. *dependency* is a list of one or more files required as input to create *target*. Each *command* is a step such as a compiler invocation or a shell command that is necessary to create *target*. Unless specified otherwise, make does all of its work in the current working directory.

Caution The first character in a *command* must be the tab character; eight spaces will not suffice. This often catches people unaware and can be a problem if your preferred editor "helpfully" translates tabs to eight spaces. If you try to use spaces instead of a tab, make displays the message `Missing separator` and stops.

Listing 28-4 shows a sample makefile for building a text editor imaginatively named editor.

Listing 28-4: **A Sample Makefile**

```
editor : editor.o screen.o keyboard.o
        gcc -o editor editor.o screen.o keyboard.o

editor.o : editor.c
        gcc -c editor.c

screen.o : screen.c
        gcc -c screen.c

keyboard.o : keyboard.c
        gcc -c keyboard.c

clean :
        rm -f *.o core *~

realclean : clean
        rm -f editor
```

To compile editor, you would simply type **make** in the directory that contains the makefile. It's that simple.

This example makefile has six rules. The first defines how to create the target named editor. The first target in every makefile is the default target (unless you specifically define one using the .DEFAULT directive, which is not covered in this chapter). The default target is the one that make builds if no target is specified as an argument to make. editor has three dependencies, editor.o, screen.o, and keyboard.o; these three files must exist to build `editor`. The second line in the first rule is the command that make must execute to create `editor`: `gcc -o editor editor.o screen.o keyboard.o`. It builds the executable from the three object files, `editor.o`, `screen.o`, and `keyboard.o`.

The next three rules tell make how to build the individual object files. Each rule consists of a one-object file target (`editor.o`, `screen,o`, `keyboard.o`); one source code file dependency (`editor.c`, `screen.c`, `keyboard.c`); and a rule that defines how to build that target.

The fifth rule defines a target named `clean` with no dependencies. When a target has no dependencies, its commands are executed whenever the target is invoked. In this case, `clean` deletes the constituent object files (`*.o`), plus any core files (`core`) as well as any Emacs backup files (`*~`) from previous builds.

The sixth rule defines a target named `realclean`. It uses the fifth rule as one of its dependencies. This causes make to build the `clean` target and then to remove the `editor` binary.

Here is where make's value becomes evident: Ordinarily, if you tried to build `editor` using the command from the second line, `gcc` would complain loudly and ceremoniously quit if the dependencies did not exist. Make, on the other hand, after determining that `editor` requires these files, first verifies that they exist and, if they don't, executes the commands to create them. After creating the dependencies, make returns to the first rule to create the editor executable. Of course, if the dependencies for the components, `editor.c`, `screen.c`, or `keyboard.c`, don't exist, make will give up because it lacks targets named, in this case, `editor.c`, `screen.c`, or `keyboard.c` (that is, no rules are defined in the makefile for creating `editor.c`, `screen.c`, and `keyboard.c`).

"All well and good," you are probably thinking, "but how does make know when to build or rebuild a file?" The answer is simple: If a specified target does not exist in a place where make can find it, make builds or rebuilds it. If the target does exist, make compares the timestamp on the target to the timestamp on the dependencies. If one or more of the dependencies are newer than the target, make rebuilds that target, assuming that the newer dependency implies some code change that must be incorporated into the target.

Library Utilities

Programming libraries are collections of code that can be reused across multiple software projects. Libraries are a classic example of software development's ardent goal, code reuse. They collect frequently used programming routines and utility code into a single location. The standard C libraries, for example, contain hundreds of frequently used routines, such as the output function `printf()` and the input function `getchar()` that would be wearisome to rewrite each time you create a new program. Beyond code reuse and programmer convenience, however, libraries provide a great deal of thoroughly debugged and well-tested utility code, such as routines for network programming, graphics handling, data manipulation, and system calls.

You need to know the tools at your disposal for creating, maintaining, and managing programming libraries. There are two types of libraries: static and shared. Static libraries are specially formatted files that contain object files, called modules or members, of reusable, precompiled code. They are stored in a special format along with a table or map that links symbol names to the members in which the symbols are defined. The map speeds up compilation and linking. Static libraries are typically named with the extension `.a`, which stands for archive.

Shared libraries, like static libraries, are files that contain other object files or pointers to other object files. They are called shared libraries because the code they contain is not linked into programs when the programs are compiled. Rather, the dynamic linker/loader links shared library code into programs at runtime. Shared libraries have several advantages over static libraries. First, they require fewer system resources. They use less disk space because shared library code is not compiled into each binary but linked and loaded from a single location dynamically at runtime. They use less system memory because the kernel shares the memory the library occupies among all the programs that use the library.

Second, shared libraries are slightly faster because they only need to be loaded into memory once. Finally, shared libraries simplify code and system maintenance. As bugs are fixed or features added, users need only obtain the updated library and install it. With static libraries, each program that uses the library must be recompiled.

The dynamic linker/loader `ld.so` links symbol names to the appropriate shared library in which they are defined at runtime. Shared libraries have a special name, the soname, that consists of the library name and the major version number. The full name of the C library on one of my systems, for example, is libc-2.3.2.so. The library name is libc.so; the major version number is 2; the minor version number is 3; and the release or patch level is 2. For historical reasons, the C library's soname is libc.so.6. Minor version numbers and patch level numbers change as bugs are fixed, but the soname remains the same and newer versions are usually compatible with older versions.

I emphasize the soname because applications link against it. How does linking work? The ldconfig utility creates a symbolic link from the actual library, say libc-2.3.2.so, to the soname, libc.so.6, and stores this information in `/etc/ld.so.cache`. At runtime, `ld.so` scans the cache file, finds the required soname and, because of the symbolic link, loads the actual library into memory and links application function calls to the appropriate symbols in the loaded library.

The nm Command

The nm command lists all of the symbols encoded in an object or binary file. It's used to see what function calls a program makes or to see if a library or object file provides a needed function. nm has the following syntax:

```
nm [options] file
```

nm lists the symbols stored in *file*, which must be a static library or archive file, as described in the preceding section. *options* controls nm's behavior. Table 28-3 describes useful options for nm.

Table 28-3	
nm Command-Line Options	
Option	**Description**
-C	Converts symbol names into user-level names. This is especially useful for making C++ function names readable.
-l	Uses debugging information to print the line number where each symbol is defined, or the relocation entry if the symbol is undefined.
-s	When used on archive (.a) files, prints the index that maps symbol names to the modules or members in which the symbol is defined.
-u	Only displays undefined symbols, symbols defined externally to the file being examined.

Here's an example that uses nm to show some of the symbols in /usr/lib/libdl.a:

```
$ nm /usr/lib/libdl.a | head

dlopen.o:
00000040 T __dlopen_check
         U _dl_open
         U _dlerror_run
00000040 W dlopen
00000000 t dlopen_doit

dlclose.o:
         U _dl_close
```

The ar Command

ar creates, modifies, or extracts archives. It is most commonly used to create static libraries, which are files that contain one or more object files. ar also creates and maintains a table that cross-references symbol names to the members in which they are defined. The ar command has the following syntax:

```
ar {dmpqrtx} [options] [member] archive file [...]
```

ar creates the archive named *archive* from the file(s) listed in *file*. At least one of d, m, p, q, r, t, and x is required. You will usually use r. Table 28-4 lists the most commonly used ar options.

	Table 28-4 ar Command-Line Options	
Option	**Description**
-c	Creates a new archive file *archive* if it doesn't exist, suppressing the warning ar would emit if *archive* doesn't already exist.
-q	Adds files to the end of *archive* without checking for replacements.
-r	Inserts files into *archive*, replacing any existing members whose name matches that being added. New members are added at the end of the archive.
-s	Creates or updates the map linking symbols to the member in which they are defined.

Tip
Given an archive created with the ar command, you can speed up access to the archive by creating an index to the archive. ranlib does precisely this, storing the index in the archive file itself. ranlib's syntax is:

```
ranlib [-v|-V] file
```

This generates a symbol map in *file*. It is equivalent to ar -s *file*.

The ldd Command

While nm lists the symbols defined in an object file, unless you know what library defines which functions, it is not terribly helpful. That is ldd's job. It lists the shared libraries that a program requires to run. Its syntax is:

```
ldd [options] file
```

lddd prints the names of the shared libraries *file* requires. Two of lddd's most useful options are -d, which reports any missing functions, and -r, which reports missing functions *and* missing data objects. For example, the following lddd reports that the mail client mutt (which may or may not be installed on your system) requires eight shared libraries.

```
$ ldd /usr/bin/mutt
        libncursesw.so.5 => /lib/libncursesw.so.5 (0x40021000)
        libssl.so.0 => /usr/lib/libssl.so.0 (0x40066000)
        libcrypto.so.0 => /usr/lib/libcrypto.so.0 (0x40097000)
        libc.so.6 => /lib/libc.so.6 (0x40195000)
        libgpm.so.1 => /lib/libgpm.so.1 (0x402c5000)
        libdl.so.2 => /lib/libdl.so.2 (0x402cb000)
        /lib/ld-linux.so.2 => /lib/ld-linux.so.2 (0x40000000)
        libncurses.so.5 => /lib/libncurses.so.5 (0x402ce000)
```

The output might be different on your system.

The ldconfig Command

ldconfig determines the runtime links required by shared libraries that are located in /usr/lib and /lib, specified in libs on the command line, and stored in /etc/ld.so.conf. It works in conjunction with ld.so, the dynamic linker/loader, to create and maintain links to the most current versions of shared libraries available on a system. It has the following syntax:

```
ldconfig [options] [libs]
```

A bare ldconfig simply updates the cache file, /etc/ld.so.cache. *options* controls ldconfig's behavior. The -v option tells ldconfig to be verbose as it updates the cache. The -p option says to print without updating the current list of shared libraries about which ld.so knows.

Environment Variables and Configuration Files

The dynamic linker/loader ld.so uses a number of environment variables to customize and control its behavior. The first variable is $LD_LIBRARY_PATH, a colon-separated list of directories in which to search for shared libraries at runtime. It is similar to the $PATH environment variable. A second important variable is $LD_PRELOAD, which is a whitespace-separated list of additional, user-specified shared libraries to load before all other libraries. It is used selectively to override functions in other shared libraries.

ld.so also uses two configuration files whose purposes parallel those environment variables. /etc/ld.so.conf contains a list of directories that the linker/loader should search for shared libraries in addition to the standard directories, /usr/lib and /lib. /etc/ld.so.preload is a disk-based version of the $LD_PRELOAD environment variable; it contains a whitespace-separated list of shared libraries to be loaded prior to executing a program. You can use $LD\_PRELOAD$ to override installed versions of a library with a specific version; this is often useful when you are testing a new (or different) library version but don't want to install the replacement library on your system.

Source Code Control

Version control is an automated process for keeping track of and managing changes made to source code files. Why bother? Because one day you *will* make that one fatal edit to a source file, delete its predecessor, and forget exactly which line or lines of code you "fixed"; because simultaneously keeping track of the current release, the next release, and eight bug fixes manually *will* become mind-numbing and confusing; because frantically searching for the backup tape because one of your colleagues overwrote a source file for the fifth time *will* drive you over the edge; because, one day, over your morning cappuccino, you will say to yourself, "Version control, it's the Right Thing to Do."

Source Code Control Using RCS

The Revision Control System (RCS) is a common solution to the version control problem. RCS, which is maintained by the GNU project, is available on almost all UNIX systems, not just on Linux. Two alternatives to RCS are the Concurrent Version System (CVS), which also is maintained by the GNU project, and the Source Code Control System (SCCS), a proprietary product.

Before proceeding, however, Table 28-5 lists a few terms that will be used throughout the chapter. Because they are so frequently used, I want to make sure you understand their meaning insofar as RCS and version control in general are concerned.

Table 28-5 Version Control Terms	
Term	**Description**
Lock	A working file retrieved for editing such that no one else can edit it simultaneously. A working file is locked by the first user against edits by other users.
RCS file	Any file located in an RCS directory, controlled by RCS, and accessed using RCS commands. An RCS file contains all versions of a particular file. Normally, an RCS file has a .v extension.
Revision	A specific, numbered version of a source file. Revisions begin with 1.1 and increase incrementally, unless forced to use a specific revision number.
Working file	One or more files retrieved from the RCS source code repository (the RCS directory) into the current working directory and available for editing.

RCS manages multiple versions of files, usually but not necessarily source code files. It automates file version storage and retrieval, change logging, access control, release management, and revision identification and merging. As an added bonus, RCS minimizes disk space requirements because it tracks only file changes.

One of RCS's attractions is its simplicity. With only a few commands, you can accomplish a great deal.

Checking Files In and Out

You can accomplish a lot with RCS using only two commands (ci and co) and a directory named RCS. ci stands for *check in*, which means storing a working file in the RCS directory; co means *check out* and refers to retrieving an RCS file from the RCS repository. To get started, you need to create an RCS directory. All RCS commands will use this directory if it is present in your current working directory. The RCS directory is also called the *repository*. When you check a file in, RCS asks for a description of the file, copies it to the RCS directory, and deletes the original. "Deletes the original?" Ack! Don't worry, you can retrieve it with the check out command, co.

Here's how to create an RCS directory:

```
$ mkdir RCS
```

Next, create the following source file shown (howdy.c) in the same directory in which you created the RCS directory.

```
/*
 * $Id$
 * howdy.c - Sample to demonstrate RCS Usage
 */
#include <stdio.h>

int main(void)
{
    fprintf(stdout,  Howdy, Linux programmer!");
    return EXIT_SUCCESS;
}
```

Now, use the command ci howdy.c to check the file into the repository:

```
$ ci howdy.c
RCS/howdy.c,v  <--  howdy.c
enter description, terminated with single '.' or end of file:
NOTE: This is NOT the log message!
>> Simple program to illustrate RCS usage
>> .
initial revision: 1.1
done
```

With the file safely checked into the repository, you can check it out and modify it. To check a file out for editing, use the `co` command. Here's an example:

```
$ co -l howdy.c
RCS/howdy.c,v  -->  howdy.c
revision 1.1 (locked)
done
```

The working file you just checked out is editable. If you do not want to edit it, omit the `-l` option.

Making Changes to Repository Files

To see version control in action, make a change to the working file. If you haven't already done so, check out and lock the `howdy.c` file. Change anything you want, but I recommend adding `\n` to the end of `fprintf()`'s string argument because Linux (and UNIX), unlike DOS and Windows, do not automatically add a newline to the end of console output. Then, check the file back in and RCS will increment the revision number to 1.2, ask for a description of the change you made, incorporate the changes you made into the RCS file, and (annoyingly) delete the original. To prevent deletion of your working files during check-in operations, use the `-l` or `-u` option with `ci`. Here's an example:

```
$ ci -l howdy.c
RCS/howdy.c,v  <--  howdy.c
new revision: 1.2; previous revision: 1.1
enter log message, terminated with single '.' or end of file:
>> Added newline
>> .
done
```

When used with `ci`, both the `-l` and `-u` options cause an implied check out of the file after the check-in procedure completes. `-l` locks the file so you can continue to edit it, while `-u` checks out an unlocked or read-only working file.

Additional Command-Line Options

In addition to `-l` and `-u`, `ci` and `co` accept two other very useful options: `-r` (for revision) and `-f` (force). Use `-r` to tell RCS which file revision you want to manipulate. RCS assumes you want to work with the most recent revision; `-r` overrides this default. The `-f` option forces RCS to overwrite the current working file. By default, RCS aborts a check-out operation if a working file of the same name already exists in your working directory. So if you really botch up your working file, use the `-f` option with `co` to get a fresh start.

RCS's command-line options are cumulative, as you might expect, and RCS does a good job of disallowing incompatible options. To check out and lock a specific revision of howdy.c, you would use a command like co -l -r2.1 howdy.c. Similarly, ci -u -r3 howdy.c checks in howdy.c, assigns it revision number 3.1, and deposits a read-only revision 3.1 working file back into your current working directory.

The following example creates revision 2.1 of howdy.c. Make sure you have checked out and changed howdy.c somehow before executing this command.

```
$ ci -r2 howdy.c
RCS/howdy.c,v  <-- howdy.c
new revision: 2.1; previous revision: 1.2
enter log message, terminated with single '.' or end of file:
>> Added something
>> .
done
```

This command is equivalent to ci -r2.1 howdy.**c**.

The next example checks out revision 1.2 of howdy.c, disregarding the presence of higher-numbered revisions in the working directory.

```
$ co -r1.2 howdy.c
RCS/howdy.c,v  --> howdy.c
revision 1.2
done
```

The handy command shown next discards all of the changes you've made and lets you start over with a known good source file.

```
$ co -l -f howdy.c
RCS/howdy.c,v  --> howdy.c
revision 2.1 (locked)
done
```

When used with ci, -f forces RCS to check in a file even if it has not changed.

Source Code Control with CVS

You may have noticed that RCS has some shortcomings that make it inadequate for use on large projects. First, without some sophisticated wrapper scripts to provide the directory handling machinery, RCS doesn't work very well with a single, centralized repository. Its repository is always the current directory unless you exert yourself to use a directory located elsewhere. More pertinent for Linux and other open source projects, RCS is utterly unsuitable for distributed development because it doesn't support network protocols. (That is, it doesn't work over the Internet.)

The Concurrent Versions System (CVS) supports both centralized repositories and network-based access. It is well-suited for use by multiple programmers, and a single CVS repository can support multiple projects. To keep the discussion simple, however, the example in this chapter deals only with a repository accessed locally. The following steps resemble the process described earlier for RCS, but they are slightly more involved and obviously use CVS concepts.

1. Create a CVS repository:

```
$ mkdir /space/cvs
$ export CVSROOT=/space/cvs
$ cvs init
```

The first command creates a directory named /space/cvs in which to establish the repository. The second command defines the environment variable $CVSROOT with this directory. Defining $CVSROOT makes using CVS much simpler. The third command initializes the repository, which creates some administrative directories CVS needs to work properly.

2. Create a top-level working directory in which to store your various projects and then cd into it:

```
$ mkdir projects
$ cd projects
```

3. Check out a copy of the CVS root directory into the top-level projects directory you just created:

```
$ cvs -d $CVSROOT co -l .
cvs checkout: Updating .
```

The -d option tells cvs the directory containing the CVS repository ($CVSROOT, or /space/cvs); co means check out (just as with RCS); the -l option, which stands for local, means to work only in the current directory rather than recursing through subdirectories; and the . specifies the current directory.

4. Create a directory to hold a project and add it to the repository:

```
$ mkdir newhello
$ cvs add newhello
Directory /space/cvs/newhello added to the repository
```

5. cd into the new directory, copy your project files into it, and then add those files (and any directories that might be present) to the repository:

```
$ cp /projects/* .
$ cvs add *
Directory /space/cvs/newhello/debugme added to the repository
cvs add: scheduling file `hello.c' for addition
cvs add: scheduling file `msg.c' for addition
cvs add: scheduling file `showit.c' for addition
cvs add: use 'cvs commit' to add these files permanently
```

6. Do as the instructions recommend; execute the command `cvs commit` to make the added files and directories permanent:

```
$ cvs commit
cvs commit: Examining .
RCS file: /space/cvs/newhello/hello.c,v
done
Checking in hello.c;
/space/cvs/newhello/hello.c,v  <--  hello.c
initial revision: 1.1
done
RCS file: /space/cvs/newhello/msg.c,v
done
Checking in msg.c;
/space/cvs/newhello/msg.c,v  <--  msg.c
initial revision: 1.1
done
RCS file: /space/cvs/newhello/showit.c,v
done
Checking in showit.c;
/space/cvs/newhello/showit.c,v  <--  showit.c
initial revision: 1.1
done
```

Notice that CVS uses RCS file-naming conventions to work with files in the repository. This is because CVS was built on top of RCS and retains compatibility with the basic RCS feature set.

CVS handles checking files in and out slightly differently than RCS. When checking a file out, it isn't necessary to specifically request a lock to get a writable copy of the file. To work on a file, you do need to use the `checkout` or `co` command:

```
$ cd ~/projects
$ cvs -d /space/cvs co newhello
cvs checkout newhello
U newhello/hello.c
U newhello/msg.c
U newhello/showit.c
```

The checkout command used in this example specifies the path to the repository using the `-d` option. This is unnecessary if you set the `$CVSROOT` environment variable. After you have made changes to files, you can check them in using the `cvs commit` command (`commit` is comparable to RCS's `ci` command):

```
$ cd ~/project/newhello
$ cvs commit .
cvs commit: Examining .
[editor session]
Checking in showit.c;
/space/cvs/newhello/showit.c,v  <--  showit.c
new revision: 1.2; previous revision: 1.1
done
```

When you check in a modified file, CVS opens an editor session to enable you to enter a log message that describes the changes you made. The editor used is the editor defined in the $EDITOR environment variable or compiled-in default (usually vi) if $EDITOR is undefined. This example did not use the -d option because the $CVSROOT environment variable is set.

To check out a specific version, or revision, of a file, use the -r option following the checkout or co command, followed by a revision number. For example, to check out revision 1.1 of the showit.c file, use the following command:

```
$ cvs checkout -r 1.1 newhello/showit.c
U newhello/showit.c
```

To see the differences between two revisions, use the diff command, using the -r m.n, where m.n indicates the revision number you want to check. If you specify -r only once, the indicated version will be diffed against the working file. If you specify -r twice, the two versions will be diffed against each other. The following example compares revision 1.2 of showit.c to the current working revision (the revision that is currently in the working directory):

```
$ cvs diff -r 1.2 newhello/showit.c
Index: newhello/showit.c
===================================================================
RCS file: /space/cvs/newhello/showit.c,v
retrieving revision 1.2
retrieving revision 1.3
diff -r1.2 -r1.3
9,10c9,10
<        char msg_hi[] = { "Hi there, programmer!\n" };
<        char msg_bye[] = { "Goodbye, programmer!\n" };
---
>        char msg_hi[] = { "Hi there, programmer!" };
>        char msg_bye[] = { "Goodbye, programmer!" };
12c12
<        printf("%s", msg_hi);
---
>        printf("%s\n", msg_hi);
```

The diff output is easier to understand than you might expect. Lines that begin with < appear in the first file (revision 1.2 of showit.c) but not in the second (revision 1.3 of showit.c. Similarly, lines beginning with > appear in the second file but not in the first. Each section of diff output begins with an alphanumeric sequence such as 9,10c9,10 or 12c12. The numeric values indicate the lines in the first and second files to which an operation must be applied to get the second file from the first. The operation to perform, such as inserting, deleting, or changing lines, is specified by the alphabetic character. So, for example, the sequence 9,10c9,10 means that to create the second file from the first you have to change (c) lines 9 and 10 of the first file to lines 9 and 10 of the second file.

Finally, if you totally botch all of your changes to your working files and want to revert to the most recent versions, use the `update` command. It updates the specified directory with the most recent versions stored in the repository, as shown in the following example:

```
$ cd ~/projects/newhello
$ cvs update .
cvs udate: Updating .
U showit.c
U msg.c
U hello.c
```

There's much more to CVS than the few examples presented here. For additional information, visit the CVS home page on the Web at `www.cvshome.org`.

Debugging with GDB

Software is buggy, and some programs have more bugs than other programs. While debugging sessions will never be aggravation-free, GDB's advanced features lighten the load and enable you to be more productive in squashing bugs. Time and effort invested in learning GDB is well spent if you can track down and fix a serious bug in just a few minutes. GDB can make this happen. Most of what you will need to accomplish with GDB can be done with a surprisingly small set of commands. The rest of this chapter explores GDB features and shows you enough GDB commands to get you going.

Effective debugging requires that your source code be compiled with `-g` option to create a binary with an extended symbol table. For example, the following command:

```
$ gcc -g file1 file2 -o prog
```

causes *prog* to be created with debugging symbols in its symbol table. If you want, you can use GCC's `-ggdb` option to generate still more (GDB-specific) debugging information. However, to work most effectively, this option requires that you have access to the source code for every library against which you link. While this can be very useful in certain situations, it can also be expensive in terms of disk space. In most cases, you can get by with the plain `-g` option.

Starting GDB

To start a debugging session, simply type **gdb *progname***, replacing ***progname*** with the name of the program you want to debug. Using a core file is optional but will enhance GDB's debugging capabilities. Of course, you'll need a program on which to try out GDB debugging, so Listing 28-5 provides one: `debugme.c`.

Listing 28-5: **A Buggy Program**

```
/*
 * debugme.c - poorly written program to debug
 */

#include <stdio.h>
#define BIGNUM 5000

void index_to_the_moon(int ary[]);

int main(int argc, char *argv[])
{
        int intary[100];

        index_to_the_moon(intary);

        return 0;
}

void index_to_the_moon(int ary[])
{
        int i;
        for (i = 0; i < BIGNUM; ++i)
                ary[i] = i;
}
```

Compile this program using the command `gcc -g debugme.c -o debugme`. Then, execute the program using the command `./debugme`.

```
$ ./debugme
Segmentation fault (core dumped)
$ file core
core: ELF 32-big LSB core file Intel 80386, version 1 (SYSV
), SVR4-style, SVR4-stylee, from 'debugme'
```

On most systems, when you execute `./debugme`, it immediately causes a segmentation fault and dumps core, as shown in the output listing. If you don't see the "core dumped" message, try executing the shell command `ulimit -c unlimited`, which allows programs to drop a memory dump in their current working directory.

The program has a bug, so you need to debug it. The first step is to start GDB, using the program name, `debugme`, and the core file, `core`, as arguments:

```
$ gdb debugme core
```

After GDB initializes, the screen should resemble the one shown in Figure 28-1.

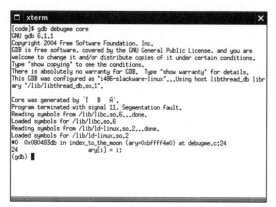

```
[code]$ gdb debugme core
GNU gdb 6.1.1
Copyright 2004 Free Software Foundation, Inc.
GDB is free software, covered by the GNU General Public License, and you are
welcome to change it and/or distribute copies of it under certain conditions.
Type "show copying" to see the conditions.
There is absolutely no warranty for GDB.  Type "show warranty" for details.
This GDB was configured as "i486-slackware-linux"...Using host libthread_db libr
ary "/lib/libthread_db.so.1".

Core was generated by `Ï Đ Ñ'.
Program terminated with signal 11, Segmentation fault.
Reading symbols from /lib/libc.so.6...done.
Loaded symbols for /lib/libc.so.6
Reading symbols from /lib/ld-linux.so.2...done.
Loaded symbols for /lib/ld-linux.so.2
#0  0x080483db in index_to_the_moon (ary=0xbffff4e0) at debugme.c:24
24                      ary[i] = i;
(gdb)
```

Figure 28-1: GDB's startup screen.

As you can see near the middle of the figure, GDB displays the name of the executable that created the core file: `Ï _ Ñ'. Obviously, the displayed name is wrong; it should be debugme. The odd characters and the incorrect program name would give an experienced developer an immediate clue that the program has a significant memory bug. The next line in the figure, the text that reads Program terminated with signal 11, Segmentation fault explains why the program terminated. A segmentation fault occurs anytime a program attempts to access memory that doesn't explicitly belong to it. GDB also helpfully displays the function it was executing, index_to_the_moon, and the line it believes caused the fault (line 24).

Tip   If you don't like the licensing messages (they annoy me), use the -q (or --quiet) option when you start GDB to suppress them. Another useful command-line option is -d dirname, where dirname is the name of a directory, which tells gdb where to find source code (it looks in the current working directory by default).

After you load the program and its core dump into the debugger, run the program in the debugger. To do so, type the command run at the GDB command prompt, (gdb), as the following example shows:

```
(gdb) run
Starting program: /home/kwall/code/debugme

Program received signal SIGSEGV, Segmentation fault.
0x0804483db in index_to_the_moon (ary=0xbffff4b0) at debugme.c:24
24                      ary[i] = i;
```

This short output listing shows that the segmentation fault occurred in the function index_to_the_moon at line 24 of debugme.c. Notice the last line of the output; GDB displays the line of code, prefixed with the line number (24), where the segmentation fault occurred. It also shows the memory address (in hexadecimal format) at which the fault occurred, 0xbffff4b0.

You can pass any arguments to the run command that your program would ordinarily accept. GDB also creates a full shell environment in which to run the program. Ordinarily, GDB uses the value of the environment variable $SHELL to create the simulated environment. If you want, however, you can use GDB's set and unset commands to set or unset arguments and environment variables before you use the run command to run the program in the debugger.

To set command-line arguments to pass to the program, type **set args *arg1 arg2***, where ***arg1*** and ***arg2*** (or any number of arguments) are options and arguments the program being debugged expects. Use **set environment *env1 env2*** to set environment variables (again, ***env1*** and ***env2*** are placeholders for the environment variables you want to set or unset).

Inspecting Code in the Debugger

What is happening in the function index_to_the_moon that's causing the error? You can execute the backtrace (or bt or back) command to generate the function tree that led to the segmentation fault. The backtrace doesn't usually show you *what* the problem is, but it does show you more precisely *where* the problem occurred. Here's how the function trace for the example looks on my system:

```
(gdb) backtrace
#0  0x080483db index_to_the_moon (ary=0x7ffffc90) at debugme.c:24
#1  0x080483a6 in main (argc=104,argv=0x69) at debugme.c:15
```

A backtrace shows the chain of function calls that resulted in the error. The backtrace starts with the most recently called function — index_to_the moon() in this case — which resides at the hexadecimal memory address shown in the second column of the display (0x0800483db). index_to_the_moon() was called by the main() function. As you can see from the output, the most recently called function was index_to_the_moon(), so, somewhere in the function, the segmentation fault occurred. Incidentally, the backtrace also shows that index_to_the_moon() was called from line 15 of the main() function in debugme.c.

Tip   It's not necessary to type complete command names while using GDB. Any sufficiently unique abbreviation works. For example, back suffices for backtrace.

It would be helpful, however, to have some idea of the context in which the offending line(s) of code exist. For this purpose, use the `list` command, which takes the general form, `list [m,n]`, where *m* and *n* are the starting and ending line numbers you want displayed. For example:

```
(gdb) list 10,32
```

would display code lines 10 through 32.

A bare `list` command displays 10 lines of code that includes the line where the error was first detected, as illustrated here:

```
(gdb) list
15                  index_to_the_moon(intary);
16
17                  exit(EXIT_SUCCESS);
18      }
19
20      void index_to_the_moon(int ary[])
21      {
22              int i;
23              for (i = 0; i < BIGNUM; ++I {
24                      ary[i] = i;
```

Examining Data

One of GDB's most useful features is its ability to display both the type and the value of almost any expression, variable, or array in the program being debugged. It can print the value of any expression legal in the language in which your program is written. The command is, predictably enough, `print`. Here are a couple of `print` commands and their results:

```
(gdb) print i
$1 = 724
(gdb) print ary[i]
Cannot access memory at address 0xc0000000.
```

This example continues the earlier examples of debugging `debugme.c` because you are still trying to identify where and why `debug me` crashed. Although in this example, the program crashed at the point when the counter variable `i` equaled 724 (the expression $1 refers to an entry in GDB's value history, explained in a moment), where it crashes on your system depends on the system's memory layout, the process's memory space (especially the kernel's stack space), the amount of available memory on your system, and other factors.

The result of the second command (`print ary[i]`) makes it pretty clear that the program does not have access to the memory location specified, although it does have legal access to the preceding one.

The expression $1 is an alias that refers to an entry in GDB's value history. GDB creates value history entries for each command you type that produces computed results. The alias numbers increment sequentially each time you execute a command that produces some sort of computed output. As a result, you can access these computed values using aliases rather than retyping the command. For example, the command $1-5 produces:

```
(gdb) print $1-5
$2 = 719
```

Notice that the alias incremented to $2. If you later need to use the value 719, you can use the alias $2. The value history is reset each time you start GDB, and the values are not accessible outside GDB.

You are not limited to using discrete values because gdb can display the addresses of data stored in an arbitrary region of memory. For example, to print the first 10 memory locations associated with ary, use the following command:

```
(gdb) print ary@10
$3 = {0xbffffc90, 0x40015580, 0x400115800, 0x0, 0x1, 0x2, 0c3, 0x4, 0x5}
```

The notation @10 means to print the 10 values that begin at ary. Say, on the other hand, that you want to print the five values stored in ary beginning with the first element. The command for this would be the following:

```
(gdb) print ary[1]@5
$4 = {1, 2, 3, 4, 5}
```

Why go to the trouble of printing variable or array values? Although it isn't necessary in this particular example because you know where the trouble occurs, it is often necessary to see the value of a variable at a particular point in a program's execution so you monitor what is happening to variables. In the case of arrays, a command that prints the values in an array, such as print ary[1]@5 in the preceding example, enables you to confirm at a glance the values are what you expect them to be. If the values don't match up with your expectations, though, that is a clue that some code is altering the array in a way you didn't intend. As a result, you can focus your bug hunting on a specific section of code.

GDB also can tell you the types of variables using the whatis command. GDB's whatis command is comparable to the man -f command, which searches the whatis database of system commands for short descriptions of those system commands (the manual page whatis database is totally separate from the whatis command used by GDB).While man's whatis database works on system commands, GDB's whatis command describes the types of variables and other data structures used in a program.

```
(gdb) whatis i
type = int
(gdb) whatis ary
type = int *
(gdb) whatis index_to_the_moon
type = void (int *)
```

This feature may seem rather useless because, of course, you know the types of all the variables in your program (yeah, right!). But, you will change your mind the first time you have to debug someone else's code or have to fix a multifile project for which you haven't seen the source files for a couple of months. The whatis command can also help you track down bugs that result from assigning an inappropriate value to a variable.

Setting Breakpoints

As you debug problematic code, it is often useful to halt execution at some point. Perhaps you want to stop execution before the code enters a section that is known to have problems. In other cases, you can set breakpoint so you can look at the values of certain variables at a given point in the execution flow. In still other situations, you might find it useful to stop execution so you can step through the code one instruction at a time. GDB enables you to set breakpoints on several different kinds of code constructs, including line numbers and function names, and also enables you to set conditional breakpoints, where the code stops only if a certain condition is met.

To set a breakpoint on a line number, use the following syntax:

```
(gdb) break linenum
```

To stop execution when the code enters a function, use:

```
(gdb) break funcname
```

In either case, GDB halts execution before executing the specified line number or entering the specified function. You can then use print to display variable values, for example, or use list to review the code that is about to be executed. If you have a multifile project and want to halt execution on a line of code or in a function that is not in the current source file, use the following forms:

```
(gdb) break filename:linenum
(gdb) break filename:funcname
```

Conditional breakpoints are usually more useful. They enable you to temporarily halt program execution if or when a particular condition is met. The correct syntax for setting conditional breakpoints is:

```
(gdb) break linenum if expr
(gdb) break funcname if expr
```

expr can be any expression that evaluates to true (nonzero). For example, the following break command stops execution at line 24 of debugme when the variable i equals 15:

```
(gdb) break 24 if i == 15
Breakpoint 1 at 0x80483cb: file debugme.c, line 24.
(gdb) run
Starting program: /home/kwall/code/debugme

Breakpoint 1, index_to_the_moon (ary=0xbffff4b0) at debugme.c:24
24                      ary[i] = i;
```

Stopping when i equals 15 is an arbitrary choice to demonstrate conditional breaks. As you can see, gdb stopped on line 24. A quick print command confirms that it stopped when the value of i reached the requested value:

```
(gdb) print i
$1 = 15
```

To resume executing after hitting a breakpoint, type **continue**. If you have set many breakpoints and have lost track of what has been set and which ones have been triggered, you can use the info breakpoints command to refresh your memory.

Working with Source Code

Locating a specific variable or function in a multifile project is a breeze with GDB, provided you use the -d switch to tell it where to find additional source code files. This is a particularly helpful option when not all of your source code is located in your current working directory or in the program's compilation directory (which GCC recorded in its symbol table). To specify one or more additional directories, start GDB using one or more -d *dirname* options, as this example illustrates:

```
$ gdb -d /source/project1 -d /oldsource/project1 -d /home/b
ubba/src killerapp
```

To locate the next occurrence of a particular *string* in the current file, use the search-*string* command. Use reverse-search *string* to find the previous occurrence of *string*. If you want to find the previous occurrence of the word "return" in debugme.c (see Listing 28-5), for example, use the command reverse-search return. GDB obliges and displays the text:

```
(gdb) reverse-search return
17                      return ret;
```

The search and reverse-search commands are especially helpful in large source files that have dozens or hundreds of lines. One common use of the reverse-search command is to find the file and/or line in which a variable is first used or in which it is defined. The search command similarly enables you to locate with relative ease each location in which a program symbol (variable, macro, or function) is used, perhaps to find the use that changes a variable unexpectedly or the place where a function is called when it shouldn't be.

Summary

This chapter took you on a whirlwind tour of a few of the most common programs and utilities used by Linux programmers. You learned how to use GCC to compile programs, how to use make to automate compiling programs, and how to find information about programming libraries using programs like ldd, nm, and ldconfig. You also learned enough about the source code control systems RCS and CVS to be comfortable with the terminology and how to use their most basic features. Finally, you learned how to use the GNU debugger GDB to figure out why, or at least where, a program fails.

✦ ✦ ✦

Media

The DVD and CD that accompany the *Linux Bible 2005 Edition* contain ten different Linux distributions. Two of those distributions can be booted directly from the DVD and run live (KNOPPIX) or installed to your hard disk (Fedora Core 3). Two can be booted and run live from the CD (Damn Small Linux) or installed to your hard disk (Debian). The others can be burned to CD-ROM from one of those two media and installed separately.

General information on installing or booting the various Linux distributions on the DVD is contained in Chapter 7. Specific instructions for using and installing each Linux distribution are contained in the other chapters in Part III (Chapters 8 to 18).

 Caution   The software contained on the CD and DVD is covered under the GNU Public License (GPL) or other licenses included on the medium for each software distribution. Use the software on this DVD (as you would any GPL software) at your own risk. Refer to README, RELEASE-NOTES, and any licensing files delivered with each distribution, and be sure that you agree with the terms they spell out before using the software.

Finding Linux Distributions on the DVD

The following sections describe the Linux distributions contained on the DVD. Fedora Core 3 and KNOPPIX are immediately bootable from the DVD. The other distributions are contained in ISO images in the `distros` directory on the DVD.

Fedora Core 3 Linux

The DVD includes the entire Fedora Core 3 distribution that normally comes on four installation CDs. This is the recommended Linux distribution for trying out most of the procedures in this book. You can install Fedora Core 3 directly from the DVD without having to create CDs from the DVD to install separately.

Because the complete Fedora Core 3 Linux distribution is included, you have access to a broad range of software packages (more than 1,600), allowing you to get a feel for using Linux as a desktop, server, or programmer's workstation.

Details on installing and using Fedora Core 3 are contained in Chapter 8.

Note   If you find that you like Fedora Core 3, consider getting the *Red Hat Fedora Linux 3 Bible* to learn more about that distribution. While some of the material overlaps with this book's, you will get more complete coverage of installation and different kinds of servers that are available with Fedora Core 3.

KNOPPIX Linux

The KNOPPIX 3.6 LiveCD Linux distribution is configured to boot by default from the DVD that comes with this book. KNOPPIX is the most popular bootable Linux and offers some unique features to set it apart from other bootable Linux distribution (such as ways of saving configuration settings and using it as a persistent desktop Linux).

Information on using KNOPPIX and configuring it in various ways is contained in Chapter 11.

SUSE Linux

The single SUSE 9.1 CD image included on the DVD contains a nice set of features that enable you to install a very usable SUSE desktop system. SUSE Linux is developed and supported by Novell, which offers SUSE as part of a wider range of Enterprise-ready Linux and NetWare software.

To install SUSE from the ISO image included on the DVD, you must first burn that image to CD, as described later in this appendix. Then, follow the installation instructions in Chapter 10.

Slackware 10

The DVD contains the first Slackware 10 CD. Slackware is the oldest surviving Linux system and continues to have a loyal following among Linux enthusiasts. The first CD contains a good mix of desktop and server software. (You can obtain the second CD from slackware.com if you want to install a full KDE or GNOME desktop for Slackware.)

Later in this appendix, you'll find out how to burn the Slackware ISO images to CD from the DVD. Chapter 14 tells how to install Slackware on your computer from that CD. Chapter 3 describes how to configure a simple window manager for Slackware.

Finding Linux Distributions on the CD

The CD that comes with this book boots directly to a Debian network install or a live boot of Damn Small Linux. An ISO image of a Gentoo minimal install CD is contained in the distros directory, as well as bootable images of INSERT and Feather Linux. Coyote Linux is contained on a tar/gzip that you copy to a hard disk and build into a floppy Linux distribution from instructions in Chapter 17.

Debian GNU/Linux

The net install ISO image of Debian GNU/Linux distribution is contained on the CD. Debian offers thoroughly tested releases that many Linux consultants and experts use because of its excellent software packaging and stability. Debian is used as the sample distribution for creating a Web server (LAMP) and mail server, as described in Chapters 23 and 24, respectively.

You can install Debian directly from the CD that comes with this book. The procedure for installing Debian is included in Chapter 9.

Gentoo Linux

The Gentoo Minimal install CD ISO image is included on the CD. With the Gentoo CD, you can install a usable Linux system, to which you can add any of the nearly 7,000 software packages that are available with Gentoo. Those packages can be obtained over a network connection or from a local CD, DVD, or hard disk. (A network install of those additional packages is described in Chapter 13.)

Procedures for burning the Gentoo ISO image from the CD that comes with this book to CD are contained later in this appendix. Then refer to Chapter 13 for information on using the Gentoo CD to install Gentoo on your computer. The procedure described in that chapter has you building much of the Gentoo operating system from scratch, specifically for your computer hardware, and downloading needed packages from the Internet.

Damn Small Linux

Damn Small Linux is set up to boot directly from the CD contained with this book. We also included an ISO image of Damn Small Linux included on the same CD that can fit on a mini-CD (less than 50MB). This distribution illustrates how a useful desktop Linux distribution, which includes full network connectivity and some useful productivity applications, can fit in a very small space.

Information on burning the Damn Small Linux distribution to CD is contained later in this appendix. See Chapter 18 for information on using Damn Small Linux.

Inside Security Rescue Toolkit

Inside Security Rescue Toolkit (INSERT) is a small, bootable Linux distribution that contains a variety of useful tools for checking, repairing, and recovering computers and networks. INSERT is small enough to fit on a bootable business card CD or mini-CD. While many of its tools are text-based, INSERT includes a simple graphical interface (using X and FluxBox window manager) and a few graphical tools.

An ISO image of INSERT is contained on the CD that comes with this book. Information on burning INSERT to CD is contained later in this appendix. Refer to Chapter 18 for descriptions of what's inside INSERT.

Feather Linux

Like Damn Small Linux, Feather Linux is a small, bootable Linux distribution that's based on KNOPPIX, with some features from Damn Small Linux as well. Burn the image from the CD that comes with this book to CD or mini-CD (it takes only 64MB of disk space). Refer to Chapter 18 for details about the contents of the Feather Linux distribution.

Coyote Linux

Although not considered a major Linux distribution, Coyote Linux is an excellent illustration of a useful Linux distribution that fits on a floppy disk (1.4MB). You'll copy the tar file of Coyote Linux on the DVD to a Linux system, configure Coyote Linux to suit your needs, and copy the resulting boot image to floppy disk.

See Chapter 17 for information on how to configure and use Coyote Linux as a firewall.

Linux Distributions Not on the DVD or CD

Not all the Linux distributions featured in this book are included on the DVD. Some of these did not encourage free redistribution of their products, while others were simply too large to include in their entirety and were not available on a single install CD or bootable Live CD.

The following Linux distributions described in the book are not on the DVD. The link shown after each distribution's name indicates the Internet site where you can find out how to purchase or otherwise obtain it.

- ✦ Yellow Dog Linux (www.terrasoftsolutions.com/store)
- ✦ Linspire Linux (www.linspire.com/product_page.php)
- ✦ Mandrakelinux (www.mandrakesoft.com/products)
- ✦ Red Hat Enterprise Linux (www.redhat.com/software/rhel/)

Some of these distributions have downloadable versions available on the Internet. I recommend that you try a Linux distribution site such as DistroWatch.com (www.distrowatch.com) to see if there is a free version of any of these distributions to try out.

Creating Linux CDs

There are several tools you can use to create bootable CDs for either installing or just running Linux from CD images contained on the DVD. Before you begin, you need to have the following:

- ✦ **DVD or CD drive** — You need a drive from which to copy the ISO image of the CD you want from the DVD or CD that come with this book, depending on which medium contains the image that you want. If you don't have a DVD drive, download and verify Linux installation CD images yourself, as described in Chapter 7. Then burn those images to CD as explained later in this appendix.

- ✦ **Linux Bible 2005 Edition DVD or CD** — The DVD contains two different CD images that you can burn to CD and use to install that particular Linux. The CD contains three live CD images and one install image you can burn to CD.

- ✦ **Blank CDs** — You need blank CDs to burn the CD images to.

- ✦ **CD burner** — You can use a different drive than your DVD/CD drive to burn CDs. Or, alternatively, you can copy a CD image to hard disk, remove the DVD/CD, and burn the new CD image to a CD in the same drive.

Unless you have two DVD/CD drives, you must copy the CD image to your hard disk before you can burn it. (If you have two drives, simply skip the steps for copying the CD image to hard disk.)

Here's how to create bootable Linux CDs from a running Linux system (such as Fedora Core 3):

1. With a Linux desktop system running, insert the *Linux Bible 2005 Edition* DVD or CD into the drive.

2. If an icon appears on the desktop for the DVD, open it (double-click). (If an icon doesn't appear, mount the DVD manually by typing something like the following as root user: **mount /dev/cdrom** or **mount /dev/hdc**, depending on the location of your DVD or CD drive. Then browse to where that image is located from your desktop window manager. It's probably mounted on /mnt/cdrom or something like /media/cdrecorder.)

3. Open the distros directory and select the Linux ISO image you want to burn to CD. Your choices are:

- **damnsmall-dsl-0.9.0.1.iso** — Contains the complete Damn Small Linux distribution. You can burn it to a regular CD, mini-CD, or bootable business card–size CD.

- **feather-0.5.6.iso** — Contains the complete Feather Linux distribution. You can burn it to a regular CD, mini-CD or bootable business card–size CD.

- **Gentoo-install-x86-universal-2004.3-rl.iso** — Contains the universal install CD image for starting a Gentoo installation. Requires 633MB of space.

- **INSERT-1.2.14.en.iso** — Contains the Inside Security Rescue Tools CD image. This is a bootable Linux CD image that requires only about 50MB of disk space. It can be burned to a regular CD, mini-CD, or bootable business card–size CD.

- **slackware-10.0-install-d1.iso** — Contains the CD image of the first of two Slackware 10 install CDs. It can be used by itself to install Slackware with a basic X desktop, some server packages, and programming tools. The second Slackware CD (`slackware-10.0-install-d2.iso`) is also on the DVD and can be used to add KDE or GNOME desktops.

- **SUSE-LiveCD-9.1.iso** — Contains the CD image of the SUSE LiveCD. You can use it to install a workable desktop SUSE Linux system that includes KDE desktop and a nice set of desktop applications.

4. Open a folder on your hard disk (such as your home directory from a desktop icon) and browse to or create a folder to copy the CD image to. (You'll need between 50MB and 700MB of hard disk space, depending on the disk image you choose.)

5. Drag-and-drop the image to the folder on your hard disk.

6. Close all folders and shells that are open on the DVD or CD, and then unmount and eject the medium (right-click the DVD or CD icon and select Eject).

7. Open a CD/DVD burning application. For this procedure, I recommend K3B CD/DVD Burning Facility (`http://www.k3b.org`). In Fedora, select the Red Hat or Applications menu and choose Sound & Video ⇨ K3b (or type **k3b** from a Terminal window). The K3b - CD Kreator window appears.

8. From the K3b window, select Tools ⇨ CD ⇨ Burn CD Image. You are asked to choose an image file.

9. Browse to the image you just copied to hard disk and select it. Once the image you want is selected, the Burn CD Image window appears and does a checksum on the image. (You can compare the checksum number that appears against the number in the MD5SUM file on the DVD for this image, to be sure that the CD image was not corrupted.) Figure A-1 shows the Burn CD Image window ready to burn an image of Damn Small Linux.

10. Insert a blank CD into the CD burner drive, which may be a combination with your DVD drive. (If a CD/DVD Creator window pops up, you can just close it.)

Figure A-1: Use K3b to burn your installation CDs.

11. Check the settings on the Burn CD Image window (often the defaults are fine, but you may want to slow down the speed if you get some bad burns) and click Start.

12. When the CD is done burning, eject it (or it may eject automatically) and mark it appropriately (information such as the distribution name, version number, and date).

Now you're ready to begin installing (or booting) the Linux distribution you just burned. Refer to Chapter 7 for general information on installing Linux. Then go to the chapter that covers your particular distribution to find its specific installation procedure.

If you don't have Linux installed or K3b available at the moment, you can burn CDs from any CD-burning application you have available. There's a nice overview of CD installation tools and how to use them to burn CDs at the Gentoo Web site (www.gentoo.org/doc/en/faq.xml). It describes disk-burning tools that are available on Windows, Mac OS X, and Linux systems.

✦   ✦   ✦

Entering the Linux Community

Using and playing with Linux is great fun. Connecting up with others who share your joy in Linux can make the whole Linux experience that much better. Some of the ways you can connect to the Linux community include:

✦ Joining a Linux User Group (LUG)

✦ Contributing to an open source project

✦ Asking or answering questions at online Linux forums

✦ Connecting to a Linux IRC chat room

Activity in the Linux and the open source communities has grown so dramatically in recent years that there are many diverse outlets for learning and getting to know other Linux enthusiasts. This appendix contains a variety of resources that you can use to help you expand your knowledge and activity in Linux and its growing communities.

General Linux Sites

While Slashdot.org is probably the news site that most Linux enthusiasts keep track of and participate in, there are many other places to look for Linux and open source news as well.

✦ **Slashdot** (www.slashdot.org) — Probably the top news site for open source devotees. People submit links to news articles, book reviews, and interviews related to technology, science, politics, or other "news for nerds." Then everyone piles on with their own commentaries. Having your book or project "slashdotted" means you have made the big time — although you are as likely to get crushed as you are to get praised.

+ **Groklaw** (www.groklaw.net) — The place to look for information regarding legal issues surrounding open source software.

+ **Linux Today** (www.linuxtoday.com) — This site gathers news that is of particular interest to software developers and IT managers.

+ **LWN.net** (www.lwn.net) — Produces a weekly newsletter covering a range of Linux topics.

+ **Newsforge** (www.newsforge.com) — Bills itself as the "Online Newspaper for Linux and Open Source." Contains many original articles, as well as links to up-to-the-minute open source stories from other locations on the Web.

+ **LinuxInsider** (www.linuxinsider.com) — Covers news articles relating to Linux issues around the world.

If you need help or have questions about Linux, here are a few sites to try:

+ **Linux Questions** (www.linuxquestions.org) — In addition to offering forums on different Linux distributions, this is a great place to ask questions relating to hardware compatibility, security, and networking. The site also has some good tutorials, as well as reviews of books and Linux distributions.

+ **Google Linux** (www.google.com/linux) — Search for Linux-specific information from this part of the Google search site.

+ **Linux Forums** (www.linuxforums.org) — Contains active forums on your favorite distributions and has active IRC channels as well.

+ **The Linux Documentation Project** (www.tldp.org) — Offers a wide range of HOWTOs, guides, FAQs, man pages, and other documentation related to Linux.

+ **Linux Help** (www.linuxhelp.net) — Offers forums, news, and current information about the Linux kernel. Also contains information about finding Linux mailing lists, newsgroups, and user groups.

+ **Linux Online** (www.linux.org) — Provides a central source of information relating to Linux distributions, documentation, books, and people.

+ **Linux Kernel Archives** (www.kernel.org) — The primary site for Linux kernel development. You can get the latest stable or testing versions of the Linux kernel. Not the first place to start with Linux, but I thought you'd want to know it was there.

Linux Distributions

Every major Linux distribution has a Web site that provides information about how to get it and use it. If you haven't chosen a distribution yet, here are some sites that can help you evaluate, find, and get a Linux distribution that interests you:

✦ **Distrowatch** (`www.distrowatch.com`) — Contains information about a few hundred different Linux distributions. The site provides an easy way to find out about different distributions, and then simply connect to the distribution's home page, download site, or related forums.

✦ **LinuxISO.org** (`www.linuxiso.org`) — Provides information about Linux distributions and how to get them. Also tells you about downloading, verifying, and burning your own CDs from ISO images.

✦ **LWN.net Linux Distributions** (`lwn.net/Distributions`) — If you want to read succinct descriptions of more than 400 Linux distributions on one page, this is the place to go.

Here are key sites associated with Linux distributions covered in this book:

✦ **Fedora** (`fedora.redhat.com`) — Community-driven Linux, supported by Red Hat. Check the Fedora Legacy Project (`http://fedoralegacy.org`) for long-term support issues. Look to Fedora Extras (`www.fedora.us`) and Livna.org (`rpm.livna.org`) for downloads of extra Fedora software.

✦ **Red Hat Enterprise Linux** (`www.redhat.com`) — Check the main Red Hat Web site for information on commercial Linux products.

✦ **Debian GNU/Linux** (`www.debian.org`) — Get news, documentation, support, and download information about Debian. To learn about packages, try the Debian Package a Day site (`www.livejournal.com/users/debaday`), which adds new descriptions of packages in the Sarge Debian distribution each day. (This site lists the 20 most recent journal entries.)

✦ **SUSE** (`www.suse.com`) — Get product and support information from this project's site. Also try the Novell site (`www.novell.com`), which owns SUSE.

✦ **Knoppix** (`www.knopper.net/knoppix/index-en.html`) — The official KNOPPIX page on its creator's (Klaus Knopper's) Web site. An English forum is at `www.knoppix.net`, and a German forum at `www.linuxtag.org/forum`.

✦ **Yellow Dog** (`www.yellowdoglinux.com`) — From this site, sponsored by Terra Soft Solutions, you can purchase Yellow Dog Linux on CDs or get it pre-installed on Mac hardware. The YDL.net site offers some extra services for Yellow Dog Linux users, such as personal e-mail accounts and Web space.

✦ **Gentoo** (`www.gentoo.org`) — The center for the very active Gentoo community. The site contains a wealth of information about Gentoo and plenty of forums and IRC channels in which to participate. You'll find a solid and growing documentation set to back up the distribution, and tons of software packages to try (in the thousands).

✦ **Slackware** (`www.slackware.org`) — Check the changelogs at this site to get a feel for the latest Slackware developments. Try LinuxPackages (`www.linux packages.net`) for a broader range of information about Slackware.

+ **Linspire** (www.linspire.com) — Purchase a computer running Linspire from this site, or just buy the boxed set. No demo copies are available, but you can get a 15-day free trial of Linspire.

+ **Mandrake** (www.mandrakelinux.com) — Developers of this distribution ask that you join the Mandrake Club to help support the project.

Companies and Groups Supporting Linux

Some companies and organizations make important contributions to Linux and open source software without producing their own Linux distribution. Here are some of the most prominent ones:

+ **VA Software** (www.vasoftware.com) — With its Open Source Technology Group (OSDG), VA Software manages many of the premier open source sites on the Web. It maintains open source development sites Freshmeat (www.freshmeat.net) and SourceForge (www.sourceforge.net). It also maintains information technology sites, such as Slashdot (www.slashdot.org), NewsForge (www.newsforge.com), Linux.com (www.linux.com), and IT Manager's Journal (www.itmanagersjournal.com).

+ **IBM** (www.ibm.com/linux) — Because IBM has taken on the lion's share of lawsuits against Linux and done a lot to further Linux, especially in the enterprise area, it deserves a mention here. There are many good resources for Linux at IBM's Web site, including some excellent white papers covering Linux in business.

+ **Ibiblio** (www.ibiblio.org) — Contains a massive archive of Linux software and documentation (www.ibiblio.org/pub/linux).

Major Linux Projects

As you know by now, the name Linux comes from the Linux kernel created by Linus Torvalds. The desktop, application, server, and other software needed to create a full Linux system are added from other open source projects. The following is a list of some of the major open source software organizations that usually have software included with Linux:

+ **Free Software Foundation** (www.fsf.org) — Supports the GNU project, which produces much of the software outside the kernel that is associated with Linux. In particular, open source versions of nearly every early UNIX command has been implemented by the GNU project.

✦ **Apache Software Foundation** (www.apache.org)—Produces the Apache (HTTP) Web server. It also manages related projects, such as SpamAssassin (spam filtering software) and a variety of modules for serving special Web content (perl, SSL, PHP, and so on).

✦ **K Desktop Environment** (www.kde.org)—Develops KDE, one of the two leading desktop environments used with Linux.

✦ **GNOME** (www.gnome.org)—Develops the other leading Linux desktop environment (used as the default desktop for Red Hat Linux systems).

✦ **X.org** (www.x.org) and **XFree86** (www.xfree86.org)—These two organizations provide different implementations of the X Window System graphical desktop framework software.

✦ **Internet Systems Consortium** (www.isc.org)—Develops several major open source software projects related to the Internet. These include Bind (domain name system server), INN (InterNetNews news server), and DHCP (dynamic host configuration protocol).

Linux User Groups

A good way to learn more about Linux and become more a part of the Linux community is to hook up with a Linux User Group (LUG). LUGs tend to come and go, so you might have to do some work to track one down in your area. Here are some places to start your search:

✦ **Google** (www.google.com/linux)—I found both of the LUGs I've been associated with by using Google to search for the word "Linux" and the city closest to where I was living.

✦ **Linux Meetup Groups** (linux.meetup.com)—Enter your ZIP Code to search for the nearest LUG in your area.

✦ **Linux Online** (www.linux.org/groups)—Offers a large, international list of Linux User Groups. Select your country to see a list of available groups.

✦ **LinuxGazette GLUE** (glue.linuxgazette.com)—The Groups of Linux Users Everywhere (GLUE) site contains lists of known LUGs.

If there is no Linux User Group in your area, you might consider starting one. To get information on what LUGs are all about and some suggestions about starting one, refer to the Linux User Group HOWTO (www.tldp.org/HOWTO/User-Group-HOWTO.html).

✦   ✦   ✦

Index

Continued

Continued

GNU General Public License

Version 2, June 1991

Copyright © 1989, 1991 Free Software Foundation, Inc.

59 Temple Place - Suite 330, Boston, MA 02111-1307, USA

Preamble

The licenses for most software are designed to take away your freedom to share and change it. By contrast, the GNU General Public License is intended to guarantee your freedom to share and change free software–to make sure the software is free for all its users. This General Public License applies to most of the Free Software Foundation's software and to any other program whose authors commit to using it. (Some other Free Software Foundation software is covered by the GNU Library General Public License instead.) You can apply it to your programs, too.

When we speak of free software, we are referring to freedom, not price. Our General Public Licenses are designed to make sure that you have the freedom to distribute copies of free software (and charge for this service if you wish), that you receive source code or can get it if you want it, that you can change the software or use pieces of it in new free programs; and that you know you can do these things.

To protect your rights, we need to make restrictions that forbid anyone to deny you these rights or to ask you to surrender the rights. These restrictions translate to certain responsibilities for you if you distribute copies of the software, or if you modify it.

For example, if you distribute copies of such a program, whether gratis or for a fee, you must give the recipients all the rights that you have. You must make sure that they, too, receive or can get the source code. And you must show them these terms so they know their rights.

We protect your rights with two steps: (1) copyright the software, and (2) offer you this license which gives you legal permission to copy, distribute and/or modify the software.

Also, for each author's protection and ours, we want to make certain that everyone understands that there is no warranty for this free software. If the software is modified by someone else and passed on, we want its recipients to know that what they have is not the original, so that any problems introduced by others will not reflect on the original authors' reputations.

Finally, any free program is threatened constantly by software patents. We wish to avoid the danger that redistributors of a free program will individually obtain patent licenses, in effect making the program proprietary. To prevent this, we have made it clear that any patent must be licensed for everyone's free use or not licensed at all.

The precise terms and conditions for copying, distribution and modification follow.

Terms and Conditions for Copying, Distribution and Modification

0. This License applies to any program or other work which contains a notice placed by the copyright holder saying it may be distributed under the terms of this General Public License. The "Program", below, refers to any such program or work, and a "work based on the Program" means either the Program or any derivative work under copyright law: that is to say, a work containing the Program or a portion of it, either verbatim or with modifications and/or translated into another language. (Hereinafter, translation is included without limitation in the term "modification".) Each licensee is addressed as "you".

Activities other than copying, distribution and modification are not covered by this License; they are outside its scope. The act of running the Program is not restricted, and the output from the Program is covered only if its contents constitute a work based on the Program (independent of having been made by running the Program). Whether that is true depends on what the Program does.

1. You may copy and distribute verbatim copies of the Program's source code as you receive it, in any medium, provided that you conspicuously and appropriately publish on each copy an appropriate copyright notice and disclaimer of warranty; keep intact all the notices that refer to this License and to the absence of any warranty; and give any other recipients of the Program a copy of this License along with the Program.

You may charge a fee for the physical act of transferring a copy, and you may at your option offer warranty protection in exchange for a fee.

2. You may modify your copy or copies of the Program or any portion of it, thus forming a work based on the Program, and copy and distribute such modifications or work under the terms of Section 1 above, provided that you also meet all of these conditions:

a) You must cause the modified files to carry prominent notices stating that you changed the files and the date of any change.

b) You must cause any work that you distribute or publish, that in whole or in part contains or is derived from the Program or any part thereof, to be licensed as a whole at no charge to all third parties under the terms of this License.

c) If the modified program normally reads commands interactively when run, you must cause it, when started running for such interactive use in the most ordinary way, to print or display an announcement including an appropriate copyright notice and a notice that there is no warranty (or else, saying that you provide a warranty) and that users may redistribute the program under these conditions, and telling the user how to view a copy of this License. (Exception: if the Program itself is interactive but does not normally print such an announcement, your work based on the Program is not required to print an announcement.)

These requirements apply to the modified work as a whole. If identifiable sections of that work are not derived from the Program, and can be reasonably considered independent and separate works in themselves, then this License, and its terms, do not apply to those sections when you distribute them as separate works. But when you distribute the same sections as part of a whole which is a work based on the Program, the distribution of the whole must be on the terms of this License, whose permissions for other licensees extend to the entire whole, and thus to each and every part regardless of who wrote it.

Thus, it is not the intent of this section to claim rights or contest your rights to work written entirely by you; rather, the intent is to exercise the right to control the distribution of derivative or collective works based on the Program.

In addition, mere aggregation of another work not based on the Program with the Program (or with a work based on the Program) on a volume of a storage or distribution medium does not bring the other work under the scope of this License.

3. You may copy and distribute the Program (or a work based on it, under Section 2) in object code or executable form under the terms of Sections 1 and 2 above provided that you also do one of the following:

   a) Accompany it with the complete corresponding machine-readable source code, which must be distributed under the terms of Sections 1 and 2 above on a medium customarily used for software interchange; or,

   b) Accompany it with a written offer, valid for at least three years, to give any third party, for a charge no more than your cost of physically performing source distribution, a complete machine-readable copy of the corresponding source code, to be distributed under the terms of Sections 1 and 2 above on a medium customarily used for software interchange; or,

   c) Accompany it with the information you received as to the offer to distribute corresponding source code. (This alternative is allowed only for noncommercial distribution and only if you received the program in object code or executable form with such an offer, in accord with Subsection b above.)

The source code for a work means the preferred form of the work for making modifications to it. For an executable work, complete source code means all the source code for all modules it contains, plus any associated interface definition files, plus the scripts used to control compilation and installation of the executable. However, as a special exception, the source code distributed need not include anything that is normally distributed (in either source or binary form) with the major components (compiler, kernel, and so on) of the operating system on which the executable runs, unless that component itself accompanies the executable.

If distribution of executable or object code is made by offering access to copy from a designated place, then offering equivalent access to copy the source code from the same place counts as distribution of the source code, even though third parties are not compelled to copy the source along with the object code.

4. You may not copy, modify, sublicense, or distribute the Program except as expressly provided under this License. Any attempt otherwise to copy, modify, sublicense or distribute the Program is void, and will automatically terminate your rights under this License. However, parties who have received copies, or rights, from you under this License will not have their licenses terminated so long as such parties remain in full compliance.

5. You are not required to accept this License, since you have not signed it. However, nothing else grants you permission to modify or distribute the Program or its derivative works. These actions are prohibited by law if you do not accept this License. Therefore, by modifying or distributing the Program (or any work based on the Program), you indicate your acceptance of this License to do so, and all its terms and conditions for copying, distributing or modifying the Program or works based on it.

6. Each time you redistribute the Program (or any work based on the Program), the recipient automatically receives a license from the original licensor to copy, distribute or modify the Program subject to these terms and conditions. You may not impose any further restrictions on the recipients' exercise of the rights granted herein. You are not responsible for enforcing compliance by third parties to this License.

7. If, as a consequence of a court judgment or allegation of patent infringement or for any other reason (not limited to patent issues), conditions are imposed on you (whether by court order, agreement or otherwise) that contradict the conditions of this License, they do not excuse you from the conditions of this License. If you cannot distribute so as to satisfy simultaneously your obligations under this License and any other pertinent obligations, then as a consequence you may not distribute the Program at all. For example, if a patent license would not permit royalty-free redistribution of the Program by all those who receive copies directly or indirectly through you, then the only way you could satisfy both it and this License would be to refrain entirely from distribution of the Program.

   If any portion of this section is held invalid or unenforceable under any particular circumstance, the balance of the section is intended to apply and the section as a whole is intended to apply in other circumstances.

   It is not the purpose of this section to induce you to infringe any patents or other property right claims or to contest validity of any such claims; this section has the sole purpose of protecting the integrity of the free software distribution system, which is implemented by public license practices. Many people have made generous contributions to the wide range of software distributed through that system in reliance on consistent application of that system; it is up to the author/donor to decide if he or she is willing to distribute software through any other system and a licensee cannot impose that choice.

   This section is intended to make thoroughly clear what is believed to be a consequence of the rest of this License.

8. If the distribution and/or use of the Program is restricted in certain countries either by patents or by copyrighted interfaces, the original copyright holder who places the Program under this License may add an explicit geographical distribution limitation excluding those countries, so that distribution is permitted only in or among countries not thus excluded. In such case, this License incorporates the limitation as if written in the body of this License.

9. The Free Software Foundation may publish revised and/or new versions of the General Public License from time to time. Such new versions will be similar in spirit to the present version, but may differ in detail to address new problems or concerns.

   Each version is given a distinguishing version number. If the Program specifies a version number of this License which applies to it and "any later version", you have the option of following the terms and conditions either of that version or of any later version published by the Free Software Foundation. If the Program does not specify a version number of this License, you may choose any version ever published by the Free Software Foundation.

10. If you wish to incorporate parts of the Program into other free programs whose distribution conditions are different, write to the author to ask for permission. For software which is copyrighted by the Free Software Foundation, write to the Free Software Foundation; we sometimes make exceptions for this. Our decision will be guided by the two goals of preserving the free status of all derivatives of our free software and of promoting the sharing and reuse of software generally.

NO WARRANTY

11. BECAUSE THE PROGRAM IS LICENSED FREE OF CHARGE, THERE IS NO WARRANTY FOR THE PROGRAM, TO THE EXTENT PERMITTED BY APPLICABLE LAW. EXCEPT WHEN OTHERWISE STATED IN WRITING THE COPYRIGHT HOLDERS AND/OR OTHER PARTIES PROVIDE THE PROGRAM "AS IS" WITHOUT WARRANTY OF ANY KIND, EITHER EXPRESSED OR IMPLIED, INCLUDING, BUT NOT LIMITED TO, THE IMPLIED WARRANTIES OF MERCHANTABILITY AND FITNESS FOR A PARTICULAR PURPOSE. THE ENTIRE RISK AS TO THE QUALITY AND PERFORMANCE OF THE PROGRAM IS WITH YOU. SHOULD THE PROGRAM PROVE DEFECTIVE, YOU ASSUME THE COST OF ALL NECESSARY SERVICING, REPAIR OR CORRECTION.

12. IN NO EVENT UNLESS REQUIRED BY APPLICABLE LAW OR AGREED TO IN WRITING WILL ANY COPYRIGHT HOLDER, OR ANY OTHER PARTY WHO MAY MODIFY AND/OR REDISTRIBUTE THE PROGRAM AS PERMITTED ABOVE, BE LIABLE TO YOU FOR DAM-AGES, INCLUDING ANY GENERAL, SPECIAL, INCIDENTAL OR CONSEQUENTIAL DAMAGES ARISING OUT OF THE USE OR INABILITY TO USE THE PROGRAM (INCLUDING BUT NOT LIMITED TO LOSS OF DATA OR DATA BEING RENDERED INACCURATE OR LOSSES SUS-TAINED BY YOU OR THIRD PARTIES OR A FAILURE OF THE PROGRAM TO OPERATE WITH ANY OTHER PROGRAMS), EVEN IF SUCH HOLDER OR OTHER PARTY HAS BEEN ADVISED OF THE POSSIBILITY OF SUCH DAMAGES.

END OF TERMS AND CONDITIONS

Please see the reverse page for licensing and warranty information regarding the Fedora Core software media. Please see Appendix A for information regarding the source code coupon offer for all other Linux distributions found on the DVD.

Fedora™ Core 3 Linux® CD-ROM Offer

If you do not have access to a PC with a DVD drive, we are offering the complete set on CD-ROMs for a nominal shipping-and-materials fee. If you'd like the CDs sent to you, please follow the instructions below to order by phone, online or coupon.

For each ordering method, please use ISBN: 0764589113 and Promo Code: RHF3B when prompted. The cost is $11.00 (USD) plus shipping.

Terms: Void where prohibited or restricted by law. Allow 2-4 weeks for delivery.

To order by phone:
1. Call toll-free in the United States: 1-877-762-2974. International customers, dial 1-317-572-3994.
2. Give the operator the appropriate ISBN and Promo Code. Please have your credit card ready.

To order online:
1. Go to http://www.wiley.com/
2. Use the Product Search feature to search for RHFLinux 3 Bible Multipack or 0764589113.
3. Place the item in the shopping cart and use the Promo Code RHF3B when prompted.

To order by coupon:
1. Complete the coupon below.
2. Include a check or money order for $11.00 (USD) plus shipping. To find out the shipping costs, call 1-877-762-2974 in the U.S. or 1-317-572-3994 for international customers.
3. Send it to us at the address listed at the bottom of the coupon.

Name _____

Company _____

Address _____

City _____ State _____ Postal Code _____ Country _____

E-mail _____ Telephone _____

Place where book was purchased _____

❑ Check here to find out what we're up to by joining our e-mail list—a convenient way to receive news about our products and events as well as about special discount offers.

Return this coupon with the appropriate U.S. funds to:

Wiley Publishing, Inc.
Customer Care
RHFLinux 3 Bible Multipack, 0764589113 Fulfillment Promo: RHF3B
10475 Crosspoint Blvd.
Indianapolis, IN 46256

Terms: Wiley is not responsible for lost, stolen, late, or illegible orders. For questions regarding this fulfillment offer, please call us at 1-877-762-2974 or 1-317-572-3994.